Food Values of Portions Commonly Used

Bowes and Church's

Food Values of Portions Commonly Used

14th edition _____ revised by

Jean A. T. Pennington, Ph.D., R.D.

_____ and

_____ Helen Nichols Church, B.S.

Harper & Row, Publishers
New York, Cambridge, Philadelphia, San Francisco
London, Mexico City, São Paulo, Singapore, Sydney

Library of Congress Cataloging in Publication Data

Pennington, Jean A. Thompson.
    Food values of portions commonly used.

    Bibliography: p.
    Includes index.
    1. Food—Composition—Tables.   2. Nutrition—Tables.
I. Church, Helen Nichols.   II. Title.   III. Title:
Food values of portions commonly used.
TX551.B64   1985   641.1   83-48373
ISBN 0-06-181679-5
ISBN 0-06-091093-3 (pbk.)

87 88 89 MPC 10 9 8 7

Dedicated to

Anna dePlanter Bowes

formerly of

the Philadelphia Child Health Society

and the University of Pennsylvania

and

Charles Frederick Church, M.D.

formerly of

the University of Pennsylvania

and Children's Hospital of Philadelphia

Preface

This edition of Bowes and Church's *Food Values of Portions Commonly Used* brings several new changes to this traditional handbook:

■ The nutrient values have been updated according to the most recent data available from the food industry, the scientific literature, and USDA food composition publications. When updated information was not available, data from previous editions were used.

■ Several nutrients have been added to the main table, including water, saturated fatty acids, vitamin B-6, folacin, vitamin B-12, pantothenic acid, cholesterol, zinc, copper, and manganese. There are now sufficient data on these "lesser known" nutrients to justify their inclusion in the main table. In addition, vitamin A is now listed in both international units (IU) and retinol equivalents (RE).

■ Information on amino acids (previously presented in the main table) is now compiled in a Supplementary Table. This change has two practical motivations. First, those who seek amino acid data can now find them neatly compacted. Second, because so many amino acid values are not yet available, much space is saved in the main table.

■ The data format for Infant Formulas has been expanded to include vitamin D, vitamin E, vitamin K, biotin, choline, myo-inositol, iodine, chloride, and amino acids. The data format for Special Dietary Formulas, Commercial and Hospital has been expanded to include the above nutrients plus molybdenum, selenium, chromium, caffeine, and saccharin. Because infant formulas and special dietary formulas are generally developed by formulation and because the manufacturers of these formulated products were able to provide such complete nutrient profiles, we thought it advisable to keep the nutrient information together. Data for vitamin D, vitamin E, vitamin K, biotin, choline, myo-inositol, iodine, chlorine, molybdenum, selenium, chromium, amino acids, and other substances in other foods are listed in the Supplementary Tables. The number of Supplementary Tables has been expanded since the previous edition.

We wish to express our gratitude to the many companies who responded to our request for food composition data. We welcome comments, corrections, and suggestions. We gratefully acknowledge the reviews provided by Judith Ashley, M.S.P.H., R.D.; Kathryn Fleming, Ph.D.; and Carolyn Miles, Ph.D. and the editorial assistance provided by Barbara Farabaugh.

Jean A. T. Pennington, Ph.D., R.D.
Helen Nichols Church, B.S.

January, 1985

Preface to the First Edition

The purpose of this book is to supply authoritative data on the nutritional values of foods in a form for quick and easy reference.

In teaching nutrition to students of medicine, dentistry, dental hygiene and public health nursing, food values based on common measures or portions frequently served have been found most useful. This basis of calculation is particularly well suited to the practical study of comparative food values, as well as to the approximate analysis of diets from records of daily food intake. For calculations of diets from weighed portions the actual weight of each food is given in grams or ounces.

Anna dePlanter Bowes
Charles F. Church

November, 1937

Contents

Supplementary Tables

Food and Nutrition Board, National Academy of Sciences—National Research Council

Recommended Daily Dietary Allowances,[a] Revised 1980

Designed for the Maintenance of Good Nutrition of Practically All Healthy People in the U.S.A.

	Age (years)	Weight (kg)	(lbs)	Height (cm)	(in)	Protein (g)	Fat-Soluble Vitamins			Water-Soluble Vitamins							Minerals					
							Vitamin A (µg)[b]	Vitamin D (µg)[c]	Vitamin E (mg α)[d]	Vitamin C (mg)	Thiamin (mg)	Riboflavin (mg)	Niacin (mg NE)[e]	Vitamin B$_6$ (mg)	Folacin[f] (µg)	Vitamin B$_{12}$ (µg)	Calcium (mg)	Phosphorus (mg)	Magnesium (mg)	Iron (mg)	Zinc (mg)	Iodine (µg)
Infants	0.0–0.5	6	13	60	24	kg × 2.2	420	10	3	35	0.3	0.4	6	0.3	30	0.5[g]	360	240	50	10	3	40
	0.5–1.0	9	20	71	28	kg × 2.0	400	10	4	35	0.5	0.6	8	0.6	45	1.5	540	360	70	15	5	50
Children	1–3	13	29	90	35	23	400	10	5	45	0.7	0.8	9	0.9	100	2.0	800	800	150	15	10	70
	4–6	20	44	112	44	30	500	10	6	45	0.9	1.0	11	1.3	200	2.5	800	800	200	10	10	90
	7–10	28	62	132	52	34	700	10	7	45	1.2	1.4	16	1.6	300	3.0	800	800	250	10	10	120
Males	11–14	45	99	157	62	45	1000	10	8	50	1.4	1.6	18	1.8	400	3.0	1200	1200	350	18	15	150
	15–18	66	145	176	69	56	1000	10	10	60	1.4	1.7	18	2.0	400	3.0	1200	1200	400	18	15	150
	19–22	70	154	177	70	56	1000	7.5	10	60	1.5	1.7	19	2.2	400	3.0	800	800	350	10	15	150
	23–50	70	154	178	70	56	1000	5	10	60	1.4	1.6	18	2.2	400	3.0	800	800	350	10	15	150
	51+	70	154	178	70	56	1000	5	10	60	1.2	1.4	16	2.2	400	3.0	800	800	350	10	15	150
Females	11–14	46	101	157	62	46	800	10	8	50	1.1	1.3	15	1.8	400	3.0	1200	1200	300	18	15	150
	15–18	55	120	163	64	46	800	10	8	60	1.1	1.3	14	2.0	400	3.0	1200	1200	300	18	15	150
	19–22	55	120	163	64	44	800	7.5	8	60	1.1	1.3	14	2.0	400	3.0	800	800	300	18	15	150
	23–50	55	120	163	64	44	800	5	8	60	1.0	1.2	13	2.0	400	3.0	800	800	300	18	15	150
	51+	55	120	163	64	44	800	5	8	60	1.0	1.2	13	2.0	400	3.0	800	800	300	10	15	150
Pregnant						+30	+200	+5	+2	+20	+0.4	+0.3	+2	+0.6	+400	+1.0	+400	+400	+150	[h]	+5	+25
Lactating						+20	+400	+5	+3	+40	+0.5	+0.5	+5	+0.5	+100	+1.0	+400	+400	+150	[h]	+10	+50

[a] The allowances are intended to provide for individual variations among most normal persons as they live in the United States under usual environmental stresses. Diets should be based on a variety of common foods in order to provide other nutrients for which human requirements have been less well defined.

[b] Retinol equivalents. 1 Retinol equivalent = 1 µg retinol or 6 µg β carotene.

[c] As cholecalciferol. 10 µg cholecalciferol = 400 IU vitamin D.

[d] α-tocopherol equivalents. 1 mg d-α-tocopherol = 1 α TE

[e] 1 NE (niacin equivalent) is equal to 1 mg of niacin or 60 mg of dietary tryptophan.

[f] The folacin allowances refer to dietary sources as determined by *Lactobacillus casei* assay after treatment with enzymes (conjugases) to make polyglutamyl forms of the vitamin available to the test organism.

[g] The RDA for Vitamin B$_{12}$ in infants is based on average concentration of the vitamin in human milk. The allowances after weaning are based on energy intake (as recommended by the American Academy of Pediatrics) and consideration of other factors such as intestinal absorption.

[h] The increased requirement during pregnancy cannot be met by the iron content of habitual American diets nor by the existing iron stores of many women; therefore the use of 30–60 mg of supplemental iron is recommended. Iron needs during lactation are not substantially different from those of non-pregnant women, but continued supplementation of the mother for 2–3 months after parturition is advisable in order to replenish stores depleted by pregnancy.

Reproduced from National Academy of Sciences: Recommended Dietary Allowances, 9th rev. ed. Washington, DC, 1980

Food and Nutrition Board, National Academy of Sciences—National Research Council

Estimated Safe and Adequate Daily Dietary Intakes of Selected Vitamins and Minerals[a]

	Age (years)	Vitamin K (µg)	Biotin (µg)	Pantothenic Acid (mg)	Copper (mg)	Manganese (mg)	Fluoride (mg)	Chromium (mg)	Selenium (mg)	Molybdenum (mg)	Sodium (mg)	Potassium (mg)	Chloride (mg)
					Vitamins			**Trace Elements**[b]				**Electrolytes**	
Infants	0–0.5	12	35	2	0.5–0.7	0.5–0.7	0.1–0.5	0.01–0.04	0.01–0.04	0.03–0.06	115–350	350–925	275–700
	0.5–1	10–20	50	3	0.7–1.0	0.7–1.0	0.2–1.0	0.02–0.06	0.02–0.06	0.04–0.08	250–750	425–1275	400–1200
Children	1–3	15–30	65	3	1.0–1.5	1.0–1.5	0.5–1.5	0.02–0.08	0.02–0.08	0.05–0.1	325–975	550–1650	500–1500
and	4–6	20–40	85	3–4	1.5–2.0	1.5–2.0	1.0–2.5	0.03–0.12	0.03–0.12	0.06–0.15	450–1350	775–2325	700–2100
Adolescents	7–10	30–60	120	4–5	2.0–2.5	2.0–3.0	1.5–2.5	0.05–0.2	0.05–0.2	0.10–0.3	600–1800	1000–3000	925–2775
	11+	50–100	100–200	4–7	2.0–3.0	2.5–5.0	1.5–2.5	0.05–0.2	0.05–0.2	0.15–0.5	900–2700	1525–4575	1400–4200
Adults		70–140	100–200	4–7	2.0–3.0	2.5–5.0	1.5–4.0	0.05–0.2	0.05–0.2	0.15–0.5	1100–3300	1875–5625	1700–5100

[a] Because there is less information on which to base allowances, these figures are not given in the main table of the RDA and are provided here in the form of ranges of recommended intakes.

[b] Since the toxic levels for many trace elements may be only several times usual intakes, the upper levels for the trace elements given in this table should not be habitually exceeded.

Reproduced from National Academy of Sciences: Recommended Dietary Allowances, 9th rev ed. Washington, DC, 1980

Food and Nutrition Board, National Academy of Sciences—National Research Council

Mean Heights and Weights and Recommended Energy Intake[a]

	Age (years)	Weight (kg)	Weight (lb)	Height (cm)	Height (in)	Energy Needs (with range) (kcal)	(MJ)
Infants	0.0–0.5	6	13	60	24	kg × 115 kg × (95–145)	kg × .48
	0.5–1.0	9	20	71	28	kg × 105 kg × (80–135)	kg × .44
Children	1–3	13	29	90	35	1300 (900–1800)	5.5
	4–6	20	44	112	44	1700 (1300–2300)	7.1
	7–10	28	62	132	52	2400 (1650–3300)	10.1
Males	11–14	45	99	157	62	2700 (2000–3700)	11.3
	15–18	66	145	176	69	2800 (2100–3900)	11.8
	19–22	70	154	177	70	2900 (2500–3300)	12.2
	23–50	70	154	178	70	2700 (2300–3100)	11.3
	51–75	70	154	178	70	2400 (2000–2800)	10.1
	76+	70	154	178	70	2050 (1650–2450)	8.6
Females	11–14	46	101	157	62	2200 (1500–3000)	9.2
	15–18	55	120	163	64	2100 (1200–3000)	8.8
	19–22	55	120	163	64	2100 (1700–2500)	8.8
	23–50	55	120	163	64	2000 (1600–2400)	8.4
	51–75	55	120	163	64	1800 (1400–2200)	7.6
	76+	55	120	163	64	1600 (1200–2000)	6.7
Pregnant						+300	
Lactating						+500	

[a] The data in this table have been assembled from the observed median heights and weights of children together with desirable weights for adults for the mean heights of men (70 inches) and women (64 inches) between the ages of 18 and 34 years as surveyed in the U.S. population (HEW/NCHS data).

The energy allowances for the young adults are for men and women doing light work. The allowances for the two older groups represent mean energy needs over these age spans, allowing for a 2% decrease in basal (resting) metabolic rate per decade and a reduction in activity of 200 kcal/day for men and women between 51 and 75 years, 500 kcal for men over 75 years and 400 kcal for women over 75. The customary range of daily energy output is shown in parentheses for adults, and is based on a variation in energy needs of ±400 kcal at any one age, emphasizing the wide range of energy intakes appropriate for any group of people.

Energy allowances for children through age 18 are based on median energy intakes of children of these ages followed in longitudinal growth studies. The values in parentheses are 10th and 90th percentiles of energy intake, to indicate the range of energy consumption among children of these ages.

Reproduced from National Academy of Sciences: Recommended Dietary Allowances, 9th rev. ed. Washington, DC, 1980

United States Recommended Daily Allowances (U.S. RDA)[a]

	Unit	Infants (birth–12 mo.)	Children under 4 yrs.	Adults and children 4 or more yrs.	Pregnant or lactating women
Protein[b]	g	25	28	65	—
Protein[c]	g	18	20	45	—
Vitamin A	IU	1500	2500	5000	8000
Vitamin D	IU	400	400	400	400
Vitamin E	IU	5	10	30	30
Vitamin C	mg	35	40	60	60
Folic Acid	mg	0.1	0.2	0.4	0.8
Thiamin (B_1)	mg	0.5	0.7	1.5	1.7
Riboflavin (B_2)	mg	0.6	0.8	1.7	2.0
Niacin	mg	8	9	20	20
Vitamin B_6	mg	0.4	0.7	2.0	2.5
Vitamin B_{12}	mcg	2	3	6	8
Biotin	mg	0.05	0.15	0.3	0.3
Pantothenic Acid	mg	3	5	10	10
Calcium	g	0.6	0.8	1.0	1.3
Phosphorus	g	0.5	0.8	1.0	1.3
Iodine	mcg	45	70	150	150
Iron	mg	15	10	18	18
Magnesium	mg	70	200	400	450
Copper	mg	0.6	1.0	2.0	2.0
Zinc	mg	5	8	15	15

[a] The U.S. RDAs are nutrient standards set by the Food and Drug Administration in 1973 using the Recommended Dietary Allowances of the National Academy of Sciences, National Research Council. The U.S. RDAs are established for four age–sex groups. Generally, the highest values in the RDA table were selected for use within each U.S. RDA category. The nutritional information on food labels is expressed as percent of the U.S. RDA.

[b] Protein efficiency ratio less than casein.
[c] Protein efficiency ratio greater than or equal to casein.

Reproduced from the FDA consumer memo, "Nutrition Labels and U.S. RDA." 81-2146, 1981.

Explanatory Notes

In the main table, entitled Nutrient Content of Foods, each food has two lines of nutrient data. The heading at the top of the page indicates the nutrients and units of measurement for the numerical values listed in the two lines. The abbreviated heading names and other abbreviations and symbols used throughout the text are listed on page xxv. Each food is identified by name, description, brand name (where applicable), and serving portion. The serving portion for most foods is listed in both household units and grams. For two food groups, Infant Formulas and Special Dietary Formulas, Commercial and Hospital, the nutrient format has four lines to include the complete nutrient profiles for these food items.

Foods are presented primarily in their table-ready form, although ingredient items (*e.g.,* flour, baking soda, herbs) are also listed. Brand names are used for some products (primarily ready-to-eat breakfast cereals, candy bars, and combination dishes) to help identify the items.

Serving portions are those suggested by the food manufacturer or USDA food-composition tables, or they are practical sizes adopted by the authors. Please note that food manufacturers may change the package or container sizes of food items, so that the portions listed here may not correspond to those currently available in grocery stores.

Foods are grouped on the basis of food type with concerns for common usage. To conserve space, each food is listed only once, although it could be applicable to several sections. Please use the index if you cannot locate an item.

There are many causes for nutrient variations in foods, such as soil content, season, geography, genetics, diet, processing, method of preparation, and method of analysis. The mean values listed here may have large standard deviations and wide ranges. Because of nutrient variation and the fact that the data are collected from various sources (the food industry, USDA food-composition tables, the scientific literature, and previous editions of Bowes and Church), inconsistencies may occur. Some of the data in the Supplementary Tables, especially those of the trace minerals, are tentative. The values are often derived from few samples and may not be representative of the entire U.S. food supply. Also, the values may represent several different analytical methodologies. Because the data are derived from various sources, portion sizes and gram weights may not be consistent among the Supplementary Tables or with the main table.

Please use these tables as approximate guides to the nutrient content of foods. Persons on special diets for various disease conditions may require more specific nutrient-composition data from food manufacturers.

Special Notes

For those unfamiliar with the use of food-composition tables, please note the following:

- Blank spaces denote lack of information. Do not assume that missing values are zeros.

- The mineral, (*e.g.,* sodium, iron) content of water varies considerably from one location to another. The mineral content of beverages made by addition of water (*e.g.,* coffee, tea, frozen concentrates, drink powders) and of foods cooked in water (*e.g.,* rice, oatmeal, pasta, vegetables) may vary considerably in mineral content depending on the mineral content of the water used. Likewise, the mineral content of commercial beverages (*e.g.,* beer, carbonated sodas, juice drinks) depends on the mineral content of the water in the area where the beverages are bottled.

Abbreviations and Symbols

am	American
amt	amount
ap	as purchased
arg	arginine
avg	average
bbq	barbeque
bio	biotin
blank space	insufficient information for nutrient values
Ca	calcium
caff	caffeine
cal	calorie(s)
calif	California
chln	choline
cho	carbohydrate
choc	chocolate
chol	cholesterol
cinn	cinnamon
ckd	cooked
Cl	chloride
cnd*	canned
combo	combination
conc	concentrate
cond	condensed
Cr	chromium
crm	cream
Cu	copper
cys	cystine
enr	enriched
Fe	iron
fibr	crude fiber
fl oz	fluid ounce
fol	folacin
frzn*	frozen
frzn bb*	frozen boil-in-bag
g	gram(s)
his	histidine
H_2O	water
hp	heaping
I	iodine
imit	imitation
inos	*myo*-inositol

inst	instant
iso	isoleucine
IU	international unit
jce	juice
jr	junior food
K	potassium
kcal	calorie(s)
lb	pound
leu	leucine
lys	lysine
marb	marbled
marg	margarine
mcg	microgram(s)
mct	medium-chain triglycerides
med	medium
met	methionine
mg	milligram(s)
Mg	magnesium
Mn	manganese
micro ckd	microwave cooked
Mo	molybdenum
Na	sodium
nfdm	nonfat dry milk solids
nia	niacin
orig	original
oz	ounce
P	phosphorus
pant	pantothenic acid
phe	phenylalanine
pkg	package
pkt	packet
prep	prepared
pro	protein
pufa	polyunsaturated fatty acids
rd	round
RE	retinol equivalents
recon	reconstituted
reg	regular
rib	riboflavin
rte	ready-to-eat
rts	ready-to-serve
sacc	saccharin
sce	sauce
Se	selenium

* *Canned (cnd)* and *frozen (frzn)* refer to commercially canned and frozen foods.

sec	second	vit B-1	vitamin B-1 (thiamine)
sfa	saturated fatty acids	vit B-2	vitamin B-2 (riboflavin)
std	standard	vit B-6	vitamin B-6 (pyridoxine)
str	strained baby food	vit B-12	vitamin B-12 (cobalamin)
sub	substitute	vit C	vitamin C (ascorbic acid)
t	teaspoon	vit D	vitamin D
T	tablespoon	vit E	vitamin E (tocopherol)
thi	thiamin	vit K	vitamin K
thr	threonine	vol	volume
tr	trace	whpd	whipped
try	tryptophan	wt	weight
tyr	tyrosine	w/	with
unenr	unenriched	w/o	without
val	valine	Zn	zinc
van	vanilla	&	and
veg	vegetable	0	zero/none
vit A	vitamin A	/	per/or

Conversion Tables

Volume Measures

$1\ t = \frac{1}{3}\ T\quad = \frac{1}{6}\ \text{fl oz}\ = 4.9\ \text{ml}$

$3\ t = 1\ T\quad = \frac{1}{2}\ \text{fl oz}\ = 14.8\ \text{ml}$

$2\ T = \frac{1}{8}\ \text{cup} = 1\ \text{fl oz}\ = 29.6\ \text{ml}$

$4\ T = \frac{1}{4}\ \text{cup} = 2\ \text{fl oz}\ = 59.1\ \text{ml}$

$5\frac{1}{3}\ T = \frac{1}{3}\ \text{cup} = 2\frac{2}{3}\ \text{fl oz} = 78.9\ \text{ml}$

$8\ T = \frac{1}{2}\ \text{cup} = 4\ \text{fl oz}\ = 118.3\ \text{ml}$

$10\frac{2}{3}\ T = \frac{2}{3}\ \text{cup} = 5\frac{1}{3}\ \text{fl oz} = 157.7\ \text{ml}$

$12\ T = \frac{3}{4}\ \text{cup} = 6\ \text{fl oz}\ = 177.4\ \text{ml}$

$14\ T = \frac{7}{8}\ \text{cup} = 7\ \text{fl oz}\ = 207.0\ \text{ml}$

$16\ T = 1\ \text{cup} = 8\ \text{fl oz}\ = 236.6\ \text{ml}$

1 ml = .034 fl oz = 1 cc = .001 liter
1 liter = 34 fl oz = 1000 ml

1 pint = 2 cups = .473 l = 473 ml
1 quart = 2 pt = .9464 l = 946 ml
1 gallon = 4 quarts = 3.785 l
1 liter = 1.057 quarts = 0.264 gallon = 1000 ml

Weight Measures

1 g = .035 oz = .001 kg = 1000 mg = 1,000,000 mcg
1 mg = .001 g = 1000 mcg
1 oz = 28.35 g (often rounded to 28 g)
1 lb = 16 oz = 453.59 g = .454 kg
1 kg = 2.21 lb = 1000 g
1 kg = 100 g = 3.52 oz

Heat Measures

1 kilojoule = 4.184 kilocalories
1 kilocalorie = .004 kilojoules

The relationship between volume measures and weight measures is variable depending on the food. For example, the weights of 1 cup of chopped almonds, cottage cheese, orange juice, canned green peas, pickle relish, chicken noodle soup, whole milk, mayonnaise, shredded wheat, puffed wheat, and peanut butter are as follows:

Food	Weight of 1 level cup
almonds, chopped	127 g
cottage cheese	233 g
orange juice	244 g
peas, green, canned	172 g
pickle relish	243 g
chicken noodle soup	230 g
milk, whole	244 g
mayonnaise	221 g
shredded wheat	35 g
puffed wheat	12 g
peanut butter	251 g

The volume weight of water is a commonly used reference point for other food measures.

1 T water = 15 g = 15 cc
1 cup water = 237 g
1 fl oz water = 29.54 g (often rounded to 30 g)
1 cc water = 1 g = 1 ml
1 liter water = 1 kg = 1000 g
1 quart water = 946 g = .946 kg

Nutrient Content of Foods

		Vitamins					Minerals			
	KCAL	**H₂O** (g)	**FAT** (g)	**PUFA** (g)	**CHOL** (mg)	**A** (RE)	**C** (mg)	**B-2** (mg)	**B-6** (mg)	**FOL** (mcg)	**Na** (mg)	**Ca** (mg)	**Mg** (mg)	**Zn** (mg)	**Mn** (mg)
	WT (g)	**PRO** (g)	**CHO** (g)	**SFA** (g)	**FIBR** (g)	**A** (IU)	**B-1** (mg)	**NIA** (mg)	**B-12** (mcg)	**PANT** (mg)	**K** (mg)	**P** (mg)	**Fe** (mg)	**Cu** (mg)	

BEVERAGES
ALCOHOLIC[a]

	KCAL / WT	H₂O / PRO	FAT / CHO	PUFA / SFA	CHOL / FIBR	A(RE) / A(IU)	C / B-1	B-2 / NIA	B-6 / B-12	FOL / PANT	Na / K	Ca / P	Mg / Fe	Zn / Cu	Mn
ale, mild	98	211.8	0.0				0	.07				30			
8 fl oz	230	1.1	8.0			0	tr	0.5				41	.20		
beer, alcohol 4.5% by vol (3.6% by wt)	148	332.5	0.0				0	.07	.18	20	18	14	36	.18	.032
12 fl oz	360	0.9	13.2				.00	1.8		.17	115	50	.11	.29	
beer, light	100[b]		0.0												
12 fl oz	360	0.4	6.0[b]												
cordials & liqueurs, 54 proof	97	15.0	0.0				0				1	0	0	.02	
(22.1% alcohol by wt)—1 fl oz	34		11.5								1	0	.02	.03	
daiquiri	122						8	tr				4			
1 cocktail glass (3½ fl oz)	100	0.1	5.2			0	.01	tr				3	.10		
eggnog	335	85.8	15.8					tr	.11			44			
1 punch cup (4 fl oz)	123	3.9	18.0			84	.04	tr				74	.70		
gin/rum/vodka/whisky															
80 proof	65	18.6	0.0				0	.00			0	30	0	.00	
1 fl oz	28		0.0	tr		0	.00	0.0			1	0	.01	.02	
86 proof	70	17.9	0.0				0	.00			0	30	0	.00	
1 fl oz	28		0.0	tr		0	.00	0.0			1	0	.01	.02	
90 proof	74	17.4	0.0				0	.00			0	30	0	.00	
1 fl oz	28		0.0	tr		0	.00	0.0			1	0	.01	.02	
94 proof	77	16.9	0.0				0	.00			0	30	0	.00	
1 fl oz	28		0.0	tr		0	.00	0.0			1	0	.01	.02	
100 proof	83	16.1	0.0				0	.00			0	30	0	.00	
1 fl oz	28		0.0	tr		0	.00	0.0			1	0	.01	.02	
gin rickey	150						4	tr				2			
4 fl oz	120	tr	1.3				.01	tr				1	tr		
manhattan	164						0	tr				1			
1 cocktail (3½ fl oz)	100	tr	7.9			35	tr	tr				1	tr		
martini	140						0	tr				5			
1 cocktail (3½ fl oz)	100	0.1	0.3			4	tr	tr				1	.10		
planter's punch	175						8	tr				4			
3½ fl oz	100	0.1	7.9			0	.01	tr				3	.10		
tom collins	180						21	tr				6			
10 fl oz	300	0.3	9.0			0	tr	tr				6	tr		
whisky sour	138		0.0				8	.00			1	2			
1 cocktail (2½ fl oz)	75	0.2	7.7			4	.02				94	3			
wine															
champagne	84														
1 wine glass (4 fl oz)	120	0.2	3.0												
dessert, dry, alcohol 18.8% by vol	126	79.0	0.0				0	.02	.05	2	7	9	4	.06	
1 wine glass (3½ fl oz)	103	0.1	4.1				.02	0.2		.02	102		1.61	.06	
dessert, sweet, alcohol 18.8% by vol	153	75.5	0.0				0	.02	.05	2	7	9	4	.06	.102
1 wine glass (3½ fl oz)	103	0.1	11.4				.02	0.2		.02	102		1.61	.06	
muscatel/port	158							.01				4	8		
1 wine glass (3½ fl oz)	100	0.2	14.0				.01	0.2			75				
sauterne	84														
1 wine glass (3½ fl oz)	100	0.2	4.0												
sherry	84							.01				2	5		
2 fl oz	60	0.2	4.8				.01	0.1			45				
table, red, alcohol 11.5% by vol	76		0.0				0	.03	.04	1	10	8	11	.10	.177
1 wine glass (3½ fl oz)	102	0.2	2.5				.01	0.1		.04	116	13	.97	.03	
table, white, alcohol 11.5% by vol	80		0.0				0	.01	.01	0	7	7	8	.17	.205
1 wine glass (3½ fl oz)	102	0.2	3.4				.00	0.1		.02	84	13	.58	.03	
vermouth, dry (french)	105							.01				4	8		
1 wine glass (3½ fl oz)	100	1.0					.01	0.2			75				

[a] Additional information on alcoholic beverages is available in the Supplementary Table "Alcoholic Beverages—Caloric, Carbohydrate, and Alcoholic Content."

[b] Values vary considerably among different brands.

3

COFFEE, TEA, CEREAL COFFEE

	KCAL / WT (g)	H₂O (g) / PRO (g)	FAT (g) / CHO (g)	PUFA (g) / SFA (g)	CHOL (mg) / FIBR (g)	A (RE) / A (IU)	C (mg) / B-1 (mg)	B-2 (mg) / NIA (mg)	B-6 (mg) / B-12 (mcg)	FOL (mcg) / PANT (mg)	Na (mg) / K (mg)	Ca (mg) / P (mg)	Mg (mg) / Fe (mg)	Zn (mg) / Cu (mg)	Mn (mg)
cereal coffee	11	177.0	tr	tr	0		0	.01	.03		3	1	10	.009	.016
1 t (3 g) in 6 fl oz water	181	0.2	2.6	tr	0.0	0	.01	0.7	tr	.03	97	21	.21	.014	
coffee															
brewed	3		tr				0	.02			2	13	13	.05	.022
6 fl oz	180	tr	0.5			0	.00	1.3			117	4	.02	.01	
from inst	3	180.0	tr				0	.00	tr		1	3	8	.02	.040
2 t (2 g) powder in 6 fl oz water	182	tr	0.8			0	.00	0.5		.01	72	7	.08	.01	
from freeze dried	4	180.2	tr								1				
1.8 g crystals in 6 fl oz water	182	tr	1.0								72				
decaffeinated, from inst	4	178.2	tr								1				
1.8 g powder in 6 fl oz water	180	tr	1.0								72				
decaffeinated, from freeze dried	4	178.2	tr								1				
1.8 g crystals in 6 fl oz	180	tr	1.0								72				
coffee, flavored, from inst															
almond mocha	85		1.4			0						0			
8 fl oz	240	0.0	15.5			0	.00						.00		
bavarian mint	82		1.4			0						0			
8 fl oz	240	0.0	16.9			0	.00						.00		
cafe, amaretto	51	173.7	2.4	tr	tr	0	.03	tr	0		26	7	9	.011	
6 fl oz	185	0.2	7.0	2.1	0.0	0	tr	0.7	.00	.00	220	50	.12	.025	
cafe capri	62		1.4			0						0			
8 fl oz	240	0.0	14.1			0	.00						.00		
cafe francais	58	173.8	3.4	0.1	tr	0	.02	tr	0		24	4	9	.011	
6 fl oz	185	0.6	6.7	2.9	0.0	tr	tr	0.7	.00	.00	248	41	.15	.027	
cafe, irish mocha mint	54	173.7	2.6	tr	tr	0	.02	tr	0		25	5	12	.006	
6 fl oz	185	0.7	7.3	2.2	0.1	tr	tr	0.2	.00	.00	236	37	.32	.014	
cafe, mocha	82		1.4			0						0			
8 fl oz	240	0.0	16.9			0	.00						.00		
cafe vienna	64	173.0	2.4	tr	tr	0	tr	tr	0		94	6	9	.013	
6 fl oz	187	0.5	10.5	2.1	0.0	0	tr	0.5	.00	tr	127	28	.06	.025	
cafe viennese	62		1.4			0	.05					0			
8 fl oz	240	0.0	12.7				.00	0.6					.00		
irish mocha	50		2.0								98				
6 fl oz	187	1.0	7.0		tr						135				
orange cappuccino	64	173.1	2.4	tr	0	0	.03	tr	0		100	4	10	.013	
6 fl oz	187	0.6	10.4	2.0	0.0	0	tr	0.4	.00	tr	124	29	.21	.027	
suisse mocha	56	173.7	2.8	tr	tr	0	.02	tr	0		23	4	9	.007	
6 fl oz	185	0.6	7.5	2.4	tr	tr	tr	0.2	.00	.00	149	35	.23	.018	
sunrise	6	178.1	tr								5				
1.89 g powder in 6 fl oz water	180	tr	1.0								64				
tea															
brewed	0		tr								19	5	5	.07	1.193
8 fl oz	240	0.0	tr				.00				58	10	.10	.03	
from inst	0	240.0	tr				.02				1	0	3	.04	.752
1 t (1 g) powder in 8 fl oz water	241	0.0	tr				.00	0.1			50	4	.04	.01	
herb, brewed	0		0.0								1				
8 fl oz	240	0.0	0.0								tr				
lemon flavored, from inst	2	179.0	0.0								8				
1 t (1 g) powder in 6 fl oz water	180	0.0	0.2								56				
sweetened, from inst	86	240.0	0.1					.04			13	1	3	.02	.667
3 t (23 g) powder in 8 fl oz water	263	0.0	22.1				.00	0.1			49	3	.04	.01	
tea, iced															
lemon flavored, from inst	2	238.7	0.0								11				
1.3 g powder in 8 fl oz water	240	0.0	0.2								81				

	KCAL	H₂O (g)	FAT (g)	PUFA (g)	CHOL (mg)	A (RE)	C (mg)	B-2 (mg)	B-6 (mg)	FOL (mcg)	Na (mg)	Ca (mg)	Mg (mg)	Zn (mg)	Mn (mg)
	WT (g)	PRO (g)	CHO (g)	SFA (g)	FIBR (g)	A (IU)	B-1 (mg)	NIA (mg)	B-12 (mcg)	PANT (mg)	K (mg)	P (mg)	Fe (mg)	Cu (mg)	
sweetened, cnd	146		0.0	0.0			0	.00			13				
12 fl oz	360	0.0	36.5			0	.00	0.0			94				

CARBONATED

	KCAL	H₂O (g)	FAT (g)	PUFA (g)	CHOL (mg)	A (RE)	C (mg)	B-2 (mg)	B-6 (mg)	FOL (mcg)	Na (mg)	Ca (mg)	Mg (mg)	Zn (mg)	Mn (mg)
	WT (g)	PRO (g)	CHO (g)	SFA (g)	FIBR (g)	A (IU)	B-1 (mg)	NIA (mg)	B-12 (mcg)	PANT (mg)	K (mg)	P (mg)	Fe (mg)	Cu (mg)	
bitter lemon	192		0.0								60				
12 fl oz	360	0.0	47.3												
cactus cooler	183		0.0												
12 fl oz	360	0.0	45.7												
coca-cola	144		0.0				0				14				
12 fl oz	370	0.0	37.5								tr	60			
cola soda	159		0.0				0	.00	.00		20	11	4	.15	
12 fl oz	369	0.0	40.7	0.0		0	.00	0.0			7	62	.18	.10	
cream soda	156		0.0				0	.00	.00		51	18	4	.26	
12 fl oz	371	0.0	40.5	0.0		0	.00	0.0			4	0	.18	.03	
fruit punch soda	182		0.0	0.0		0	0	.00			16	0	0		
12 fl oz	330	0.0	45.6	0.0		0	.00	0.0			0	0	.00		
ginger ale	113		0.0				0	.00	.00		30	11	4	.04	
12 fl oz	366	0.0	29.0			0	.00	0.0			5	0	.15	.01	
grape soda	179		0.0				0	.00	.00		50	15	4	.30	
12 fl oz	372	0.0	45.8	0.0		0	.00	0.0			4	0	.37	.09	
lemon-lime soda	144		0.0								43				
12 fl oz	360	0.0	39.6								2	1			
mello yello	173		0.0				tr				27				
12 fl oz	370	0.0	45.0								9	tr			
mountain dew	171		0.0								31	tr			
12 fl oz	360	0.0	42.8								9	0	.10		
mr. pibb	143		0.0				0				21				
12 fl oz	370	0.0	37.5								tr	42			
orange soda	179		0.0				0	.00	.00		52	15	4	.26	
12 fl oz	372	0.0	45.8	0.0		0	.00	0.0			37	13	.26	.07	
peach soda	184		0.0	0.0		0	0	.00			33	0	0		
12 fl oz	330	0.0	46.1	0.0		0	.00	0.0			0	0	.00		
pepper type soda	159		0.0				0	.00	.00		36	11	0	.15	
12 fl oz	369	0.0	40.7	0.0		0	.00	0.0			3	42	.15	.02	
pepsi cola	156		0.0								9	tr			
12 fl oz	360	0.0	39.4								13	54	.10		
quinine water[a]	37	110.4									8	12			
4 fl oz	120	0.0	9.6												
RC 100 (caffeine-free cola)	156		0.0	0.0		0	0	.00			1	0	0		
12 fl oz	330	0.0	38.9	0.0	0.0	0	.00	0.0				47	.00		
root beer	163		0.0				0	.00	.00		49	15	4	.22	
12 fl oz	370	0.0	42.2	0.0		0	.00	0.0			4	2	.18	.02	
royal crown cola	156		0.0	0.0		0	0	.00			1	0	0		
12 fl oz	330	0.0	38.9	0.0	0.0	0	.00	0.0			1	47	.00		
seven-up	144		0.0								4	0			
12 fl oz	360	0.0	36.0								0	0	.00		
sprite	144						0				47	11			
12 fl oz	360	0.0	36.0								0	0			
strawberry soda	174		0.0	0.0		0	0	.00			14	0	0		
12 fl oz	330	0.0	43.6	0.0		0	.00	0.0			0	94	.00		
teem	150		0.0								31	tr			
12 fl oz	360	0.0	37.0									0	tr		
tonic water	42		0.0								2	0			
4 fl oz	122	0.0	10.4								1				
upper 10	152		0.0	0.0		0	0	.00			40	0			
12 fl oz	300	0.0	38.0		0.0	0	.00	0.0			0	0			
van cream	204		0.0								27				
12 fl oz	360	0.0	51.1												
vernors	139		0.0								12				
12 fl oz	360	1.4	33.3												
wink	193		0.0								31	0			
12 fl oz	360	0.0	48.3								0	0			

[a] Sweetened carbonated water

	KCAL	H₂O (g)	FAT (g)	PUFA (g)	CHOL (mg)		A (RE)	C (mg)	B-2 (mg)	B-6 (mg)	FOL (mcg)		Na (mg)	Ca (mg)	Mg (mg)	Zn (mg)	Mn (mg)
	WT (g)	PRO (g)	CHO (g)	SFA (g)	FIBR (g)		A (IU)	B-1 (mg)	NIA (mg)	B-12 (mcg)	PANT (mg)		K (mg)	P (mg)	Fe (mg)	Cu (mg)	

CARBONATED, LOW CALORIE

Item	KCAL / WT	H₂O / PRO	FAT / CHO	PUFA / SFA	CHOL / FIBR	A(RE) / A(IU)	C / B-1	B-2 / NIA	B-6 / B-12	FOL / PANT	Na / K	Ca / P	Mg / Fe	Zn / Cu	Mn
club soda/seltzer/sparkling water^a	0		0.0			0	.00	.00			78	18	4		
12 fl oz	355	0.0	0.0		0.0	0	.00	0.0			1	0			
diet coke	1		0.0			0					33				
12 fl oz	370	0.0	0.4								tr	27			
diet mr. pibb	1		0.0			0					39				
12 fl oz	370	0.0	0.4								tr	39			
diet pepsi	1		0.0								63	tr			
12 fl oz	360	0.0	0.2								12	51	.10		
diet rite	1		0.0	0.0		0	0	.00			37	0	0		
12 fl oz	355	0.0	0.1	0.0	0.0		.00	0.0			1	38	.00		
diet RC 100 (caffeine-free cola)	1		0.0	0.0		0	0	.00			37	0	0		
12 fl oz	355	0.0	0.1	0.0	0.0	0	.00	0.0			1	38	.00		
diet root beer	1		0.0			0					59				
12 fl oz	370	0.0	0.4								tr	0			
diet seven-up	4		0.0												
12 fl oz	360	0.0	0.0												
diet soda, all flavors	0		0.0			0	.00	.00			76	14	4	.78	
12 fl oz	355	0.0	0.4	0.0		0	.00	0.0			6	15	.46	.06	
diet sprite	3		0.0			0					45				
12 fl oz	370	0.0	0.0								tr	0			
fresca	4		0.0			0					36				
12 fl oz	360	0.0	0.1								tr	0			
mineral water, Perrier	0		0.0			0	.00	.00			5	33	0		
8 fl oz	236	0.0	0.0	0.0		0	.00	0.0			0	0	.00		
pepsi light	1		0.0								42	tr			
12 fl oz	360	0.0	0.1								12	27	.10		
tab	1		0.0			0					27				
12 fl oz	360	0.0	0.1								tr	45			

NONCARBONATED (PUNCHES, JUICE DRINKS,^b FRUIT ADES, ETC.)

Item	KCAL / WT	H₂O / PRO	FAT / CHO	PUFA / SFA	CHOL / FIBR	A(RE) / A(IU)	C / B-1	B-2 / NIA	B-6 / B-12	FOL / PANT	Na / K	Ca / P	Mg / Fe	Zn / Cu	Mn
apple jce drink, cnd	92	157.7	tr				60				12				
6 fl oz	180	0.7	23.0		tr						21		.39		
awake,^c from frzn conc	91	163.2	0.3	0.2	0		90	.01			15	59	tr	.007	
6 fl oz	186	0.1	21.9	0.1	0.1	0	.15	tr	.00		237	33	.71	.061	
bright & early,^c from frzn conc	90	162.2	0.7				60				15				
6 fl oz	186	0.1	21.6		tr						340				
cherry jce drink, cnd	93	157.5	tr				60				4				
6 fl oz	180	0.6	23.0		tr						24				
citrus cooler fruit drink, cnd	93	157.5	tr				60				4				
6 fl oz	180	0.7	23.0		0.2						36				
cranberry-apple jce drink, cnd	135		1.0				61	.04			13	10	4	.34	
6 fl oz	190	0.1	34.5		0.0		.01	0.1			53	4	.23	.02	
five alive citrus, from frzn conc	85	166.3	0.1				55	.02	.04	3	1	11	13		
6 fl oz	189	0.9	20.8		0.1	232	.10	0.4		.19	227	18	.14		
five alive fruit punch, from frzn conc	87	170.7	tr				6	.02	.02	22	1	8	6		
6 fl oz	194	0.2	22.7		0.1	20	.02	0.1		.12	123	10	.83		
florida punch jce drink, cnd	95	157.0	tr				60				3				
6 fl oz	180	0.6	24.0		0.2						35				
fruit jce drink, from mix^d	70	163.2					60				18	25			
6 fl oz	181		17.6									12			
fruit punch jce drink, cnd	99		tr				64	.05			27	6	4	.10	
6 fl oz	190	0.1	25.2		0.0		.04	tr			36	0	.11	.02	
gatorade	39		0.0								123	23			
8 fl oz	230	0.0	10.5								23	0			
grape jce drink, cnd	89	158.2	tr				60				tr				
6 fl oz	180	0.1	22.0								10				

^a All are unsweetened carbonated water
^b Juice drinks contain 10%–50% fruit jce and may have vit C added as a preservative or nutrient.
^c Imitation orange jce
^d Values are averages for 9 flavors.

	KCAL / WT (g)	H₂O (g) / PRO (g)	FAT (g) / CHO (g)	PUFA (g) / SFA (g)	CHOL (mg) / FIBR (g)	A (RE) / A (IU)	C (mg) / B-1 (mg)	B-2 (mg) / NIA (mg)	B-6 (mg) / B-12 (mcg)	FOL (mcg) / PANT (mg)	Na (mg) / K (mg)	Ca (mg) / P (mg)	Mg (mg) / Fe (mg)	Zn (mg) / Cu (mg)	Mn (mg)
hawaiian punch, cnd	120	tr					40	.08			50	20			
8 fl oz	250	0.1	29.3			125	.05	0.1			63	8	.30		
kool-aid, from mix, all flavors[a]	95	221.0	0.0	0.0	0		6	.00	.00	0	4	3	tr	tr	
8 fl oz	246	0.0	24.2	0.0	0.0	0	.00	0.0	.00	.00	7	21	.02	tr	
lemonade,[b] cnd	138	330.9	0.0	0.0	0		33	.00	.00	0	92	tr	tr	.02	
12 fl oz	368	0.0	34.4	0.0	0.0	0	.00	0.0	.00	.00	11	tr	.03	.007	
lemonade,[b] from frzn conc	94	220.2	tr	tr	0		15	.00	tr		26	80	tr	.010	
8 fl oz	246	tr	23.9	tr	tr	1	.03	tr	.00	tr	100	92	.80	.68	
lemonade,[b] from mix	89	220.3	tr	tr	0		9	.00	.00	0	30			tr	
8 fl oz	244	0.0	22.1	tr	tr	0	.00	.00	.00	.00	16	tr	.02		
lemon-lime, from mix	91	219.8	tr	tr	0		9	.00	.00	0	30			tr	
8 fl oz	244	0.0	22.6	tr	tr	0	.00	0.0	.00	.00	10	tr	.02		
limeade, from frzn conc	75	163.6	tr				5	tr			tr	2			
6 fl oz	184	0.1	20.1		tr		tr	tr			23	2	.04		
orange jce drink, cnd	92	157.7	tr				60				58				
6 fl oz	180	0.8	23.0								35				
orange plus,[c] from frzn conc	97	162.1	0.4	0.2	0		90	.76	.08	60	9	41	16	.009	
6 fl oz	187	0.2	23.6	0.1	0.1	31	.15	0.4	.00	.20	281	64	.64	.160	
orange-pineapple jce drink, cnd	94	157.3	tr				60				1				
6 fl oz	180	0.6	23.0		0.1	576					64				
peach jce drink, cnd	90	157.3	tr				60		.01	tr	tr	2	2		
6 fl oz	180	0.2	23.0		0.1	145	.01	0.1		.03	38	3	.06		
pineapple-grapefruit jce drink, cnd	95		0.1				51	.04		20	41	11	11	.09	
6 fl oz	187	0.4	23.8		0.0	4	.04	0.5			103	7	.60	.06	
pineapple-orange jce drink, cnd	99		0.0				46	.04	.09		6	9	11	.11	
6 fl oz	187	0.4	23.9		0.0	993	.06	0.4		.09	90	7	.50	.08	
strawberry jce drink, cnd	89	158.4	tr				60				tr				
6 fl oz	180	0.6	22.0								7				
tang, grape	89	162.5	0.0	0.0	0		60	.00	.00	0	5	40	0	tr	
3 rd t in 6 fl oz water	186	0.0	22.9	0.0	tr	500	.00	0.0	.00	.00	1	77	.02		
tang, grapefruit	87	162.5	0.0	0.0	0		60	.00	.00	0	1	40		tr	
3 rd t in 6 fl oz water	186	0.0	21.5	0.0	0	500	.00	0.0	.00	.00	1	38	.02		
tang, orange	89	162.5	tr	tr	0		60	.00	.00	0	1	40	tr	tr	
3 rd t in 6 fl oz water	186	0.0	22.2	tr	tr	500	.00	0.0	.00	.00	50	31	.02		
tangerine jce drink, cnd	90	157.5	tr				60	tr	.01	tr	tr	2	2		
6 fl oz	180	0.1	23.0		tr	43	.02	0.1		.03	38	3	.02		
wild berry jce drink, cnd	88	158.6	tr				60				5				
6 fl oz	180	0.6	22.0		tr						32		.39		

CANDY & CANDY BARS
CANDY

	KCAL / WT (g)	H₂O (g) / PRO (g)	FAT (g) / CHO (g)	PUFA (g) / SFA (g)	CHOL (mg) / FIBR (g)	A (RE) / A (IU)	C (mg) / B-1 (mg)	B-2 (mg) / NIA (mg)	B-6 (mg) / B-12 (mcg)	FOL (mcg) / PANT (mg)	Na (mg) / K (mg)	Ca (mg) / P (mg)	Mg (mg) / Fe (mg)	Zn (mg) / Cu (mg)	Mn (mg)
butterscotch	116	0.4	2.5				0	tr			19	6			
6 pieces	28	0.0	24.3			39	0	tr			1	2	.50		
butterscotch chips	150		7.0		tr		20								
1 oz	28	1.0	19.0								50				
caramels, plain/choc	112	2.1	2.9					.05			63	41	1		
3 pieces	28	1.1	21.5		0.1	3	.01	0.1			54	34	.40		
caramels, plain/choc w/nuts	120	2.0	4.6					.05			57	39			
2 pieces	28	1.3	19.7		0.1	6	.03	0.1			65	39	.40		
choc chips, dark	148		8.0					tr			64	8			
1 oz	28	1.7	17.5		0.4	6	tr	0.1			81	50	1.23		
choc chips, milk choc	218		11.0		7			.11			55	80	23	.38	.13
¼ cup	42	3.0	26.9		0.1	25	.03	0.1			34	113	.50	.13	
choc chips, semi-sweet	220		12.2					.04			8	13	46	.71	.34
¼ cup	42	2.4	25.5		1.2	25	.02	0.1			126	44	1.26	.29	
choc chips, choc flavored	195	0.3	8.4	3.9	tr		0	.05			10	13	20		
¼ cup	43	1.4	31.9	1.7	0.2	1	.01	0.1			57	43	.52	.005	

[a] Values are averages for 12 flavors.
[b] Includes pink lemonade
[c] Imitation orange jce

	KCAL	H₂O (g)	FAT (g)	PUFA (g)	CHOL (mg)	A (RE)	C (mg)	B-2 (mg)	B-6 (mg)	FOL (mcg)	Na (mg)	Ca (mg)	Mg (mg)	Zn (mg)	Mn (mg)
	WT (g)	PRO (g)	CHO (g)	SFA (g)	FIBR (g)	A (IU)	B-1 (mg)	NIA (mg)	B-12 (mcg)	PANT (mg)	K (mg)	P (mg)	Fe (mg)	Cu (mg)	
choc covered															
almonds	159	0.6	12.2				tr	.15			17	57	11		
1 oz	28	3.4	11.1		0.4	15	.03	0.5			153	96	.80		
brazil nuts	162		14.1								13	57			
1 oz	28	3.1	8.9		0.5						154	137			
choc fudge center	129	1.9	4.8				0	.04			68	30			
1 piece	30	1.1	21.9		0.1		.01	0.1			58	33	.40		
choc fudge w/nuts center	127	1.7	5.8					.04			57	28			
1 piece	28	1.4	18.8		0.1		.02	0.1			61	38	.40		
coconut center	123	1.8	4.9				0	.02			55	13			
1 piece	28	0.8	20.2		0.2	0	.01	0.1			46	22	.30		
cream center	102		3.6								2				
1 piece	28	1.0	18.8		0.0						30				
fondant center	115	1.6	2.9					.02			52	16			
1 piece	28	0.5	22.7		tr		.01	tr			26	15	.30		
peanuts	153	0.9	9.0					.06				23			
1 oz	28	4.6	13.3			51	.02	2.1					.68		
raisins	115	3.7	3.7					.12				27			
1 oz	28	1.0	19.5			49	.02	0.2					.54		
van cream center	114	2.1	4.4					.02			48	34			
1 piece	28	1.0	18.2		tr		.02	tr			46	28	.20		
choc kisses	154		9.0					.08			25	53	18	.36	.08
6 pieces	28	2.1	15.9		0.3	17	.02	0.1			115	87	.50	.11	
choc stars	145		8.1								26	64			
7 pieces	28	2.2	17.0		0.1						108	65			
creme eggs, Cadbury	136		6.0												
1 oz	28	1.3	19.2												
english toffee	193		16.7				0	.04			79	0			
1 oz	28	0.9	9.7		0.1	21	.05	0.1			44	0	.18		
fondant	40	0.8	0.2				0				23	2			
1 piece	11	tr	9.9			0					1	1	.10		
food sticks,ᵃ Pillsbury	180		6.0								130				
4 sticks		4.0	27.0												
fudge, choc	112	2.3	3.4				tr	.03			53	22	14		
1 oz	28	0.8	21.0		0.1	66	.01	0.1			41	24	.30		
fudge, choc w/nuts	119	2.2	4.9					.03			48	22			
1 oz	28	1.1	19.3		0.1		.01	0.1			50	32	.30		
fudge, van	111	2.8	3.1					.04			58	31	14		
1 oz	28	0.8	20.9		0.0		.01	tr			36	23	.10		
fudge, van w/nuts	119	2.6	4.6					.04			52	31			
1 oz	28	1.2	19.3		0.1		.01	tr			32	32	.20		
good & fruity	160		tr									3			
1.5 oz pkg	43	0.3	40.0									4			
good & plenty	151		0.1									69			
1.5 oz pkg	43	tr	37.4									tr			
gum drops	97	3.3	0.2				0	.00			10	2			
28 pieces	28	tr	24.5		0.0	0	.00	0.0			1	0	.10		
hard candy	108	0.4	0.3				0	.00			9	6			
6 pieces	28	0.0	27.2		0.0	0		0.0			1	2	.50		
jelly beans	66	1.8	0.0				0				3	3			
10 pieces	28	0.0	16.7		0.0	0	.00				tr	1	.30		
life savers	39		0.1				0	.00			3	2			
5 pieces	10	0.0	9.7		0.0	0	.00	0.0			tr	1	.20		
lollipop	108		0.0				0	.00				0			
1 med	28	0.0	28.0		0.0	0	.00					0	.00		
m & ms	220		10.0												
1.59 oz pkg	45	3.0	31.0												
m & ms, peanut	240		12.0												
1.67 oz pkg	47	5.0	28.0												
malted milk balls	135		7.0								28	63			
14 pieces	28	2.3	17.8		0.1						113	86			

ᵃ Avg values for caramel, choc, choc malt, choc mint, orange & peanut butter; contains 6% of the U.S. RDA for vit A, vit C, vit B-1, vit B-2, niacin, vit B-6, vit B-12, folacin, vit D, vit E, Ca, P, Mg, Fe & I.

	KCAL / WT (g)	H₂O (g) / PRO (g)	FAT (g) / CHO (g)	PUFA (g) / SFA (g)	CHOL (mg) / FIBR (g)	A (RE) / A (IU)	C (mg) / B-1 (mg)	B-2 (mg) / NIA (mg)	B-6 (mg) / B-12 (mcg)	FOL (mcg) / PANT (mg)	Na (mg) / K (mg)	Ca (mg) / P (mg)	Mg (mg) / Fe (mg)	Zn (mg) / Cu (mg)	Mn (mg)
marshmallow	25	1.4	0				0				4	1			
1 large	8	0.2	6.2		0.0	0	.00				1	1	.10		
mints	104		0.6								47	2			
14 pieces	28	0.0	25.6		0.0						1	tr			
peanut brittle	123	0.6	4.4				0	.01			9	11			
1 oz	28	2.4	20.4			8	.02	1.3			43	35	.56		
peanut butter cups, Reese's	184		10.7	3.0	5			.06			109	29	29	.48	.27
2 pieces	34	4.4	17.4	6.0	0.3	7	.01	1.6			136	82	.48	.14	
peanut butter flavored chips, Reese's	223		12.5					.08			90	46	46	.84	.59
¼ cup	42	8.7	18.9		0.5	8	.02	3.4			212	130	.71	.17	
reese's pieces	240		10.0					.12			74	69	42	.69	.294
1.7 oz pkg	49	7.1	30.0		0.3		.02	2.8			191	118	.78	.20	
rolo	139		6.4					.02			62	73	8	.20	.06
5 pieces	28	1.3	19.0		0.1	17	.06	0.1			73	45	.34	.03	
sno-caps	132	0.7	4.3					.15				7			
1 oz	28	1.0	22.2			47	.01	0.1					.53		
sugar-coated almonds	128	0.6	5.2				0	.08			6	28			
7 pieces	28	2.2	19.7		0.1	0	.01	0.3			71	47	.50		

CANDY BARS

	KCAL / WT (g)	H₂O (g) / PRO (g)	FAT (g) / CHO (g)	PUFA (g) / SFA (g)	CHOL (mg) / FIBR (g)	A (RE) / A (IU)	C (mg) / B-1 (mg)	B-2 (mg) / NIA (mg)	B-6 (mg) / B-12 (mcg)	FOL (mcg) / PANT (mg)	Na (mg) / K (mg)	Ca (mg) / P (mg)	Mg (mg) / Fe (mg)	Zn (mg) / Cu (mg)	Mn (mg)
almond joy	151		7.8												
1 oz	28	1.7	18.5												
bit-o-honey	121	2.3	3.6					.13				13			
1 oz	28	0.9	21.2				tr	1.4					.25		
bit-o-honey	220	4.2	6.6					.24				24			
1.8 oz	51	1.3	38.6				tr	2.6					.46		
butter nut	250		12.0												
1.8 oz	51	5.0	29.0												
caramello	144		7.8												
1 oz	28	1.7	16.7												
caravelle	137		5.1												
1 oz	28	1.7	21.0												
choc almond, Cadbury	155		9.0												
1 oz	28	2.9	15.5												
choc brazil nut, Cadbury	156		9.3												
1 oz	28	2.6	15.3												
choc, german sweet, Baker's	140	0.1	9.3	0.3	tr	0	.02		tr	1	1	8	29		
1 oz	28	1.0	17.0	5.5	0.2	6	tr	0.1	.00	.02	82	38	.67	.264	
choc hazelnut, Cadbury	155		9.0												
1 oz	28	2.5	16.0												
choc krisp, Cadbury	146		7.1												
1 oz	28	2.3	18.3												
choc, semi-sweet, Baker's	132	0.2	9.0	0.3	tr	0	.03		tr	1	1	11	42		
1 oz	28	1.5	16.5	5.5	0.4	8	.01	0.2	.00	.03	120	58	.98	.387	
choc, special dark, Hershey	157		8.6	0.0	0			.03			1	9	33	.44	.23
1.02 oz	29	1.7	17.9	6.0	0.3	6	.02	0.1			97	46	.87	.23	
choc, special dark, Hershey	222		12.2	0.0	0			.04			1	13	47	.62	
1.45 oz	41	2.4	25.3	8.5	0.4	8	.03	0.1			137	65	1.23	.33	
chunky, milk choc	120	3.6	4.4					.14				51			
1 oz	28	1.7	18.3			44	.02	0.1					.37		
chunky, original	143	1.1	7.1					.14				35			
1 oz	28	1.9	17.9			59	.02	0.3					.54		
chunky, peanut	151	0.7	8.5			56		.10				47			
1 oz	28	2.8	15.9				.02	0.8					.64		
chunky, pecan	148	0.6	7.6					.09				33			
1 oz	28	1.6	18.2			49	.01	0.1					.62		
crunch, Nestle	160		8.0		5						50				
1.06 oz	30	2.0	19.0								110				
fruit & nut, Cadbury	152		8.7												
1 oz	28	2.4	16.0												
golden almond, Hershey	161		11.0					.11			17	60	34	.50	.25
1 oz	28	3.2	12.2		0.6	11	.01	0.3			140	90	.67	.14	

	KCAL	H₂O (g)	FAT (g)	PUFA (g)	CHOL (mg)	A (RE)	C (mg)	B-2 (mg)	B-6 (mg)	FOL (mcg)	Na (mg)	Ca (mg)	Mg (mg)	Zn (mg)	Mn (mg)
	WT (g)	PRO (g)	CHO (g)	SFA (g)	FIBR (g)	A (IU)	B-1 (mg)	NIA (mg)	B-12 (mcg)	PANT (mg)	K (mg)	P (mg)	Fe (mg)	Cu (mg)	
kit kat	162		8.5					.08			28	48	14	.32	.10
1.13 oz	32	2.3	18.9		0.1	22	.02	0.1			96	58	.42	.06	
kit kat	210		11.0					.11			38	65	19	.43	.13
1.5 oz	43	3.0	25.0		0.1	30	.03	0.1			129	78	.56	.08	
krackel, Hershey	179		9.7					.09			49	60	20	.37	.10
1.2 oz	34	2.4	20.3		0.2	24	.02	0.1			116	82	.48	.14	
marathon	179		7.3								114				
1.38 oz	39	2.1	26.5								120				
mars bar	230		10.0												
1.7 oz	48	4.0	29.0												
milk choc, Cadbury	151		8.3												
1 oz	28	2.2	16.9												
milk choc, Hershey	160		9.4	1.0	10			.08			26	55	19	.38	.09
1.02 oz	29	2.2	16.5	7.0	0.3	17	.02	0.1			119	90	.52	.12	
milk choc, Nestle	160		9.0		5						25				
1.07 oz	30	2.0	19.0												
milk choc w/almonds, Hershey	160		9.5	1.0	5			.11			23	58	26	.46	.17
1.05 oz	29	2.7	15.7	6.0	0.3	26	.02	0.2			125	87	.44	.15	
milk choc w/almonds, Nestle	150		9.0		5						20				
1 oz	28	2.0	16.0								125				
milk mounds	138		7.6												
1 oz	28	1.4	16.1												
milk shake	250		8.0												
2 oz	56	2.0	43.0												
milky way	260		9.0												
2.1 oz	60	3.0	43.0												
mounds	147		6.9												
1 oz	28	1.2	19.9												
mr. goodbar	198		11.9	2.0	5			.09			16	50	34	.65	.29
1.27 oz	36	4.7	17.6	6.0	0.4	14	.04	1.6			162	101	.72	.18	
mr. goodbar	250		15.0	2.6	7			.12			21	65	45	.85	.38
1.65 oz	47	6.0	23.0	7.8	0.5	18	.05	2.1			212	132	.94	.24	
mr. goodbar, big block	300		18.0	3.2	8			.14			25	79	54	1.03	
2 oz	57	8.0	28.0	9.5	0.6	22	.06	2.5			257	160	1.14	.29	
oh henry	139	1.9	7.1				1	.10				19			
1 oz	28	3.4	15.5				.03	1.3					.40		
oh henry	278	3.8	14.2				2	.20				38			
2 oz	57	6.8	31.0				.06	2.6					.80		
pay day	250		12.0												
1.9 oz	54	9.0	28.0												
peppermint pattie	124		2.3												
1 oz	28	0.9	25.1												
powerhouse	131		5.1												
1 oz	28	2.5	18.9												
snickers	270		13.0												
2 oz	57	6.0	33.0												
starbar	141		7.1												
1 oz	28	3.2	16.2												
summit	100		6.0												
0.76 oz	22	1.0	11.0												
thousand dollar bar	200		8.0								75				
1.5 oz	43	2.0	31.0								70				
three musketeers	280		8.0												
2.28 oz	65	2.0	49.0												
twix	120		6.0												
1.73 oz	49	1.0	16.0												
whatchamacallit	173		9.3					.07			80	45	21	.45	.192
1.13 oz	32	3.6	18.0		0.1		.02	1.1			112	64	.26	.10	
zero	250		8.0												
2 oz	56	2.0	42.0												

	KCAL / WT (g)	H₂O (g) / PRO (g)	FAT (g) / CHO (g)	PUFA (g) / SFA (g)	CHOL (mg) / FIBR (g)	A (RE) / A (IU)	C (mg) / B-1 (mg)	B-2 (mg) / NIA (mg)	B-6 (mg) / B-12 (mcg)	FOL (mcg) / PANT (mg)	Na (mg) / K (mg)	Ca (mg) / P (mg)	Mg (mg) / Fe (mg)	Zn (mg) / Cu (mg)	Mn (mg)

CEREALS, COOKED

Food / Measure	KCAL/WT	H₂O/PRO	FAT/CHO	PUFA/SFA	CHOL/FIBR	A(RE)/A(IU)	C/B-1	B-2/NIA	B-6/B-12	FOL/PANT	Na/K	Ca/P	Mg/Fe	Zn/Cu	Mn
barley, pearled, dry	98	2.8	tr			0	0	.01		6	1	6	13	.577	.43
1 oz	28	2.9	22.1		0.1	0	.03	0.9		.14	45	53	.56	.272	
barley, pearled, reg/quick, dry	172	5.0	0.5					.06	.13	32	4	11	34	.00	.00
¼ cup (1.7 oz)	48	5.5	36.3		0.5	11	.11	2.2	.00	.00	127	116	1.24	.21	
buckwheat groats, dry	98	2.8				0	0							.73	.45
1 oz	28	3.0				0							.36	.22	
bulgar wheat, cnd	227	75.6	0.9				0	.04			809	27			
1 cup	135	8.4	47.3		0.8	0	.07	3.2			117	270	1.80		
corn grits, reg/quick, enr, ckd	146	206.5	0.5					.15	.06	1	0ᵃ	1	11	.17	.041
1 cup	242	3.5	31.4		0.2	ᵇ	.24	2.0			54	29	1.55	.029	
corn grits, reg/quick, unenr, ckd	146	206.4	0.5					.02	.06	1	0ᵃ	1	11	.17	.041
1 cup	242	3.5	31.4		0.2	ᵇ	.05	0.5			54	29	.48	.029	
corn grits, inst	82	116.4	0.2					.09	.05	1	344	7	5	.09	
1 pkt prep	137	2.1	17.8		0.1	0	.17	1.3	.00	.43	29	17	1.02	.014	
corn grits w/cheese flavor, inst	107	115.6	0.9					.13			481	14			
1 pkt prep	142	2.8	21.3		0.2	0	.17	1.5			40		1.16		
corn grits w/imit bacon bits, inst	104	114.2	0.5					.12	.05	8	531	6	9	.18	
1 pkt prep	141	3.0	21.5		0.2	0	.20	1.6	.00	.06	60	28	1.29	.034	
corn grits w/imit ham bits, inst	103	114.2	0.4					.15	.06	10	657	7	9	.17	
1 pkt prep	141	2.9	21.4		0.2	0	.25	1.7	.00	.74	52	33	1.51	.027	
cream of rice, ckd	95	160.1	0.1					.00	.05	6	1ᶜ	6	6	.29	.264
¾ cup	183	1.6	21.1		0.1		.10	0.8			37	32	.30	.062	
cream of wheat, reg, ckd	100	163.8	0.4					.10		7	2ᵈ	38	7	.24	
¾ cup	188	2.9	20.8				.10	1.1		.14	33	31	7.70	.056	
cream of wheat, quick, ckd	96	155.1	0.4					.10		7	104ᵉ	38	9	.26	
¾ cup	179	2.7	20.0				.10	1.1		.13	35	75	7.60	.050	
cream of wheat, inst, ckd	115	152.8	0.4					.10		8	5ᶠ	44	11	.31	
¾ cup	181	3.3	23.8				.20	1.3			36	32	9.00	.069	
cream of wheat, mix & eat	102	116.4	0.3			375		.30	.50	100	241	20	8	.24	
1 pkt prep	142	2.8	21.4			1250	.40	5.0		.13	38	20	8.10	.041	
cream of wheat, mix & eat, flavoredᵍ	132	117.2	0.4			375		.20	.50	100	241	40	9	.23	
1 pkt prep	150	2.5	28.9			1250	.40	5.0			55	20	8.10	.057	
farina, enr, ckd	87	153.8	0.1					.09	.02	4	1ʰ	3	3	.12	.00
¾ cup	175	2.5	18.5		0.1	0	.14	1.0	.00	.10	22	21	.88	.019	
farina, unenr, ckd	87	153.8	0.1					.02	.02	4	1ʰ	3	3	.12	.00
¾ cup	175	2.5	18.5		0.1	0	.02	0.1	.00	.098	22	21	.04	.019	
maltex, ckd	135	151.5	0.8					.07	.06	16	7ⁱ	14	43	1.40	
¾ cup	187	4.3	29.7		0.6		.19	1.8		.17	200	134	1.35	.252	
malt-o-meal, plain/choc, ckd	92	157.6	0.2			0	0	.20	.01		2ʲ	4		.13	
¾ cup	180	2.6	19.4		0.2	0	.30	4.4		.104	35	18	7.10	.020	
maypo, ckd	128	148.9	1.8			527	21	.60	.70	7	6ᵏ	94	38	1.12	
¾ cup	180	4.4	23.9		0.3	1754	.50	7.0	2.10	.25	158	186	6.30	.119	
oats, reg/quick, ckd	108	149.3	1.8	0.7	0			.04	.04	7	1ᵐ	15	42	.86	1.024
*¾ cup*ˡ	175	4.5	18.9	0.3	0.3	29	.19	0.2	.00	.35	99	133	1.19	.096	
oats, inst	104	151.8	1.7		0	455		.29	.74	150	286	163	35	1.00	1.00
1 pkt prep	177	4.4	18.1		0.3	1514	.53	5.5	.00	.35	100	133	6.32	.13	
oats w/apples & cinn, inst	135	115.9	1.6			435		.28	.70	137	222	158	31	1.00	1.00
1 pkt prep	149	3.9	26.3		0.4	1450	.48	5.1	.00	.35	107	117	6.07	.12	
oats w/bran & raisins, inst	158	155.7	1.9			479		.63	.76	155	247	173	57	1.35	1.587
1 pkt prep	195	4.9	30.4		0.9	1596	.56	8.1	.00	.45	236	206	7.61	.284	

ᵃ Na is 540 mg if salt is added according to label directions.
ᵇ White corn grits contain only a trace of vitamin A; yellow corn grits contain 145 IU.
ᶜ Na is 317 mg if salt is added according to label directions.
ᵈ Na is 252 mg if salt is added according to label directions.
ᵉ Na is 347 mg if salt is added according to label directions.
ᶠ Na is 273 mg if salt is added according to label directions.

ᵍ Apple w/cinn, banana & spice, or maple & brown sugar
ʰ Na is 576 mg if salt is added according to label directions.
ⁱ Na is 142 mg if salt is added according to label directions.
ʲ Na is 243 mg if salt is added according to label directions.
ᵏ Na is 194 mg if salt is added according to label directions.
ˡ ⅓ cup (1 oz) dry
ᵐ Na is 280 mg if salt is added according to label directions.

	KCAL / WT (g)	H₂O (g) / PRO (g)	FAT (g) / CHO (g)	PUFA (g) / SFA (g)	CHOL (mg) / FIBR (g)	A (RE) / A (IU)	C (mg) / B-1 (mg)	B-2 (mg) / NIA (mg)	B-6 (mg) / B-12 (mcg)	FOL (mcg) / PANT (mg)	Na (mg) / K (mg)	Ca (mg) / P (mg)	Mg (mg) / Fe (mg)	Zn (mg) / Cu (mg)	Mn (mg)
oats w/cinn & spice, inst	177	118.0	1.9			475		.34	.77	153	280	172	51	.97	1.476
1 pkt prep	161	4.8	35.1		0.4	1581	.56	5.7	.00	.38	104	146	6.65	.119	
oats w/maple & brown sugar, inst	163	115.3	1.9			451		.32	.74	145	280	162	85	1.00	1.00
1 pkt prep	155	4.6	31.9		0.3	1503	.53	5.4	.00	.32	102	143	6.35	.20	
oats w/raisins & spice, inst	161	118.4	1.8			440		.36	.75	150	225	165	57	1.00	1.00
1 pkt prep	158	4.3	31.8		0.4	1466	.51	5.5	.00	.37	150	133	6.58	.16	
ralston, ckd	100	163.5	0.6				1	.13	.09	13	3[b]	10	45	1.06	
¾ cup[a]	190	4.2	21.2		0.6	35	.15	1.5	.08	.25	115	111	1.24	.150	
roman meal, ckd	111	149.7	0.7					.09	.09	18	2[c]	22	82	1.34	
¾ cup	181	4.9	24.8		1.1		.18	2.3		.28	227	162	1.59	.241	
roman meal w/oats, ckd	127	146.8	1.5					.16	.28		7[d]	21	56		
¾ cup	180	5.4	25.6		0.9		.23	2.4		.19		176	1.05	.112	
wheatena, ckd	101	155.4	0.8					.04	.04	13	4[e]	8	37	1.26	1.496
¾ cup	182	3.7	21.5		0.5		.02	1.0		.08	140	109	1.02	.095	
wheat hearts, ckd	110		1.0					.06			410[f]				
¾ cup	180	4.0	21.0				.20	0.4			94		.64		
whole wheat hot natural cereal, ckd, Quaker—¾ cup	113	152.1	0.7					.09	.05	19	1[g]	13	40	.87	1.061
	182	3.7	24.9		0.7	0	.13	1.6	.00	.30	129	126	1.13	.151	

CEREALS, READY-TO-EAT

	KCAL / WT (g)	H₂O (g) / PRO (g)	FAT (g) / CHO (g)	PUFA (g) / SFA (g)	CHOL (mg) / FIBR (g)	A (RE) / A (IU)	C (mg) / B-1 (mg)	B-2 (mg) / NIA (mg)	B-6 (mg) / B-12 (mcg)	FOL (mcg) / PANT (mg)	Na (mg) / K (mg)	Ca (mg) / P (mg)	Mg (mg) / Fe (mg)	Zn (mg) / Cu (mg)	Mn (mg)
all bran	71	0.9	0.5			375	15	.40	.50	100	320	23	106	3.70	
⅓ cup (1 oz)	28	4.0	21.1		2.0	1250	.40	5.0		.49	350	264	4.50	.32	
alpen	110		5.0												
1 oz	28	3.7	19.0								61				
alpha-bits	111	0.4	0.6			375		.40	.50	100	219	8	17	1.50	
1 cup (1 oz)	28	2.2	24.6		0.2	1250	.40	5.0	1.50	.15	110	51	1.80	.07	
apple jacks	110	0.7	0.1			375	15	.40	.50	100	125	3	6	3.70	
1 cup (1 oz)	28	1.5	25.7		0.1	1250	.40	5.0		.10	23	30	4.50	.10	
banana flavored frosted flakes	110		1.0				15	.43	.50	100	180	1	2	.10	
1 oz	28	1.0	25.0		tr	1250	.30	5.0			23	6	1.80	.04	
body buddies, brown sugar & honey	110		1.0								290				
1 cup (1 oz)	28	2.0	24.0												
body buddies, fruit flavor	110		1.0								285				
1 cup (1 oz)	28	2.0	24.0												
boo berry	109		1.0				15	.42			210	20			
1 cup (1 oz)	28	1.0	23.7			1236	.37	4.9					4.50		
bran, 100%	76	0.8	1.4	0.8			27	.80	.90		196	20	134	2.46	
½ cup (1 oz)	28	3.5	20.7	0.3	2.1		.70	9.0	2.70	.55	354	344	3.49	.447	
bran buds	73	0.8	0.7			375	15	.40	.50	100	174	19	90	3.70	
⅓ cup (1 oz)	28	3.9	21.6		2.0	1250	.40	5.0		.55	474	246	4.50	.30	
bran chex	91	0.7	0.8			6	15	.15	.50	100	263	17	73	1.24	
⅔ cup (1 oz)	28	2.9	22.6		1.3	62	.40	5.0	1.50	.29	228	189	4.50	.22	
bran flakes, 40%, Kellogg's	93	0.9	0.5			375		.40	.50	100	264	14	52	3.70	
¾ cup (1 oz)	28	3.6	22.2		1.0	1250	.40	5.0	1.50		180	139	8.10	.210	
bran flakes, 40%, Post	92	0.9	0.5			375		.40	.50	100	260	12	61	1.50	
⅔ cup (1 oz)	28	3.2	22.5		1.1	1250	.40	5.0	1.50		151	178	4.50	.194	
bran flakes, 40%, Ralston	92	0.7	0.4			375	15	.40	.50	100	264	22	68	1.18	
¾ cup (1 oz)	28	3.3	22.6		1.2	1250	.40	5.0	1.50	.12	184	158	4.50	.207	
buc wheats	108		1.0				27	.77			235				
¾ cup (1 oz)	28	2.0	22.7			2224	.67	8.9					8.00		
cap'n crunch	119	0.7	2.6	0.4				.55	.77	182	213	5	12	3.07	.150
¾ cup (1 oz)	28	1.5	22.9	1.7	0.2	0	.50	6.6	1.79	3.86	36	36	7.53	.034	
cap'n crunch's crunchberries	118	0.7	2.4	0.4				.54	.75	103	197	9	11	2.88	.00
¾ cup (1 oz)	28	1.5	23.1	1.6	0.2	0	.48	6.6	2.03	2.42	40	38	7.32	.01	

[a] ¼ cup (1 oz) dry
[b] Na is 357 mg if salt is added according to label directions.
[c] Na is 148 mg if salt is added according to label directions.
[d] Na is 405 mg if salt is added according to label directions.
[e] Na is 433 mg if salt is added according to label directions.
[f] Prep w/added salt
[g] Na is 424 mg if salt is added according to label directions.

	KCAL / WT (g)	H₂O (g) / PRO (g)	FAT (g) / CHO (g)	PUFA (g) / SFA (g)	CHOL (mg) / FIBR (g)	A (RE) / A (IU)	C (mg) / B-1 (mg)	B-2 (mg) / NIA (mg)	B-6 (mg) / B-12 (mcg)	FOL (mcg) / PANT (mg)	Na (mg) / K (mg)	Ca (mg) / P (mg)	Mg (mg) / Fe (mg)	Zn (mg) / Cu (mg)	Mn (mg)
cap'n crunch's peanut butter	124	0.5	3.7	0.8				.57	.84	197	217	6	15	3.07	.00
¾ cup (1 oz)	28	2.0	21.5	1.5	0.2	0	.49	7.3	1.86	3.87	46	40	7.38	.05	
cap'n crunch's punch crunch	116		1.7				0	.25						8	
1 oz	28	5.2	23.8		0.1	0	1.32	4.9				20	4.50		
cap'n crunch's vanilly	116		1.8					.60			143	21			
1 oz	28	1.5	23.4		0.1		.49	4.7			44	31	4.70		
cheerios	111	1.4	1.8	0.8		375	15	.42	.50	6	307	48	39	.79	.765
1¼ cups (1 oz)	28	4.3	19.6	0.3	0.4	1250	.37	5.0	1.50	.29	101	134	4.45	.143	
cocoa krispies	110	0.7	0.4			375	15	.40	.50	100	217	5	9	1.50	
¾ cup (1 oz)	28	1.5	25.2		0.1	1250	.40	5.0			42	37	1.80	.09	
cocoa pebbles	116	0.6	1.5			375		.40	.50	100	136	5	12	1.50	
⅞ cup (1 oz)	28	1.3	24.3		0.1	1250	.40	5.0	1.50		47	22	1.80	.062	
cocoa puffs	109		1.0								205				
1 cup (1 oz)	28	1.0	24.7												
cookie crisp, choc chip/van	114	0.5	1.0			375	15	.40	.50	3	195	5	8	.27	
1 cup (1 oz)	28	1.4	24.8		0.1	1250	.40	5.0	1.50	.06	28	23	4.50	.085	
corn bran	98	0.7	1.0			0		.55	.68	183	244	33	14	3.15	
⅔ cup (1 oz)	28	1.9	23.9		1.1	0	.30	8.6	1.10	3.39	55	41	9.64		
corn chex	111	0.5	0.1			14	15	.07	.50	100	271	3	4	.10	.024
1 cup (1 oz)	28	2.0	24.9		0.1	143	.40	5.0	1.50	.05	23	11	1.80	.024	
corn flakes, Kellogg's	110	0.7	0.1			375	15	.40	.50	100	351	1	3	.08	.023
1¼ cups (1 oz)	28	2.3	24.4		0.1	1250	.40	5.0		.05	26	18	1.80	.019	
corn flakes, Post Toasties	110	0.8	0.1			375		.40	.50	100	297	1	4	.08	
1 cup (1 oz)	28	2.3	24.3		0.2	1250	.40	5.0	1.50		33	13	.75	.030	
corn flakes, Ralston	111	0.8	0.1			11	15	.00	.02	2	271	2	3	.07	
1 cup (1 oz)	28	2.2	24.6		0.1	108	.10	1.2	.10	.02	25	11	.70	.025	
corn flakes, low Na	113	0.9	0.1					.05				3	12	4	.08
1 cup (1 oz)	28	2.2	25.2		0.2		.00	0.1			21	14	.63	.025	
corn total	109		1.0								310				
1 cup (1 oz)	28	2.0	23.7												
count chocula	109		1.0				15	.42			205	0			
1 cup (1 oz)	28	2.0	23.7			1236	.37	4.9					4.50		
cracklin bran	108	1.0	4.1			375	15	.40	.50	100	230	19	55	1.50	
⅓ cup (1 oz)	28	2.6	19.4		1.0	1250	.40	5.0		.32	168	114	1.80	.159	
crazy cow, choc	110		1.0								185				
1 cup (1 oz)	28	1.0	25.0												
crazy cow, strawberry	110		1.0								190				
1 cup (1 oz)	28	1.0	25.0												
crisp rice, low Na	114	0.9	0.1					.05			3	19	11	.43	
1 cup (1 oz)	28	1.6	25.8		0.1		.00	0.4			22	29	.87	.069	
crispy rice	112	0.7	0.1				1	.00	.05	3	208	5	12	.47	
1 cup (1 oz)	28	1.8	25.1		0.8	1250	.10	2.0	.08	.11	27	31	.70	.062	
crispy wheats & raisins	99	2.0	0.5			375		.40	.50		135	47	23	.34	
¾ cup (1 oz)	28	2.0	23.1		0.4	1250	.40	5.0	1.50		115	77	4.50	.085	
c.w. post	126	0.7	4.4	0.4		375		.40	.50	100	49	14	20	.48	
¼ cup (1 oz)	28	2.6	20.3	3.3	0.3	1250	.40	5.0	1.50		58	66	4.50	.11	
c.w. post w/raisins	123	1.1	4.0	0.4		375		.40	.50	100	44	14	20	.45	
¼ cup (1 oz)	28	2.4	20.3	3.0	0.3	1250	.40	5.0	1.50		72	64	4.50	.11	
donutz, choc flavor	120		2.0								185				
1 cup (1 oz)	28	2.0	23.0												
donutz, powdered	120		3.0								185				
1 cup (1 oz)	28	2.0	22.0												
fortified oat flakes	105	0.9	0.4			375		.40	.50	100	253	40	34	.89	
⅔ cup (1 oz)	28	5.3	20.5		0.4	1250	.40	5.0	1.50		203	104	8.10	.151	
franken berry	110		1.0				15	.42			205	20			
1 cup (1 oz)	28	1.0	23.7			1236	.37	4.9					4.50		
froot loops	111	0.7	0.5			375	15	.40	.50	100	145	3	7	3.70	
1 cup (1 oz)	28	1.7	25.0		0.3	1250	.40	5.0		.10	26	24	4.50	.060	
frosted mini-wheats[a]	102	1.4	0.3			375	15	.40	.50	100	8	9	23	1.50	
4 biscuits (1 oz)	28	2.9	23.4		0.5	1250	.40	5.0			97	74	1.80	.130	
fruit & fibre w/apples & cinn	87	1.9	0.3	0.2	0		0	.42	.49	99	193	14	53	1.48	
½ cup (1 oz)	28	2.7	22.0	tr	1.1	1235	.37	4.9	1.48		151	151	4.44	.19	

[a] Sugar frosted, brown sugar-cinn, or apple flavored

	KCAL / WT (g)	H₂O (g) / PRO (g)	FAT (g) / CHO (g)	PUFA (g) / SFA (g)	CHOL (mg) / FIBR (g)	A (RE) / A (IU)	C (mg) / B-1 (mg)	B-2 (mg) / NIA (mg)	B-6 (mg) / B-12 (mcg)	FOL (mcg) / PANT (mg)	Na (mg) / K (mg)	Ca (mg) / P (mg)	Mg (mg) / Fe (mg)	Zn (mg) / Cu (mg)	Mn (mg)
fruit & fibre w/dates, raisins & walnuts	87	2.4	0.7	0.4	0		0	.42	.49	99	168	15	54	1.48	
½ cup (1 oz)	28	2.9	21.0	0.1	1.0	1235	.37	4.9	1.48		149	115	4.44	.18	
fruit brute	109		1.0				15	.42			215	40			
1 cup (1 oz)	28	2.0	23.7			1236	.37	4.9				5			
fruity pebbles	115	0.8	1.5			375		.40	.50	100	157	3	8	1.50	
⅞ cup (1 oz)	28	1.1	24.4		0.0	1250	.40	5.0	1.50		21	17	1.80	.036	
golden grahams	109	0.6	1.1	0.2		375	15	.42	.50		346	17	12	.25	
¾ cup (1 oz)	28	1.6	24.1	0.8	0.2	1250	.37	5.0	1.50	.12	63	41	4.45	.226	
graham crackos	102	0.9	0.2			375	15	.40	.50	100	185	13	24	1.50	
¾ cup (1 oz)	28	2.1	24.5		0.4	1250	.40	5.0			102	62	1.80	.074	
granola, homemade	138	0.9	7.7	4.0			0	.07	.10	23	3	18	33	1.04	
¼ cup (1 oz)	28	3.5	15.6	1.4	0.4	10	.17	0.5		.17	142	115	1.13	.162	
granola, Nature Valley[a]	126	1.1	4.9	0.7				.05		21	58	18	29	.55	
⅓ cup (1 oz)	28	2.9	18.9	3.3	0.3		.10	0.2		.23	98	89	.95	.092	
grape-nuts	101	0.9	0.1			375		.40	.50	100	197	11	19	.62	
¼ cup (1 oz)	28	3.3	23.2		0.5	1250	.40	5.0	1.50	.27	95	71	1.23	.094	
grape-nuts flakes	102	1.0	0.3			375		.40	.50	100	218	11	31	.57	
⅞ cup (1 oz)	28	3.0	23.2		0.4	1250	.40	5.0	1.50	.29	99	84	4.50	.115	
heartland natural	123	1.2	4.4					.04		16	72	19	36	.75	
¼ cup (1 oz)	28	2.9	19.4		0.3		.09	0.4			95	103	1.07		
heartland natural w/coconut	125	0.9	4.6					.04		15	57	18	37	.74	
¼ cup (1 oz)	28	3.0	19.2		0.3		0.9	0.5			104	103	1.45		
heartland natural w/raisins	120	1.4	4.0					.04		11	58	17	36	.73	
¼ cup (1 oz)	28	2.8	19.6		0.3		.08	0.4			107	97	1.04		
honey & nut corn flakes	113	1.1	1.5			375	15	.40	.50	100	225	3	6	.11	
¾ cup (1 oz)	28	1.8	23.3		0.1	1250	.40	5.0			36	13	1.80	.05	
honey bran	97	0.7	0.6			375	15	.40	.50	19	164	13	37	.73	
⅞ cup (1 oz)	28	2.5	23.2		1.3	1250	.40	5.0	1.50	.16	122	107	4.50	.135	
honeycomb	111	0.4	0.5			375		.40	.50	100	213	5	10	1.50	
1⅓ cups (1 oz)	28	1.6	25.3		0.1	1250	.40	5.0	1.50	.11	91	28	1.80	.049	
honeynut cheerios	107	0.9	0.7	0.3		375	15	.42	.50		257	20	33	.74	
¾ cup (1 oz)	28	3.1	22.8	0.1		1250	.37	5.0	1.50		99	105	4.45	.198	
kaboom	108		1.0				27	.76			370	20			
1 cup (1 oz)	28	2.0	23.7			2224	.67	8.9					8.00		
king vitaman	115	0.5	1.6	0.3		968	45	1.43	1.59	386	218	5	10	.22	.125
1¼ cups (1 oz)	28	1.5	24.1	1.0	0.2	3223	1.25	17.4	5.57	.06	35	23	17.20	.038	
kix	110	0.9	0.7	0.3		375	15	.42	.50		339	35	12	.25	
1½ cups (1 oz)	28	2.5	23.4	0.2	0.2	1250	.37	5.0	1.50		44	39	8.10	.047	
life, plain/cinn	104	1.3	0.5			0		.64	.03	24	148	99	9	.93	.975
⅔ cup (1 oz)	28	5.2	20.3		0.4	0	.61	7.5	.00	.32	127	153	7.49	.152	
lucky charms	110	0.8	1.1	0.4		375	15	.40	.50		201	32	24	.50	
1 cup (1 oz)	28	2.6	23.2	0.2	0.2	1250	.40	5.0	1.50	.18	59	78	4.50	.098	
marshmallow krispies	140		0.0				15	.43	.50	100	285	3	12	.43	
1¼ cups (1.3 oz)	37	2.0	33.0		tr	1250	.38	5.0			32	35	1.80	.07	
most	95	1.3	0.3			1502	60	1.70	2.00	400	150	43	56	1.50	
⅔ cup (1 oz)	28	4.0	21.6		1.0	5000	1.50	20.0	6.00		185	197	18.00	.159	
nutri-grain, barley	106	0.8	0.2			375	15	.40	.50	100	192	8	22	3.70	
¾ cup (1 oz)	28	3.1	23.5		0.4	1250	.40	5.0	1.50		75	87	1.00	.170	
nutri-grain, corn	108	0.8	0.7			375	15	.40	.50	100	187	1	18	3.70	
⅔ cup (1 oz)	28	2.3	23.9		0.5	1250	.40	5.0	1.50		66	81	.60	.082	
nutri-grain, rye	102	0.9	0.2			375	15	.40	.50	100	193	6	22	3.70	
¾ cup (1 oz)	28	2.5	24.0		0.4	1250	.40	5.0	1.50		51	74	.80	.097	
nutri-grain, wheat	102	0.9	0.3			375	15	.40	.50	100	193	8	22	3.70	
¾ cup (1 oz)	28	2.5	24.0		0.5	1250	.40	5.0	1.50		77	106	.80	.153	
nutri-grain, wheat & raisins	140		0.0				tr	.43	.50	100	165	13	31	3.75	
⅔ cup (1.4 oz)	40	3.0	33.0		1.0	1250	.38	5.0	1.5		149	98	1.10	.17	
product 19	108	0.9	0.2			1502	60	1.70	2.00	400	325	3	11	.43	
¾ cup (1 oz)	28	2.8	23.5		0.1	5000	1.50	20.0	6.00	.18	44	40	18.00	.079	
puffa puffa rice	118		3.0				15	.42			25	5	5		
1 cup (1 oz)	28	0.8	23.7		0.1	1235	.37	4.8			23	16	1.80		
puffed rice	57	0.4	0.1					.01	.01	3	0	1	3	.15	.213
1 cup (½ oz)	14	0.9	12.8		0.0		.02	0.4		.05	16	14	.15	.024	

[a] Cinn & raisin, coconut & honey, fruit & nut, or toasted oat

	KCAL	H₂O (g)	FAT (g)	PUFA (g)	CHOL (mg)	A (RE)	C (mg)	B-2 (mg)	B-6 (mg)	FOL (mcg)	Na (mg)	Ca (mg)	Mg (mg)	Zn (mg)	Mn (mg)
	WT (g)	PRO (g)	CHO (g)	SFA (g)	FIBR (g)	A (IU)	B-1 (mg)	NIA (mg)	B-12 (mcg)	PANT (mg)	K (mg)	P (mg)	Fe (mg)	Cu (mg)	
puffed rice, Kellogg's	40		0.0					.02			0	1	2	.13	
⅜ oz	11	1.0	9.0		tr		.06	tr			10	10	.40	.02	
puffed rice, Malt-O-Meal	50		0.0				0	.26			1	3			
1 cup (½ oz)	14	1.0	12.0		0.1	0	.38	5.0			15	13	4.50		
puffed rice, Quaker Oats	55	0.4	0.1					.02	.01	3	1	3	6	.00	.00
1 cup (½ oz)	14	0.9	12.7		0.1	0	.10	1.2	.00	.00	15	26	.41	.02	
puffed wheat	52	0.4	0.2					.03	.02	5	1	4	21	.33	
1 cup (½ oz)	14	2.1	11.3		0.3		.03	1.5		.07	49	50	.67	.058	
puffed wheat, Malt-O-Meal	50		0.0				0	.26			1	4			
1 cup (½ oz)	14	2.0	11.0		0.2	0	.38	5.0			50	45	4.50		
puffed wheat, Quaker Oats	54	0.4	0.2					.10	.01	5	1	3	13	.00	.00
1 cup (½ oz)	14	2.2	10.8		0.3	0	.08	2.0	.00	.00	47	48	.67	.06	
quaker 100% natural	133	0.6	6.1	0.6				.15	.05	9	12	49	34	.64	.488
¼ cup (1 oz)	28	3.3	17.8	4.1	0.3	0	.08	0.7	.00	.23	140	104	.84	.125	
quaker 100% natural w/apples & cinn	130	0.5	5.3	0.4				.16	.03	5	14	43	19	.55	.513
¼ cup (1 oz)	28	2.9	19.0	4.2	0.4	0	.09	0.5	.08	.30	140	96	.79	.115	
quaker 100% natural w/raisins & dates	128	1.0	5.2	0.4		0		.17	.04	12	12	41	32	.54	.473
¼ cup (1 oz)	28	2.9	18.7	3.5	0.4	0	.08	0.5	.00	.24	139	89	.80	.125	
quisp	117	0.6	2.1	0.3				.72	.86	8	228	9	12	.17	.136
1 cup (1 oz)	28	1.4	23.6	1.4	0.2	0	.51	5.5	2.44	.04	42	24	5.97	.010	
raisin bran, Kellogg's	115	3.1	0.7			375		.40	.50	100	269	13	48	3.80	
¾ cup (1.3 oz)	37	4.0	27.9		1.1	1250	.40	5.0	1.50		192	137	4.50	.214	
raisin bran, Post	87	2.6	0.5			375		.40	.50	100	185	13	48	1.50	
½ cup (1 oz)	28	2.6	21.4		0.9	1250	.40	5.0	1.50		175	119	4.50	.155	
raisin bran, Ralston	120	2.8	0.2			375	1	.40	.50	100	328	18	57	1.13	
¾ cup (1.3 oz)	38	3.0	31.4		1.1	1250	.40	5.0	1.50	.28	194	167	4.50	.206	
raisins, rice & rye	124	2.2	0.1			375	0	.40	.50	100	280	8	16	3.80	
1 cup (1.3 oz)	37	2.1	31.5		0.4	1250	.40	5.0	1.50		115	40	4.50	.13	
rice chex	112	0.7	0.1				15		.50	100	237	4	7	.39	
1⅛ cups (1 oz)	28	1.5	25.3		0.1	17	.40	5.0	1.50	.10	33	28	1.80	.075	
rice krispies	112	0.7	0.2			375	15	.40	.50	100	340	4	10	.48	.281
1 cup (1 oz)	28	1.9	24.8		0.1	1250	.40	5.0		.20	30	34	1.80	.071	
rice krispies, frosted	109	0.7	0.1			375	15	.40	.50	100	240	1	5	.31	
1 cup (1 oz)	28	1.3	25.7		0.1	1250	.40	5.0		.13	21	27	1.80	.071	
ruskets biscuits, Loma Linda	110	2.2						.43			84	14		.59	
2 biscuits	31	3.7	24.0				.31	3.0			100		3.10		
shredded wheat	102	1.5	0.6					.08	.07	14	3	11	37	.93	
1 oz	28	3.1	22.6		0.6		.07	1.5		.24	102	100	1.20	.188	
shredded wheat	83	1.5	0.3					.06	.06	12	0	10	40	.59	.725
1 biscuit	24	2.6	18.8		0.5		.07	1.1		.19	77	86	.74	.118	
shredded wheat, Quaker Oats	104	1.8	0.4					.08	.05	19	2	11	32	1.00	.00
2 small biscuits (1.3 oz)	37	3.1	22.0		0.6	0	.07	1.3	.00	.00	96	116	.86	.14	
sir grapefellow	109		1.0				15	.42				20			
1 oz	28	2.0	23.7			1236	.37	4.9					4.50		
special K	111	0.6	0.1			375	15	.40	.50	100	265	8	16	3.70	
1⅓ cups (1 oz)	28	5.6	21.3		0.1	1250	.40	5.0		.15	49	55	4.50	.128	
sugar corn pops	108	1.0	0.1			375	15	.40	.50	100	103	1	2	1.50	
1 cup (1 oz)	28	1.4	25.6		0.1	1250	.40	5.0		.06	17	28	1.80	.060	
sugar frosted flakes, Kellogg's	108	0.7	0.1			375	15	.40	.50	100	230	1	2	.04	
¾ cup (1 oz)	28	1.4	25.7		0.1	1250	.40	5.0			18	21	1.80	.060	
sugar frosted flakes, Ralston	111	0.4	0.4			375	15	.40	.50	2	184	3	2	.61	
¾ cup (1 oz)	28	1.5	25.5		0.1	1250	.40	5.0	1.50	.01	18	7	.70	.019	
sugar frosted rice	110		0.4				15	.43	.50	100	151	5	7	.41	
1 cup (1 oz)	28	1.6	26.0		0.1	1250	.38	5.0	1.50	.06	21	24	1.80		
sugar puffs	110		0.0					.43	.50	100	40		16	.30	
⅞ cup (1 oz)	28	2.0	26.0		0.3	1250	.38	5.0	1.50			60	4.50	.08	
sugar smacks	106	0.9	0.5			375	15	.40	.50	100	75	3	13	.28	
¾ cup (1 oz)	28	2.0	24.7		0.2	1250	.40	5.0		.13	42	31	1.80	.079	
sugar sparkled flakes	109	0.5	0.1			375		.40	.50	100	160	4	3	.05	
1 oz	28	1.5	25.8		0.1	1250	.40	5.0	1.50		64	7	.40	.053	
super sugar crisp	106	0.4	0.3			375		.40	.50	100	25	6	17	1.50	
⅞ cup (1 oz)	28	1.8	25.6		0.3	1250	.40	5.0	1.50	.10	105	51	1.80	.077	

	KCAL	H₂O (g)	FAT (g)	PUFA (g)	CHOL (mg)	A (RE)	C (mg)	B-2 (mg)	B-6 (mg)	FOL (mcg)	Na (mg)	Ca (mg)	Mg (mg)	Zn (mg)	Mn (mg)
	WT (g)	PRO (g)	CHO (g)	SFA (g)	FIBR (g)	A (IU)	B-1 (mg)	NIA (mg)	B-12 (mcg)	PANT (mg)	K (mg)	P (mg)	Fe (mg)	Cu (mg)	
tasteeos	111	0.6	0.8			375	15	.40	.50	11	216	13	31	.81	
1¼ cups (1 oz)	28	3.6	22.4		0.4	1250	.40	5.0	1.50	.14	84	113	4.50	.167	
team	111	1.1	0.5			375	15	.40	.50		175	4	13	.39	
1 cup (1 oz)	28	1.8	24.3		0.3	1250	.40	5.0	1.50	.21	48	44	1.74	.146	
toasty o's	110		2.0				15	.43	.50		280	40	40	.90	
1¼ cups (1 oz)	28	4.0	20.0		0.3	1250	.38	5.0	1.50		90	150	4.50	.16	
total	100	1.1	0.6	0.3		1502	60	1.68	2.00	400	352	48	32	.67	.425
1 cup (1 oz)	28	2.8	22.3	0.1	0.5	5000	1.48	19.8	6.20	.20	106	118	18.00	.122	
trix	109		0.4			375	15	.42	.50		181	6	6	.13	
1 cup (1 oz)	28	1.5	25.2		0.1	1250	.37	5.0	1.50	.08	27	19	4.45	.045	
waffelos	115	0.7	1.2			375	15	.40	.50	3	118	8	6	.23	
1 cup (1 oz)	28	1.6	24.5		0.1	1250	.40	5.0	1.50	.05	25	231	4.50	.032	
wheat chex	104	0.7	0.7				15	.10	.50	100	190	11	36	.76	
⅔ cup (1 oz)	28	2.8	23.3		0.6		.40	5.0	1.50	.13	107	112	4.50	.166	
wheat & raisin chex	130		0.3				1	.13	.50	164	216	24	36	.96	
¾ cup (1.3 oz)	38	3.7	31.0		0.6		.38	5.0	1.50	.11	149	119	4.50	.20	
wheat germ, toasted	108	1.6	3.0	1.8			2	.23	.28	100	1	13	91	4.73	5.658
¼ cup (1 oz)	28	8.3	14.1	0.5	0.7		.47	1.6		.39	268	325	2.58	.176	
wheat germ, toasted w/brown sugar	107	1.6	2.3	1.4				.18	.21	75	1	9	68	3.54	4.243
& honey—¼ cup (1 oz)	28	6.2	17.2	0.4	0.5		.35	1.2		.30	201	244	1.93	.132	
wheaties	99	1.3	0.5	0.2	2.0	375	15	.42	.50	9	354	43	31	.63	.425
1 cup (1 oz)	28	2.7	22.6	0.1	0.5	1250	.37	5.0	1.50	.21	106	98	4.45	.131	

CHEESE & CHEESE PRODUCTS
NATURAL CHEESE

	KCAL	H₂O (g)	FAT (g)	PUFA (g)	CHOL (mg)	A (RE)	C (mg)	B-2 (mg)	B-6 (mg)	FOL (mcg)	Na (mg)	Ca (mg)	Mg (mg)	Zn (mg)	Mn (mg)
	WT (g)	PRO (g)	CHO (g)	SFA (g)	FIBR (g)	A (IU)	B-1 (mg)	NIA (mg)	B-12 (mcg)	PANT (mg)	K (mg)	P (mg)	Fe (mg)	Cu (mg)	
blue	100	12.0	8.2	0.2	21	65	0	.11	.05	10	396	150	7	.75	
1 oz	28	6.1	0.7	5.3	0.0	204	.01	0.3	.35	.49	73	110	.09		
brick	105	11.7	8.4	0.2	27	86	0	:10	.02	6	159	191	7	.74	
1 oz	28	6.6	0.8	5.3	0.0	307	tr	tr	.36	.08	38	128	.07		
brie	95	13.7	7.9		28		0	.15	.07	18	178	52			
1 oz	28	5.9	0.1		0.0	189	.02	0.1	.47	.20	43	53	.14		
camembert	85	14.7	6.9	0.2	20	71	0	.14	.06	18	239	110	6	.68	
1 oz	28	5.6	0.1	4.3	0.0	262	.01	0.2	.37	.39	53	98	.09		
caraway	107	11.1	8.3			82	0	.13			196	191	6		
1 oz	28	7.1	0.9		0.0	299	.01	0.1	.08	.05		139			
cheddar	114	10.4	9.4	0.3	30	86	0	.11	.02	5	176	204	8	.88	
1 oz	28	7.1	0.4	6.0	0.0	300	.01	tr	.23	.12	28	145	.19		
cheddar	403	36.8	33.1	0.9	105	303	0	.38	.07	18	620	721	28	3.11	
3½ oz	100	24.9	1.3	21.1	0.0	1059	.03	0.1	.83	.41	98	512	.68		
cheddar, grated	455	41.5	37.5	1.1	119	342	0	.42	.08	21	701	815	31	3.51	
1 cup, not packed	113	28.1	1.5	23.8	0.0	1197	.03	0.1	.94	.47	111	579	.77		
cheshire	110	10.7	8.7		29	69	0	.08			198	182	6		
1 oz	28	6.6	1.4		0.0	279	.01				27	131	.06		
colby	112	10.8	9.1	0.3	27	78	0	.11	.02		171	194	7	.87	
1 oz	28	6.7	0.7	5.7	0.0	293	tr	tr	.23	.06	36	129	.22		
cottage cheese, creamed	29	22.3	1.3	tr	4	14	tr	tr	.02	4	114	17	2	.20	
1 rd T	28	3.5	0.8	0.8	0.0	48	tr	tr	.18	.06	24	37	.07		
cottage cheese, creamed	117	89.2	5.1	0.2	17	54	tr	.18	.08	14	457	68	6	.42	
4 oz	113	14.1	3.0	3.2	0.0	184	.02	0.1	.70	.24	95	149	.16		
cottage cheese, creamed	217	165.8	9.5	0.3	31	101	tr	.34	.14	26	850	126	11	.78	
1 cup, not packed	210	26.2	5.6	6.0	0.0	342	.04	0.3	1.31	.45	177	277	.29		
cottage cheese, creamed w/fruit	279	163.0	7.7	0.2	25		tr	.29	.12	22	915	108	9	.66	
1 cup	226	22.4	30.1	4.9	tr	139	.04	0.2	1.12	.38	151	236	.25		
cottage cheese, dry curd	123	115.7	0.6	tr	10	12	0	.21	.12	21	19	46	6	.68	
1 cup, not packed	145	25.0	2.7	0.4	0.0	44	.04	0.2	1.20	.24	47	151	.33		
cottage cheese, low fat, 1% fat	164	186.4	2.3	tr	10	25	tr	.37	.15	28	918	138	12	.80	
1 cup	226	28.0	6.2	1.5	0.0	84	.05	0.3	1.43	.49	193	302	.32		
cottage cheese, low fat, 2% fat	203	179.2	4.4	0.1	19	45	tr	.42	.17	30	918	155	14	.95	
1 cup	226	31.1	8.2	2.8	0.0	158	.05	0.3	1.61	.55	217	340	.36		

	KCAL / WT (g)	H₂O (g) / PRO (g)	FAT (g) / CHO (g)	PUFA (g) / SFA (g)	CHOL (mg) / FIBR (g)	A (RE) / A (IU)	C (mg) / B-1 (mg)	B-2 (mg) / NIA (mg)	B-6 (mg) / B-12 (mcg)	FOL (mcg) / PANT (mg)	Na (mg) / K (mg)	Ca (mg) / P (mg)	Mg (mg) / Fe (mg)	Zn (mg) / Cu (mg)	Mn (mg)
cream cheese	99	15.2	9.9	0.4	31	124	0	.06	.01	tr	84	23	2	.15	
1 oz (2 T)	28	2.1	0.8	6.2	0.0	405	.01	tr	.12	.08	34	30	.34		
edam	101	11.8	7.9	0.2	25	72	0	.11	.02	5	274	207	8	1.06	
1 oz	28	7.1	0.4	5.0	0.0	260	.01	tr	.44	.08	53	152	.12		
feta	75	15.7	6.0	0.2	25		0				316	140	5	.82	
1 oz	28	4.0	1.2	4.2	0.0						18	96	.18		
fontina	110	10.8	8.8	0.5	33		0	.06				156	4	.99	
1 oz	28	7.3	0.4	5.4	0.0	333	.01	tr					.06		
gjetost	132	3.8	8.4	0.3							170	113			
1 oz	28	2.7	12.1	5.4	0.0			0.2				126			
gouda	101	11.8	7.8	0.2	32	49	0	.10	.02	6	232	198	8	1.11	
1 oz	28	7.1	0.6	5.0	0.0	183	.01	tr		.10	34	155	.07		
gruyere	117	9.4	9.2	2.4	31		0	.08	.02	3	95	287			
1 oz	28	8.5	0.1	5.4	0.0	346	.02	tr	.45	.16	23	172			
liederkranz	85		7.4	0.2			0					178			
1 oz	28	4.6			0.0							120			
limburger	93	13.7	7.7	0.1	26		0	.14	.02	16	227	141	6	.60	
1 oz	28	5.7	0.1	4.8	0.0	363	.02	0.1	.30	.33	36	111	.04		
monterey	106	11.6	8.6				0	.11			152	212	8	.85	
1 oz	28	6.9	0.2		0.0	269					23	126	.20		
mozzarella	80	15.4	6.1	0.2	22	68	0	.07	.02	2	106	147	5	.63	
1 oz	28	5.5	0.6	3.7	0.0	225	.00	tr	.19	.02	19	105	.05		
mozzarella, low moisture	90	13.7	7.0	0.2	25	78	0	.08	.02	2	118	163	6	.70	
1 oz	28	6.1	0.7	4.4	0.0	256	.01	tr	.21	.02	21	117	.06		
mozzarella, part skim	72	15.3	4.5	0.1	16	50	0	.09	.02	2	132	183	7	.78	
1 oz	28	6.9	0.8	2.9	0.0	166	.01	tr	.23	.02	24	131	.06		
mozzarella, part skim, low moisture	79	13.8	4.9	0.1	15	54	0	.10	.02	3	150	207	7	.89	
1 oz	28	7.8	0.9	3.1	0.0	178	.01	tr	.26	.03	27	149	.07		
muenster	104	11.8	8.5	0.2	27	90	0	.09	.02	3	178	203	8	.80	
1 oz	28	6.6	0.3	5.4	0.0	318	tr	tr	.42	.05	38	133	.12		
mysost[a]	70		0.4				0	.14				297			
1 oz	28	1.6	15.4		0.0		.01	0.1				173	.20		
neufchatel	74	17.6	6.6	0.2	22	75	0	.06	.01	3	113	21	2	.15	
1 oz	28	2.8	0.8	4.2	0.0	321	tr	tr	.08	.16	32	39	.08		
parmesan, grated	33	0.9	1.5	tr	4		0	.02	.01	tr	93	69	3	.16	
1 T	5	2.1	0.2	1.0	0.0	35	tr	tr		.03	5	40	.05		
parmesan, hard	111	8.3	7.3	0.2	19		0	.09	.03	2	454	336	12	.78	
1 oz	28	10.1	0.9	4.7	0.0	171	.01	0.1		.13	26	197	.23		
port du salut	100	12.9	8.0	0.2	35		0	.07	.02	5	151	184			
1 oz	28	6.7	0.2	4.7	0.0	378		tr	.43	.06		102			
provolone	100	11.6	7.6	0.2	20	75	0	.09	.02	3	248	214	8	.92	
1 oz	28	7.3	0.6	4.8	0.0	231	.01	tr	.42	.14	39	141	.15		
ricotta, part skim	171	92.3	9.8	0.3	38	140	0	.23	.03		155	337	18	1.66	
½ cup	124	14.1	6.4	6.1	0.0	536	.03	0.1	.36		155	226	.55		
ricotta, whole milk	216	88.9	16.1	0.5	63	166	0	.24	.05		104	257	14	1.44	
½ cup	124	14.0	3.8	10.3	0.0	608	.02	0.1	.42		130	196	.47		
romano	110	8.8	7.6		29		0	.11		2	340	302			
1 oz	28	9.0	1.0		0.0	162		tr				215			
roquefort, sheep milk	105	11.2	8.7	0.4	26		0	.17	.04	14	513	188	8	.59	
1 oz	28	6.1	0.6	5.5	0.0	297	.01	0.2	.18	.49	26	111	.16		
swiss	107	10.6	7.8	0.3	26	72	0	.10	.02	2	74	272	10	1.11	
1 oz	28	8.1	1.0	5.0	0.0	240	.01	tr	.48	.12	31	171	.05		
tilsit, whole milk	96	12.2	7.4	0.2	29		0	.10			213	198	4	.99	
1 oz	28	6.9	0.5	4.8	0.0	296	.02	0.1	.60	.10	18	142	.06		

PROCESSED CHEESE

	KCAL / WT (g)	H₂O (g) / PRO (g)	FAT (g) / CHO (g)	PUFA (g) / SFA (g)	CHOL (mg) / FIBR (g)	A (RE) / A (IU)	C (mg) / B-1 (mg)	B-2 (mg) / NIA (mg)	B-6 (mg) / B-12 (mcg)	FOL (mcg) / PANT (mg)	Na (mg) / K (mg)	Ca (mg) / P (mg)	Mg (mg) / Fe (mg)	Zn (mg) / Cu (mg)	Mn (mg)
american	106	11.1	8.9	0.3	27	82	0	.10	.02	2	406	174	6	.85	
1 oz	28	6.3	0.5	5.6	0.0	343	.01	tr	.20	.14	46	211	.11		
american & swiss	102		8.4	0.3	26		0	.09			439	181			
1 oz	28	6.2	0.4	5.3		277	.01	tr			32	263	.16		
american, extra melt process	105		8.8	0.3	26		0	.10			400	172			
1 oz	28	6.2	0.4	5.5		339	.01	tr			45	209	.11		

[a] Scandinavian cheese made from whey

	KCAL / WT (g)	H₂O (g) / PRO (g)	FAT (g) / CHO (g)	PUFA (g) / SFA (g)	CHOL (mg) / FIBR (g)	A (RE) / A (IU)	C (mg) / B-1 (mg)	B-2 (mg) / NIA (mg)	B-6 (mg) / B-12 (mcg)	FOL (mcg) / PANT (mg)	Na (mg) / K (mg)	Ca (mg) / P (mg)	Mg (mg) / Fe (mg)	Zn (mg) / Cu (mg)	Mn (mg)
american, low cal	52		2.2												
1 oz	28	7.3	0.6												
pimento	106	11.1	8.8	0.3	27			.10	.02	2	405	174	6	.84	
1 oz	28	6.3	0.5	5.6	tr	358	.01	tr	.20	.14	46	211	.12		
swiss	95	12.0	7.1	0.1	15	65	0	.08	.01		388	219	8	1.02	
1 oz	28	7.0	0.6	2.9	0.0	229	tr	tr	.35	.07	61	216	.17		

CHEESE PRODUCTS

	KCAL / WT (g)	H₂O (g) / PRO (g)	FAT (g) / CHO (g)	PUFA (g) / SFA (g)	CHOL (mg) / FIBR (g)	A (RE) / A (IU)	C (mg) / B-1 (mg)	B-2 (mg) / NIA (mg)	B-6 (mg) / B-12 (mcg)	FOL (mcg) / PANT (mg)	Na (mg) / K (mg)	Ca (mg) / P (mg)	Mg (mg) / Fe (mg)	Zn (mg) / Cu (mg)	Mn (mg)
cheese fondue, homemade	170	15.2	11.7		30			.22			347	203			
¼ cup	64	9.5	6.4	2.5		563	.04	0.1			106	188	.80		
cheese food															
american	93	12.2	7.0	0.2	18		0	.13			337	163	9	.85	
1 oz	28	5.6	2.1	4.4	0.0	259	.01	tr	.32	.16	79	130	.24		
american, cold pack	94	12.2	6.9	0.2	18		0	.13	.04	2	274	141	8	.85	
1 oz	28	5.6	2.4	4.4	0.0	200	.01	tr	.36	.28	103	113	.24		
blue cheese, cold pack	100		7.0								265				
1 oz	28	6.0	2.0								85				
caraway	91		6.9	0.3	18		0	.11			318	167			
1 oz	28	5.5	1.8	4.3		215	tr	0.1			74		.10		
cheddar, sharp, cold pack	93		6.9	0.2	18		0	.12			270	139			
1 oz	28	5.5	2.3	4.3		197	.01	tr			102	112	.24		
cheese & salami	97		7.6	0.3	20		0	.10			395	155			
1 oz	28	5.3	1.8	4.7		120	.01	0.1					.17		
hot pepper	92		6.9	0.3	18		0	.13			357	169			
1 oz	28	5.6	1.9	4.3		126	.01	0.1					.18		
onion	92		6.6	0.3	17		0	.15			326	183			
1 oz	28	5.9	2.2	4.1		112	.01	tr					.15		
pepperoni	93		7.2	0.3	18		0	.11			389	158			
1 oz	28	5.5	1.4	4.5		355	tr	0.1			62		.14		
pimento	106		8.9	0.3	23		0	.09			316	163			
1 oz	28	5.7	0.7	5.5		318	tr	tr			23		.09		
port wine, cold pack	100		9.0		20						250				
1 oz	28	5.0	tr								75				
smoked	91		6.7	0.3	17		0	.10			377	157			
1 oz	28	5.2	2.4	4.2		115	.01	tr			98		.11		
swiss	92	12.4	6.8		23		0	.11			440	205	8	1.01	
1 oz	28	6.2	1.3		0.0	243	tr	tr	.65	.14	81	149	.17		
cheese sce															
homemade	66	26.9	4.9	2.0	27		0	.08	.02	3	197	89	6	.30	
2 T	38	3.0	2.4	3.0	0.0	209	.01	tr	.15	.08	40	65	.10		
homemade	132	53.8	9.8	4.0	54		0	.16	.04	6	394	178	12	.60	
¼ cup	76	6.0	4.8	6.0	0.0	418	.02	tr	.30	.16	80	130	.20		
cnd	39		2.8				0	.07			263	106			
1 oz	28	1.7	2.0			32	.01	tr			24	62	.39		
cnd, aged cheddar	50		3.7		8		0	.05			232	69			
1 oz	28	2.3	1.8			84	.01	tr			29	124	.06		
from dry mix	158	108.0	8.5	0.8	26		1	.28			783	285	23	.48	
½ cup	139	8.0	11.6	4.6	0.0		.07	0.1			277	218	.13		
cheese spread															
american	47	7.7	3.4	0.1	9		0	.03	.01	1	218	91	5	.16	
1 T	16	2.7	1.4	2.2	0.0	127	tr	tr	.06	.11	39	115	.05		
american	82	13.5	6.0	0.2	16		0	.12	.03	2	381	159	8	.73	
1 oz	28	4.7	2.5	3.8	0.0	223	.01	tr	.11	.19	69	202	.09		
pimento	80		6.0		15						335				
1 oz	28	3.0	2.0								30				

	KCAL / WT (g)	H₂O (g) / PRO (g)	FAT (g) / CHO (g)	PUFA (g) / SFA (g)	CHOL (mg) / FIBR (g)	A (RE) / A (IU)	C (mg) / B-1 (mg)	B-2 (mg) / NIA (mg)	B-6 (mg) / B-12 (mcg)	FOL (mcg) / PANT (mg)	Na (mg) / K (mg)	Ca (mg) / P (mg)	Mg (mg) / Fe (mg)	Zn (mg) / Cu (mg)	Mn (mg)

CHIPS & SNACKS

Food	KCAL/WT	H₂O/PRO	FAT/CHO	PUFA/SFA	CHOL/FIBR	A(RE)/A(IU)	C/B-1	B-2/NIA	B-6/B-12	FOL/PANT	Na/K	Ca/P	Mg/Fe	Zn/Cu	Mn
bac-o-chips	116		4.5					.01			840	73			
1 oz	28	11.5	7.6				0.5				512		1.88		
bacon nips	148		9.2	0.8			0	.04			700	14	3		
1 oz	28	2.5	14.3	0.1		0	0.2				38	30	.10		
barley snack, cheese flavored	80		2.0												
0.7 oz	20	3.0	14.0												
bugles	150		8.0					.01			335	2			
1 oz	28	2.0	18.0				.02	0.3			14	13	.20		
cheese puffed balls, Cheetos	161	0.4	10.6	1			1	.11			366	17	5	.10	.021
1 oz	28	1.8	14.8			86	.09	1.1			41	31	.81	.04	
cheese puffs, Cheetos	159	0.3	10.0	1			1	.11	.03		368	17	5	.10	.019
1 oz	28	1.8	15.4	0.1		83	.08	1.1			41	30	.75	.04	
cheese puffs w/bacon flavor, Cheetos	159	0.4	9.9	tr			1	.08	.04		323	12	7	.13	.037
1 oz	28	1.9	15.4	0.2		86	.10	0.7			43	28	.55	.01	
cheese snacks, Cheetos	158	0.4	10.0	1			1	.10	.03		294	15	6	.10	.020
1 oz	28	1.9	15.4	0.2		97	.09	1.0			39	29	.67	.03	
cheese straws	109	5.2	7.2				0	.04			173	64			
4 pieces	24	2.7	8.3	tr		94	tr	0.1			15	49	.10		
cheese twists	153		9.5				tr	.07			329	40			
1 oz	28	2.4	14.6			107	.03	0.2				52	.20		
corn chips	153	0.3	8.8				0	.03			218	2	22	.43	
1 oz	28	1.7	16.6			65	.05	tr	.00			31		.04	
corn chips, Fritos	155	0.2	9.7	tr			0	.03	.06	2	183	29	19	.19	.399
1 oz	28	1.9	15.8	0.3		19	.01	0.3		.03	38	47	.41	.10	
corn chips, bbq flavor, Fritos	151	0.3	9.2	0			1	.06	.06		286	36	22	.26	.250
1 oz	28	2.2	15.9	0.4		178	.03	0.5			55	59	.46	.06	
corn chips, king size, Fritos	152	0.3	9.2	tr			tr	.04	.06		178	39	22	.33	.124
1 oz	28	1.9	16.3	0.4		37	.02	0.3			43	60	.34	.03	
corn chips, lights, Fritos	155	0.2	9.7	0				.04	.05		194	25	21	.31	.135
1 oz	28	1.9	15.9	0.4		37	.02	0.4			48	52	.31	.03	
cracker jacks	114		1.0				3	.05				9	22		
1 oz	28	0.8	25.5			38	.01	0.3				46	.30		
funyuns	140	0.6	6.4	tr			1	.09	.04		267	8	8	.09	.119
1 oz	28	2.2	18.4	0.1		34	.06	0.9			39	20	1.06	.03	
on-yo bits	153		9.5					.04			230	11			
1 oz	28	2.8	14.0				.04	1.2			108		.64		
popcorn	54	0.6	0.7				0	.02			tr	2	24		
1 cup	14	1.8	10.7	0.3		0	.06	0.3			28	39	.40		
popcorn w/sugar coating	134	1.4	1.2				0	.02			tr	2			
1 cup	35	2.1	29.9					0.4				47	.50		
pork rinds, fried, Frito-Lay	151	0.5	9.3		24		tr	.04	.01		715	10	3	.14	.037
1 oz	28	14.9	2.1	0.2		13	.17	0.4			37	20	.24	.06	
potato chips	113	0.4	8.0				3	.01				8			
10 pieces	20	1.1	10.0	0.3		tr	.04	1.0			226	28	.40		
potato chips	318	1.0	22.3				9	.04				22			
2 oz	56	3.0	28.0	0.9		tr	.12	2.7			633	78	1.01		
potato chips, Lay's	153	0.6	9.8	tr			10	.04	.20	3	207	8	21	.18	.292
1 oz	28	2.0	14.7	0.4			.05	1.1		.23	393	54	.55	.18	
potato chips, Pringles	171	0.5	12.9	0			6	.02			213	8	15	.17	
1 oz	28	1.7	11.8	0.3			.04	1.0			308	39	.39	.03	
potato chips, Ruffles	151	0.5	9.8	tr			11	.05	.20		213	8	21	.22	.206
1 oz	28	2.0	14.6	0.5		39	.05	1.3			366	44	.49	.13	
potato chips, bacon & sour cream flavor, Ruffles—1 oz	152	0.5	9.2	1			11	.06	.16		253	20	21	.22	.314
	28	2.5	14.8	0.4		33	.06	1.2			409	46	.42	.17	
potato chips, bbq flavor, Lay's	149	0.5	9.5	tr			11	.07	.17		317	17	22	.25	.253
1 oz	28	2.3	14.5	0.6		160	.07	1.3			368	58	.60	.12	
potato chips, bbq flavor, Ruffles	147	0.6	9.1	tr			10	.07	.16		278	15	24	.25	.385
1 oz	28	2.4	14.9	0.7		46	.06	1.5			347	49	.59	.19	

	KCAL / WT (g)	H₂O (g) / PRO (g)	FAT (g) / CHO (g)	PUFA (g) / SFA (g)	CHOL (mg) / FIBR (g)	A (RE) / A (IU)	C (mg) / B-1 (mg)	B-2 (mg) / NIA (mg)	B-6 (mg) / B-12 (mcg)	FOL (mcg) / PANT (mg)	Na (mg) / K (mg)	Ca (mg) / P (mg)	Mg (mg) / Fe (mg)	Zn (mg) / Cu (mg)	Mn (mg)
potato chips, cheese flavor, Lay's	153	0.6	9.5		1		12	.07	.17		237	21	22	.24	.257
1 oz	28	2.2	14.8		0.5	117	.05	1.2			370	55	.41	.11	
potato chips, cheese flavor, Ruffles	154	0.8	9.4		1		10	.05	.13		212	18	15	.39	.114
1 oz	28	2.5	14.9			78	.05	1.2			346	56	.38	.09	
potato chips, chipsters	130		6.0					.11			420	9			
1 oz	28	1.0	18.0				.10	0.9			31	31	.30		
potato chips, light style, Pringles	144	0.5	7.8		0		6	.02			141	7	16	.20	
1 oz	28	1.9	16.5		0.3		.05	1.2			297	48	.56	.03	
potato chips, no salt added, Lay's	156	0.5	10.5		0		12	.04	.18		4	6	19	.23	.119
1 oz	28	2.1	14.3			8	.06	1.1			380	50	.44	.06	
potato chips, rippled, Pringles	157	0.6	10.4		0		6	.02			244	10	18	.20	
1 oz	28	1.8	14.0		0.3		.03	1.4			283	48	.39	.06	
potato chips, salt & vinegar flavor, Lay's	146	1.0	9.2				12	.05	.18		392	5	20	.34	.135
1 oz	28	2.2	14.5			0	.07	1.4			388	45	.56	.12	
potato chips, sour cream & onion, Lay's	153	0.5	9.5		1		11	.06	.17		267	20	21	.23	.223
1 oz	28	2.4	14.6		0.7	39	.06	1.1			371	51	.47	.13	
potato chips, sour cream & onion, Ruffles	153	0.5	9.4		1		8	.07	.21		235	22	23	.26	.282
1 oz	28	2.4	14.6		1.2	5.2	.05	1.2			362	52	.48	.14	
potato crisps, Munchos	154	0.8	9.4		0		1	.04			251	8	12	.10	.183
1 oz	28	1.5	15.8		0.2	0	.04	0.8			134	31	.37	.07	
potato fries	158		10.1												
1 oz	28	1.5	14.8		0.4										
potato sticks	152	0.4	10.2				11	.02			280	12			
1 oz	28	1.8	14.2		0.4		.06	1.3			316	39	.50		
pretzels	111	0.7	1.0				0	.07	.01	4	451	7	7	.30	
1 oz	28	2.6	22.4		0.1	0	.09	1.2	.00	.08	28	25	.55	.04	
pretzel gems, Pepperidge Farm	70		1.0				0	.01			235	5			
12 gems	18	1.0	14.0			0	.02	0.2			28	28	.30		
pretzel nuggets, Pepperidge Farm	150		3.0				0	.13			490	23			
1¼ oz	35	3.0	26.0			0	.07	2.1			40	73	1.90		
pretzel rods, Rold Gold	110	1.2	1.0				0	.20			618	12	11	.22	.689
1 oz	28	3.0	21.7		0.2	0	.14	1.5			40	26	1.24	.09	
pretzel sticks, Rold Gold	109	0.5	0.8				0	.18	.04		875	15	12	.21	.739
1 oz	28	2.9	22.0		0.2	0	.13	1.4			39	23	1.04	.10	
pretzels, tiny tim, Rold Gold	112	0.8	1.1				0	.23			649	11	11	.24	.688
1 oz	28	3.0	21.9		0.1	0	.14	1.6			43	31	1.21	.08	
pretzel tiny twists, Pepperidge Farm	100		2.0				0	.09			610	17			
1 oz	28	2.0	19.0			0	.06	1.7			34	55	1.50		
pretzel twists, Rold Gold	112	0.9	0.9		0		0	.25			487	10	10	.17	.578
1 oz	28	2.9	22.5		0.2	0	.13	1.4			42	26	1.27	.11	
tortilla chips, Doritos	139	0.4	6.6	0			0	.03	.10	4	180	30	21	.24	.397
1 oz	28	2.0	18.6		0.3	52	.03	0.4		.07	51	59	.50	.12	
tortilla chips, cheese flavor, Doritos	144	0.4	6.9	tr			tr	.04	.08		166	37	23	.31	.231
1 oz	28	2.2	18.2		0.5	131	.04	0.4			64	69	.41	.06	
tortilla chips, extra crispy, Doritos	145	0.3	7.6	tr			1	.04	.07		156	48	25	.34	.100
1 oz	28	1.9	17.9			109	.02	0.4			47	56	.39	.03	
tortilla chips, extra crispy, cheese flavor, Doritos—*1 oz*	148	0.3	7.7		1		1	.06	.07		167	53	24	.35	.089
	28	2.2	17.4			49	.03	0.4			62	66	.37	.03	
tortilla chips, round, Tostitos	145	0.4	7.7	tr			0	.04	.07		149	44	23	.34	.173
1 oz	28	2.0	17.6		0.3	52	.02	0.3			47	64	.39	.05	
tortilla chips, round, cheese flavor, Tostitos—*1 oz*	148	0.4	7.8		1			.04	.07		180	53	23	.34	.282
	28	2.2	17.2		0.4	101	.03	0.3			54	70	.37	.05	
tortilla chips, taco flavor, Doritos	139	0.5	6.8		0		1	.06			238	42	24	.35	.162
1 oz	28	2.3	17.8		0.5	257	.08	0.5			61	67	.58	.06	

	KCAL	H₂O (g)	FAT (g)	PUFA (g)	CHOL (mg)	A (RE)	C (mg)	B-2 (mg)	B-6 (mg)	FOL (mcg)	Na (mg)	Ca (mg)	Mg (mg)	Zn (mg)	Mn (mg)
	WT (g)	PRO (g)	CHO (g)	SFA (g)	FIBR (g)	A (IU)	B-1 (mg)	NIA (mg)	B-12 (mcg)	PANT (mg)	K (mg)	P (mg)	Fe (mg)	Cu (mg)	

COMBINATION FOODS (ENTREES & FROZEN MEALS)

	KCAL	H₂O	FAT	PUFA	CHOL	A(RE)	C	B-2	B-6	FOL	Na	Ca	Mg	Zn	Mn
beans & beef in tomato sce, cnd,	260		6.0				5	.09			1150	113			
Campbell's—*8 oz*	224	12.0	37.0			340	.11	1.8			728	184	3.50		
beans & franks, cnd, Stokely van Camp	340		16.0								1030				
1 cup	250	16.0	35.0	2.3							600				
beans & franks in tomato sce, cnd, Heinz	332	151.1	14.5				6	.14			1118	117			
7¾ oz	220	15.6	35.2	1.5		713	.12	2.0			476		3.30		
beans & franks in tomato & molasses	355		14.0				5	.11			1050	122			
sce, cnd, Campbell's—*8 oz*	224	15.0	42.0			265	.09	2.1			596	260	4.20		
beans, refried & sausage, cnd, Old El	194		13.0								312				
Paso—*½ cup*	100	7.0	13.0								300				
beef goulash, cnd, Heinz	213	167.2	8.1				1	.16			753	49			
7½ oz	213	13.2	21.7			722	.05	1.7			357		1.70		
beef oriental in sce w/veg & rice, frzn,	280		9.0		45						1175				
Stouffer's[a]—*9⅛ oz*	259	18.0	30.0								300				
beef pie															
frzn, Banquet	409		20.0				2	.09			908	27			
8 oz	227	16.3	40.9			749	.16	1.2			14	125	5.20		
frzn, Stouffer's	550		36.0								1600				
10 oz	284	20.0	38.0								315				
frzn, Swanson	430		23.0						.18		1124	34	191	2.22	.27
8 oz	227	12.0	44.0						.79		227	102	4.31	.30	
frzn, Swanson Hungry-Man	770		44.0						.18		2157	77	304	2.86	.45
16 oz	454	30.0	65.0						1.18		545	250	4.99	.54	
homemade	558	125.1	32.9				7	.27			645	32			
8 oz	227	22.7	42.7	0.9		1861	.25	4.5			361	161	4.10		
beef, sliced w/gravy & whpd potatoes,	200		6.0								875				
frzn, Swanson Hungry-Man—*8 oz*	227	18.0	17.0												
beef veg stew															
cnd, Bounty	145		4.0				6	.10			830	23			
7½ oz	210	12.0	16.0			3645	.03	2.3			407	66	2.20		
cnd, Heinz	166	174.0	3.6				5	.16			1182	26			
7½ oz	213	13.2	17.3	1.1		6100	.03	1.9			347		2.34		
cnd, Swanson	150		4.0								965				
7⅝ oz	216	12.0	16.0												
frzn, Banquet	175		3.6				1	.09			1320	32			
8 oz	227	12.7	22.7			291	.05	2.2			164	94	2.20		
frzn, Campbell's	180		3.0				7	.02			795	11			
8 oz	224	14.0	24.0			662	.16	4.2			391	163	2.30		
frzn bb, Green Giant	160		2.8				15	.28			938	50			
9 oz	252	14.5	20.5	0.5		3625	.08	2.8			248		2.00		
frzn, Stouffer's	310		17.0								1675				
10 oz	284	22.0	16.0								480				
homemade	218	201.9	10.5	4.9			17	.17			91	29	49		
1 cup	245	15.7	15.2		1.0	2401	.15	4.7			613	184	2.90		
beef stew & biscuits, frzn, Green Giant	180		5.1				12	.16			847	49			
7 oz	196	13.9	20.0		0.4	1705	.14	2.2			145		1.96		
beef stroganoff, frzn, Campbell's	192		9.0				2	.32			785	24			
6 oz	168	20.0	9.0			340	.05	2.9			310	160	2.90		
beef stroganoff w/noodles, frzn, Stouffer's	390		20.0								1300				
9¾ oz	276	22.0	31.0								320				
beef style pot pie,[b] frzn, Worthington	470		25.0		0										
8 oz	227	10.0	51.0												
beef teriyaki w/rice & veg, frzn,	365		11.0								1450				
Stouffer's—*10 oz*	284	26.0	41.0								360				
burrito & guacamole, frzn,	354		16.0								652				
Van de Kamp's—*6 oz*	168	14.0	40.0												

[a] Stouffer's Lean Cuisine

[b] Vegetarian item made w/meat analogue

						Vitamins					Minerals				
	KCAL	H_2O (g)	FAT (g)	PUFA (g)	CHOL (mg)	A (RE)	C (mg)	B-2 (mg)	B-6 (mg)	FOL (mcg)	Na (mg)	Ca (mg)	Mg (mg)	Zn (mg)	Mn (mg)
	WT (g)	PRO (g)	CHO (g)	SFA (g)	FIBR (g)	A (IU)	B-1 (mg)	NIA (mg)	B-12 (mcg)	PANT (mg)	K (mg)	P (mg)	Fe (mg)	Cu (mg)	
cabbage rolls, stuffed w/beef & tomato	170		7.0				48	.14			829	55			
sce, frzn, Campbell's—*8 oz*	224	11.0	18.0			642	.16	2.9			462	127	2.00		
cabbage rolls, stuffed w/beef & tomato	206		11.0				14	.10			947	33			
sce, frzn, Green Giant—*7 oz*	196	10.4	16.3		1.2	1842	.06	2.2			386		1.57		
cannelloni, beef w/tomato sce, frzn,	430		22.0		90		12	.94			1660	298			
Mrs. Smith's—*8¼ oz*	234	19.0	39.0			305	.12	3.0			555		2.60		
cannelloni, chicken w/cheese sce, frzn,	540		33.0		80		0	.61			1440	389			
Mrs. Smith's—*8¼ oz*	234	23.0	37.0			490	.18	3.3			435		1.30		
cannelloni, shrimp w/cheese sce, frzn,	500		31.0		70		91	.56			1370	490			
Mrs. Smith's—*8¼ oz*	234	19.0	35.0			795	.12	0.5			425		1.40		
chicken a la king															
cnd, Swanson	180		12.0								681				
5¼ oz	149	10.0	9.0												
frzn bb, Banquet	138		4.7				1	.10			892	61			
5 oz	142	13.6	10.4			166	.04	1.7			166	94	1.70		
frzn, Campbell's	220		9.0				0	.16			897	46			
8 oz	224	23.0	11.0			0	.16	5.5			307	182	1.20		
frzn bb, Green Giant	170		9.1				8	.14			840	109			
5 oz	140	11.9	7.6			259	.04	1.5			171		.70		
homemade	468	167.1	34.3				12	.42			760	127			
1 cup	245	27.4	12.3		tr	1127	.10	5.4			404	358	2.50		
chicken a la king w/rice, frzn, Stouffer's	330		11.0								900				
9½ oz	269	21.0	38.0								280				
chicken & biscuits, frzn, Green Giant	192		5.5				8	.12				88			
7 oz	196	17.4	18.4		0.4	1372	.08	4.9					.59		
chicken & dumplings, cnd, Bounty	195		9.0				0	.11			1214	26			
7½ oz	210	9.0	19.0			3045	.03	2.6			145	92	100		
chicken & dumplings, cnd, Swanson	220		12.0								1030				
7½ oz	213	11.0	18.0												
chicken & dumplings, frzn, Banquet	302		10.5				2	.16			1298	68			
8 oz	227	19.8	32.1			196	.09	3.5			241	159	2.55		
chicken & noodles															
frzn, Banquet	191		5.2				tr	.18			1411	34			
8 oz	227	16.4	19.8			409	.09	4.3			218	164	1.85		
frzn, Campbell's	220		10.0				0	.16			795	30			
8 oz	224	15.0	18.0			569	.08	3.0			132	142	1.50		
frzn bb, Green Giant	250		9.6				10	.26			1186	130			
9 oz	252	18.7	21.8			273	.13	3.6			260		1.82		
frzn, Stouffer's	250		15.0								720				
5¾ oz	163	13.0	16.0								155				
homemade	367	170.6	18.5					.17			600	26			
1 cup	240	22.3	25.7		tr	432	.05	4.3			149	247	2.20		
chicken & rice, homemade	234		12.6				0	.12				122			
7 oz	200	15.0	14.6			34	.06	3.4				44	1.40		
chicken & veg w/vermicelli, frzn,	260		7.0		50						1230				
Stouffer's[a]—*12¾ oz*	361	22.0	28.0								375				
chicken cacciatore w/spaghetti, frzn,	310		11.0								1135				
Stouffer's—*11¼ oz*	319	25.0	29.0								300				
chicken fricassee, homemade	328	142.6	18.6				0	.14			308	12	22		
7 oz	200	30.9	6.5		0.0	142	.42	1.3			280	226	1.80		
chicken, fried w/whpd potatoes, Swanson	410		23.0						.25		1050				
Hungry-Man—*7¼ oz*	206	22.0	28.0						.49						
chicken, glazed w/veg rice, frzn,	270		7.0		85						760				
Stouffer's[a]—*8½ oz*	241	29.0	23.0								355				
chicken nibbles w/french fries, frzn,	360		20.0								725				
Swanson—*5 oz*	142	15.0	30.0												
chicken paprikash w/egg noodles, frzn,	385		15.0								1325				
Stouffer's—*10½ oz*	298	30.0	32.0								210				
chicken parmigiana, homemade	308		14.8				16	.18			358	174			
7 oz	200	21.6	22.1			1388	.16	4.8			342	293	6.30		

[a] Stouffer's Lean Cuisine

	KCAL	H₂O (g)	FAT (g)	PUFA (g)	CHOL (mg)	A (RE)	C (mg)	B-2 (mg)	B-6 (mg)	FOL (mcg)	Na (mg)	Ca (mg)	Mg (mg)	Zn (mg)	Mn (mg)
	WT (g)	PRO (g)	CHO (g)	SFA (g)	FIBR (g)	A (IU)	B-1 (mg)	NIA (mg)	B-12 (mcg)	PANT (mg)	K (mg)	P (mg)	Fe (mg)	Cu (mg)	
chicken pie															
frzn, Banquet	427		23.2				2	.11			999	50			
8 oz	227	15.4	39.0			531	.11	3.4			16	148	3.20		
frzn, Stouffer's	500		28.0								1530				
10 oz	284	21.0	40.0								280				
frzn, Swanson	450		25.0							.14	1112	64	177	.66	.386
8 oz	227	14.0	41.0							.41	204	114	2.04	.25	
frzn, Swanson Hungry-Man	780		44.0							.18	2020	95	277	1.68	.50
16 oz	454	32.0	66.0							.68	454	250	4.54	.59	
frzn, Van de Kamp's	520		29.0								890				
7½ oz	210	16.0	47.0												
homemade	273	65.7	15.7				2	.13			297	35			
4 oz	116	11.7	21.2		0.5	1543	.13	2.1			172	116	1.50		
chicken pie filling, frzn, Campbell's	180		6.0				0	.16			885	34			
8 oz	224	18.0	14.0			3524	.08	4.3			209	148	1.80		
chicken stew, cnd, Bounty	160		7.0				5	.10			905	31			
7½ oz	210	11.0	15.0			6845	.04	2.9			320	109	1.10		
chicken stew, cnd, Swanson	170		7.0								965				
7⅝ oz	216	9.0	16.0												
chicken stew w/dumplings, cnd, Heinz	196	171.9	8.7				tr	.11			489	49			
7½ oz	213	9.8	19.8			2390	.04	1.7			70		.85		
chicken style pot pie,ᵃ vegetarian, frzn, Worthington—*8 oz*	450		27.0		0										
	227	9.0	42.0												
chili con carne															
w/beans, cnd, Bounty	305		15.0				3	.11			1110	90			
7¾ oz	217	17.0	27.0			1270	.09	1.6			807	201	3.70		
w/beans, cnd, Heinz	326	155.5	17.2				1	.16			786	90			
7¾ oz	220	14.7	28.4			1569	.09	1.3			311		3.52		
w/beans, cnd, Stokely van Camp	390		26.0								1260				
1 cup	250	15.0	24.0								550				
w/beans, frzn, Stouffer's	270		10.0								1265				
8¾ oz	248	20.0	26.0								700				
w/beans, homemade	133	72.4	6.1					.07			531	32			
3½ oz	100	7.5	12.2		0.6	60	.03	1.3			233	126	1.70		
w/beans, hot, cnd, Bounty	305		15.0				3	.11			940	70			
7¾ oz	217	17.0	27.0			1270	.09	1.6			603	216	3.70		
w/beans, hot, cnd, Heinz	326	156.2	17.4				2	.17			904	101			
7¾ oz	220	15.4	27.1			1778	.09	1.5			340		3.08		
w/o beans, cnd, Stokely van Camp	430		35.0								1360				
1 cup	245	15.0	14.0								380				
w/o beans, homemade	200	66.9	14.8					.12				38			
3½ oz	100	10.3	5.8		0.2	150	.02	2.2				152	1.40		
chili, meatless,ᵃ cnd, Worthington	190		7.0		0										
½ cup	140	11.0	20.0												
chili w/franks, cnd, Stokely van Camp	320		17.0								1080				
1 cup	250	15.0	31.0		2.4						530				
chop suey, beef, frzn, Banquet	105		3.0				2	.07			1334	32			
8 oz	227	9.8	9.8			161	.05	1.1			136	68	2.08		
chop suey, beef, frzn bb, Banquet	73		1.4				2	.06			1140	32			
7 oz	198	5.7	9.5			251	.04	1.1			107	61	1.50		
chop suey, beef, homemade	300	188.5	17.0				33	.38			1053	60			
1 cup	250	26.0	12.8		1.3	600	.28	5.0			425	248	4.80		
chop suey, beef w/rice, frzn, Stouffer's	355		10.0								2040				
12 oz	340	18.0	48.0								260				
chow mein															
beef, cnd, La Choy	72		2.3								976				
1 cup	227	7.3	5.7												
beef, cnd bipack, La Choy	83		1.1								1009				
1 cup	227	7.9	10.3												

ᵃ Vegetarian item made w/meat analogue

	KCAL	H₂O (g)	FAT (g)	PUFA (g)	CHOL (mg)	Vitamins A (RE)	C (mg)	B-2 (mg)	B-6 (mg)	FOL (mcg)	Minerals Na (mg)	Ca (mg)	Mg (mg)	Zn (mg)	Mn (mg)
	WT (g)	PRO (g)	CHO (g)	SFA (g)	FIBR (g)	A (IU)	B-1 (mg)	NIA (mg)	B-12 (mcg)	PANT (mg)	K (mg)	P (mg)	Fe (mg)	Cu (mg)	
beef, frzn, La Choy	97		1.6								1226				
1 cup	227	9.1	11.6												
chicken, cnd, La Choy	68		2.3								924				
1 cup	227	6.8	5.0												
chicken, cnd, bipack, La Choy	101		3.4								928				
1 cup	227	8.1	9.3												
chicken, frzn, Banquet	86		1.6				1.8	.09			1245	41			
8 oz	227	9.1	9.1			93	.05	2.4			132	109	1.33		
chicken, frzn bb, Banquet	89		1.6				2	.08			1188	36			
7 oz	198	9.1	9.7			152	.04	2.4			135	113	.60		
chicken, frzn, Campbell's	90		2.0				0	.00			1362	41			
8 oz	224	8.0	11.0			0	.08	3.2			289	118	.90		
chicken, frzn bb, Green Giant	130		1.3				18	.26			1836	47			
9 oz	252	14.0	15.1		0.8	541	.08	3.4			260		1.56		
chicken, frzn, La Choy	108		4.1								1026				
1 cup	227	8.6	9.1												
chicken, frzn, Stouffer's	145		6.0								1115				
8 oz	227	13.0	10.0								225				
chicken, homemade	224	171.6	8.8	4.0			9	.20			631	51	40		
1 cup	220	27.3	8.8		0.7	242	.07	3.7			416	259	2.20		
mushroom, cnd bipack, La Choy	85		3.4								1161				
1 cup	227	2.8	10.7												
pepper oriental, cnd, La Choy	89		1.4								1024				
1 cup	227	8.9	10.2												
pepper oriental, cnd bipack, La Choy	89		1.0								1559				
1 cup	227	8.8	11.1												
pork, cnd bipack, La Choy	120		6.0								1675				
1 cup	227	5.8	10.6												
shrimp, cnd, La Choy	61		1.6								951				
1 cup	227	5.9	5.7												
shrimp, cnd bipack, La Choy	110		5.8								1079				
1 cup	227	4.7	9.7												
shrimp, frzn, La Choy	73		0.7								985				
1 cup	227	5.9	10.9												
veg, cnd, La Choy	47		1.4								835				
1 cup	227	2.7	5.9												
chow mein, chicken w/rice, frzn,	240		4.0		30						1115				
Stouffer's[a]—*11¼ oz*	319	15.0	36.0								290				
egg rolls															
beef & shrimp, frzn, La Choy	108		4.0								322				
4 rolls	48	3.6	14.0												
chicken, frzn, La Choy	120		5.2								262				
4 rolls	48	4.0	14.4												
lobster, frzn, La Choy	108		3.6								248				
4 rolls	48	3.6	14.2												
shrimp, frzn, La Choy	104		3.2								254				
4 rolls	48	3.6	14.8												
enchiladas															
beef, frzn, Van de Kamp's	342		16.0								1481				
4 enchiladas	266	16.0	33.0												
beef, shredded, frzn, Van de Kamp's	214		10.0								648				
6 oz	168	12.0	20.0												
beef & cheese w/gravy, frzn, Banquet	280		13.6				2	.14			1584	309			
8 oz	227	9.8	29.6			3029	.05	2.0			448	207	3.35		
beef w/sce, frzn bb, Banquet	207		6.6				2	.10			1219	269			
2 enchiladas	170	8.0	28.9			1105	.03	1.4			342	153	3.00		
cheese, frzn, Van de Kamp's	366		21.0								1177				
4 enchiladas	266	15.0	29.0												
cheese ranchero, frzn, Van de Kamp's	262		15.0								731				
6 oz	168	11.0	22.0												

[a] Stouffer's Lean Cuisine

	KCAL / WT (g)	H₂O (g) / PRO (g)	FAT (g) / CHO (g)	PUFA (g) / SFA (g)	CHOL (mg) / FIBR (g)	A (RE) / A (IU)	C (mg) / B-1 (mg)	B-2 (mg) / NIA (mg)	B-6 (mg) / B-12 (mcg)	FOL (mcg) / PANT (mg)	Na (mg) / K (mg)	Ca (mg) / P (mg)	Mg (mg) / Fe (mg)	Zn (mg) / Cu (mg)	Mn (mg)
chicken, frzn, Van de Kamp's	247		11.0								1108				
7½ oz	210	14.0	24.0												
fish & chips, frzn, Swanson	290		15.0								447				
5 oz	142	13.0	25.0								440	213			
fish & chips, batter-dipped, frzn,	500		30.0								551				
Van de Kamp's—8 oz	224	16.0	45.0												
fish creole,ª homemade	86		2.7	0.4			11	.06			84	12	24		
3½ oz	100	11.6	3.4			327	.06	1.6			62	131	.50		
fritter, clam	311	40.3	15.0					.12				76			
3½ oz	100	11.4	30.9				.03	0.9			147	195	3.50		
fritter, corn	377	29.1	21.5				2	.20			477	64			
3½ oz	100	7.8	39.7		0.5	400	.16	1.6			133	155	1.70		
fritter, pork	300		27.0					.07			1403	15			
3½ oz	100	12.0	2.0			11	.26	1.3			302	142	.80		
frzn breakfasts															
french toast & sausage, Swanson	300		17.0						.15				67	23	1.55
Hungry-Man—4½ oz meal	127	16.0	22.0						.86					2.16	.18
pancakes & sausage, Swanson	500		25.0						.20		1050	109	26	.02	.002
Hungry-Man—6 oz meal	170	15.0	50.0						.75					2.72	tr
scrambled eggs, sausage & hash	460		31.0						.09				53	7	.97
browns, Swanson—6½ oz meal	177	16.0	22.0						.76					1.06	.23
frzn dinnersᵇ															
beans & franks, Banquet	591		30.2				8	.21			2153	131			
10¾ oz meal	305	16.8	63.1			1995	.31	2.8			537	397	4.00		
beans & franks, Swanson	550		19.0						.26		1372	112	64	3.96	.57
11¼ oz meal	319	16.0	75.0						1.08		702	303	3.83	.54	
beef, Banquet	312		11.9				8	.25			1925	37			
11 oz meal	312	30.3	20.9			175	.12	5.6			456	246	5.10		
beef, Swanson	290		10.0						.37		983	37	66	4.49	.37
11 oz meal	312	27.0	22.0						3.62		577	265	4.37	.34	
beef, 3 course, Swanson	490		17.0						.30		1360	51	47	4.04	.26
15 oz meal	425	29.0	57.0						1.70		914	276	5.53	.51	
beef, chopped, Banquet	443		26.5				7	.22			1934	68			
11 oz meal	312	18.1	32.8			4505	.12	4.5			374	206	3.60		
beef, chopped steak, Swanson	730		41.0								2065				
Hungry-Man—18 oz meal	510	20.0	70.0												
beef, sliced, Swanson Hungry-Man	540		18.0												
17 oz meal	482	44.0	51.0												
chicken, Banquet Man-Pleaser	1026		51.6				7	.34			3562	439			
17 oz meal	482	51.1	89.2			4473	.24	10.5			1340	636	6.50		
chicken, boneless, Swanson	730		29.0								1660				
Hungry-Man—19 oz meal	539	43.0	74.0								857	480			
chicken, breast, Swanson Hungry-Man	870		43.0								1806				
14 oz meal	397	43.0	78.0												
chicken, drumsticks, Swanson	870		48.0								1350				
Hungry-Man—14 oz meal	397	41.0	68.0												
chicken, fried, Banquet	530		25.0				22	.25			2371	284			
11 oz meal	312	27.8	48.4			5107	.16	7.0			393	415	4.60		
chicken, fried, bbq flavor, Swanson	390		14.0								1102				
11½ oz meal	326	12.0	55.0								691	359			
chicken, fried, breast, Swanson	590		31.0						.22		1544	90	56	1.93	.37
11 oz meal	312	32.0	46.0						.50		655	328	3.12	.44	
chicken, fried, dark meat, Swanson	570		33.0								1118				
10½ oz meal	298	27.0	40.0												
chicken, fried, 3 course, Swanson	630		31.0						.30		1488	94	51	1.57	.43
15 oz meal	425	24.0	65.0						1.06		786	383	3.83	.43	
chicken & dumplings, Banquet	282		8.2				5	.20			1914	112			
12 oz meal	340	16.0	36.4			5032	.24	4.5			347	255	4.10		
chicken & noodles, Banquet	374		10.5				2	.24			1710	58			
12 oz meal	340	18.7	50.7			3223	.20	4.9			258	184	2.60		

ª Contains fish, okra, tomatoes, peppers & seasoning

ᵇ Usually includes the main item, a veg & potatoes/rice; meal weight refers to edible portion

	KCAL / WT (g)	H₂O (g) / PRO (g)	FAT (g) / CHO (g)	PUFA (g) / SFA (g)	CHOL (mg) / FIBR (g)	A (RE) / A (IU)	C (mg) / B-1 (mg)	B-2 (mg) / NIA (mg)	B-6 (mg) / B-12 (mcg)	FOL (mcg) / PANT (mg)	Na (mg) / K (mg)	Ca (mg) / P (mg)	Mg (mg) / Fe (mg)	Zn (mg) / Cu (mg)	Mn (mg)
chop suey, beef, Banquet	282		8.2				4	.14			1802	44			
12 oz meal	340	13.6	38.8			340	.10	3.0			173	116	2.40		
chow mein, beef,[a] La Choy	342		6.9								1892				
11 oz meal	308	12.9	55.6												
chow mein, chicken, Banquet	282		8.5				4	.14			2268	51			
12 oz meal	340	12.2	38.8			190	.10	3.4			241	180	1.20		
chow mein, chicken,[a] La Choy	354		7.6								1776				
11 oz meal	308	12.7	55.0												
chow mein, shrimp,[a] La Choy	325		5.6								1752				
11 oz meal	308	11.1	56.1												
corned beef hash, Banquet	372		13.3				13	.14			1752	65			
10 oz meal	284	19.9	42.6			352	.20	3.1			318	148	4.00		
enchilada, beef, Banquet	479		17.3				15	.20			2326	371			
12 oz meal	340	17.0	63.6			1965	.20	2.7			673	313	5.40		
enchilada, beef, Swanson	570		27.0								1573				
15 oz meal	425	19.0	72.0								829	319			
enchilada, beef, Van de Kamp's	391		15.0								2177				
12 oz meal	336	18.0	45.0												
enchilada, cheese, Banquet	459		16.7				7	.24			2356	425			
12 oz meal	340	18.4	58.8			2489	.20	1.7			615	388	4.40		
enchilada, cheese, Van de Kamp's	449		22.0								1664				
12 oz meal	336	19.0	44.0												
fillet of fish, Van de Kamp's	300		11.0								1822				
12 oz meal	336	25.0	27.0												
fish, Banquet	382		14.6				11	.15			1473	55			
8¾ oz meal	248	19.3	43.6			2470	.30	4.1			290	300	1.70		
fish, batter-dipped, Van de Kamp's	540		34.0												
11 oz meal	308	20.0	39.0												
fish & chips, Swanson	450		22.0						.20		696	58	67	.64	.32
10¼ oz meal	290	25.0	38.0						.52		856	421	3.77	.38	
fish & chips, Swanson Hungry-Man	820		39.0								1115				
15¾ oz meal	447	30.0	87.0												
german style, Swanson	430		17.0						.40		1465				
11¾ oz meal	333	28.0	40.0						1.60						
haddock, Banquet	419		16.9				17	.17			1770	52			
8¾ oz meal	248	21.3	45.4			402	.42	4.5			300	317	2.20		
ham, Banquet	369		12.2				57	.23			1590	151			
10 oz meal	284	16.8	47.7			6555	.57	3.4			125	278	2.50		
ham, Swanson	380		13.0						.31		1079	17	17	.80	.14
10 oz meal	284	19.0	47.0						.71		426	270	1.70	.17	
italian style, Banquet	446		20.9				10	.28			2156	66			
11 oz meal	312	19.7	44.6			4649	.50	3.0			374	200	4.90		
lasagna, Swanson	390		14.0								825				
13 oz meal	369	13.0	54.0												
lasagna w/meat, Swanson Hungry-Man	790		34.0								1554				
17¾ oz meal	503	30.0	91.0								739	453			
macaroni & beef, Banquet	394		13.6				21	.24			2254	75			
12 oz meal	340	12.6	55.1			7014	.37	4.0			452	156	3.40		
macaroni & beef, Swanson	400		15.0						.10		1054	119	31	2.82	.41
12 oz meal	340	12.0	55.0				.		.78		459	170	2.72	.65	
macaroni & cheese, Banquet	326		10.2				21	.27			1768	224			
12 oz meal	340	13.3	45.6			5977	.34	2.5			190	227	6.10		
macaroni & cheese, Swanson	390		14.0						.07		1062	209	28	1.38	.319
12½ oz meal	354	12.0	55.0						tr		35	25	4.25	.42	
meatloaf, Banquet	412		23.7				8	.22			1991	84			
11 oz meal	312	20.9	29.0			2134	.16	4.2			468	243	4.30		
meatloaf, Banquet Man-Pleaser	916		57.7				15	.38			3649	162			
19 oz meal	539	35.6	63.6			8004	.27	5.8			997	372	7.20		
meatloaf, Swanson	530		29.0						.37		1214	82	49	3.97	.427
10¾ oz meal	305	19.0	48.0						1.89		543	287	3.36	.67	
mexican, Banquet	608		25.4				13	.27			3114	390			
16 oz meal	454	21.3	73.5			3550	.23	3.5			540	381	8.70		

[a] Includes main dish, sweet & sour veg & fried rice

	KCAL	H₂O (g)	FAT (g)	PUFA (g)	CHOL (mg)	A (RE)	C (mg)	B-2 (mg)	B-6 (mg)	FOL (mcg)	Na (mg)	Ca (mg)	Mg (mg)	Zn (mg)	Mn (mg)
	WT (g)	PRO (g)	CHO (g)	SFA (g)	FIBR (g)	A (IU)	B-1 (mg)	NIA (mg)	B-12 (mcg)	PANT (mg)	K (mg)	P (mg)	Fe (mg)	Cu (mg)	
mexican, Van de Kamp's	521		30.0								1282				
12 oz meal	336	22.0	41.0												
mexican combo, Banquet	571		21.4				10	.20			2346	527			
12 oz meal	340	22.1	72.1			1193	.24	2.9			452	418	6.40		
mexican combo, Swanson	700		35.0						.59		1793	154	127	2.95	.863
16 oz meal	454	22.0	75.0						1.14		953	386	5.90	.68	
mexican combo, Van de Kamp's	430		16.0								1504				
11 oz meal	308	22.0	49.0												
mexican, 3 course, Swanson	630		29.0								1938				
18 oz meal	510	21.0	72.0								893	332			
noodles & chicken, Swanson	390		13.0						.09		1106	76	26	1.37	.35
10¼ oz meal	291	14.0	53.0						.55		306	189	2.04	.61	
ocean perch, Banquet	434		17.6				10	.12			1416	45			
8¾ oz meal	248	19.1	49.8			200	.22	3.2			300	295	1.60		
pepper oriental,[a] La Choy	349		7.3								1798				
11 oz meal	308	13.6	56.0												
polynesian style, Swanson	490		17.0								1734				
13 oz meal	369	20.0	65.0								332	240			
pork loin, Swanson	470		22.0						.41		798	70	22	1.88	.128
11¼ oz meal	319	24.0	48.0						.51		359	319	3.19	.38	
salisbury steak, Banquet	390		24.6				7	.19			2059	90			
11 oz meal	312	18.1	24.0			3956	.16	3.6			387	206	3.50		
salisbury steak, Banquet Man-Pleaser	873		48.0				8	.27			3741	146			
19 oz meal	539	37.7	71.7			4582	.22	5.3			927	323	5.20		
salisbury steak, Swanson	500		29.0								1055				
11½ oz meal	326	20.0	40.0												
salisbury steak, 3 course, Swanson	490		23.0						.32		1680	91	41	3.72	.318
16 oz meal	454	23.0	47.0						2.00		545	272	4.54	.45	
salisbury steak, Swanson Hungry-Man—*17 oz meal*	890		53.0								1759				
	482	39.0	63.0								868	506			
shrimp, Van de Kamp's	370		17.0								880				
10 oz meal	280	15.0	40.0												
sirloin, chopped, Swanson	460		25.0						.11		1108	45	31	3.69	.45
10 oz meal	284	22.0	36.0						3.07		568	241	4.54	.48	
spaghetti & meatballs, Banquet	450		15.3				23	.20			1851	82			
11½ oz meal	326	14.7	62.9			3645	.36	3.8			365	166	3.70		
spaghetti & meatballs, Swanson	340		14.0						.18		1151	92	28	2.44	.53
12½ oz meal	354	10.0	42.0						.53		513	177	3.19	.50	
swiss steak, Swanson	350		13.0						.34		966	57	54	7.04	.28
10 oz meal	284	19.0	40.0						1.76		497	170	3.69	.51	
turkey, Banquet	293		9.7				20	.19			1797	81			
11 oz meal	312	23.4	27.8			3962	.16	6.5			365	228	2.90		
turkey, Banquet Man-Pleaser	620		18.9				14	.32			3649	135			
19 oz meal	539	39.3	73.8			7417	.27	9.1			771	334	4.30		
turkey, Swanson	360		11.0						.26		1060	91	39	2.18	.59
11½ oz meal	326	21.0	45.0						1.43		554	196	2.61	.46	
turkey, 3 course, Swanson	520		19.0						.41		1703	123	59	2.27	.45
16 oz meal	454	27.0	62.0						1.77		817	295	5.45	.59	
turkey, Swanson Hungry-Man	740		26.0								1623				
18¾ oz meal	532	48.0	79.0								931	452			
veal parmagian, Banquet	421		19.0				12	.22			2527	181			
11 oz meal	312	20.6	42.1			7013	.19	4.0			440	287	2.90		
veal parmagian w/tomato sce, Banquet—*8 oz meal*	391		21.8				3	.32			1650	205			
	227	18.4	29.8			438	.18	5.0			268	243	2.73		
veal parmigiana, Swanson	510		25.0						.31		1110	180	38	4.09	.486
12¼ oz meal	347	22.0	51.0						1.74		555	312	3.12	.52	
veal parmigiana, Swanson Hungry-Man—*20½ oz meal*	990		48.0								2063				
	581	42.0	75.0								901	523			
western, Banquet	417		24.0				8	.22			2178	153			
11 oz meal	312	17.8	32.4			1376	.16	4.3			459	243	4.00		
western, Swanson	440		21.0								1335				
11¾ oz meal	333	24.0	42.0								709	283			

[a] Includes main dish, sweet & sour veg & fried rice

	KCAL	H₂O (g)	FAT (g)	PUFA (g)	CHOL (mg)	A (RE)	C (mg)	B-2 (mg)	B-6 (mg)	FOL (mcg)	Na (mg)	Ca (mg)	Mg (mg)	Zn (mg)	Mn (mg)
	WT (g)	PRO (g)	CHO (g)	SFA (g)	FIBR (g)	A (IU)	B-1 (mg)	NIA (mg)	B-12 (mcg)	PANT (mg)	K (mg)	P (mg)	Fe (mg)	Cu (mg)	
western, Swanson Hungry-Man	820		40.0								2419				
17¾ oz meal	503	48.0	67.0								951	624			
green pepper steak w/rice, frzn,	350		13.0								1500				
Stouffer's—*10½ oz*	298	25.0	35.0								430				
green pepper, stuffed															
w/beef & breadcrumbs, homemade	315		10.2				74	.81			581	78			
1 avg	185	24.1	31.1			520	.17	4.6			477	224	3.90		
w/beef & sce, Campbell's	190		9.0				30	.13			995	19			
6½ oz	182	10.0	18.0			860	.13	2.9			454	96	2.00		
w/beef & creole sce, frzn, Green Giant	198		10.6				31	.08			906	27			
7 oz	196	8.2	17.8		0.8	500	.08	2.4			394		1.76		
w/beef & tomato sce, frzn, Stouffer's	225		11.0								960				
7¾ oz	220	10.0	18.0								420				
hamburger helper, prepared[a]															
beef noodle	320		15.0								970				
1 serving	b	20.0	25.0												
beef romanoff	340		16.0								1095				
1 serving	b	21.0	28.0												
cheeseburger macaroni	360		18.0								1025				
1 serving	b	21.0	28.0												
chili tomato	320		14.0								1230				
1 serving	b	19.0	29.0												
hamburger hash	300		15.0								920				
1 serving	b	18.0	24.0												
hamburger pizza	340		14.0								960				
1 serving	b	20.0	33.0												
hamburger stew	290		14.0								945				
1 serving	b	18.0	23.0												
lasagna	330		14.0								1000				
1 serving	b	19.0	33.0												
potatoes au gratin	320		15.0								890				
1 serving	b	18.0	27.0												
potato stroganoff	320		15.0								965				
1 serving	b	18.0	27.0												
rice oriental	340		14.0								1085				
1 serving	b	18.0	35.0												
spaghetti	330		14.0								1045				
1 serving	b	20.0	31.0												
tamale pie	190		2.0								865				
1 serving	b	4.0	39.0												
ham croquette, fried	163	35.1	9.8					.14			222	45			
2⅓ oz	65	10.6	7.6		0.1	169	.18	1.6			54	104	1.40		
ham & lima bean casserole, homemade	476		18.8				6	.30			709	213			
10 oz	280	30.4	46.2			565	.48	6.6			1313	459	6.70		
hash, corned beef, cnd	184		12.5	5.5		tr	2	.11			589	14	13		
3½ oz	100	8.2	9.3		0.5	tr	.02	1.4			174	68	.98		
hash, corned beef, homemade	290		9.9	0.5			21	.21			40	28			
1 cup	225	21.7	28.7		0.6	30	.15	4.6				171	2.90		
hash, roast beef, frzn, Stouffer's	265		16.0								760				
5¾ oz	163	19.0	11.0								365				
hopping john, frzn bb, Green Giant	118		3.6				2	.03			447	22			
⅔ cup	100	5.0	17.8		0.5	21	.50	0.3			112	81	1.00		
lasagna															
cheese, frzn, Campbell's	300		12.0				0	.27			670	227			
8 oz	224	12.0	35.0			837	.18	2.2			331	250	2.50		
cheese, frzn, Stouffer's	385		14.0								1200				
10½ oz	298	28.0	36.0								580				
vegetarian,[c] frzn, Worthington	280		7.0		0						1175				
9 oz	255	16.0	37.0								780				

[a] 1 serving = ⅕ pkg + ⅕ lb hamburger.
[b] Gram wt not available

[c] Vegetarian item made w/meat analogue

	KCAL / WT (g)	H₂O (g) / PRO (g)	FAT (g) / CHO (g)	PUFA (g) / SFA (g)	CHOL (mg) / FIBR (g)	A (RE) / A (IU)	C (mg) / B-1 (mg)	B-2 (mg) / NIA (mg)	B-6 (mg) / B-12 (mcg)	FOL (mcg) / PANT (mg)	Na (mg) / K (mg)	Ca (mg) / P (mg)	Mg (mg) / Fe (mg)	Zn (mg) / Cu (mg)	Mn (mg)
w/meat, frzn, Campbell's	300		14.0				6	.33			806	353			
8 oz	224	19.0	32.0			1359	.42	4.2			477	435	4.50		
w/meat, frzn, Green Giant	290		11.2				16	.22			743	249			
7 oz	196	20.0	27.4		0.6	1005	.16	3.5			416		2.35		
w/meat, frzn bb, Green Giant	310		10.3				14	.27			1318	302			
9 oz	252	20.5	34.0		0.8	1377	.14	4.6			440		2.70		
w/meat, frzn, Swanson	490		20.0						.17		1090	285	52	3.37	.451
12¼ oz	347	25.0	54.0						1.32		458	316	2.78	.42	
w/meat, frzn, Swanson Hungry-Man	540		28.0								1108				
12¾ oz	361	20.0	51.0								545	292			
zucchini, frzn, Stouffer's[a]	260		6.0		25						1180				
11 oz	312	20.0	34.0								620				
lima beans w/smoked pork, frzn,	235		5.0				19	.11			680	27			
Campbell's—8 oz	224	14.0	32.0			417	.20	1.6			479	201	2.30		
linguini w/clam sce, frzn, Stouffer's	285		8.0								1010				
10½ oz	298	17.0	36.0								115				
macaroni & beef in chili sce															
cnd, Bounty chili-mac	240		11.0				2	.14			1210	76			
7¾ oz	217	10.0	25.0			350	.11	2.2			481	148	2.60		
cnd, Heinz chili-mac	247	161.7	11.3				2	.16			827	77			
7½ oz	213	10.2	26.4			1110	.07	1.5			139		2.34		
macaroni & beef in tomato sce															
cnd, Franco-Am	220		8.0				6	.19			1220	32			
7½ oz	210	8.0	30.0			790	.18	3.2			375	113	2.30		
cnd, Franco-Am beefy o's	220		7.0								1214				
7½ oz	213	9.0	29.0												
cnd, Heinz	196	164.4	8.2				1	.15			819	21			
7¼ oz	206	8.7	21.6			595	.11	2.5			157		2.06		
frzn, Banquet	250		10.2				tr	.18			1336	39			
8 oz	227	13.0	26.6			2209	.27	3.2			252	139	2.28		
frzn, Campbell's	210		7.0				6	.16			1067	66			
8 oz	224	10.0	29.0			2258	.24	3.8			500	170	3.90		
frzn bb, Green Giant	240		7.4				13	.13			660	63			
9 oz	252	11.9	31.7		0.5	1135	.13	3.2			314		2.11		
frzn, Stouffer's	190		8.0								810				
5¾ oz	163	10.0	20.0								320				
macaroni & cheese															
cnd, Franco-Am	170		6.0				0	.22	.02		926	102	15	1.38	.48
7⅜ oz	209	6.0	24.0			885	.22	1.9	tr		115	117	.42	.25	
cnd, Franco-Am cheese Os	170		6.0								852				
7½ oz	213	8.0	21.0												
cnd, Heinz	170	173.8	5.1				tr	.17			973	96			
7½ oz	213	7.2	23.9		1.1	360	.13	1.1			23	132	1.70		
frzn, Banquet	279		10.0				tr	.16			1310	200			
8 oz	227	11.8	35.9			983	.07	1.2			173	179	1.10		
frzn bb, Banquet	261		10.2				3	.20			1171	220			
8 oz	227	13.6	28.6			170	.16	1.8			136	197	5.00		
frzn, Campbell's	260		12.0				0	.20			885	197			
8 oz	224	10.0	29.0			926	.11	0.7			114	154	1.60		
frzn, Green Giant	282		12.1				4	.34			1163	143			
8 oz	224	12.5	31.1		0.0	101	.13	1.3			190		1.34		
frzn bb, Green Giant	330		13.3				3	.30			1263	233			
9 oz	252	13.9	38.8		0.0	197	.17	1.9			199		1.39		
frzn, Stouffer's	260		12.0								780				
6 oz	170	12.0	24.0								140				
frzn, Swanson	420		21.0						.03		1377	282	17	1.53	.204
12 oz	340	20.0	40.0						tr		765	231	2.04	.34	
frzn, Van de Kamp's	150		4.0								590				
5 oz	140	6.0	23.0												

[a] Stouffer's Lean Cuisine

	KCAL / WT (g)	H_2O (g) / PRO (g)	FAT (g) / CHO (g)	PUFA (g) / SFA (g)	CHOL (mg) / FIBR (g)	Vitamins A (RE) / A (IU)	C (mg) / B-1 (mg)	B-2 (mg) / NIA (mg)	B-6 (mg) / B-12 (mcg)	FOL (mcg) / PANT (mg)	Minerals Na (mg) / K (mg)	Ca (mg) / P (mg)	Mg (mg) / Fe (mg)	Zn (mg) / Cu (mg)	Mn (mg)
manicotti, cheese & spinach w/sce, frzn,	505		31.0		80		48	.58			1325	602			
Mrs. Smith's—*8¼ oz*	234	22.0	34.0			645	.12	0.5			390		1.90		
manicotti, cheese w/meat sce, frzn,	320		13.0				6	.26			843	333			
Campbell's—*8¾ oz*	245	13.0	36.0			1313	.18	2.1			289	298	1.80		
manicotti, cheese w/meat sce, frzn,	500		30.0		130		10	.68			1270	552			
Mrs. Smith's—*8¼ oz*	234	24.0	33.0			715	.12	3.5			490		2.40		
meatball stew, frzn, Stouffer's[a]	240		9.0		70						1540				
10 oz	284	20.0	19.0								490				
meatballs, gravy & whpd potatoes, frzn,	330		19.0								1090				
Swanson Hungry-Man—*9¼ oz*	262	18.0	26.0												
meatballs & noodles, frzn, Stouffer's	475		27.0								1620				
11 oz	312	25.0	33.0								395				
meatloaf, tomato sce & whpd potatoes,	330		17.0						.20		1020				
frzn, Swanson Hungry-Man—*9 oz*	255	16.0	30.0						.99		536	179			
noodles & beef, frzn, Banquet	189		6.6				1	.18			1395	50			
8 oz	227	11.6	20.9			382	.27	3.4			302	132	2.53		
noodles & beef w/sce, cnd, Heinz	145	179.1	4.0				1	.09			835	28			
7½ oz	213	8.9	17.7		0.4	554	.03	1.1			168	89	1.28		
noodles & chicken, cnd, Bounty	215		13.0				0	.17			1065	58			
7½ oz	210	9.0	16.0			922	.09	2.3			150	110	1.90		
noodles & chicken, cnd, Heinz	153	179.1	6.0				tr	.07			926	34			
7½ oz	213	7.2	18.1			1759	.04	1.3			78		1.28		
noodles & tuna, cnd, Heinz	170	173.0	4.3				1	.08			703	43			
7½ oz	213	11.5	21.1			603	.04	3.8			80		1.28		
pepper oriental,[b] **frzn, La Choy**	110		2.3								1065				
1 cup	227	10.2	12.3												
pizza															
cheese, frzn, Celeste	320	71.8	12.8					.24				277			
¼ pizza	133	14.4	36.2		0.6	739	.12	1.5					1.43		
cheese, homemade	153	31.4	5.4				5	.13			456	144			
1 piece	65	7.8	18.4			410	.04	0.7			85	127	.70		
combination, frzn, Van de Kamp's	310		17.0								614				
¼ pizza	165	16.0	24.0												
deluxe, frzn, Celeste	367	92.9	18.6					.34				258			
¼ pizza	165	16.2	33.9		1.0	1126	.28	2.4					2.41		
italiana,[c] frzn, Worthington	420		17.0		0						1135				
7½ oz	212	20.0	45.0								575				
mexican, frzn, Van de Kamp's	416		28.0								568				
5½ oz	154	14.0	27.0												
pepperoni, frzn, Celeste	356	70.7	18.2					.38				266			
¼ pizza	140	16.3	31.7		0.7	883	.27	2.0					2.21		
pepperoni, frzn, Van de Kamp's	370		17.0								651				
¼ pizza	154	16.0	38.0												
sausage, frzn, Celeste	375	81.6	19.5					.31				290			
¼ pizza	154	16.0	33.9		0.7	1085	.31	2.2					2.21		
sausage & mushroom, frzn, Celeste	379	94.0	19.3					.48				257			
¼ pizza	168	16.9	34.3		1.0	1338	.52	3.0					2.95		
pizza, french bread, frzn, Stouffer's															
cheese	330		13.0								850				
5⅛ oz	145	10.0	43.0								220				
deluxe	400		18.0								1150				
6³⁄₁₆ oz	177	15.0	46.0								325				
hamburger	400		20.0								1100				
6⅛ oz	174	17.0	39.0								265				
pepperoni	410		20.0								1190				
5⅝ oz	163	12.0	44.0								290				
sausage	420		20.0								1320				
6 oz	170	17.0	44.0								315				
sausage & mushroom	395		18.0								1220				
6¼ oz	177	17.0	40.0								365				

[a] Stouffer's Lean Cuisine
[b] Contains bean sprouts, red peppers, beef, green peppers, onions & carrots
[c] Vegetarian item made w/meat analogue

	KCAL / WT (g)	H₂O (g) / PRO (g)	FAT (g) / CHO (g)	PUFA (g) / SFA (g)	CHOL (mg) / FIBR (g)	A (RE) / A (IU)	C (mg) / B-1 (mg)	B-2 (mg) / NIA (mg)	B-6 (mg) / B-12 (mcg)	FOL (mcg) / PANT (mg)	Na (mg) / K (mg)	Ca (mg) / P (mg)	Mg (mg) / Fe (mg)	Zn (mg) / Cu (mg)	Mn (mg)
pizza, sicilian, frzn, Celeste															
cheese	329	69.2	10.6					.32				269			
¼ pizza	140	15.4	42.5		0.8	618	.37	2.0					2.10		
deluxe	425	96.8	19.5					.48				267			
¼ pizza	182	18.6	43.8		1.1	868	.34	2.5					1.97		
sausage	399	85.6	16.5					.46				267			
¼ pizza	168	18.2	44.5		1.2	1066	.31	2.1					1.65		
potato stew w/beef, cnd, Bounty	140		2.0				9	.10			1191	24			
7½ oz	210	10.0	21.0			0	.04	2.2			356	107	1.60		
ravioli, beef, in sce, cnd, Franco-Am	230		6.0								1165				
7½ oz	213	9.0	36.0								362	109			
ravioli, beef, in sce, frzn, Campbell's	60		2.0				0	.05			80	12			
1 ravioli (1 oz)	28	2.0	7.0			0	.07	0.8			40	34	.70		
raviolios, beef, in sce, cnd, Franco-Am	210		5.0				2	.17			990	34			
7¾ oz	217	8.0	34.0			1845	.17	2.8			162	111	2.30		
raviolios, cheese, in sce, cnd, Franco-Am	260		8.0												
7½ oz	213	7.0	39.0												
rice, fried w/chicken, frzn, La Choy	209		1.9								1153				
4 oz	114	7.0	40.1												
rice, fried w/pork, frzn, La Choy	216		5.6								1514				
5 oz	150	7.2	34.2												
salisbury steak w/fries, frzn, Swanson	350		22.0						.19		715				
Hungry-Man—*5½ oz*	156	13.0	27.0						1.20						
sandwiches															
bacon, lettuce, tomato, mayo on white	282		15.6				13	.14				53			
bread—*1 sandwich*	148	6.8	28.8		0.6	870	.16	1.6				89	1.50		
chicken & gravy on white bread	356		15.3				0	.21				49			
1 sandwich	160	21.9	29.8		0.1	0	.18	6.5				219	2.40		
chicken, lettuce, mayo on white bread	303		14.4				2	.17				52			
1 sandwich	131	15.8	26.6		0.3	320	.16	4.6				165	1.80		
chicken salad on white bread	245		8.6				1	.14				50			
1 sandwich	110	14.3	26.6		0.1	10	.14	3.2				101	1.50		
club sandwich[a]	590		20.8				27	.41				103			
1 sandwich	315	35.6	41.7		1.2	1705	.38	10.2				394	4.30		
corned beef on rye bread	296		10.8				0	.24			1214	51	43		
1 sandwich	130	25.7	24.0		0.2	17	.10	3.5			140	158	4.50		
cream cheese & jelly on white bread	368		16.0				2	.14				60			
1 sandwich	119	6.6	50.4		0.1	575	.12	1.0				74	1.10		
egg salad on white bread	279		12.5				2					68			
1 sandwich	138	10.5	30.6		0.3	580	.16	1.0				153	2.40		
ham & mayo on white bread	281		15.4				0	.14				40			
1 sandwich	81	10.9	23.9		0.1	165	.28	2.3				93	1.70		
ham salad on white bread	321		16.9				2	.14				45			
1 sandwich	114	11.3	30.4		0.4	30	.28	2.3				102	2.00		
frank in roll (hot dog)	260	38.5	15.2		22		12	.15			731	68			
1 sandwich	87	8.5	22.2		0.1		.26	2.9	.58				1.78		
liverwurst & mayo on rye bread	251		12.3				0	.38				38			
1 sandwich	91	9.4	26.8		0.1	1745	.13	2.2				143	2.50		
peanut butter on white bread	328		19.5				0	.80				61			
1 sandwich	83	11.8	30.0		0.8	165	.10	5.4				177	1.00		
peanut butter & jelly on white bread	374		15.1	11.0			1	.17			475	72	61		
1 sandwich	100	12.3	50.0		0.6	2	.19	5.7			257	169	2.30		
peanut butter & jelly on whole wheat	385		15.2	11.0			2	.12			418	72	71		
bread—*1 sandwich*	114	12.6	55.0		1.3	4	.16	5.6			344	220	2.20		
roast beef & mayo on white bread	328		22.6				0	.08				61			
1 sandwich	83	11.8	19.5		0.8	165	.10	5.4				177	1.00		
roast beef & gravy on white bread	429		24.5				0	.21				43			
1 sandwich	160	19.3	29.8		0.1	0	.17	4.9				163	2.90		
roast pork & mayo on white bread	288		14.7				2	.17				46			
1 sandwich	116	11.4	26.6		0.3	155	.38	2.5				123	1.90		

[a] Bacon, chicken, tomato, lettuce & mayo on 3 slices white bread

| | KCAL | H₂O (g) | FAT (g) | PUFA (g) | CHOL (mg) | A (RE) | C (mg) | B-2 (mg) | B-6 (mg) | FOL (mcg) | Na (mg) | Ca (mg) | Mg (mg) | Zn (mg) | Mn (mg) |
	WT (g)	PRO (g)	CHO (g)	SFA (g)	FIBR (g)	A (IU)	B-1 (mg)	NIA (mg)	B-12 (mcg)	PANT (mg)	K (mg)	P (mg)	Fe (mg)	Cu (mg)	
roast pork & gravy on white bread	503		30.9				0	.29				46			
1 sandwich	180	23.3	29.8		0.1	0	.79	5.1				239	3.50		
tuna salad on white bread	278		14.2				1	.11				48			
1 sandwich	105	11.0	25.8		0.1	231	.14	4.1				135	1.20		
turkey & mayo on white bread	402		18.4				0	.22				62			
1 sandwich	156	29.2	28.0		0.1	45	.18	6.8				370	5.80		
scallops & shrimp mariner w/rice, frzn, Stouffer's—10¼ oz	400		16.0								1120				
	291	23.0	40.0								355				
scallops, oriental & veg w/rice, frzn, Stouffer's—11 oz	230		2.0		35						1290				
	312	21.0	32.0								335				
shad creole, homemade[a]—3½ oz	152		8.7				8	.16			73	19			
	100	15.0	1.6			450	.09	5.1			280	190	.60		
spaghetti & meat sce															
cnd, Franco-Am	230		10.0								869				
7½ oz	213	9.0	26.0								422	138			
cnd, Heinz	168	175.1	6.2				1	.05			827	32			
7½ oz	213	8.7	19.8			976	.08	1.7			186		2.34		
frzn, Banquet	311		14.5				15	.11			1426	100			
8 oz	227	13.8	31.3			2265	.18	2.5			225	188	3.00		
frzn, Stouffer's	445		12.0								1970				
14 oz	397	22.0	62.0								750				
homemade	396		20.7				24	.12				27			
10 oz	292	12.7	39.4	0.7		901	.12	3.0				148	2.10		
w/mushrooms, frzn, Stouffer's[b]	280		7.0		40						1445				
11½ oz	326	15.0	38.0								645				
spaghetti & tomato sce															
w/beef, cnd, Franco-Am	215		9.0				4	.20			1171	30			
7¾ oz	217	9.0	26.0			755	.20	3.0			473	113	2.30		
w/meatballs, cnd, Franco-Am	210		8.0						.10		1137	75	2	2.01	.32
7⅜ oz	209	10.0	26.0						.50		355	117	2.32	.27	
w/meatballs, frzn, Banquet	282		11.1				3	.16			1334	57			
8 oz	227	13.2	32.3			4570	.16	3.1			277	168	2.73		
w/meatballs, frzn bb, Green Giant	280		11.2				34	.18			1235	75			
9 oz	252	13.5	29.6	0.8		2254	.16	3.4			333		2.90		
w/meatballs, homemade	134	70.0	4.7				9	.12			407	50			
3½ oz	100	7.5	15.6	0.3		640	.10	1.6			268	95	1.50		
spaghettios & franks in tomato sce, cnd, Franco-Am—7⅜ oz	210		10.0						.13		911	48	19	1.55	.46
	209	7.0	26.0						.42		314	109	1.46	.29	
spaghettios & meatballs in tomato sce, cnd, Franco-Am—7⅜ oz	210		9.0						.10		1198	56	17	2.01	.40
	209	9.0	24.0						.69		334	125	1.46	.27	
spanish rice, homemade	130	117.8	2.6				2	.04			475	21			
5 oz	150	2.7	24.9	0.8		990	.06	1.1			347	58	.90		
steak & green peppers, frzn, Campbell's	190		8.0				16	.36			1249	34			
8 oz	224	20.0	11.0			0	.11	4.1			415	220	4.30		
steak & green peppers w/sce, frzn, Swanson—8½ oz	200		9.0								855				
	241	23.0	11.0												
stew, vegetarian,[c] cnd, Worthington	240		12.0		0						410				
9½ oz	269	12.0	20.0								255				
sweet & sour chicken, cnd, La Choy	320		1.0								1428				
¾ cup	227	9.0	67.0												
sweet & sour pork, cnd, La Choy	340		6.0								1547				
¾ cup	227	6.0	65.0												
sweet & sour pork, frzn, La Choy	245		3.2								1693				
1 cup	227	5.9	48.3												
sweet & sour pork, homemade	386		21.7				10	.24			856	25	2.90		
7 oz	200	19.1	28.7	0.5		49	.71	8.8			400	209			
sukiyaki gravy & veg, cnd, La Choy	98		1.4								1467				
¾ cup	227	8.8	12.6												
tamales,[d] cnd	217		11.0			0					1031	31	14		
2 tamales	155	7.0	22.0		0.0	0					60		1.90		

[a] Prep w/shad, tomatoes, onion, green peppers, butter & flour
[b] Stouffer's Lean Cuisine
[c] Vegetarian item made w/meat analogue
[d] Soft corn dough (masa) rolled around chili flavored meat, wrapped in parchment paper & steamed in red chili sce

	KCAL / WT (g)	H₂O (g) / PRO (g)	FAT (g) / CHO (g)	PUFA (g) / SFA (g)	CHOL (mg) / FIBR (g)	A (RE) / A (IU)	C (mg) / B-1 (mg)	B-2 (mg) / NIA (mg)	B-6 (mg) / B-12 (mcg)	FOL (mcg) / PANT (mg)	Na (mg) / K (mg)	Ca (mg) / P (mg)	Mg (mg) / Fe (mg)	Zn (mg) / Cu (mg)	Mn (mg)
tuna, creamed w/peas, frzn bb, Green	140		7.0				13	.14				109			
Giant—*5 oz*	140	8.1	9.7			297	.07	2.7					.42		
tuna helper, prepared[a]															
dumplings, noodles & tuna	230		6.0								1020				
1 serving	b	13.0	31.0												
noodles, cheese sce & tuna	230		7.0						'		745				
1 serving	b	14.0	28.0												
noodles, cream sce & tuna	280		11.0								880				
1 serving	b	13.0	31.0												
tuna noodle casserole, frzn, Stouffer's	200		9.0								670				
5¾ oz	163	10.0	18.0								210				
tuna noodle casserole, homemade	280		11.8												
1 cup	200	17.8	25.0												
tuna pie, frzn, Banquet	434		22.9				2	.16			958	93			
8 oz	227	14.1	42.7			1498	.18	3.6			15	175	2.40		
turkey a la king, homemade	212		11.7				6	.14			497	15			
6 oz	180	16.6	9.5		0.2	486	.07	4.2			28	142	1.30		
turkey w/gravy & dressing, frzn,	310		11.0						.10		1396				
Swanson—*9¼ oz*	262	32.0	21.0						1.02		529	419			
turkey, gravy, dressing, whpd potatoes,	260		9.0						.12		880				
frzn, **Swanson Hungry-Man**—*8¾ oz*	248	20.0	26.0						.77		397	186			
turkey pie															
frzn, Banquet	415		21.6				2	.11			1017	107			
8 oz	227	14.5	40.6			788	.11	3.7			18	168	2.60		
frzn, Stouffer's	460		26.0								1735				
10 oz	284	20.0	35.0								270				
frzn, Swanson	460		25.0						.07		1146	39	27	1.84	.39
8 oz	227	13.0	47.0						.64		182	102	2.27	.30	
frzn, Swanson Hungry-Man	800		47.0						.18		2020	77	395	2.72	.50
16 oz	454	30.0	64.0						1.14		386	204	4.99	.50	
homemade	538	127.6	30.6				5	.30			620	61			
8 oz	227	23.6	42.0		0.9	3019	.25	5.7			449	229	3.20		
turkey tetrazzini, frzn, Stouffer's	240		14.0								620				
6 oz	170	12.0	17.0								200				
turkey w/dressing & gravy, frzn,	250		11.0				0	.15			809	32			
Campbell's—*7½ oz*	210	19.0	19.0			0	.15	5.3			325	209	1.50		
veal, breaded w/spaghetti & tomato sce,	290		15.0						.19		995				
frzn, **Swanson Hungry-Man**—*8¼ oz*	234	14.0	24.0						2.48		421	164			
veal scallopini, homemade	199		11.3				tr	.29			918	106			
4 oz	116	20.4	2.7		0.1	94	.05	10.1			385	228	2.10		
veal & veg (carrot & onion) stew,	242		15.6				0	.17				32			
homemade—*1 cup*	238	17.6	7.1		0.6	3253	.07	2.9				191	2.90		
welsh rarebit, frzn bb, Green Giant	220		14.6				4	.21				175			
5 oz	140	10.1	11.2			126	.06	0.4					.28		
welsh rarebit, frzn, Stouffer's	355		29.0								660				
5 oz	142	8.0	17.0								155				
welsh rarebit, homemade	415	162.9	31.6					.53			770	582			
1 cup	232	18.8	14.6		0.0	1230	.09	2.3			320	432	.70		

CREAMS, CREAM SUBSTITUTES & WHIPPED TOPPINGS
CREAMS

	KCAL / WT (g)	H₂O (g) / PRO (g)	FAT (g) / CHO (g)	PUFA (g) / SFA (g)	CHOL (mg) / FIBR (g)	A (RE) / A (IU)	C (mg) / B-1 (mg)	B-2 (mg) / NIA (mg)	B-6 (mg) / B-12 (mcg)	FOL (mcg) / PANT (mg)	Na (mg) / K (mg)	Ca (mg) / P (mg)	Mg (mg) / Fe (mg)	Zn (mg) / Cu (mg)	Mn (mg)
half & half	20	12.1	1.7	tr	6	16	tr	.02	.01	tr	6	16	2		.08
1 T	15	0.4	0.6	1.1	0.0	65	.01	tr	.05	.04	19	14	.01		
light (coffee/table)	29	11.1	2.9	0.1	10	27	tr	.02	.01	tr	6	14	1		.04
1 T	15	0.4	0.6	1.8	0.0	108	.01	tr	.03	.04	18	12	.01		
medium (25% fat)	37	10.3	3.8	0.1	13	35	tr	.02	.01	tr	6	14	1		.04
1 T	15	0.4	0.5	2.3	0.0	141	tr	tr	.03	.04	17	11	.01		

[a] 1 serving = ⅕ pkg + 1⅓ oz tuna   [b] Gram wt not available

	KCAL	H₂O (g)	FAT (g)	PUFA (g)	CHOL (mg)	A (RE)	C (mg)	B-2 (mg)	B-6 (mg)	FOL (mcg)	Na (mg)	Ca (mg)	Mg (mg)	Zn (mg)	Mn (mg)
	WT (g)	PRO (g)	CHO (g)	SFA (g)	FIBR (g)	A (IU)	B-1 (mg)	NIA (mg)	B-12 (mcg)	PANT (mg)	K (mg)	P (mg)	Fe (mg)	Cu (mg)	
sour, cultured	26	8.5	2.5	tr	5	23	tr	.02	tr	1	6	14	1	.03	
1 T	12	0.4	0.5	1.6	0.0	95	tr	tr	.04	.04	17	10	.01		
sour, half & half, cultured	20	12.0	1.8	tr	6	17	tr	.02	tr	2	6	16	2	.08	
1 T	15	0.4	0.6	1.1	0.0	68	.01	tr	.05	.05	19	14	.01		
sour, imitation	59	20.2	5.5	tr	0	0	0	.00	.00	0	29	1			
1 oz	28	0.7	1.9	5.0	0.0	0	.00	0.0	.00	.00	46	13			
whipped, pressurized	8	1.8	0.7	tr	2	6	0	tr	tr		4	3	tr	.01	
1 T	3	0.1	0.4	0.4	0.0	27	tr	tr	.01	.01	4	3	tr		
whipping, heavy, fluid	52	8.7	5.6	0.2	21	63	tr	.02	tr	1	6	10	1	.03	
1 T	15	0.3	0.4	3.5	0.0	220	tr	tr	.03	.04	11	9	tr		
whipping, light, fluid	44	9.5	4.6	0.1	17	44	tr	.02	tr	1	5	10	1	.04	
1 T	15	0.3	0.4	2.9	0.0	169	tr	tr	.03	.04	15	9	tr		

CREAM SUBSTITUTES

	KCAL	H₂O (g)	FAT (g)	PUFA (g)	CHOL (mg)	A (RE)	C (mg)	B-2 (mg)	B-6 (mg)	FOL (mcg)	Na (mg)	Ca (mg)	Mg (mg)	Zn (mg)	Mn (mg)
liquid/frzn[a]	20	11.6	1.5	tr	0	1	0	.00	.00	0	12	1	tr	tr	
½ fl oz	15	0.2	1.7	0.3	0.0	13	.00	0.0	.00	.00	29	10	tr		
liquid/frzn[b]	20	11.6	1.5	tr	0	1	0	.00	.00	0	12	1	tr	tr	
½ fl oz	15	0.2	1.7	1.4	0.0	13	.00	0.0	.00	.00	29	10	tr		
powdered[b]	11	tr	0.7	tr	0	tr	0	tr	.00	0	4	tr	tr	tr	
1 t	2	0.1	1.1	0.7	0.0	4	.00	0.0	.00	.00	16	8	tr		
Mrs. Smith's	15		0.1		0		0	.00			10	tr			
1 T	6	0.1	3.0			0	.00	0.0			15		.00		
Pet, powdered	10		1.0								5				
1 t	2	0.0	1.0								23				

WHIPPED TOPPINGS

	KCAL	H₂O (g)	FAT (g)	PUFA (g)	CHOL (mg)	A (RE)	C (mg)	B-2 (mg)	B-6 (mg)	FOL (mcg)	Na (mg)	Ca (mg)	Mg (mg)	Zn (mg)	Mn (mg)
frzn	13	2.0	1.0	tr	0	3	0	.00	.00	0	1	tr	tr	tr	
1 T	4	0.1	0.9	0.9	0.0	34	.00	0.0	.00	.00	1	tr	tr		
frzn, Cool Whip	13	1.9	1.0	tr	tr		0	tr	tr	tr	1	tr	tr	tr	
1 T	4	0.1	1.0	1.0	0.0	28	tr	tr	.00	tr	tr	1	.01	.001	
frzn, Dover Farms	17	2.3	1.3	tr	1		tr	tr	tr	tr	2	1	tr	.002	
1 T	5	0.1	1.3	1.2	0.0	46	tr	tr	tr	tr	1	1	.02	.002	
from mix, prep w/whole milk	8	2.7	0.5	tr	tr	2	tr	.01	tr	tr	3	4	tr	.01	
1 T	4	0.1	0.7	0.4	0.0	14	tr	.01	.01		6	3	tr		
from mix, Dream Whip	10		0.5	tr	1		tr	.01	tr	tr	4	5	1	.015	
1 T	5	0.2	1.0	0.4	tr	11	tr	tr	.01	.01	6	4	tr	.001	
from mix, low cal, D-Zerta	7	1.9	0.6	tr	tr		tr	.01	tr	tr	7	3	1	.008	
1 T	3	0.1	0.3	0.5	tr	8	tr	tr	.01	.02	8	5	tr	tr	
from mix, Whip n Top	3		0.0		0		0	.00			2	tr			
1 T	4	0.0	1.0			0	.00	0.0			0		.00		
pressurized	11	2.4	0.9	tr	0	2	0	.00	.00	0	2	tr	tr	tr	
1 T	4	tr	0.6	0.8	0.0	19	.00	0.0	.00	.00	1	1	tr		

DESSERTS & DESSERT SAUCES, SYRUPS & TOPPINGS
DESSERTS

brownies	KCAL	H₂O (g)	FAT (g)	PUFA (g)	CHOL (mg)	A (RE)	C (mg)	B-2 (mg)	B-6 (mg)	FOL (mcg)	Na (mg)	Ca (mg)	Mg (mg)	Zn (mg)	Mn (mg)
butterscotch	115		5.0			0		.02			98	31			
1 brownie	30	1.3	16.3		tr		.01	tr			88	45	.50		
choc, from mix	130		5.0								95				
1 brownie	32	1.0	20.0												
choc w/nuts & icing	81	2.6	3.5				tr	.05	.03	2	47	10	8	.29	
1 brownie	20	0.9	12.7		0.1	59	.06	0.3	.04	.10	40	21	.48	.09	
choc, Hostess	151	3.2	6.0		11		0	.05			75	15			
1 small	35	1.4	23.8			24	.00	0.4					.53		
choc, Hostess	241	5.0	9.5		17		0	.08			120	25			
1 large	56	2.2	38.1			39	.00	0.6					.84		
choc, Little Debbie	219		7.3					.10				11			
2 small	52	2.3	36.0				.19	0.5					1.16		

[a] Contains hydrogenated veg oil & soy pro; veg oils are usually soybean, cottonseed, safflower, or blends thereof.

[b] Contains lauric acid oil & Na caseinate; lauric oils include modified coconut oil, hydrogenated coconut oil &/or palm kernel oil.

	KCAL	H_2O (g)	FAT (g)	PUFA (g)	CHOL (mg)	Vitamins A (RE)	C (mg)	B-2 (mg)	B-6 (mg)	FOL (mcg)	Minerals Na (mg)	Ca (mg)	Mg (mg)	Zn (mg)	Mn (mg)
	WT (g)	PRO (g)	CHO (g)	SFA (g)	FIBR (g)	A (IU)	B-1 (mg)	NIA (mg)	B-12 (mcg)	PANT (mg)	K (mg)	P (mg)	Fe (mg)	Cu (mg)	
choc, Sara Lee	192	7.5	9.7				0	.06			108	11	1		
1 brownie	46	2.0	26.0		0.3	144	.06	0.4			97	29			
cake															
angel food, homemade	161	18.9	0.1				tr	.14	.01	5	161	7	7	.12	
1 piece	60	4.8	35.7	tr		0	.07	0.7	.02	.14	59	17	.51	.02	
angel food, from mix	126	20.0	0.2				0	.11	.01	4	269	44	4	.05	
1/12 cake	53	3.2	28.6		0.1	0	.03	0.1	.00	.12	70	91	.23	.03	
apple cinn, from mix	260		11.0								275				
1/12 cake	a	3.0	36.0												
applesce spice, from mix	250		11.0								290				
1/12 cake	a	3.0	34.0												
apple streusel crumb, Sara Lee	200	13.1	8.3				15	.08			210	11	5		
1 piece	54	2.5	29.3		0.3	65	.11	0.9			43	31	.81		
apple walnut, Sara Lee	212	15.6	10.2				1	.20			179	18	10		
1/8 cake	57	2.3	27.7		0.3	201	.04	0.4			60	20	.51		
banana, from mix	260		11.0								305				
1/12 cake	a	3.0	36.0												
banana, Sara Lee	175	12.9	6.9				0	.05			154	7	6		
1/8 cake	49	1.3	26.8		0.1	146	.04	0.5			56	37	.39		
banana nut, Sara Lee	111	10.9	5.4				1	.05			72	7	7		
1/10 cake	33	1.4	14.4		0.1	63	.06	0.4			49	20	.46		
banana w/buttercream icing	181		6.7				tr	.02			122	32			
1 piece	50	1.2	29.4		tr	288	tr	0.4			77	47	tr		
black forest, Sara Lee	194	32.7	9.3				10	.08			133	34	10		
1/8 cake	71	1.8	27.9		0.3	158	.02	0.4			80	75	.57		
blueberry crumb, Sara Lee	169	13.7	6.0				1	.09			192	19	4		
1 piece	50	2.0	26.8		0.6	136	.07	0.6			33	58	.85		
boston cream pie[b]	332	38.0	10.3				tr	.12			205	74			
1 piece	110	5.5	54.9		0.0	230	.03	0.2			98	111	.50		
boston cream pie,[b] frzn, Mrs. Smith's	260		8.0		20		0	.18			225	26			
1/8 cake	120	2.0	44.0			95	.01	0.7			40		.60		
butter brickle, from mix	260		11.0								255				
1/12 cake	a	3.0	37.0												
butter pecan, from mix	250		11.0								250				
1/12 cake	a	3.0	35.0												
butter recipe, from mix	230		8.0								295				
1/12 cake	a	3.0	36.0												
caramel, from mix	173		7.8				tr	.04			137	35			
1 piece	45	2.0	24.2		0.1	81	.01	0.1			31	48	.60		
caramel, w/caramel icing, from mix	208		8.1				tr	.04			139	46			
1 piece	55	2.0	32.5		0.0	110	.01	0.1			35	52	.80		
carrot, from mix	250		11.0								255				
1/12 cake	a	3.0	35.0												
carrot, Pepperidge Farm	249		12.0				2	.02			211	22			
1 piece	80	2.4	32.0			1453	.02	0.2			166	0	.80		
carrot, Sara Lee	238	22.2	12.1				0	.18			194	20	14		
1/8 cake	67	2.5	29.4		0.5	1187	.03	0.5			76	64	.74		
cheesecake	257	39.0	16.3				4	.11	.05	15	189	48	9	.36	
1 piece	85	4.6	24.3		0.4	216	.03	0.4	.42	.49	83	75	.41	.05	
cheesecake, from mix	300	43.0	14.3	1.1	30		1	.27	.05	7	366	181	22	.427	
1/8 cake	103	6.0	37.8	8.9	0.1	366	.11	0.6	.31	.35	241	193	.36	.059	
cheesecake, Sara Lee	230	35.5	11.3				1	0.2			153	61	10		
1/6 cake	80	5.1	27.0		0.7	363	.06	0.6			79	76	.48		
cheesecake, blueberry, Sara Lee	228	40.4	7.9				11	.16			178	36	10		
1/6 cake	90	3.8	35.3		1.6	248	.07	0.6			73	66	.72		
cheesecake, cherry, Sara Lee	243	41.5	7.8				12	.14			184	37	10		
1/6 cake	90	4.3	35.2		1.0	432	.06	0.5			70	74	.81		
cheesecake, strawberry, Sara Lee	222	42.0	8.2				6	.14			171	41	12		
1/6 cake	90	3.7	33.6		1.5	205	.04	0.5			87	68	.54		
cherry chip, from mix	180		3.0								265				
1/12 cake	a	2.0	36.0												

[a] Gram wt not available   [b] Yellow cake w/yellow cream filling & choc icing

	KCAL	H₂O (g)	FAT (g)	PUFA (g)	CHOL (mg)	A (RE)	C (mg)	B-2 (mg)	B-6 (mg)	FOL (mcg)	Na (mg)	Ca (mg)	Mg (mg)	Zn (mg)	Mn (mg)
	WT (g)	PRO (g)	CHO (g)	SFA (g)	FIBR (g)	A (IU)	B-1 (mg)	NIA (mg)	B-12 (mcg)	PANT (mg)	K (mg)	P (mg)	Fe (mg)	Cu (mg)	
choc, from mix	250		11.0								450				
¹/₁₂ cake	a	3.0	35.0												
choc, Sara Lee	185	10.4	8.9				2	.11			135	16	12		
⅛ cake	47	1.9	24.4		0.6	170	.01	0.4			96	53	1.36		
choc chip, from mix	190		4.0								240				
¹/₁₂ cake	a	3.0	35.0												
choc chip, Sara Lee	143	9.4	6.8				tr	.09			75	18	11		
¹/₁₀ cake	37	2.0	17.4			81	.06	1.1			89	31	.88		
choc, devil's food, homemade	227	13.8	11.3				tr	.11	.02	6	160	68	23	.48	
1 piece	60	3.4	30.4		0.2	53	.08	0.7	.13	.24	95	76	1.03	.14	
choc, devil's food, from mix	191	21.7	9.3				0	.08	.03	6	341	54	16	.41	
1 piece	60	2.9	24.8		0.2	47	.06	0.8	.26	.12	129	128	1.21	.10	
choc, devil's food, w/choc icing, homemade—1 piece	233	11.6	10.8				tr	.08	.02	4	108	50	21	.40	
	60	2.6	34.2		0.2	39	.05	0.5	.10	.17	87	62	.83	.14	
choc fudge & nut torte, Sara Lee	200	19.0	11.8				2	.13			144	40	21		
⅛ cake	56	2.4	21.0		0.7	108	.04	0.4			128	94	1.23		
choc fudge bundt ring, from mix	270		12.0								315				
¹/₁₆ cake	a	3.0	37.0												
choc fudge w/van icing, from mix	280		10.0								295				
¹/₆ cake	a	2.0	46.0												
choc macaroon bundt ring, from mix	250		11.0								315				
¹/₁₆ cake	a	3.0	35.0												
choc mint, from mix	250		12.0								375				
¹/₁₂ cake	a	4.0	33.0												
choc pudding, from mix	230		5.0								255				
¹/₆ cake	a	2.0	45.0												
cinn raisin crumb, Sara Lee	196	13.4	7.8				15	.08			199	12	7		
1 piece	54	2.4	29.7		0.3	61	.11	0.8			62	32	.86		
coconut, Sara Lee	246	30.5	13.1				1	.09			96	44	10		
⅛ cake	78	2.3	29.9		0.7	144	.06	0.4			73	55	.55		
cottage pudding, homemade	172	13.3	5.6				tr	.08			150	45			
1 piece	50	3.2	27.2		0.1	70	.07	0.6			44	58	.70		
cottage pudding w/choc sce, homemade—1 piece	223	19.5	6.2				tr	.10			163	50			
	70	3.7	39.6		0.2	70	.08	0.7			98	76	1.00		
cottage pudding w/fruit sce, homemade—1 piece	204	25.6	6.2				8	.10			163	51			
	70	3.6	33.8		0.2	84	.08	0.8			6.5	65	.80		
french crumb, Sara Lee	188	8.8	6.7				tr	.11			171	17	4		
1 piece	48	2.1	29.9		0.3	137	.08	0.6			29	60	.62		
fruitcake, dark	152	7.2	6.1				tr	.06			63	29	6		
1 piece	40	1.9	23.9		0.2	48	.05	0.4			198	45	1.00		
fruitcake, light	156	7.5	6.6				tr	.05			77	27	6		
1 piece	40	2.4	23.0		0.3	28	.04	0.3			93	46	.60		
german choc, from mix	260		11.0								420				
¹/₁₂ cake	a	3.0	36.0												
german choc, Pepperidge Farm	297		16.0				0	.06			244	26			
1 piece	80	3.2	35.2			0	.03	0.4			151	0	.72		
german choc, Sara Lee	198	12.6	11.4				0	.13			153	28	14		
⅛ cake	50	2.5	22.1		0.6	189	.04	0.3			93	63	.90		
gingerbread, homemade	267	17.1	12.9				tr	.11	.05	6	99	48	15	.32	
1 piece	70	3.0	35.0		0.1	28	.13	1.1	.07	.27	237	41	2.11	.13	
gingerbread, from mix	210	28.1	6.0					.06			325	68			
¹/₉ cake	76	2.0	36.0		tr		.02	0.6			208	76	1.22		
lemon, from mix	260		11.0								260				
¹/₁₂ cake	a	3.0	36.0												
lemon bundt ring, from mix	270		10.0								290				
¹/₁₆ cake	a	2.0	43.0												
lemon chiffon, from mix	190		4.0								190				
¹/₁₂ cake	a	4.0	35.0												
lemon pudding, from mix	230		5.0								270				
¹/₆ cake	a	2.0	45.0												
marble, from mix	270		11.0								280				
¹/₁₂ cake	a	3.0	40.0												

a Gram wt not available

	KCAL / WT (g)	H₂O (g) / PRO (g)	FAT (g) / CHO (g)	PUFA (g) / SFA (g)	CHOL (mg) / FIBR (g)	A (RE) / A (IU)	C (mg) / B-1 (mg)	B-2 (mg) / NIA (mg)	B-6 (mg) / B-12 (mcg)	FOL (mcg) / PANT (mg)	Na (mg) / K (mg)	Ca (mg) / P (mg)	Mg (mg) / Fe (mg)	Zn (mg) / Cu (mg)	Mn (mg)
marble, w/white icing, from mix	165	11.8	4.3				45	.04			129	39			
1 piece	50	2.2	31.0		tr		.01	0.1			61	85	.40		
marble streusel w/icing, from mix	224	19.0	9.8				tr	.08	.03	6	278	34	9	.26	
1 piece	65	2.5	32.7		0.2	38	.07	0.6	.13	.22	71	129	.88	.06	
orange, from mix	260		11.0								280				
¹/₁₂ cake	a	3.0	36.0												
orange, Pepperidge Farm	244		8.8								252				
1 piece	80	2.4	39.2			63					109	0			
orange, Sara Lee	192	11.2	7.6				3	.03			157	15	4		
1 piece	50	1.6	29.2		0.2	223	.05	0.4			30	29	.40		
orange w/icing, homemade	183		6.6				tr	.02			141	37			
1 piece	50	1.5	29.9		tr	286	.01	0.4			79	56	.10		
pineapple, Pepperidge Farm	247		9.6				1	.05			220	14			
1 piece	80	2.4	38.4			0	.04	0.2			90	0	.72		
pineapple upside-down, homemade	236	25.0	9.1				4	.08	.05	9	179	54	13	.41	
1 piece	75	2.5	37.4		0.2	291	.12	0.8	.06	.25	128	47	1.19	.09	
pineapple upside-down, from mix	270		10.0								215				
¹/₉ cake	a	2.0	43.0												
plum pudding cake, cnd	270		1.0								150				
2 inch wedge	101	4.0	61.0												
pound (old-fashioned), homemade	142	5.2	8.8				0	.03			33	6			
1 piece	30	1.7	14.1		tr	84	.01	0.1			18	24	.20		
pound (modified), homemade	123	5.8	5.6				tr	.03			53	12			
1 piece	30	1.9	16.4		tr	87	.01	0.1			23	31	.20		
pound, from mix	200		9.0								155				
¹/₁₂ cake	a	2.0	27.0												
pound, Sara Lee	125	7.4	6.9				tr	.08			104	11	3		
¹/₁₀ cake	31	1.6	14.2		0.1	193	.06	0.5			22	33	.53		
pound, banana nut, Sara Lee	117	8.4	5.6				0	.05			104	9	6		
¹/₁₀ cake	31	1.6	15.1		0.1	139	.04	0.4			51	42	.43		
pound, choc, Sara Lee	122	7.3	6.4				1	.07			134	11	8		
¹/₁₀ cake	30	1.5	14.5		0.5	149	.04	0.3			52	37	.80		
pound, choc swirl, Sara Lee	130	7.3	5.7				1	.08			116	12	9		
¹/₁₀ cake	33	1.8	17.9		0.5	98	.04	0.4			57	40	.92		
pound, raisin, Sara Lee	126	9.9	4.5				1	.11			108	15	5		
¹/₁₀ cake	37	1.8	19.6		0.3	169	.07	0.5			61	52	.56		
shortcake	86		2.0				tr	.03				10			
1 piece	25	1.0	12.2			85	.03	0.1				13	.10		
shortcake w/blackberries	347		8.3				30	.08				105			
1 serving	149	4.6	57.7			490	.04	0.4				101	.90		
shortcake w/peaches	266		6.3				8	.13				31			
1 serving	150	3.2	42.4			1109	.12	1.6				66	1.20		
shortcake w/raspberries	290		6.7				29	.16				72			
1 serving	160	4.2	47.4			389	.12	1.1				90	1.70		
shortcake w/strawberries	344		8.9				89	.21				73			
1 serving	175	4.8	61.2			429	.17	1.3				84	2.00		
snack cake,[b] from mix, Duncan Hines—*¹/₉ cake*	187		5.3								248				
	a	2.3	31.7												
snackin cake,[c] from mix, General Mills—*¹/₉ cake*	186		5.8								245				
	a	2.0	31.5												
sour cream choc, from mix	260		11.0								420				
¹/₁₂ cake	a	3.0	36.0												
sour cream white, from mix	180		3.0								260				
¹/₁₂ cake	a	3.0	36.0												
spice, from mix	175		5.9				0	.09			175	31	6		
1 piece	50	2.2	28.3			60	.07	0.6				115	.50		
spice w/van icing, from mix	176		5.4				0	.80			193	35	9		
1 piece	50	2.0	30.4		tr	80	.06	0.5			102	96	.60		
sponge, homemade	188	21.6	3.1				tr	.13	.04	15	164	25	7	.80	
1 piece	66	4.8	35.7		tr	125	.09	0.7	.33	.53	59	65	1.11	.03	
sponge, Sara Lee	113	8.5	4.2				tr	.09			94	12	3		
1 piece	32	1.5	17.0		0.1	200	.06	0.5			22	35	.54		

ᵃ Gram wt not available
ᵇ Avg of apple raisin, banana nut & choc chip

ᶜ Avg of applesce raisin, banana walnut, choc almond, golden choc chip, choc fudge chip, coconut pecan, date nut, spice raisin, german choc coconut pecan & carrot nut

	KCAL / WT (g)	H₂O (g) / PRO (g)	FAT (g) / CHO (g)	PUFA (g) / SFA (g)	CHOL (mg) / FIBR (g)	A (RE) / A (IU)	C (mg) / B-1 (mg)	B-2 (mg) / NIA (mg)	B-6 (mg) / B-12 (mcg)	FOL (mcg) / PANT (mg)	Na (mg) / K (mg)	Ca (mg) / P (mg)	Mg (mg) / Fe (mg)	Zn (mg) / Cu (mg)	Mn (mg)
sponge w/strawberries & whipped cream—1 serving	328		7.8				45	.13				45			
	153	4.1	60.4			485	.04	0.3				77	1.20		
strawberry, from mix	260		11.0								260				
¹⁄₁₂ cake	a	3.0	36.0												
strawberry, Pepperidge Farm	240		8.0				4	.06			216	17			
1 piece	80	2.4	39.2			0	.05	0.4			93	0	.64		
strawberry layer, Sara Lee	277	50.7	12.7				28	.17			179	50	13		
¹⁄₁₀ cake	107	2.3	38.6		1.9	178	.06	0.5			78	103	.64		
streusel swirl,b from mix	260		11.0								257				
¹⁄₁₆ cake	a	3.0	37.6												
van, Pepperidge Farm	283		12.8				0	.06			288	15			
1 piece	80	2.4	39.2			0	.06	0.4			63	0	.56		
walnut, Sara Lee	148	8.4	8.2				0	.04			73	17	6		
¹⁄₁₀ cake	36	2.3	16.4		0.1	64	.03	0.2			36	35	.29		
white, homemade	285	19.4	11.6				tr	.16	.02	5	346	87	11	.27	
1 piece	78	4.6	40.9		0.1	29	.12	1.1	.08	.22	80	66	.84	.03	
white, from mix	219	26.6	9.8				tr	.08	.01	4	293	34	4	.11	
1 piece	71	2.5	31.2		0.1	tr	.06	0.7	.04	.21	34	115	.46	.03	
white mountain devil's food, Sara Lee—1 piece	220	10.7	11.1				0	.13			155	19	11		
	53	1.7	28.3		0.3	127	.02	0.4			90	60	.74		
white w/choc icing, homemade	298	15.8	12.1				tr	.12	.02	4	219	62	15	.29	
1 piece	78	3.3	45.8		0.1	23	.08	0.7	.06	.15	84	58	.75	.09	
yellow, homemade	283	17.9	12.4				tr	.15	.03	9	329	89	11	.41	
1 piece	75	4.3	38.9		0.1	74	.13	1.1	.19	.35	72	80	1.02	.03	
yellow, from mix	231	23.6	10.8				0	.11	.02	7	299	43	5	.41	
1 piece	69	3.1	30.5		0.1	56	.12	1.0	.18	.23	39	139	.87	.07	
yellow, Sara Lee	170	13.3	6.6				tr	.07			144	22	6		
¹⁄₈ cake	50	1.9	27.5		0.2	158	.06	0.4			47	35	.60		
yellow w/choc icing, homemade	292	14.6	12.3				tr	.11	.02	6	208	62	14	.37	
1 piece	75	3.2	43.8		0.1	52	.08	0.7	.13	.24	79	66	.86	.08	
cake, coffee cake															
from mix	232		6.9					.12			310	44			
1 piece	72	4.5	37.7		0.1	115	.13	1.0			78	125	1.20		
almond ring, Sara Lee	165	9.7	8.1				tr	.14			157	14	10		
¹⁄₈ ring	42	2.9	20.0		0.3	85	.12	1.1			27	42	.88		
apple, Little Debbie	221		5.4					.08							
2 oz	57	2.6	40.4				.10	1.3					1.31		
apple, Sara Lee	161	16.7	7.0				4	.08			194	14	5		
¹⁄₈ cake	50	2.3	22.4		0.2	245	.10	0.8			38	30	.70		
apple cinn, from mix	240		7.0								155				
¹⁄₈ cake	a	3.0	40.0												
blueberry ring, Sara Lee	133	8.3	6.2				tr	.08			135	6	5		
¹⁄₈ ring	35	1.8	17.6		0.2	49	.05	0.8			29	22	.56		
butter pecan, from mix	310		15.0								335				
¹⁄₈ cake	a	4.0	39.0												
butter streusel, Sara Lee	164	9.0	8.0				tr	.14			179	11	7		
¹⁄₈ cake	41	2.7	20.3		0.3	303	.12	0.8			34	40	.86		
cinn streusel, from mix	250		8.0								225				
¹⁄₈ cake	a	3.0	41.0												
cinn streusel, Sara Lee	146	10.0	7.1				tr	.10			134	12	6		
¹⁄₈ cake	39	2.2	19.4		0.3	256	.10	0.8			36	28	.74		
maple crunch ring, Sara Lee	138	7.8	6.7				tr	.09			131	7	6		
¹⁄₈ ring	35	2.1	17.2		0.2	34	.09	0.9			29	25	.60		
pecan, Sara Lee	153	9.1	8.6				0	.08			159	8	8		
¹⁄₈ cake	40	2.3	19.1		0.2	256	.11	0.8			31	29	.64		
raspberry ring, Sara Lee	133	7.9	5.8				tr	.10			120	8	5		
¹⁄₈ ring	35	1.9	18.5		0.2	39	.09	0.6			26	23	.67		
sour cream, from mix	270		12.0								235				
¹⁄₈ cake	a	4.0	35.0												

a Gram wt not available

b Avg for cinn, devil's food, fudge marble, german choc, lemon, rich butter & banana

	KCAL / WT (g)	H₂O (g) / PRO (g)	FAT (g) / CHO (g)	PUFA (g) / SFA (g)	CHOL (mg) / FIBR (g)	A (RE) / A (IU)	C (mg) / B-1 (mg)	B-2 (mg) / NIA (mg)	B-6 (mg) / B-12 (mcg)	FOL (mcg) / PANT (mg)	Na (mg) / K (mg)	Ca (mg) / P (mg)	Mg (mg) / Fe (mg)	Zn (mg) / Cu (mg)	Mn (mg)
cake, cupcake/snack cake															
apple delight, Little Debbie	227		7.1					.12				8			
2 oz	57	2.7	38.0				.13	0.8					1.14		
apple spice cake, Little Debbie	248		10.3					.05				7			
2 oz	57	1.6	37.2				.05	0.4					.42		
banana twin, Little Debbie	227		8.1					.07				9			
2 oz	57	2.0	36.6				.09	0.6					.60		
cherry bar, Little Debbie	175		4.6					.08							
2 bars	47	2.2	31.4				.07	0.8					.04		
choco-dile, Hostess	492	20.9	22.1		43		0	.15			443	48			
2 cakes	123	3.7	73.8			87	.15	1.2					1.72		
coco-jel, Little Debbie	266		12.3					.09				6			
2 oz	57	1.7	37.2				.09	0.6					.82		
coconut crunch, Little Debbie	318		19.0					.08							
2 oz	57	1.6	35.1				.01	0.2					.64		
coconut round, Little Debbie	264		11.8					.07				4			
2 oz	57	2.0	37.4				.05	0.7					.98		
crumb cake, Hostess	259	20.7	8.4		21		0	.12			193	31			
2 cakes	70	2.8	42.7			43	.11	1.1					1.19		
cupcake, choc, Hostess	314	24.5	8.8		10		0	.14			490	43			
2 cakes	98	2.9	58.8			2	.00	1.3					1.37		
cupcake, choc w/icing, from mix	129		4.5					.04			121	47			
1 cake	36	1.6	21.3		0.1	61	.01	0.1			42	71	.30		
cupcake, orange, Hostess	294	18.5	8.4		25		0	.12			298	38			
2 cakes	84	2.5	52.9			48	.11	1.0					.92		
cupcake, yellow w/choc icing	155		5.3					.07							
1 cake	40	1.6	25.2				.04	0.2							
cupcake, yellow w/van icing	160		6.2					.08			184	16			
1 cake	40	1.3	24.8			96	tr	0.1					.20		
devil square, Little Debbie	263		10.4					.09				6			
2 squares	61	2.2	40.2				.06	0.8					.96		
devil twin, Little Debbie	224		6.8					.08				10			
2 pieces	59	2.2	38.6				.06	0.8					.80		
ding dongs/big wheels, Hostess	345	8.3	20.3		14		0	.08			191	35			
2 cakes	75	2.3	42.8			16	.00	0.5					.90		
dutch apple bar, Little Debbie	207		5.3					.06				9			
2 oz	57	1.8	38.1				.05	0.6					.70		
fudge frostee, Little Debbie	248		9.3					.02							
2 oz	57	3.2	37.8				.02	1.4					2.79		
fudge krispy, Little Debbie	256		7.1					.11							
2 oz	57	1.9	46.1				.03	0.6					1.70		
fudge round, Little Debbie	315		12.5					.14				10			
2 pieces	71	2.6	47.9				.11	1.5					1.66		
ho hos, Hostess	235	8.4	11.8		25		0	.04			157	24			
2 cakes	56	2.2	32.5			45	.00	0.1					.56		
honey bun, Hostess	572	26.6	33.3		33		0	.19			818	32			
1 bun	133	5.3	62.5			11	.23	2.1					1.60		
jel-creme roll, Little Debbie	221		7.0					.05				6			
2 oz	57	1.5	38.1				.06	0.8					.51		
loco lemon, Little Debbie	266		12.8					.01							
2 oz	57	3.2	34.7				.01	1.5					2.39		
nutty bar, Little Debbie	312		18.6					.08				13			
2 bars	57	3.8	32.3				.01	1.7					.83		
oatmeal cremes, Little Debbie	332		12.6					.13				16			
2 pieces	76	3.7	51.1				.11	0.8					1.18		
peanut butter bar, Little Debbie	265		13.5					.12				13			
2 bars	52	5.8	30.1				.07	2.6					.95		
shortcake snack, Cadbury	144		6.9												
1 oz	28	1.6	19.1												
snoballs, Hostess	269	22.7	7.6		4		0	.08			323	24			
2 cakes	84	2.5	49.6			1	.00						1.01		

	KCAL / WT (g)	H₂O (g) / PRO (g)	FAT (g) / CHO (g)	PUFA (g) / SFA (g)	CHOL (mg) / FIBR (g)	A (RE) / A (IU)	C (mg) / B-1 (mg)	B-2 (mg) / NIA (mg)	B-6 (mg) / B-12 (mcg)	FOL (mcg) / PANT (mg)	Na (mg) / K (mg)	Ca (mg) / P (mg)	Mg (mg) / Fe (mg)	Zn (mg) / Cu (mg)	Mn (mg)
star crunch, Little Debbie	290		11.8					.09					12		
2 pieces	61	2.2	43.9				.07	0.6					.95		
strawberry wafer, Little Debbie	302		16.6					.09							
2 oz	57	2.9	35.2				.07	1.0					.91		
super-stix, Little Debbie	285		14.0					.71					19		
2 oz	57	8.5	31.2				.60								
suzy q's, banana, Hostess	479	25.2	17.6		44		0	.23			384	91			
2 cakes	126	5.0	75.6			67	.16	1.5					1.51		
suzy q's, choc, Hostess	466	29.0	18.9		32		0	.11			617	42			
2 cakes	126	2.5	71.8			8	.00	1.0					1.64		
swiss cake roll, Little Debbie	264		12.0					.08				8			
2 rolls	61	1.9	37.2				.07	0.5					.80		
tiger tail, Hostess	418	28.3	13.5		52		1	.16			480	54			
2 cakes	123	3.7	75.0			106	.17	1.4					1.85		
twinkies, Hostess	286	20.2	8.4		42		0	.12			378	38			
2 cakes	84	2.5	51.2			81	.11	1.0					1.09		
twinkies, devil's food, Hostess	286	21.0	10.1		21		0	.12			420	31			
2 cakes	84	2.5	48.7			32	.00	1.0					1.26		
white cake w/choc icing, Little Debbie—*2 cakes*	317		14.2					.09				9			
	71	2.4	45.0				.10	1.2					1.24		
white cake, w/white icing, Little Debbie—*2 cakes*	320		15.1					.05							
	71	1.9	44.1				.07	0.4					.35		
cake icing															
homemade, boiled	128	7.2	0.0				0				56				
amt for ¹/₁₂ cake	40	0.4	32.0	0.0							8				
from mix[a]	167		6.2								91				
amt for ¹/₁₂ cake	39	0.0	28.2												
ready-to-spread,[b] General Mills	169		6.9								97				
¹/₁₂ tub	39	0.0	26.5												
ready-to-spread,[c] Pillsbury	160		6.3								69				
amt for ¹/₁₂ cake	39	0.2	25.8												
low calorie, Baker's Joy	4		tr		0										
amt for ¹/₁₀ cake	0.4	0.0	0.0												
caramel	140	5.5	5.0								35	39			
amt for ¹/₁₂ cake	39	tr	24.0	0.0		109					20	23	.39		
choc	148	5.6	5.5					.04			23	23			
amt for ¹/₁₂ cake	39	1.2	26.1		tr	82					78	43	.39		
choc, double dark	150		4.0								80				
amt for ¹/₁₂ cake	36	tr	26.0												
choc fudge	150	6.0	4.0				0				70	8	8		
amt for ¹/₁₂ cake	39	tr	27.0			105					23	27	.39		
coconut	140	5.9	3.1				0				47	4			
amt for ¹/₁₂ cake	39	0.8	29.3	0.4		0					66	12	.39		
coconut almond	170		10.0								95				
amt for ¹/₁₂ cake	35	2.0	17.0												
coconut pecan	150		8.0								105				
amt for ¹/₁₂ cake	33	1.0	20.0												
lemon	140		5.0								15				
amt for ¹/₁₂ cake	33	tr	25.0												
milk choc	150		5.0								55				
amt for ¹/₁₂ cake	32	tr	26.0												
strawberry	140		5.0								55				
amt for ¹/₁₂ cake	32	1.0	25.0												
van	150		5.0								30				
amt for ¹/₁₂ cake	36	0.0	25.0												
white, fluffy	70		0.0								85	4			
amt for ¹/₁₂ cake	18	0.0	17.0	0.0		49					4				

[a] Avg for sour cream white, lemon, choc fudge, dark choc fudge, milk choc, sour cream choc, coconut almond, butter brickle, butter pecan, banana, coconut pecan, cherry, white & choc almond fudge

[b] Avg for butter pecan, cherry, orange, sour cream white, lemon, van, choc, choc nut, choc chip, dark dutch fudge, milk choc, sour cream choc & cream cheese

[c] Avg for choc fudge, double dutch, lemon, milk choc, strawberry, van, sour cream van, sour cream choc & cream cheese

	KCAL	H₂O (g)	FAT (g)	PUFA (g)	CHOL (mg)	A (RE)	C (mg)	B-2 (mg)	B-6 (mg)	FOL (mcg)	Na (mg)	Ca (mg)	Mg (mg)	Zn (mg)	Mn (mg)
	WT (g)	PRO (g)	CHO (g)	SFA (g)	FIBR (g)	A (IU)	B-1 (mg)	NIA (mg)	B-12 (mcg)	PANT (mg)	K (mg)	P (mg)	Fe (mg)	Cu (mg)	
cookies (commercial unless otherwise indicated)															
animal	120		2.9				0	.13	.01	4	113	3	3	.14	
15 cookies	28	1.9	22.0		0.1	0	.08	1.1	.01	.06	26	17	.92	.024	
arrowroot	47		1.7					.03			24	6			
2 cookies	10	0.6	7.3				.04	0.2			11	13	.30		
bordeaux, Pepperidge Farm	78		3.5				34	.02			50	11			
2 cookies	16	0.8	11.0		tr		.03	0.2			26	13	.30		
brownie, Pepperidge Farm	336	1.3	17.3				0	.06			234	18			
2 large cookies	64	3.8	40.3			0	.03	0.7			172		.83		
capri, Pepperidge Farm	82		4.6					.01			39	6	7		
1 cookie	16	0.8	9.7		0.1		.02	0.2			36	16	.30		
cherry coolers	58		2.1									3			
2 cookies	12	0.5	8.7									11	.20		
choc	93	0.8	3.3					.02			29	11	3		
1 cookie	21	1.5	15.0		0.1	34	.01	0.1			27	27	.20		
choc chip, homemade	46	0.3	2.7				0	.02	tr	1	21	3	4	.04	
1 cookie	10	0.5	6.4		tr	4	.02	0.1	.01	.03	21	8	.25	.03	
choc chip, from mix	120		6.0								75				
2 cookies	25	1.0	16.0												
choc chip, from refrig dough	47	0.5	2.3				0	.02	tr	1	36	3	2	.05	
1 cookie	10	0.5	6.6		tr	6	.01	0.2		.02	13	7	.22	.01	
choc chip, Pepperidge Farm	321	1.3	14.7				0	.04			182	15			
2 large cookies	64	3.2	44.2			0	.03	0.3			141		.83		
choc chip coconut	82		4.4									8			
1 cookie	16	0.9	10.0									22	.30		
choc sandwich	49	0.2	2.1					.02	tr	tr	63	3	5	.09	
1 cookie	10	0.5	7.1		tr		.02	0.2	.00		22	10	.36	.04	
choc snaps	53		1.8									5			
4 cookies	12	0.7	8.8									15	.30		
coconut bars	109	0.6	5.4				0	.01			33	16	3		
1 bar	22	1.4	14.1		0.1	35	.01	0.1			50	26	.30		
fig bars	53	1.7	1.0				tr	.02	.02	1	45	10	4	.09	
1 bar	14	0.5	10.6		0.2	16	.02	0.2	tr	.05	41	8	.34	.04	
gingersnaps	50	0.4	1.1					tr			69	9	2		
3 small	12	0.7	9.6		tr	8	tr	tr			55	6	.30		
gingersnaps, homemade	34	0.2	1.6				tr	.01	tr	1	20	3	1	.03	
1 cookie	7	0.3	4.7		tr	3	.01	0.1	.01	.02	14	4	.16	.01	
golden fruit	63		0.6									13			
1 cookie	19	0.8	14.8									21	.60		
graham crackers, choc covered	62		3.1				0	.04			53	15			
1 cookie	13	0.7	8.8		0.1	8	.01	0.2			42	27	.30		
granola, Pepperidge Farm	318	2.8	15.4				0	.04			230	21			
2 large cookies	64	3.8	41.0			0	.08	0.4			147		.83		
lemon coolers	57		2.2									4			
2 cookies	12	0.5	8.7									8	.20		
lemon nut, Pepperidge Farm	336	1.5	17.9				0	.06			189	22			
2 large cookies	64	3.8	40.3			0	.03	0.3			97		.38		
lido, Pepperidge Farm	90		5.3					.02			32	tr	5		
1 cookie	17	0.9	9.9		tr		.02	0.3			23	17	.30		
macaroons	67		3.2				0	.02			5	4			
1 cookie	14	0.7	9.3		0.3	0	.01	0.1			65	12	.10		
milano, Pepperidge Farm	63		3.6					.01			22	5	4		
1 cookie	12	0.7	7.3		tr		.02	0.2			18	12	.20		
molasses	71		2.9				0	.02			58	15			
1 cookie	15	0.8	10.2		tr	14	.03	0.2			21	11	.50		
oatmeal	80		3.2					.03			69	7			
1 cookie	18	1.1	12.2				.05	0.3			20	22	.40		
oatmeal, homemade	62	0.4	2.6				0	.02	.01	2	45	11	5	.13	
1 cookie	13	0.8	8.9		tr	5	.03	0.2	.01	.07	31	18	.41	.01	
oatmeal, from mix	130		6.0								80				
2 cookies	28	1.0	17.0												

	KCAL	H₂O (g)	FAT (g)	PUFA (g)	CHOL (mg)	A (RE)	C (mg)	B-2 (mg)	B-6 (mg)	FOL (mcg)	Na (mg)	Ca (mg)	Mg (mg)	Zn (mg)	Mn (mg)
	WT (g)	PRO (g)	CHO (g)	SFA	FIBR (g)	A (IU)	B-1 (mg)	NIA (mg)	B-12 (mcg)	PANT (mg)	K (mg)	P (mg)	Fe (mg)	Cu (mg)	
oatmeal choc chip	57		2.7								23				
1 cookie	13	0.7	7.3												
oatmeal raisin, from refrig dough	61	0.6	2.6				0	.02	.01	2	37	4	4	.08	
1 cookie	13	0.7	8.9		0.1	10	.02	0.2		.06	23	14	.28	.01	
oatmeal, Pepperidge Farm	305	2.7	12.8				0	.04			262	15			
2 large cookies	64	3.8	44.2			0	.06	0.3			102		.64		
orleans, Pepperidge Farm	61		3.6					.01			15	4	6		
2 cookies	12	0.6	7.3		0.1		.02	0.2			23	13	.20		
peanut	57	0.3	2.3				tr	.01			21	5			
1 cookie	12	1.2	8.0		0.1	24	.01	0.3			21	14	.10		
peanut butter, from refrig dough	50	0.5	2.6				0	.02	tr	2	57	12	4	.08	
1 cookie	10	0.8	5.9		tr	15	.02	0.4		.01	19	24	.19	.02	
peanut butter bar	198		9.7				0	.06			116	28			
1 bar	50	4.4	26.1		0.2	97	.06	1.8			119	87	.60		
rochelle, Pepperidge Farm	82		4.6					.02			39	7	8		
1 cookie	16	0.8	9.7		0.1		.03	0.3			29	18	.30		
shortbread, homemade	42	0.2	2.3				tr	.02	tr	1	36	2	1	.04	
1 cookie	8	0.5	4.9		tr	85	.02	0.2	tr	.02	5	9	.15	tr	
social tea	43		1.1					.03			33	2			
2 cookies	10	0.7	7.5				.03	0.2			6	8	.20		
sugar, homemade	89	1.6	3.4				tr	.03			64	16			
1 cookie	20	1.2	13.6		tr	22	.03	0.3			15	21	.30		
sugar, from mix	120		5.0								75				
2 cookies	24	1.0	18.0												
sugar, from refrig dough	35	0.3	1.7				0	.01	tr	1	38	7	1	.02	
1 cookie	7	0.3	4.6		tr	5	.01	0.2		.02	5	13	.14	tr	
sugar, Pepperidge Farm	312	2.4	13.4				0	.05			202	15			
2 large cookies	64	3.8	44.2			0	.03	0.3			83		.38		
sugar wafers	53	0.2	2.1				0	tr			21	4	2		
2 wafers	11	0.5	8.0		tr	15	tr	0.1			7	9	tr		
toy	41		1.5				11				160	1	4		
3 cookies	10	0.6	7.4		tr						7	9	tr		
van creme sandwich	69		3.1				0	.01			68	4	2		
1 cookie	14	0.7	9.7		tr	0	.01	0.1			5	34	.10		
van wafers	51	0.3	1.8				0	.01			28	4	2		
3 wafers	11	0.6	8.2		tr	14	tr	tr			8	7	tr		
vienna dream bar, from mix	90		5.0								65				
1 bar	ᵃ	1.0	10.0												
vienna finger sandwich	72		3.0									6			
1 cookie	15	0.7	10.7									14	.30		
custard															
homemade, baked	153	102.7	7.3				tr	.25			104	148			
½ cup	133	7.1	14.7			465	.05	0.1			193	150	.55		
homemade, boiled	164		7.3				0	.25			103	131	18		
½ cup	130	7.1	18.2		0.0	486	.07	0.1			190	151	.80		
from mix	161	107.5	5.4	0.3	80		1	.28	.09	12	219	194	23	.645	
½ cup	143	5.4	22.9	3.0	0.0	199	.08	0.2	.71	.78	254	174	.47	.060	
banana	143		4.6								125	142			
½ cup	112	5.6	19.9								180				
choc	142		4.4								153	144			
½ cup	112	5.9	19.6								186				
coconut	144		4.4								124	141			
½ cup	112	5.7	20.3								174				
lemon	143		4.6								92	142			
½ cup	112	5.6	19.8								179				
van	143		4.6								128	142			
½ cup	112	5.6	19.7								174				
danish pastry															
apple, Sara Lee	121	11.9	4.9				5	.09			110	8	4		
1 pastry	37	1.8	17.4		0.4	86	.06	0.5			28	20	.48		

ᵃ Gram wt not available

	KCAL / WT (g)	H₂O (g) / PRO (g)	FAT (g) / CHO (g)	PUFA (g) / SFA (g)	CHOL (mg) / FIBR (g)	A (RE) / A (IU)	C (mg) / B-1 (mg)	B-2 (mg) / NIA (mg)	B-6 (mg) / B-12 (mcg)	FOL (mcg) / PANT (mg)	Na (mg) / K (mg)	Ca (mg) / P (mg)	Mg (mg) / Fe (mg)	Zn (mg) / Cu (mg)	Mn (mg)
caramel w/nuts, from refrig dough	300		14.0								485				
2 pastries	86	4.0	39.0												
cheese, Sara Lee	131	12.4	7.2				tr	.11			125	18	5		
1 pastry	37	2.5	13.9		0.3	172	.07	0.6			36	31	.52		
cherry, Sara Lee	123	12.1	5.6				4	.09			103	10	5		
1 pastry	37	1.8	16.4		0.4	247	.06	0.5			41	20	.67		
cinn raisin, from refrig dough	270		11.0								450				
2 pastries	78	3.0	40.0												
cinn raisin, Sara Lee	147	8.4	7.6				tr	.12			132	18	7		
1 pastry	37	2.5	17.3		0.3	135	.09	0.7			55	38	.74		
custard streusel, Sara Lee	303	18.7	15.1				tr	.16			285	21	9		
1 pastry	77	4.6	37.1		0.5	52	.22	1.7			58	51	1.16		
orange, from refrig dough	270		11.0								485				
2 pastries	80	3.0	39.0												
orange, Sara Lee	149	7.8	7.5				5	.08			149	15	4		
1 pastry	37	2.1	18.6		0.2	143	.09	0.7			35	27	.56		
pecan, Sara Lee	148	7.8	7.3				tr	.11			119	21	8		
1 pastry	37	2.3	18.3		0.3	128	.09	1.0			46	37	.67		
plain	161	11.2	8.8				tr	.10			161	45	6		.35
1 pastry	42	2.6	18.8		0.2	45	.10	0.9			39	43	.78		
plain, Little Debbie	245		9.8					.06							
2 oz	57	1.7	37.5				.06	0.6					.46		
raspberry, Sara Lee	287	18.0	10.7				2	.13			243	13	10		
1 pastry	78	3.7	44.1		0.5	73	.17	1.5			56	40	1.17		
strawberry, Sara Lee	115	14.9	6.2				3	.06			122	12	3		
1 pastry	37	1.7	13.2		0.2	117	.07	0.6			26	22	.41		
doughnut															
cake	105	5.3	5.8				tr	.05	.01	2	139	11	6		.13
1 doughnut	25	1.3	12.2	tr		14	.06	0.4		.10	27	55	.37	.03	
cake, Hostess	115	6.2	7.0		7		0	.04			133	12			
1 doughnut	28	1.1	12.6			3	.05	0.5					.39		
cake w/sugar icing	151		6.5	0.3			tr	.06				12	8		
1 doughnut	37	2.1	21.7	tr		41	.07	0.5				26	.60		
choc covered, Hostess	129	4.5	8.4		4		0	.03			95	10			
1 doughnut	28	1.1	13.4			3	.03	0.3					.39		
cinn, Hostess	109	5.9	5.6		6		0	.03			109	10			
1 doughnut	28	0.8	14.3			3	.04	0.4					.28		
cream filled	122		4.7	0.2			0	.05				15	9		
1 doughnut	35	1.8	16.2		0.0	65	.06	0.5				23	.40		
krunch, Hostess	101	6.4	3.9		4		0	.03			105	17			
1 doughnut	28	0.8	16.2			2	.04	0.4					.31		
old fashioned, Hostess	172	10.1	10.1		10		0	.06			164	11			
1 doughnut	42	1.7	19.3			3	.09	0.7					.55		
powdered sugar, Hostess	112	5.9	5.9		7		0	.03			109	9			
1 doughnut	28	0.8	14.8			3	.04	0.4					.28		
raised/yeast	124	8.5	8.0	0.3			0	.05			70	11	6		
1 doughnut	30	1.9	11.3		0.1	18	.05	0.4			24	23	.50		
raised, jelly center	226		8.8	0.3			tr	.10				28	16		
1 doughnut	65	3.4	30.0		tr	121	.12	0.9				42	.80		
sugar	153		9.5				tr	.02			64	23			
1 doughnut	30	1.4	16.2			31	.02	0.1				21	.20		
fruit betty/cobbler/crisp/dumpling															
apple brown betty	211	90.3	4.9				1	.06			214	25	7		
½ cup	140	2.2	41.6		0.7	140	.08	0.6			140	31	.80		
apple crisp	302		8.1				2	.03			228	10			
½ cup	145	0.9	58.0		0.4	357	.05	0.4			79	15	.70		
apple dumpling	280		17.0				2	.05			210	1			
1 dumpling	85	2.0	31.0			8	.16	0.5			45	16	.90		
cherry crisp	226		0.1					.05				26			
½ cup	140	1.2	55.0				.06	0.4					1.50		

	KCAL / WT (g)	H₂O(g) / PRO(g)	FAT(g) / CHO(g)	PUFA(g) / SFA(g)	CHOL(mg) / FIBR(g)	A(RE) / A(IU)	C(mg) / B-1(mg)	B-2(mg) / NIA(mg)	B-6(mg) / B-12(mcg)	FOL(mcg) / PANT(mg)	Na(mg) / K(mg)	Ca(mg) / P(mg)	Mg(mg) / Fe(mg)	Zn(mg) / Cu(mg)	Mn(mg)
peach cobbler	160		6.4				26	.07			158	7			
⅓ cup	100	1.0	25.4		0.2	479	.03	0.9			88	15	.50		
peach crisp	249		9.3				38	.06			235	10	1		
½ cup	145	5.8	36.7		0.3	695	.04	1.3			128	22	.73		
gelatin dessert															
all flavors[a]	81	118.9	tr	tr	0		0	.00	.00	0	55	tr	tr	.011	
½ cup	140	1.6	18.7	tr	0.0	0	.00	0.0	.00	.00	1	31	.02	.004	
all flavors, low cal, D-Zerta[b]	8	118.8	tr	tr	0		0	.00	.00	0	9	tr	tr	tr	
½ cup	121	1.6	tr	tr	0.0	0	.00	0.0	.00	.00	45	tr	tr	tr	
bavarian,[c] choc	347	41.9	24.5				0	.15			103	61	24		
1 serving	99	3.6	28.1		0.4	446	.04	0.5			187	70	1.40		
bavarian,[c] choc mint	331	39.9	23.3				0	.14			98	58	23		
1 serving	95	3.4	26.7		0.4	424	.04	0.5			178	67	1.33		
bavarian,[c] dutch apple	194	39.2	8.0				1	.12			130	45	10		
1 serving	79	2.1	28.6		0.6	111	.05	0.3			104	41	.40		
bavarian,[c] lime	278	42.8	17.7				0	.08			76	40	7		
1 serving	91	2.3	27.9		0.5	353	.05	0.5			52	47	.27		
bavarian,[c] strawberry	277	51.4	17.9				50	.13			79	50	11		
1 serving	99	3.2	25.8		0.5	439	.04	0.6			92	60	.50		
granola dessert															
granola bar	109		4.2					.03			67	14			
1 bar	24	2.3	16.0		0.2		.07		.00	.13	78	66	.76		
granola bar, Little Debbie	133		5.5					.05				16			
1 bar	28	2.4	18.3				.08	0.1					.77		
granola bar,[d] Nature Valley	110		5.0								65				
1 bar	24	2.0	16.0												
granola bar, choc chip, chewy, Quaker—1 bar	130		5.0								95				
1 bar	28	2.0	19.0								75				
granola & fruit bar,[e] Nature Valley	140		4.0								150				
1 bar	33	2.0	25.0												
granola clusters,[f] Nature Valley	150		3.0								115				
1 roll	34	2.0	28.0												
granola snack, light & crunchy,[g]	140		7.0								175				
Nature Valley—1 pouch	28	2.0	18.0												
ice cream															
choc	295		16.0					.27			75	186	18		
1 cup	133	5.0	32.8			567	.07	0.2				168			
french custard	257		14.4				1	.28			84	194	10		
1 cup	133	6.0	27.7		0.0	585	.05	0.1			241	153	.10		
french van, soft serve	377	103.4	22.5	1.0	153	199	1	.45	.10	9	153	236	25	1.99	
1 cup	173	7.0	38.3	13.5	0.0	794	.08	0.2	1.00	1.07	338	199	.43		
strawberry	250		12.0					.20			59	146	19		
1 cup	133	4.3	31.3			503	.05	0.1				124			
van, reg (10% fat)	269	80.9	14.3	0.5	59	133	1	.33	.06	3	116	176	18	1.41	
1 cup	133	4.8	31.7	8.9	0.0	543	.05	0.1	.63	.65	257	134	.12		
van, rich (16% fat)	349	87.1	23.7	0.9	88	219	1	.28	.05	2	108	151	16	1.21	
1 cup	148	4.1	32.0	14.7	0.0	897	.04	.12	.54	.56	221	115	.10		
ice cream/ice milk bars/novelties															
creamsicle	103		3.1					.08			27	46	5		
1 bar	66	1.2	17.6			125	.02	0.3			82	37	.00		
drumstick	186		9.9					.09			57	67	7		
1 drumstick	60	2.6	21.5			185	.02	0.5			99	59	.10		
fudgsicle	91		0.2					.18			55	129	14		
1 bar	73	3.8	18.6			0	.03	0.7			173	99	.10		

[a] Apricot, blackberry, cherry, concord grape, lemon, lime, mixed fruit, orange, orange pineapple, peach, raspberry, strawberry, strawberry banana, or wild strawberry

[b] Cherry, lemon, lime, orange, raspberry, or strawberry

[c] Flavored whipped gelatin mixture w/whipped cream

[d] Almond, coconut, cinn, oat & honey, or peanut

[e] Apple, date, or raspberry

[f] Almond, caramel, or raisin

[g] Cinn, oats & honey, or peanut butter

	KCAL	H₂O (g)	FAT (g)	PUFA (g)	CHOL (mg)	A (RE)	C (mg)	B-2 (mg)	B-6 (mg)	FOL (mcg)	Na (mg)	Ca (mg)	Mg (mg)	Zn (mg)	Mn (mg)
	WT (g)	PRO (g)	CHO (g)	SFA (g)	FIBR (g)	A (IU)	B-1 (mg)	NIA (mg)	B-12 (mcg)	PANT (mg)	K (mg)	P (mg)	Fe (mg)	Cu (mg)	
ice cream cone (cone only)	45	1.1	0.3				tr	.02			28	19			
1 cone	12	1.2	9.3		tr	tr	.01	0.1			29	24	.10		
ice cream sandwich	167		6.2	0.3				.10			92	73	7		
1 sandwich	62	3.1	26.1			193	.02	0.5			102	72	.10		
van ice cream bar w/choc coating	162		10.6					.10			28	70	8		
1 bar	60	2.1	14.5			209	.02	0.1			107	52			
van ice milk bar w/choc coating	144		7.6					.14			38	98	8		
1 bar	60	2.8	16.0			83	.04	0.1			126	73			
ice milk															
choc	137		4.6	0.1			1	.20			61	140	12		
⅔ cup	90	4.3	20.2		0.0	190	.04	0.1			175	111	.10		
strawberry	133		3.1					.23			64	161	12		
⅔ cup	90	4.3	22.1			129	.06	0.1				121			
van	184	89.9	5.6	0.2	18	52	1	.35	.09	3	105	176	19	.55	
1 cup	131	5.2	29.0	3.5	0.0	214	.08	0.1	.88	.66	265	129	.18		
van, soft serve	223	121.9	4.6	0.2	13	44	1	.54	.13	5	162	274	29	.86	
1 cup	175	8.0	38.4	2.9	0.0	175	.12	0.2	1.37	1.03	412	202	.28		
ices[a]															
lime/orange	247	129.1	tr				2	tr			tr	tr			
1 cup	193	0.8	62.9			tr	tr	tr			6	tr	tr		
lime/orange	165	86.3	tr				1	tr			tr	tr			
⅔ cup	129	0.5	41.9		.	tr	tr	tr			4	tr	tr		
pastry															
cream puff w/custard filling	245	61.2	14.6				0	.18			87	85	14		
1 cream puff	105	6.8	21.5		0.0	368	.04	0.1			127	120	.70		
eclair w/choc icing & custard filling	316		15.4				0	.24				90			
1 eclair	110	7.6	39.1		0.0	730	.12	1.0				150	1.30		
eclair w/choc icing & custard filling, frzn—*1 eclair*	205	19.3	9.7		35			.08			113	10	10	.26	
	57	2.3	27.2		0.0		.03	0.4			47	33	.84	.12	
eclair w/choc icing & whipped filling	296		25.7				0	.12				48			
1 eclair	105	3.9	15.0		0.0	1120	.07	0.3				70	.70		
lady finger w/whipped cream filling	326	51.9	16.6					.11			49	52			
1 lady finger	114	6.7	38.2			844	.03	0.1				104	.80		
pie															
apple, homemade	282	60.0	11.9				tr	.09	.03	6	181	11	9	.20	
⅛ pie	118	2.4	43.0		0.5	22	.13	1.1	.00	.17	100	27	1.06	.06	
apple, frzn, Banquet	240		9.7				1	.02			298	8			
⅙ pie	95	2.7	35.5			27	.02	0.3			73	17	.25		
apple, frzn, Mrs. Smith's	390		17.0		10		0	.06			590	15			
⅛ pie	163	3.0	56.0			230	.03	0.5			120		.70		
apple lattice, frzn, Mrs. Smith's	350		13.0		5		0	.05			440	14			
⅛ pie	128	2.0	58.0			195	.09	0.9			80		.60		
apple natural jce, frzn, Mrs. Smith's	420		22.0		5		0	.06			370	13			
1/7 pie	149	3.0	52.0			230	.01	0.3			60		1.40		
apple, old fashioned, frzn, Mrs. Smith's—*⅛ pie*	515		27.0		10		0	.08			620	10			
	177	4.0	64.0			315	.03	1.3			105		1.00		
apple streusel, frzn, Mrs. Smith's	420		16.0		5		0	.05			365	21			
1/7 pie	167	3.0	67.0			250	.01	0.3			85		.70		
banana cream, frzn, Banquet	258		14.4				1	.16			116	136			
¼ pie	99	8.9	29.9			123	.03	0.2			158	137	.12		
banana cream, frzn, Mrs. Smith's	240		12.0		5		0	.14			180	39			
⅛ pie	85	2.0	31.0			85	.04	0.6			70		.70		
banana custard, homemade	353	87.0	14.8				2	.20			310	106	21		
1 piece	160	7.2	49.2		0.3	400	.06	0.5			325	131	.80		
blackberry, homemade	389	81.6	17.6				6	.03			429	30	10		
1 piece	160	4.2	55.0		3.0	144	.03	0.5			160	42	.80		
blueberry, homemade	387	81.6	17.3				5	.03			429	18	10		
1 piece	160	3.8	56.0		1.1	48	.03	0.5			104	37	1.00		

[a] Sweet frzn dessert containing fruit jce or other flavoring

	KCAL / WT (g)	H_2O (g) / PRO (g)	FAT (g) / CHO (g)	PUFA (g) / SFA (g)	CHOL (mg) / FIBR (g)	Vitamins: A (RE) / A (IU)	C (mg) / B-1 (mg)	B-2 (mg) / NIA (mg)	B-6 (mg) / B-12 (mcg)	FOL (mcg) / PANT (mg)	Minerals: Na (mg) / K (mg)	Ca (mg) / P (mg)	Mg (mg) / Fe (mg)	Zn (mg) / Cu (mg)	Mn (mg)
blueberry, frzn, Banquet	253		10.1				3	.02			263	11			
1/6 pie	95	3.1	37.5			26	.02	0.3			71	18	.53		
blueberry, frzn, Mrs. Smith's	380		17.0		10		0	.05			535	12			
1/8 pie	163	4.0	54.0			230	.01	0.5			80		.50		
butterscotch, homemade	427	72.2	17.6				tr	.16			342	120	21		
1 piece	160	7.0	61.3		tr	416	.05	0.3			152	130	1.40		
butterscotch cream, homemade	264		15.3				tr	.11			139	69			
1 piece	100	3.1	29.0		tr	319	.06	0.9			124	69	1.00		
cherry, homemade	418	74.6	18.1				tr	.03			486	22	10		
1 piece	160	4.2	61.5		0.2	705	.03	0.8			168	40	.50		
cherry, frzn, Banquet	228		9.1				tr	.02			294	10			
1/6 pie	95	2.7	33.8			377	.02	0.4			108	19	.25		
cherry, frzn, Mrs. Smith's	400		16.0		10		0	.06			445	34			
1/8 pie	163	4.0	60.0			165	.03	0.3			140		1.00		
cherry lattice, frzn, Mrs. Smith's	350		11.0		5		0	.13			490	12			
1/8 pie	128	3.0	59.0			540	.01	0.0			125		.60		
cherry natural jce, frzn, Mrs. Smith's	410		18.0		10		0	.06			380	15			
1/7 pie	149	4.0	59.0			140	.06	0.6			140		1.10		
choc chiffon, homemade	262	26.4	12.2				0	.08			201	19			
1 piece	80	5.4	35.0		0.1	248	.03	0.1			88	77	.90		
choc cream, homemade	301	56.4	17.3				tr	.19	.05	10	311	96	29	.75	
1/8 pie	114	5.2	33.6		0.2	301	.11	0.8	.42	.55	162	124	1.23	.14	
choc cream, frzn, Banquet	266		13.7				1	.16			95	147			
1/4 pie	99	3.0	32.8			111	.03	0.2			162	110	.13		
choc cream, frzn, Mrs. Smith's	270		13.0		5		0	.06			235	23			
1/8 pie	85	2.0	35.0			130	.01	0.9			115		.60		
choc meringue, homemade	378	72.6	18.0				tr	.18			385	103			
1 piece	150	7.2	50.0		0.3	286	.05	0.3			209	147	1.00		
coconut cream, frzn, Banquet	261		15.3				1	.16			97	120			
1/4 pie	99	2.3	28.7			134	.03	0.2			145	127	.13		
coconut cream, frzn, Mrs. Smith's	270		14.0		5		0	.07			220	25			
1/8 pie	85	2.0	33.0			80	.04	0.2			55		.70		
coconut custard, homemade	365	85.9	19.4				0	.29			284	145	20		
1 piece	155	9.4	38.5		0.2	357	.09				253	180	1.10		
coconut custard, from mix	203		7.9					.14			235	93			
1 piece	100	4.3	29.1		0.3	210	.03	0.2			154	103	.40		
coconut custard, frzn, Banquet	203		7.9				tr	.15			297	78			
1/6 pie	95	4.8	28.3			198	.04	0.3			112	88	.55		
coconut custard, frzn, Mrs. Smith's	330		15.0		50		0	.32			550	123			
1/8 pie	156	9.0	40.0			170	.03	0.7			270		1.30		
custard, homemade	327	87.2	16.6				0	.24			430	144			
1 piece	150	9.2	35.1		tr	345	.08	0.4			205	170	.90		
custard, frzn, Banquet	206		6.6				tr	.16			289	76			
1/6 pie	95	4.8	31.8			185	.04	0.3			120	85	.65		
custard, frzn, Mrs. Smith's	300		9.0		65		0	.42			490	156			
1/8 pie	156	9.0	45.0			75	.06	0.0			240		.80		
lemon chiffon, homemade	335	38.1	13.5				3	.08			279	25			
1 piece	107	7.5	46.9		tr	182	.03	0.2			87	89	1.00		
lemon chiffon, from pudding mix	288		9.6				3	.08			261	23			
1 piece	100	2.5	45.0			170	.03	0.2			81	83	.90		
lemon cream, frzn, Banquet	252		12.7				2	.15			99	145			
1/4 pie	99	1.2	32.8			126	.03	3.3			169	115	.20		
lemon cream, frzn, Mrs. Smith's	245		12.0		5		0	.07			185	16			
1/8 pie	85	2.0	32.0			175	.03	0.7			60		.60		
lemon meringue, homemade	350	66.4	13.1				4	.14	.03	13	260	18	8	.39	
1/6 pie	140	4.5	55.1		0.1	195	.11	0.8	.22	0.4	62	56	1.05	.03	
lemon meringue, from pudding mix	227		7.5				3	.08			282	14			
1 piece	100	2.7	36.4			170	.03				50	49	.50		
lemon meringue, frzn, Mrs. Smith's	310		10.0		35		1	.06			315	15			
1/8 pie	120	2.0	52.0			215	.08	0.5			35		.60		
mincemeat, homemade	434	68.8	18.4				2	.06			716	45	29		
1 piece	160	4.0	66.0		0.6	tr	.11	0.6			285	61	1.60		

	KCAL	H₂O (g)	FAT (g)	PUFA (g)	CHOL (mg)	A (RE)	C (mg)	B-2 (mg)	B-6 (mg)	FOL (mcg)	Na (mg)	Ca (mg)	Mg (mg)	Zn (mg)	Mn (mg)
	WT (g)	PRO (g)	CHO (g)	SFA (g)	FIBR (g)	A (IU)	B-1 (mg)	NIA (mg)	B-12 (mcg)	PANT (mg)	K (mg)	P (mg)	Fe (mg)	Cu (mg)	
mincemeat, frzn, Banquet	252		9.6				1	.04			459	28			
⅙ pie	95	3.0	38.5			10	.06	0.4			154	45	.90		
peach, homemade	421	78.4	17.7				5	.07			246	16	10		
1 piece	165	4.0	63.0		0.7	1200	.03	1.2				48	.80		
peach, frzn, Banquet	219		9.8				2	.04			274	10			
⅙ pie	95	2.8	29.9			665	.02	0.7			154	31	.50		
peach, frzn, Mrs. Smith's	365		16.0		10		0	.03			435	13			
⅛ pie	163	4.0	53.0			170	.06	0.3			205		.80		
pecan, homemade	334	15.6	18.3				tr	.05			177	37			
1 piece	80	4.1	41.0		0.4	128	.12	0.2			98	82	2.20		
pecan, frzn, Mrs. Smith's	510		23.0		30		0	.13			510	15			
⅛ pie	128	5.0	70.0			335	.05	0.8			95		1.00		
pineapple, homemade	404	76.8	17.1				2	.03			434	21			
1 piece	160	3.5	61.0		0.3	32	.06	0.6			115	34	.80		
pineapple cheese, homemade	270		9.5				1	.16				81			
1 piece	160	7.1	39.9		0.1	286	.08	0.2				107	.90		
pineapple chiffon, homemade	308	44.0	12.9				1	.09			274	26			
1 piece	107	7.0	41.8		0.1	374	.04	0.4			105	81	1.00		
pineapple custard, homemade	330	81.5	13.0				2	.14			279	75	20		
1 piece	150	6.0	48.1		0.2	270	.06	0.6			145	98	.60		
pumpkin, homemade	317	88.8	16.8				tr	.15			321	76	20		
1 piece	150	6.0	36.7		0.8	3700	.04	0.8			240	104	.80		
pumpkin, frzn, Banquet	206		6.9				tr	.08			221	45			
⅙ pie	95	3.6	32.3			2025	.03	0.4			170	57	.38		
pumpkin custard, frzn, Mrs. Smith's	310		11.0		30		0	.26			495	97			
⅛ pie	163	6.0	46.0			1540	.06	0.0			210		.80		
raisin, homemade	325	51.0	12.9				1	.04			342	22			
1 piece	120	3.1	51.6		0.4	tr	.04	0.4			231	48	1.10		
rhubarb, homemade	405	75.8	17.1				5	.06			432	102			
1 piece	160	4.0	61.2		1.0	80	.03	0.5			254	42	1.10		
shoofly, homemade	441	20.6	16.4				0	.07				129			
1 piece	110	4.0	70.6		0.1	411	.11	0.9				65	3.20		
strawberry, homemade	228	67.2	9.1				29	.05			227	18			
1 piece	115	2.2	35.6		0.9	46	.02	0.4			138	29	.80		
strawberry cream, frzn, Banquet	254		12.3				1	.16			125	149			
¼ pie	99	2.0	33.8			135	.03	0.2			170	145	.28		
strawberry w/whipped cream, homemade—1 piece	378		16.8				22	.05				47			
	145	2.9	56.2		0.9	485	.03	0.3				52	.70		
sweet potato, homemade	342	94.9	18.2				6	.19			349	110			
1 piece	160	7.2	37.8		0.3	3840	.08	0.5			261	134	.80		
piecrust/pastry crust															
crumb crust	866		64.4				0	.20				113			
1 crust	165	10.9	64.1		0.3	2460	.24	2.8				126	2.30		
graham cracker crust	159		10.0				0	.03			184	8	3		
1 serving	32	1.2	17.5		0.2	326	.01	0.2			57	24	.20		
pastry crust, enr	675	20.1	45.2				0	.19			825	19	19		
1 crust	135	8.2	59.1		0.3	0	.27	2.4			67	67	2.30		
pastry crust, unenr	675	20.1	45.2				0	.04			825	19	19		
1 crust	135	8.2	59.1		0.3		.04	0.7			67	67	.70		
pastry crust, from mix	626		39.3				0	.04			1098	55			
1 crust	135	8.6	59.4		0.3	0	.04	0.7			76		.50		
pastry crust, from sticks	290		18.0				0				400				
⅙ double crust	58	4.0	27.0												
pastry crust, frzn	130		8.0		5		0	.01			270	3			
¹⁄₁₆ crust	28	2.0	14.0			62	.02	0.0			25		.20		
pastry puff dough	129		10.0				0	.01			117	3			
1 oz	28	1.0	8.0			0	.01	0.1			10	11	.10		
patty shell	240		19.0				0	.06			210	0			
1 shell	71	2.0	15.0			5	.20	0.4			27	12	.90		

	KCAL	H_2O (g)	FAT (g)	PUFA (g)	CHOL (mg)	A (RE)	C (mg)	B-2 (mg)	B-6 (mg)	FOL (mcg)	Na (mg)	Ca (mg)	Mg (mg)	Zn (mg)	Mn (mg)
	WT (g)	PRO (g)	CHO (g)	SFA (g)	FIBR (g)	A (IU)	B-1 (mg)	NIA (mg)	B-12 (mcg)	PANT (mg)	K (mg)	P (mg)	Fe (mg)	Cu (mg)	
pie filling															
banana cream, from mix	103	72.2	2.7	0.1	11		1	.13	.03	4	167	99	11	.323	
amt for ⅙ pie	96	2.7	17.4	1.7	tr	102	.03	.07	.29	.26	124	76	.05	.036	
choc, cnd	123		3.0					.07			165	53			
amt for ⅙ pie	100	2.0	22.0								135				
coconut cream, from mix	111	72.1	4.3	0.1	11		1	.04	.03	4	139	102	14	.320	
amt for ⅙ pie	96	2.9	15.8	3.1	0.1	102	.03	0.1	.29	.26	140	81	.13	.024	
lemon w/meringue, from mix	175		1.9	0.3	91		0	.06	.02	10	92	11	2	.197	
amt for ⅙ pie	145	2.1	37.9	0.6	0.1	105	.01	tr	.22	.28	22	30	.37	.014	
pumpkin, cnd	350		0.0								840				
1 cup	270	2.0	87.0		3.2						350				
van, cnd	120		4.0					.06			165	40			
amt for ⅙ pie	100	1.0	20.0								55				
pie, snack pie															
apple, fried	258	40.6	13.1				0	.11			288	9	10	.24	
1 snack pie	90	2.7	32.6		0.2		.18	1.2			74	68	1.25	.05	
apple, Hostess	403	47.9	20.2		19		1	.14			410	26			
1 snack pie	126	2.5	52.9			6	.15	1.6					1.39		
berry, Hostess	391	50.4	20.2		19		4	.16			410	33			
1 snack pie	126	3.8	51.0			52	.16	1.9					1.76		
blueberry, Hostess	378	52.9	20.2		19		2	.14			410	28			
1 snack pie	126	2.5	49.1			23	.16	1.8					1.51		
cherry, Hostess	416	42.8	20.2		19		2	.14			410	29			
1 snack pie	126	3.8	58.0			134	.16	1.6					1.39		
lemon, Hostess	416	46.6	21.4		32		0	.13			416	26			
1 snack pie	126	2.5	51.7			26	.15	1.5					1.26		
peach, Hostess	403	47.9	20.2		19		1	.20			441	37			
1 snack pie	126	3.8	51.7			256	.19	2.3					2.02		
pecan, Little Debbie	376		4.0					.08							
4 oz	113	4.6	80.4				.06	0.2					1.02		
raisin creme, Little Debbie	492		20.6					.20					12		
4 oz	113	3.8	73.0				.16	2.0					1.64		
popsicle															
popsicle	65		0.0				0	.00					0		
1 bar	88	0.0	16.7			0	.00	0.0							
popsicle, kool pop	24		0.0								9				
1 bar	33	0.0	6.3												
popsicle, twin pop	95		tr												
1 bar	128	tr	23.7												
pudding															
banana, cnd	107		3.0					.07			205	61			
⅖ cup	100	1.0	19.0								60				
banana cream, from inst mix	172	108.4	4.3	0.2	17		1	.20	.05	6	441	147	17	.475	
½ cup	149	4.0	30.3	2.6	tr	154	.05	0.1	.44	.39	187	312	.09	.018	
bread w/raisins, homemade	314	96.7	10.0					.31				191			
¾ cup	165	8.9	47.8		0.2	457	.15	0.9				194	1.70		
butter pecan, from inst mix	174	107.8	4.8	0.3	17		1	.21	.05	7	443	150	19	.478	
½ cup	148	4.2	29.1	2.6	tr	154	.05	0.1	.44	.39	195	317	.14	.027	
butterscotch, homemade	207		4.7				0	.21				165			
½ cup	140	4.3	37.4		0.0	194	.04	0.1				124			
butterscotch, cnd	107		3.0					.07			215	60			
⅖ cup	100	1.0	19.0								65				
butterscotch, from inst mix	171	108.4	4.3	0.2	17		1	.20	.05	6	478ᵃ	147	17	.475	
½ cup	149	4.0	30.2	2.6	0.1	154	.05	0.1	.44	.39	187	338	.09	.018	
butterscotch, from mix, low cal,	69	111.8	0.2	tr	2		1	.20	.06	7	147	165	17	.52	
D-Zerta—½ cup	130	4.4	12.2	0.2	tr	250	.05	0.1	.50	.48	234	137	.06	.027	
choc, homemade	219	94.8	6.6				0	.22			81	147			
½ cup	144	4.5	37.1		0.1	196	.04	0.2			246	129	.20		

ᵃ Noninstant contains 245 mg Na.

Food	KCAL / WT (g)	H₂O / PRO (g)	FAT / CHO (g)	PUFA / SFA (g)	CHOL / FIBR (mg/g)	A (RE) / A (IU)	C / B-1 (mg)	B-2 / NIA (mg)	B-6 / B-12 (mg/mcg)	FOL / PANT (mcg/mg)	Na / K (mg)	Ca / P (mg)	Mg / Fe (mg)	Zn / Cu (mg)	Mn (mg)
choc, cnd	111		3.0					.07			150	60			
⅖ cup	100	1.0	20.0								110				
choc, from inst mix	179	107.6	4.5	0.2	17		1	.21	.05	6	527ᵃ	150	26	.476	
½ cup	151	4.4	31.3	2.2	0.1	154	.05	0.1	.44	.39	202	279	.34	.019	
choc, from mix, low cal, D-Zerta	65	112.2	0.5	tr	2		1	.18	.05	6	82	161	22	.495	
½ cup	130	4.6	11.5	0.3	0.1	251	.05	0.2	.07	.41	227	138	.29	.027	
choc fudge, from inst mix	178	107.6	4.6	0.2	17		1	.21	.05	6	495ᵇ	151	30	.474	
½ cup	151	4.6	31.6	2.8	0.2	154	.05	0.2	.44	.38	208	385	.44	.019	
choc mousse, low cal	200		6.0												
½ cup	226	8.0	28.0												
coconut cream, from inst mix	184	108.4	6.7	0.2	17		1	.20	.05	6	354	148	20	.474	
½ cup	149	4.3	27.8	4.7	0.1	154	.05	0.1	.44	.38	210	292	.22	.039	
french van, from inst mix	172	108.4	4.3	0.2	17		1	.20	.05	6	437ᶜ	149	17	.475	
½ cup	149	4.0	30.3	2.6	tr	154	.05	0.1	.44	.39	187	313	.09	.018	
indian, baked	161		5.6				0	.26			221				
⅔ cup	158	5.4	22.6			395	.08	0.4				151	1.40		
lemon, cnd	138		2.0								170				
⅖ cup	100	0.0	30.0								10				
lemon, from inst mix	178	107.9	4.3	0.2	17		1	.20	.05	6	387	147	17	.480	
½ cup	149	4.0	31.1	2.6	0.1	154	.05	0.1	.44	.39	192	326	.10	.019	
lemon snow, homemade	114		tr				10	.02				4			
½ cup	130	3.1	26.5		0.0	0	.01	tr				5	.10		
lemon snow w/custard sce, homemade—1 serving	249		6.0				10	.24				129			
	225	8.9	41.3		0.0	370	.06	0.1				136	.70		
milk choc, from mix	170		4.0								180				
½ cup	140	5.0	29.0		0.1						210				
pineapple cream, from inst mix	172	108.4	4.3	0.2	17		1	.20	.05	6	393	147	17	.475	
½ cup	149	4.0	30.4	2.6	tr	154	.05	0.3	.44	.39	187	312	.09	.018	
pistachio, from inst mix	182	107.9	5.1	0.4	17		1	.20	.06	7	424	149	19	.478	
½ cup	149	4.2	29.9	2.6	tr	154	.05	0.1	.44	.38	201	312	.15	.027	
rice, cnd	115		3.0					.07			120	65			
⅖ cup	100	2.0	20.0								85				
rice, from mix	175	108.9	4.1	0.2	17		1	.20	.05	6	158	150	20	.553	
½ cup	149	4.8	30.0	2.6	tr	154	.11	0.6	.44	.41	187	125	.54	.016	
rice pineapple	217		5.1				3	.01			15	10			
½ cup	130	0.9	43.0		0.2	24	.08	1.2			55	12	.40		
rice w/raisins, homemade	212	95.4	4.5				tr	.20			103	142			
¾ cup	145	5.2	38.7		0.1	160	.04	0.3			257	136	.60		
tapioca, homemade	133	75.4	5.0				1	.19				105			
½ cup	105	4.9	17.3		0.0	313	.05	0.1				109	.50		
tapioca, cnd	116		4.0					.09			140	55			
⅖ cup	100	2.0	18.0								125				
tapioca, from mix	160	108.3	4.1	0.2	17		1	.20	.05	6	170	147	17	.481	
½ cup	145	4.0	27.4	2.6	tr	154	.05	0.1	.44	.38	186	115	.09	.055	
tapioca, choc, from mix	169	108.5	4.6	0.2	17		1	.21	.05	6	169	151	29	.465	
½ cup	147	4.9	27.6	2.9	0.2	155	.05	0.2	.44	.38	204	143	.49		
van, homemade	152	95.0	4.7				0	.21				144			
½ cup	125	4.2	23.8	tr		195	.04	0.1				113	.10		
van, cnd	107		3.0					.07			305	40			
⅖ cup	100	1.0	19.0								50				
van, from inst mix (w/skim milk)	147		0.3	tr			2	.19			422ᶜ	157	14		
½ cup	148	4.1	31.2		0.0	254	.06	0.1			207	314	.10		
van, from inst mix (w/whole milk)	177	107.9	4.3	0.2	17		1	.20	.05	6	422ᶜ	148	17	.480	
½ cup	149	4.0	30.9	2.6	tr	154	.05	0.1	.59	.38	189	314	.10	.019	
van, from mix, low cal, De Zerta	71	111.5	0.2	tr	2		1	.20	.06	7	132	166	17	.525	
½ cup	130	4.4	12.6	0.2	tr	251	.05	0.1	.50	.50	238	139	.07	.027	
pudding pops															
banana	94	35.8	2.6	tr	1		tr	.11	.03		63	76	7	.244	
1 pop	57	2.4	15.7	2.5	tr	99	.03	tr	.16	.22	83	63	.04		
butterscotch	94	35.8	2.6	tr	1		tr	.11	.03		63	76	7	.245	
1 pop	57	2.4	15.7	2.5	tr	99	.03	tr	.17	.22	83	63	.04		tr

ᵃ Noninstant contains 190 mg Na.
ᵇ Noninstant contains 195 mg Na.
ᶜ Noninstant contains 200 mg Na.

	KCAL	H₂O (g)	FAT (g)	PUFA (g)	CHOL (mg)	A (RE)	C (mg)	B-2 (mg)	B-6 (mg)	FOL (mcg)	Na (mg)	Ca (mg)	Mg (mg)	Zn (mg)	Mn (mg)
	WT (g)	PRO (g)	CHO (g)	SFA (g)	FIBR (g)	A (IU)	B-1 (mg)	NIA (mg)	B-12 (mcg)	PANT (mg)	K (mg)	P (mg)	Fe (mg)	Cu (mg)	
choc	99	34.4	2.7	tr	1		tr	.11	.02		103	86	15	.353	
1 pop	57	2.7	16.5	2.5	0.1	67	.03	0.1	.05	.22	123	75	.36	.059	
choc fudge	99	34.2	2.7	tr	1		tr	.11	.02	3	105	88	16	.357	
1 pop	57	2.8	16.5	2.5	0.1	62	.03	0.1	.05	.23	127	79	.39	.059	
van	93	36.0	2.6	tr	1		tr	.11	.03		63	76	7	.245	
1 pop	57	2.4	15.7	2.5	tr	100	.03	tr	.17	.22	83	63	.04	tr	
rennin dessert															
homemade	113	103.0	4.4				1	.19			104	141			
½ cup	127	3.9	14.7		0.0	178	.04	0.1			160	105			
choc, from mix (w/skim milk)	95		0.5					.23			63	163	19		
½ cup	135	4.5	17.8		0.1		.08	0.7			186	128	.30		
choc, from mix (w/whole milk)	127	105.2	4.5	0.0				.22			59	159	19		
½ cup	135	4.3	17.4		0.1	169	.07	0.7			185	124	.30		
fruit/van, from mix (w/skim milk)	88		0.1				1	.19			58	143	16		
½ cup	135	4.9	17.1		0.1		.05	0.3			159	106	.20		
fruit/van, from mix (w/whole milk)	140	107.6	4.5	0.0				.22			65	161	19		
½ cup	135	5.5	19.4		0.1	169	.04	0.3			182	119	.30		
sherbet															
lemon, homemade	241		5.4				5	.25				168	19		
¾ cup	135	5.0	44.9			274	.04	0.1				135	.10		
orange	270	127.5	3.8	0.1	14	39	4	.09	.03	14	88	103	15	1.33	
1 cup	193	2.2	58.7	2.4	tr	185	.03	0.1	.16	.06	198	74	.31		
various flavors	236		0.0				0	.14				96			
1 cup	192	2.8	57.6			0	.04	0.0				76	.00		
strudel															
apple, Pepperidge Farm	250		13.0				3	.08			175	3			
1 piece	83	2.0	39.0			10	.16	0.6			74	19	1.00		
apple, Sara Lee	282	21.0	17.3				7	.11			189	11	8		
1 piece	71	2.7	28.9		0.2	36	.12	1.1			53	23	.99		
cherry, Sara Lee	279	21.0	17.2				3	.11			198	10	9		
1 piece	71	2.9	28.2		0.9	166	.16	1.2			71	26			
sweet roll															
sweet roll	154	10.5	6.8				tr	.13	.04	13	170	11	8	.20	
1 roll	42	2.6	21.4		0.2	tr	.16	0.9		.16	47	30	.76	.02	
apple crunch, Sara Lee	102	8.2	4.7				0	.06			105	5	4		
1 roll	28	1.5	13.5		0.1	17	.05	0.6			30	18	.48		
caramel sticky, Sara Lee	116	6.3	5.4				tr	.07			111	10	5		
1 roll	29	1.7	15.2		0.1	53	.08	0.7			37	22	.61		
caramel pecan, Sara Lee	161	7.3	8.9				1	.13			148	17	11		
1 roll	37	2.8	17.5		0.3	295	.13	0.7			50	40	.96		
cinn, Sara Lee	100	5.9	4.2				tr	.08			96	8	5		
1 roll	26	1.5	13.9		0.1	22	.07	0.5			36	22	.49		
cinn w/icing, refrig dough	230		8.0								500				
2 rolls	60	3.0	35.0												
honey, Sara Lee	112	6.4	4.7				0	.05			119	5	3		
1 roll	28	1.5	15.2		0.1	20	.08	0.6			24	15	.45		
toaster pastry															
blueberry	210		6.0				tr	.17	.20	40	220	14	9	.37	
1 pastry	52	3.0	36.0			500	.15	2.0			61	54	1.80	.10	
blueberry, frosted	200		5.0				tr	.17	.20	40	220	13	9	.37	
1 pastry	52	3.0	38.0			500	.15	2.0			52	51	1.80	.13	
brown sugar cinn	210		8.0					.17	.20	40	215		9	.35	
1 pastry	50	3.0	33.0			500	.15	2.0			77		1.80	.07	
brown sugar cinn, frosted	210		7.0					.17	.20	40	205		9	.47	
1 pastry	50	3.0	34.0			500	.15	2.0			70		1.80	.06	
cherry	210		6.0				tr	.17	.20	40	230	15	11	.37	
1 pastry	52	3.0	36.0			500	.15	2.0			67	53	1.80	.15	

	KCAL / WT (g)	H₂O (g) / PRO (g)	FAT (g) / CHO (g)	PUFA (g) / SFA (g)	CHOL (mg) / FIBR (g)	A (RE) / A (IU)	C (mg) / B-1 (mg)	B-2 (mg) / NIA (mg)	B-6 (mg) / B-12 (mcg)	FOL (mcg) / PANT (mg)	Na (mg) / K (mg)	Ca (mg) / P (mg)	Mg (mg) / Fe (mg)	Zn (mg) / Cu (mg)	Mn (mg)
cherry, frosted	210		5.0				tr	.17	.20	40	230	15	11	.37	
1 pastry	52	3.0	37.0			500	.15	2.0			59	53	1.80	.15	
choc chip	200		6.0					.17	.20	40	255		12	.37	
1 pastry	50	3.0	34.0			500	.15	2.0			87		1.80	.10	
choc fudge, frosted	200		4.0					.17	.20	40	255		15	.55	
1 pastry	52	3.0	36.0			500	.15	2.0			96		1.80	.11	
choc van creme, frosted	220		6.0					.17	.20	40	285		13	.18	
1 pastry	52	3.0	37.0			500	.15	2.0			85		1.80	.09	
concord grape, frosted	210		6.0				tr	.17	.20	40	215	14	9	.36	
1 pastry	52	3.0	36.0			500	.15	2.0			68	53	1.80	.06	
dutch apple, frosted	210		6.0				tr	.17	.20	40	215	14	8	.32	
1 pastry	52	3.0	36.0			500	.15	2.0			63	53	1.80	.06	
raspberry, frosted	210		6.0				tr	.17	.20	40	215	14	8	.36	
1 pastry	52	3.0	36.0			500	.15	2.0			66	53	1.80	.07	
strawberry	200		4.0				tr	.17	.20	40	225	13	10	.37	
1 pastry	52	3.0	37.0			500	.15	2.0			60	53	1.80	.15	
strawberry, frosted	200		6.0				tr	.17	.20	40	215	12	9	.37	
1 pastry	52	3.0	38.0			500	.15	2.0			49	48	1.80	.07	
various flavors	195	6.4	5.7					.17	.19	40	229	96	9	.29	
1 pastry	50	1.9	35.2		0.1	482	.16	2.1	.00	.11	84	96	2.00	.07	
turnover															
from mix[a]	173		8.0								307				
1 turnover	45	2.0	23.0												
apple, Pepperidge Farm	310		21.0				2	.06			240	2			
1 turnover	84	2.0	30.0			8	.16	0.6			55	18	1.10		
blueberry, Pepperidge Farm	320		20.0				4	.09			255	3			
1 turnover	84	2.0	32.0			8	.16	0.6			34	20	.90		
cherry, Pepperidge Farm	340		20.0				0	.06			255	4			
1 turnover	85	3.0	30.0			240	.16	0.6			47	20	1.20		
peach, Pepperidge Farm	320		20.0				11	.05			250	3			
1 turnover	84	2.0	33.0			362	.20	0.8			63	21	1.10		
raspberry, Pepperidge Farm	340		20.0				2	.05			255	1			
1 turnover	85	3.0	37.0			8	.18	0.5			48	20	.90		
yogurt, frozen															
danny on a stick	65		1.0		5						15				
1 bar	75	2.0	12.5												
danny on a stick, choc/carob coated	135		7.5		5						15				
1 bar	75	2.0	12.5												
danny-yo	110		1.0		5						25				
½ cup	127	4.0	21.0												
fruit varieties	108		1.0				tr	.13				100	12		
½ cup	113	3.5	20.9			0	.01	0.0				100	.00		
raspberry bar, choc coated	127		6.9				0	.07				98			
1 bar	70	2.0	14.7			0	.00	0.0				59	.00		
strawberry bar	69		1.0				0	.07				78			
1 bar	70	2.0	12.7				.00	0.0				59	.00		

DESSERT SAUCES, SYRUPS & TOPPINGS

	KCAL / WT (g)	H₂O (g) / PRO (g)	FAT (g) / CHO (g)	PUFA (g) / SFA (g)	CHOL (mg) / FIBR (g)	A (RE) / A (IU)	C (mg) / B-1 (mg)	B-2 (mg) / NIA (mg)	B-6 (mg) / B-12 (mcg)	FOL (mcg) / PANT (mg)	Na (mg) / K (mg)	Ca (mg) / P (mg)	Mg (mg) / Fe (mg)	Zn (mg) / Cu (mg)	Mn (mg)
butterscotch sce, homemade	203		7.2				tr	.02				41			
2 T	44	0.5	40.5			296	tr	tr				23	1.40		
butterscotch topping	156		0.1				0	.04			111	24	3		
3 T	50	0.7	39.5			1	.00	0.0			34	23	.10		
caramel topping	155		tr				0	.05			152	28	3		
3 T	50	0.8	39.0			1	.00	0.0			33	23	.10		
cherry topping	147		0.1				tr	.01			17	14	2		
3 T	50	0.2	37.5				tr	tr			380	8	.10		
choc fudge topping	97		3.8					.06			32	28	13	.22	.08
2 T	28	1.3	14.3		0.7	25	tr	tr			60	48	.34	.08	

[a] Avg of apple, blueberry & cherry

	KCAL / WT (g)	H_2O (g) / PRO (g)	FAT (g) / CHO (g)	PUFA (g) / SFA (g)	CHOL (mg) / FIBR (g)	A (RE) / A (IU)	C (mg) / B-1 (mg)	B-2 (mg) / NIA (mg)	B-6 (mg) / B-12 (mcg)	FOL (mcg) / PANT (mg)	Na (mg) / K (mg)	Ca (mg) / P (mg)	Mg (mg) / Fe (mg)	Zn (mg) / Cu (mg)	Mn (mg)
choc mint topping	151	0.7					0	.05			75	30	6		
3 T	50	1.4	36.0			tr	.00	0.0			44	26	.20		
choc syrup, Hershey	73	0.4						.01			20	4	20	.22	.11
2 T	28	0.9	16.4		0.1	6	tr	0.1			48	36	.50	.14	
custard sce, homemade	85	3.8					tr	.24				78			
4 T	72	3.7	9.3			235	.04	0.1				82	.40		
hard sce, homemade	193	11.3					0	tr				3			
4 T	42	0.1	23.9			462	tr	tr				2	.00		
lemon sce, homemade	133	2.8					3	tr				3			
4 T	54	0.1	27.8			124	tr	tr				2	tr		
marshmallow creme topping	158	0.0					5				29	16			
3 T	50	0.5	40.3	0.0							16	6			
milk choc fudge topping	104	4.0					tr	.07			35	33	5		
2 T	30	1.3	15.3		0.7	27	.01	0.1			65	51	.40		
peanut butter caramel topping	168	2.1					0	.06			175	20	2		
3 T	50	3.8	34.5			tr	.02	1.6			101	63	.40		
pecans in syrup topping	168	0.8					0	.06			0	15	29		
3 T	50	2.3	39.0			27	.13	0.2			125	60	.50		
pineapple topping	146	0.2					1	tr			17	14	1		
3 T	50	0.1	37.0			11	.01	tr			28	5	.20		
raisin sce, homemade	126	3.0					5	.02				15			
4 T	48	0.6	25.9			161	.03	0.6				24			
strawberry topping	139	0.1					tr	.00			17	12	0		
3 T	50	0.2	35.5			1	.00	0.0			4	4	.20		
walnuts in syrup topping	169	1.3					0	.04			tr	19	25		
3 T	50	2.9	37.5			6	.04	0.1			88	74	.50		

EGGS, EGG DISHES & EGG SUBSTITUTES

EGGS, CHICKEN

	KCAL / WT (g)	H_2O (g) / PRO (g)	FAT (g) / CHO (g)	PUFA (g) / SFA (g)	CHOL (mg) / FIBR (g)	A (RE) / A (IU)	C (mg) / B-1 (mg)	B-2 (mg) / NIA (mg)	B-6 (mg) / B-12 (mcg)	FOL (mcg) / PANT (mg)	Na (mg) / K (mg)	Ca (mg) / P (mg)	Mg (mg) / Fe (mg)	Zn (mg) / Cu (mg)	Mn (mg)
boiled, hard/soft	79	37.3	5.6	0.7	274	78	0	.14	.06	24	69	28	6	.72	
1 large	50	6.1	0.6	1.7	0.0	260	.04	tr	.66	.86	65	90	1.04		
fried	83	33.1	6.4	0.7	246	83	0	.13	.05	22	144	26	5	.64	
1 large	46	5.4	0.5	2.4	0.0	286	.03	tr	.58	.76	58	80	.92		
omelet, plain	95	48.8	7.1	0.7	248	89	tr	.16	.06	22	155	47	8	.70	
1 large egg	64	6.0	1.4	2.8	0.0	311	.04	tr	.64	.82	85	97	.93		
poached	79	37.1	5.6	0.7	273	78	0	.13	.05	24	146	28	6	.72	
1 large	50	6.0	0.6	1.7	0.0	259	.04	tr	.62	.86	65	90	1.04		
scrambled w/milk & fat	95	48.8	7.1	0.7	248	89	tr	.16	.06	22	155	47	8	.70	
1 large egg	64	6.0	1.4	2.8	0.0	311	.04	tr	.64	.82	85	97	.93		
white, fresh/frzn	16	29.1	tr	0.0	0	0	0	.09	.00	5	50	4	3	.01	
white of 1 large egg	33	3.4	0.4	0.0	0.0	0	tr	tr	.02	.08	45	4	.01		
whole, dried, stabilized	31	0.1	2.2	0.3	101	31	0	.06	.02	10	27	11	2	.28	
(glucose reduced)—1 T	5	2.4	0.1	0.7	0.0	102	.02	tr	.53	.34	26	86	.41		
whole, fresh/frzn	79	37.3	5.6	0.7	274	78	0	.15	.06	32	69	28	6	.72	
1 large	50	6.1	0.6	1.7	0.0	260	.04	tr	.77	.86	65	90	1.04		
yolk, fresh/frzn	63	8.3	5.6	0.7	272	94	0	.07	.05	26	8	26	3	.58	
yolk of 1 large egg	17	2.8	tr	1.7	0.0	313	.04	tr	.65	.75	15	86	.95		

EGGS, OTHER

	KCAL / WT (g)	H_2O (g) / PRO (g)	FAT (g) / CHO (g)	PUFA (g) / SFA (g)	CHOL (mg) / FIBR (g)	A (RE) / A (IU)	C (mg) / B-1 (mg)	B-2 (mg) / NIA (mg)	B-6 (mg) / B-12 (mcg)	FOL (mcg) / PANT (mg)	Na (mg) / K (mg)	Ca (mg) / P (mg)	Mg (mg) / Fe (mg)	Zn (mg) / Cu (mg)	Mn (mg)
duck, whole	130	49.6	9.6	0.9	619		0	.28	.18	56	102	45	12	.99	
1 egg	70	9.0	1.0	2.6	0.0	930	.11	0.1	3.78		156	154	2.70		
goose, whole	267	101.4	19.1	2.4			0								
1 egg	144	20.0	1.9	5.2	0.0										
quail, whole	14	6.7	1.0	0.1	76		0	.07	.01			6			
1 egg	9	1.2	tr	0.3	0.0	27	.01	tr				20	.33		
turkey, whole	135	57.3	9.4	1.3	737		0	.37				78			
1 egg	79	10.8	0.9	2.9	0.0		.09	tr				134	3.24		
turtle, whole	115	80.2	6.3					.31				62			
3–5 eggs	100	12.6	0.9		0.0	65	.28	0.1				180	1.60		

	KCAL / WT (g)	H₂O / PRO (g)	FAT / CHO (g)	PUFA / SFA (g)	CHOL (mg) / FIBR (g)	A (RE) / A (IU)	C (mg) / B-1 (mg)	B-2 (mg) / NIA (mg)	B-6 (mg) / B-12 (mcg)	FOL (mcg) / PANT (mg)	Na (mg) / K (mg)	Ca (mg) / P (mg)	Mg (mg) / Fe (mg)	Zn (mg) / Cu (mg)	Mn (mg)

EGG DISHES

crepes

apple, frzn, Mrs. Smith's	195		5.0		15		0	.09			210	45			
1 crepe	85	3.0	34.0			75	.04	0.0			130		.80		
beef burgundy, frzn, Stouffer's	335		17.0								830				
6¼ oz	177	23.0	24.0								465				
chicken continental, frzn, Mrs. Smith's	320		15.0		65		0	.30			1235	38			
2 crepes	184	22.0	23.0			175	.08	5.2			160		2.00		
chicken maison, frzn, Mrs. Smith's	350		20.0		70		32	.28			1087	160			
2 crepes	184	19.0	24.0			235	.10	4.2			480		1.80		
chicken w/mushroom sce, frzn, Stouffer's—8¼ oz	390		22.0								1040				
	234	30.0	19.0								420				
ham & asparagus, frzn, Stouffer's	325		20.0								840				
6¼ oz	177	17.0	21.0								345				
ham & veg, frzn, Mrs. Smith's	305		16.0		70		32	.40			1000	131			
2 crepes	184	11.0	29.0			210	.36	3.0			410		1.60		
mushroom, frzn, Stouffer's	255		13.0								865				
6¼ oz	177	10.0	27.0								325				
shrimp, frzn, Mrs. Smith's	305		16.0		105		38	.24			1335	178			
2 crepes	184	13.0	26.0			300	.10	0.2			220		1.30		
strawberry, frzn, Mrs. Smith's	150		5.0		15		0	.05			210	50			
1 crepe	85	3.0	23.0			50	.03	0.0			130		.80		
omelet w/cheese sce & ham, frzn, Swanson Hungry-Man—8 oz	380		28.0								851				
	227	20.0	12.0												
omelet, spanish style, frzn, Swanson Hungry-Man—8 oz	250		18.0								783				
	227	10.0	13.0												
quiche florentine, frzn, Mrs. Smith's	625		34.0		70		0	.72			1800	535			
9½ oz	269	27.0	53.0			990	.13	0.8			480		2.00		
quiche lorraine, frzn, Mrs. Smith's	720		41.0		95		0	1.01			1965	97			
9½ oz	269	34.0	54.0			335	.33	6.0			610		2.70		
quiche, mushroom, frzn, Mrs. Smith's	595		30.0		75		0	.75			1565	79			
9½ oz	269	24.0	57.0			380	.15	3.4			670		2.80		

souffle

asparagus, frzn, Stouffer's	115		7.0								440				
4 oz	113	6.0	8.0								190				
cheese, frzn, Stouffer's	355		26.0								1360				
6 oz	170	18.0	14.0								275				
cheese, homemade	240	71.5	18.8				tr	.26			400	221			
4 oz serving	113	10.9	6.8		tr	880	.06	0.2			133	215	1.10		
corn, frzn, Stouffer's	155		7.0								510				
4 oz	113	4.0	19.0								190				
spinach, frzn, Green Giant	116		6.8				3	.16				106			
²/₅ cup	100	5.0	8.7		0.2	800	.05	0.3					.90		
spinach, frzn, Stouffer's	135		7.0								600				
4 oz	113	5.0	12.0								250				

EGG SUBSTITUTES

frzn[a]	96	43.9	6.7	3.7	1	81		.23	.08		120	44		.59	
¼ cup	60	6.8	1.9	1.2	0.0	810	.07			1.00	128	43	1.19		
liquid[b]	40	38.9	1.6	0.8	tr	102	0	.14			33	25			.61
1½ fl oz	47	5.6	0.3	0.3	0.0	1015	.05	.05	.14	1.27	155	57	.99		
powdered[c]	44	0.4	1.3	0.2	57		tr	.17			79	32			
0.35 oz	10	5.5	2.2	0.4	0.0	122	.02	tr			74	47	.31		
country morning, Land O Lakes	173		12.1		594		0	.52			180	52			
½ cup	121	14.6	1.3			1338	.06				133	197	2.07		
egg beaters, Fleischmann	30		0.0		0						90				
¼ cup	60	6.0	1.0												

[a] Contains egg white, corn oil & nfdm
[b] Contains egg white, hydrogenated soybean oil & soy protein
[c] Contains egg white solids, whole egg solids, sweet whey solids, nfdm & soy protein

	KCAL / WT (g)	H₂O (g) / PRO (g)	FAT (g) / CHO (g)	PUFA (g) / SFA (g)	CHOL (mg) / FIBR (g)	A (RE) / A (IU)	C (mg) / B-1 (mg)	B-2 (mg) / NIA (mg)	B-6 (mg) / B-12 (mcg)	FOL (mcg) / PANT (mg)	Na (mg) / K (mg)	Ca (mg) / P (mg)	Mg (mg) / Fe (mg)	Zn (mg) / Cu (mg)	Mn (mg)
egg replacer, Ener-G Foods	95	4.0	tr								27				
1 oz	28	0.1			0.2						266				
eggstra, prep, Tillie Lewis	43		1.0		58		tr	.15			80	32			
1 serving	50	5.5	2.2		0.0	123	.02	tr			74	47	.30		
eggtime, prep, Nestle	90		5.0								120				
1 serving	55	7.0	3.0												
scramblend, Land O Lakes	143		9.1		466		0	.38			173	77			
½ cup	121	12.1	3.0			1071	.06				150	190	1.67		
scramblers, Morningstar Farms	61	44.5	2.7	1.6	0			.63	.19		120	4	10	.80	.03
¼ cup	57	6.7	2.4	0.4		426	.52	0.4		1.14	90	42	2.00	.05	

FAST FOODS[a]
ARBY'S®

	KCAL / WT (g)	H₂O (g) / PRO (g)	FAT (g) / CHO (g)	PUFA (g) / SFA (g)	CHOL (mg) / FIBR (g)	A (RE) / A (IU)	C (mg) / B-1 (mg)	B-2 (mg) / NIA (mg)	B-6 (mg) / B-12 (mcg)	FOL (mcg) / PANT (mg)	Na (mg) / K (mg)	Ca (mg) / P (mg)	Mg (mg) / Fe (mg)	Zn (mg) / Cu (mg)	Mn (mg)
club sandwich	560		30.0		100			.43			1610	200			
	252	30.0	43.0				.68	7.0					3.60		
ham & cheese sandwich	380		17.0		60			.34			1350	200			
	154	23.0	33.0				.75	5.0					2.70		
junior roast beef sandwich	220		9.0		35			.17			530	40			
	74	12.0	21.0				.15	3.0					1.80		
roast beef sandwich	350		15.0		45			.34			880	80			
	140	22.0	32.0				.30	5.0					3.60		
roast beef & cheese sandwich	450		22.0		55			.43			1220	200			
	168	27.0	36.0				.38	6.0					4.50		
super roast beef sandwich	620		28.0		85			.43			1420	100			
	263	30.0	61.0				.53	7.0					5.40		
turkey sandwich	510		24.0		70			.34			1220	80			
	236	28.0	46.0				.45	8.0					2.70		

ARTHUR TREACHER®

	KCAL / WT (g)	H₂O (g) / PRO (g)	FAT (g) / CHO (g)	PUFA (g) / SFA (g)	CHOL (mg) / FIBR (g)	A (RE) / A (IU)	C (mg) / B-1 (mg)	B-2 (mg) / NIA (mg)	B-6 (mg) / B-12 (mcg)	FOL (mcg) / PANT (mg)	Na (mg) / K (mg)	Ca (mg) / P (mg)	Mg (mg) / Fe (mg)	Zn (mg) / Cu (mg)	Mn (mg)
chicken, fried filet	369		21.6	5.6			1	.15			326	11	27		
	136	27.1	16.5			102	.07	11.0			326	192	.80		
chicken sandwich	413		19.2	6.7			19	.24			708	59	27		
	156	16.2	44.0			123	.17	8.1			279	147	1.70		
chips (fried potatoes)	275		13.1	2.7			6	.03			392	12	29		
	113	4.0	34.8			85	.17	2.4			597	85	.50		
coleslaw	118		8.0	4.3			57	.02			256	22	7		
	82	1.0	10.7			164	.02	0.4			157	21	.20		
fish chowder	112		5.4	0.9			2	.14			835	61	12		
	117	4.6	11.2			340	.07	0.4			228	87	.10		
fish, fried	354		19.7	5.6			2	.02			448	15	9		
	147	19.1	25.3			110	.10	2.1			407	197	.60		
fish sandwich	440		19.2	6.9			2	.22			836	89	22		
	156	16.4	44.0			117	.27	4.1			248	170	1.30		
krunch pup (hot dog)	204		14.9	2.2			3	.05			448	8	7		
	57	5.4	12.1			48	.05	1.2			71	50	.60		
shrimp, fried	381		24.4	6.2			1	.05			537	57	29		
	115	13.1	27.1			86	.08	1.7			99		.60		

BURGER CHEF®

	KCAL / WT (g)	H₂O (g) / PRO (g)	FAT (g) / CHO (g)	PUFA (g) / SFA (g)	CHOL (mg) / FIBR (g)	A (RE) / A (IU)	C (mg) / B-1 (mg)	B-2 (mg) / NIA (mg)	B-6 (mg) / B-12 (mcg)	FOL (mcg) / PANT (mg)	Na (mg) / K (mg)	Ca (mg) / P (mg)	Mg (mg) / Fe (mg)	Zn (mg) / Cu (mg)	Mn (mg)
cheeseburger	290	46.0	13.0		39		1	.21	.17			132	9	1.90	
	104	14.0	29.0	0.2		267	.18	2.8	.36		218	202	2.20	.08	
cheeseburger, double	420	67.0	22.0		77		1	.32	.31			223	15	3.60	
	145	24.0	30.0	0.2		431	.20	4.4	.73		360	355	3.20	.10	
fish filet sandwich	547	72.0	31.0		43		1	.22	.04			145	19	1.20	
	179	21.0	46.0	0.4		400	.23	2.7	.10		271	302	2.20	.04	
french fries, small	250	29.0	19.0		0		12	.04				9	16		
	68	2.0	20.0	0.6		0	.07	1.7	.00		473	62	.70	.16	
french fries, large	351	40.0	26.0		0		16	.06				13	22		
	85	3.0	28.0	0.9		0	.10	2.4	.00		661	86	.90	.23	

[a] Portions are those commonly served by the restaurant.

	KCAL	H_2O (g)	FAT (g)	PUFA (g)	CHOL (mg)	A (RE)	C (mg)	B-2 (mg)	B-6 (mg)	FOL (mcg)	Na (mg)	Ca (mg)	Mg (mg)	Zn (mg)	Mn (mg)
	WT (g)	PRO (g)	CHO (g)	SFA (g)	FIBR (g)	A (IU)	B-1 (mg)	NIA (mg)	B-12 (mcg)	PANT (mg)	K (mg)	P (mg)	Fe (mg)	Cu (mg)	
funmeal feast	545	70.0	30.0		27		13	.21	.16			61	26	1.60	
	170	15.0	55.0		0.8	123	.25	4.6	.26		688	183	2.80	.24	
hamburger, reg chef	244	41.0	9.0		27		1	.16	.16		496	45	9	1.60	
	91	11.0	29.0		0.2	114	.17	2.7	.26		208	106	2.00	.08	
hamburger, big chef	569	80.0	36.0		81		1	.31	.31			152	14	3.40	
	186	23.0	38.0		0.3	279	.26	4.7	.63		382	280	3.60	.05	
hamburger, super chef	563	143.0	30.0		105		9	.40	.45			205	25	4.50	
	252	29.0	44.0		0.5	754	.31	6.0	.87		578	377	4.50	.21	
hamburger, top chef	661	91.0	38.0		134		0	.47	.56			194	26	5.90	
	206	41.0	36.0		0.1	273	.35	8.1	1.16		612	445	5.40	.13	
hot chocolate	198		8.0		30		2	.39	.10			271	50	1.10	
	250	8.0	23.0			288	.93	0.3	.79		436	245	.70	.09	
mariner platter[a]	734	195.0	34.0		35		24	.23	.09			63	49	1.20	
	373	32.0	78.0		1.8	2069	.34	5.2	.56		996	397	3.30	.32	
rancher platter[a]	640	209.0	42.0		106		24	.38	.61			66	53	5.60	
	316	32.0	33.0		1.3	1750	.29	8.6	1.01		1237	326	5.30	.38	
shake, choc	403		9.0		36		0	.76	.10			449	54	1.60	
	336	10.0	72.0			292	.16	0.4	1.07		762	429	1.10		
shake, van	380		10.0		40		0	.66	.10		307	497	40		
	336	13.0	60.0			387	.10	0.5	1.77		622	392	.30		
skippers treat	604		37.0				1	.30			201				
	179	21.0	47.0			303	.29	3.7					2.50		

BURGER KING®

	KCAL	H_2O (g)	FAT (g)	PUFA (g)	CHOL (mg)	A (RE)	C (mg)	B-2 (mg)	B-6 (mg)	FOL (mcg)	Na (mg)	Ca (mg)	Mg (mg)	Zn (mg)	Mn (mg)
	WT (g)	PRO (g)	CHO (g)	SFA (g)	FIBR (g)	A (IU)	B-1 (mg)	NIA (mg)	B-12 (mcg)	PANT (mg)	K (mg)	P (mg)	Fe (mg)	Cu (mg)	
cheeseburger	350		17.0				1	.02			730	141	24		
	124	18.0	30.0			195	.01	2.2			230	274	2.00		
cheeseburger, double	530		32.0								990				
	179	30.0	31.0								360				
french fries, reg	210		11.0								230				
	68	3.0	25.0								380				
hamburger	290		13.0				1	.01			525	45	17		
	110	15.0	29.0			21	.01	2.2			240	96	2.00		
hamburger, whopper	630		36.0				13	.03			990	37			
	261	26.0	50.0			641	.02	5.2			520		6.00		
hamburger, whopper w/cheese	740		45.0								1435				
	289	32.0	52.0								590				
hamburger, whopper, double beef	850		52.0								1080				
	337	44.0	52.0								760				
hamburger, whopper, double beef w/cheese	950		60.0								1535				
	365	50.0	54.0								730				
hamburger, whopper junior	370		20.0								560				
	144	15.0	31.0								280				
hamburger, whopper junior w/cheese	420		25.0								785				
	158	18.0	32.0								270				
onion rings, reg	270		16.0								450				
	76	3.0	29.0								140				
pie, apple	240		12.0								335				
	85	2.0	32.0								50				
shake, choc	340		10.0								280				
	282	8.0	57.0								340				
shake, van	340		11.0								320				
	282	8.0	52.0								210				

CHURCH'S FRIED CHICKEN®

	KCAL	H_2O (g)	FAT (g)	PUFA (g)	CHOL (mg)	A (RE)	C (mg)	B-2 (mg)	B-6 (mg)	FOL (mcg)	Na (mg)	Ca (mg)	Mg (mg)	Zn (mg)	Mn (mg)
	WT (g)	PRO (g)	CHO (g)	SFA (g)	FIBR (g)	A (IU)	B-1 (mg)	NIA (mg)	B-12 (mcg)	PANT (mg)	K (mg)	P (mg)	Fe (mg)	Cu (mg)	
chicken, dark meat, fried	305	48.0	21.0				1	.27			475	15			
3½ oz	100	22.0	7.0		0.2	140	.10	5.3			206		1.30		
chicken, white meat, fried	327	45.0	23.0				1	.18			498	94			
3½ oz	100	21.0	10.0		0.1	160	.10	7.2			186		1.00		

[a] Includes salad

	KCAL	H₂O (g)	FAT (g)	PUFA (g)	CHOL (mg)	A (RE)	C (mg)	B-2 (mg)	B-6 (mg)	FOL (mcg)	Na (mg)	Ca (mg)	Mg (mg)	Zn (mg)	Mn (mg)
	WT (g)	PRO (g)	CHO (g)	SFA (g)	FIBR (g)	A (IU)	B-1 (mg)	NIA (mg)	B-12 (mcg)	PANT (mg)	K (mg)	P (mg)	Fe (mg)	Cu (mg)	

DAIRY QUEEN®

	KCAL/WT	H₂O/PRO	FAT/CHO	PUFA/SFA	CHOL/FIBR	A(RE)/A(IU)	C/B-1	B-2/NIA	B-6/B-12	FOL/PANT	Na/K	Ca/P	Mg/Fe	Zn/Cu	Mn
cheeseburger	318		14.0					.29			871	163			
	121	18.0	30.0				.29	5.7					3.50		
cheeseburger, big	553		30.0					.53				268			
	213	32.0	38.0			495	.34	9.5					5.20		
cheese dog	330		19.0					.18	.07			168	24	1.90	
	113	15.0	24.0					3.3	1.22			182	1.60	.08	
cheese dog, super	593		36.0				14	.48	.18		1986	297	42	3.50	
	203	26.0	43.0				.43	8.1	2.34			312	4.40	.18	
chili dog	330		20.0				11	.23	.17		939	86	38	1.80	
	128	13.0	25.0				.15	3.9	1.29			139	2.00	.13	
chili dog, super	555		33.0				18	.48	.27		1640	158	48	2.80	
	210	23.0	42.0				.42	8.8	2.67			231	4.00	.21	
desserts															
banana split	540		15.0		30		18	.60				350			
	383	10.0	91.0			750	.60	0.8	.90			250	1.80		
buster bar	390		22.0				tr	.34				200			
	140	10.0	37.0			300	.09	1.6					.70		
dilly bar	240		15.0		10		tr	.17				100			
	85	4.0	22.0			100	.06	tr	.50			100	.40		
float	330		8.0		20		tr	.17				200			
	397	6.0	59.0			100	.12	tr	.60			200	tr		
float, mr. misty	440		8.0		20		tr	.17				200			
	404	6.0	85.0			100	.12	tr	.60			200	tr		
freeze	520		13.0		35		tr	.34				300			
	397	11.0	89.0			200	.15	tr	1.20			250	tr		
freeze, mr. misty	500		12.0		35		tr	.34				300			
	411	10.0	87.0			200	.15	tr	.12			200	tr		
frozen dessert	180		6.0		20		tr	.17				150			
	113	5.0	27.0			100	.09	tr	.60			100	tr		
hot fudge brownie delight	570		22.0				tr	.43				300			
	266	11.0	83.0			500	.45	0.8					1.10		
ice cream in cone															
small	110		3.0		10		tr	.14				100			
	71	3.0	18.0			100	.03	tr	.40			60	tr		
med	230		7.0		20		tr	.26				200			
	142	6.0	35.0			300	.09	tr	.60			150	tr		
large	340		10.0		30		tr	.43				300			
	213	10.0	52.0			400	.15	tr	1.20			200	tr		
dipped in choc, small	150		7.0		10		tr	.17				100			
	78	3.0	20.0			100	.03	tr	.40			80	tr		
dipped in choc, med	300		13.0		20		tr	.34				200			
	156	7.0	40.0			300	.09	tr	.60			150	.40		
dipped in choc, large	450		20.0		30		tr	.51				300			
	234	10.0	58.0			400	.12	tr	.90			200	.40		
ice cream parfait	460		11.0		30		tr	.43				300			
	284	10.0	81.0			400	.12	0.4	1.20			250	1.80		
ice cream sandwich	140		4.0		10		tr	.14				60			
	60	3.0	24.0			100	.03	0.4	.20			60	.04		
kiss, mr. misty	70		0.0		0		tr	tr				tr			
	89	0.0	17.0			tr	tr	tr	tr			tr	tr		
shake, small	340		11.0		30		2	.34				300			
	241	10.0	51.0			400	.06	0.4	1.20			200	1.80		
shake, med	600		20.0		50		4	.60				500			
	418	15.0	89.0			750	.12	0.8	1.80			400	3.60		
shake, large	840		28.0		70		6	.85				600			
	588	22.0	125.0			750	.15	1.2	2.40			600	5.40		

	KCAL	H₂O (g)	FAT (g)	PUFA (g)	CHOL (mg)	A (RE)	C (mg)	Vitamins B-2 (mg)	B-6 (mg)	FOL (mcg)	Na (mg)	Ca (mg)	Minerals Mg (mg)	Zn (mg)	Mn (mg)
	WT (g)	PRO (g)	CHO (g)	SFA (g)	FIBR (g)	A (IU)	B-1 (mg)	NIA (mg)	B-12 (mcg)	PANT (mg)	K (mg)	P (mg)	Fe (mg)	Cu (mg)	
sundae, choc, small	170		4.0		15		tr	.17				100			
	106	4.0	30.0			100	.03	tr	.50			100	.70		
sundae, choc, med	290		7.0		20		tr	.26				200			
	177	6.0	51.0			300	.06	tr	.60			150	1.10		
sundae, choc, large	400		9.0		30		tr	.43				300			
	248	9.0	71.0			400	.09	0.4	1.20			250	1.80		
sundae, fiesta	570		22.0				tr	.26				200			
	269	9.0	84.0			200	.23	tr					tr		
fish sandwich	400		17.0				tr	.26	.16			60	24	.30	
	170	20.0	41.0			tr	.15	3.0	1.20			200	1.10	.08	
fish sandwich w/cheese	440		21.0				tr	.26	.16			150	24	.30	
	177	24.0	39.0			100	.15	3.0	1.50			250	.40	.08	
french fries, reg	200		10.0				4	tr	.16			tr	16	tr	
	71	2.0	25.0			tr	.06	0.8				100	.40	.04	
french fries, large	320		16.0				5	.03	.30			tr	24	.30	
	113	3.0	40.0			tr	.09	1.2				150	.40	.08	
hamburger	260		9.0					.26			572	70			
	106	13.0	28.0				.28	5.0					3.50		
hamburger, big	457		23.0					.39			909	113			
	184	27.0	37.0				.37	9.6					5.20		
hamburger, big deluxe	470		24.0					.37				111			
	213	28.0	36.0				.34	9.6					5.20		
hamburger, super	783		48.0					.69			1624	282			
	298	53.0	35.0				.39	15.6					7.30		
hot dog	273		15.0				11	.15	.08		868	75	21	1.40	
	99	11.0	23.0				.12	2.6	1.05			104	1.50	.79	
hot dog, super	518		30.0				14	.44	.17		1552	158	37	2.80	
	182	20.0	41.0			tr	.42	7.0	2.09			195	4.30	.18	
onion rings	300		17.0				2	tr	.08			20	16	.30	
	85	6.0	33.0			tr	.09	0.4				60	.40	.08	

JACK IN THE BOX®

breakfast															
breakfast jack sandwich	301	59.0	13.0		182		3	.47	.14		1037	177	24	1.80	
	121	18.0	28.0	0.1		442	.41	5.1	1.10		190	310	2.50	.11	
french toast	537	78.0	29.0		115		9	.30	.47		1130	119	27	1.80	
	180	15.0	54.0	0.9		522	.56	4.4	1.62		194	256	3.00	.11	
omelette, double cheese	423	88.0	25.0		370		2	.68	.14		899	276	26	2.10	
	166	19.0	30.0	0.2		797	.33	2.5	1.33		208	370	3.60	.13	
omelette, ham & cheese	425	94.0	23.0		355			.70	.18		975	260	29	2.30	
	174	21.0	32.0	0.2		766	.45	3.0	1.44		237	397	4.00	.14	
omelette, ranchero style	414	117.0	23.0		343			.74	.18		1098	278	29	2.00	
	196	20.0	33.0	0.4		853	.33	2.6	1.51		260	372	3.80	.14	
pancakes	626	104.0	27.0		87			.44	.19		1670	106	36	1.90	
	232	16.0	79.0	0.7		488	.63	4.6	.56		237	633	2.80	.12	
scrambled eggs	719	137.0	44.0		259			.56	.34		1110	257	55	3.00	
	267	26.0	55.0	1.3		694	.69	5.2	1.31		635	483	5.00	.24	
cheeseburger	310	47.0	15.0		32			.21	.12		877	172	22	2.30	
	109	16.0	28.0	0.2		338	.27	5.4	.87		177	194	2.60	.10	
cheeseburger, jumbo jack	628	153.0	35.0		110		5	.38	.31		1666	273	49	4.80	
	272	32.0	45.0	0.8		734	.52	11.3	3.05		499	411	4.60	.24	
french fries	270	29.0	15.0		13		4	.02	.22		128	19	27	.30	
	80	3.0	31.0	0.6			.12	1.9	.17		423	88	.70	.10	
hamburger	263	43.0	11.0		26		1	.18	.11		566	82	20	1.80	
	97	13.0	29.0	0.2		49	.27	5.6	.73		165	115	2.30	.10	
hamburger, jumbo jack	551	139.0	29.0		80		4	.34	.30		1134	134	44	4.20	
	246	28.0	45.0	0.7		246	.47	11.6	2.68		492	261	4.50	.22	
moby jack sandwich	455	57.0	26.0		56		1	.21	.12		837	167	30	1.10	
	141	17.0	38.0	0.1		240	.30	4.5	1.10		246	263	1.70	.08	
onion rings	351	24.0	23.0		24			.12	.07		318	26	16	.40	
	85	5.0	32.0	0.3			.24	3.1	.26		109	69	1.40	.07	

	KCAL / WT (g)	H₂O (g) / PRO (g)	FAT (g) / CHO (g)	PUFA (g) / SFA (g)	CHOL (mg) / FIBR (g)	A (RE) / A (IU)	C (mg) / B-1 (mg)	B-2 (mg) / NIA (mg)	B-6 (mg) / B-12 (mcg)	FOL (mcg) / PANT (mg)	Na (mg) / K (mg)	Ca (mg) / P (mg)	Mg (mg) / Fe (mg)	Zn (mg) / Cu (mg)	Mn (mg)
shake, choc	365	235.0	10.0		35			.60	.18		294	350	57	1.20	
	317	11.0	59.0		0.3	380	.16	0.6	.98		633	332	1.20	.16	
shake, choc[a]	325	247.0	7.0		26			.64	.19		270	348	53	1.10	
	322	11.0	55.0		0.3		.16	0.6	1.55		676	328	.70	.13	
shake, strawberry	380	242.0	10.0		33			.62	.18		268	351	47	1.00	
	328	11.0	63.0		0.3	426	.16	0.5	.92		556	316	.30	.07	
shake, strawberry[a]	323	253.0	7.0		26			.46	.15		241	371	40	1.10	
	328	11.0	55.0		0.3		.16	0.6	1.25		613	328	.60	.10	
shake, van	342	238.0	9.0		36		4	.47	.18		263	349	48	1.00	
	314	10.0	54.0		0.3	440	.16	0.5	1.10		536	318	.40	.06	
shake, van[a]	317	243.0	6.0		26			.38	.20		229	349	38	1.00	
	317	10.0	57.0		0.3		.16	0.5	1.36		599	312	.20	.06	
taco	189	47.0	11.0		22			.08	.14		460	116	36	1.30	
	83	8.0	15.0		0.6	356	.07	1.8	.50		264	150	1.20	.11	
taco, super	285	92.0	17.0		37		2	.12	.22		968	196	53	2.10	
	146	12.0	20.0		1.0	599	.10	2.8	.77		415	235	1.90	.18	
turnover, apple	411	45.0	24.0		17			.12	.03		352	11	10	.20	
	119	4.0	45.0		0.2		.23	2.5	.17		69	33	1.40	.06	

KENTUCKY FRIED CHICKEN®

	KCAL / WT (g)	H₂O (g) / PRO (g)	FAT (g) / CHO (g)	PUFA (g) / SFA (g)	CHOL (mg) / FIBR (g)	A (RE) / A (IU)	C (mg) / B-1 (mg)	B-2 (mg) / NIA (mg)	B-6 (mg) / B-12 (mcg)	FOL (mcg) / PANT (mg)	Na (mg) / K (mg)	Ca (mg) / P (mg)	Mg (mg) / Fe (mg)	Zn (mg) / Cu (mg)	Mn (mg)
chicken breast filet sandwich	436	71.6	22.5				4				2732				
	157	24.8	33.8		0.5	47									
chicken, fried															
1 piece															
drumstick, extra crispy	155	29.5	9.0		59		tr	.11	.16	6	263	11	14	1.32	.058
	58	13.3	5.1	2.3	tr	tr	.07	3.1	.43	.17	147	100	.95	.04	
drumstick, orig recipe	117	25.0	6.5		63		tr	.09	.09	4	207	12	13	1.29	.047
	47	12.1	2.6	1.7	tr	tr	.04	2.4	.41	.22	122	95	.80	.04	
keel, extra crispy	297	48.0	16.4		79		tr	.11	.30	11	584	62	29	.77	.125
	104	23.6	13.6	4.3	0.1	tr	.11	7.9	.48	.28	244	218	1.29	.06	
keel, orig recipe	236	49.0	12.3		87		tr	.11	.31	8	631	30	28	.72	.104
	95	23.9	7.4	3.4	tr	tr	.08	7.6	.40	.54	267	205	1.17	.05	
side breast, extra crispy	286	33.1	17.8		65		tr	.13	.24	9	564	57	21	.88	.135
	85	17.2	14.1	4.9	0.2	tr	.12	5.4	.54	.30	188	157	1.12	.06	
side breast, orig recipe	199	32.1	11.7				tr	.08	.20	6	558	50	19	.77	.097
	69	16.2	7.1		0.1	tr	.06	5.7	.46	.39	176	151	.98	.04	
thigh, extra crispy	343	48.1	23.4		109		tr	.19	.17	11	549	49	24	1.73	.128
	107	20.4	12.6	6.4	0.2	tr	.12	5.4	.97	.57	228	185	1.49	.09	
thigh, orig recipe	257	43.5	17.5		109		tr	.16	.17	9	566	34	22	1.65	.106
	88	18.4	6.5	4.4	0.1	tr	.08	4.0	.97	.56	217	169	1.45	.07	
wing, extra crispy	201	18.8	13.5		59		tr	.09	.11	5	312	16	12	.67	.091
	53	11.2	8.7	3.7	0.1	tr	.06	2.9	.34	.28	100	77	.65	.02	
wing, orig recipe	136	18.3	9.0		55		tr	.04	.10	4	302	22	9.8	.58	.059
	42	9.6	4.2	2.3	0.2	tr	.03	2.3	.32	.20	86	76	.68	.04	
coleslaw	121	68.9	7.5		7		32	tr	.08	11	225	32	11	.15	.127
	91	0.9	12.7	1.1	0.5	255	.03	0.2	.05	tr	132	23	.53	.02	
corn on the cob	169	94.9	2.8		tr		3	.07	.08	11	225	32	11	.15	.283
	135	4.6	31.2	0.2	0.7	162	.12	1.2	.05	tr	132	23	.53	.02	
dinner[b]															
drumstick & thigh, extra crispy	765	233.0	44.0		183		37	.38	.54	46	1480	130	70	3.58	.514
	375	38.3	54.7	10.5	1.0	255	.32	10.4	1.56	1.04	776	383	4.09	.39	
drumstick & thigh, orig recipe	643	223.0	35.2		180		37	.32	.46	42	1441	116	66	3.47	.481
	346	35.1	46.2	7.8	0.8	255	.25	8.5	1.53	1.08	720	363	3.90	.20	
wing & side breast, extra crispy	755	207.0	42.6		132		37	.29	.56	43	1544	143	65	2.08	.554
	348	33.0	59.9	10.3	1.0	255	.31	10.4	1.03	.88	689	333	6.03	1.60	
wing & side breast, orig recipe	604	205.0	32.1		133		37	.19	.50	39	1528	142	61	1.88	.484
	322	30.4	48.3	7.3	1.0	255	.22	10.0	.93	.89	643	326	3.31	.17	
wing & thigh, extra crispy	812	222.0	48.2		176		37	.35	.49	45	1529	135	68	2.93	.547
	371	36.2	58.4	11.9	1.0	255	.31	10.3	1.46	1.14	729	361	6.40	1.63	
wing & thigh, orig recipe	661	216.0	37.8		172		37	.27	.47	41	1536	126	64	2.76	.493
	341	32.6	47.8	8.4	1.0	255	.24	8.4	1.44	1.06	684	344	3.78	.20	

[a] Formula for California, Arizona, Texas, and Washington   [b] Includes 2 pieces chicken, mashed potatoes, gravy, coleslaw & roll

	KCAL / WT (g)	H_2O / PRO (g)	FAT / CHO (g)	PUFA / SFA (g)	CHOL / FIBR (mg)/(g)	A (RE) / A (IU)	C / B-1 (mg)	B-2 / NIA (mg)	B-6 / B-12 (mg)/(mcg)	FOL / PANT (mcg)/(mg)	Na / K (mg)	Ca / P (mg)	Mg / Fe (mg)	Zn / Cu (mg)	Mn (mg)
french fries	184	58.9	6.7				14				434				
	99	3.2	27.7		0.8	tr									
gravy	23	10.6	1.8		tr		tr	.01	tr	tr	57	2	1	.01	.009
	14	0.4	1.3	0.2	tr	tr	tr	0.1	.02	.02	8	4	.13	tr	
mashed potatoes	64	68.9	0.9		tr		5	.02	.11	11	268	16	15	.17	.077
	85	1.5	12.2	0.2	0.2	tr	tr	0.8	.06	.21	232	44	.46	.04	
roll	61	6.5	1.1		tr		tr	.04	.01	7	118	21	6	.20	.115
	21	1.8	10.9	0.2	tr	tr	.10	1.0	.02	.07	29	28	.53	.03	

LONG JOHN SILVER®

	KCAL / WT	H_2O / PRO	FAT / CHO												
chicken planks	457		23.0												
4 pieces	166	27.0	35.0												
clam chowder	107		3.0												
	170	5.0	15.0												
clams, breaded	617		34.0												
	142	18.0	61.0												
coleslaw	138		8.0												
	113	1.0	16.0												
corn on the cob	176		4.0												
	150	5.0	29.0												
fish sandwich	560		31.0												
	193	22.0	49.0												
fish w/batter	366		22.0												
2 pieces	136	22.0	21.0												
fish w/batter	549		32.0												
3 pieces	207	32.0	32.0												
french fries	288		16.0												
	85	4.0	33.0												
hush puppies	153		7.0												
3 pieces	45	3.0	20.0												
ocean scallops	283		13.0												
6 pieces	120	11.0	30.0												
oysters, breaded	441		19.0												
6 pieces	156	13.0	53.0												
peg leg w/batter	440		28.0												
5 pieces	125	22.0	26.0												
shrimp w/batter	268		13.0												
6 pieces	88	8.0	30.0												
treasure chest	540		33.0												
4 pieces	143	30.0	32.0												

MCDONALD'S®

	KCAL / WT	H_2O / PRO	FAT / CHO	PUFA / SFA	CHOL / FIBR	A(RE) / A(IU)	C / B-1	B-2 / NIA	B-6 / B-12	FOL / PANT	Na / K	Ca / P	Mg / Fe	Zn / Cu	Mn
breakfast															
egg mcmuffin	327	70.7	14.8		229		1	.44	.21	29	885	226	26	1.90	
	138	18.5	31.0		0.1	97	.47	3.8	.75	.77	168	322	2.90	.12	
english muffin w/butter	186	21.7	5.3		13		1	.49	.04	17	318	117	13	.50	
	63	5.0	29.5		0.1	164	.28	2.6	.02	.14	71	74	1.50	.69	
hash brown potatoes	125	30.9	7.0		7		4	.01	.13	6	325	5	3	.20	
	55	1.5	14.0		0.3	13	.06	0.8	.01	.26	247	67	.40	.04	
hotcakes w/butter & syrup	500	97.8	10.3		47		5	.36	.12	9	1070	103	28	.70	
	214	7.9	93.9		0.2	257	.26	2.3	.19	.24	187	501	2.20	.11	
sausage, pork	206	22.9	18.6		43		tr	.11	.18	1	615	16	9	1.50	
	53	8.8	0.6		0.1	30	.27	2.1	.53	.29	127	95	.80	.05	
scrambled eggs	180	68.1	13.0		349		1	.47	.20	65	205	61	13	1.70	
	98	13.2	2.5			652	.08	0.2	.93	1.12	135	264	2.50	.06	
big mac	563	100.4	33.0		86		2	.37	.27	21	1010	157	38	4.70	
	204	25.7	40.6		0.6	530	.39	6.5	1.80	.29	237	314	4.00	.18	
cheeseburger	307	108.4	14.1		37		2	.23	.12	21	767	132	23	2.68	
	115	15.1	29.8		0.2	345	.25	3.8	.91	.33	156	205	2.40	11	

	KCAL / WT (g)	H₂O (g) / PRO (g)	FAT (g) / CHO (g)	PUFA (g) / SFA (g)	CHOL (mg) / FIBR (g)	A (RE) / A (IU)	C (mg) / B-1 (mg)	B-2 (mg) / NIA (mg)	B-6 (mg) / B-12 (mcg)	FOL (mcg) / PANT (mg)	Na (mg) / K (mg)	Ca (mg) / P (mg)	Mg (mg) / Fe (mg)	Zn (mg) / Cu (mg)	Mn (mg)
chicken mcnuggets	314		19.0		76		2	.16			525	11			
6 pieces	111	20.3	15.4				.12	8.6					1.07		
chicken mcnugget sauce															
barbeque	60		0.4								309				
	32	0.4	13.7												
honey	50		tr								tr				
	14	tr	12.4												
hot mustard	63		2.1								259				
	30	0.6	10.5												
sweet & sour	64		0.3								186				
	32	0.2	15.0												
desserts															
cookies, chocolaty chip	342		16.3		18		1	.21	.03	6	313	29	29	.50	
	69	4.2	44.8			76	.12	1.7	.08	.12		108	1.60	.17	
cookies, mcdonaldland	308		10.8		10		1	.23	.03	6	358	12	11	.30	
	67	4.2	48.7		0.1	27	.23	2.9	.03	.10	52	74	1.50	.07	
ice cream in cake cone	185		5.2		24		1	.36	.06	3	109	183	17	.60	
	115	4.3	30.2			218	.06	0.4	.03	.14		160	.10	tr	
ice cream in sugar cone	170		4.5		19		1	.18	.05	1	110	129	14	.50	
	93	4.2	28.2			205	.05	0.2	.35	.18		122	.19	.02	
pie, apple	253	38.3	14.3		12		1	.02	.02	5	398	14	6	.20	
	85	1.9	29.3		0.3	34	.02	0.2	.03	.21	39	27	.60	.05	
pie, cherry	260	38.9	13.6		13		1	.02	.02	3	427	12	7	.20	
	88	2.0	32.1		0.1	114	.03	0.2	.04	.27	35	27	.60	.06	
shake, choc	383	203.0	9.0		30		2	.44	.13	7	300	320	49	1.40	
	291	9.9	65.5		0.3	349	.12	0.5	1.16	.64	580	335	.80	.19	
shake, strawberry	362	207.9	8.7		32		4	.44	.14	8	207	322	31	1.20	
	290	9.0	62.1			377	.12	0.3	1.16	.67	423	313	.20	.07	
shake, van	352	211.3	8.4		31		3	.70	.12	73	201	329	31	1.20	
	291	9.3	59.6			349	.12	0.3	1.19	.64	422	314	.20	.09	
sundae, caramel	328	93.2	10.0		26		4	.31	.05	13	195	200	30	.90	
	165	7.2	52.2			279	.07	1.0	.64	.39	338	230	.20	.09	
sundae, hot fudge	310	97.9	10.8		18		3	.31	.13	11	175	215	35	1.00	
	164	7.0	46.2		0.2	230	.07	1.1	.67		410	236	.60	.13	
sundae, strawberry	289	101.0	8.7		20		3	.30	.05	20	96	174	28	.80	
	164	6.6	46.1		0.2	230	.07	1.0	.61	.41	290	180	.40	.11	
filet-o-fish sandwich	432	59.5	25.0		47		1	.20	.10	20	781	93	27	.90	
	139	14.3	37.4		0.1	42	.26	2.6	.82	.22	150	229	1.70	.10	
french fries, reg	220	25.4	11.5		9		13	.02	.22	19	109	9	27	.30	
	68	3.0	26.1		0.5	17	.12	2.3	.03	.27	564	101	.60	.03	
hamburger	255	48.0	9.8		25		2	.18	.12	17	520	51	19	2.10	
	102	12.3	29.5		0.3	82	.25	4.0	.81	.30	142	126	2.30	.10	
quarter pounder	424	83.7	21.7		67		1	.28	.27	23	735	63	37	5.10	
	166	24.4	32.7		0.7	133	.32	6.5	1.88	.53	322	249	4.10	.17	
quarter pounder w/cheese	524	96.0	30.7		96		3	.37	.23	23	1236	219	41	5.70	
	194	29.9	32.2		0.8	660	.31	7.4	2.15	.60	341	382	4.30	.18	

PIZZA

	KCAL / WT (g)	H₂O (g) / PRO (g)	FAT (g) / CHO (g)	PUFA (g) / SFA (g)	CHOL (mg) / FIBR (g)	A (RE) / A (IU)	C (mg) / B-1 (mg)	B-2 (mg) / NIA (mg)	B-6 (mg) / B-12 (mcg)	FOL (mcg) / PANT (mg)	Na (mg) / K (mg)	Ca (mg) / P (mg)	Mg (mg) / Fe (mg)	Zn (mg) / Cu (mg)	Mn (mg)
cheese, regular crust	653	127.7	12.4				5	.13			1347	581	78	3.30	1.40
½ of 12-inch pizza	282	39.0	96.2		0.5	410	.04	0.7			474	529	2.60	.40	
cheese, thin crust	359	85.2	9.8								1116	355	39	2.40	.550
½ of 10-inch pizza	168	18.8	48.9		0.9						285	334	1.10	.20	
cheese, thick crust	460	95.6	6.2								1132	290	53	2.60	.75
½ of 10-inch pizza	208	23.1	77.9		0.8						368	318	1.30	.35	

SUBMARINE SANDWICHES

	KCAL / WT (g)	H₂O (g) / PRO (g)	FAT (g) / CHO (g)	PUFA (g) / SFA (g)	CHOL (mg) / FIBR (g)	A (RE) / A (IU)	C (mg) / B-1 (mg)	B-2 (mg) / NIA (mg)	B-6 (mg) / B-12 (mcg)	FOL (mcg) / PANT (mg)	Na (mg) / K (mg)	Ca (mg) / P (mg)	Mg (mg) / Fe (mg)	Zn (mg) / Cu (mg)	Mn (mg)
ham, salami, cheese[a]	449	132.2	16.6								1032	50	44	1.60	.500
6-inch sandwich	228	13.7	61.2		0.6						145	240	2.10	.30	

[a] Contains lettuce, tomato, onion, oil & vinegar

	KCAL / WT (g)	H2O (g) / PRO (g)	FAT (g) / CHO (g)	PUFA (g) / SFA (g)	CHOL (mg) / FIBR (g)	Vitamins A (RE) / A (IU)	C (mg) / B-1 (mg)	B-2 (mg) / NIA (mg)	B-6 (mg) / B-12 (mcg)	FOL (mcg) / PANT (mg)	Minerals Na (mg) / K (mg)	Ca (mg) / P (mg)	Mg (mg) / Fe (mg)	Zn (mg) / Cu (mg)	Mn (mg)
ham, salami, cheese[a]	639	186.6	23.4								3528	378	116	5.20	.700
8-inch sandwich	326	41.3	65.7		0.6						704	578	4.80	.60	
roast beef[a]	368	161.3	6.6								482	39	30	1.90	.400
6-inch-sandwich	249	21.6	55.7		0.8						294	147	1.50	.30	
roast beef[b]	611	165.5	22.5								1442	62	120	6.20	.700
8-inch sandwich	295	46.4	55.7		0.8						590	307	5.00	.60	
tuna[a]	581	141.5	28.0								824	83	27	1.60	.400
6-inch sandwich	256	21.0	61.2		0.6						160	168	1.20	.10	
tuna[a]	685	171.1	33.6								1760	77	123	2.15	.700
8-inch sandwich	306	41.2	54.8		0.7						532	280	4.00	.55	
TACO BELL®															
burrito, bean[c]	350	91.8	10.8				15	.22						78	1.40 / .400
	169	15.1	48.3		1.1	1657	.37	2.2				200	1.20	.30	
burrito, beef	466		21.0				15	.39			327	83			
	184	30.0	37.0			1675	.30	7.0			320	288	4.60		
burrito, combination	404		16.0				15	.31			300	91			
	175	21.0	43.0			1666	.34	4.6			278	230	3.70		
burrito, supreme	457		22.0				16	.35			367	121			
	222	21.0	43.0			3462	.33	4.7			350	245	3.80		
cheeseburger	278		12.0				10	.27			330	147			
	137	19.0	23.0			3146	.16	3.7			195	208	2.70		
enrichito[d]	373	129.0	16.9				10	.37			1304	203	76	2.60	.400
	206	19.2	35.6		1.4	1178	.31	4.7			626	238	1.90	.20	
frijoles & cheese[e]	232	134.1	6.0				11	.20				234	116	1.80	.500
	193	13.0	29.9		1.9	3815	.32	1.1				271	2.00	.40	
hamburger	221		7.0				10	.20			231	40			
	123	15.0	23.0			2961	.15	3.7			183	140	2.60		
taco[f]	162	43.3	8.6				0	.16				111	37	2.00	.200
	75	11.8	8.9		0.4	120	.09	2.9			203	115	1.00	.10	
tostada	179		6.0				10	.15			101	191			
	138	9.0	25.0			3152	.18	0.8			172	186	2.30		
tostada w/beef	291		15.0				13	.27			138	208			
	184	19.0	21.0			3450	.16	3.3			277	265	3.40		
WENDY'S®															
cheeseburger, single	580	133.4	34.0	9.0			1	.43			1085	228		5.50	
	240	33.0	34.0	1.0		221	.38	6.3				315	5.40		
cheeseburger, double	800	179.2	48.0		155		2	.75			1414	177		10.10	
	325	50.0	41.0	1.3		439	.49	11.4				489	10.20		
cheeseburger, triple	1040	216.4	68.0		225		3	.84			1848	371		14.30	
	400	72.0	35.0	1.6		472	.80	15.1				712	10.90		
chili con carne	230	195.9	8.0		25		3	.25			1065	83		3.70	
	250	19.0	21.0	2.3		1188	.22	3.4				168	4.40		
french fries	330	54.9	16.0		5		6	.07			112	16		.50	
	120	5.0	41.0	1.2		40	.14	3.0				196	1.20		
hamburger, single	470	110.6	26.0		70		1	.36			774	84		4.80	
	200	26.0	33.0	0.8		94	.24	5.8				239	5.30		
hamburger, double	670	162.1	40.0		125		2	.54			980	138		8.40	
	285	44.0	34.0	1.1		128	.43	10.6				364	8.20		
hamburger, triple	850	204.6	51.0		205		2	.68			1217	104		13.50	
	360	65.0	33.0	1.4		220	.47	14.7				525	10.70		
shake, choc (frozen dessert)	390	169.8	16.0		45		0	.60	.00		247	270		1.00	
	250	9.0	54.0	0.0		355	.20	tr	tr			278	.90		

[a] Contains lettuce, tomato, onion, oil & vinegar
[b] Contains lettuce, tomato & mayonnaise
[c] Pinto beans, shredded cheese, onion & mild sce in flour tortilla
[d] Ground beef, cheese, black olives & milk sce in flour tortilla
[e] Whipped pinto beans & cheddar cheese w/red sce
[f] Crisp, folded corn tortilla w/ground beef, lettuce, shredded cheese & red sce

	KCAL	H₂O (g)	FAT (g)	PUFA (g)	CHOL (mg)	A (RE)	C (mg)	Vitamins B-2 (mg)	B-6 (mg)	FOL (mcg)	Na (mg)	Ca (mg)	Minerals Mg (mg)	Zn (mg)	Mn (mg)
	WT (g)	PRO (g)	CHO (g)	SFA (g)	FIBR (g)	A (IU)	B-1 (mg)	NIA (mg)	B-12 (mcg)	PANT (mg)	K (mg)	P (mg)	Fe (mg)	Cu (mg)	

FATS, SHORTENINGS & OILS
ANIMAL FATS

	KCAL	H₂O	FAT	PUFA	CHOL	A(RE)	C	B-2	B-6	FOL	Na	Ca	Mg	Zn	Mn
bacon fat	126		14.0	0.8											
1 T	14	0.0													
beef separable fat, raw	216		23.3					.01			18	1	tr		
1 oz	28	1.3	0.0			48	.01	0.3			99	10	.20		
beef tallow, raw	116	0.0	12.8	0.5	14						0				
1 T	13	0.0	0.0	6.4	0.0						0				
butter, anhydrous	123	tr	13.9	0.5	36	130	0								
1 T	14	tr	0.0	8.7	0.0	525									
chicken fat, raw	115	0.0	12.8	2.7	11									.002	
1 T	13	0.0	0.0	3.8											
duck fat, raw	115	0.0	12.8	1.7	13										
1 T	13	0.0	0.0	4.3	0.0										
goose fat, raw	115	0.0	12.8	1.4	13										
1 T	13	0.0	0.0	3.5	0.0										
lamb separable fat, raw	199		21.2				0	.02			20	1			
1 oz	28	1.8	0.0		0.0	0	.02	0.5			81	9	.00		
mutton tallow, raw	116	0.0	12.8	1.0	13										
1 T	13	0.0	0.0	6.1	0.0										
pork backfat, raw	232		25.4	2.8			0	.01			20	tr			
1 oz	28	0.6	0.0		0.0	0	.03	0.1			80	0	.10		
pork fat (lard), raw	116	0.0	12.8	1.4	12						0	tr	0	.01	
1 T	13	0.0	0.0	5.0	0.0						0				
pork separable fat, raw	192		20.5				0	.02			20	1			
1 oz	28	1.6	0.0		0.0	0	.08	0.4			80	12	.30		
pork separable fat, ckd	216		23.4				0				18				
1 oz	28	1.3	0.0		0.0	0		0.0			109				
salt pork, raw	219	2.2	23.8	2.7			0	.01			339				
1 oz	28	1.1	0.0		0.0	0	.05	0.3			12		.20		
salt pork, fried	191		19.6	2.4			0	.03				2			
1 oz	28	3.4	0.0		0.0	0	.08	0.6				34	.50		
suet (beef kidney fat), raw	120	0.6	13.1	0.3											
1 T	14	0.2	0.0												
turkey fat, raw	115	0.0	12.8	3.0	13										
1 T	13	0.0	0.0	3.8	0.0										

SHORTENINGS

	KCAL	H₂O	FAT	PUFA	CHOL	A(RE)	C	B-2	B-6	FOL	Na	Ca	Mg	Zn	Mn
Crisco	106	0.0	12.0	3.5	0						0				
1 T	12	0.0	0.0	3.2	0.0										
Fluffo	106	0.0	12.0	2.9	0						0				
1 T	12	0.0	0.0	4.0	0.0										
soybean & cottonseed	113	0.0	12.8	3.3											
1 T	13	0.0	0.0	3.2	0.0										
soybean & palm	113	0.0	12.8	1.8											
1 T	13	0.0	0.0	3.9	0.0										
lard & veg oil	115	0.0	12.8	1.4											
1 T	13	0.0	0.0	5.2	0.0										

VEGETABLE OILS

	KCAL	H₂O	FAT	PUFA	CHOL	A(RE)	C	B-2	B-6	FOL	Na	Ca	Mg	Zn	Mn
almond oil	120	0.0	13.6	2.4											
1 T	14	0.0	0.0	1.1	0.0										
coconut oil	120	0.0	13.6	0.2											
1 T	14	0.0	0.0	11.8	0.0										
corn oil	120	0.0	13.6	8.0											
1 T	14	0.0	0.0	1.7	0.0										
cottonseed oil	120	0.0	13.6	7.1											
1 T	14	0.0	0.0	3.5	0.0										
crisco oil	124	0.0	14.0	5.6	0						0				
1 T	14	0.0	0.0	1.7	0.0										

	KCAL / WT (g)	H₂O (g) / PRO (g)	FAT (g) / CHO (g)	PUFA (g) / SFA (g)	CHOL (mg) / FIBR (g)	A (RE) / A (IU)	C (mg) / B-1 (mg)	B-2 (mg) / NIA (mg)	B-6 (mg) / B-12 (mcg)	FOL (mcg) / PANT (mg)	Na (mg) / K (mg)	Ca (mg) / P (mg)	Mg (mg) / Fe (mg)	Zn (mg) / Cu (mg)	Mn (mg)
mazola no-stick spray	8	0.0	0.8	0.4	0			.00							
2-sec spray	1	0.0	0.0	0.1	0.0	0	.00	0.0							
olive oil	119	0.0	13.5	1.1							0	tr	0	.01	
1 T	14	0.0	0.0	1.8	0.0							tr	.05		
palm oil	120	0.0	13.6	1.3											
1 T	14	0.0	0.0	6.7	0.0							tr	.00		
palm kernel oil	120	0.0	13.6	0.2											
1 T	14	0.0	0.0	11.1	0.0										
peanut oil	119	0.0	13.5	4.3							tr	tr	tr	.00	
1 T	14	0.0	0.0	2.3	0.0						0	0	.00		
puritan oil	124	0.0	14.0	9.5	0						0				
1 T	14	0.0	0.0	1.7	0.0										
safflower oil	120	0.0	13.6	10.1											
1 T	14	0.0	0.0	1.2	0.0										
sesame oil	120	0.0	13.6	5.7											
1 T	14	0.0	0.0	1.9	0.0										
soybean oil	120	0.0	13.6	7.9							0	tr	0	.00	
1 T	14	0.0	0.0	2.0	0.0							tr	.00		
soybean oil, hydrogenated	120	0.0	13.6	5.1											
1 T	14	0.0	0.0	2.0	0.0										
soybean (hydrogenated) &	120	0.0	13.6	6.5											
cottonseed oil—*1 T*	14	0.0	0.0	2.4	0.0										
soybean lecithin[a]	120	0.0	13.6	6.1											
1 T	14	0.0	0.0	2.1	0.0										
sunflower oil	120	0.0	13.6	8.9											
1 T	14	0.0	0.0	1.4	0.0										
wheat germ oil	120	0.0	13.6	8.5										.50	
1 T	14	0.0	0.0	2.6	0.0										

FISH, SHELLFISH & SEAFOOD

	KCAL / WT (g)	H₂O (g) / PRO (g)	FAT (g) / CHO (g)	PUFA (g) / SFA (g)	CHOL (mg) / FIBR (g)	A (RE) / A (IU)	C (mg) / B-1 (mg)	B-2 (mg) / NIA (mg)	B-6 (mg) / B-12 (mcg)	FOL (mcg) / PANT (mg)	Na (mg) / K (mg)	Ca (mg) / P (mg)	Mg (mg) / Fe (mg)	Zn (mg) / Cu (mg)	Mn (mg)
abalone, raw	98	75.8	0.5					.14				37			
3½ oz	100	18.7	3.4		0.0		.18					191	2.40		
abalone, cnd	80	80.2	0.3									14			
3½ oz	100	16.0	2.3		0.0		.12					128			
alewife, raw	127	79.4	4.9												
3½ oz	100	19.4	0.0		0.0							218			
alewife, cnd	141	73.0	8.0												
3½ oz	100	16.2	0.0		0.0										
anchovy, cnd	21		1.2	0.7								20			
3 fillets	12	2.3	tr		0.0							25			
anchovy paste	14		0.8	0.5											
1 t	7	1.4	0.3		0.0										
anchovy, pickled	49	16.4	2.9									47			
1 oz	28	5.4	0.1		tr							59			
barracuda, pacific, raw	113	75.4	2.6												
3½ oz	100	21.0	0.0		0.0										
bass, freshwater, small/largemouth,	104	77.3	2.6					.03							
raw—*3½ oz*	100	18.9	0.0		0.0		.10	2.1				192			
bass, saltwater															
black, raw	93	79.3	1.2								68				
3½ oz	100	19.2	0.0		0.0						256				
black, baked	287		19.4				0	.16			68	96			
1 serving	115	23.6	3.0		0.0	97	.07	3.5			256	269	1.20		
black, baked, stuffed[b]	259	52.9	15.8												
3½ oz	100	16.2	11.4		0.0										
striped, raw	105	77.7	2.7												
3½ oz	100	18.9	0.0		0.0						212				
striped, broiled	228		12.8				0	.14				47	43		
3½ oz	100	20.2		7.9	0.0	116	.15	2.9			230		1.90		

[a] 70% soybean phosphatide in 30% soybean oil [b] Stuffed w/bacon, butter, celery, onion & bread cubes

	KCAL	H₂O (g)	FAT (g)	PUFA (g)	CHOL (mg)	A (RE)	C (mg)	B-2 (mg)	B-6 (mg)	FOL (mcg)	Na (mg)	Ca (mg)	Mg (mg)	Zn (mg)	Mn (mg)
	WT (g)	PRO (g)	CHO (g)	SFA (g)	FIBR (g)	A (IU)	B-1 (mg)	NIA (mg)	B-12 (mcg)	PANT (mg)	K (mg)	P (mg)	Fe (mg)	Cu (mg)	
striped, oven-fried[a]	196	60.8	8.5												
3½ oz	100	21.5	6.7												
bluefish															
raw	117	75.4	3.3					.09			74	23			
3½ oz	100	20.5	0.0	0.0			.12	1.9				243	.60		
baked fillet	199	85.0	6.5					.13			130	36			
1 fillet	125	32.8	0.0	0.0		62	.14	2.4				359	.90		
broiled	192	83.0	6.3					.12			127	35			
½ fish	122	32.0	0.0	0.0		61	.13	2.3				350	.80		
fried[b]	205	60.8	9.8					.11			146	35			
3½ oz	100	22.7	4.7				.11	1.8				257	.90		
bonito, cnd	257		19.1					.09			514	8	28		
3½ oz	100	19.8	0.0	0.0			.01	9.8			302	193	1.00		
buffalofish, raw	113	77.4	4.2								52				
3½ oz	100	17.5	0.0	0.0							293				
bullhead, black, raw	84	81.3	1.6												
3½ oz	100	16.3	0.0	0.0											
burbot, raw	82	81.1	0.9					.14							
3½ oz	100	17.4	0.0	0.0			.39	1.5				190			
burbot, fried	156	60.5	1.2					.23							
3½ oz	100	37.0	0.0	0.0			.54	3.7							
butterfish, northern, raw	169	71.4	10.2												
3½ oz	100	18.1	0.0	0.0											
butterfish, gulf, raw	95	78.2	2.9												
3½ oz	100	16.2	0.0	0.0											
butterfish, fried	211		19.1					.03				10			
1 fish	50	9.1	0.0				.03	2.0				104			
carp, raw	115	77.8	4.2				1	.04			50	50			
3½ oz	100	18.0	0.0	0.0		170	.01	1.5			286	253	.90		
catfish, raw	103	78.0	3.1					.03			60				
3½ oz	100	17.6	0.0	0.0			.04	1.7			330		.40		
caviar, sturgeon, granular	26	4.6	1.5		25						220	28			
1 rd t	10	2.7	3.3								18	36	1.18		
caviar, sturgeon, pressed	32	3.6	1.7												
1 rd t	10	3.4	0.5												
chub, raw	145	74.9	8.8		50										
3½ oz	100	15.3	0.0	0.0											
clams, soft, raw, meat only	82	80.8	1.9								36				
4 large	100	14.0	1.3								235	183	3.40		
clams, hard/round, meat only	80	79.8	0.9								205	69			
5 large	100	11.1	5.9								311	151	7.50		
clams, cnd, solids & liquid	52	86.3	0.7					.11				55			
½ cup	100	7.9	2.8				.01	1.0			140	137	4.10		
clams, cnd, solids only	98	77.0	2.5		80										
½ cup	100	15.8	1.9												
clams, cnd, liquor only	19	93.6	0.1												
½ cup	100	2.3	2.1		0.0										
cod															
raw	78	81.2	0.3		50		2	.07			70	10	28		
3½ oz	100	17.6	0.0	0.0		0	.06	2.2			382	194	.40		
broiled	162	61.4	5.0					.10			105	29			
3½ oz	95	26.1	0.0	0.0		170	.08	2.8			386	260	.90		
cnd	85	78.6	0.3					.08							
3½ oz	100	19.2	0.0	0.0											
dried, salted	130	52.4	0.7		82			.45				225			
3½ oz	100	29.0	0.0	0.0		0	.08								
dried, salted, creamed	267		11.7				0	.27				115			
4¾ oz	135	30.7	8.1			436	.06	3.3			216	378	1.40		
crab cake	46		2.5				0	.03				15	10		
1 oz	28	5.4	0.5			82	.02	0.5				59	.30		

[a] Prep w/milk, breadcrumbs, butter & salt   [b] Prep w/egg, milk & breadcrumbs

	KCAL / WT (g)	H₂O (g) / PRO (g)	FAT (g) / CHO (g)	PUFA (g) / SFA (g)	CHOL (mg) / FIBR (g)	A (RE) / A (IU)	C (mg) / B-1 (mg)	B-2 (mg) / NIA (mg)	B-6 (mg) / B-12 (mcg)	FOL (mcg) / PANT (mg)	Na (mg) / K (mg)	Ca (mg) / P (mg)	Mg (mg) / Fe (mg)	Zn (mg) / Cu (mg)	Mn (mg)
crab, cnd	86	65.6	2.1		86			.07			850	38	34		
½ cup	85	14.8	0.9				.07	1.6			94	155	.70		
crab, deviled[a]	188	63.3	9.9				6	.11			867	47	26		
3½ oz	100	11.4	13.3			540	.08	1.5			166	137	1.20		
crab, fried	185		12.0												
2⅓ oz	65	10.7	8.6												
crab imperial[b]	294	143.8	15.2				10	.24			1456	120			
7 oz	200	29.2	7.8				.12	2.2			262	332	1.80		
crab salad	145		8.5				2	.06				38	26		
3½ oz	100	11.8	4.9			97	.06	1.3				129	.60		
crab, steamed	93	78.5	1.9		100			.08				43	34		
3½ oz	100	17.3	0.5			2170	.16	2.8				175	.80		
crappie, white, raw	79	81.8	0.8					.03							
3½ oz	100	16.8	0.0		0.0		tr	1.4							
crayfish, freshwater, raw	72	82.5	0.5					.04					77		
3½ oz	100	14.6	1.2				.01	1.9				201	1.50		
croaker, atlantic, raw	96	79.2	2.2					.08			87				
3½ oz	100	17.8	0.0		0.0	60	.12	5.5			234				
croaker, atlantic, baked	133	71.3	3.2					.10			12				
3½ oz	100	24.3	0.0		0.0	70	.13	6.5			323				
croaker, white, raw	84	79.7	0.8												
3½ oz	100	18.0	0.0		0.0										
croaker, yellowfin, raw	89	79.0	0.8												
3½ oz	100	19.2	0.0		0.0										
cusk, raw	75	81.3	0.2												
3½ oz	100	17.2	0.0		0.0										
cusk, steamed	106	74.3	0.7					.10			74	27			
3½ oz	100	23.4	0.0		0.0		.03	2.7			386	283	1.00		
dogfish, spiny, raw	156	72.3	9.0												
3½ oz	100	17.6	0.0		0.0		.05								
dolly varden, raw	144	73.1	6.5					.06							
3½ oz	100	19.9	0.0		0.0		.06								
drum, freshwater, raw	121	77.0	5.2								70				
3½ oz	100	17.3	0.0		0.0						286				
drum, red (redfish), raw	80	80.2	0.4					.05			55				
3½ oz	100	18.0	0.0		0.0		.15	3.5			273				
eel, am, raw	233	64.6	18.3					.36					18		
3½ oz	100	15.9	0.0		0.0	1610	.22	1.4				202	.70		
eel, am, smoked	165	25.1	13.9		35										
1¾ oz	50	9.3	0.0		0.0										
eulachon (smelt), raw	118	79.6	6.2					.04							
3½ oz	100	14.6	0.0		0.0		.04								
filet of fish divan, frzn, Stouffer's[c]	240		3.0								1115				
12⅜ oz	351	30.0	23.0								835				
filet of fish florentine, frzn, Stouffer's[c]	200		6.0		105						815				
9 oz	255	25.0	11.0								510				
fish cakes, cnd	111	72.1	0.6									49			
3½ oz	100	24.7	0.0		0.0							232	.80		
fish cakes, fried[d]	172	66.0	8.0												
3½ oz	100	14.7	9.3												
fish cakes, fried, frzn	270	52.9	17.9												
3½ oz	100	9.2	17.2												
fish fillets															
batter-dipped, frzn, Van de Kamp's	440		31.0								704				
2 pieces (6 oz)	168	17.0	25.0												
country seasoned, frzn, Van de Kamp's—*2 pieces (4¾ oz)*	360		25.0								668				
	133	14.0	21.0												
light & crispy, frzn, Van de Kamp's	311		23.0								722				
2 pieces (4 oz)	112	11.0	20.0												

[a] Prep w/bread cubes, butter, parsley, egg, lemon jce & catsup
[b] Prep w/butter, flour, milk, onion, green peppers, egg & lemon jce
[c] Stouffer's Lean Cuisine
[d] Made w/cnd flaked fish, potato & egg

						Vitamins					Minerals				
	KCAL	H_2O (g)	FAT (g)	PUFA (g)	CHOL (mg)	A (RE)	C (mg)	B-2 (mg)	B-6 (mg)	FOL (mcg)	Na (mg)	Ca (mg)	Mg (mg)	Zn (mg)	Mn (mg)
	WT (g)	PRO (g)	CHO (g)	SFA (g)	FIBR (g)	A (IU)	B-1 (mg)	NIA (mg)	B-12 (mcg)	PANT (mg)	K (mg)	P (mg)	Fe (mg)	Cu (mg)	
fish kabobs															
batter-dipped, frzn, Van de Kamp's	260		17.0								577				
10 pieces (4 oz)	112	11.0	16.0												
country seasoned, frzn, Van de	290		19.0								490				
Kamp's—*10 pieces (4 oz)*	112	12.0	19.0												
fish loaf, ckd[a]	124	72.2	3.7		99										
3½ oz	100	14.1	7.3												
fish, ocean, almondine, frzn,	240		18.0				0	.17			418	25			
Campbell's—*4 oz*	112	16.0	4.0			tr	.12	1.9			327	209	.80		
fish, ocean w/lemon sce, frzn,	270		21.0				0	.15			418	14			
Campbell's—*4 oz*	112	14.0	4.0			tr	.11	1.9			357	209	.70		
fish sticks															
frzn	176	65.8	8.9		70		2	.07			180	11	18		
4½ sticks	100	16.6	6.5		0.0	0	.04	1.6			390	167	.40		
frzn, batter-dipped, Van de Kamp's	288		14.0								982				
5 pieces (5 oz)	140	15.0	26.0												
frzn, country seasoned, Van de	410		29.0												
Kamp's—*5 oz*	140	14.0	22.0												
frzn, light & crispy, Van de Kamp's	286		18.0								769				
5 pieces (3¾ oz)	105	11.0	21.0												
flatfishes, raw	79	81.3	0.8		61			.05			78	12			
3½ oz	100	16.7	0.0		0.0		.05	1.7			342	195	.80		
flounder/sole, raw	68		0.5					.05			56	61	30		
3½ oz	100	14.9	0.0		0.0		.06	1.7			366	195	.80		
flounder/sole, baked	202	58.1	8.2				2	.08			237	23	30		
3½ oz	100	30.0	0.0		0.0		.07	2.5			587	344	1.40		
gizzard shad, raw	200	67.8	14.0												
3½ oz	100	17.2	0.0		0.0										
grouper, raw	87	79.2	0.5												
3½ oz	100	19.3	0.0		0.0		.17								
haddock															
raw	79	80.5	0.1		60			.07			61	23	24		
3½ oz	100	18.3	0.0		0.0		.04	3.0			304	197	.70		
batter-dipped, frzn, Van de Kamp's	330		23.0								529				
2 pieces (4 oz)	112	14.0	16.0												
broiled	141		6.6				3	.07			71	13	32		
3½ oz	100	20.1	0.3		0.0	276	.03	2.1			356	230	.50		
filet almondine, frzn, Swanson	370		24.0								1044				
7½ oz	213	29.0	9.0												
fried[b]	165	66.3	6.4		60			.07			177	40			
3½ oz	100	19.6	5.8				.04	3.2			348	247	1.20		
smoked/cnd	103	72.6	0.4					.05							
3½ oz	100	23.2	0.0		0.0		.06	2.1							
hake (including whiting), raw	74	81.8	0.4					.20			74	41			
3½ oz	100	16.5	0.0		0.0		.10				363	142			
halibut															
atlantic/pacific, raw	100	76.5	1.2		50			.07			54	13			
3½ oz	100	20.9	0.0		0.0	440	.07	8.3			449	211	.70		
atlantic/pacific, broiled	214	83.3	8.8		75			.09			168	20			
1 serving	125	31.5	0.0		0.0	850	.06	10.4			656	310	1.00		
atlantic/pacific, smoked	224	49.4	15.0												
3½ oz	100	20.8	0.0		0.0										
batter-dipped, frzn, Van de Kamp's	270		17.0								618				
3 pieces (4 oz)	112	12.0	17.0												
calif, raw	97	77.8	1.2		50							13	23		
3½ oz	100	19.8	0.0		0.0										
greenland, raw	146	74.5	8.4		50							13	23		
3½ oz	100	16.4	0.0		0.0		.01					210			

[a] Prep w/cnd flaked fish, bread cubes, egg, tomato, onion & fat

[b] Dipped in egg, milk & breadcrumbs

	KCAL / WT (g)	H₂O (g) / PRO (g)	FAT (g) / CHO (g)	PUFA (g) / SFA (g)	CHOL (mg) / FIBR (g)	A (RE) / A (IU)	C (mg) / B-1 (mg)	B-2 (mg) / NIA (mg)	B-6 (mg) / B-12 (mcg)	FOL (mcg) / PANT (mg)	Na (mg) / K (mg)	Ca (mg) / P (mg)	Mg (mg) / Fe (mg)	Zn (mg) / Cu (mg)	Mn (mg)
herring															
atlantic, raw	176	69.0	11.3	2.0	85			.15							
3½ oz	100	17.3	0.0		0.0	110	.02	3.6				256	1.10		
atlantic, broiled	217		14.2				0	.15							
1 fish	85	20.8	0.0		0.0	130	.01	3.3				290	1.20		
cnd, solids & liquid	208	62.9	13.6	2.0	98							147			
3½ oz	100	19.9	0.0		0.0		.18					297	1.80		
cnd, tomato sce	176	66.7	10.5	tr				.11							
3½ oz	100	15.8	3.7		0.0			3.5				243			
pacific, raw	98	79.4	2.6	tr				.16			74				
3½ oz	100	17.5	0.0		0.0	100	.02	3.5			420	225	1.30		
pickled, bismarck type	223	59.4	15.1												
3½ oz	100	20.4	0.0		0.0										
smoked bloaters	196	64.0	12.4												
3½ oz	100	19.6	0.0		0.0										
smoked, kippered	211	61.0	12.9					.28				66			
3½ oz	100	22.2	0.0		0.0	30		3.3				254	1.40		
inconnu (sheepfish), raw	146	72.0	6.8												
3½ oz	100	19.9	0.0		0.0										
jack mackerel, raw	143	71.4	5.6												
3½ oz	100	21.6	0.0		0.0										
kingfish, raw	105	77.3	3.0								83				
3½ oz	100	18.3	0.0								250				
kingfish, ckd	255		13.4				0	.13			101	80	56		
3½ oz	100	22.3	11.7		0.0	93	.11	2.9			293	287	1.90		
lake herring (cisco), raw	96	79.7	2.3					.10			47	12			
3½ oz	100	17.7	0.0		0.0		.09	3.3			319	206	.50		
lake trout (under 6.5 lb), raw	241	64.9	19.9												
3½ oz	100	14.3	0.0		0.0										
lake trout (6.5 lb & over), raw	524	36.8	54.4												
3½ oz	100	7.9	0.0		0.0										
lingcod, raw	84	80.0	0.8					.04			59				
3½ oz	100	17.9	0.0		0.0	0	.05				433				
lobster															
northern, raw	91	78.5	1.9		200			.05				29	22		
3½ oz	100	16.9	0.5		0.0		.40	1.5				183	.60		
northern, boiled/broiled w/butter	308		24.9				0	.06			210	80			
¾ lb	334	20.0	0.8		0.0	920	.11	2.3			180	229	.70		
northern, cnd	75	65.3	1.1					.06			55				
½ cup	85	15.4	0.0				.03	1.9				161	.70		
lobster newburg[a]	388	128.0	21.2					.22			458	174			
7 oz	200	37.0	10.2				.14				342	384	1.80		
lobster paste	13	4.3	0.7					.02				5			
1 t	7	1.5	0.1				.01					13	.10		
lobster salad[b]	110	80.3	6.4	0.9			18	.08			124	36			
3½ oz	100	10.1	2.3					.09			264	95	.90		
lobster thermidor	405		26.6				0	.51				290			
5½ oz	157	28.5	14.8		0.5	984	.15	4.8				451	1.90		
lobster, spiny	72	82.5	0.5					.04			77				
3½ oz	100	14.6	1.2				.01	1.9				201	1.50		
mackerel															
atlantic, raw	191	67.2	12.2		95			.33					28		
3½ oz	100	19.0	0.0			450	.15	8.2							
atlantic, broiled fillet	300	80.1	20.5												
1 fillet	130	28.3	0.0		0.0										
atlantic, cnd	192	69.3	11.7					.22				194			
½ cup	105	20.2	0.0		0.0	460	.06	6.0				287	2.20		
pacific, raw	159	69.8	7.3									8			
3½ oz	100	21.9	0.0		0.0	120						274	2.10		

[a] Prep w/butter, egg yolks, sherry & cream

[b] Prep w/onion, sweet pickle, celery, egg, mayo & tomato

	KCAL	H_2O (g)	FAT (g)	PUFA (g)	CHOL (mg)	A (RE)	C (mg)	B-2 (mg)	B-6 (mg)	FOL (mcg)	Na (mg)	Ca (mg)	Mg (mg)	Zn (mg)	Mn (mg)
	WT (g)	PRO (g)	CHO (g)	SFA (g)	FIBR (g)	A (IU)	B-1 (mg)	NIA (mg)	B-12 (mcg)	PANT (mg)	K (mg)	P (mg)	Fe (mg)	Cu (mg)	
pacific, cnd	180	66.4	10.0					.33				260			
3½ oz	100	21.1	0.0		0.0	30	.03	8.8				288	2.20		
salted	305	43.0	25.1												
3½ oz	100	18.5	0.0		0.0										
smoked	219	59.4	13.0												
3½ oz	100	23.8	0.0		0.0										
menhaden, atlantic, cnd	172	67.9	10.2												
3½ oz	100	18.7	0.0		0.0										
mullet, striped, raw	146	72.6	6.9					.08			81	26	32		
3½ oz	100	19.6	0.0		0.0		0.7	5.2			292	220	1.80		
mullet, striped, breaded, fried	296		17.4				0	.10			99	53	38		
3½ oz	100	22.6	12.2		0.0	95	.10	5.1			341	258	2.30		
muskellunge, raw	109	76.3	2.5												
3½ oz	100	20.2	0.0		0.0							227	.60		
mussels, atlantic & pacific, meat &	66	83.8	1.4										23		
liquid—3½ oz	100	9.6	3.¹												
mussels, atlantic & pacific, meat only	95	78.6	2.2					.21			289	88	25		
3½ oz	100	14.4	3.3				.16				315	236	3.40		
mussels, pacific, cnd	114	74.6	3.3		150										
3½ oz	100	18.2	1.5												
ocean perch (rosefish/red perch/															
pacific perch)															
atlantic, raw	88	79.7	1.2					.08			79	20	32		
3½ oz	100	18.0	0.0		0.0		.10	1.9			269	207	1.00		
atlantic, fried, breaded, frzn	319	43.2	18.9												
3½ oz	100	18.9	16.5												
atlantic, fried[a]	227	59.0	13.3					.11			153	33			
3½ oz	100	19.0	6.8		0.0		.10	1.8			284	226	1.30		
batter-dipped, frzn, Van de Kamp's	290		16.0												
2 pieces (2 oz)	56	16.0	20.0												
pacific, raw	95	79.0	1.5								63				
3½ oz	100	19.0	0.0		0.0						390				
octopus, raw	73	82.2	0.8					.06				29			
3½ oz	100	15.3	0.0		0.0		.02	1.8				173			
oysters															
cnd, solids & liquid	76	82.2	2.2		230			.29			206	152			
3½ oz	100	8.5	4.9		0.1	440	.17	3.2			203	241	8.10		
eastern, raw	66	84.6	1.8		200			.18			73	94	32		
5–8 med	100	8.4	3.4			310	.14	2.5			121	143	5.50		
fried[a]	239	54.7	13.9		230			.29			206	152			
3½ oz	100	8.6	18.6		tr	440	.17	3.2			203	241	8.10		
frzn	46	87.4	1.3					.18			380				
3½ oz	100	6.1	2.5			310	.14	2.5			210				
pacific & western, raw	91	79.1	2.2				30					85	24		
2–4 med	100	10.6	6.4				.12	1.3				153	7.20		
scalloped	356		18.0				0	.28				158			
6 med	143	15.9	31.6			894	.14	1.5				232	7.00		
perch, freshwater, yellow, raw	91	79.2	0.9					.17			68				
3½ oz	100	19.5	0.0		0.0		.06	1.7			230	180	.60		
pickerel, raw	84	79.7	0.5												
3½ oz	100	18.7	0.0		0.0								.70		
pike, blue, raw	90	78.8	0.9												
3½ oz	100	19.1	0.0		0.0										
pike, northern, raw	88	80.0	1.1												
3½ oz	100	18.3	0.0		0.0										
pike, walleye, raw	93	78.3	1.2					.16			51				
3½ oz	100	19.3	0.0		0.0		.25	2.3			319	214	.40		
pollack, raw	95	77.4	0.9					.10			48				
3½ oz	100	20.4	0.0		0.0		.05	1.6			350				
pollack, ckd, creamed[b]	128	74.7	5.9				tr	.13			111				
3½ oz	100	13.9	4.0		0.0		.03	0.7			238				

[a] Dipped in egg, milk & breadcrumbs   [b] Prep w/flour, butter & milk

	KCAL / WT (g)	H₂O (g) / PRO (g)	FAT (g) / CHO (g)	PUFA (g) / SFA (g)	CHOL (mg) / FIBR (g)	A (RE) / A (IU)	C (mg) / B-1 (mg)	B-2 (mg) / NIA (mg)	B-6 (mg) / B-12 (mcg)	FOL (mcg) / PANT (mg)	Na (mg) / K (mg)	Ca (mg) / P (mg)	Mg (mg) / Fe (mg)	Zn (mg) / Cu (mg)	Mn (mg)
pompano, raw	166	70.9	9.5					.22			47				
3½ oz	100	18.8	0.0		0.0	tr	.41				191				
pompano, broiled	284		15.4					.27			57				
3½ oz	100	23.0	0.0		0.0		.50				223				
porgy/scup, raw	112	76.2	3.4								63	54			
3½ oz	100	19.0	0.0		0.0						287	250			
porgy/scup, fried	279		15.5				0	.08			58	24			
1 serving	93	22.7	10.8			75	.07	3.7			266	258	1.50		
red snapper, raw	93	78.5	0.9					.02			67	16			
3½ oz	100	19.8	0.0		0.0		.17				323	214	.80		
redhorse, silver, raw	98	78.6	2.3												
3½ oz	100	18.0	0.0		0.0										
rockfish, raw	97	78.9	1.8					.12			60				
3½ oz	100	18.9	0.0		0.0		.06				388				
rockfish, oven-steamed	107	75.4	2.5					.12			68				
3½ oz	100	18.1	1.9				.05				446				
roe, raw (carp/cod/herring/haddock/pike/shad)—3½ oz	130	70.1	2.3		360		14	.76							
	100	24.4	1.5				.10	1.4					.60		
roe, raw (salmon/sturgeon/turbot)	207	61.3	10.4				18	.72							
3½ oz	100	25.2	1.4				.38	2.3							
roe, baked/broiled (cod/shad)ᵃ	126	71.3	2.8								73	13			
3½ oz	100	22.0	1.9								132	402	2.30		
roe, cnd (cod/haddock/herring)	118	72.4	2.8									15			
3½ oz	100	21.5	0.3									346	1.20		
sablefish (black cod), raw	190	71.6	14.9					.09			56				
3½ oz	100	13.0	0.0		0.0		.11				358				
salmon															
atlantic, raw	217	63.6	13.4	tr	35		9	.08				79			
3½ oz	100	22.5	0.0		0.0			7.2				186	.90		
atlantic, cnd	203	64.2	12.2	tr	35										
3½ oz	100	21.7	0.0		0.0										
chinook, raw	222	64.2	15.6	tr				.23			45				
3½ oz	100	19.1	0.0		0.0	310	.10				399	301			
chinook, cnd	210	64.4	14.0	tr	60			.14				154	27		
⅖ cup	100	19.6	0.0		0.0	230	.03	7.3			366	289	.90		
chum, cnd	139	70.8	5.2					.16			53	249	30		
3½ oz	100	21.5	0.0		0.0	60	.02	7.1			336	352	.70		
coho (silver), raw	153	69.3	8.2				1	.11			48	175	29		
3½ oz	100	18.8	0.0		0.0		.09				421	231			
coho (silver), cnd	153	69.3	8.2				0	.06			351	185	30		
3½ oz	100	18.8	0.0		0.0	19	.03	7.4			339	249	.60		
pink (humpback), raw	119	76.0	3.7	tr				.05			64				
3½ oz	100	20.0	0.0		0.0		.14				306				
pink (humpback), cnd	141	70.8	5.9	tr				.18			387	196	30		
⅖ cup	100	20.5	0.0		0.0	70	.03	8.0			361	286	.80		
sockeye (red), raw	171	67.2	9.3		36			.07			48				
3½ oz	100	20.3	0.0		0.0		.14				391				
sockeye (red), cnd	171	67.2	9.3		36			.16			522	259	29		
⅖ cup	100	20.3	0.0		0.0	230	.04	7.3			344	344	1.20		
broiled/baked	182	63.4	7.4		47			.06			116	414			
3½ oz	100	27.0	0.0		0.0	160	.16	9.8			443		1.20		
smoked	176	58.9	9.3		60							14			
3½ oz	100	21.6	0.0		0.0							245			
salmon patty	239		12.4		64		4	.22	.07	13	96	78	34	.84	
3½ oz	100	15.8	16.1		0.8	66	.12	4.0	3.00	.66	89	104	1.24		
salmon rice loaf	122	74.4	4.5												
3½ oz	100	12.0	7.3												
sardines, atlantic, cnd in oil	311	50.6	24.4		120			.16			510	354			
8 med	100	20.6	0.6			180	.02	4.4			560	434	3.50		
sardines, pacific, raw	160	70.7	8.6									33	24		
3½ oz	100	19.2	0.0		0.0							215	1.80		

ᵃ Prep w/butter or margarine & lemon jce or water

	KCAL	H₂O (g)	FAT (g)	PUFA (g)	CHOL (mg)	A (RE)	C (mg)	B-2 (mg)	B-6 (mg)	FOL (mcg)	Na (mg)	Ca (mg)	Mg (mg)	Zn (mg)	Mn (mg)
	WT (g)	PRO (g)	CHO (g)	SFA (g)	FIBR (g)	A (IU)	B-1 (mg)	NIA (mg)	B-12 (mcg)	PANT (mg)	K (mg)	P (mg)	Fe (mg)	Cu (mg)	
sardines, pacific, cnd															
in brine	196	64.1	12.0				30				760	303			
3½ oz	100	18.8	1.7								260	354	5.20		
in mustard sce	230		17.0								850				
1 can	105	18.0													
in soy oil	380		34.0		140			.30			800				
1 can	105	18.0					.01	7.4							
in tomato sce	230		17.0					.27			850	449			
1 can	105	18.0	1.0			30	.01	5.3			320	478	4.10		
sauger, raw	84	80.8	0.8												
3½ oz	100	17.9	0.0		0.0										
scallops, bay & sea															
raw	81	79.8	0.2		35			.06			255	26			
3½ oz	100	15.3	3.3					1.3			396	208	1.80		
steamed	112	73.1	1.4		53						265	115			
3½ oz	100	23.2	1.8								476	338	3.00		
frzn, breaded, fried	194	60.2	10.5												
3½ oz	100	18.0	8.4												
sea bass, white, raw	96	76.3	0.5												
3½ oz	100	21.4	0.0		0.0										
shad, am, raw	170	70.4	10.0					.24			54	20			
3½ oz	100	18.6	0.0				.15	8.4			330	260	.50		
shad, am, baked[a]	201	64.0	11.3					.26			79	24			
3½ oz	100	23.2	0.0			30	.13	8.6			377	313	.60		
shad, am, cnd	152	71.1	8.8					.16							
3½ oz	100	16.9	0.0										.70		
sheepshead, atlantic, raw	113	75.9	2.8								101				
3½ oz	100	20.6	0.0								234	197			
shrimp															
raw	91	78.2	0.8		150			.03			140	63	42		
3½ oz	100	18.8	1.5				.02	3.2			220	166	1.60		
cnd, dry pack	116	70.4	1.1					.03			115				
3½ oz	100	24.2	0.7			60	.01	1.8			122	263	3.10		
cnd, wet pack	80	78.2	0.8		150			.03			59				
½ cup	100	16.2	0.8			50	.01	1.5			152		1.80		
french fried[b]	225	56.9	10.8		120			.08			186	72	51		
3½ oz	100	20.3	10.0				.04	2.7			229	191	2.00		
frzn, breaded, raw	139	65.0	0.7					.03				38			
3½ oz	100	12.3	19.9		0.1		.03	2.0				111	1.00		
shrimp paste	180	61.3	9.4												
3½ oz	100	20.8	1.5											.26	
skate (rajah fish), raw	98	77.8	0.7												
3½ oz	100	21.5	0.0				.02								
smelt, atlantic, raw	98	79.0	0.0					.12							
4–5 med	100	18.6	2.1		0.0		.01	1.4				272	.40		
smelt, atlantic, cnd	200	62.7	13.5									358			
4–5 med	100	18.4	0.0									370	1.70		
sole, raw	68		0.5					.05			56	61	30		
3½ oz	100	14.9	0.0				.06	1.7			366	195	.80		
sole, batter-dipped, frzn, Van de Kamp's—*2 pieces (4 oz)*	280		14.0								578				
	112	14.0	24.0												
sole fillet	80		0.8								162				
1 serving	113	17.7	0.6								281				
spanish mackerel, raw	177	68.9	10.4					.14			68	71			
3½ oz	100	19.5	0.0				.13	4.8			264	249	1.00		
spot, raw	219	65.3	15.9					.22			61				
3½ oz	100	17.6	0.0				.16								
spot, baked	295	53.8	21.9								312				
3½ oz	100	22.8	0.0		0.0										

[a] Prep w/butter or margarine & bacon slices

[b] Dipped in egg & flour/breadcrumbs or in batter

	KCAL	H_2O (g)	FAT (g)	PUFA (g)	CHOL (mg)	A (RE)	C (mg)	B-2 (mg)	B-6 (mg)	FOL (mcg)	Na (mg)	Ca (mg)	Mg (mg)	Zn (mg)	Mn (mg)
	WT (g)	PRO (g)	CHO (g)	SFA (g)	FIBR (g)	A (IU)	B-1 (mg)	NIA (mg)	B-12 (mcg)	PANT (mg)	K (mg)	P (mg)	Fe (mg)	Cu (mg)	
squid, raw	84	80.2	0.9					.12				12			
3½ oz	100	16.4	1.5				.02					119	.50		
sturgeon, raw	94	78.7	1.9												
3½ oz	100	18.1	0.0		0.0										
sturgeon, smoked	149	63.7	1.8												
3½ oz	100	31.2	0.0		0.0										
sturgeon, steamed	160	67.5	5.7								108	40			
3½ oz	100	25.4	0.0		0.0						235	263	2.00		
sucker, white, raw	104	76.4	1.8								56				
3½ oz	100	20.6	0.0		0.0		tr	1.2			336	220			
sucker, carp, raw	111	76.2	3.2												
3½ oz	100	19.2	0.0		0.0										
swordfish, raw	118	75.9	4.0					.05				19			
3½ oz	100	19.2	0.0		0.0	1580	.05	8.0				195	.90		
swordfish, broiled[a]	174	64.6	6.0					.05				27			
3½ oz	100	28.0	0.0		0.0	2050	.04	10.9				275	1.30		
swordfish, cnd	102	78.0	3.0					.05							
3½ oz	100	17.5	0.0		0.0	1580	.01	11.4							
tautog (blackfish), raw	89	79.3	1.1												
3½ oz	100	18.6	0.0		0.0							227			
terrapin (diamond back), raw	111	77.0	3.5												
3½ oz	100	18.6	0.0		0.0								3.20		
tilefish, raw	79	80.3	0.5												
3½ oz	100	17.5	0.0		0.0										
tilefish, baked	138	71.6	3.7												
3½ oz	100	24.5	0.0		0.0										
tomcod, atlantic, raw	77	81.5	0.4					.17							
3½ oz	100	17.2	0.0		0.0										
trout															
brook, raw	101	77.7	2.1		55										
3½ oz	100	19.2	0.0		0.0							266			
brook, ckd	196		11.2				1	.06				218	35		
3½ oz	100	23.5	0.4			319	.12	2.5				272	1.10		
rainbow, raw	195	66.3	11.4		55			.20							
3½ oz	100	21.5	0.0		0.0		.08	8.4							
rainbow/steelhead, cnd	209	63.2	13.4												
3½ oz	100	20.6	0.0		0.0										
tuna															
albacore, raw	177	66.2	7.6	tr	60						40	26			
3½ oz	100	25.3	0.0		0.0						293				
bluefin, raw	145	70.5	4.1	tr	60										
3½ oz	100	25.2	0.0		0.0								1.30		
yellowfin, raw	133	71.5	3.0	tr	60						37				
3½ oz	100	24.7	0.0		0.0										
cnd, flakes/grated in oil	440		29.0								731				
6¼ oz	177	43.0	0.0												
cnd, light in oil	386	111.9	22.1	7.9	48			.17	.74	6	883	19	61	1.58	.074
6½ oz	184	46.9	0.2		0.0	[b]	.06	21.2	5.06	.22	442	340	2.58	.120	
cnd, light in water	204	113.4	1.7	.61	110			.13	.61	6	745	19	52	1.66	
6½ oz	184	47.3	0.2		0.0		.04	20.2	7.73	.17	523	342	1.84	1.104	
cnd, white (albacore) in oil	381	111.0	19.9	6.6	42			.12	.92	6	1159	8	59	.79	.074
6½ oz	184	50.6	0.1		0.0	[c]	.06	22.3	3.50	.18	506	506	1.29	.092	
cnd, white (albacore) in water	237	126.6	3.5	1.3	64			.09	.68	6	865	9	59	.92	.074
6½ oz	184	51.5	0.1		0.0	[d]	.06	22.8	2.58	.14	478	405	2.21	.110	
cnd, white (albacore) in water, low Na	230	128.1	3.5	1.3	64			.09	.68	6	72	9	59	.92	.074
6½ oz	184	49.7	0.1		0.0	[d]	.06	22.8	2.58	.14	478	405	2.21	.110	
tuna patty	209		10.6	0.7	47		1	.16			154	56	25		
3½ oz	100	19.8	7.4		tr	78	.08	7.4			64	173	1.70		
tuna salad[e]	170	69.8	10.5				1	.11				20			
½ cup	100	14.6	3.5			290	.04	5.0				142	1.30		

[a] Prep w/butter or margarine
[b] 55 to 129 IU
[c] 46 to 110 IU
[d] 74 to 184 IU
[e] W/celery, mayo, pickle, onion & egg

	KCAL	H₂O (g)	FAT (g)	PUFA (g)	CHOL (mg)	A (RE)	C (mg)	B-2 (mg)	B-6 (mg)	FOL (mcg)	Na (mg)	Ca (mg)	Mg (mg)	Zn (mg)	Mn (mg)
	WT (g)	PRO (g)	CHO (g)	SFA (g)	FIBR (g)	A (IU)	B-1 (mg)	NIA (mg)	B-12 (mcg)	PANT (mg)	K (mg)	P (mg)	Fe (mg)	Cu (mg)	
weakfish (sea trout), raw	121	76.5	5.6					.06			75				
3½ oz	100	16.5	0.0		0.0		.09	2.7			317				
weakfish (sea trout), broiled	208	61.4	11.4					.08			560				
3½ oz	100	24.6	0.0		0.0		.10	3.5			465				
whitefish, lake, raw	155	71.7	8.2				tr	.12			52				
3½ oz	100	18.9	0.0		0.0	2260	.14	3.0			299	270	.40		
whitefish, lake, baked, stuffed[a]	215	63.2	14.0				tr	.11			195				
3½ oz	100	15.2	5.8			2000	.11	2.3			291	246	.50		
whitefish, lake, smoked	155	68.2	7.3									22			
3½ oz	100	20.9	0.0		0.0							274			
white perch, raw	118	75.7	4.0												
3½ oz	100	19.3	0.0		0.0							192			
white perch, fried fillet	108		5.3				0	.05				9			
1 serving	65	12.5	0.0		0.0	0	.04	2.7				113	.70		
wreckfish, raw	114	76.5	3.9								47				
3½ oz	100	18.4	0.0		0.0						282	171	3.20		
yellowtail, pacific, raw	138	72.7	5.4												
3½ oz	100	21.0	0.0		0.0										

FLOUR & GRAIN FRACTIONS

	KCAL	H₂O (g)	FAT (g)	PUFA (g)	CHOL (mg)	A (RE)	C (mg)	B-2 (mg)	B-6 (mg)	FOL (mcg)	Na (mg)	Ca (mg)	Mg (mg)	Zn (mg)	Mn (mg)
	WT (g)	PRO (g)	CHO (g)	SFA (g)	FIBR (g)	A (IU)	B-1 (mg)	NIA (mg)	B-12 (mcg)	PANT (mg)	K (mg)	P (mg)	Fe (mg)	Cu (mg)	
arrowroot flour	29		0.0				0	.00			4	0			
1 T	8	0.0	7.0			0	.00	0.0			1	0	.00		
barley flour	28		0.1								tr				
1 T	8	0.8	6.1		0.1						13				
barley flour	401		1.9								3				
1 cup	112	11.4	86.1		0.8						179				
bisquick mix	240		8.0								700				
½ cup	56	4.0	38.0												
buckwheat flour, dark	92	3.4	0.7			0	0	.04			tr	9			
1 oz	28	3.3	20.2		0.4	0	.16	0.8			184	97	.78		
buckwheat flour, light	97	3.4	0.3				0	.01			tr	3			
1 oz	28	1.8	22.3		0.1	0	.02	0.1			90	25	.28		
carob flour	452	15.7	2.0									493			
1 cup	140	6.3	113.0		10.8							113			
corn flake crumbs	110		0.0				15	.43	.50	100	305	1	3	.12	
1 oz	28	2.0	25.0		tr	250	.38	5.0			28	12	1.80	.02	
corn flour	405	13.2	2.9	1.1			0	.06			1	7			
1 cup sifted	110	8.6	84.5		0.8	374	.22	1.5				180	2.00		
corn flour, masa harina	137	3.2	1.5					.29	.19	17	3	77	41	1.00	.00
⅓ cup	36	3.5	27.4		0.7		.52	3.5	.00	.00	120	86	2.93	.08	
corn flour, masa trigo	149	3.7	4.0					.24	.01	29	294	66	8	.00	.00
⅓ cup	37	3.5	24.7		0.1	0	.39	3.1	.00	.00	35	77	2.60	.04	
corn flour, white, tortilla, lime-treated	103		1.6				tr	.04				25			
1 oz	28	2.3	20.7		0.9	1	.10	0.5				107	.70		
corn flour, yellow, tortilla, untreated	101		1.1				0	.03				4			
1 oz	28	2.7	20.9		0.4	48	.07	0.5				49	1.00		
corn germ, toasted	130	1.2	7.1				1	.21	.39	26	3	188	2.97		
1 oz	28	4.8	11.7		1.2	17	.47	0.6		.28		444	2.18	.14	
corn meal, white/yellow, enr, dry	102	3.0	0.5				0	.07	.10	15	1	1	12	.00	.00
1 oz (3 T)	28	2.4	22.2		0.2	0	.12	1.0	.00	.00	54	37	.81	.02	
corn meal, white/yellow, enr, dry	364	10.7	1.8				0	.25	.36	54	4	4	43	.00	.00
3½ oz	100	8.6	79.3		0.7	0	.43	3.6	.00	.00	193	132	2.89	.07	
corn meal, white/yellow, enr, ckd	120	210.5	0.4				0	.10			0	2	20		
1 cup	240	2.6	25.6		0.2	144	.14	1.2			38	34	1.00		
corn meal, white, self-rising, dry	98	3.0	0.5					.07	.11		352	109	14		
1 oz (⅙ cup)	28	2.3	21.1		0.2	0	.12	1.0			45	179	.81		
corn meal, white, self-rising, bolted, dry—1 oz (⅙ cup)	99	3.0	0.9					.07	.15	16	350	109	24	1.00	.00
	28	2.3	20.4		0.3	0	.12	1.0	.00	.00	69	207	.81	.04	

[a] Prep w/bacon, butter, onion, celery & breadcrumbs

	KCAL	H₂O (g)	FAT (g)	PUFA (g)	CHOL (mg)	A (RE)	C (mg)	B-2 (mg)	B-6 (mg)	FOL (mcg)	Na (mg)	Ca (mg)	Mg (mg)	Zn (mg)	Mn (mg)
	WT (g)	PRO (g)	CHO (g)	SFA (g)	FIBR (g)	A (IU)	B-1 (mg)	NIA (mg)	B-12 (mcg)	PANT (mg)	K (mg)	P (mg)	Fe (mg)	Cu (mg)	
corn meal, whole ground, dry	409	14.2	3.8	1.1			0	.13			1628	354	125		
1 cup	118	10.0	84.5		1.1	531	.45	2.4			276	756	2.80		
corn starch	35	1.1	tr		0										
1 T	10	tr	8.3		0.0										
manioc (casava) flour	320		0.5				14	.07			5	148			
3½ oz	100	1.6	81.0		1.8	0	.08	1.6			19	104	5.40		
rice bran	80	2.8	0.4		0						5	16	408		
1 oz	28	5.0	15.6		2.2						593	119	4.56		
rice flour	479		0.4		0		0	.14			13	11	35		
1 cup	125	7.5	107.4			0	.52	7.2			170	120	3.60		
rice polish	101	2.8	2.1		0						2	17	199		
1 oz	28	2.9	17.4		0.8						288	391	3.11		
rye flour, light	357	11.0	1.0				0	.07			1	22	73		
3½ oz	100	9.4	78.0		0.5	0	.15	0.6			156	185	1.14		
rye flour, med	350	11.1	1.7				0	.13		39	1	27	73	1.14	2.129
3½ oz	100	11.4	74.8		1.0	0	.30	2.5		.63	203	263	2.61	.57	
rye flour, dark	327	11.0	2.6				0	.22			1	54	115		
3½ oz	100	16.3	68.1		2.3	0	.61	2.7			860	536	4.53		
rye & wheat flour	400		1.0								tr				
1 cup	112	11.0	86.0												
soybean flour	380	8.0	12.0	6.0			0	.36			1	240	272		
3½ oz	100	41.1	33.3		2.2		.89	2.3			1775	650	8.98		
soybean flour, defatted	326	8.0	0.9	tr			0	.04			1	265			
3½ oz	100	47.0	38.1		2.3	40	.11	2.6			1820	655	11.09		
wheat flour															
all-purpose, enr	25	0.8	0.1				0	.03			tr	1	2		
1 T	7	0.7	5.4		tr	0	.04	0.4			8	6	.22		
all-purpose, enr	400	13.4	1.1				0	.43			2	20	28		
1 cup	112	11.6	86.2		0.3	0	.67	5.9			129	96	3.58		
all-purpose, unenr	25	0.8	0.1				0	tr			tr	1	2		
1 T	7	0.7	5.4		tr	0	tr	0.1			8	6	tr		
all-purpose, unenr	400	13.4	1.1				0	.06			2	20	28		
1 cup	112	11.6	86.2		0.3	0	.07	1.0			129	96	.90		
bread flour, enr	409	13.4	1.2				0	.29			2	18	28		
1 cup sifted	112	13.2	83.7		0.3	0	.49	3.9			106	106	3.20		
bread flour, unenr	409	13.4	1.2				0	.07			2	18	28		
1 cup sifted	112	13.2	83.7		0.3	0	.09	1.1			106	106	1.00		
cake/pastry flour	364	12.0	0.8				0	.03			2ª	17	26		
1 cup sifted	100	7.5	79.4		0.2	0	.03	0.7			95	73	.50		
gluten flour (55% white & 45%	529	11.9	2.7				0				3	56			
gluten)—*1 cup*	140	58.0	66.1		0.6	0					84	196			
self-rising	436	12.4	1.2				0	.44			1420	240	24		
1 cup	112	12.0	94.4		0.4	0	.72	6.0			116	612	3.24		
whole wheat	400	13.8	2.4				0	.14			4	49	136		
1 cup	120	16.0	85.2		2.8	0	.66	5.2			444	446	4.00		
whole wheat, 80% extraction	402	13.2	1.4				0	.08			2	26	27		
1 cup sifted	110	13.2	81.5		0.5	0	.28	2.2			104	210	1.40		
whole wheat, straight hard	365	12.0	1.2				0	.07			2	20	27		
3½ oz	100	11.8	74.5		0.4	0	.12	1.4			95	97	1.40		
whole wheat, straight soft	364	12.0	1.0				0	.05			2	20	27		
3½ oz	100	9.7	76.9		0.4	0	.08	1.2			95	97	1.10		
whole wheat & soy flour	365		6.8					.59			297	684	169		
3½ oz	100	21.4	57.3		1.3		2.02	8.2			642	533			

ª Self-rising cake/pastry flour would contain 1143 mg Na/100 g; other nutrients are similar.

	KCAL / WT (g)	H₂O (g) / PRO (g)	FAT (g) / CHO (g)	PUFA (g) / SFA (g)	CHOL (mg) / FIBR (g)	A (RE) / A (IU)	C (mg) / B-1 (mg)	B-2 (mg) / NIA (mg)	B-6 (mg) / B-12 (mcg)	FOL (mcg) / PANT (mg)	Na (mg) / K (mg)	Ca (mg) / P (mg)	Mg (mg) / Fe (mg)	Zn (mg) / Cu (mg)	Mn (mg)

FRUITS

	KCAL / WT	H₂O / PRO	FAT / CHO	PUFA / SFA	CHOL / FIBR	A(RE) / A(IU)	C / B-1	B-2 / NIA	B-6 / B-12	FOL / PANT	Na / K	Ca / P	Mg / Fe	Zn / Cu	Mn
acerola, raw	31	89.6	0.3		0	75	1644	.06	.01		7	12	18		
1 cup	98	0.4	7.5		0.4	751	.02	0.4	.00	.30	143	11	.20		
amaranth (purple heart), raw	36	86.9	0.5				80	.16				267			
3½ oz	100	3.5	6.5		1.3	6100	.08	1.4			411	67	3.90		
apples															
raw, w/skin	81	115.8	0.5	0.1	0	7	8	.02	.07	4	1	10	6	.05	.062
1 med	138	0.3	21.1	0.1	1.1	74	.02	0.1	.00	.08	159	10	.25	.057	
raw, w/o skin	72	108.1	0.4	0.1	0	6	5	.01	.06	1	0	5	4	.05	.029
1 med	128	0.2	19.0	0.1	0.7	56	.02	0.1	.00	.07	144	9	.09	.040	
boiled, w/o skin	91	146.2	0.6	0.2	0	7	tr	.02	.08	1	1	8	5	.07	.202
1 cup	171	0.5	23.3	0.1	0.9	75	.03	0.2	.00	.08	150	13	.32	.060	
cnd, sliced, sweetened	68	84.0	0.5	0.1	0	5	tr	.01	.05	tr	3	4	2	.03	.156
½ cup	102	0.2	17.0	0.1	0.6	52	.01	0.1	.00	.03	69	6	.23	.054	
dried, sulfured	155	20.3	0.2	0.1	0	0	3	.10	.08		56	9	10	.13	.058
10 rings	64	0.6	42.4	tr	1.8	0	.00	0.6	.00		288	25	.90	.122	
frzn, sliced, sweetened	93	75.1	0.1				7	.03			14	5			
½ cup	100	0.2	24.3		0.7	20	.01	0.2			68	6	.50		
micro ckd, w/o skin	96	143.9	0.7	0.2	0	7	1	.02	.08	1	1	8	6	.06	.241
1 cup	170	0.5	24.5	0.1	0.9	68	.03	0.1	.00	.08	159	14	.28	.078	
applesce, cnd, sweetened	97	101.9	0.2	0.1	0	1	2	.04	.03	1	4	5	4	.05	.096
½ cup	128	0.2	25.5	tr	0.5	14	.02	0.2	.00	.07	78	9	.45	.055	
applesce, cnd, unsweetened	53	107.8	0.1				2	.02			2	4	4	.03	.092
½ cup	122	0.2	13.8		0.7	29	.01	tr			91	9	.15	.032	
apricots															
raw	51	91.5	0.4	0.1	0	277	11	.04	.06	9	1	15	8	.28	.084
3 med	106	1.5	11.8	tr	0.6	2769	.03	0.6	.00	.25	313	21	.58	.094	
cnd, heavy syrup	75	69.9	0.1	tr	0	112	3	.02	.05	2	9	8	7	.09	.046
4 halves	90	0.5	19.3	tr	0.3	1116	.02	0.4	.00	.08	120	12	.38	.059	
cnd, jce pack	40	72.8	tr	tr	0	142	4	.02			3	10	8	.09	.044
3 halves	84	0.5	10.4	tr	0.3	1421	.02	0.3	.00		139	17	.25	.045	
cnd, light syrup	54	70.2	tr	tr	0	112	2	.02	.05	1	3	10	7	.09	.044
3 halves	85	0.5	14.0	tr	0.4	1124	.01	0.3	.00	.08	117	11	.33	.067	
cnd, water pack	20	84.1	tr	tr	0	163	2	.02	.05	2	10	8	8	.10	.048
4 halves	90	0.6	4.9	tr	0.3	1629	.02	0.4	.00	.08	139	15	.49	.061	
dried, sulfured	83	10.9	0.2	tr	0	253	1	.05	.06	4	3	16	16	.26	.096
10 halves	35	1.3	21.6	tr	1.0	2534	tr	1.0	.00	.26	482	41	1.65	.150	
frzn, sweetened	119	88.7	0.1	tr	0	203	11	.05	.07		5	12	11	.12	.061
½ cup	121	0.9	30.4	tr	0.7	2033	.02	1.0	.00	.24	277	23	1.09	.077	
banana, raw	105	84.7	0.6	0.1	0	9	10	.11	.66	22	1	7	33	.19	.173
1 med	114	1.2	26.7	0.2	0.6	92	.05	0.6	.00	.30	451	22	.35	.119	
banana flakes	170	1.5	0.5				4	.12			2	16			
½ cup	50	2.0	44.5			380	.09	1.4			738	52	1.40		
blackberries															
raw	37	61.7	0.3		0	12	15	.03	.04		0	23	14	.20	.930
½ cup	72	0.5	9.2		3.0	119	.02	0.3	.00	.17	141	15	.41	.101	
cnd, heavy syrup	118	96.1	0.2		0	28	4	.05	.05	34	3	27	22	.23	.892
½ cup	128	1.7	29.6		3.3	280	.04	0.4	0	.19	127	18	.83	.170	
frzn, unsweetened	97	124.1	0.7		0	17	5	.07	.09	51	2	44	33	.37	1.847
1 cup	151	1.8	23.7		4.1	172	.04	1.8	.00	.23	211	46	1.21	.181	
blueberries															
raw	82	122.7	0.6		0	15	19	.07	.05	9	9	9	7	.16	.409
1 cup	145	1.0	20.5		1.9	145	.07	0.5	.00	.14	129	15	.24	.088	
cnd, heavy syrup	112	98.3	0.4		0	8	1	.07	.05	2	4	7	4	.09	.260
½ cup	128	0.8	28.2		1.2	82	.04	0.1	0	.11	51	13	.42	.068	

	KCAL / WT (g)	H₂O (g) / PRO (g)	FAT (g) / CHO (g)	PUFA (g) / SFA (g)	CHOL (mg) / FIBR (g)	A (RE) / A (IU)	C (mg) / B-1 (mg)	B-2 (mg) / NIA (mg)	B-6 (mg) / B-12 (mcg)	FOL (mcg) / PANT (mg)	Na (mg) / K (mg)	Ca (mg) / P (mg)	Mg (mg) / Fe (mg)	Zn (mg) / Cu (mg)	Mn (mg)
frzn, sweetened	187	178.0	0.3		0	10	2	.12	.14	16	3	13	6	.14	.603
1 cup	230	0.9	50.5		2.1	102	.05	0.6	.00	.29	137	16	.90	.090	
boysenberries															
cnd, heavy syrup	113	97.6	0.2		0	5	8	.04	.05	44	4	23	14	.24	.320
½ cup	128	1.3	28.6		2.4	21	.03	0.3	.00	.17	115	13	.55	.090	
cnd, jce pack	88	219.1	0.2				17	.24			2	46			
1 cup	244	1.7	22.2		4.6	32	.02	1.7			207	46	2.90		
frzn, unsweetened	66	113.4	0.4		0	9	4	.05	.07	84	2	36	21	.29	.722
1 cup	132	1.5	16.1		3.6	89	.07	1.0	.00	.33	183	36	1.12	.106	
breadfruit, raw	99	67.8	0.2		0	4	28	.03			2	17	24	.11	.058
¼ small	96	1.0	26.0		1.4	38	.11	0.9	.00	.44	470	29	.52	.081	
cantaloupe, raw	57	143.6	0.4		0	516	68	.03	.18	27	14	17	17	.25	.075
1 cup pieces	160	1.4	13.4		0.6	5158	.06	0.9	.00	.21	494	27	.34	.067	
cantaloupe, frzn	31	91.0	tr				6	.02			10	11	8.0	.08	
³⁄₅ cup	100	0.8	7.7		0.3	2295	.08	0.7			325	10	.11	.04	
carambola, raw	42	115.5	0.4		0	62	27	.03			2	6	12	.14	.104
1 med	127	0.7	9.9		1.2	626	.04	0.5	.00		207	20	.33	.152	
carissa, raw	12	16.8	0.3		0	1	8	.01			1	2	3		
1 med	20	0.1	2.7		0.2	8	.01	tr	.00		52	1	.26	.042	
casaba melon, raw	45	156.4	0.2		0	5	27	.03			20	9	14		
1 cup pieces	170	1.5	10.5		0.9	51	.10	0.7	.00		357	12	.68		
cherimoya, raw	515	402.1	2.2		0	5	49	.60				126			
1 med	547	7.1	131.3		12.0	55	.55	7.1	.00			219	2.74		
cherries															
sour, cnd, heavy syrup	116	96.8	0.1	tr	0	91	3	.05	.06	10	9	13	7	.08	.092
½ cup	128	0.9	29.8	tr	0.1	914	.02	0.2	.00	.13	119	12	1.70	.084	
sour, cnd, water pack	43	109.7	0.1	tr	0	92	3	.05	.05	10	9	13	7	.08	.093
½ cup	122	0.9	10.9	tr	0.1	920	.02	0.2	.00	.13	120	12	1.67	.085	
sweet, raw	49	54.9	0.7	0.2	0	15	5	.04	.02	3	0	10	8	.04	.063
10 cherries	68	0.8	11.3	0.1	0.3	146	.03	0.3	.00	.09	152	13	.26	.065	
sweet, cnd, heavy syrup	107	100.1	0.2	0.1	0	20	5	.05	.04		3	12	11	.13	.076
½ cup	129	0.8	27.4	tr	0.4	199	.03	0.5	.00		187	23	.46	.183	
sweet, cnd, jce pack	68	106.2	tr	tr	0	16	3	.03			3	17	16	.12	.076
½ cup	125	1.1	17.3	tr	0.3	156	.02	0.5	.00		163	27	.73	.091	
sweet, cnd, water pack	57	107.9	0.2	tr	0	20	3	.05	.04		2	13	11	.09	.077
½ cup	124	1.0	14.6	tr	0.3	198	.03	0.5	.00		162	19	.45	.093	
sweet, frzn, sweetened	232	195.6	0.3	0.1	0	49	3	.12			3	31	26	.10	.282
1 cup	259	3.0	57.9	0.1	1.0	489	.07	0.5	.00		514	41	.90	.062	
crabapples, raw	83	86.8	0.3	0.1	0	4	9	.02			1	20	7		.127
1 cup slices	110	0.4	21.9	0.1	0.7	44	.03	0.1	.00		213	17	.39	.074	
cranberries, raw	46	82.2	0.2		0	4	13	.02	.06	2	1	7	5	.12	.149
1 cup whole	95	0.4	12.1		1.1	44	.03	0.1	.00	.21	67	8	.19	.055	
cranberries, frzn	46	87.9	0.2				13				1	8	5		
3½ oz	100	0.4	10.7		1.2						74	11			
cranberry sce, jelled, cnd	209	83.7	0.2		0	3	3	.03	.02		40	5	4	.07	.083
½ cup	138	0.3	53.7		0.4	28	.02	0.1	.00		35	8	.30	.028	
cranberry sce, whole berries, cnd	89	34.2	0.1								16	2	2		
2 oz	57	0.1	22.0		0.2						16	4	.13	.01	
cranberry orange relish, cnd	246	73.4	0.1			10	25	.03		0	44	15	6		
½ cup	138	0.4	63.8		0.8	97	.04	0.1	.00		53	11	.28	.055	
cranberry raspberry sce, cnd	89	34.2	0.2								14	3	2	.03	
2 oz	57	0.1	20.8		0.3						19	3	.30	.01	
currants, european black, raw	36	45.9	0.2	0.1	0	13	101	.03	.04		1	31	14	.15	.143
½ cup	56	0.8	8.6	tr	1.3	129	.03	0.2	.00	.22	180	33	.86	.048	
currants, red & white, raw	31	47.0	0.1	tr	0	7	23	.03	.04		1	18	7	.13	.104
½ cup	56	0.8	7.7	tr	1.9	67	.02	0.1	.00	.04	154	24	.56	.060	
currants, zante,[a] dried	204	13.8	0.2	0.1	0	5	3	.10	.21	7	6	62	30	.47	.338
½ cup	72	2.9	53.3	tr	1.1	52	.12	1.2	.00	.03	642	90	2.34	.337	
custard apple, raw	101	71.5	0.6		0		19	.10	.22		4	30	18		
3½ oz	100	1.7	25.2		3.4		.08	0.5	.00	.14	382	21	.71		

[a] Dried black Corinth grapes; not related to European black, red or white currants

	KCAL / WT (g)	H_2O (g) / PRO (g)	FAT (g) / CHO (g)	PUFA (g) / SFA (g)	CHOL (mg) / FIBR (g)	A (RE) / A (IU)	C (mg) / B-1 (mg)	B-2 (mg) / NIA (mg)	B-6 (mg) / B-12 (mcg)	FOL (mcg) / PANT (mg)	Na (mg) / K (mg)	Ca (mg) / P (mg)	Mg (mg) / Fe (mg)	Zn (mg) / Cu (mg)	Mn (mg)
dates, dried	228	18.7	0.4		0	4	0	.08	.16	10	2	27	29	.24	.247
10 dates	83	1.6	61.0		1.8	42	.08	1.8	.00	.65	541	33	.96	.239	
elderberries, raw	105	115.7	0.7		0	87	52	.09	.33			55			
1 cup	145	1.0	26.7		10.2	870	.10	0.7	.00	.20	406	57	2.32		
figs, raw	37	39.6	0.2	0.1	0	7	1	.03	.06		1	18	8	.07	.064
1 med	50	0.4	9.6	tr	0.6	71	.03	0.2	.00	.15	116	7	.18	.035	
figs, cnd, heavy syrup	75	64.9	0.1	tr	0	3	1	.03			1	23	8	.09	.071
3 figs	85	0.3	19.5	tr	0.5	31	.02	0.4	.00	.06	85	9	.24	.090	
figs, dried	477	53.2	2.2	1.0	0	25	2	.17	.42	14	20	269	111	.94	.726
10 figs	187	5.7	122.2	0.4	9.0	248	.13	1.3	.00	.81	1332	128	4.18	.585	
fruit cocktail[a]															
cnd, heavy syrup	93	102.9	0.1	tr	0	26	2	.02	.06		7	8	7	.11	
½ cup	128	0.5	24.2	tr	0.6	262	.02	0.5	.00	.08	112	14	.36	.088	
cnd, jce pack	56	108.4	tr	tr	0	38	3	.02			4	10	9	.11	
½ cup	124	0.6	14.7	tr	0.4	376	.02	0.5	.00		118	17	.26	.077	
cnd, water pack	40	110.7	0.1	tr	0	30	3	.01	.06		5	6	8	.11	
½ cup	122	0.5	10.4	tr	0.6	305	.02	0.4	.00	.08	115	14	.31	.087	
fruit roll-ups[b]	50		0.0												
1 roll	14		12.0												
fruit salad,[c] **cnd, heavy syrup**	94	102.7	0.1	tr	0	65	3	.03	.04		7	8	7	.09	
½ cup	128	0.4	24.5	tr	0.8	646	.02	0.4	.00		103	12	.36	.082	
fruit salad,[c] **cnd, jce pack**	62	106.8	tr	tr	0	74	4	.02			7	14	10	.18	
½ cup	124	0.6	16.2	tr	0.4	744	.01	0.4	.00		144	18	.31	.062	
fruit salad, tropical,[d] **cnd, heavy syrup**	110	98.3	0.1		0	16	22	.06			3	17	17	.14	
½ cup	128	0.5	28.6		0.6	162	.07	0.7	.00		168	10	.66	.102	
gooseberries, raw	67	131.8	0.9	tr	0	44	42	.05	.12		1	38	15	.18	.216
1 cup	150	1.3	15.3	0.1	2.9	435	.06	0.5	.00	.43	297	40	.47	.105	
gooseberries, cnd, light syrup	93	100.9	0.3	0.1	0	17	13	.07	.02	4	3	20	8	.14	.223
½ cup	126	0.8	23.6	tr	1.5	174	.03	0.2	.00	.17	97	9	.42	.273	
grapefruit															
raw, pink & red	37	112.4	0.1	tr	0	32	47	.03	.05	15	0	13	10	.09	.012
½ med	123	0.7	9.5	tr	0.3	318	.04	0.2	.00	.35	158	11	.15	.054	
raw, white	39	106.8	0.1	tr	0	1	39	.02	.05	12	0	14	11	.08	.015
½ med	118	0.8	9.9	tr	0.2	12	.04	0.3	.00	.33	175	9	.07	.059	
cnd, jce pack	46	111.2	0.1	tr	0	0	42	.02			9	19	13	.09	.009
½ cup	124	0.9	11.4	tr	0.2	0	.04	0.3	.00		209	15	.26	.046	
cnd, light syrup	76	106.2	0.1	tr	0	0	27	.03	.03	11	2	18	13	.11	.009
½ cup	127	0.7	19.6	tr	0.4	0	.05	0.3	.00	.15	164	13	.51	.084	
grapes															
american (slip skin), raw	58	74.8	0.3	0.1	0	9	4	.05	.10	4	2	13	5	.04	.661
1 cup	92	0.6	15.8	0.1	0.7	92	.09	0.3	.00	.02	176	9	.27	.037	
european (adherent skin), raw	114	128.9	0.9	.03	0	12	17	.09	.18	6	3	17	10	.09	.093
1 cup	160	1.1	28.4	0.3	0.7	117	.15	0.5	.00	.04	296	21	.41	.144	
thompson seedless, cnd, heavy syrup	94	101.8	0.1	tr	0	8	1	.03			7	13	8	.06	.049
½ cup	128	0.6	25.2	tr	0.3	81	.04	0.2	.00		132	22	1.20	.069	
groundcherries, raw[e]	74	119.6	1.0			101	15	.06		0		13			
1 cup	140	2.7	15.7		3.9	1008	.15	3.9	.00			56	1.40		
guava, raw	45	77.5	0.5	0.2	0	71	165	.05	.13		2	18	9	.21	.130
1 med	90	0.7	10.7	0.2	5.0	713	.05	1.1	.00	.14	256	23	.28	.093	
guava, strawberry, raw	169	196.8	1.5	0.6	0	22	90	.07			89	52	41		
1 cup	244	1.4	42.4	0.4	15.6	220	.07	1.5	.00		713	67	.53		
haws, scarlet, raw	87	75.8	0.7												
3½ oz	100	2.0	20.8		2.1										
honeydew melon, raw	33		0.3				23	.03			12	14			
¼ small	100	0.8	7.7		0.6	40	.04	0.6			251	16	.40		

[a] Peaches, pears, grapes, pineapples & cherries
[b] Apple, apricot, cherry, or strawberry
[c] Peaches, pears, apricots, pineapple & cherries
[d] Pineapples, papayas, pineapple jce, bananas, guava puree, cherries & passionfruit jce
[e] Roundish yellow berries, ¾ inches across, sweet & slightly acid; enclosed within the lanternlike, light brown calyx or husk; native to eastern & central North America

	KCAL	H₂O (g)	FAT (g)	PUFA (g)	CHOL (mg)	A (RE)	C (mg)	B-2 (mg)	B-6 (mg)	FOL (mcg)	Na (mg)	Ca (mg)	Mg (mg)	Zn (mg)	Mn (mg)
	WT (g)	PRO (g)	CHO (g)	SFA (g)	FIBR (g)	A (IU)	B-1 (mg)	NIA (mg)	B-12 (mcg)	PANT (mg)	K (mg)	P (mg)	Fe (mg)	Cu (mg)	
honeydew melon, frzn	60	152.4	0.2		0	7	42	.03	.10		17	10	12		.031
1 cup	170	0.8	15.6		1.0	68	.13	1.0	.00	.35	461	17	.12	.070	
indian fig	67		0.4				18	.02				57			
3½ oz	100	1.1	16.6		1.1		.01	0.3				32	1.20		
jackfruit, raw	94	72.3	0.3			30	7		.11	0	3	34	37	.42	.197
3½ oz	100	1.5	24.0		1.0	297	.03	0.4	.00		303	36	.60	.187	
java plum, raw	82	112.2	0.3			0	19	.02	.05		18	25	21		
1 cup	135	1.0	21.0		0.4	5	.01	0.4	.00		106	23	.25		
jujube, raw	79	77.9	0.2			4	69	.04	.08	0	3	21	10	.05	.084
3½ oz	100	1.2	20.2		1.4	40	.02	0.9	.00		250	23	.48	.073	
jujube, dried	287	19.7	1.1				13	.36		0	9	79	37	.19	.305
3½ oz	100	3.7	73.6		3.0		.21	0.5	.00		531	100	1.80	.265	
kiwifruit, raw	46	63.1	0.3			13	75	.04		0	4	20	23		
1 med	76	0.8	11.3		0.8	133	.02	0.4	.00		252	31	.31		
kumquats, raw	12	15.5	tr		0	6	7	.02			1	8	2	.02	.016
1 med	19	0.2	3.1		0.7	57	.02		.00		37	4	.07	.020	
lemon, raw	17	51.6	0.2	tr	0	2	31	.01	.05	6	1	15		.04	
1 med	58	0.6	5.4	tr	0.2	17	.02	.06	.00	.11	80	9	.35	.021	
lemon peel	ᵃ	4.9	tr	tr	0	0	8	.01	.01		0	8	1		
1 T	6	0.1	1.0	tr		3	tr	tr	.00	.02	10	1	.05		
lime, raw	20	59.1	0.1	tr	0	1	20	.01		6	1	22		.07	
1 med	67	0.5	7.1	tr	0.3	7	.02	0.1	.00	.15	68	12	.40	.044	
loganberries, cnd, heavy syrup	89	76.5	0.4				8	.02			1	22			
½ cup	100	0.6	22.2		1.9	130	.01	0.2			109	11	.80		
loganberries, frzn	80	124.4	0.5		0	5	23	.05	.10	38	1	38	32	.50	1.833
1 cup	147	2.2	19.1			52	.07	1.2	.00	.36	213	38	.94	.172	
longans, raw	60	82.8	0.1		0		84	.14			0	1	10	.05	.052
31 fruits	100	1.3	15.1		0.4		.03	0.3	.00		266	21	.13	.169	
longans, dried	286	17.6	0.4		0	0	28				48	45	46	.22	.248
3½ oz	100	4.9	74.0		2.0	0	.04		.00		658	196	5.40	.807	
loquats, raw	47	86.7	0.2	0.1	0	153	1	.02			1	16	13	.05	.148
10 med	100	0.4	12.1	tr	0.5	1528	.02	0.2	.00		266	27	.28	.040	
lychees, raw	66	81.8	0.4		0	0	72	.07			1	5	10	.07	.055
10 med	100	0.8	16.5		0.2	0	.01	0.6	.00		171	31	.31	.148	
lychees, dried	277	22.3	1.2		0	0	183	.57			3	33	42	.28	.234
3½ oz	100	3.8	70.7		1.4	0	.01	3.1	.00		1110	181	1.70	.631	
mammy apple, raw	51	86.2	0.5		0	23	14	.04			15	11			
⅛ med	100	0.5	12.5		1.00	230	.02	0.4	.00	.10	47	11	.70		
mandarin oranges, cnd, jce pack	46	111.0	.03	tr	0	106	43	.04			7	14	14	.63	
½ cup	124	0.8	11.9	tr	0.1	1056	.10		.00		165	13	.33	.041	
mandarin oranges, cnd, light syrup	76	104.7	0.1	tr	0	106	25	.06			8	9	10	.30	
½ cup	126	0.6	20.4	tr	0.2	1058	.07	0.6	.00		99	12	.46	.055	
mangos, raw	135	169.1	0.6	0.1	0	806	57	.12	.28		4	21	18	.07	.056
1 med	207	1.1	35.2	0.1	1.7	8060	.12	1.2	.00	.33	322	22	.26	.228	
melon balls (cantaloupe & honeydew), frzn—1 cup	55	156.1	0.4		0	307	11	.04	.18	45	53	17	24	.29	.069
	173	1.5	13.7			3069	.29	1.1	.00	.28	484	22	.50	.104	
mixed fruit,ᵇ cnd, heavy syrup	92	103.1	0.1	tr	0	25	88ᶜ	.05			5	1	6	.09	
½ cup	128	0.5	24.0	tr	0.5	248	.02	0.8	.00		108	13	.46	.074	
mixed fruit,ᵇ cnd, jce pack	45		0.1				2	.02			8	8	8		
3½ oz	100	0.5	10.8			355	tr	0.7			129	12	.50		
mixed fruit, dried	243	31.2	0.5	0.1	0	244	4	.16	.16		18	38	39	.50	.227
3½ oz	100	2.5	64.1	tr	2.9	2442	.04	1.9	.00		796	77	2.71	.385	
mixed fruit,ᵈ frzn, sweetened	245	184.3	0.5	0.2	0	81	188ᶜ	.09	.25	9	8	18	14	.12	.160
1 cup	250	3.5	60.6	0.1	1.1	806	.04	1.0	.00	.41	327	30	.70	.085	
mulberries, raw	61	122.8	0.6		0	4	51	.14			14	55	25		
1 cup	140	2.0	13.7		1.3	35	.04	0.9	.00		271	53	2.59		
nectarines, raw	67	117.3	0.6		0	100	7	.06	.03	5	0	6	11	.12	.060
1 med	136	1.3	16.0		0.5	1001	.02	1.3	.00	.22	288	22	.21	.099	
oheloberries, raw	39	129.2	0.3		0	116	8	.05			2	10	9		
1 cup	140	0.5	9.6		1.9	1162	.02	0.4	.00		54	14	.13		
orange, navel, raw	65	121.5	0.1	tr	0	26	80	.06	.10	47	1	56	15	.08	.038
1 med	140	1.4	16.3	tr	0.6	256	.12	0.4	.00	.35	250	27	.17	.078	

ᵃ Cannot be calculated; no digestibility value for peel
ᵇ Peaches, pears & pineapple
ᶜ Added vit C
ᵈ Peaches, sweet cherries, red sour cherries, red raspberries, boysenberries & grapes

	KCAL / WT (g)	H₂O (g) / PRO (g)	FAT (g) / CHO (g)	PUFA (g) / SFA (g)	CHOL (mg) / FIBR (g)	A (RE) / A (IU)	C (mg) / B-1 (mg)	B-2 (mg) / NIA (mg)	B-6 (mg) / B-12 (mcg)	FOL (mcg) / PANT (mg)	Na (mg) / K (mg)	Ca (mg) / P (mg)	Mg (mg) / Fe (mg)	Zn (mg) / Cu (mg)	Mn (mg)
orange, valencia, raw	59	104.5	0.4	0.1	0	28	59	.05	.08	47	0	48	12	.07	.028
1 med	121	1.3	14.4	tr	0.6	278	.11	0.3	.00	.30	217	21	.11	.045	
orange peel	a	4.4	tr	tr	0	3	8	.01	.01		0	10	1		
1 T	6	0.1	1.5	tr		25	.01	0.1	.00	.03	13	1	.05		
papaws, raw	85	76.6	0.9												
3½ oz	100	5.2	16.8												
papayas, raw	117	270.0	0.4	0.1	0	612	188	.10	.06		8	72	31	.22	.033
1 med	304	1.9	29.8	0.1	2.4	6122	.08	1.0	.00	.66	780	16	.30	.049	
passionfruit (purple grandilla), purple,	18	13.1	0.1		0	13	5	.02			5	2	5		
raw—*1 med*	18	0.4	4.2		2.0	126		0.3	.00		63	12	.29		
peach															
raw	37	76.3	0.1	tr	0	47	6	.04	.02	3	0	5	6	.12	.041
1 med	87	0.6	9.7	tr	0.6	465	.02	0.9	.00	.15	171	11	.10	.059	
cnd, heavy syrup	190	203.0	0.3	0.1	0	85	7	.06	.05	8	16	8	13	.22	.115
1 cup	256	1.2	51.0	tr	0.7	849	.03	1.6	.00	.13	235	29	.69	.131	
cnd, heavy syrup, spiced	66	69.7	0.1	tr	0	28	5	.03			3	5	6	.07	
1 med	88	0.4	17.7	tr	0.2	279	.01	0.5	.00		75	8	.25	.086	
cnd, jce pack	109	217.0	0.1		0	95	9	.04			11	15	18	.26	
1 cup	248	1.6	28.7	tr	0.6	945	.02	1.4	.00		317	43	.66	.124	
cnd, light syrup	136	212.6	0.1	tr	0	89	6	.06	.05	8	13	9	12	.22	.115
1 cup	251	1.1	36.5	tr	0.8	888	.02	1.5	.00	.13	244	27	.90	.131	
cnd, water pack	58	227.2	0.1	tr	0	130	7	.05	.05	8	8	6	12	.22	.117
1 cup	244	1.1	14.9	tr	0.8	1298	.02	1.3	.00	.12	241	25	.77	.132	
dried, sulfured	311	41.3	1.0	0.5	0	281	6	.28	.09		9	37	54	.75	.397
10 halves	130	4.7	79.7	0.1	3.8	2812	tr	5.7	.00		1295	155	5.28	.473	
frzn, sweetened	235	186.8	0.3	0.2	0	71	235c	.09	.05	24	16	6	12	.13	.073
1 cup	250	1.6	59.9	tr	1.0	709	.03	1.6	.00	.33	325	28	.93	.060	
pears															
raw	98	139.1	0.7	0.2	0	3	7	.07	.03	12	1	19	9	.20	.126
1 med	166	0.7	25.1	tr	2.3	33	.03	0.2	.00	.12	208	18	.41	.188	
cnd, heavy pack	188	204.9	0.3	0.1	0	0	3	.06	.04	3	13	12	11	.21	.082
1 cup	255	0.5	48.9	tr	1.5	0	.03	0.6	.00	.06	165	17	.56	.125	
cnd, jce pack	123	214.5	0.2	tr	0	1	4	.03			10	21	17	.22	
1 cup	248	0.9	32.1	tr	1.2	14	.03	0.5	.00		238	29	.71	.131	
cnd, light syrup	144	212.0	0.1	tr	0	0	2	.04	.04	3	13	13	11	.21	.083
1 cup	251	0.5	38.1	tr	1.5	0	.03	0.4	.00	.06	165	17	.70	.123	
cnd, water pack	71	224.0	0.1	tr	0	0	3	.02	.03	3	5	9	9	.21	.083
1 cup	244	0.5	19.1	tr	1.5	0	.02	0.1	.00	.05	130	17	.52	.124	
dried, sulfured	459	46.7	1.1	0.3	0	1	12	.25			10	59	58	.68	.572
10 halves	175	3.3	122.0	0.1	10.0	6	.01	2.4	.00		932	103	3.68	.649	
persimmons, raw	32	16.1	0.1		0		17				0	7			
1 med	25	0.2	8.4		0.4				.00		78	7	.63		
persimmons, japanese, raw	118	134.9	0.3		0	364	13	.03		13	3	13	15	.18	.596
1 med	168	1.0	31.2		2.5	3640	.05	0.2	.00		270	28	.26	.190	
persimmons, japanese, dried	93	7.8	0.2		0	19	0	.01			1	8	11	.14	.473
1 med	34	0.5	25.0		1.2	190		0.1	.00		273	27	.25	.150	
pineapple															
raw	77	135.1	0.7	0.2	0	4	24	.06	.14	16	1	11	21	.12	2.556
1 cup pieces	155	0.6	19.2	tr	0.8	35	.14	0.7	.00	.25	175	11	.57	.171	
cnd, heavy syrup	199	201.4	0.3	0.1	0	4	19	.06	.19	12	3	35	40	.29	2.754
1 cup pieces	255	0.9	51.5	tr	1.1	37	.23	0.7	.00	.26	264	17	.98	.258	
cnd, jce pack	150	208.8	0.2	0.1	0	9	24	.05			4	34	35	.24	
1 cup pieces	250	1.0	39.2	tr	0.9	95	.24	0.7	.00		304	16	.70	.215	
pitanga, raw	57	157.1	0.7		0	260	46	.07			5	16	21		
1 cup	173	1.4	13.0		1.0	2595	.05	0.5	.00		178	19	.35		
plantain, ckd	179	103.6	0.3		0	140	17	.08	.37	40	8	3	49	.20	
1 cup slices	154	1.2	48.0			1400	.07	1.2	.00	.36	716	43	.89	.102	

a Cannot be calculated; no digestibility value for peel

	KCAL	H₂O (g)	FAT (g)	PUFA (g)	CHOL (mg)	A (RE)	Vitamins C (mg)	B-2 (mg)	B-6 (mg)	FOL (mcg)	Na (mg)	Minerals Ca (mg)	Mg (mg)	Zn (mg)	Mn (mg)
	WT (g)	PRO (g)	CHO (g)	SFA (g)	FIBR (g)	A (IU)	B-1 (mg)	NIA (mg)	B-12 (mcg)	PANT (mg)	K (mg)	P (mg)	Fe (mg)	Cu (mg)	
plum															
raw	36	56.2	0.4	0.1	0	21	6	.06	.05	1	0	2	4	.06	.032
1 med	66	0.5	8.6	tr	0.4	213	.03	0.3	.00	.12	113	7	.07	.028	
cnd, heavy syrup	119	101.2	0.1	tr	0	34	1	.05	.04	3	26	12	7	.10	.041
3 plums	133	0.5	30.9	tr	0.4	344	.02	0.4	.00	.10	121	17	1.12	.049	
cnd, jce pack	55	79.8	tr	tr	0	96	3	.06			1	9	8	.10	
3 plums	95	0.5	14.4	tr	0.3	958	.02	0.5	.00		147	15	.32	.051	
pomegranates, raw	104	124.7	0.5		0		9	.05	.16		5	5			
1 med	154	1.5	26.4		0.3		.05	0.5	.00	.92	399	12	.46		
pricklypears, raw	42	90.2	0.5		0	5	14	.06			6	58	88		
1 med	103	0.8	9.9		1.9	53	.01	0.5	.00		226	25	.31		
prunes															
cnd, heavy syrup	90	60.8	0.2	tr	0	69	2	.11			2	15	13	.16	.084
5 prunes	86	0.8	23.9	tr	0.6	686	.03	0.7	.00		194	22	.35	.101	
dried	201	27.2	0.4	0.1	0	167	3	.14	.22	3	3	43	38	.45	.185
10 prunes	84	2.2	52.7	tr	1.7	1669	.07	1.6	.00	.39	626	66	2.08	.361	
dried, ckd	113	73.9	0.2	tr	0	32	3	.11	.23	tr	2	24	21	.25	.104
½ cup	106	1.2	29.8	tr	1.0	324	.03	0.8	.00	.11	354	37	1.18	.205	
pummelo, raw	71	169.3	0.1		0	0	116	.05	.07		2	7	12	.15	.032
1 cup pieces	190	1.4	18.3		0.3	0	.07	0.4	.00		411	32	.22	.091	
quinces, raw	53	77.1	0.1	tr	0	4	14	.03	.04		4	10	7		
1 med	92	0.4	14.1	tr	1.6	38	.02	0.2	.00	.08	181	16	.64	.120	
raisins															
golden seedless	302	14.9	0.5	0.1	0	4	3	.19	.32	3	12	53	35	.32	.308
⅔ cup	100	3.4	79.5	0.2	1.4	44	.01	1.1	.00	.14	746	115	1.79	.363	
seeded	296	16.6	0.5	0.2	0	0	5	.18	.19	3	28	28	30	.18	.267
⅔ cup	100	2.5	78.5	0.2	0.7	0	.11	1.1	.00		825	75	2.59	.302	
seedless	300	15.4	0.5	0.1	0	1	3	.09	.25	3	12	49	33	.27	.308
⅔ cup	100	3.2	79.1	0.2	1.3	8	.16	0.8	.00	.05	751	97	2.08	.309	
raspberries															
raw	61	106.5	0.7	0.4	0	16	31	.11	.07		0	27	22	.57	1.246
1 cup	123	1.1	14.2	tr	3.7	160	.04	1.1	.00	.30	187	15	.70	.091	
cnd, heavy syrup	117	96.4	0.2	0.1	0	4	11	.04	.05	13	4	14	16	.20	.298
½ cup	128	1.1	29.9	tr		43	.03	0.6	.00	.31	120	12	.54	.073	
frzn, sweetened	103	72.8	0.2	0.1	0	6	17	.05	.03	26	1	15	13	.18	.650
⅖ cup	100	0.7	26.2	tr	2.2	60	.02	0.2	.00	.15	114	17	.65	.11	
rose apples, raw	25	93.0	0.3		0	34	22	.03			0	29	5	.06	.029
3½ oz	100	0.6	5.7		1.1	339	.02	0.8	.00		123	8	.07	.016	
roselle, raw	28	49.4	0.4		0	16	7	.02			3	123	29		
1 cup	57	0.6	6.5		0.7	163	.01	0.2	.00		118	21	.84		
sapodilla, raw	140	132.6	1.9		0	10	25	.03	.06		20	36			
1 med	170	0.7	33.9		2.4	102		0.3	.00	.43	328	20	1.36		
sapotes, raw	301	140.5	1.4		0	92	45	.05			21	88	68		
1 med	225	4.8	76.0		4.3	923	.02	4.1	.00		773	63	2.25		
soursop, raw	150	182.6	0.7		0	1	46	.11	.13		31	32	46		
1 cup	225	2.3	37.9		2.5	5	.16	2.0	.00	.57	626	61	1.35		
strawberries															
raw	45	136.4	0.6	0.3	0	4	85	.10	.09	26	2	21	16	.19	.432
1 cup	149	0.9	10.5	tr	0.8	41	.03	0.3	.00	.51	247	28	.57	.073	
frzn, sweetened	245	186.6	0.3	0.2	0	6	106	.13	.08	38	8	28	18	.14	.638
1 cup	255	1.4	66.1	tr	1.6	61	.04	1.02	.00	.28	249	32	1.49	.051	
frzn, unsweetened	52	134.1	0.2	0.1	0	7	61	.06	.04	25	3	23	16	.19	.432
1 cup	149	0.6	13.6	tr	1.2	66	.03	0.7	.00	.16	220	20	1.12	.073	
sugar apples, raw	146	113.5	0.5		0	1	56	.18	.31		15	37	33		
1 med	155	3.2	36.6		2.3	9	.17	1.4	.00	.35	384	50	.93		
tamarinds, raw	287	37.7	0.7	0.1	0	4	4	.18	.08		33	89	110		
1 cup	120	3.4	75.0	0.3	6.1	36	.51	2.3	.00	.17	753	136	3.36		

	KCAL	H₂O (g)	FAT (g)	PUFA (g)	CHOL (mg)	A (RE)	C (mg)	B-2 (mg)	B-6 (mg)	FOL (mcg)	Na (mg)	Ca (mg)	Mg (mg)	Zn (mg)	Mn (mg)
	WT (g)	PRO (g)	CHO (g)	SFA (g)	FIBR (g)	A (IU)	B-1 (mg)	NIA (mg)	B-12 (mcg)	PANT (mg)	K (mg)	P (mg)	Fe (mg)	Cu (mg)	
tangelos, raw	39		0.1				26					2	27	19	
1 med	170	0.5	9.2									296	20	.20	
tangerines, raw	37	73.6	0.2	tr	0	77	26	.02	.06	17	1	12	10		.027
1 med	84	0.5	9.4	tr	0.3	773	.09	0.1	.00	.17	132	8	.09	.024	
watermelon, raw	50	146.4	0.7		0	58	15	.03	.23	3	3	13	17	.11	.059
1 cup	160	1.0	11.5		0.5	585	.13	0.3	.00	.34	186	14	.28	.051	

GRAIN PRODUCTS (BREADS, CRACKERS, ROLLS, ETC.)

	KCAL	H₂O (g)	FAT (g)	PUFA (g)	CHOL (mg)	A (RE)	C (mg)	B-2 (mg)	B-6 (mg)	FOL (mcg)	Na (mg)	Ca (mg)	Mg (mg)	Zn (mg)	Mn (mg)
	WT (g)	PRO (g)	CHO (g)	SFA (g)	FIBR (g)	A (IU)	B-1 (mg)	NIA (mg)	B-12 (mcg)	PANT (mg)	K (mg)	P (mg)	Fe (mg)	Cu (mg)	
bagel	163	16.0	1.4				0	.16	.02	13	198	23	11	.29	
1 bagel	55	6.0	30.9	0.1		0	.21	1.9	.00	.20	41	37	1.46	.05	
biscuits															
from mix	93	8.0	3.3				tr	.11	.01	2	262	58	7	.18	
1 biscuit	28	2.1	13.6	tr		16	.12	0.8	.05	.10	56	128	.57	.03	
from refrig dough	91	8.4	3.1				0	.07	.01		349	6	4	.12	
1 biscuit	28	2.0	13.6	tr		0	.11	0.9	.00	.07	25	110	.66	.02	
baking powder, enr, homemade	103	7.7	4.8				tr	.06			175	34			
1 biscuit	28	2.1	12.8			tr	.06	0.5			33	49	.40		
baking powder, from refrig dough	110		4.0								350				
2 biscuits	34	2.0	15.0												
buttermilk, from refrig dough	130		6.0								410				
2 biscuits	40	2.0	18.0												
butter tastin, from refrig dough	190		10.0								550				
2 biscuits	50	3.0	22.0												
flaky, from refrig dough	180		9.0								580				
2 biscuits	50	3.0	23.0												
bread															
brown, cnd	80		tr								220				
½ inch slice	45	2.0	18.0												
brown w/raisins, cnd	80		tr								220				
½ inch slice	45	2.0	18.0												
corn bread, from mix	160		4.0								720				
⅛ prep mix	58	4.0	26.0												
corn bread w/enr cornmeal, homemade—*1 piece*	198	41.7	7.3				tr	.15	.06	8	232	90	15	.39	
	83	4.1	28.7		0.1	114	.15	1.2	.14	.32	78	81	1.24	.03	
corn bread w/whole ground cornmeal, homemade—*1 piece*	172	42.0	6.9				tr	.11	.08	6	209	83	20	.46	
	78	3.7	24.1		0.2	104	.11	0.8	.13	.28	88	90	.83	.05	
corn pone[a] w/whole ground cornmeal	92		2.4	1.0			0	.02			178	28	9		
1 cake	45	2.0	16.3		0.4	0	.07	0.4			27	73	.50		
cracked wheat	66	8.8	0.9				tr	.10	.02		108	16	9		
1 slice	25	2.3	12.5		0.1	tr	.10	0.8	.00	.15	33	32	.67		
cracked wheat, toasted	63	5.5	0.8				tr	.09	.02		104	16	8		
1 slice	21	2.2	12.0		0.1	tr	.07	0.8	.00	.14	32	30	.64		
french/vienna	70	8.5	1.0	0			tr	.09	.01	9	138	28	5	.16	
1 slice	25	2.4	12.6	tr		tr	.12	1.0	.00	.09	22	20	.77	.04	
fresh horizons, wheat[b]	49	12.6	0.5	0			0	.07			145	42			
1 slice	28	2.5	9.5	2.1		0	.11	1.1					.98		
fresh horizons, white	50	12.6	0.5	0			0	.08			140	42			
1 slice	28	2.5	9.5	2.1		0	.11	1.0					.98		
fruit/nut[c] quick bread, from mix	118	13.0	2.4					.09			126	12	6	.16	
1 slice	40	1.8	22.3		0.1		.10	1.1			40	48	.69	.04	
hillbilly	68	10.6	0.8				0	.08			168	28			
1 slice	28	2.5	12.9	0.1		0	.11	1.1					.84		
hollywood, dark[b]	68	10.6	1.1				0	.11			159	36			
1 slice	28	2.8	12.3	0.2		0	.12	1.1					.98		
hollywood, light	68	10.6	0.9				0	.09			168	36			
1 slice	28	2.8	12.9	0.1		0	.11	1.1					.98		

[a] Corn bread often made w/o milk or eggs, shaped in irregular ovals by the palm of the hand & baked or fried on a griddle
[b] Made w/white enr flour & colored brown; not the same as whole wheat bread
[c] Applesce spice, apricot nut, banana nut, cherry nut, cranberry, or date nut

	KCAL	H₂O (g)	FAT (g)	PUFA (g)	CHOL (mg)	A (RE)	C (mg)	B-2 (mg)	B-6 (mg)	FOL (mcg)	Na (mg)	Ca (mg)	Mg (mg)	Zn (mg)	Mn (mg)
	WT (g)	PRO (g)	CHO (g)	SFA (g)	FIBR (g)	A (IU)	B-1 (mg)	NIA (mg)	B-12 (mcg)	PANT (mg)	K (mg)	P (mg)	Fe (mg)	Cu (mg)	
honey wheatberry	70	10.6	1.1				0	.11			161	35			
1 slice	28	2.5	13.1		0.1	0	.11	1.1					.98		
italian, enr	55	6.4	0.2				0	.05			117	3			
1 slice	20	1.8	11.3		tr	0	.06	0.5			15	15	.40		
matzoᵃ	117		0.3								tr				
1 piece	30	3.0	25.4												
mixed grain	64	9.4	0.9				tr	.10	.03	16	103	26	12	.30	
1 slice	25	2.5	11.7		0.2	tr	.10	1.0	.00	.16	55	53	.82	.07	
mixed grain, toasted	63	5.8	0.9				tr	.09	.03	16	100	25	12	.29	
1 slice	21	2.4	11.4		0.2	tr	.08	1.0	.00	.15	53	52	.79	.07	
raisin	70	8.3	1.0				tr	.16	.01	9	94	26	4	.16	
1 slice	25	2.1	13.2		0.2	tr	.08	1.0	.00	.11	60	22	.78	.03	
raisin, toasted	66	5.1	0.9				tr	.15	.01	8	90	24	6	.15	
1 slice	21	1.9	12.6		0.2	tr	.06	1.0	.00	.10	57	21	.74	.03	
roman meal	68	10.6	1.0				0	.08			140	31			
1 slice	28	2.8	12.3		0.4	0	.11	1.1					.98		
rye, am	66	9.4	0.9				tr	.08	.02	10	174	20	6	.32	
1 slice	25	2.1	12.0		0.1	0	.10	0.8	.00	.11	51	36	.68	.03	
rye, am, toasted	66	6.3	0.9				0	.08	.02	10	175	20	6	.32	
1 slice	22	2.1	12.0		0.1	0	.08	0.8	.00	.11	51	37	.68	.03	
rye, pumpernickel	82	11.9	0.8				0	.17	.05		173	23	22	.36	
1 slice	32	2.9	15.4		0.3	0	.11	1.1	.00	.15	139	70	.88		
rye, pumpernickel, toasted	82	7.9	1.1				0	.17	.05		174	23	22	.36	
1 slice	28	2.9	15.4		0.3	0	.09	1.1	.00	.15	139	70	.88		
sourdough	68	10.6	0.5		0		0	.06			154	28			
1 slice	28	2.5	13.4		0.1	0	.11	1.0					.70		
spoon breadᵇ w/whole ground	187		10.9	0.9			tr	.17			463	92			
cornmeal—3²⁄₅ oz	96	6.4	16.2		0.2	278	.09	0.4			127	157	1.00		
wheatᶜ	61	8.9	1.0		0		tr	.08	.03	11	129	30	11	.25	
1 slice	24	2.3	11.3		0.2	tr	.11	1.1	1.1	.10	33	44	.84	.06	
wheat,ᶜ toasted	64	5.9	0.9				tr	.08	.01	8	123	30	5	.15	
1 slice	21	2.0	11.7		0.1	tr	.09	0.9	.00	.10	27	26	.68	.03	
wheatberry	70	10.6	1.1		0		0	.06			148	29			
1 slice	28	2.5	12.3		0.4	0	.11	1.0					.70		
white	64	8.9	0.9				tr	.07	.01	8	123	30	5	.15	
1 slice	24	2.0	11.7		tr	tr	.11	0.9	.00	.10	27	26	.68	.03	
white, toasted	64	5.9	0.9				tr	.08	.01	8	123	30	5		
1 slice	21	2.0	11.7		0.1	tr	.03	0.9	.00	.10	27	26	.68		
white, homemade	72	9.0	1.7				tr	.08	.01	9	102	16	6	.16	
1 slice	25	1.9	12.0		tr	13	.08	0.7	.03	.12	33	25	.54	.02	
white, homemade, toasted	70	5.5	1.6				tr	.08	.01	9	98	16	5	.16	
1 slice	21	1.8	11.7		tr	12	.06	0.7	.03	.11	32	24	.52	.02	
white, low Na	68	10.6	1.0				0	.06			3	21			
1 slice	28	2.2	13.4		0.1	0	.11	1.0					.70		
white w/buttermilk	71	10.6	1.1				0	.08			163	40			
1 slice	28	2.2	13.1		0.1	0	.11	1.1					.84		
whole wheat	61	9.6	1.1				tr	.05	.05	14	159	18			
1 slice	25	2.4	11.4		0.4	tr	.09	1.0	.00	.18	44	23	.86		
whole wheat, toasted	59	6.1	1.1				tr	.05	.04	13	153	17	23	.40	
1 slice	21	2.3	10.9		0.4	tr	.07	0.9	.00	.18	42	63	.82	.08	
whole wheat, homemade	67	9.0	1.6				tr	.04	.05	12	89	20	23	.56	
1 slice	25	2.2	11.6		0.3	11	.07	0.8	.03	.20	85	63	.67	.06	
whole wheat, homemade, toasted	65	5.5	1.6				tr	.04	.05	12	87	19	23	.55	
1 slice	21	2.2	11.3		0.3	11	.05	0.8	.03	.20	83	61	.65	.06	
bread crumbs	345	5.7	4.0	0.6			tr	.26			648	107	30		
1 cup	88	11.1	64.6		0.3	tr	.19	3.1			134	124	3.20		
bread sticks															
reg	23	0.3	0.2				tr				100	2			
1 piece	6	0.7	4.5		tr	tr	0.1				6	6	tr		
garlic	24		0.3												
1 piece	6	tr	4.3												

ᵃ Flat, thin unleavened bread
ᵇ Bread made of cornmeal w/ or w/o added rice & hominy & mixed w/ milk, eggs, shortening & leavening to a consistency that must be served w/a spoon
ᶜ Made w/white enr flour & colored brown; not the same as whole wheat bread

	KCAL / WT (g)	H₂O (g) / PRO (g)	FAT (g) / CHO (g)	PUFA (g) / SFA (g)	CHOL (mg) / FIBR (g)	A (RE) / A (IU)	C (mg) / B-1 (mg)	B-2 (mg) / NIA (mg)	B-6 (mg) / B-12 (mcg)	FOL (mcg) / PANT (mg)	Na (mg) / K (mg)	Ca (mg) / P (mg)	Mg (mg) / Fe (mg)	Zn (mg) / Cu (mg)	Mn (mg)
sesame	56		3.7												
1 piece	10	1.1	4.4												
vienna	18	1.5	0.2				tr				94	3			
1 piece	6	0.6	3.5	tr		tr	tr				6	5	tr		
crackers															
cheese	81	0.6	4.9				0	.06			180	16	3	.15	
5 pieces	15	1.4	7.8	tr			.06	1.2			28	32	.53	.07	
cheese crackers w/peanut butter	283	1.4	13.5					.11							
2 oz	57	9.5	30.9				.13	2.9					1.88		
cheese crackers w/peanut butter, Frito-Lay—*1.5 oz*	205	1.8	9.5	tr				.17			477	53	27	.50	.285
1.5 oz	43	6.4	23.4				.20	3.2			130	150	1.33	.09	
cheese snacks, Dixie Bells	140		6.1				0	.14	.03	7	263	24	5	.24	
25 crackers	28	2.8	18.0		0.1	46	.13	1.2	1.31	.07	43	35	1.40	.016	
crackers w/cheese, Frito-Lay	198	1.7	8.8		5			.31			596	117	15	.26	.123
1.5 oz	43	4.3	25.6		0.2	40	.19	1.6			205	173	1.02	.04	
goldfish, Pepperidge Farm	30		2.0				0	.02			50	4			
12 crackers	6	tr	4.0			1	.04	0.2			12	6	.20		
goldfish, cheese, Pepperidge Farm	30		2.0				0	.02			70	2			
12 crackers	6	tr	4.0			11	.03	0.2			10	8	.20		
goldfish, pizza, Pepperidge Farm	30		1.0				0	.02			70	3			
12 crackers	6	tr	4.0			25	.04	0.2			10	5	.30		
goldfish, pretzel, Pepperidge Farm	30		1.0				0	.02			130	2			
12 crackers	7	tr	5.0			1	.03	0.2			10	6	.30		
graham	60	0.5	1.5				0	.04	.01	2	66	5	5	.11	
2 squares	14	1.0	10.8		0.1	tr	.05	0.4	.00	.07	23	17	.37	.02	
graham cracker crumbs (not packed)	180	1.5	4.5				0	.12	.03	6	198	15	15	.33	
½ cup	42	3.0	32.4		0.3	tr	.15	1.2	.00	.21	69	51	1.11	.06	
hi ho, Sunshine	82		4.4									21			
4 crackers	16	1.1	9.5									40	.50		
melba toast	15		0.2								3				
1 piece	4	0.5	2.7								9				
oyster	120		3.3				0	.14	.01	8	356	4	5	.20	
33 crackers	28	2.7	20.0		0.1	0	.10	1.5	.01	.06	34	25	1.20	.045	
rich & crisp, Dixie Belle	140		5.6				0	.14	.00	4	183	12	5	.15	
10 crackers	28	2.4	19.0		0.1	14	.16	1.4	.10	.10	14	30	1.40	.054	
rice wafer	31		0.0								8				
3 wafers	10	0.8	6.7								3				
ritz, Nabisco	54		2.9								97	15			
3 crackers	10	0.7	6.4				.04	0.3			8	24	.30		
ritz, cheese, Nabisco	52		2.9					.05			104	20			
3 crackers	10	0.6	5.5				0.8	0.3			9	24	.30		
rusk	42		0.9					.02			25	2			
1 piece	10	1.4	7.1	tr		23	.01	0.1			16	12	.10		
rye crackers w/cheese, Frito-Lay	205	1.6	9.5		4		1	.22	.08		474	102	16	.30	.270
1.5 oz	43	4.1	25.7		0.2	71	.28	1.4			172	144	.99	.041	
ryekrisp	50		0.2					.05	.04	7	97	5	15	.36	
2 triple crackers	12	1.3	10.0		0.2		.02	0.3		.07	64	42	.58	.06	
ryekrisp, seasoned	60		0.9					.02	.03	6	131	5	13	.30	
2 triple crackers	13	1.3	9.0		0.2		.03	0.6		.06	64	36	.45	.053	
ryekrisp, sesame	60		1.5				0	.04	.03	9	151	15	19	.42	
2 triple crackers	15	1.3	10.0		0.1	19	.03	0.3	.00	.10	71	48	.58	.07	
saltines	26	0.2	0.6				0	.03	tr	1	80	4	2	.04	
2 crackers	6	0.6	4.4	tr		0	.02	0.4	.00	.02	8	6	.16	.01	
sesame,[a] Ak-Mok	117		2.3				2	.04				21	41		
1 oz	28	4.6	18.9			14	.06	1.1				0	.50		
snackers, Dixie Belle	140		6.4				0	.15	.02	4	187	6	3	.16	
8 crackers	28	2.1	18.0		0.1	9	.04	1.2	.04	.06	26	22	.89	.021	
soda (unsalted tops)	120	1.1	3.2				0	.15	.01	17	208	5	5	.21	
10 crackers	28	2.7	20.0		0.0	0	.15	1.5	.00	.07	35	23	1.26	.018	
toast crackers w/peanut butter	212	1.4	10.5	tr				.17			352	60	27	.51	.302
1.5 oz	43	5.9	23.5				.20	3.1			129	141	1.26	.12	

[a] Armenian cracker bread

	KCAL	H₂O (g)	FAT (g)	PUFA (g)	CHOL (mg)	A (RE)	C (mg)	B-2 (mg)	B-6 (mg)	FOL (mcg)	Na (mg)	Ca (mg)	Mg (mg)	Zn (mg)	Mn (mg)
	WT (g)	PRO (g)	CHO (g)	SFA (g)	FIBR (g)	A (IU)	B-1 (mg)	NIA (mg)	B-12 (mcg)	PANT (mg)	K (mg)	P (mg)	Fe (mg)	Cu (mg)	
triscuits, Nabisco	42		1.5												
2 crackers	9	0.8	6.2												
uneeda, Nabisco	42		1.0					.03			69	3			
2 crackers	10	1.0	7.0				.04	0.3			11	8	.40		
waverly wafers, Nabisco	36		1.6					.02			96	13			
2 crackers	8	0.5	5.0				.05	0.3			7	22	.30		
wheat crackers w/cheese, Frito-Lay	212	1.4	10.9		4			.25			488	104	23	.37	
1.5 oz	43	4.3	24.1		0.3	30	.14	1.5			184	162	1.06	.07	
wheat crackers w/peanut butter, Frito-Lay—*1.5 oz*	166	1.0	1.1					.14	.06		449	102	16	.35	.299
	43	6.2	32.9				.20	2.7			175	148	1.04	.02	
wheat snacks, Dixie Belle	140		5.5				0	.10	.04	5	183	7	14	.46	
15 crackers	28	2.6	18.0		0.2	14	.16	1.3	.12	.09	49	49	1.15	.137	
wheat thins, Nabisco	36		1.4												
4 crackers	7	0.5	5.0												
zwieback	31	0.4	0.7				0	tr			18	1			
1 piece	7	0.9	5.4				tr				11	5	tr		
croutons, herb-seasoned	70		0.0					.14	tr	tr	260	20	8	.21	
⁷/₁₀ oz	20	3.0	14.0		0.2	tr	.09	1.2			27	20	1.08	.04	
english muffin	135	23.9	1.1		0	0		.18	.02	18	364	92	11	.41	
1 muffin	57	4.5	26.2		0.3	0	.26	2.1	.00	.29	319	64	1.61	.18	
english muffin, toasted	145	14.5	1.2		0	0		.19	.02	19	391	99	12	.44	
1 muffin	50	4.8	28.1		0.3	0	.22	2.3	.00	.31	343	68	1.73	.19	
english muffin w/raisins	146	21.8	2.2		0	0		.17			224	78			
1 muffin	56	4.5	27.4		0.2		.22	1.6					1.68		
english muffin, sourdough	129	24.1	1.1		0	0		.14			252	112			
1 muffin	56	4.5	25.2		0.2		.22	2.2					1.40		
french toast															
homemade	153	34.3	6.7				tr	.16	.04	18	257	72	12	.55	
1 slice	65	5.7	17.2		0.1	111	.12	1.0	.29	.53	86	85	1.34	.06	
frzn, Aunt Jemima	170	46.2	4.3					.17	.30	37	430	94	12	1.00	.00
2 slices	84	6.4	26.4		0.1	173	.15	1.6	.90	1.00	97	120	1.44	.08	
frzn, Campbell's	130		5.0				0	.18			330	49			
1 slice	67	6.0	15.0			110	.08	1.0			77	70	1.60		
cinn swirl, frzn, Aunt Jemima	193	43.4	6.4					.17	.30	48	360	94	16	1.00	.00
2 slices	84	6.4	27.3		0.3	183	.15	1.6	.90	1.00	126	126	1.44	.06	
macaroni, enr, ckd	102	64.8	0.4					.13	.02	3	2	6	13	.28	.147
*³/₅ cup*ᵃ	90	3.6	21.0		0.1		.30	2.3			43	41	1.15	.069	
macaroni in pizza sce (pizza Os), Franco Am—*7½ oz*	170		1.0								980				
	213	5.0	34.0												
muffin															
blueberry, from mix	126	13.0	4.3				tr	.07			200	14	4	.20	
1 muffin	40	2.4	19.5		0.2	40	.10	1.0			48	80	.48	.03	
bran, homemade	112	14.2	5.1				2	.11	.11	17	168	54	35	1.08	
1 muffin	40	3.0	16.7		0.5	206	.10	1.3	.09	.24	99	111	1.26	.09	
corn w/enr cornmeal, from mix	130	13.2	4.2					.08			315	96			
1 muffin	40	2.8	20.0		tr	96	.07	0.6			44	152	.60		
corn w/enr cornmeal, homemade	141	14.7	4.5	0.4			tr	.10			216	47	22		
1 muffin	45	3.2	21.6		0.1	135	.09	0.7			61	76	.80		
corn w/whole ground cornmeal, homemade—*1 muffin*	130	17.0	4.6	0.4			tr	.08			223	50	48		
	45	3.2	19.1		0.2	140	.08	0.5			59	97	.60		
soyᵇ	119		4.4	0.4			0	.10				35	52		
1 muffin	40	3.9	16.7		tr	196	.08	0.5				56	.90		
white, enr	118	15.2	4.0	0.4			tr	.09			176	42	11		
1 muffin	40	3.1	16.9		0.1	40	.07	0.6			50	60	.60		
whole wheat, homemade	103		1.1				tr	.05			226	42	45		
1 muffin	40	4.0	20.9		0.6	tr	.14	1.2			117	112	1.00		
noodles, enr, ckd	107	65.3	1.2					.14	.02	4	6	9	20	.49	.193
*³/₅ cup*ᵃ	92	3.9	20.1		0.1		.30	2.2			53	60	1.37	.073	
noodles almondine, from mix	240		12.0								835				
¼ pkg prep w/butter & milk	ᶜ	6.0	27.0												

ᵃ From 1 oz dry
ᵇ Soy flour replaces ¼ of the white flour.
ᶜ Gram wt not available

	KCAL / WT (g)	H₂O (g) / PRO (g)	FAT (g) / CHO (g)	PUFA (g) / SFA (g)	CHOL (mg) / FIBR (g)	A (RE) / A (IU)	C (mg) / B-1 (mg)	B-2 (mg) / NIA (mg)	B-6 (mg) / B-12 (mcg)	FOL (mcg) / PANT (mg)	Na (mg) / K (mg)	Ca (mg) / P (mg)	Mg (mg) / Fe (mg)	Zn (mg) / Cu (mg)	Mn (mg)
noodles, chow funn,ª dry	102	2.0	0.4								260		13		
1 oz	28	3.4	21.2								325		1.37		
noodles, chow mein, cnd	153	0.3	8.8								201				
½ cup	28	2.7	15.8												
noodles, ramen, beef, ckd, La Choy	225		7.5								865				
1 cup	227	6.1	33.4												
noodles, ramen, chicken, ckd, La Choy	202		6.8								738				
1 cup	227	6.1	29.1												
noodles, ramen, oriental, ckd, La Choy	207		8.6								829				
1 cup	227	5.9	30.7												
noodles, rice, dry	130	2.7	0.6					.01	.01	6			1		
1 oz	28	2.0	22.7				.01	0.1				18	.59		
noodles romanoff, frzn, Stouffer's	170		9.0								675				
4 oz	113	6.0	16.0								95				
noodles romanoff, from mix	230		12.0								705				
¼ pkg prep w/butter & milk	ᵇ	7.0	23.0												
noodles, saimin,ª dry	95	3.2	0.1								261				
1 oz	28	2.8	20.6								251				
noodles, soba,ª dry	99	3.2	0.6										23		
1 oz	28	3.2	20.1										1.12		
noodles stroganoff, from mix	240		12.0								605				
¼ pkg prep w/butter & milk	ᵇ	7.0	26.0												
pancakes															
plain, from batter, Aunt Jemima	210	60.2	1.6					.24				68			
3 med ᶜ	112	6.6	42.2		0.2	53	.35	2.1				329	1.51		
plain, from batter, Mrs. Smith's	230		4.0		40	0		.12			660	56			
3 med ᶜ	113	7.0	41.0			115	.06	1.1			125		.70		
plain, from mix	159	39.1	5.9				tr	.16	.15	8	431	96	14	.52	
1 large (7 T batter)	73	5.0	21.3		0.1	104	.10	0.7	.96	.26	117	191	.72	.04	
plain, homemade	104	22.5	3.2	0.5			tr	.10			191	45	11		
1 med	45	3.2	15.3		0.1	54	.08	0.6			55	63	.60		
frzn, Campbell's	75		3.0			0		.10			195	21			
1 small	28	2.0	10.0			28	.04	0.5			32	65	.40		
blueberry, from batter, Aunt Jemima	205	61.2	1.6					.23				68			
3 med ᶜ	112	6.2	41.5		0.2	54	.32	2.0				329	1.44		
blueberry, from mix	330		15.0								925				
3 med ᶜ	ᵇ	7.0	42.0												
buckwheat, from mix	90	26.1	4.1	tr							209	99	22		
1 med	45	3.1	10.7		0.2						110	152	.60		
buttermilk, from batter, Aunt Jemima	212	59.2	1.5					.28				91			
3 med ᶜ	112	7.1	42.6		0.1	56	.34	2.2				340	1.70		
buttermilk, from mix	280		10.0								810				
3 med ᶜ	ᵇ	8.0	39.0												
cornmeal, homemade	68		1.3	tr		0		.07				23	23		
1 med	48	2.3	11.4		0.1	95	.05	0.4				36	.50		
extra light, from mix	200		7.0								495				
3 med ᶜ	ᵇ	6.0	28.0												
soyᵈ	68		1.9	tr		0		.07				26	55		
1 med	45	2.9	10.2		tr	90	.07	0.4				42	.60		
popover, from mix	170		5.0												
1 popover	28	7.0	25.0												
popover, homemade	112	27.5	4.6	0.5			tr	.12			110	48	12		
1 popover	50	4.4	12.9		0.1	165	.07	0.5			75	70	.80		
rolls															
brown & serve	92	7.5	2.2				1	.06			157	14	6		
1 roll	28	2.4	15.3		tr	0	.07	0.6			28	25	.60		
butterflake, from refrig dough	110		3.0								445				
1 roll	ᵇ	3.0	17.0												
butterfly, Sara Lee	105	6.5	4.2				0	.12			189	17	8		
1 roll	28	2.6	14.3		0.2	20	.25	1.5			48	33	1.04		

ª Asian noodles; chow funn & saimin are wheat products; soba is a buckwheat product.

ᵇ Gram wt not available.

ᶜ 1 med pancake is 4 inches in diameter.

ᵈ Soy flour replaces ¼ of the white flour.

								Vitamins					Minerals		
	KCAL	H₂O (g)	FAT (g)	PUFA (g)	CHOL (mg)	A (RE)	C (mg)	B-2 (mg)	B-6 (mg)	FOL (mcg)	Na (mg)	Ca (mg)	Mg (mg)	Zn (mg)	Mn (mg)
	WT (g)	PRO (g)	CHO (g)	SFA (g)	FIBR (g)	A (IU)	B-1 (mg)	NIA (mg)	B-12 (mcg)	PANT (mg)	K (mg)	P (mg)	Fe (mg)	Cu (mg)	
buttermilk, from mix	113		4.9								343				
1 roll	35	2.0	14.8												
buttermilk, Wonder	168	20.2	5.0				0	.13			280	84			
2 rolls	56	4.5	25.8		0.2	0	.22	2.0					1.40		
cloverleaf, Sara Lee	89	7.7	3.2				0	.14			157	24	8		
1 roll	27	2.4	12.4		0.2	17	.21	1.3			41	36	.92		
crescent, from refrig dough	200		10.0								665				
2 rolls	ᵃ	4.0	24.0												
croissants, Sara Lee	109	5.9	6.1				0	.10			140	12	7		
1 roll	26	2.3	11.2		0.1	41	.28	1.2			40	32	1.04		
dinner/pan	85	9.0	2.1				tr	.09	.02	11	155	33	6	.20	
1 roll	28	2.4	14.0		0.1	tr	.14	1.1		.15	36	44	.83	.02	
finger, Sara Lee	59	5.1	2.1				0	.09			105	22	5		
1 roll	18	1.6	8.3		0.1	11	.14	0.8			26	25	.59		
french, enr	137	16.0	0.4				0	.18	.03	29	287	8	12	.30	
1 roll	50	4.3	28.3		0.1	tr	.20	2.0	.00	.24	50	41	1.48	.05	
french, unenr	137	16.0	0.4				0	.06	.03	29	287	8	12	.30	
1 roll	50	4.3	28.3		0.1	tr	.05	0.6	.00	.25	50	41	.63	.05	
gem style, Wonder	160	20.2	4.5				0	.14			308	84			
2 rolls	56	4.5	25.8		0.2	0	.22	2.0					1.68		
half & half, Wonder	157	20.2	4.5				0	.14			143	95			
2 rolls	56	4.5	25.2		0.2	0	.22	2.0					1.68		
hamburger	114	13.6	2.1				tr	.13	.01	15	241	54	8	.25	
1 roll	40	3.4	20.1		0.1	tr	.20	1.6	.00	.21	37	33	1.19	.07	
home bake, Wonder	146	20.2	2.8				0	.14			224	62			
2 rolls	56	4.5	25.2		0.2	0	.22	2.0					1.40		
hotdog	116	14.3	2.1				0	.13			227	63			
1 roll	42	3.4	21.0		0.1	0	.17	1.7					1.26		
kaiser/hoagie	470	60.5	8.4				0	.50			857	252			
1 large roll	168	15.1	80.6		0.5	0	.67	6.7					5.04		
kaiser/hoagie	93	7.7	1.8				0	.13			192	7	9		
1 small roll	29	3.0	16.0		0.2	0	.17	1.2			30	31	1.28		
parkerhouse	59	5.1	2.1				0	.09			105	15	5		
1 roll	18	1.6	8.3		0.1	11	.14	0.8			26	23	.59		
raisin	165	19.2	1.7					.06			230	45	12		
1 large roll	60	4.1	33.8		0.5		.04	0.4			147	55	.80		
rye	55	5.7	1.6				0	.06			120	6	3		
1 roll	18	1.4	8.6		0.1	7	.21	0.8			16	14	.52		
rye, dark, hard	80	8.3	1.0				0	.17			254	5	14		
1 roll	28	3.1	14.6		0.1	0	.13	1.1			48	43	1.26		
rye, light, hard	79	8.4	1.0				0	.08			247	8	15		
1 roll	28	3.1	14.4		0.1	0	.11	1.1			50	45	.90		
sandwich	162	13.4	3.1				0	.22			335	13	16		
1 roll	51	5.3	27.9		0.3	0	.31	2.1			52	55	2.24		
sesame seed	59	5.1	2.1				0	.09			105	15	5		
1 roll	18	1.6	8.3		0.1	11	.14	0.8			26	25	.59		
wheatᵇ	52	6.4	1.7				0	.05			126	6	2		
1 roll	18	1.3	7.9		0.1	7	.22	0.8			15	13	.49		
wheat,ᵇ from refrig dough	90		1.0								295				
1 roll	29	4.0	16.0												
white, enr, from mix	190		4.0								255				
2 rolls	63	6.0	31.0												
white, enr, from refrig dough	90		1.0								335				
1 roll	29	3.0	18.0												
white, enr, homemade	119	9.1	3.1	0.1			tr	.09			98	16	13		
1 roll	35	2.9	19.6		0.1	28	.09	0.8			41	36	.70		
white, enr, hard	88	7.3	1.7				0	.12			182	7	9		
1 roll	28	2.9	15.2		0.1	0	.17	1.1			29	30	1.23		
white, enr, hard, homemade	109	8.9	1.1	0.1			tr	.08			219	16	8		
1 roll	35	3.4	20.8		0.1	tr	.09	0.9			34	32	.80		
whole wheat, homemade	90	11.2	1.0	tr			tr	.05			197	34	40		
1 roll	35	3.5	18.3		0.6	tr	.12	1.1			102	98	.80		

ᵃ Gram wt not available

ᵇ Made from white, enr flour colored brown; not the same as whole wheat

	KCAL	H₂O (g)	FAT (g)	PUFA (g)	CHOL (mg)	A (RE)	C (mg)	Vitamins B-2 (mg)	B-6 (mg)	FOL (mcg)	Minerals Na (mg)	Ca (mg)	Mg (mg)	Zn (mg)	Mn (mg)
	WT (g)	PRO (g)	CHO (g)	SFA (g)	FIBR (g)	A (IU)	B-1 (mg)	NIA (mg)	B-12 (mcg)	PANT (mg)	K (mg)	P (mg)	Fe (mg)	Cu (mg)	
spaghetti, enr, ckd	216	92.9	0.7				0	.15				1	16	29	
1 cup	146	7.3	44.0		0.1	0	.26	2.0			115	95	1.60		
spaghetti, w/tomato sce, homemade	179	169.4	1.5				0	.24			840	35			
8 oz	220	7.0	34.3		0.4	807	.31	4.0				95	2.40		
spaghetti w/tomato cheese sce, cnd, Franco-Am—7⅜ oz	170		2.0						.11		790	27	13	.94	.38
	209	5.0	33.0					tr			219	79	1.25	.27	
spaghetti w/tomato cheese sce, cnd, Heinz—7¾ oz	156	180.2	2.0				1	.09			717	33			
	220	4.4	29.9			596	.09	1.3			326		1.54		
spaghetti w/tomato cheese sce, homemade—10⁷⁄₁₀ oz	315	233	10.6				15	.21			1150	97			
	302	10.6	44.8		0.6	1300	.31	2.7			493	163	2.70		
spaghetti hoops in tomato sce, cnd, Heinz—7¾ oz	169	178.2	3.1				tr	.13			957	40			
	220	4.6	30.6			473	.18				83		1.32		
spaghettiOs in tomato sce, cnd, Franco-Am—7⅜ oz	160		2.0						.06		834	50	15	1.00	.49
	209	4.0	33.0					tr			219	71	.84	.38	
stuffing, bread, from mix	198		12.2				1	.09			479	38			
½ cup	95	4.2	18.7		0.2	399	.05	0.8			55	63	1.00		
stuffing, cornbread, from mix	117		1.8					.08			434	45			
½ cup	90	4.1	22.9		0.3	23	.10	1.0			62	77	1.00		
stuffing, flavored,ᵃ from mix, Stove Top—½ cup	176	72.0	8.9	0.7	21		1	.13	.06	22	632	41	13	.272	
	108	4.3	20.7	5.0	0.4	358	.15	1.5	.02	.34	103	62	1.17	.083	
taco/tostada shells (from corn tortillas)	50	0.4	2.2					.02			72	16	11	.14	
1 shell	11	1.0	7.2		0.2		.03	0.2	.00		25	25	.29	.04	
tortilla															
corn, enr	67	13.6	1.1				0	.14	.09	6	53	42	20	.43	
1 tortilla	30	2.1	12.8		0.3		.20	1.5	.00	.06	52	55	1.42	.09	
corn, unenr	67	13.6	1.1				0	.03	.09	6	53	42	20	.43	
1 tortilla	30	2.1	12.8		0.3		.05	0.4	.00	.06	52	55	.57	.09	
corn, cnd	75		0.8								191				
1 tortilla	34	1.7	15.1								55				
flour	95		1.8				tr	.08				46	7		
1 tortilla	30	2.5	17.3			2	.01	1.0				25	1.10		
waffles															
homemade	245	27.6	12.6				tr	.24	.05	14	445	154	17	.65	
1 large waffle	75	6.9	25.7		0.1	140	.18	1.5	.36	.60	129	135	1.48	.05	
from batter, Mrs. Smith's	285		13.0		25		0	.19			495	27			
1 large waffle	113	5.0	36.0			105	.15	2.1			95		.90		
frzn	95	13.7	3.2				tr	.18	.09	1	235	28	7	.28	
1 waffle	34	2.0	14.2		0.1	436	.15	1.8		.12	71	130	1.65	.02	
frzn, Aunt Jemima	86	16.0	2.5					.19	.29	15	349	85	7	.00	.00
1 waffle	35	2.2	13.6		0.1		.17	1.7	.18	.00	39	135	1.69	.02	
frzn, Campbell's	116		6.0				0	.07			150	13			
1 waffle	35	2.0	15.0			311	.06	0.7			40	112	.40		
frzn, Eggo	120		5.0					.17			265	20			
1 waffle	39	3.0	17.0		0.1	500	.15	2.0			61		1.80		
frzn, Mrs. Smith's	120		5.0				0	.17				20			
1 waffle	39	3.0	16.0			500	.15	2.0					1.80		
blueberry, frzn, Mrs. Smith's	120		5.0				0	.17				20			
1 waffle	39	3.0	16.0			500	.15	2.0					1.80		
blueberry (imit), frzn, Eggo	130		5.0					.17			260	20			
1 waffle	39	3.0	18.0		0.1	500	.15	2.0			60		1.80		
buttermilk, frzn, Aunt Jemima	86	16.0	2.5					.19	.29	15	357	85	7	.00	.00
1 waffle	35	2.2	13.6		0.1		.17	1.7	.18		39	135	1.69	.02	
buttermilk, frzn, Mrs. Smith's	110		5.0				0	.17				20			
1 waffle	39	3.0	15.0			500	.15	2.0					1.80		
strawberry (imit), frzn, Eggo	130		5.0					.17			265	20			
1 waffle	39	3.0	18.0		0.1	500	.15	2.0			60		1.80		
weiner wrap, plain/cheese	60		2.0								413				
1 wrap	20	1.0	10.0												

ᵃ New England style, San Francisco style, chicken, cornbread, for beef, for pork, or with rice

	KCAL	H₂O (g)	FAT (g)	PUFA (g)	CHOL (mg)	A (RE)	C (mg)	B-2 (mg)	B-6 (mg)	FOL (mcg)	Na (mg)	Ca (mg)	Mg (mg)	Zn (mg)	Mn (mg)
	WT (g)	PRO (g)	CHO (g)	SFA (g)	FIBR (g)	A (IU)	B-1 (mg)	NIA (mg)	B-12 (mcg)	PANT (mg)	K (mg)	P (mg)	Fe (mg)	Cu (mg)	

INFANT, JUNIOR & TODDLER FOODS
BAKED PRODUCTS

	KCAL/WT	H₂O/PRO	FAT/CHO	PUFA/SFA	CHOL/FIBR	A(RE)/A(IU)	C/B-1	B-2/NIA	B-6/B-12	FOL/PANT	Na/K	Ca/P	Mg/Fe	Zn/Cu	Mn
arrowroot cookies	24	0.3	0.9	tr	0.1		tr	.03	tr		22	2	1	.03	
1 cookie	6	0.4	4.3	0.2			.03	0.3	tr		9	7	.18		
baby cookies	28	0.4	0.9	0.0		0	1	.21	.38		12	7	3	.07	
1 cookie	7	0.8	4.4	0.2	0.0	2	.10	1.0	.30		33	12	.27		
baby pretzels	24	0.2	0.1					.03	tr		16	1	2	.05	
1 pretzel	6	0.7	4.9		0.0		.04	0.4			8	7	.23		
teething biscuits	43	0.7	0.5			1	1	.06	.01		40	29	4	.10	
1 biscuit	11	1.2	8.4		0.1	13	.03	0.5	.01		35	18	.39		
zwieback	30	0.3	0.7	0.1	1	0	tr	.02	.01		16	1	1	.04	
1 piece	7	0.7	5.2	0.3	0.0	4	.02	0.1			21	4	.04		

CEREALS

	KCAL/WT	H₂O/PRO	FAT/CHO	PUFA/SFA	CHOL/FIBR	A(RE)/A(IU)	C/B-1	B-2/NIA	B-6/B-12	FOL/PANT	Na/K	Ca/P	Mg/Fe	Zn/Cu	Mn
barley, dry	9	0.2	0.1				tr	.07	.01	1	1	19	3	.08	
1 T	2.4	0.3	1.8		0.0		.07	0.9			9	11	1.80	.01	
barley, prep w/whole milk	31	21.2	0.9				tr	.16	.03	3	14	65	8	.24	
1 oz	28	1.3	4.6		0.1	30	.14	1.7			54	43	3.50		
cereal & egg yolks, str	66	113.7	2.3	0.2	81	52	1	.06	.03	4	42	30	4	.37	
1 jar	128	2.5	9.0	0.8	0.2	181	.01	0.1	.09		50	51	.60	.03	
cereal & egg yolks, jr	110	189.0	3.8	0.3		88	2	.10	.04	7	70	51	6	.62	
1 jar	213	4.1	15.1	1.3	0.2	306	.02	0.1	.13		75	84	1.09	.05	
cereal, egg yolks & bacon, str	101	109.9	6.4				1	.10		5	62	36	6	.35	
1 jar	128	3.2	8.0			121	.06	0.3			44		.60	.03	
cereal, egg yolks & bacon, jr	178	180.9	11.0				3	.11		9	97	54	10	.61	
1 jar	213	5.4	15.1			142	.04	0.3			79		1.06	.05	
grits & egg yolks, str	76	112.7	2.9			39	1	.09	.03	4		36	6	.29	
1 jar	128	2.3	10.1			156	.04	0.4	.05		71	46	.64		
high protein, dry	9	0.1	0.1				tr	.07	.01	5	1	17	5	.11	
1 T	2.4	0.9	1.1		0.1		.06	0.8			32	15	1.77	.03	
high protein, prep w/whole milk	31	21.1	1.1				tr	.16	.03	10	14	62	14	.30	
1 oz	28	2.5	3.3		0.1	30	.13	1.6			99	50	3.44		
high protein w/apple & orange, dry	9	0.1	0.2				tr	.05	.01		2	15			
1 T	2.4	0.6	1.3	tr		1	.04	0.3			29	13	1.14		
mixed, dry	9	0.2	0.1				tr	.07	.01	1	1	18	2	.06	
1 T	2.4	0.3	1.8		0.0		.06	0.8			10	9	1.52	.01	
mixed, prep w/whole milk	32	21.2	1.0				tr	.17	.02	3	13	62	8	.20	
1 oz	28	1.3	4.5		0.0	30	.12	1.6			56	40	2.96		
mixed w/applesce & bananas, str	111	108.0	0.7			2	35	.47	.19	5	3	9	11	.26	
1 jar	135	1.6	24.2		0.4	24	.38	5.4			55	32	8.94		
mixed w/applesce & bananas, jr	183	175.1	0.9			4	20	.78	.31	8	78	9	16	.48	
1 jar	220	2.6	40.5		0.6	41	.63	8.9			70	63	12.33		
mixed w/bananas, dry	9	0.1	0.1			0	tr	.09	.10		3	17	2	.03	
1 T	2.4	0.3	1.9		0.0	3	.09	0.5	.01		16	9	1.62		
mixed w/bananas, prep w/whole milk	33	21.1	1.0			8	tr	.20	.03		17	61	7	.16	
1 oz	28	1.3	4.7		0.0	31	.19	1.0	.10		67	39	3.16		
mixed w/honey, dry	9	0.1	0.1			0	0	.07			1	28			
1 T	2.4	0.3	1.8			1	.06	0.9			6	16	1.64		
mixed w/honey, prep w/whole milk	33	21.0	1.0			7	tr	.17			14	83			
1 oz	28	1.4	4.5			26	.13	1.8			49	52	3.20		
oatmeal, dry	10	0.1	0.2				tr	.06	tr	1	1	18	3	.09	
1 T	2.4	0.3	1.7		0.0		.07	0.9			11	12	1.77	.01	
oatmeal, prep w/whole milk	33	21.1	1.2				tr	.16	.02	3	13	62	10	.26	
1 oz	28	1.4	4.3		0.1	30	.14	1.7			58	45	3.44		
oatmeal w/applesce & bananas, str	99	110.9	0.9			4	29	.49	.27	5	2	11	15	.47	
1 jar	135	1.8	20.8		1.0	40	.57	6.8			63	56	7.63	.10	
oatmeal w/applesce & bananas, jr	165	179.9	1.6				42	.11	.53	8	69	12	24	.73	
1 jar	220	2.9	34.6		0.9		.53	7.4			106	89	12.13	.17	
oatmeal w/bananas, dry	9	0.1	0.1			0	tr	.09	.01		3	16	3	.05	
1 T	2.4	0.3	1.8		0.0	2	.09	0.5	.01		18	11	1.63		

	KCAL	H₂O (g)	FAT (g)	PUFA (g)	CHOL (mg)	A (RE)	C (mg)	B-2 (mg)	B-6 (mg)	FOL (mcg)	Na (mg)	Ca (mg)	Mg (mg)	Zn (mg)	Mn (mg)
	WT (g)	PRO (g)	CHO (g)	SFA (g)	FIBR (g)	A (IU)	B-1 (mg)	NIA (mg)	B-12 (mcg)	PANT (mg)	K (mg)	P (mg)	Fe (mg)	Cu (mg)	
oatmeal w/bananas, prep w/whole milk	33	21.1	1.1			8	tr	.21	.03		17	59	9	.18	
1 oz	28	1.3	4.5		0.0	28	.18	1.0	.09		70	43	3.18		
oatmeal w/honey, dry	9	0.1	0.2			0	0	.07			1	28			
1 T	2.4	0.3	1.7			1	.07	0.9			6	18	1.61		
oatmeal w/honey, prep w/whole milk	33	21.1	1.1			7	tr	.17			14	82			
1 oz	28	1.4	4.3			26	.14	1.7			48	56	3.14		
rice, dry	9	0.2	0.1				tr	.05	.01	1	1	20	5	.05	
1 T	2.4	0.2	1.9		0.0		.06	0.8			9	14	1.77	.01	
rice, prep w/whole milk	33	21.2	1.0				tr	.14	.03	2	13	68	13	.18	
1 oz	28	1.1	4.7		0.0	30	.13	1.5			54	50	3.46		
rice w/applesce & bananas, str	107	109.4	0.5			3	43	.57	.32	3	38	23	4	.11	
1 jar	135	1.6	23.1		0.2	28	.35	5.4			38	16	9.09		
rice w/bananas, dry	10	0.1	0.1			0	0	.09	.02		2	17	3	.04	
1 T	2.4	0.2	1.9		0.0	1	.10	0.6	.01		18	10	1.61		
rice w/bananas, prep w/whole milk	33	21.1	1.0			7	tr	.22	.04		16	60	10	.16	
1 oz	28	1.2	4.8		0.0	26	.19	1.1	.09		72	41	3.13		
rice w/honey, dry	9	0.1	0.1			0	0	.07			1	28			
1 T	2.4	0.2	1.9			1	.07	0.9			2	15	1.57		
rice w/honey, prep w/whole milk	33	21.1	0.9			7	tr	.17			14	83			
1 oz	28	1.1	4.9			26	.14	1.7			40	51	3.07		
rice w/mixed fruit, jr	186	175.2	0.5			3	45	1.31	.54		24	43	10	.40	
1 jar	220	2.3	41.0		0.5	33	.55	6.0			72	51	10.36		

DESSERTS

	KCAL	H₂O (g)	FAT (g)	PUFA (g)	CHOL (mg)	A (RE)	C (mg)	B-2 (mg)	B-6 (mg)	FOL (mcg)	Na (mg)	Ca (mg)	Mg (mg)	Zn (mg)	Mn (mg)
	WT (g)	PRO (g)	CHO (g)	SFA (g)	FIBR (g)	A (IU)	B-1 (mg)	NIA (mg)	B-12 (mcg)	PANT (mg)	K (mg)	P (mg)	Fe (mg)	Cu (mg)	
apple betty, str	97	107.9	0.0			2	47	.05		1	14	25			
1 jar	135	0.5	26.5			23	.02	0.1			68		.24		
apple betty, jr	153	177.1	0.0			3	60	.11		1	19	36			
1 jar	220	0.8	41.7			35	.02	0.1			117		.44		
banana apple, str	96	110.6	0.2				16	.02	.14		3	3			
1 jar	135	0.9	22.7		0.4	30	.02	0.3			88	20	.14		
banana apple, jr	165	178.0	0.4				16	.02	.18		9	9			
1 jar	220	2.0	38.5		0.7	48	.02	0.5			172	35	.22		
banana pudding, str	76	116.6	0.8				12	.03	.13		9	9		.12	
1 jar	135	0.7	16.7			89	.01	0.1			73		.30	.04	
caramel pudding, str	104	108.5	0.9			5	3	.11		1	37	60			
1 jar	135	1.8	23.2			49	.01	.05			70		.23		
caramel pudding, jr	167	171.2	1.9			7	5	.15		2	60	116			
1 jar	213	2.9	36.2			69	.02	0.1			124		.34		
cherry van pudding, str	91	110.0	0.4			27	2	.02	.02	tr	22	7	3	.05	
1 jar	135	0.3	24.1		0.2	270	.01	0.1			46	10	.26		
cherry van pudding, jr	152	178.2	0.4			44	2	.02	.03	1	32	11	5	.07	
1 jar	220	0.4	40.5		0.3	440	.02	0.1			73	15	.38		
choc custard pudding, str	107	102.2	2.1			6	2	.13	.02	6	30	78	13	.41	
1 jar	128	2.4	20.6			58	.02	0.1			110	63	.48		
choc custard pudding, jr	195	172.7	3.5			10	2	.24	.03	11	55	134	23	.73	
1 jar	220	4.2	38.3			101	.03	0.2			196	112	.88		
cottage cheese w/bananas, str	71	111.0	0.8				12	.05	.04		34	24		.10	
1 jar	128	2.2	13.6			38	.02	0.1			47		.10	.03	
cottage cheese w/bananas, jr	71	203.0	0.8				7	.05	.04		34	24		.10	
1 jar	220	2.2	13.6			38	.02	0.1			47		.10	.03	
cottage cheese w/pineapple, str	94	111.5	1.1			4	31	.07	.02	6	70	35	5	.21	
1 jar	135	4.0	17.8		1.7	39	.02	0.1	.10		58	51	.14		
cottage cheese w/pineapple, jr	172	176.5	1.5			3	52	.11	.02	11	113	68	8	.39	
1 jar	220	6.5	35.1		2.1	35	.03	0.1	.16		92	86	.28		
custard pudding, str	78	109.9	1.5				tr	.08	.02		27	72		.27	
1 jar	128	2.1	14.0			94	.02	0.1			57		.20	.03	
custard pudding, jr	78	201.9	1.5				tr	.08							
1 jar	220	2.1	14.0			94	.02	0.1							
dutch apple, str	92	111.0	1.2	tr		7	29	.02	.02	1	21	6	2	.01	
1 jar	135	0.0	22.6	0.8	0.3	66	.02	0.1			44	5	.27		
dutch apple, jr	151	180.6	2.1	tr		11	47	.03	.03	2	36	10	4	.06	
1 jar	220	0.0	37.0	1.4	0.6	110	.03	0.1			82	8	.44		

	KCAL / WT (g)	H₂O (g) / PRO (g)	FAT (g) / CHO (g)	PUFA (g) / SFA (g)	CHOL (mg) / FIBR (g)	A (RE) / A (IU)	C (mg) / B-1 (mg)	B-2 (mg) / NIA (mg)	B-6 (mg) / B-12 (mcg)	FOL (mcg) / PANT (mg)	Na (mg) / K (mg)	Ca (mg) / P (mg)	Mg (mg) / Fe (mg)	Zn (mg) / Cu (mg)	Mn (mg)
fruit dessert, str	79	112.6	0.0			34	3	.01	.05	4	18	11	7		.05
1 jar	135	0.4	21.6		0.3	338	.02	0.2			127	9	.29	.04	
fruit dessert, jr	138	180.9	0.0			53	66	.03	.07	8	29	19	11		.11
1 jar	220	0.6	37.9		0.7	525	.05	0.3			208	17	.46	.07	
hawaiian delight, str	111	100.4	0.8				15	.05	.05		23	44			
1 jar	128	1.8	24.3			31	.04	0.2			83	44	.13		
hawaiian delight, jr	185	172.3	1.3				16	.11	.09		40	77			
1 jar	220	3.1	40.7		1.5	73	.07	0.3			152	77	.22		
orange pudding, str	108	107.7	1.2			16	12	.08	.04	11		43	7		.23
1 jar	135	1.5	23.8		0.5	155	.05	0.2			117	38	.14		
peach cobbler, str	88	110.4	0.0			19	28	.02	.01	2	10	6			.41
1 jar	135	0.4	24.0			192	.01	0.4			73	7		.26	
peach cobbler, jr	147	178.6	0.0			31	45	.03	.02	3	20	9			.07
1 jar	220	0.7	40.3			312	.02	0.6			123	13	.22		
peach melba, str	81	111.9	0.0			25	42	.05		3	12	13			
1 jar	135	0.3	22.3			249	.01	0.5			112		.45		
peach melba, jr	132	182.5	0.0			43	57	.07		4	19	23			
1 jar	220	0.6	36.1			430	.02	0.6			205		.66		
pineapple orange dessert, str	89	103.0	0.0			7	18	.03		3	13	14	5		
1 jar	128	0.3	24.4			73	.02	0.1			61	5	.23	.03	
pineapple pudding, str	104	99.3	0.4			5	35	.06	.05	7	24	40	11		.26
1 jar	128	1.6	26.0		0.9	52	.05	0.1	.08		104	39	.23		
pineapple pudding, jr	192	167.4	0.9			8	59	.11	.09	12	48	75	20		.42
1 jar	220	3.1	47.4		1.7	80	.09	0.3	.14		198	67	.41		
raspberry w/nonfat yogurt, str	87	106.0	0.1				1	.06	.01		29	44			
1 jar	128	1.4	20.2			5	.03	0.1			70		.13		
raspberry w/nonfat yogurt, jr	145	175.9	0.4				1	.11	.02		51	72			
1 jar	213	2.3	33.7			19	.04	0.1			126		.21		
tropical fruit dessert, jr	131	183.1	0.0			4	41	.07			16	22			
1 jar	220	0.4	36.1			43	.02	0.2			128		.57		
van custard pudding, str	109	102.2	2.5	0.1		8	1	.10	.03	8	36	71	7		.36
1 jar	128	2.0	20.6	1.3		82	.02	0.1		.32	85	57	.31	.06	
van custard pudding, jr	196	174.7	5.0	0.2		8	2	.17	.04	14	64	123	11		.61
1 jar	220	3.5	35.7	2.6		79	.03	0.1		.56	136	99	.57	.11	

DINNERS

	KCAL / WT (g)	H₂O (g) / PRO (g)	FAT (g) / CHO (g)	PUFA (g) / SFA (g)	CHOL (mg) / FIBR (g)	A (RE) / A (IU)	C (mg) / B-1 (mg)	B-2 (mg) / NIA (mg)	B-6 (mg) / B-12 (mcg)	FOL (mcg) / PANT (mg)	Na (mg) / K (mg)	Ca (mg) / P (mg)	Mg (mg) / Fe (mg)	Zn (mg) / Cu (mg)	Mn (mg)
beef & egg noodles, str	68	113.4	2.2			141	2	.05	.06	7	37	12	9		.48
1 jar	128	2.9	9.0		.04	1053	.05	0.9	.12	.27	61	37	.53	.04	
beef & egg noodles, jr	122	186.9	4.0			187	3	.08	.07	12	37	18	16		.85
1 jar	213	5.4	15.7		0.4	1397	.06	1.2	.20	.49	99	64	.92	.07	
beef & egg noodles w/veg, str	84	109.4	2.6				2	.05	.06		19	8			
1 jar	128	3.6	11.9		0.4	1256	.04	0.9			96	42	.51		
beef & egg noodles w/veg, jr	138	182.3	4.0				4	.06	.09		36	15			
1 jar	213	6.2	19.0		0.4	2769	.06	1.3			200	77	.85		
beef & rice, toddler	146	144.9	5.1				7	.12	.25		632	20	15	1.62	
1 jar	177	8.9	15.5		0.5	889	.03	2.4			212	62	1.23	.10	
beef & rice w/tomato sce, toddler	131	145.7	3.5				7	.07	.18		678	23			
1 jar	177	7.6	17.0		0.5	428	.05	1.8			212	71	1.24		
beef lasagna, toddler	137	145.7	3.8				3	.16	.13		804	32	20	1.24	
1 jar	177	7.4	17.7		0.4	2058	.13	2.4			216	70	1.55		
beef stew, toddler	90	153.8	2.1	tr	22		5	.12	.13		611	16	20	1.54	
1 jar	177	9.1	9.6	1.0	0.5	2918	.03	2.3			251	78	1.27		
chicken & noodles, str	67	113.3	1.9			144	1	.07	.04	7	20	29	11		.38
1 jar	128	2.7	9.6		0.4	1158	.04	0.6			50	31	.58	.05	
chicken & noodles, jr	109	189.0	3.0			229	3	.07	.06	11	36	36	19		.63
1 jar	213	4.1	16.1		1.3	1907	.06	1.1			75	51	.84	.08	
chicken soup, cream of, str	74	111.5	2.0			149	2	.06	.06		24	44	7		.33
1 jar	128	3.2	10.8		0.4	929	.01	0.5	.07		100	38	.38		
chicken soup, str	64	114.1	2.2				1	.04		7	20	47			
1 jar	128	2.0	9.2			1772	.02	0.4					.35		
chicken stew, toddler	132	141.5	6.4	0.1	49		3	.13	.08		683	60	18		.70
1 jar	170	8.9	10.9	1.9	0.5	1718	.05	2.0			156	87	1.13	.03	

	KCAL	H₂O (g)	FAT (g)	PUFA (g)	CHOL (mg)	A (RE)	C (mg)	B-2 (mg)	B-6 (mg)	FOL (mcg)	Na (mg)	Ca (mg)	Mg (mg)	Zn (mg)	Mn (mg)
	WT (g)	PRO (g)	CHO (g)	SFA (g)	FIBR (g)	A (IU)	B-1 (mg)	NIA (mg)	B-12 (mcg)	PANT (mg)	K (mg)	P (mg)	Fe (mg)	Cu (mg)	
egg noodles & beef, jr	50	201.3	0.9				tr	.03	.02		22	15		.31	
1 jar	213	2.3	8.2			451	.04	0.5			34		.40	.06	
green beans, potatoes & ham casserole, toddler—*1 jar*	131	147.1	5.0				7	.09	.12		536	39			
	177	7.3	14.5			327	.07	1.5			269	81	1.06		
lamb & noodles, jr	138	184.3	4.7				4	.14			39	39			
1 jar	213	4.8	18.6			1667	.08	1.4			165		.78		
macaroni & bacon, jr	160	181.2	7.1				5	.18			166	152			
1 jar	213	5.4	18.2			2471	.10	1.3			180		.80		
macaroni & cheese, str	76	111.5	2.7			7	2	.09	.02	2	93	69	11	.44	
1 jar	128	3.3	9.6		0.1	35	.07	0.6	.04		59	73	.40	.03	
macaroni & cheese, jr	130	184.2	4.3			6	3	.14	.03	3	163	108	14	.68	
1 jar	213	5.5	17.5		0.2	28	.12	1.2	.06		94	125	.64	.05	
macaroni & ham, jr	127	184.2	2.9				5	.21			101	159			
1 jar	213	6.8	18.0			1120	.12	1.7			225		.81		
macaroni, tomato & beef, str	71	111.7	1.4			116	2	.08	.06	26	21	21	12	.40	
1 jar	128	2.9	11.3		0.5	679	.09	1.1	.29		123	54	.63	.05	
macaroni, tomato & beef, jr	125	184.6	2.4			233	3	.12	.10		35	30	15	.77	
1 jar	213	5.3	20.1		0.6	1471	.10	1.6	.51		153	94	.76	.08	
mixed veg dinner, str	52	113.6	0.1			349	4	.04		10	10	29			
1 jar	128	1.5	12.2			3492	.02	0.6			155		.42		
mixed veg dinner, jr	71	193.0	0.1			520	7	.05		14	19	37			
1 jar	213	2.1	16.8			5205	.03	0.9			240		.65		
spaghetti, tomato & meat, jr	135	182.1	2.7			284	5	.15	.13		42	39		.90	
1 jar	213	5.4	21.6		0.9	1477	.14	2.3		.38	230	79	1.16		
spaghetti, tomato & meat, toddler	133	144.4	1.8				7	.18	.15		634	39	26	.85	
1 jar	177	9.4	19.1		0.7	784	.11	2.8			289	79	1.59	.04	
split peas & ham, jr	152	177.8	2.8			170	4	.10	.09		30	49			
1 jar	213	7.0	24.1		0.6	1284	.10	1.0			291	104	1.06		
turkey & rice, str	63	114.0	1.7	0.2	13	122	2	.03	.04	4	21	27			
1 jar	128	2.4	9.4	0.5	0.1	783	.01	0.4			53	26	.33		
turkey & rice, jr	104	190.2	2.9	0.4		316	3	.06	.06	7	33	50			
1 jar	213	3.8	15.3	0.9	0.4	2256	.02	0.6			71	36	.62		
turkey & rice w/veg, str	76	111.7	2.8				2	.06	.08		23	26			
1 jar	128	2.4	9.9		0.1	1523	.01	0.9			88	44	.38		
turkey & rice w/veg, jr	130	183.6	4.3				4	.06	.11		36	43			
1 jar	213	5.8	17.5		0.4	3472	.02	1.4			147	75	.64		
veg & bacon, str	88	110.0	4.2	0.1	4	382	2	.04	.10	12	55	17			
1 jar	128	2.0	11.0	1.5	0.5	3409	.04	0.7	.13		115	40	.45		
veg & bacon, jr	150	183.5	8.2	0.1		463	2	.06	.14	19	96	23			
1 jar	213	3.9	16.1	3.0	0.4	3356	.11	1.2			184	81	.88		
veg & beef, str	67	113.3	2.6			219	2	.04	.07	6	27	16	7	.42	
1 jar	128	2.5	9.0		0.3	1520	.03	0.7	.32	.15	129	52	.49	.01	
veg & beef, jr	113	187.3	3.6			410	3	.07	.14	10	52	22	13	.88	
1 jar	213	5.0	15.8		0.4	3011	.07	1.4	.56	.27	224	91	1.01	.08	
veg & chicken, str	55	115.2	1.4			176	1	.02	.03	4	14	18			
1 jar	128	2.5	8.5		0.3	1416	.02	0.2		.26	38	32	.35		
veg & chicken, jr	106	187.9	2.3			316	3	.04	.08	8	18	30			
1 jar	213	4.0	18.0		0.4	2546	.03	0.7		.50	54	55	.64		
veg & ham, str	62	114.2	2.2			122	2	.04	.04	6	15	11	6	.25	
1 jar	128	2.2	8.8		0.2	872	.04	0.5			109	29	.38	.04	
veg & ham, jr	110	188.2	3.6			173	3	.05	.07	11	37	16	15	.48	
1 jar	213	5.2	14.9		0.4	1310	.08	0.7			197	55	.47	.07	
veg & ham, toddler	128	148.0	5.2	0.3	14		7	.10	.15		531	41	30	.83	
1 jar	177	7.4	13.9	1.9		629	.08	1.2			271	71	1.23	.07	
veg & lamb, str	67	113.4	2.6			363	2	.04	.06	5	26	15	9	.28	
1 jar	128	2.5	8.9		0.4	2554	.02	0.7	.20	.21	120	63	.44	.04	
veg & lamb, jr	108	188.8	3.7			423	4	.07	.09	8	28	27	16	.47	
1 jar	213	4.4	15.1		0.4	3158	.05	1.2	.34	.34	202	104	.72	.06	
veg & liver, str	50	115.2	0.6			940	2	.34	.11	37	24	9			
1 jar	128	2.8	8.8		0.2	3981	.02	1.5			120	51	2.83		
veg & liver, jr	93	189.4	1.2			1524	4	.48	.21	68	27	20			
1 jar	213	3.9	17.5		0.6	8368	.05	2.5			189	81	3.86		

	KCAL	H₂O (g)	FAT (g)	PUFA (g)	CHOL (mg)	A (RE)	C (mg)	B-2 (mg)	B-6 (mg)	FOL (mcg)	Na (mg)	Ca (mg)	Mg (mg)	Zn (mg)	Mn (mg)
	WT (g)	PRO (g)	CHO (g)	SFA (g)	FIBR (g)	A (IU)	B-1 (mg)	NIA (mg)	B-12 (mcg)	PANT (mg)	K (mg)	P (mg)	Fe (mg)	Cu (mg)	
veg & turkey, str	54	115.4	1.5			143	1	.02	.04	3	17	21			.29
1 jar	128	2.1	8.4		0.3	1068	.01	0.4		.24	56	24	.34	.03	
veg & turkey, jr	101	189.5	2.7			244	2	.04	.05	6	36	27			.54
1 jar	213	3.6	16.4		0.4	1909	.03	0.5		.45	53	40	.68	.06	
veg & turkey, toddler	141	145.7	6.1				6	.16	.11		591	82	29		.55
1 jar	177	8.5	14.2		0.9	3715	.04	1.0			294	102	1.07		
veg, dumplings & beef, str	61	113.8	1.2				1	.05		9	62	18	8		.51
1 jar	128	2.6	9.8			533	.06	0.7					.49		
veg, dumplings & beef, jr	103	188.7	1.7				2	.08		16	110	30	14		.70
1 jar	213	4.4	17.0			1407	.08	1.0					1.00		
veg, noodles & chicken, str	81	111.6	3.3				1	.06	.03	4	26	35			.32
1 jar	128	2.6	10.1		0.2	1813	.04	0.5	.10	.24	70	39	.45	.07	
veg, noodles & chicken, jr	137	183.7	4.8				2	.08	.05	7	54	54			.68
1 jar	213	3.7	19.4		0.4	2238	.09	1.4	.19	.44	126	70	1.04	.12	
veg, noodles & turkey, str	56	115.6	1.6				1	.06	.02	3	27	41	10		.35
1 jar	128	1.5	8.7		0.3	1268	.02	0.3	.13		81	32	.25		
veg, noodles & turkey, jr	110	189.0	3.2				2	.09	.04	6	37	67	20		.64
1 jar	213	3.9	16.1		0.5	2118	.05	0.6	.25		156	62	.55		

DINNERS, HIGH MEAT/CHEESE

	KCAL	H₂O (g)	FAT (g)	PUFA (g)	CHOL (mg)	A (RE)	C (mg)	B-2 (mg)	B-6 (mg)	FOL (mcg)	Na (mg)	Ca (mg)	Mg (mg)	Zn (mg)	Mn (mg)
	WT (g)	PRO (g)	CHO (g)	SFA (g)	FIBR (g)	A (IU)	B-1 (mg)	NIA (mg)	B-12 (mcg)	PANT (mg)	K (mg)	P (mg)	Fe (mg)	Cu (mg)	
beef w/veg, str	96	109.3	5.3			141	3	.08	.11	7	46	15	10	1.66	
1 jar	128	7.3	5.3		0.4	1003	.04	1.7	.65	.31	179	62	.93	.10	
beef w/veg, jr	108	106.5	5.9			126	2	.10	.11	8	42	15	10	1.79	
1 jar	128	8.1	6.7		0.3	1014	.05	1.8	.75	.35	191	66	1.01	.12	
chicken w/veg, str	100	107.2	4.6			106	1	.09	.08	1	35	66	9	1.21	
1 jar	128	8.0	7.6		0.3	737	.04	1.3	.18	.41	76	69	1.27		
chicken w/veg, jr	117	105.8	7.0			167	1	.09	.05	2	33	56	9	1.28	
1 jar	128	9.0	5.4		0.3	1071	.04	1.3	.20	.44	79	68	.95		
cottage cheese w/pineapple, str	157	97.2	3.0			10	2	.19	.06		201	88	9	.39	
1 jar	135	8.5	25.4		1.2	104	.05	0.1	.30		128	98	.14		
ham w/veg, str	97	107.6	4.4	0.3		52	2	.11	.14	8	29	14	11	1.28	
1 jar	128	8.0	7.1	1.5	0.3	214	.13	1.8	.34	.50	198	72	.75		
ham w/veg, jr	98	107.0	4.2	0.3	23	85	2	.11	.12	8	28	12	12	1.39	
1 jar	128	8.2	7.9	1.4	0.2	332	.14	1.5	.36	.52	208	71	.76		
turkey w/veg, str	111	106.3	6.1			119	2	.09	.05	12	38	80	10	1.28	
1 jar	128	7.2	7.7		0.1	419	.01	1.3	.56		153	90	.88	.05	
turkey w/veg, jr	115	105.6	6.4			143	2	.09	.05	13	56	91	10	1.16	
1 jar	128	7.6	7.5		0.3	810	.01	1.0	.58		137	81	1.00	.05	
veal w/veg, str	89	108.2	3.4			96	2	.10	.11		30	12	10	1.28	
1 jar	128	7.6	7.8		0.4	349	.03	2.1	.58	.32	196	69	.76	.13	
veal w/veg, jr	93	107.9	4.0			101	2	.11	.09		32	14	12	1.41	
1 jar	128	7.8	7.4		0.2	545	.03	2.0	.59	.32	201	69	1.13	.13	

FRUITS

	KCAL	H₂O (g)	FAT (g)	PUFA (g)	CHOL (mg)	A (RE)	C (mg)	B-2 (mg)	B-6 (mg)	FOL (mcg)	Na (mg)	Ca (mg)	Mg (mg)	Zn (mg)	Mn (mg)
	WT (g)	PRO (g)	CHO (g)	SFA (g)	FIBR (g)	A (IU)	B-1 (mg)	NIA (mg)	B-12 (mcg)	PANT (mg)	K (mg)	P (mg)	Fe (mg)	Cu (mg)	
apple blueberry, str	82	112.2	0.3			3	38	.05	.05	5	2	5			
1 jar	135	0.3	22.0		0.3	27	.02	0.2			93	11	.27		
apple blueberry, jr	137	182.2	0.4			9	31	.10	.09	8	28	10			
1 jar	220	0.4	36.5		0.4	92	.04	0.2			143	15	.88		
apple raspberry, str	79	113.1	0.2			3	36	.04	.05	5	3	7			
1 jar	135	0.3	21.2			29	.02	0.1		.12	108	11	.30		
apple raspberry, jr	127	184.7	0.4			7	64	.06	.08	7	4	11			
1 jar	220	0.4	34.1			66	.03	0.2		.19	158	17	.48		
applesce, str	53	113.4	0.2			2	49	.04	.04	2	3	5	4		.03
1 jar	128	0.2	14.0		0.7	22	.02	0.1		.14	91	9	.28	.05	
applesce, jr	79	190.7	0.0			2	81	.06	.06	4	5	10	6		.09
1 jar	213	0.1	21.9		1.2	20	.03	0.1		.21	164	13	.46	.08	
applesce & apricots, str	60	118.3	0.3			52	26	.04	.04	2	4	8	5		.06
1 jar	135	0.3	15.7		0.9	523	.02	0.2			162	13	.34		
applesce & apricots, jr	104	191.1	0.5			74	39	.07	.07	3	6	13	8		.07
1 jar	220	0.5	27.3		1.5	745	.03	0.3			240	23	.57		
applesce & cherries, str	65	116.6	0.0			5	45	.06		1	3	14			
1 jar	135	0.4	17.7			53	.02	0.1			130		.52		

	KCAL / WT (g)	H₂O (g) / PRO (g)	FAT (g) / CHO (g)	PUFA (g) / SFA (g)	CHOL (mg) / FIBR (g)	A (RE) / A (IU)	C (mg) / B-1 (mg)	B-2 (mg) / NIA (mg)	B-6 (mg) / B-12 (mcg)	FOL (mcg) / PANT (mg)	Na (mg) / K (mg)	Ca (mg) / P (mg)	Mg (mg) / Fe (mg)	Zn (mg) / Cu (mg)	Mn (mg)
applesce & cherries, jr	106	189.9	0.0			9	51	.10		1	6	20			
1 jar	220	0.6	28.9			91	.03	0.2			214		.89		
applesce & pineapple, str	48	114.6	0.1			3	36	.03	.05	3	3	5	4	.02	
1 jar	128	0.1	12.9			26	.03	0.1			100	8	.13		
applesce & pineapple, jr	83	189.8	0.2			4	57	.06	.08	4	4	8	7	.64	
1 jar	213	0.2	22.3			45	.05	0.2			162	13	.21		
apricots w/tapioca, str	80	112.2	0.0			98	29	.02	.04	2	11	12	5	.06	
1 jar	135	0.4	22.0		0.4	979	.01	0.3		.18	163	14	.40	.05	
apricots w/tapioca, jr	139	180.5	0.0			159	39	.03	.06	4	14	18	9	.09	
1 jar	220	0.6	38.0		1.0	1590	.02	0.4		.30	274	22	.58		
bananas & pineapple w/tapioca, str	91	109.5	0.1			5	29	.03	.12	7	10	9	8	.04	
1 jar	135	0.3	24.8			55	.02	0.2			105	7	.18	.05	
bananas & pineapple w/tapioca, jr	143	179.8	0.0			9	42	.04	.18	12	13	15	14	.09	
1 jar	220	0.5	39.3			90	.04	0.4			149	11	.51	.09	
bananas w/tapioca, str	77	113.4	0.1			6	23	.04	.16	7	12	6	14	.08	
1 jar	135	0.5	20.6		0.2	58	.02	0.2		.20	118	9	.26	.05	
bananas w/tapioca, jr	147	179.3	0.4			10	57	.04	.31	14	21	17	25	.15	
1 jar	220	0.8	39.1		0.4	97	.03	0.5		.38	237	20	.66	.10	
guava & papaya w/tapioca, str	80	105.6	0.1			24	104	.03	.02		5	9	6	.08	
1 jar	128	0.3	21.8		0.7	236	.01	0.3			95	7	.26		
guava w/tapioca, str	86	103.9	0.0			38	97	.09	.05		2	9	3	.10	
1 jar	128	0.4	23.4		1.3	383	.02	0.5			94	6	.26		
mango w/tapioca, str	109	104.9	0.3			90	168	.04	.16		6	5	5	.08	
1 jar	135	0.4	29.2		0.2	898	.03	0.3			80	8	.14		
papaya & applesce w/tapioca, str	89	103.2	0.1			10	145	.04	.03		6	9	7	.04	
1 jar	128	0.3	24.2		0.5	97	.01	0.1			101	7			
peaches, str	96	108.1	0.2			22	42	.05	.02	5	8	8	8	.12	
1 jar	135	0.7	25.5		1.0	217	.02	0.8		.18	219	16	.32	.07	
peaches, jr	157	176.1	0.4			39	42	.07	.04	9	10	11	12	.13	
1 jar	220	1.2	41.6		1.6	392	.03	1.4		.29	342	24	.59	.11	
pears, str	53	113.2	0.2			4	31	.04	.01	5	3	11	10	.10	
1 jar	128	0.4	13.9			43	.02	0.2		.12	166	15	.30	.08	
pears, jr	93	187.0	0.2			7	47	.06	.02	8	4	18	19	.17	
1 jar	213	0.6	24.7			72	.03	0.4		.20	246	26	.54	.17	
pears & pineapple, str	52	113.3	0.1			4	35	.04	.02	4	5	13	9	.08	
1 jar	128	0.4	13.9		0.3	37	.03	0.3			148	11	.32	.18	
pears & pineapple, jr	93	187.0	0.4			7	36	.05	.03	6	2	21	16	.27	
1 jar	213	0.6	24.4		0.5	68	.05	0.4			251	21	.44	.22	
plums w/tapioca, str	96	108.0	0.0			13	1	.04	.03	1	8	8	5	.11	
1 jar	135	0.2	26.6			128	.01	0.3		.15	115	8	.27	.05	
plums w/tapioca, jr	163	174.3	0.0			21	2	.07	.06	2	18	12	9	.18	
1 jar	220	0.3	45.0			207	.01	0.5		.25	182	14	.48	.08	
prunes w/tapioca, str	94	108.4	0.1			61	1	.10	.11	tr	6	20	14	.12	
1 jar	135	0.8	25.0		0.4	612	.03	0.7		.19	238	21	.47	.08	
prunes w/tapioca, jr	155	176.1	0.2			90	2	.18	.19	1	5	33	21	.22	
1 jar	220	1.3	41.2		0.7	895	.05	1.2		.31	357	32	.72		

FRUIT JUICES

	KCAL / WT (g)	H₂O (g) / PRO (g)	FAT (g) / CHO (g)	PUFA (g) / SFA (g)	CHOL (mg) / FIBR (g)	A (RE) / A (IU)	C (mg) / B-1 (mg)	B-2 (mg) / NIA (mg)	B-6 (mg) / B-12 (mcg)	FOL (mcg) / PANT (mg)	Na (mg) / K (mg)	Ca (mg) / P (mg)	Mg (mg) / Fe (mg)	Zn (mg) / Cu (mg)	Mn (mg)
apple	61	114.3	0.1			2	75	.02	.04	tr	4	6	4	.04	
1 jar	130	0.0	15.2			24	.01	0.1			118	7	.73		
apple & nonfat yogurt	97	103.0	0.3				16	.09	.05		22	58			
1 jar	128	2.6	21.2			41	.03	0.3			165	68	.26		
apple banana	64	113.1	0.1				42	.03	.08		4	8			
1 jar	130	0.3	15.0		0.1	161	.01	0.2			208	10	.13		
apple cherry	53	116.3	0.3			1	76	.02	.04	tr	4	7	4	.04	
1 jar	130	0.2	12.9			7	.01	0.1			127	7	.86		
apple grape	60	114.5	0.2			1	70	.03	.04	tr	4	7	4	.05	
1 jar	130	0.1	14.8			7	.01	0.1			118	7	.51		
apple peach	55	115.7	0.1			8	76	.01	.03	2		4	4	.03	
1 jar	130	0.2	13.6			82	.01	0.3			126	6	.73		
apple plum	63	113.5	0.0			6	76	.02	.04	tr		6	4	.04	
1 jar	130	0.1	16.0			55	.03	0.3			131	4	.81		

	KCAL / WT (g)	H₂O (g) / PRO (g)	FAT (g) / CHO (g)	PUFA (g) / SFA (g)	CHOL (mg) / FIBR (g)	A (RE) / A (IU)	C (mg) / B-1 (mg)	B-2 (mg) / NIA (mg)	B-6 (mg) / B-12 (mcg)	FOL (mcg) / PANT (mg)	Na (mg) / K (mg)	Ca (mg) / P (mg)	Mg (mg) / Fe (mg)	Zn (mg) / Cu (mg)	Mn (mg)
apple prune	94	105.7	0.2				88	tr	.05	tr	7	12			
1 jar	130	0.3	23.4				.01	0.4			192	20	1.24		
banana & nonfat yogurt	79	107.4	0.3				16	.10	.12		22	55			
1 jar	128	2.6	16.8		0.4	67	.03	0.4			182	68	.13		
mixed fruit	61	114.3	0.1			5	83	.02	.06	9	5	10	7	.04	
1 jar	130	0.2	15.1			54	.03	0.2			131	7	.44		
mixed fruit & nonfat yogurt	101	102.7	0.3				16	.09	.06		23	63			
1 jar	128	2.9	21.6		0.3	52	.04	0.4			192	74	.26		
orange	58	115.0	0.3			7	81	.04	.07	34	2	16	11	.07	
1 jar	130	0.8	13.3			72	.06	0.3			240	14	.22		
orange apple	56	115.5	0.3			9	100	.04	.05	16	4	13	6	.03	
1 jar	130	0.5	13.2			95	.05	0.2			179	9	.26		
orange apple banana	61	113.9	0.1			4	42	.04	.08	13	6	6	7	.03	
1 jar	130	0.5	15.0			35	.06	0.3			174	10	.45		
orange apricot	60	114.1	0.1			28	112	.04	.07	26	7	8	9	.05	
1 jar	130	1.0	14.2			281	.08	0.3			259	15	.49		
orange banana	65	113.0	0.1			6	44	.06		32	4	22			
1 jar	130	0.9	15.4			60	.07	0.2			261		.14		
orange pineapple	63	113.5	0.1			4	69	.03	.08	24	2	10	12	.05	
1 jar	130	0.7	15.2			40	.07	0.3			183	11	.55		
prune orange	91	106.5	0.4			17	83	.16	.08	17	2	16	10	.05	
1 jar	130	0.8	21.8			170	.06	0.5			236	14	1.13		

MEAT/EGG YOLKS

	KCAL / WT (g)	H₂O (g) / PRO (g)	FAT (g) / CHO (g)	PUFA (g) / SFA (g)	CHOL (mg) / FIBR (g)	A (RE) / A (IU)	C (mg) / B-1 (mg)	B-2 (mg) / NIA (mg)	B-6 (mg) / B-12 (mcg)	FOL (mcg) / PANT (mg)	Na (mg) / K (mg)	Ca (mg) / P (mg)	Mg (mg) / Fe (mg)	Zn (mg) / Cu (mg)	Mn (mg)
beef, str	106	79.8	5.3	0.2		55	2	.14	.14	6	80	7	17	2.43	
1 jar	99	13.5	0.0	2.6		183	.01	2.8	1.41	.34	218	83	1.46	.04	
beef, jr	105	79.1	4.9	0.2		31	2	.16	.12	6	65	8	9	1.98	
1 jar	99	14.3	0.0	2.6		102	.01	3.3	1.46	.35	189	71	1.63	.09	
beef w/beef heart, str	93	81.7	4.4	0.2		37	2	.35	.12	5	62	4	12	1.82	
1 jar	99	12.6	0.0	2.1	0.1	124	.02	3.8			198	93	1.97	.13	
chicken, str	128	76.7	7.8	1.9		40	2	.15	.20	10	47	63	13	1.20	
1 jar	99	13.6	0.1	2.0		133	.01	3.2		.67	139	96	1.39	.05	
chicken, jr	148	75.2	9.5	2.3		55	2	.16	.19	11	50	54	11	1.00	
1 jar	99	14.6	0.0	2.4		184	.01	3.4		.72	121	89	.98	.05	
chicken sticks, jr	134	48.5	10.2			678	1	.14	.07		340	52			
1 jar	71	10.4	1.0		0.1	2257	.01	1.4			75	86	1.11		
egg yolks, str	191	66.3	16.3	1.8	739	353	1	.25	.15	.87	37	72	6	1.80	
1 jar	94	9.4	0.9	4.9		1176	.07	tr	1.45	2.01	73	270	2.60	.07	
ham, str	110	78.6	5.7	0.8		11	2	.15	.25	2	40	6	13	2.22	
1 jar	99	13.7	0.0	1.9		38	.14	2.6		.51	202	80	1.02	.06	
ham, jr	123	77.8	6.6	0.9		9	2	.19	.20	2	66	5	11	1.68	
1 jar	99	14.9	0.0	2.2		31	.14	2.8		.53	208	88	1.00		
lamb, str	102	79.5	4.7	0.2		25	1	.20	.15	2	62	7	13	2.73	
1 jar	99	13.9	0.1	2.3		85	.02	2.9	2.17	.41	203	96	1.48	.05	
lamb, jr	111	78.8	5.2	0.2		8	2	.20	.18	2	73	7	10	2.57	
1 jar	99	15.0	0.0	2.5		27	.02	3.2	2.25	.42	209	90	1.65	.06	
liver, str	100	78.5	3.7	0.1	182	11337	19	1.8	.34	334	73	3	13	2.95	
1 jar	99	14.2	1.4	1.4		37754	.05	8.2	2.14		224	201	5.23	2.00	
meat sticks, jr	130	49.3	10.4	1.1		15	2	.12	.06		388	24			
1 jar	71	9.5	0.8	4.1	0.1	49	.04	1.1			81	73	.98		
pork, str	123	77.6	7.1	0.8		11	2	.20	.20	2	42	5	10	2.25	
1 jar	99	13.8	0.0	2.4		38	.15	2.2	.98		221	93	.99	.07	
turkey, str	113	78.1	5.8	1.4		166	2	.21	.18	11	54	23	14	1.81	
1 jar	99	14.1	0.0	1.9		554	.02	3.6	.99	.56	229	125	1.19	.04	
turkey, jr	128	76.7	7.0	1.7		169	2	.25	.16	12	72	28	11	1.78	
1 jar	99	15.2	0.0	2.3		563	.02	3.4	1.06	.60	178	94	1.34		
turkey sticks, jr	129	49.6	10.1			49	1	.11	.05		343	51			
1 jar	71	9.7	1.0		0.4	162	.01	1.2			65	73	.88		
veal, str	100	80.0	4.7	0.2		14	2	.16	.15	6	64	7	12	1.98	
1 jar	99	13.4	0.0	2.3	0.1	45	.02	3.5		.43	214	97	1.26	.04	
veal, jr	109	79.0	4.9	0.2		15	2	.18	.12	7	68	6	11	2.49	
1 jar	99	15.1	0.0	2.4	0.2	50	.02	3.8		.45	234	97	1.24	.07	

	KCAL	H₂O (g)	FAT (g)	PUFA (g)	CHOL (mg)	A (RE)	C (mg)	B-2 (mg)	B-6 (mg)	FOL (mcg)	Na (mg)	Ca (mg)	Mg (mg)	Zn (mg)	Mn (mg)
	WT (g)	PRO (g)	CHO (g)	SFA (g)	FIBR (g)	A (IU)	B-1 (mg)	NIA (mg)	B-12 (mcg)	PANT (mg)	K (mg)	P (mg)	Fe (mg)	Cu (mg)	

VEGETABLES

	KCAL / WT	H₂O / PRO	FAT / CHO	PUFA / SFA	CHOL / FIBR	A(RE) / A(IU)	C / B-1	B-2 / NIA	B-6 / B-12	FOL / PANT	Na / K	Ca / P	Mg / Fe	Zn / Cu	Mn
beans, green, str	32	117.8	0.1			57	7	.11	.05	44	2	49	30	.26	
1 jar	128	1.7	7.6		1.3	574	.03	0.4		.21	202	26	.96	.07	
beans, green, jr	51	190.5	0.3			89	17	.21	.07	67	3	133	46	.40	
1 jar	206	2.5	11.8		2.0	892	.04	0.7		.31	263	39	2.23	.10	
beans, green, buttered, str	42	116.3	1.0			58	11	.14		36	4	82			
1 jar	128	1.6	8.5			584	.02	0.4			205		1.64		
beans, green, buttered, jr	67	187.9	1.8			79	18	.23		56	4	143			
1 jar	206	2.7	12.5			787	.03	0.7			351		2.38		
beans, green, creamed, jr	68	193.6	0.9			32	6	.12	.03		26	68	16	.34	
1 jar	213	2.1	15.3			320	.05	0.5			139	39	.56		
beets, str	43	115.3	0.1			4	3	.06	.03	39	106	18	18	.15	
1 jar	218	1.7	9.8		1.0	43	.01	0.2			233	17	.41	.09	
carrots, str	34	118.1	0.2			1467	7	.05	.09	19	48	29	12	.20	
1 jar	128	1.0	7.7		1.0	14670	.03	0.6		.31	251	25	.47	.05	
carrots, jr	67	193.9	0.4			2516	12	.09	.17	37	104	49	23	.38	
1 jar	213	1.7	15.4		1.7	25156	.05	1.1		.59	429	43	.82	.10	
carrots, buttered, str	46	116.0	0.8			1386	12	.07		12	24	45			
1 jar	128	1.1	9.4			13860	.02	0.8			292		.36		
carrots, buttered, jr	70	194.6	1.2			2096	16	.12		18	34	76			
1 jar	213	1.7	14.3			20960	.04	1.1			310		.66		
corn, creamed, str	73	107.0	0.5			10	3	.06	.05	14	55	25	11	.24	
1 jar	128	1.8	18.1		0.4	96	.02	0.7	.02	.37	115	43	.36	.04	
corn, creamed, jr	138	173.5	0.8			16	5	.10	.09	27	111	39	17	.49	
1 jar	213	3.1	34.7		0.2	165	.03	1.1	.05	.70	172	71	.58	.08	
garden veg, str	48	115.2	0.3			777	7	.09	.13	52	45	36	27	.33	
1 jar	128	2.9	8.7		1.2	7766	.08	1.0			215	35	1.06	.09	
mixed veg, str	52	114.9	0.6			511	2	.03	.07	5	6	17	13	.19	
1 jar	128	1.6	10.2		0.5	5109	.03	0.4		.32	163	29	.41	.05	
mixed veg, jr	88	190.4	0.8			894	5	.07	.17	9	77	24	23	.58	
1 jar	213	3.1	17.4		1.1	8935	.06	1.4		.55	362	53	.87	.09	
peas, str	52	112.0	0.4			72	9	.08	.09	33	5	26	19	.45	
1 jar	128	4.5	10.4		1.5	723	.10	1.3		.36	144	55	1.23	.08	
peas, jr	128	179.3	1.3				12	.13	.15		11	32			
1 jar	213	7.2	21.5		2.6	746	.13	1.7			243	64	3.41		
peas, buttered, str	72	107.8	1.4			42	15	.09		44	10	49			
1 jar	128	4.7	13.6			422	.10	1.8			124		1.41		
peas, buttered, jr	123	172.0	2.6			84	26	.16		75	11	93			
1 jar	206	7.3	23.3			845	.15	2.8			240		2.14		
peas, creamed, str	68	110.7	2.4			11	2	.07	.06	29	18	16		.50	
1 jar	128	2.8	11.4		0.5	110	.11	1.0	.10		113	40	.72	.07	
spinach, creamed, str	48	114.7	1.7			534	11	.13	.10	78	62	113	71	.40	
1 jar	128	3.2	7.3		0.6	5338	.02	0.3			244	70	.80	.08	
spinach, creamed, jr	90	187.9	3.0			783	8	.18	.12	147	117	240	134	.85	
1 jar	213	6.4	13.7		1.1	7830	.05	0.6			471	104	2.98	.15	
squash, str	30	118.7	0.2			259	10	.07	.08	20	3	30	16	.18	
1 jar	128	1.1	7.2		0.9	2590	.01	0.5		.28	229	20	.38	.07	
squash, jr	51	197.6	0.4			429	17	.14	.15	33	3	50	25	.17	
1 jar	213	1.8	12.0		1.5	4291	.02	0.8		.47	393	34	.74	.11	
squash, buttered, str	37	117.4	0.4			212	10	.09		15	2	42			
1 jar	128	0.8	8.8			2123	.01	0.5			163		.53		
squash, buttered, jr	63	195.5	1.3			326	16	.14		25	3	65			
1 jar	213	1.5	13.7			3259	.02	0.7			288		.89		
sweet potatoes, str	77	114.5	0.2			869	13	.05	.13	13	27	21	18	.28	
1 jar	135	1.5	17.8		0.9	8691	.04	0.5		.53	355	32	.50	.11	
sweet potatoes, jr	133	185.0	0.3			1460	21	.08	.25	23	49	35	26	.24	
1 jar	220	2.4	30.7		1.4	14600	.06	0.8		.90	535	52	.85	.22	
sweet potatoes, buttered, str	76	115.9	1.0			920	12	.05		18	11	28			
1 jar	135	1.3	15.9			9199	.02	0.4			281		.60		
sweet potatoes, buttered, jr	126	188.3	1.6			1330	21	.10		29	17	61			
1 jar	220	1.8	26.8			13295	.04	0.7			474		.87		

KCAL / WT (g) / / try (mg)	H₂O (g) / PRO (g) / / thr (mg)	FAT (g) / CHO (g) / / iso (mg)	PUFA (g) / SFA (g) / / leu (mg)	CHOL (mg) / FIBR (g) / INOS (mg) / lys (mg)	**Vitamins** A (RE) / A (IU) / D (IU) / met (mg)	C (mg) / B-1 (mg) / E (mg) / cys (mg)	B-2 (mg) / NIA (mg) / K (mcg) / phe (mg)	B-6 (mg) / B-12 (mcg) / BIO (mcg) / tyr (mg)	FOL (mcg) / PANT (mg) / CHLN (mg) / val (mg)	**Minerals** Na (mg) / K (mg) / Cl (mg) / arg (mg)	Ca (mg) / P (mg) / I (mcg) / his (mg)	Mg (mg) / Fe (mg) / Mo (mg)	Zn (mg) / Cu (mg)	Mn (mg)

INFANT FORMULAS

advance, Ross
1 fl oz

KCAL	H₂O	FAT	PUFA	CHOL	A	C	B-2	B-6	FOL	Na	Ca	Mg	Zn	Mn
16	27.0	0.8	0.4			1	.02	.02	3	9	15	2	.18	tr
30	0.6	1.6	0.1		71	.02	0.3ᵃ	.07	.10		11	.35	.026	
					12	0.5ᵇ	0.6	0.4		16	2			
7	24	25	52	39	13	6	29		27		13			

cho free soy protein formula base, Ross
1 fl oz

12	26.0	1.1	0.4	0.0		2	.02	.01	3	9	21	1	.15	.006
30	0.6	0.0	0.5		74	.01	0.3ᵃ	.09	.10	21	15	.35	.015	
					12	0.6ᵇ	4	9		16	3			
6	21	26	47	35	12	6	31		27		15			

enfamil, Mead Johnson
20 cal/oz
1 fl oz

20	26.1	1.1	0.3	0.5	19	2	.03	.01	3	6	14	2	.16	.003
30	0.5	2.1	0.5		50	.02	0.3	.05	.09	20	9	.03ᶜ	.02	
				0.9	13	0.6	3	tr	3.1	13	3			
7	24	28	47	31	9	3	18	18	28		11			

24 cal/oz
1 fl oz

24	26.1	1.3	0.4	0.6	22	2	.04	.01	4	8	17	2	.19	.038
30	0.5	2.5	0.6			.02	0.3	.06	.11	24	11	.04	.02	
				1.1	15	0.8	1		3.8	15	4			
8	29	34	56	37	11	4	21	22	34		13			

powder, 20 cal/oz
1.05 oz

156		8.7	2.9	1	149	13	.25	.10	25	50	108	12	1.23	.025
30	3.6	16.0	3.8			.12	2.0	.37	.75	162	75	.25ᵈ	.15	
				7.5	99	5.0		4	25	99	25			
54	192	220	375	250	72	27	141	144	220		86			

premature formula, 20 cal/oz
1 fl oz

20	26.2	1.0	0.3	tr	19	2	.02	.01	6	8	23	2	.20	.005
30	0.6	2.2	0.2		74	.02	0.3	.06	.09	22	12	.03	.02	
				0.9	13	0.4	2	1	1.4	17	2			
9	13	33	58	45	13	6	23	27	36		12			

premature formula, 24 cal/oz
1 fl oz

24	25.4	1.2	0.3	tr	23	2	.02	.01	7	9	28	3	.24	.006
30	0.7	2.6	0.3		74	.02	0.3	.07	.11	26	14	.04	.02	
				1.1	15	0.5	2	1	1.7	20	2			
11	40	40	70	54	16	8	28	32	43		14			

isomil,ᵉ 20 cal/oz, Ross
1 fl oz

20	26.5	1.1	0.4	0.0		2	.02	.01	3	9	21	1	.15	.006
30	0.6	2.0	0.5		74	.01	0.3ᵃ	.09	.15	21	15	.36	.015	
					12	0.6ᵇ	4	0.9		16	3			
6	21	26	47	35	12	6	31		27		15			

isomilᵉ SF, 20 cal/oz, Ross
1 fl oz

20	26.5	1.1	0.4	0.0		2	.02	.01	3	9	21	1	.15	.006
30	0.6	2.0	0.5		74	.01	0.3ᵃ	.09	.15	21	15	.35	.015	
					12	0.6ᵇ	4	0.9		16	3			
6	21	26	47	35	12	6	31		27		15			

lofenalac,ᶠ 20 cal/oz, Mead Johnson
1 fl oz

20	26.7	0.8	0.5	tr	15	2	.02	.01	3	9	19	2	.13	.031
30	0.7	2.6	0.1		50	.02	0.3	.06	.09	20	14	.38	.02	
				0.9	13	0.3	3		2.6	14	1			
8	34	38	72	72	24	3	3	35	60		21			

meat base formula (MBF), Gerber
1 fl oz

20	26.2	1.0				2	.03	.03	1	8	30	1	.10	1.00
30	0.8	1.9			53	.02	0.1	.26	.10	16	20	.40	.01	
				5.0	12	0.2ᵃ	0.8	0.3	3.0	15	1			
9	32	36	68	63	29	8	38	30	40	59	23			

nursoy,ᵉ 20 cal/oz, Wyeth
1 fl oz

20		1.1	0.2			2	.03	.01	2	6	19	2	.11	.031
30	0.6	2.0	0.5		78	.02	0.2	.06	.09	22	13	.38	.01	
					13	0.3ᵃ	3.1	1.1	2.7	11	2			
7	21	35	53	39	16	7	36	27	35	50	17			

ᵃ Niacin equivalent
ᵇ Vit E value in IUs
ᶜ Enfamil w/Fe contains .38 mg Fe/fl oz.
ᵈ Enfamil powder w/Fe contains 3.00 mg/1.05 oz.
ᵉ Soy-based formula
ᶠ Low phe formula for infants & children w/PKU

	KCAL	H₂O (g)	FAT (g)	PUFA (g)	CHOL (mg)	A (RE)	C (mg)	B-2 (mg)	B-6 (mg)	FOL (mcg)	Na (mg)	Ca (mg)	Mg (mg)	Zn (mg)	Mn (mg)
						(Vitamins)					*(Minerals)*				
	WT (g)	PRO (g)	CHO (g)	SFA (g)	FIBR (g)	A (IU)	B-1 (mg)	NIA (mg)	B-12 (mcg)	PANT (mg)	K (mg)	P (mg)	Fe (mg)	Cu (mg)	
					INOS (mg)	D (IU)	E (mg)	K (mcg)	BIO (mcg)	CHLN (mg)	Cl (mg)	I (mcg)	Mo (mg)		
	try (mg)	thr (mg)	iso (mg)	leu (mg)	lys (mg)	met (mg)	cys (mg)	phe (mg)	tyr (mg)	val (mg)	arg (mg)	his (mg)			
nutramigen,[a] Mead Johnson	20	27.0	0.8	0.5	tr	15	2	.02	.01	3	9	19	2	.13	.006
1 fl oz	30	0.7	2.6	0.1		50	.02	0.3	.06	.09	20	14	.38	.019	
					0.9	13	0.3	3	1.3	2.6	14	1			
	7	32	39	66	56	20	3	32	11	49		20			
nutramigen,[a] Mead Johnson	160	216.3	6.2	3.8	0	120	13	.15	.10	25	75	150	18	1.00	.050
8 fl oz	250	5.2	21.0	0.9		400	.13	2.0	.50	.70	162	112	3.00	.15	
					7.5	100	2.5	25	10	21	112	11			
	58	260	310	520	450	162	22	250	86	400		163			
pregestimil,[b] Mead Johnson	20	27	0.8	0.3	tr	19	2	.02	.01	3	9	19	2	.13	.006
1 fl oz	30	0.6	2.7	0.1		62		0.3	.06	.06	22	13	.38	.019	
					0.9	13	0.5	3.3	1.3	2.6	17	1			
	9	28	34	58	48	17	9	27	15	42		17			
pregestimil,[b] Mead Johnson	160	215.8	6.4	2.3	tr	150	13	.15	.10	25	75	150	18	1.00	.05
8 fl oz	250	4.5	22.0	0.6		499	.13	2.0	.50	.50	175	100	3.00	.15	
					7.5	100	3.8	26	10	21	138	11			
	72	220	270	460	390	135	72	220	120	340		136			
prosobee,[c] 20 cal/oz, Mead Johnson	20	26.3	1.1	0.3		19	2	.02	.01	3	9	19	2	.16	.006
1 fl oz	30	0.6	2.0	0.5		62	.02	0.3	.06	.09	24	15	.38	.02	
					0.9	13	0.6	3	1	1.6	16	2			
	7	19	28	46	36	11	5	29	20	28		14			
prosobee,[c] 20 cal/oz, Mead Johnson	160	218.8	8.5	2.5	0	150	13	.15	.10	25	69	150	18	1.25	.05
8 fl oz	250	4.8	16.0	4.0		499	.13	2.0	.50	.75	185	119	3.00	.15	
					7.5	100	5.0	25	12	12.5	130	16			
	58	152	220	360	290	88	42	230	163	220		112			
similac, Ross	13	27.5	0.7	0.2			1	.02	.01	2	6	12	1	.10	.001
13 cal/oz	30	0.4	1.4	0.3		48	.01	0.1[d]	.03	.06	18	9	.03[e]	.011	
1 fl oz					8		0.4[f]	0.9	.24		12	2			
	4	15	17	33	25	10	3	17		19		7			
20 cal/oz	20	27	1.1	0.4			2	.03	.01	3	7	15	1	.15	.001
1 fl oz	30	0.5	2.1	0.5		74	.02	0.2[d]	.04	.09	23	11	.04[g]	.018	
					12		0.6[f]	0.9	0.3		16	3			
	6	19	22	43	32	13	4	22		25		9			
24 cal/oz	24	26	1.3	0.4			2	.04	.01	4	11	21	2	.18	.001
1 fl oz	30	0.6	2.5	0.6		88	.02	0.2[d]	.05	.11	32	16	.05[h]	.021	
					14		0.7[f]	1.2	0.4		22	4			
	8	29	31	60	45	18	5	29		35		13			
27 cal/oz	27	25.5	1.4	0.5			2	.04	.02	4	11	24	2	.20	.001
1 fl oz	30	0.7	2.8	0.6		99	.03	0.3[d]	.06	.12	35	18	.06	.024	
					16		0.8[f]	1.2	0.4		24	4			
	9	32	34	66	49	20	6	33		39		15			
low birth weight (LBW), 24 cal/oz	24	25.9	1.3	0.2			3	.04	.01	3	11	21	2	.24	.001
1 fl oz	30	0.6	2.5	0.9		88	.03	0.2[d]	.06	.11	36	16	.09	.024	
					14		0.7[f]	1.2	0.4		26	4			
	8	29	31	60	45	18	5	29		35		13			
pm, 60/40	20	27.0	1.1	0.3			2	.03	.01	1	5	12	1	.12	tr
1 fl oz	30	0.5	2.0	0.6		74	.02	0.2[d]	.04	.09	17	6	.08	.012	
					12		0.4[f]	0.8	0.3		7	1			
	10	27	24	46	32	11	7	18		26		8			
special care, 20 cal/oz	20	26.5	1.1	0.2			7	.12	.05	7	9	35	2	.29	.005
1 fl oz	30	0.5	2.1	0.6		135	.05	1.0[d]	.11	.37	24	18	.07	.050	
					29		0.7[f]	2	7.4		16	4			
	6	30	26	55	44	13	9	21		28		10			

[a] Hypoallergenic formula for infants & children sensitive to intact proteins of milk & other foods

[b] Pro hydrolysate formula w/MCTs & added amino acids

[c] Milk-free, lactose-free & sucrose-free infant formula w/soy pro for infants w/milk sensitivity

[d] Niacin equivalent

[e] Similac w/Fe contains .23 mg Fe/fl oz.

[f] Vit E value in IUs

[g] Similac w/Fe contains .35 mg Fe/fl oz.

[h] Similac w/Fe contains .44 mg Fe/fl oz.

	KCAL	H₂O (g)	FAT (g)	PUFA (g)	CHOL (mg)	A (RE)	C (mg)	B-2 (mg)	B-6 (mg)	FOL (mcg)	Na (mg)	Ca (mg)	Mg (mg)	Zn (mg)	Mn (mg)
	WT (g)	PRO (g)	CHO (g)	SFA (g)	FIBR (g)	A (IU)	B-1 (mg)	NIA (mg)	B-12 (mcg)	PANT (mg)	K (mg)	P (mg)	Fe (mg)	Cu (mg)	
					INOS (mg)	D (IU)	E (mg)	K (mcg)	BIO (mcg)	CHLN (mg)	Cl (mg)	I (mcg)	Mo (mg)		
	try (mg)	thr (mg)	iso (mg)	leu (mg)	lys (mg)	met (mg)	cys (mg)	phe (mg)	tyr (mg)	val (mg)	arg (mg)	his (mg)			
special care, 24 cal/oz	24	26.0	1.3	0.2			9	.15	.06	9	10	42	3	.35	.006
1 fl oz	30	0.6	2.5	0.8		162	.06	1.2[a]	.13	.44	29	21	.09	.059	
						35	0.9[b]	2.9	9		19	4			
	8	36	32	66	52	16	11	25		34		12			
SMA, Wyeth	13		0.7	0.1			1	.02	.01	1	3	9	1	.07	.003
13 cal/oz	30	0.3	1.4	0.3		51	.01	0.1	.02	.04	11	6	.24	.01	
1 fl oz						8	0.2[b]	1.12	.29	2.6	7	1			
	5	20	20	35	30	7	5	15	16	21	10	7			
20 cal/oz	20		1.1	0.2			2	.03	.01	2	4	13	2	.11	.005
1 fl oz	30	0.4	2.1	0.5		78	.02	0.2	.03	.06	17	10	.38	.01	
						13	0.3[b]	1.7	.44	4.1	11	2			
	8	31	30	55	46	10	8	24	24	32	16	11			
24 cal/oz	24		1.3	0.2			2	.04	.02	2	5	16	2	.13	.006
1 fl oz	30	0.5	2.6	0.6		94	.03	0.2	.04	.08	20	12	.45	.02	
						15	0.3[b]	2.1	.53	4.9	13	2			
	9	37	37	66	55	12	10	28	29	39	19	14			
27 cal/oz	27		1.4	0.2			2	.04	.02	2	6	18	2	.15	.006
1 fl oz	30	0.6	2.9	0.6		105	.03	0.2	.04	.08	22	13	.51	.02	
						17	0.4[b]	2.3	.59	5.5	15	3			
	11	42	41	74	62	14	11	32	32	43	21	15			

[a] Niacin equivalent
[b] Vit E value in IUs

	KCAL	H₂O (g)	FAT (g)	PUFA (g)	CHOL (mg)	A (RE)	C (mg)	B-2 (mg)	B-6 (mg)	FOL (mcg)	Na (mg)	Ca (mg)	Mg (mg)	Zn (mg)	Mn (mg)
	WT (g)	PRO (g)	CHO (g)	SFA (g)	FIBR (g)	A (IU)	B-1 (mg)	NIA (mg)	B-12 (mcg)	PANT (mg)	K (mg)	P (mg)	Fe (mg)	Cu (mg)	

JUICES, FRUIT & VEGETABLE

Food	KCAL / WT	H₂O / PRO	FAT / CHO	PUFA / SFA	CHOL / FIBR	A(RE) / A(IU)	C / B-1	B-2 / NIA	B-6 / B-12	FOL / PANT	Na / K	Ca / P	Mg / Fe	Zn / Cu	Mn
acerola jce, fresh	51	228.2	0.7			123	3872	.15	.01		7	24	29		
8 fl oz	242	1.0	11.6		0.7	1232	.05	1.0	.00	.50	235	22	1.21		
apple jce, cnd/bottled	116	218.1	0.3	0.1	0	0	2	.04	.07	tr	7	16	8	.07	.280
8 fl oz	248	0.2	29.0	tr	0.5	2	.05	0.2	.00		296	18	.92	.055	
apple jce, from frzn conc	111	210.1	0.3	0.1	0		1	.04	.08	1	17	14	12	.09	.151
8 fl oz	239	0.3	27.6	tr			.01	0.1	.00	.15	301	16	.61	.033	
apricot nectar, cnd	141	213.0	0.2	tr	0	330	1	.04		3	9	17	13	.23	
8 fl oz	251	0.9	36.1	tr	0.5	3304	.02	0.7	.00		286	23	.96	.183	
blackberry jce, fresh	93	227.3	1.5				25	.08			3	30			
8 fl oz	250	0.8	19.5		tr		.05	0.1			425	30	2.25		
black currant jce, fresh	138		0.0				405					50			
8 fl oz	250	1.3	34.3									40			
blueberry jce, fresh	135		0.0								3				
8 fl oz	250	0.3	34.3								278				
carrot jce, cnd	96		0.2												
8 fl oz	240	1.9	21.4			11520									
coconut cream [a]	48	7.6	4.5	0.3							1	2			
1 T	14	0.6	1.2			0		0.1			45	18	.30		
coconut milk [b]	307	80.2	30.4				2				64	19			
4 fl oz	122	3.9	6.3	0.0			.03	1.0			232	122	1.95		
coconut water [c]	53	226.1	0.5				5				60	48			
8 fl oz	240	0.7	11.3			0		0.2			353	31	.70		
cranberry jce cocktail, bottled	147	215.1	0.1		0		108	.04		1	10	8	8	.05	.397
8 fl oz	253	0.1	37.7				.01	0.1	.00	.17	61	3	.40	.033	
cranberry jce cocktail, low cal, bottled	36	171.6	0.4				60				6	17	3	.03	
6 fl oz	180	0.2	8.3								40	2	.07	.02	
cranberry apple jce, bottled	129	155.5	0.2				60				4	13	4	.07	
6 fl oz	188	0.2	32.1								51	5	.10	.014	
cranberry apple jce, low cal, bottled	32	172.1	0.2				60				8	17	5	.027	
6 fl oz	180	0.2	7.4								80	2	.11	.016	
cranberry apricot jce, bottled	123	160.3	0.2				0				4	18	6	.08	
6 fl oz	189	0.3	30.4								115	10	.29	.03	
cranberry grape jce, bottled	108	160.5	0.2				60				5	15	6	.08	
6 fl oz	188	0.3	26.3								45	8	.03	.015	
grape jce, cnd/bottled	155	212.8	0.2	0.1	0	2	tr	.09	.16	7	7	22	24	.13	.911
8 fl oz	253	1.4	37.9	0.1		20	.07	0.7	.00	.10	334	27	.60	.071	
grape jce, from frzn conc, sweetened	128	217.3	0.2	0.1	0	2	60	.07	11	3	5	9	11	.10	.443
8 fl oz	250	0.5	31.9	0.1		19	.04	0.3	.00	.06	53	11	.26	.033	
grapefruit jce, fresh	96	222.3	0.3	0.1	0		94	.05			2	22	30	.13	.049
8 fl oz	247	1.2	22.7	tr		[d]	.10	0.5	.00		400	37	.49	.082	
grapefruit jce, bottled	64	167.1	0.2				30	.03			7	17	15		
6 fl oz	185	1.0	14.5				.02	0.4			212	24	.11	.038	
grapefruit jce, cnd	93	222.6	0.2	0.1	0	2	72	.05	.05	26	3	18	24	.21	.049
8 fl oz	247	1.3	22.1	tr	0.0	18	.10	0.6	.00	.32	378	27	.50	.094	
grapefruit jce, cnd, sweetened	116	218.4	0.2	0.1	0	0	67	.06	.05	26	4	20	24	.15	.050
8 fl oz	250	1.5	27.8	tr	0.0	0	.10	0.8	.00	.33	405	27	.89	.120	
grapefruit jce, from frzn conc	102	220.6	0.3	0.1	0	2	83	.05	.11	9	2	19	26	.13	.049
8 fl oz	247	1.4	24.0	tr		22	.10	0.5	.00	.47	337	34	.34	.082	
grapefruit, pink jce cocktail, bottled	84	163.7	0.2				60				15	14	8	.11	
6 fl oz	185	0.5	20.0								125	16	.24	.06	
lemon jce, fresh	4	13.8	0.0		0	0	7	tr	.01	2	0	1	1	.01	.001
1 T	15	0.1	1.3			3	.01	tr	.00	.02	19	1	.00	.004	
lemon jce, fresh	60	221.4	0.0		0	5	112	.02	.12	32	2	18	16	.12	.020
8 fl oz	244	0.9	21.1			49	.07	0.2	.00	.25	303	14	.08	.071	
lemon jce, cnd/bottled	3	14.1	tr	tr	0	0	4	tr	.01	2	3	2	1	.01	.003
1 T	15	0.1	1.0	tr		2	.01	tr	.00	.01	15	1	.02	.006	
lemon jce, frzn, single-strength	3	14.0	0.1	tr	0	0	5	tr	.01	1	0	1	1	.01	.005
1 T	15	0.1	1.0	tr		2	.01	tr	.00	.02	14	1	.02	.005	

[a] Liquid expressed from grated coconut
[b] Liquid expressed from grated coconut & coconut water
[c] Liquid from coconut
[d] 25 IU for white grapefruit jce; 1087 IU for pink or red grapefruit jce

	KCAL	H₂O (g)	FAT (g)	PUFA (g)	CHOL (mg)	Vitamins A (RE)	C (mg)	B-2 (mg)	B-6 (mg)	FOL (mcg)	Minerals Na (mg)	Ca (mg)	Mg (mg)	Zn (mg)	Mn (mg)
	WT (g)	PRO (g)	CHO (g)	SFA (g)	FIBR (g)	A (IU)	B-1 (mg)	NIA (mg)	B-12 (mcg)	PANT (mg)	K (mg)	P (mg)	Fe (mg)	Cu (mg)	
lime jce, fresh	4	13.9	tr	tr	0	0	5	tr	.01		0	1	1	.01	.001
1 T	15	0.1	1.4	tr		2	tr	tr	.00	.02	17	1	.00	.005	
lime jce, fresh	66	221.9	0.3	0.1	0	2	72	.03	.11		2	22	14	.15	.020
8 fl oz	246	1.1	22.2	tr		25	.05	0.2	.00	.34	268	18	.08	.074	
lime jce, cnd/bottled	3	14.3	tr	tr	0	0	1	.00	tr	1	2	2	1	.01	.001
1 T	15	tr	1.0	tr		3	.01	tr	.00	.01	12	1	.03	.005	
loganberry jce, fresh	100	0.0										16			
8 fl oz	246	1.4	24.8		0.0							8	.20		
orange jce, fresh	111	219.0	0.5	0.1	0	50	124	.07	.01		2	27	27	.13	.035
8 fl oz	248	1.7	25.8	0.1	0.3	496	.22	0.1	.00	.47	496	42	.50	.109	
orange jce, cnd	104	221.6	0.4	0.1	0	44	86	.07	.22		6	21	27	.17	.035
8 fl oz	249	1.5	24.5	tr	0.3	437	.15	0.8	.00	.37	436	36	1.10	.142	
orange jce, from frzn conc	112	219.4	0.1	tr	0	19	97	.05	.11	109	2	22	24	.13	.035
8 fl oz	249	1.7	26.8	tr	0.1	194	.20	0.5	.00	.39	474	40	.24	.110	
orange grapefruit jce, cnd	107	218.9	0.2	tr	0	29	72	.07	.06		8	21	24	.18	.042
8 fl oz	247	1.5	25.4	tr		293	.14	0.8	.00	.35	390	34	1.15	.188	
orange grapefruit jce, from frzn conc	101	217.3	0.1				107	.04	.07	7	1	24	25		
8 fl oz	245	1.6	25.5		0.1	281	.16	0.7	.00	.40	459	41	.28		
papaya nectar, cnd	142	212.5	0.4	0.1	0	28	8	.01	.02	5	14	24	8	.38	.033
8 fl oz	250	0.4	36.3	0.1		277	.02	0.4	.00	.14	78	1	.86	.033	
passionfruit jce, purple, fresh	126	211.5	0.1	0		177	74	.32				9			
8 fl oz	247	1.0	33.6		0.1	1771		3.6	.00			31	.59		
passionfruit jce, yellow, fresh	149	208.0	0.4		0	595	45	.25			15	9	41		
8 fl oz	247	1.7	35.7		0.4	5953		5.5	.00		687	61	.89		
peach nectar, cnd	134	213.2	0.1	tr	0	64	13	.04			17	13	11	.20	.047
8 fl oz	249	0.7	34.7	tr	0.4	643	.01	0.7	.00		101	16	.47	.172	
pear nectar, cnd	149	210.0	tr	tr	0	0	3	.03			9	11	6	.16	.075
8 fl oz	250	0.3	39.4	tr	0.8	1	.01	0.3	.00		33	7	.65	.168	
pineapple jce, cnd	139	213.8	0.2	0.1	0	1	27	.06	.24	58	2	42	34	.29	2.475
8 fl oz	250	0.8	34.4	tr	0.3	12	.14	0.6	.00	.25	334	20	.65	.225	
pineapple jce, from frzn conc	129	216.3	0.1	tr	0	3	30	.05	.19		3	28	23	.29	2.475
8 fl oz	250	1.0	31.9	tr	0.3	25	.18	0.5	.00	.31	340	20	.75	.225	
pineapple orange jce, from frzn conc	125	216.0	0.1				37	.04	.19	1	3	31	28		
8 fl oz	248	1.1	30.7		0.3	130	.15	0.5	.00	.28	357	23	.65		
prune jce, cnd	181	208.0	0.1	tr	0	1	11	.18		1	11	30	36	.52	.387
8 fl oz	256	1.6	44.7	tr	tr	9	.04	2.0	.00		706	64	3.03	.174	
raspberry jce, fresh	98	0.0					36					58			
8 fl oz	240	0.4	25.6		tr	240	.40					28	2.00		
tangelo jce, fresh	103		0.3				68								
8 fl oz	250	1.3	24.3		tr										
tangerine jce, fresh	106	219.6	0.5	0.1	0	104	77	.05			2	44	20	.06	.091
8 fl oz	247	1.2	25.0	tr	0.3	1037	.15	0.2	.00		440	35	.49	.062	
tangerine jce, cnd, sweetened	125	216.6	0.5	0.1	0	105	55	.05	.80		2	45	20	.06	.092
8 fl oz	249	1.3	29.9	tr	0.3	1046	.15	0.2	.00		443	35	.50	.062	
tangerine jce, from frzn conc, sweetened—*8 fl oz*	110	212.3	0.3	tr	0	138	58	.05	.10	11	2	18	19	.06	.089
	241	1.0	27.7	tr		1382	.13	0.2	.00	.30	273	20	.23	.060	
tomato jce, cnd	41	228.2	0.2				102	.07	.46		676	19	29	.36	
8 fl oz	243	1.9	10.0		0.5	909	.10	1.7		.61	598	46	1.60	.365	
tomato veg jce cocktail, bottled	44	169.0	0.2					.05			599	20	22	.20	
6 fl oz	182	1.5	9.1		0.6	711	.06	1.4			388	33	.69	.14	
V-8 veg jce cocktail, cnd	53		0.1				48	.04	.37		715ᵃ	35	27	.40	.270
8 fl oz	242	1.3	10.7			3427	.04	1.6	tr		527	51	1.47	.400	

MEATS
BEEF

	KCAL	H₂O (g)	FAT (g)	PUFA (g)	CHOL (mg)	A (RE)	C (mg)	B-2 (mg)	B-6 (mg)	FOL (mcg)	Na (mg)	Ca (mg)	Mg (mg)	Zn (mg)	Mn (mg)
arm/blade, lean & marb, pot-roasted	218		11.2	0.6			0	.19			45	7	16		
2 slices	83	27.4	0.0		0.0	0	.08	3.6			320	158	4.10		
arm/blade, lean only, pot-roasted	90		3.1	0.2			0	.10			20	3	9		
2 slices	41	14.4	0.0		0.0	0	.04	1.8			169	80	2.20		
beef breakfast strips, ckd, Oscar	40	2.4	3.0	0.1	11		3	.02	.03		202	2	2	.56	
Mayerᵇ—*1 strip*	9	2.8	0.2	1.3			.01	0.6	.35		38	21	.29	.01	

ᵃ Low Na V-8 veg jce contains 47 mg Na; spicy hot V-8 veg jce contains 759 mg Na.

ᵇ Cured, chopped, formed beef w/added smoke flavoring

	KCAL	H₂O (g)	FAT (g)	PUFA (g)	CHOL (mg)	A (RE)	C (mg)	B-2 (mg)	B-6 (mg)	FOL (mcg)	Na (mg)	Ca (mg)	Mg (mg)	Zn (mg)	Mn (mg)
	WT (g)	PRO (g)	CHO (g)	SFA (g)	FIBR (g)	A (IU)	B-1 (mg)	NIA (mg)	B-12 (mcg)	PANT (mg)	K (mg)	P (mg)	Fe (mg)	Cu (mg)	
beef burgundy, frzn, Campbell's	150		6.0				3	.24			653	11			
5 oz	140	17.0	7.0			611	.04	0.3			280	140	2.40		
beef jerky	38		1.7					.08						4	
1 piece	10	4.2	1.4				.02	0.8					.60		
beef, sliced															
frzn, Swanson Hungry-Man	330		9.0								850				
12¼ oz	347	38.0	23.0												
w/bbq sce, frzn bb, Banquet	126		2.6				2	.11			885	17			
5 oz	142	13.5	12.5			2586	.04	2.5			199	126	2.70		
w/gravy, frzn, Banquet	196		10.5				tr	.18			1345	27			
8 oz	227	16.6	8.6			50	.09	4.4			286	202	2.88		
w/gravy, frzn bb, Banquet	116		4.3				tr	.11			852	14			
5 oz	142	14.6	4.8			68	.04	2.6			196	138	2.70		
w/gravy, frzn bb, Green Giant	130		3.1				8	.24			504	17			
5 oz	140	17.6	5.6			407	.03	2.7			284		1.68		
brisket, lean, marb & fat, ckd	411		37.4	1.9		0		.21			52	11	13		
3 slices	95	17.3	0.0		0.0	0	.04	3.7			285	123	2.60		
chipped	57		1.8	0.1		0		.09			1253	6			
2 slices	28	9.6	0.0		0.0	0	.02	1.1			56	113	1.40		
chipped	173		5.4	0.3		0		.27			3660	17			
3 oz	85	29.1	0.0		0.0	0	.06	3.2			170	343	4.3		
chipped, creamed	209		13.1	0.7	32	0		.26			1161	106			
½ cup	120	16.1	6.1		0.0	437	.06	1.6			184	232	2.10		
chipped, creamed, frzn bb, Banquet	124		4.1				tr	.09			949	85			
5 oz	142	11.2	10.5			72	.04	1.4			172	82	1.90		
chipped, creamed, frzn, Stouffer's	235		16.0								900				
5½ oz	156	12.0	10.0								290				
chipped, creamed, frzn, Swanson	350		24.0						.09		1401	298	21	4.59	
10½ oz	298	18.0	15.0						1.25				2.68	.27	
chuck, lean & fat, braised	327	49.4	23.9					.20			60	11	15		
3½ oz	100	26.0	0.0		0.0	40	.05	4.0			370	140	3.30		
chuck, separable lean, braised	214	59.7	9.5					.23			60	13	18		
3½ oz	100	30.0	0.0		0.0	20	.05	4.6			370	160	3.80		
chuck, ground, ckd	327		23.9					.20			60	11	15		
3½ oz	100	26.0	0.0		0.0	40	.05	4.0			370	140	3.30		
chuck stew meat, raw	476		40.7	2.0			0	.28			68	15			
4 oz	113	25.4	0.0		0.0	0	.11	5.8			563	190	3.70		
club steak, lean, marb & fat, ckd	260		17.5	0.9		0		.11			48	10	18		
1 steak	93	23.9	0.0		0.0	0	.09	5.7			370	151	3.60		
club steak, lean only, ckd	108		4.5	0.2		0		.05			27	4	11		
1 steak	55	16.0	0.0		0.0	0	.07	3.7			236	100	2.40		
corned beef, med fat, ckd	372		30.4			0		.18			1740	9	29		
3½ oz	100	22.9	0.0		0.0		.02	1.5			150	93	2.90		
corned beef, cnd	141		8.7				tr	.10			608	7	8		
2 oz	57	15.0	1.7		0.0	69	tr	1.4			74	70	1.45		
cubed steak, ckd	261		15.4	0.7		0		.22			60	12	21		
3½ oz	100	28.6	0.0		0.0	30	.08	5.6			370	250	3.50		
flank steak, lean & marb, ckd	331		14.4	0.7		0		.22			67	20	30		
1 steak	141	47.1	0.0		0.0	0	.07	3.9			344	299	7.10		
flank steak, lean only, ckd	158		5.2	0.3		0		.02			47	6	16		
1 steak	75	25.7	0.0		0.0	0	.04	3.8			281	176	3.90		
hamburger, med fat, ckd	224		14.5	0.7		0		.15			40	6	18		
1 patty	85	21.8	0.0		0.0	0	.13	4.8			382	187	3.30		
hamburger, lean, ckd	140		3.4	0.2		0		.11			41	14	22		
1 patty	86	25.9	0.0		0.0	0	.18	7.1			480	233	3.90		
hindshank, separable lean, ckd	176	63.4	4.8					.23			60	14	18		
3½ oz	100	31.0	0.0		0.0	10	.06	4.7			370	151	3.90		
meatballs, homemade	78		5.5			0		.04				11	6		
1 oz	28	5.0	1.9			14	.02	0.8				42	.60		
meatballs, frzn, Campbell's	70		5.0			0		.03			150	6			
1 oz	28	3.0	4.0			0	.01	0.8			46	46	.60		

Food	KCAL / WT (g)	H₂O (g) / PRO (g)	FAT (g) / CHO (g)	PUFA (g) / SFA (g)	CHOL (mg) / FIBR (g)	A (RE) / A (IU)	C (mg) / B-1 (mg)	B-2 (mg) / NIA (mg)	B-6 (mg) / B-12 (mcg)	FOL (mcg) / PANT (mg)	Na (mg) / K (mg)	Ca (mg) / P (mg)	Mg (mg) / Fe (mg)	Zn (mg) / Cu (mg)	Mn (mg)
meatloaf, homemade	160		7.6		92		2	.19			653	38			
3½ oz	100	17.0	4.6		0.1	179	.07	8.0			374	162	2.30		
meatloaf, frzn, Banquet	361		27.1				2	.09			1355	75			
8 oz	227	18.0	11.6			2968	.07	2.6			318	177	2.60		
meatloaf, frzn bb, Banquet	224		15.6				2	.06			951	37			
5 oz	142	7.2	13.6			1808	.04	1.4			196	109	1.50		
meatloaf, frzn, Campbell's	50		3.0				0	.05			167	6			
1 oz	28	3.0	3.0			0	.02	1.2			71	36	.60		
meatloaf w/beef gravy, frzn, Campbell's	230		13.0				0	.33			1049	48			
6½ oz	182	14.0	13.0			0	.07	5.5			259	155	3.00		
meatloaf w/texturized veg pro	285		15.9												
3½ oz	100	20.2	15.3												
neck, lean & marb, pot-roasted	325		16.9	0.8			0	.03			72	15	27		
2 slices	132	40.3	0.0		0.0	0	.06	5.1			396	230	6.10		
neck, lean only, pot-roasted	60		1.8	0.1			0	.09			19	3	7		
2 slices	30	10.3	0.0		0.0	0	.01	1.5			112	57	1.60		
porterhouse steak, lean & marb, broiled	242		14.7	0.7			0	.12			52	11	20		
1 steak	100	25.4	0.0		0.0	0	.10	6.1			398	183	3.80		
porterhouse steak, lean only, broiled	102		4.4	0.2			0	.04			26	4	12		
1 steak	54	14.7	0.0		0.0	0	.07	3.6			232	106	2.20		
rib roast, lean & marb, ckd	264		16.7	0.3			0	.22			57	8	24		
2 slices	106	28.4	0.0		0.0	0	.06	4.2			438	217	3.50		
rib roast, lean only, ckd	70		2.6	0.1			0	.09			17	4	9		
2 slices	41	11.0	0.0		0.0	0	.03	2.3			169	84	1.40		
rib steak, lean & marb, ckd	246		16.0	0.8			0	.20			50	7	22		
1 steak	94	24.0	0.0		0.0	0	.06	3.8			388	159	3.60		
rib steak, lean only, ckd	73		2.2	0.1			0	.10			23	4	12		
1 steak	43	12.3	0.0		0.0	0	.05	1.9			205	68	1.80		
ribeye steak, ckd	440		39.4				0	.15			60	9	20		
3½ oz	100	19.9	0.0		0.0	80	.05	3.6			370	186	2.60		
round, bottom, lean & marb, broiled	271		10.8	0.5			0	.38			51	14	28		
1 slice	114	40.5	0.0		0.0	0	.15	6.5			552	260	6.10		
round, bottom, lean only, broiled	205		8.2	0.4			0	.28			38	12	21		
1 slice	86	30.5	0.0		0.0	0	.11	4.9			437	196	4.60		
round, top, lean & marb, broiled	254		5.9	0.3			0	.34			46	9	28		
1 slice	111	43.1	0.0		0.0	0	.11	6.3			547	268	6.50		
round, top, lean only, broiled	173		4.2	0.2			0	.26			34	8	29		
1 slice	80	31.4	0.0		0.0	0	.09	4.5			369	193	4.70		
round heel, lean & marb, pot-roasted	261		11.4	0.6			0	.27			64	10	28		
1 slice	118	36.8	0.0		0.0	0	.12	5.1			455	204	5.50		
round heel, lean only	100		2.9	0.1			0	.13			26	5	13		
1 slice	53	17.4	0.0		0.0	0	.06	2.3			218	109	2.60		
round stew meat, raw	294		15.3	0.8			0	.28			68	15	24		
4 oz	113	36.7	0.0		0.0	0	.11	5.8			563	215	5.50		
rump, lean & marb, pot-roasted	188		8.7	0.4			0	.18			43	7	16		
2 slices	80	25.6	0.0		0.0	0	.08	3.4			309	158	3.80		
rump, lean only, pot-roasted	77		2.8	0.1			0	.09			18	3	8		
2 slices	37	12.0	0.0		0.0	0	.04	1.6			152	68	1.80		
salisbury steak															
frzn, Swanson Hungry-Man	640		39.0								1495				
12½ oz	354	31.0	40.0												
w/gravy, frzn, Banquet	364		27.3				tr	.18			1380	75			
8 oz	227	17.3	12.1			46	.11	3.0			246	209	2.43		
w/gravy, frzn bb, Banquet	246		18.5				tr	.10			941	38			
5 oz	142	12.1	7.8			65	.06	2.0			172	118	1.70		
w/gravy, frzn, Green Giant	270		16.3				10	.27			1004	22			
7 oz	196	17.1	13.7		0.4	559	.12	3.9			276		2.35		
w/gravy, frzn, Swanson	430		29.0						.14		1267	43	23	5.48	.028
10 oz	284	26.0	16.0						1.93		469	256	3.41	.48	
w/mushroom gravy, frzn, Campbell's—6½ oz	280		19.0				0	.20			892	18			
	182	20.0	8.0			0	.20	4.4			370	204	3.30		

	KCAL	H₂O (g)	FAT (g)	PUFA (g)	CHOL (mg)	A (RE)	C (mg)	B-2 (mg)	B-6 (mg)	FOL (mcg)	Na (mg)	Ca (mg)	Mg (mg)	Zn (mg)	Mn (mg)
	WT (g)	PRO (g)	CHO (g)	SFA (g)	FIBR (g)	A (IU)	B-1 (mg)	NIA (mg)	B-12 (mcg)	PANT (mg)	K (mg)	P (mg)	Fe (mg)	Cu (mg)	
w/onion gravy, frzn, Stouffer's	250		15.0								1150				
6 oz	170	20.0	5.0								340				
w/tomato sce, frzn bb, Green Giant	390		24.8				29	.24					75		
9 oz	252	20.8	21.1		0.8	1736	.13	4.8					2.94		
short plate, separable lean, simmered	199	61.1	7.7					.23			60	13	18		
3½ oz	100	30.3	0.0		0.0	10	.05	4.6			370	149	3.80		
short ribs, lean & marb, ckd	290		23.9	1.2			0	.15			39	5	14		
1 serving	72	17.6	0.0		0.0	0	.04	2.9			297	106	2.60		
short ribs, lean only, ckd	46		2.5	0.1			0	.04			9	1	4		
1 serving	17	5.5	0.0		0.0	0	.01	0.9			81	32	.80		
short ribs w/veg gravy, frzn, Stouffer's	350		25.0								560				
5¾ oz	163	29.0	2.0								345				
sirloin, lean & marb, broiled	260		13.8	0.7			0	.58			57	18	26		
1 slice	125	31.9	0.0		0.0	0	.13	4.1			545	282	4.80		
sirloin, lean only, broiled	128		4.4	0.2			0	.46			34	12	18		
1 slice	77	20.8	0.0		0.0	0	.09	2.2			349	178	3.10		
sirloin tip, lean & marb, roasted	141		5.1	0.3			0	.35			35	11	17		
1 slice	76	22.3	0.0		0.0	0	.08	2.5			331	179	3.50		
sirloin tip, lean only, roasted	74		1.8	0.1			0	.26			19	7	10		
1 slice	44	13.4	0.0		0.0	0	.05	1.3			199	108	2.00		
sirloin, ground, ckd	408		34.7				0	.18			60	10	21		
3½ oz	100	22.2	0.0		0.0	60	.06	4.6			370	186	2.90		
sloppy joe (beef & tomato sce), frzn bb, Banquet—*5 oz*	199		12.4				2	.10			903	41			
	142	10.5	11.2			301	.04	1.7			153	95	1.80		
sloppy joe (beef & tomato sce), frzn bb, Green Giant—*5 oz*	160		5.6				13	.14			1120	27			
	140	11.2	14.1			707	.07	2.7			372		1.54		
steak, chicken-fried	389		30.0					.14			815	11			
3½ oz	100	17.9	12.3			26	.11	2.7			126	110	2.30		
steak, teriyaki, ckd	453		40.3				0	.16			85	9			
3½ oz	100	20.4	0.2		0.0	70	.06	4.3			371	175	2.60		
T-bone, lean & marb, broiled	235		14.7	0.7			0	.11			49	10	19		
1 steak	95	24.0	0.0		0.0	0	.10	5.8			378	172	3.60		
T-bone, lean only, broiled	116		5.4	0.3			0	.05			29	4	12		
1 steak	59	15.6	0.0		0.0	0	.08	4.0			253	105	2.30		
tenderloin, lean & marb, broiled	148		8.3	0.4			0	.30			30	10	15		
1 steak	66	17.2	0.0		0.0	0	.07	2.2			288	137	2.60		
tenderloin, lean only, broiled	107		4.6	0.2			0	.31			23	8	12		
1 steak	52	15.2	0.0		0.0	0	.06	1.5			236	112	2.30		

LAMB

	KCAL	H₂O (g)	FAT (g)	PUFA (g)	CHOL (mg)	A (RE)	C (mg)	B-2 (mg)	B-6 (mg)	FOL (mcg)	Na (mg)	Ca (mg)	Mg (mg)	Zn (mg)	Mn (mg)
	WT (g)	PRO (g)	CHO (g)	SFA (g)	FIBR (g)	A (IU)	B-1 (mg)	NIA (mg)	B-12 (mcg)	PANT (mg)	K (mg)	P (mg)	Fe (mg)	Cu (mg)	
arm chop, lean, marb & fat, ckd	339		27.0	1.1	70		0	.26			66	7	2		
3½ oz	100	22.4	0.0		0.0	0	.16	6.3			388	210	2.20		
arm chop, lean & marb, ckd	144		8.9	0.4			0	.17			43	4	14		
1 chop	57	14.6	0.0		0.0	0	.10	4.1			252	135	1.30		
arm chop, lean & marb, ckd	287		17.9	0.7			0	.34			87	9	28		
2 chops	114	29.3	0.0		0.0	0	.22	8.3			509	269	3.40		
arm chop, lean only, ckd	110		4.4	0.2			0	.19			49	5	16		
2 chops	59	16.5	0.0		0.0	0	.12	4.7			286	151	1.80		
blade chop, lean, marb & fat, ckd	340		26.1	1.0	70		0	.28			70	7	22		
3½ oz	100	24.6	0.0		0.0	0	.17	6.7			412	227	3.00		
blade chop, lean & marb, ckd	260		16.8	0.7			0	.28			72	11	22		
1 chop	93	25.4	0.0		0.0	0	.18	6.9			422	226	2.80		
blade chop, lean only, ckd	128		6.4	0.3			0	.18			46	5	14		
1 chop	56	16.3	0.0		0.0	0	.11	4.4			272	149	1.70		
leg, lean, marb & fat, roasted	242		14.5	0.6	70		0	.22			61	6	22		
3½ oz	100	20.6	0.0		0.0	0	.16	5.3			369	199	3.10		
leg, lean & marb, roasted	96		4.1	0.2			0	.14			41	4	10		
1 slice	49	13.8	0.0		0.0	0	.11	3.5			246	105	1.50		
leg, lean & marb, roasted	192		8.2	0.3			0	.29			82	8	24		
2 slices	98	27.6	0.0		0.0	0	.22	7.0			492	210	3.00		
leg, lean only, roasted	107		3.5	0.1			0	.18			52	5	14		
2 slices	61	17.6	0.0		0.0	0	.14	4.5			312	134	1.90		

	KCAL / WT (g)	H₂O (g) / PRO (g)	FAT (g) / CHO (g)	PUFA (g) / SFA (g)	CHOL (mg) / FIBR (g)	A (RE) / A (IU)	C (mg) / B-1 (mg)	B-2 (mg) / NIA (mg)	B-6 (mg) / B-12 (mcg)	FOL (mcg) / PANT (mg)	Na (mg) / K (mg)	Ca (mg) / P (mg)	Mg (mg) / Fe (mg)	Zn (mg) / Cu (mg)	Mn (mg)
loin chop, lean, marb & fat, ckd	302		22.5	0.9	70		0	.27			49	10	20		
3½ oz	100	23.0	0.0		0.0	0	.17	6.5			466	193	3.00		
loin chop, lean & marb, ckd	103		5.5	0.2			0	.14			37	4	11		
1 chop	46	12.5	0.0		0.0	0	.09	3.6			218	98	1.40		
loin chop, lean & marb, ckd	205		10.9	0.4				.29			75	7	22		
2 chops	92	24.9	0.0		0.0	0	.18	7.1			437	197	2.80		
loin chop, lean only, ckd	130		5.2	0.2			0	.23			58	6	15		
2 chops	70	19.6	0.0		0.0	0	.14	5.5			340	160	2.20		
rib chop, lean, marb & fat, ckd	423		37.2	1.5	70		0	.33			83	8	17		
3½ oz	100	20.3	0.0		0.0	0	.21	7.9			485	182	3.00		
rib chop, lean & marb, ckd	119		8.3	0.3			0	.13			34	3	8		
1 chop	41	10.5	0.0		0.0	0	.08	3.2			199	90	1.20		
rib chop, lean & marb, ckd	238		16.6	0.7			0	.27			68	6	16		
2 chops	82	21.0	0.0		0.0	0	.17	6.4			398	180	2.40		
rib chop, lean only, ckd	102		4.3	0.2			0	.17			43	4	11		
2 chops	52	14.9	0.0		0.0	0	.10	4.1			252	125	1.60		

PORK

bacon

	KCAL / WT (g)	H₂O (g) / PRO (g)	FAT (g) / CHO (g)	PUFA (g) / SFA (g)	CHOL (mg) / FIBR (g)	A (RE) / A (IU)	C (mg) / B-1 (mg)	B-2 (mg) / NIA (mg)	B-6 (mg) / B-12 (mcg)	FOL (mcg) / PANT (mg)	Na (mg) / K (mg)	Ca (mg) / P (mg)	Mg (mg) / Fe (mg)	Zn (mg) / Cu (mg)	Mn (mg)
bits (real bacon), Oscar Mayer	20	2.7	1.0	0.2	6		1	.03	.02		189	1	2.0	.36	
¼ oz	7	2.4	0.2	0.3			.04	0.6	.16		37	39	.15	.01	
canadian, broiled/fried	65		4.2	0.6	19		0	.03			442	4	5		
1 slice	21	6.2	3.0		0.0	0	.18	1.1			91	59	.90		
cured, raw	156		16.2	2.4			0	.05			71	1	2		
1 slice	28	2.3	0.2		0.0	0	.17	0.9			16	22	.20		
cured, broiled/fried crisp	35	0.8	3.1	0.5	5		2	.02	.02		114	tr	1	.18	
1 slice	6	1.6	0.1	1.1	0.0	0	.04	0.4	.09		24	22	.11	.01	
cured, broiled/fried crisp	105	2.4	9.3	1.5	15		6	.06	.06		342	12	3	.54	
3 slices	18	4.8	0.3	3.3	0.0	0	.12	1.2	.27		72	66	.33	.03	
cured, cnd, ckd	193		20.3	3.1			0	.03			304	4	7		
1 oz	28	2.4	0.2		0.0	0	.07	0.4			67	26	.39		
fresh, fat class, raw	177	7.4	18.6		20		0	.02			20	1			
1 oz	28	2.0	0.0		0.0	0	.10	0.5			80	17	.30		
fresh, med fat class, raw	165	8.5	14.3	1.6	20		0	.03			20	1			
1 oz	28	2.3	0.0		0.0	0	.11	0.6			80	21	.30		
fresh, thin class, raw	153	9.6	15.7		20		0	.03			20	1			
1 oz	28	2.6	0.0		0.0	0	.13	0.7			80	26	.40		
blade, lean, marb & fat, ckd	366		28.8	4.9			0	.22			50	5	20		
3½ oz	100	24.9	0.0		0.0	0	.46	3.7			352	199	3.70		
blade, lean & marb, ckd	150		9.2	1.6			0	.17			39	4	13		
1 slice	54	15.7	0.0		0.0	0	.36	2.9			275	123	2.40		
blade, lean & marb, ckd	299		18.4	3.1			0	.34			78	8	26		
2 slices	108	31.3	0.0		0.0	0	.73	5.7			551	245	4.70		
blade, lean only, ckd	134		5.9	1.0			0	.19			44	5	15		
2 slices	61	18.8	0.0		0.0	0	.41	3.2			311	159	2.80		
boston butt, lean, marb & fat, ckd	348		28.0	4.8			0	.16			37	4	21		
3½ oz	100	22.5	0.0		0.0	0	.34	2.7			260	210	3.40		
boston butt, lean & marb, roasted	164		11.2	1.9			0	.18			42	4	13		
1 slice	58	14.7	0.0		0.0	0	.39	3.1			296	131	2.20		
boston butt, lean & marb, roasted	328		22.4	3.8			0	.37			83	8	25		
2 slices	116	29.5	0.0		0.0	0	.78	6.1			592	261	4.40		
boston butt, lean only, roasted	82		3.5	0.6			0	.13			29	3	10		
2 slices	41	11.8	0.0		0.0	0	.27	2.2			209	102	1.80		
ham, fresh, lean, marb & fat, ckd	306		18.3	3.1			0	.27			61	6	26		
3½ oz	100	32.9	0.0		0.0	0	.57	4.5			434	263	2.30		
ham, fresh, lean & marb, ckd	126		4.7	0.8			0	.16			37	4	15		
1 slice	53	19.6	0.0		0.0	0	.34	2.7			260	146	1.20		
ham, fresh, lean & marb, ckd	254		9.4	1.6			0	.32			73	7	30		
2 slices	107	39.6	0.0		0.0	0	.69	5.4			520	295	2.50		

	KCAL	H₂O (g)	FAT (g)	PUFA (g)	CHOL (mg)	A (RE)	C (mg)	B-2 (mg)	B-6 (mg)	FOL (mcg)	Na (mg)	Ca (mg)	Mg (mg)	Zn (mg)	Mn (mg)
	WT (g)	PRO (g)	CHO (g)	SFA (g)	FIBR (g)	A (IU)	B-1 (mg)	NIA (mg)	B-12 (mcg)	PANT (mg)	K (mg)	P (mg)	Fe (mg)	Cu (mg)	
ham, fresh, lean only, ckd	167		4.8	0.8			0	.24			54	5	21		
2 slices	75	29.0	0.0		0.0	0	.51	4.0			382	202	1.70		
ham, cured butt, lean, marb & fat, ckd	348		28.0	4.8			0	.22			718	5	21		
3½ oz	100	22.5	0.3		0.0	0	.70	3.6			332	210	2.50		
ham, cured butt, lean & marb, ckd	123		6.5	1.1			0	.14			518	5	13		
1 slice	60	15.1	0.2		0.0	0	.46	2.5			239	123	1.50		
ham, cured butt, lean & marb, ckd	246		13.0	2.2				.28			1036	10	26		
2 slices	120	30.2	0.4		0.0	0	.93	5.0			478	246	3.00		
ham, cured butt, lean only, ckd	102		2.9	0.5				.18			589	4	14		
2 slices	64	17.7	0.2		0.0	0	.57	2.9			272	140	1.60		
ham, cured shank, lean, marb & fat, ckd—3½ oz	371		31.4	5.3				.21			672	5	16		
	100	20.4	0.3		0.0	0	.65	3.4			310	157	2.50		
ham, cured shank, lean & marb, ckd	91		5.4	0.9				.09			336	3	8		
1 slice	39	10.0	0.1		0.0	0	.30	.16			155	73	1.00		
ham, cured shank, lean & marb, ckd	185		10.9	1.9				.19			682	6	15		
2 slices	79	20.2	0.2		0.0	0	.61	3.2			314	147	2.00		
ham, cured shank, lean only, ckd	76		2.7	0.5				.12			396	3	9		
2 slices	43	12.1	0.1		0.0	0	.38	2.0			183	89	1.10		
ham, cured, cnd	142		8.5	1.4			23	.21			837	4	13		
3 oz	85	15.7	0.4		0.0		.66	3.9			281	139	.51		
ham, cured, cnd, chopped	257		20.5					.17			1020	10			
3½ oz	100	16.1	2.0				.62	3.4			236	145	.90		
ham, sectioned & formed, cnd	110	74.0	4.0	0.4	41		28	.23	.41		1219	tr	18	1.92	
3½ oz	100	18.0	0.3	1.6			.82	5.5	.85		354	245	1.05	.11	
ham, sectioned & formed, smoked, cnd	115	72.0	4.0	0.4	49		31	.22	.43		1333	tr	19	1.98	
3½ oz	100	20.0	0.0	1.5			.89	4.8	.78		335	260	.95	.09	
ham, smoked, ckd	175	66.0	11.0	1.4	58		28	.25	.32		1377	tr	17	2.02	
3½ oz	100	18.0	0.8	4.1			.83	5.2	1.00		343	257	.87	.12	
hamloaf, glazed	247		14.7		81	1		.18			326	49			
3½ oz	100	13.3	14.3		tr	153	.27	4.0			262	148	2.10		
ham steaks, sectioned & formed	120	72.0	5.0	0.4			33	.21	.38		1300	tr	19	1.98	
3½ oz	100	19.0	0.0	1.4			.81	5.1	.80		332	256	1.02	tr	
loin chop, lean & fat, ckd	357		25.6	4.4			0	.19			60	12	22		
3½ oz	100	29.4	0.0		0.0	0	1.18	5.5			568	229	4.40		
loin chop, lean & fat, ckd	314		22.5	3.8			0	.16			52	10	19		
1 chop	88	25.9	0.0		0.0	0	1.03	4.8			500	202	3.90		
loin chop, lean only, ckd	170		7.7	1.3			0	.12			41	8	17		
1 chop	68	23.5	0.0		0.0	0	.80	3.7			386	179	3.50		
picnic, fresh, separable lean, simmered	150		7.4				0	.23			70	11	22		
3½ oz	100	19.4	0.0		0.0	0	.94	5.0			285	225	2.90		
picnic, cured, separable lean, roasted	211		9.9	1.0				.26			930	13			
3½ oz	100	28.4	0.0		0.0	0	.65	5.0			326	220	3.70		
picnic shoulder, lean, marb & fat, ckd	312		23.5	4.0			0	.13			30	3	20		
3½ oz	100	23.3	0.0		0.0	0	.28	2.2			214	197	3.50		
picnic shoulder, lean & marb, roasted	116		7.0	1.2			0	.15			34	3	10		
1 slice	47	12.2	0.0		0.0	0	.31	2.5			240	102	1.80		
picnic shoulder, lean & marb, roasted	234		14.3	2.4			0	.30			68	7	21		
2 slices	95	24.6	0.0		0.0	0	.64	5.0			485	207	3.70		
picnic shoulder, lean only, roasted	81		2.7	0.5			0	.14			32	3	11		
2 slices	45	13.1	0.0		0.0	0	.30	2.4			229	108	2.00		
pig's feet, pickled	56		4.1												
1 oz	28	4.7	0.0		0.0										
pork & gravy, cnd	256	56.9	17.8					.17				13			
3½ oz	100	16.4	6.3		0.0	0	.49	3.5				183	2.40		
pork, sweet & sour, homemade	386		21.7				10	.24			856	25			
1 serving	200	19.1	28.7		0.5	49	.71	8.8			400	209	2.90		
sausage															
pork, brown & serve, browned	118		10.6												
1 oz	28	4.6	0.8		0.0										
pork, cnd	299		25.9				0	.24			740	9	16		
2 patties	100	15.4	0.0		0.0	0	.20	3.0			140	166	2.30		

	KCAL / WT (g)	H₂O (g) / PRO (g)	FAT (g) / CHO (g)	PUFA (g) / SFA (g)	CHOL (mg) / FIBR (g)	A (RE) / A (IU)	C (mg) / B-1 (mg)	B-2 (mg) / NIA (mg)	B-6 (mg) / B-12 (mcg)	FOL (mcg) / PANT (mg)	Na (mg) / K (mg)	Ca (mg) / P (mg)	Mg (mg) / Fe (mg)	Zn (mg) / Cu (mg)	Mn (mg)
pork, fresh, ckd	48	5.8	4.1	0.5	11		0	.03	.04		168	4	2	.30	.009
1 link	13	2.6	0.1	1.4	0.0		.10	0.6	.22	.09	47	24	.20	.02	
pork, fresh, ckd	100	12.0	8.4	1.0	22		0	.07	.09		349	9	5	.68	.019
1 patty	27	5.3	0.3	2.9	0.0		.20	1.2	.47	.20	97	50	.34	.04	
pork & beef, fresh, ckd	52	5.8	4.7	0.5				.02	.01		105		1	.24	
1 link	13	1.8	0.4	1.7	0.0		.05	0.4	.06	.06		14	.15	.00	
shoulder butt, cured, lean, marb & fat, ckd—*3½ oz*	385		33.4	5.7				.19			699	6	19		
	100	19.6	0.0		0.0	0	.63	3.3			322	168	3.00		
shoulder butt, cured, lean & marb, roasted—*1 slice*	238		18.4	3.1				.18			647	6	15		
	75	17.0	0.0		0.0	0	.58	3.1			298	142	2.60		
shoulder butt, cured, lean & marb, roasted—*2 slices*	477		36.8	6.3				.36			1294	12	30		
	150	33.9	0.0		0.0	0	1.17	6.2			597	285	5.20		
shoulder butt, cured, lean only, roasted	109		5.1	0.9				.16			507	4	12		
2 slices	55	14.7	0.0		0.0	0	.49	2.5			234	115	2.20		
sirloin, lean & marb, roasted	297		20.0	3.4				.19			32	3	25		
3½ oz	100	27.3	0.0		0.0	0	.73	2.6			295	244	4.20		
sirloin, lean & marb, roasted	161		7.8	1.3				.24			39	4	17		
3 slices	71	21.3	0.0		0.0	0	.90	3.3			361	186	3.20		
sirloin, lean only, roasted	91		3.3	0.6				.15			25	2	11		
3 slices	46	14.3	0.0		0.0	0	.58	2.1			234	123	2.20		
spareribs, roasted	198	88.2	17.5				0	.09				4			
3 med ribs	45	9.4	0.0		0.0	0	.19	1.5				54	1.17		
spareribs, roasted	396	176.4	35.0				0	.18				8			
6 med ribs	90	18.8	0.0		0.0	0	.38	3.0				108	2.34		
tenderloin, lean only, roasted	239		12.1	2.1				.34			55	5	26		
3½ oz	100	30.6	0.0		0.0	0	1.27	4.6			509	301	4.70		

VEAL

	KCAL / WT (g)	H₂O (g) / PRO (g)	FAT (g) / CHO (g)	PUFA (g) / SFA (g)	CHOL (mg) / FIBR (g)	A (RE) / A (IU)	C (mg) / B-1 (mg)	B-2 (mg) / NIA (mg)	B-6 (mg) / B-12 (mcg)	FOL (mcg) / PANT (mg)	Na (mg) / K (mg)	Ca (mg) / P (mg)	Mg (mg) / Fe (mg)	Zn (mg) / Cu (mg)	Mn (mg)
arm steak, lean & fat, ckd	298		19.0	0.6	90		0	.31			51	10	20		
3½ oz	100	29.6	0.0		0.0	0	.12	6.1			503	242	3.80		
arm steak, lean only, ckd	180		4.8	0.2			0	.27			46	8	20		
1 steak	90	32.0	0.0		0.0	0	.10	5.4			452	252	4.00		
blade, lean & fat, ckd	276		16.6	0.5	90		0	.33			55	11	22		
3½ oz	100	29.7	0.0		0.0	0	.13	6.5			539	244	3.80		
blade, lean only, ckd	228		8.4	0.2			0	.35			60	12	26		
1 steak	108	36.0	0.0		0.0	0	.14	7.0			582	290	4.60		
breast, stew meat, raw	346		25.2	0.8	90		0	.18			87	11	19		
3½ oz	100	27.9	0.0		0.0	0	.11	7.2			491	233	3.50		
breast, stewed w/gravy	256		18.6	0.6			0	.13			64	8	14		
4 pieces	74	20.6	0.0		0.0	0	.08	5.3			363	172	2.60		
chuck, med fat, braised	235	58.5	12.8		90		0	.29			80	121			
3½ oz	100	27.9	0.0		0.0	0	.09	6.4			500	151	3.50		
cutlet, round, lean & fat, ckd	277		15.0	0.4	90		0	.32			54	10	23		
3½ oz	100	33.2	0.0		0.0	0	.12	6.4			527	288	4.20		
cutlet, round, lean only, ckd	194		12.8	0.4			0	.27			46	9	20		
1 cutlet	70	23.2	0.0		0.0	0	.10	5.4			448	245	3.60		
cutlet, breaded, ckd	319		15.0	0.4			0	.32			54	0	23		
3½ oz	100	34.2	10.5		0.0	0	.12	6.4			527	288	4.20		
flank, med fat, stewed	390	43.8	32.3		90		0	.22			80	11			
3½ oz	100	23.2	0.0		0.0	0	.05	4.2			500	117	3.00		
foreshank, med fat, stewed	216	60.1	10.4		90		0	.26			80	12			
3½ oz	100	28.7	0.0		0.0	0	.05	5.0			500	154	3.60		
loin, med fat, broiled	234	58.9	13.4		90		0	.25			80	11			
3½ oz	100	26.4	0.0		0.0	0	.07	5.4			500	225	3.20		
loin chop, lean & fat, ckd	421		35.9	1.1	90		0	.21			44	6	16		
3½ oz	100	22.7	0.0		0.0	0	.14	4.7			314	187	2.90		
loin chop, lean & fat, ckd	514		43.8				0	.26			54	7	20		
1 chop	122	27.6	0.0		0.0	0	.17	5.8			384	228	3.50		
loin chop, lean only, ckd	149		4.8				0	.23			47	6	15		
1 chop	72	24.6	0.0		0.0	0	.15	5.1			342	188	3.10		
plate, med fat, stewed	303	52.1	21.2		90		0	.24			80	12			
3½ oz	100	26.1	0.0		0.0	0	.05	4.6			500	138	3.30		

	KCAL	H₂O (g)	FAT (g)	PUFA (g)	CHOL (mg)	A (RE)	C (mg)	B-2 (mg)	B-6 (mg)	FOL (mcg)	Na (mg)	Ca (mg)	Mg (mg)	Zn (mg)	Mn (mg)
	WT (g)	PRO (g)	CHO (g)	SFA (g)	FIBR (g)	A (IU)	B-1 (mg)	NIA (mg)	B-12 (mcg)	PANT (mg)	K (mg)	P (mg)	Fe (mg)	Cu (mg)	
rib, med fat, roasted	269	54.6	16.9		90		0	.31			80	12	20		
3½ oz	100	27.2	0.0		0.0	0	.13	7.8			500	248	3.40		
rib chop, lean & fat, ckd	318		22.2		90		0	.26			49	10	17		
3½ oz	100	27.6	0.0		0.0	0	.17	5.8			466	192	3.50		
rib chop, lean & fat, ckd	264		18.4		90		0	.22			41	8	14		
1 chop	83	22.9	0.0		0.0	0	.14	4.8			387	159	2.90		
rib chop, lean only, ckd	125		4.6				0	.19			35	7	11		
1 chop	58	19.5	0.0		0.0	0	.12	4.1			329	132	2.50		
round w/rump, med fat, broiled	216	60.4	11.1				0	.25			80	11			
3½ oz	100	27.1	0.0		0.0	0	.07	5.4			500	231	3.20		
rump, lean, marb & fat, ckd	232		12.3				0	.18			68	8	19		
3½ oz	100	28.3	0.0		0.0	0	.15	7.5			468	230	3.60		
rump, lean & marb, roasted	169		4.8				0	.20			73	8	20		
2 slices	97	29.5	0.0		0.0	0	.15	7.9			492	240	3.70		
rump, lean only, roasted	78		1.1				0	.22			66	8	11		
2 slices	50	15.9	0.0		0.0	0	.19	8.9			521	132	2.00		
sirloin, lean, marb & fat, ckd	274		19.1				0	.21			53	8	19		
3½ oz	100	23.9	0.0		0.0	0	.15	7.1			476	221	3.00		
sirloin, lean & marb, roasted	172		6.2				0	.24				8	22		
2 slices	98	27.4	0.0		0.0	0	.17	8.2				246	3.50		
sirloin, lean only, roasted	90		1.9				0	.15			38	5	13		
2 slices	59	17.1	0.0		0.0	0	.11	5.1			342	152	2.20		
sirloin steak, lean & fat, ckd	266		17.4				0	.23			39	8	15		
½ steak	88	25.3	0.0		0.0	0	.09	4.7			384	199	3.20		
sirloin steak, lean only, ckd	139		4.1				0	.25			42	8	14		
½ steak	68	23.7	0.0		0.0	0	.10	5.0			412	180	3.00		
stew meat, marb, raw	346		25.2				0	.18			87	11	19		
3½ oz	100	27.9	0.0		0.0	0	.11	7.2			491	233	3.50		
veal parmagian, frzn bb, Banquet	287		16.2				2	.17			1014	136			
5 oz	142	15.9	19.5			2366	.11	2.8			197	168	1.60		
veal parmigiana, frzn, Campbell's	295		14.0				8	.38			1825	99			
7½ oz	210	25.0	17.0			618	.30	6.9			468	289	2.40		
veal parmigiana, frzn, Green Giant	306		16.7				31	.14			1266	235			
7 oz	196	21.0	18.0		0.6	739	.14	3.3			543		1.18		

ORGAN MEATS

	KCAL	H₂O (g)	FAT (g)	PUFA (g)	CHOL (mg)	A (RE)	C (mg)	B-2 (mg)	B-6 (mg)	FOL (mcg)	Na (mg)	Ca (mg)	Mg (mg)	Zn (mg)	Mn (mg)
	WT (g)	PRO (g)	CHO (g)	SFA (g)	FIBR (g)	A (IU)	B-1 (mg)	NIA (mg)	B-12 (mcg)	PANT (mg)	K (mg)	P (mg)	Fe (mg)	Cu (mg)	
brains, all kinds, raw	106	67.1	7.3		1785		15	.22			106	9	11		
3 oz	85	8.8	0.7		0.0	0	.20	3.7			186	265	2.00		
heart															
beef, lean, braised	188	61.3	5.7	1.1	274		1	1.22			104	6	18		
3½ oz	100	31.3	0.7		0.0	30	.25	7.6			232	181	5.90		
beef, lean w/fat, braised	372	44.4	29.0		150						102		35		
3½ oz	100	25.8	0.1		0.0						329	169			
calf, braised	208	60.3	9.1		180	40	1	1.44			113	4	35		
3½ oz	100	27.8	1.8		0.0		.29	8.1			250	148	4.40		
hog, braised	195	61.0	6.9	1.5	150		1	1.89			65	4			
3½ oz	100	30.8	0.3		0.0	40	.64	6.7			128	121	4.90		
lamb, braised	260	54.1	14.4		150		1	1.62			102	14	35		
3½ oz	100	29.5	1.0		0.0	100	.93	6.4			329	231			
kidneys															
beef, braised	252	53.0	12.0		375		0	4.58			253	18	18		
3½ oz	100	33.0	0.8		0.0	1150	.67	10.7			324	244	13.10		
calf, raw	113	77.4	4.6		375		6	2.40			238	9	10		
3½ oz	100	16.6	0.1		0.0	1200	.26	7.4			240	171	4.00		
hog, raw	106	77.8	3.6	0.5	375		12	1.73			115	11	17		
3½ oz	100	16.3	1.1		0.0	130	.58	9.8			178	218	6.70		
lamb, raw	105	77.7	3.3		375		15	2.42			200	13	16		
3½ oz	100	16.8	0.9		0.0	690	.51	7.4			230	218	7.60		

	KCAL / WT (g)	H₂O (g) / PRO (g)	FAT (g) / CHO (g)	PUFA (g) / SFA (g)	CHOL (mg) / FIBR (g)	A (RE) / A (IU)	C (mg) / B-1 (mg)	B-2 (mg) / NIA (mg)	B-6 (mg) / B-12 (mcg)	FOL (mcg) / PANT (mg)	Na (mg) / K (mg)	Ca (mg) / P (mg)	Mg (mg) / Fe (mg)	Zn (mg) / Cu (mg)	Mn (mg)
liver															
beef, raw	140	69.7	3.8	0.6			31	3.26			136	8	8		
3½ oz	100	19.9	5.3		0.0	43900	.25	13.6			281	352	6.50		
beef, fried	229	56.0	10.6				27	4.19			184	11			
3½ oz	100	26.4	5.3		0.0	53400	.26	16.5			380	476	8.80		
calf, raw	140	70.7	4.7	0.1	300		36	2.72			73	8	16		
3½ oz	100	19.0	4.0		0.0	22500	.20	11.4			281	333	8.80		
calf, fried	261	51.4	13.2	0.3	438		37	4.17			118	13	26		
3½ oz	100	29.5	4.0		0.0	32700	.24	16.5			453	537	14.20		
hog, raw	131	71.6	3.7	0.6	300		23	3.02			73	10	16		
3½ oz	100	20.6	2.6		0.0	10900	.30	16.4			261	356	19.20		
hog, fried	241	54.0	11.5	1.8	438		22	4.36			111	15	24		
3½ oz	100	29.9	2.5		0.0	14900	.34	22.3			395	539	29.1		
lamb, raw	136	70.8	3.9				33	3.28			52	10			
3½ oz	100	21.0	2.9		0.0	50500	.40	16.9			202	349	10.90		
lamb, broiled	261	50.4	12.4	0.3	438		36	5.11			85	16	23		
3½ oz	100	32.3	2.8		0.0	74500	.49	24.9			331	572	17.90		
lungs															
beef, raw	96	78.8	2.3												
3½ oz	100	17.6	0.0		0.0			6.2				216			
calf, raw	106	77.4	3.8												
3½ oz	100	16.8	0.0		0.0										
lamb, raw	103	76.7	2.3												
3½ oz	100	19.3	0.0		0.0							180			
pancreas															
beef, med fat, raw	283	60.0	25.0					.55			67	9	17		
3½ oz	100	13.5	0.0		0.0			5.8			276	270	1.20		
beef, lean only, raw	141	73.0	7.3								67	8			
3½ oz	100	17.6	0.0		0.0						276	330	2.80		
calf, raw	161	69.7	8.8												
3½ oz	100	19.2	0.0		0.0							326			
hog, raw	242	63.4	19.9								44	11	17		
3½ oz	100	14.7	0.0		0.0						217	282	1.00		
spleen															
beef & calf, raw	104	76.9	3.0					.37							
3½ oz	100	18.1	0.0		0.0			8.2				272	10.60		
hog, raw	107	77.4	3.8												
3½ oz	100	17.1	0.0		0.0							298	29.40		
lamb, raw	115	74.4	3.9												
3½ oz	100	18.8	0.0		0.0										
stomach, pork, scalded	152	74.0	9.0												
3½ oz	100	16.5	0.0		0.0							118			
sweetbread (thymus)															
beef (yearling), braised	320	49.6	23.2				44	.40			116				
3½ oz	100	25.9	0.0		0.0		.04	3.1			433	364			
calf, braised	168	62.7	3.2		466		44	.27			98				
3½ oz	100	32.6	0.0		0.0	17	.09	2.9			360	400	1.20		
lamb, braised	175	64.6	6.1		466		44	.40			96				
3½ oz	100	28.1	0.0		0.0	17	.04	3.1			360	204			
tongue															
beef, lamb, etc, cnd/pickled	75	15.8	5.7												
1 oz	28	5.4	tr		0.0										
beef, lamb, etc, potted/deviled	81	14.8	6.4					.03							
1 oz	28	5.2	0.2		0.0		.01	0.4							
beef, med fat, braised	244	60.8	16.7	0.7	140		0	.29			61	7	16		
3½ oz	100	21.5	0.4		0.0	0	.05	3.5			164	117	2.20		

	KCAL	H₂O (g)	FAT (g)	PUFA (g)	CHOL (mg)	A (RE)	C (mg)	B-2 (mg)	B-6 (mg)	FOL (mcg)	Na (mg)	Ca (mg)	Mg (mg)	Zn (mg)	Mn (mg)
	WT (g)	PRO (g)	CHO (g)	SFA (g)	FIBR (g)	A (IU)	B-1 (mg)	NIA (mg)	B-12 (mcg)	PANT (mg)	K (mg)	P (mg)	Fe (mg)	Cu (mg)	
beef, smoked	330	48.9	28.8		210			.21							
3½ oz	100	17.2	0.4		0.0		.04	3.0							
calf, braised	160	68.5	6.0												
3½ oz	100	23.9	1.0		0.0										
hog, braised	247	59.4	17.4	2.3				.29				26			
3½ oz	100	22.0	0.5		0.0		.07	3.50				119	1.40		
lamb, braised	254	60.2	18.2												
3½ oz	100	20.5	0.5		0.0							102			
sheep, braised	323	51.6	25.3												
3½ oz	100	19.8	2.4		0.0								3.40		
tripe, beef, raw	100	79.1	2.0				0	.15			72	127			
3½ oz	100	19.1	0.0		0.0	0		1.6			9	86	1.60		
tripe, beef, pickled	17	24.2	0.4								13				
1 oz	28	3.3	0.0		0.0						5				

OTHER MEATS

	KCAL	H₂O (g)	FAT (g)	PUFA (g)	CHOL (mg)	A (RE)	C (mg)	B-2 (mg)	B-6 (mg)	FOL (mcg)	Na (mg)	Ca (mg)	Mg (mg)	Zn (mg)	Mn (mg)
	WT (g)	PRO (g)	CHO (g)	SFA (g)	FIBR (g)	A (IU)	B-1 (mg)	NIA (mg)	B-12 (mcg)	PANT (mg)	K (mg)	P (mg)	Fe (mg)	Cu (mg)	
alligator, raw	232		4.2				0	.30			1231				
3½ oz	100	45.6	0.0		0.0	45	.10	6.3				767	11.40		
armadillo, raw	172		5.4				0	.40			30				
3½ oz	100	29.0	0.0		0.0	0	.10	6.0				208	10.90		
beaver, roasted	248	56.2	13.7					.38							
3½ oz	100	29.2	0.0		0.0		.08								
frog legs, raw	73	81.9	0.3		50			.25			55	18	147		
4 large	100	16.4	0.0		0.0	0	.14	1.2			308	147	1.50		
frog legs, flour coated & fried	418		28.6					.35				28			
6 large	144	25.8	12.2		0.0	0	.17	1.8				231	2.00		
goat, raw	165		9.4				0	.32				11			
3½ oz	100	18.7	0.0			0	.17	5.6					2.20		
guinea pig, raw	96		1.6					.14				29			
3½ oz	100	19.0	0.0				.06	6.5				253	1.90		
hare, raw	135	73.0	5.0					.19				12			
3½ oz	100	21.0	0.0		0.0		.09	5.0				157	3.20		
horse, raw	118		4.1	1.2				.12				10			
3½ oz	100	18.1	0.9		0.0		.07	4.3				150	2.70		
muskrat, roasted	153	67.3	4.1					.21							
3½ oz	100	27.2	0.0		0.0		.16								
opossum, roasted	221	57.3	10.2					.38							
3½ oz	100	30.2	0.0		0.0		.12								
rabbit, baked	177		5.0				0	.15							
3½ oz	100	30.9	0.0				.11	7.0							
rabbit, stewed	216	59.8	10.1		65		0	.07			41	21			
3½ oz	100	29.3	0.0		0.0		.05	11.3			368	259	1.50		
raccoon, roasted	255	54.8	14.5				0	.52							
3½ oz	100	29.2	0.0		0.0		.59								
reindeer, forequarter, raw	178	67.4	9.4												
3½ oz	100	21.8	0.0		0.0										
reindeer, hindquarter, raw	256	59.6	19.2												
3½ oz	100	19.4	0.0		0.0										
reindeer, side, raw	217	63.3	14.4												
3½ oz	100	20.5	0.0		0.0										
snail, raw	90	79.2	1.4												
3½ oz	100	16.1	2.0										3.50		
snail, giant african, raw	73	82.2	1.4												
3½ oz	100	9.9	4.4												
turtle, green, raw	89	78.5	0.5												
3½ oz	100	19.8	0.0		0.0										
turtle, green, cnd	106	75.0	0.7												
3½ oz	100	23.4	0.0		0.0										
venison, roasted	146		2.2	0.2			0	.28			70	20	29		
3½ oz	100	29.5	0.0		0.0	0	.37	7.4			336	264	3.50		
venison, salted, dried	142		0.9	0.1				.34				60			
3½ oz	100	31.4	0.0				.09	10.0				298	1.90		

	KCAL	H₂O (g)	FAT (g)	PUFA (g)	CHOL (mg)	A (RE)	C (mg)	Vitamins B-2 (mg)	B-6 (mg)	FOL (mcg)	Na (mg)	Ca (mg)	Minerals Mg (mg)	Zn (mg)	Mn (mg)
	WT (g)	PRO (g)	CHO (g)	SFA (g)	FIBR (g)	A (IU)	B-1 (mg)	NIA (mg)	B-12 (mcg)	PANT (mg)	K (mg)	P (mg)	Fe (mg)	Cu (mg)	
whale meat, raw	156	70.9	7.5		15		6	.08			78	12			
3½ oz	100	20.6	0.0		0.0	1860	.09				22	144			

MEATS: LUNCHEON MEATS, FRANKS, SANDWICH SPREADS

	KCAL	H₂O (g)	FAT (g)	PUFA (g)	CHOL (mg)	A (RE)	C (mg)	B-2 (mg)	B-6 (mg)	FOL (mcg)	Na (mg)	Ca (mg)	Mg (mg)	Zn (mg)	Mn (mg)
	WT (g)	PRO (g)	CHO (g)	SFA (g)	FIBR (g)	A (IU)	B-1 (mg)	NIA (mg)	B-12 (mcg)	PANT (mg)	K (mg)	P (mg)	Fe (mg)	Cu (mg)	
bbq loaf, (pork & beef)	40	14.9	2.1	0.2	9		4	.06	.06		307	13	4	.60	.009
1 slice	23	3.6	1.5	0.7			.08	0.5	.39	.36	76	30	.27	.02	
beef, loaved lunchmeat	87	14.9	7.4	0.3	18		4	.06	.05		377	13	4	.72	.013
1 slice	28	4.1	0.8	3.2	0.0		.03	1.0	1.10	.15	59	34	.66	.03	
beef, thinly sliced lunchmeat	26	14.7	0.7	tr	9		3	.04	.07		348		4	.84	.008
5 slices	21	4.6	0.1	0.3	0.0		.02	1.1	.54	.12	86	35	.45	.02	
berliner (pork & beef)	53	14.0	4.0	0.4	11		2	.05	.05		298	3	3	.57	.009
1 slice	23	3.5	0.6	1.4	0.0		.09	0.7	.61		65	30	.27	.02	
blood sausage (blood pudding)ᵃ	95	11.8	8.6	0.9	30										
1 slice	25	3.7	0.3	3.3											
bockwurst (pork, veal, milk, etc.), raw	200	36.5	17.9	1.9											
1 link	65	8.7	0.3	6.6											
bologna															
beef	72	12.6	6.5	0.2	13		4	.03	.04	1	230	3	2	.46	.009
1 slice	23	2.7	0.5	2.7	0.0		.01	0.6	.32	.06	36	19	.32	.01	
beef & pork	73	12.5	6.5	0.6	13		5	.03	.04	1	234	3	3	.45	.01
1 slice	23	2.7	0.6	2.5	0.0		.04	0.6	.31	.06	41	21	.35	.02	
beef & pork w/cheese	75	12.2	6.7	0.8	14		4	.03	.03		245	15	3	0.4	
1 slice	23	2.8	0.6	2.7			.05	0.6	.32		39	43	0.3	.01	
pork	57	13.9	4.6	0.5	14		8	.04	.06	1	272	3	3	.47	.01
1 slice	23	3.5	0.2	1.6	0.0		.12	0.9	.21	.17	65	32	.18	.02	
turkey	60	18.5	4.5	1.1	20			.05	.05		222	26	4	.64	
1 slice	28	3.9	0.6	1.4			.01	1.1	.44		53	44	.36	.01	
bratwurst (pork), ckd	256	47.7	22.0	2.3	51		1	.16	.18		473	38	12	1.96	.039
1 link	85	12.0	1.8	7.9			.43	2.7	.81	.27	180	126	1.09	.08	
braunschweiger (pork liver sausage)	65	8.6	5.8	0.7	28	760	2	.28	.06		206	2	2	.51	.028
1 slice	18	2.4	0.6	2.0	0.0	2529	.05	1.5	3.62	.61	36	30	1.68	.04	
brotwurst (pork & beef w/nfdm)	226	35.9	19.5	2.0	44		20	.16	.09		778	34	11	1.47	.027
1 link	70	10.0	2.1	7.0			.18	2.3	1.44	.04	197	94	.72	.05	
canadian style bacon	40	19.3	2.0	0.1	12		8	.04	.10		393		5	.36	
1 slice	28	5.6	0.0	0.6			.20	1.6	.19		84	57	.16	.01	
chicken roll, light meat	90	38.9	4.2	0.9	28			.07			331	24	10	.41	
2 slices	57	11.1	1.4	1.2			.04	3.0			129	89	.55	.02	
chorizo (pork & beef)	265	19.1	23.0	2.1											
1 link	60	14.5	0.0	8.6											
corned beef loaf, jellied	46	19.1	1.9	0.1	12		2	.03	.04		294	3	3	1.08	.009
1 slice	28	6.7	0.0	0.8			tr	0.5	.33	.05	25	18	.58	.02	
frankfurter															
beef	145	24.3	13.2	0.5	22		11	.05	.05	2	461	6	4	.95	.015
1 frank	45	5.1	1.1	5.4	0.0		.02	1.1	.74	.13	71	37	.60	.03	
beef & pork	144	24.2	13.1	1.2	22		12	.05	.06	2	504	5	5	.83	.01
1 frank	45	5.1	1.2	4.8	0.0		.09	1.2	.58	.16	75	38	.52	.04	
chicken	116	25.9	8.8	1.8	45			.05			617	43			
1 frank	45	5.8	3.1	2.5			.03	1.4					.90		
pork & beef, battered & fried	330	50.0	20.0	1.4	37		3	.17	.11		1252	34	22	1.44	
(corn dog)—*1 frank*	111	10.0	27.3	8.4			.28	3.3	.58		164	303	1.94	.09	
pork & beef w/am cheese	145	23.9	13.5	1.0	31		9	.07	.04		551	29	5	.89	
1 frank	45	5.4	0.7	5.3			.08	1.0	.57		56	77	.43	.02	
turkey	100	28.8	8.1	2.1	39			.08	.09		472	58	8	1.00	
1 frank	45	5.8	0.6	2.7			.03	1.7	.58		72	83	.71	.02	

ᵃ Sausage containing a large proportion of blood so that it is very dark in
color

	KCAL	H₂O (g)	FAT (g)	PUFA (g)	CHOL (mg)	A (RE)	C (mg)	B-2 (mg)	B-6 (mg)	FOL (mcg)	Na (mg)	Ca (mg)	Mg (mg)	Zn (mg)	Mn (mg)
	WT (g)	PRO (g)	CHO (g)	SFA (g)	FIBR (g)	A (IU)	B-1 (mg)	NIA (mg)	B-12 (mcg)	PANT (mg)	K (mg)	P (mg)	Fe (mg)	Cu (mg)	
ham															
chopped, cnd	50	12.8	4.0	0.4	10		0	.04	.07		287	1	3	.38	.009
1 slice	21	3.4	0.1	1.3	0.0		.11	0.7	.15		60	29	.20	.01	
chopped, packaged	48	13.4	3.6	0.4	11		4	.04	.07	0	288	1	3	.41	.009
1 slice	21	3.6	0.0	1.2	0.0		.13	0.8	.19	.06	67	33	.17	.01	
minced	55	12.0	4.3	0.5	15		6	.04	.06		261	2	3	.40	.009
1 slice	21	3.4	0.4	1.5	0.0		.15	0.9	.20	.04	65	33	.16	.02	
sliced, lean (5% fat)	37	20.0	1.4	0.1	13		7	.06	.13	1	405	2	5	.55	.009
1 slice	28	5.5	0.3	0.5	0.0		.26	1.4	.21	.13	99	62	.22	.02	
sliced, reg (11% fat)	52	18.3	3.0	0.3			8	.07	.10	1	373	2	5	.61	.009
1 slice	28	5.0	0.9	1.0	0.0		.24	1.5	.24	.13	94	70	.28	.03	
ham & cheese loaf/roll	73	16.4	5.7	0.6	16		7	.05	.07		381	16	5	.57	.008
1 slice	28	4.7	0.4	2.1			.17	1.0	.23	.15	83	72	.26	.02	
ham roll sausage	35	15.6	1.8	0.3	11		5	.05	.07		270	3	5	.46	
1 slice	23	4.1	0.5	0.7			.20	1.0	.19		78	52	.29	.03	
headcheese (pork)	60	18.4	4.5	0.5	23		6	.05	.05	1	356	4	3	.37	.005
1 slice	28	4.5	0.1	1.4	0.0		.01	0.3	.30	.06	9	17	.33	.03	
honey loaf (pork & beef)	36	20.0	1.3	0.1	10		6	.07	.09		374	5	5	.69	.009
1 slice	28	4.5	1.5	0.4			.14	0.9	.31	.19	97	41	.38	.02	
honey roll sausage (beef)	42	14.9	2.4	0.1	12		4	.04	.06		304	2	4	.75	.008
1 slice	23	4.3	0.5	0.9	0.0		.02	1.0	.54	.11	67	31	.51	.02	
italian sausage (pork), ckd	216	33.5	17.2	2.2	52		1	.16	.22		618	16	12	1.60	.055
1 link	67	13.4	1.0	6.1	0.0		.42	2.8	.87	.30	204	114	1.00	.05	
kielbasa/kolbassy (pork & beef	81	14.0	7.1	0.8	17		6	.06	.05		280	11	4	.53	.010
w/nfdm)—*1 slice*	26	3.5	0.6	2.6	0.0		.06	0.7	.42	.21	70	38	.38	.03	
knackwurst/knockwurst (pork & beef)	209	37.7	18.9	2.0	39		18	.10	.11		687	7	8	1.13	
1 link	68	8.1	1.2	6.9	0.0		.23	1.9	.80	.22	136	67	.62	.04	
lebanon balogna (beef)	52	13.6	3.4	0.2	15		8	.05	.06	1	291	3	4	.90	.013
1 slice	23	4.5	0.5	1.4	0.0		.01	1.1	.64	.12	70	34	.55	.02	
livercheese (pork liver)	115	20.4	9.7	1.3	66	1996	1	.85	.18		465	3	4	1.41	.076
1 slice	38	5.8	0.8	3.4		6646	.08	4.5	9.33	1.34	86	79	4.11	.15	
liver pate															
chicken, cnd	57		3.7				3	.40				3			
1 oz	28	3.8	1.9			205	.02	2.1					2.60		
goose, smoked, cnd	131	10.5	12.4		43			.09							
1 oz	28	3.2	1.3		0.0		.03	0.7	2.66						
unspecified, cnd	90	15.3	7.9				0	.17	.02	17	198	20	4		.034
1 oz	28	4.0	0.4			936	.01	0.9	.91	.34	39	57	1.56	.11	
liver sausage/liverwurst (pork)	59	9.4	5.1	0.5	28			.19		5		5			
1 slice	18	2.5	0.4	1.9			.05		15.41	.53		41	1.15		
luxury loaf (pork)	40	19.4	1.4	0.1	10		6	.08	.09		347	10	6	.86	.012
1 slice	28	5.2	1.4	0.5			.20	1.0	.39	.15	107	52	.30	.03	
mortadella (beef & pork)	47	7.9	3.8	0.5	8		4	.02	.02		187	3	2	.32	.004
1 slice	15	2.5	0.5	1.4			.02	0.4	.22		24	15	.21	.01	
mother s loaf (pork)	59	11.5	4.7	0.5	9		0	.04	.04		237	9	3	.30	.014
1 slice	21	2.5	1.6	1.7			.12	0.7	.22	.10	47	27	.28	.02	
new england brand sausage	37	15.4	1.7	0.2	11		5	.06	.08	2	281	2	4	.62	.008
(pork & beef)—*1 slice*	23	4.0	1.1	1.6	0.0		.15	0.8	.31	.16	74	31	.22	.02	
old fashioned loaf (pork & beef)	68	16.8	5.1	0.5	13		5	.08	.06		354	24	6	.49	.009
1 slice	28	3.8	1.6	1.8			.09	0.7	.37	.17	107	46	.35	.02	
olive loaf (pork)	67	16.5	4.7	0.6	11		2	.07	.07		421	31	5	.39	.010
1 slice	28	3.4	2.6	1.7			.08	0.5	.36	.22	84	36	.15	.01	
peppered loaf (pork & beef)	42	19.1	1.8	0.1	13		7	.09	.08		432	15	6	.92	.018
1 slice	28	4.9	1.3	0.7			.11	0.9	.56	.15	112	48	.30	.03	
pepperoni (pork & beef)	27	1.5	2.4	0.2				.01	.01		112	1	1	.14	
1 slice	6	1.2	0.2	0.9	0.0		.02	0.3	.14	.10	19	7	.08	.00	
pickle & pimento loaf (pork)	74	16.2	6.0	0.7	10		4	.07	.05		394	27	5	.40	.008
1 slice	28	3.3	1.7	2.2			.08	0.6	.33	.22	96	40	.29	.04	
picnic loaf (pork & beef)	66	17.1	4.7	0.5	11		5	.07	.09		330	13	4	.62	.008
1 slice	28	4.2	1.4	1.7			.11	0.7	.42	.19	76	36	.29	.02	

	KCAL / WT (g)	H₂O / PRO (g)	FAT / CHO (g)	PUFA / SFA (g)	CHOL / FIBR	A (RE) / A (IU)	C / B-1 (mg)	B-2 / NIA (mg)	B-6 / B-12	FOL / PANT	Na / K (mg)	Ca / P (mg)	Mg / Fe (mg)	Zn / Cu (mg)	Mn (mg)
polish sausage (pork)	92	15.1	8.1	0.9	20	0	.04	.05			248	3	4	.55	.014
1 oz	28	4.0	0.5	2.9	0.0		.14	1.0	.28	.13	67	39	.41	.03	
pork & beef lunchmeat	100	14.0	9.1	1.1	15	4	.04	.06		2	367	3	4	.47	.008
1 slice	28	3.6	0.7	3.3	0.0		.09	0.8	.36	.18	57	24	.24	.01	
pork & beef luncheon sausage	60	13.5	4.8	0.5	15	4	.05	.05			272	3	3	.56	.01
1 slice	23	3.5	0.4	1.8	0.0		.05	0.8	.45	.09	56	28	.33	.02	
pork lunchmeat, cnd	70	10.8	6.4	0.8	13	0	.04	.04		1	271	1	2	.31	.005
1 slice	21	2.6	0.4	2.3	0.0		.08	0.7	.19	.10	45	17	.15	.01	
prem, cnd	92		8.2								341				
1 oz	28	3.2	1.4												
salami															
ckd, beef	58	13.7	4.6	0.2	14	3	.06	.05		0	266	2	3	.49	.01
1 slice	23	3.4	0.6	1.9	0.0		.03	0.8	1.11	.22	52	23	.46	.02	
ckd, beef & pork	57	13.9	4.6	0.5	15	3	.09	.05		0	245	3	3	.49	.013
1 slice	23	3.2	0.5	1.9	0.0		.06	0.8	0.8	.20	46	27	.61	.05	
ckd, turkey	50	19.0	3.4	1.1	20		.08	.07			251	7	5	.72	
1 slice	28	4.5	0.3	1.0			.02	1.2	.60		63	45	.38	.03	
dry/hard, pork	41	3.6	3.4	0.4			.03	.06			226	1	2	.42	.007
1 slice	10	2.3	0.2	1.2	0.0		.09	0.6	.28			23	.13	.02	
dry/hard, pork & beef	42	3.5	3.4	0.3	8	3	.03	.05			186	1	2	.32	tr
1 slice	10	2.3	0.3	1.2	0.0		.06	0.5	.19	.11	38	14	.15	.01	
for beer (beerwurst), beef	75	12.4	6.8	0.2	13	3	.03	.05		1	214	2	3	.61	
1 slice	23	2.8	0.4	2.8	0.0		.03	0.7	.49	.08	42	24	.31	.01	
for beer (beerwurst), pork	55	14.1	4.3	0.5	13	7	.04	.08		1	285	2	3	.40	.007
1 slice	23	3.3	0.5	1.4	0.0		.13	0.7	.20	.11	58	24	.17	.01	
sandwich spread															
chicken, cnd	55		3.3					.03				35			
1 oz	28	4.4	1.5				tr	0.8					.66		
chicken, cnd, Swanson	70		5.0								265				
1 oz	28	4.0	1.0								45	48			
chicken, chunky, cnd, Underwood	150		11.0								575				
½ can	67	10.0	3.0												
corned beef, cnd, Underwood	120		10.0								605				
½ can	67	6.0	1.5												
deviled ham, cnd, Underwood	220		20.0								640				
½ can	63	9.0	1.0												
ham & cheese	69	16.8	5.3	0.4	17	2	.06	.04			339	62	5	.64	.010
1 oz	28	4.6	0.6	2.4			.09	0.6	.21	.17	46	140	.22	.03	
ham salad	61	17.8	4.4	0.8	10	2	.03	.04			259	2	3	.31	
1 oz	28	2.5	3.0	1.4			.12	0.6	.22	.09	42	34	.17	.02	
liverwurst, cnd, Underwood	220		19.0								570				
½ can	67	10.0	3.0												
pork & beef	67	17.1	4.9	0.7	11	0	.04	.03			287	3	2	.29	.01
1 oz	28	2.2	3.4	1.7			.05	0.5	.32	.12	31	17	.22	.04	
poultry (chicken/turkey) salad	57		3.8	1.8	9	0	.02	.03		1	107	3			
1 oz	28	3.3	2.1	1.0		39	.01	0.5	.11	.08	52	9	.17		
potted meat, cnd	115		8.8			tr	tr	.14			347	20	8		
2 oz	57	7.9	0.5			tr	.02	1.2			79	67	.83		
roast beef, cnd, Underwood	140		10.0								515				
½ can	67	11.0	1.5												
smoked link sausage															
beef	130	23.2	11.6	0.5	30	5	.06	.05			455	6	6	1.20	
1 link	43	6.0	0.9	5.2			.02	1.3	.83		78	46	.78	.04	
pork	265	26.7	21.6	2.6	46	1	.18	.24			1020	20	13	1.92	
1 link	68	15.1	1.4	7.7	0.0		.48	3.1	1.11	.53	228	110	.79	.05	
pork & beef	229	35.5	20.6	2.2	48	13	.12	.12			642	7	8	1.44	.03
1 link	68	9.1	1.0	9.2	0.0		.18	2.2	1.03	.30	129	73	.99	.04	
pork & beef w/am cheese	141	22.6	12.5	1.3	29	8	.07	.05			465	25	5	.97	.01
1 link	43	6.0	0.6	4.5			.11	1.2	.74	.33	89	76	.46	.03	

	KCAL / WT (g)	H₂O (g) / PRO (g)	FAT (g) / CHO (g)	PUFA (g) / SFA (g)	CHOL (mg) / FIBR (g)	A (RE) / A (IU)	C (mg) / B-1 (mg)	B-2 (mg) / NIA (mg)	B-6 (mg) / B-12 (mcg)	FOL (mcg) / PANT (mg)	Na (mg) / K (mg)	Ca (mg) / P (mg)	Mg (mg) / Fe (mg)	Zn (mg) / Cu (mg)	Mn (mg)
pork & beef w/flour & nfdm	182	39.0	14.6	1.5	59	2	.12	.09			741	12	9	1.36	.035
1 link	68	9.5	2.7	5.3			.16	1.8	.89		105	74	1.05	.06	
pork & beef w/nfdm	213	36.7	18.8	2.1	44	14	.15	.12			798	28	11	1.33	.026
1 link	68	9.0	1.3	6.6	0.0		.13	1.9	1.07	.41	194	92	1.00	.06	
spam, cnd	87		7.4					.04			336	3			
1 oz	28	3.9	1.1		tr		.11	0.6			59	35	.50		
thuringer (cervelat/summer sausage), beef—1 slice	70	11.7	6.2	0.3	17	5	.07	.06			317		3	.48	
	23	3.4	0.7	2.8			.03	1.0	1.29		53	24	.52	.02	
thuringer (cervelat/summer sausage), beef & pork—1 slice	80	11.0	6.9	0.4	16	5	.07	.07			334	2	3	.47	.007
	23	3.7	0.5	2.8	0.0		.04	0.9	1.06	.13	53	23	.47	.02	
treet	83		7.3			0		.04			360	5			
1 oz	28	3.9	0.3				.10	0.8				35	.35		
turkey breast meat	23	15.1	0.3	0.1	9	0	.02	.07			301	1	4	.24	
1 slice	21	4.7	0.0	0.1			.01	1.7	.42	.12	58	48	.08	.01	
turkey ham (cured thigh meat)	73	40.5	2.9	0.9	34			.14	.14		565	5	10	1.50	
2 slices	57	10.7	0.2	1.0			.03	2.0	1.02		184	108	1.57	.06	
turkey loaved lunchmeat	40	19.9	2.5	0.7	13			.03	.07		274	2	5	.45	
1 slice	28	4.5	0.3	0.8			.01	1.6	.19		57	65	.14	.01	
turkey pastrami	80	40.1	3.5	0.9	30			.14	.16		593	5	8	1.22	
2 slices	57	10.4	0.9	1.0			.03	2.0	1.14		147	113	.94	.03	
turkey roll, light & dark meat	84	39.8	4.0	1.0	31			.16			332	18	10	1.13	
2 slices	57	10.3	1.2	1.2			.05	2.7			153	95	.76	.04	
turkey roll, light meat	83	40.6	4.1	1.0	24			.13			277	23	9	.88	
2 slices	57	10.6	0.3	1.1			.05	4.0			142	104	.72	.02	
turkey summer sausage	50	18.5	3.1	0.8	22			.12	.08		333	3	5	.74	
1 slice	28	4.8	0.6	1.1			.03	1.4	1.15		68	80	.58	.04	
vienna sausage, cnd (beef & pork)	45	9.6	4.0	0.3	8	0	.02	.02			152	2	1	.26	.005
1 sausage	16	1.7	0.3	1.5	0.0		.01	0.3	.16		16	8	.14	.00	

MEAT ANALOGUES

	KCAL / WT (g)	H₂O (g) / PRO (g)	FAT (g) / CHO (g)	PUFA (g) / SFA (g)	CHOL (mg) / FIBR (g)	A (RE) / A (IU)	C (mg) / B-1 (mg)	B-2 (mg) / NIA (mg)	B-6 (mg) / B-12 (mcg)	FOL (mcg) / PANT (mg)	Na (mg) / K (mg)	Ca (mg) / P (mg)	Mg (mg) / Fe (mg)	Zn (mg) / Cu (mg)	Mn (mg)
bac o bits, General Mills	33		1.3					tr			189	18			
1 T	8	3.3	2.2					0.1			218		.54		
bacon, imit crumbles, French's	6										55				
1 t	2	1.0													
beef style roll, frzn, Worthington	140		9.0		0										
2½ oz	70	11.0	4.0												
beef style roll, smoked, frzn, Worthington—2½ oz	170		10.0		0										
	70	12.0	7.0												
beef style slices, smoked, frzn, Worthington—6 slices	130		7.0		0										
	56	10.0	6.0												
big franks,[a] cnd, Loma Linda	95	31.0	4.6					.66	.51		280	20		.56	
1 frank	51	10.0	3.1		1.0		.30	7.1	1.20	1.8	92		.92		
bologna, frzn, Loma Linda	140	27.0	8.0					.29	.57		520	25		1.00	
2 slices	57	14.0	3.4		2.3		.63	6.8	1.70	2.30	160		1.70		
bolono, frzn, Worthington	70		3.0		0						730				
2 slices		7.0	3.0												
breakfast links, Morningstar Farms	190	35.3	13.3		0			.28	.54		600	29	23	.48	
5 links	68	14.5	3.2				.88	5.7	2.64		85		3.1	.13	
breakfast patties, Morningstar Farms	224	36.1	14.9	7.1	0			.39	.93		836	45	23	.68	
2 patties	76	15.7	6.8	3.4			1.01	12.2	2.71		99		4.32	.11	
breakfast strips, Morningstar Farms	92	9.9	8.5	5.1	0			.08	.06		298	7	6	.10	
3 strips	24	2.8	1.1	1.2			.12	1.9	.67		43		.55	.02	
chicken, fried, frzn, Loma Linda	140	33.0	10.0					.57	.54		250	26		.86	
1 piece	57	9.1	3.4				.80	4.0	1.00	1.10	68		1.10		
chicken, fried w/gravy, cnd, Loma Linda—2 pieces	190	51	12.0					.30	.55		380	18		1.70	
	85	14.0	6.8				.54	4.7	2.10	2.00	140		1.60		
chicken style, diced, frzn, Worthington	220		17.0		0										
½ cup	84	14.0	2.0												
chicken style roll, frzn, Worthington	170		13.0		0										
2½ oz	70	11.0	2.0												

[a] Resembles Polish sausage

	KCAL / WT (g)	H₂O (g) / PRO (g)	FAT (g) / CHO (g)	PUFA (g) / SFA (g)	CHOL (mg) / FIBR (g)	A (RE) / A (IU)	C (mg) / B-1 (mg)	B-2 (mg) / NIA (mg)	B-6 (mg) / B-12 (mcg)	FOL (mcg) / PANT (mg)	Na (mg) / K (mg)	Ca (mg) / P (mg)	Mg (mg) / Fe (mg)	Zn (mg) / Cu (mg)	Mn (mg)
chicken style slices, frzn, Worthington	140		11.0		0										
2 slices	57	9.0	2.0												
chic-ketts, frzn, Worthington	180		10.0		0										
½ cup	84	17.0	6.0												
chik stiks, frzn, Worthington	120		8.0		0						425				
1 piece	47	8.0	4.0								70				
choplets, cnd, Worthington	110		3.0		0						770				
2 slices	92	14.0	7.0								35				
corned beef style roll, frzn, Worthington—2½ oz	188		12.0		0										
	70	11.0	9.0												
cutlets, cnd, Worthington	100		2.0		0						430				
1½ slices	92	14.0	7.0								20				
dinner cuts (wheat pro) w/sce, cnd, Loma Linda—2 cuts	110	72.0	1.0					.32	.52		650	16		1.00	
	100	20.0	4.0		1.0		.21	0.8	2.00	.19	200	2.00			
dinner roast, frzn, Worthington	140		10.0		0						495				
2 oz	57	7.0	4.0								70				
fillets, frzn, Worthington	180		10.0		0						855				
2 pieces	85	14.0	9.0												
fri chik, cnd, Worthington	190		16.0		0										
2 pieces	90	9.0	2.0												
fri pats, frzn, Worthington	160		12.0		0						470				
1 piece	64	11.0	3.0								55				
granburger, dry, Worthington	110		1.0		0										
6 T	33	20.0	6.0												
griddle steaks, frzn, Loma Linda	160	26.0	11.0					.67	.84		530	67		.62	
1 steak	56	12.0	3.9		1.1		.46	8.4	2.20	2.60	340	2.00			
grillers, Morningstar Farms	184	31.1	11.6	4.4	0			.22	.48		294	67	21	1.04	
1 patty	64	14.6	5.5	2.6			.78	5.3	2.16		115	3.39	.14		
linketts,ª cnd, Loma Linda	140	44.0	4.4					.44	.74		410	30		1.10	
2 links	74	16.0	8.1				.52	8.9	2.20	1.60	160	2.10			
little links,ᵇ cnd, Loma Linda	85	29.0	4.6					.46	.14		280	9		.64	
2 links	46	7.8	3.2				.60	6.4	2.00	1.60	92	1.10			
meatless meatballs, frzn, Loma Linda	190	40.0	5.1					.55	.71		480	52		1.40	
4 pieces	85	26.0	9.4		3.4		1.00	6.4	1.40	1.90	320	1.60			
non-meat balls, cnd, Worthington	120		8.0		0										
3 pieces	54	6.0	7.0												
numete, cnd, Worthington	160		11.0		0										
½ inch slice	68	7.0	9.0												
nuteena (peanuts & soy flour), cnd, Loma Linda—½ inch slice	160	38.0	12.0					.74	4.0		340	23		.80	
	67	8.0	6.0		1.3		.57	16.0	1.30	2.30	390	1.20			
ocean fillet, frzn, Loma Linda	180	22.0	11.0					.50	.62		500	73		.84	
1 fillet	56	14.0	5.6		1.1		.52	9.0	1.90	2.70	170	2.20			
prime stakes, cnd, Worthington	160		11.0		0						570				
1 piece	92	10.0	5.0								85				
proteena (lowfat nut loaf), cnd, Loma Linda—½ inch slice	140	40.0	5.7					.64	.50		470	17		1.10	
	71	17.0	5.0		2.1		.71	8.5	1.60	2.80	230	1.80			
protose, cnd, Worthington	190		10.0		0										
½ inch slice	76	17.0	7.0												
prosage links, frzn, Worthington	210		17.0		0						810				
3 links	68	12.0	3.0												
prosage patties, frzn, Worthington	250		17.0		0						1130				
2 patties	76	17.0	6.0												
prosage roll, frzn, Worthington	180		11.0		0										
2 slices	70	12.0	6.0												
redi-burger, cnd, Loma Linda	120	38.0	4.7					.44	.45		470	21		1.10	
½ inch slice	67	14.0	5.4		2.7		.15	7.4	1.70	1.20	210	1.90			
salami, meatless, frzn, Worthington	100		6.0		0						645				
2 slices	43	8.0	3.0												
sandwich spread,ᶜ cnd, Loma Linda	69	34.0	3.8					.43	.53		290	25		.53	
3 T	48	4.3	4.3		1.0		.58	8.6	.91	1.10	240	.96			
saucettes, cnd, Worthington	130		9.0		0										
2 links	67	9.0	3.0												

ª Resembles frankfurters
ᵇ Resembles breakfast sausage
ᶜ Minced olives, veg proteins & seasonings

	KCAL / WT (g)	H$_2$O (g) / PRO (g)	FAT (g) / CHO (g)	PUFA (g) / SFA (g)	CHOL (mg) / FIBR (g)	A (RE) / A (IU)	C (mg) / B-1 (mg)	B-2 (mg) / NIA (mg)	B-6 (mg) / B-12 (mcg)	FOL (mcg) / PANT (mg)	Na (mg) / K (mg)	Ca (mg) / P (mg)	Mg (mg) / Fe (mg)	Zn (mg) / Cu (mg)	Mn (mg)
savorex (veg seasoning paste),	16		0.0					.43	.20			40			.05
plastic tub, Loma Linda—1 T	7	3.0	1.0				.09	3.0		.40			2.20		
savory dinner loaf, cnd, Loma Linda	140	33.0	9.7					.34	.86		540	63			.37
1 slice	57	9.1	2.9				.63	3.0	1.20	1.70			.74		
sizzle burger, frzn, Loma Linda	190	30.0	11.0					.38	.70		600	51			.78
1 burger	71	15.0	7.8	5.7			.50	6.2	1.80	1.70	470		1.80		
sizzle franks, cnd, Loma Linda	160	42.0	13.0					.41	.43		420	21			.77
2 franks	70	9.1	2.8	2.1			.39	4.0	1.50	2.70	180		1.50		
skallops, veg, cnd, Worthington	70		2.0		0										
½ cup	85	10.0	3.0												
soymeat, beef-like, sliced, cnd,	110		7.0		0										
Worthington—2 slices	56	8.0	3.0												
soymeat, chicken-like, sliced, cnd,	130		10.0		0										
Worthington—2 slices	60	8.0	2.0												
stakelets, frzn, Worthington	150		9.0		0						570				
1 piece	71	10.0	7.0								40				
stakes au sce, frzn, Worthington	280		17.0		0						960				
7 oz	199	16.0	16.0								170				
stew pac (veg pro chunks) in sce, cnd,	66	38.0	1.1					.28	.62		340	18			.31
Loma Linda—2 oz	56	10.0	3.9	1.7			.25	3.0	.90	1.60	110		.84		
stripples, frzn, Worthington	100		7.0		0						550				
4 strips	[a]	5.0	3.0												
super-links, cnd, Worthington	100		7.0		0						495				
1 link	48	6.0	3.0												
swiss steak w/gravy, cnd, Loma Linda	130	46.0	7.4					.44	.41		520	22			.74
1 steak	74	9.6	6.7	2.2			.56	4.6	1.50	1.70	270		1.60		
tender bits, cnd, Loma Linda	74	40.0	2.9					.29	.43		430	14			.63
4 pieces	57	8.0	4.0				.17	5.7	.63	2.40	63		1.00		
tender rounds w/gravy, cnd,	100	50.0	3.0					.30	.40		380	23			.74
Loma Linda—3 pieces	76	14.0	5.3	1.5			.55	3.1	.71	1.00	170		1.10		
tuno roll, frzn, Worthington	90		7.0		0										
2 oz	57	4.0	3.0												
turkey-like slices, cnd, Worthington	150		11.0		0										
2½ slices	63	9.0	3.0												
turkey style roll, smoked, frzn,	160		11.0		0										
Worthington—2½ oz	70	12.0	3.0												
turkey style slices, smoked, frzn,	170		11.0		0										
Worthington—4 slices	76	12.0	5.0												
veelets parmesano, frzn, Worthington	340		21.0		0						1125				
7 oz	199	19.0	17.0								380				
vege-burger, cnd, Loma Linda	110	79.0	1.0					.86	.65		420	27			1.10
½ cup	108	23.0	3.2	1.1			.67	6.2	1.80	1.60	220		2.50		
vegelona,[b] cnd, Loma Linda	95	42.0	1.3					.54	.50		340	20			1.40
½ inch slice	67	16.0	4.7	2.0			.50	10.0	1.00	1.40	170		1.70		
veg steaks, cnd, Worthington	100		2.0		0										
2½ pieces	90	14.0	7.0												
vegetarian burger, cnd, Worthington	160		6.0		0						850				
½ cup	113	17.0	9.0								45				
veja-links, cnd/frzn, Worthington	130		10.0		0										
2 links	62	6.0	4.0												
wham, Worthington	130		8.0		0						1155				
3 slices	68	10.0	4.0								140				

[a] Gram wt not available

[b] Resembles bologna

	KCAL	H₂O (g)	FAT (g)	PUFA (g)	CHOL (mg)	A (RE)	C (mg)	B-2 (mg)	B-6 (mg)	FOL (mcg)	Na (mg)	Ca (mg)	Mg (mg)	Zn (mg)	Mn (mg)
	WT (g)	PRO (g)	CHO (g)	SFA (g)	FIBR (g)	A (IU)	B-1 (mg)	NIA (mg)	B-12 (mcg)	PANT (mg)	K (mg)	P (mg)	Fe (mg)	Cu (mg)	

MILK, MILK BEVERAGES & YOGURT
MILK, COW

	KCAL	H₂O	FAT	PUFA	CHOL	A(RE)/A(IU)	C/B-1	B-2/NIA	B-6/B-12	FOL/PANT	Na/K	Ca/P	Mg/Fe	Zn/Cu	Mn
buttermilk, cultured	99	220.8	2.2	tr	9	20	2	.38	.08		257	285	27	1.03	
1 cup	245	8.1	11.7	1.3	0.0	81	.08	0.1	.54	.67	371	219	.12		
buttermilk, dry	25	0.2	0.4	tr	5	4	tr	.10	.02	3	34	77	7	.26	
1 T	7	2.2	3.2	0.2	0.0	14	.03	0.1	.25	.21	103	61	.02		
condensed, sweetened, cnd	123	10.4	3.3	0.1	13	31	1	.16	.02	4	49	108	10	.49	
1 fl oz	38	3.0	20.8	2.1	0.0	125	.03	0.1	.17	.29	142	97	.07		
evaporated, filled, cnd	150		8.0	3.0	5						120				
½ cup	128	9.0	12.0	1.0							376				
evaporated, skim, cnd	25	25.3	0.1	tr	1	37	tr	.10	.02	3	37	92	9	.29	
1 fl oz	32	2.4	3.6	tr	0.0	125	.01	0.1	.08	.24	106	62	.09		
evaporated, whole, cnd	42	23.3	2.4	0.1	9	17	1	.10	.02	2	33	82	8	.24	
1 fl oz	32	2.1	3.2	1.5	0.0	77	.02	0.1	.05	.20	95	64	.06		
evaporated, whole, cnd	169	93.3	9.5	0.3	37	68	2	.40	.06	10	133	329	30	.97	
½ cup	126	8.6	12.7	5.8	0.0	306	.06	0.2	.21	.80	382	255	.24		
lowfat, 1% fat	102	219.8	2.6	0.1	10	145	2	.41	.11	12	123	300	34	.95	
1 cup	244	8.0	11.7	1.6	0.0	500	.10	0.2	.90	.79	381	235	.12		
lowfat, 1% fat w/nfdm	104	220.0	2.4	0.1	10	145	2	.42	.11	13	128	313	35	.98	
1 cup	245	8.5	12.2	1.5	0.0	500	.10	0.2	.94	.82	397	245	.12		
lowfat, 1% fat, pro fortified	119	218.3	2.9	0.1	10	145	3	.47	.12	15	143	349	39	1.11	
1 cup	246	9.7	13.6	1.8	0.0	500	.11	0.3	1.05	.92	444	273	.15		
lowfat, 2% fat	121	217.7	4.7	0.2	18	140	2	.40	.11	12	122	297	33	.95	
1 cup	244	8.1	11.7	2.9	0.0	500	.10	0.2	.89	.78	377	232	.12		
lowfat, 2% fat w/nfdm	125	217.7	4.7	0.2	18	140	2	.42	.11	13	128	313	35	.98	
1 cup	245	8.5	12.2	2.9	0.0	500	.10	0.2	.94	.82	397	245	.12		
lowfat, 2% fat, pro fortified	137	215.8	4.9	0.2	19	140	3	.48	.13	15	145	352	40	1.11	
1 cup	246	9.7	13.5	3.0	0.0	500	.11	0.3	1.05	.93	447	276	.15		
skim	86	222.5	0.4	tr	4	149	2	.34	.10	13	126	302	28	.98	
1 cup	245	8.4	11.9	0.3	0.0	500	.09	0.2	.93	.81	406	247	.10		
skim w/nfdm	90	221.4	0.6	tr	5	149	2	.43	.11	13	130	316	36	1.00	
1 cup	245	8.8	12.3	0.4	0.0	500	.10	0.2	.95	.83	418	255	.12		
skim, pro fortified	100	219.8	0.6	tr	5	149	3	.48	.12	15	144	352	40	1.11	
1 cup	246	9.7	13.7	0.4	0.0	500	.11	0.3	1.05	.93	446	275	.15		
skim, dry	109	1.0	0.2	tr	6	2	2	.47	.11	15	161	377	33	1.22	
¼ cup	30	10.9	15.6	0.2	0.0	11	.12	.29	1.21	1.07	538	290	.10		
skim, dry, Ca reduced	100	1.4	0.1	tr	1	1		.47	.08		646	79	17		
1 oz	28	10.1	14.7	tr	0.0	2	.05	0.2	1.13	.94	193	287			
skim, dry, inst	326	3.6	0.7	tr	17	646	5	1.59	.31	45	499	1120	107	4.01	
1⅓ cup (3.2 oz envelope)[a]	91	31.9	47.5	0.4	0.0	2157	.38	0.8	3.63	2.94	1552	896	.28		
whole, 3.3% fat	150	214.7	8.2	0.3	33	76	2	.40	.10	12	120	291	33	.93	
1 cup	244	8.0	11.4	5.1	0.0	307	.09	0.2	.87	.77	370	228	.12		
whole, 3.5% fat	150	213.3	8.0	0.2	34		5	.42	.02	37	122	288	24	1.00	
1 cup	244	8.0	11.0	4.9	0.0		.10	0.2	1.34	.85	351	227			
whole, 3.7% fat	157	214.0	8.9	0.3	35	83	4	.39	.10	12	119	290	33	.93	
1 cup	244	8.0	11.4	5.6	0.0	337	.09	0.2	.87	.76	368	227	.12		
whole, low Na	149	215.2	8.4	0.3	33	78		.26	.08		6	246	12		
1 cup	244	7.6	10.9	5.3	0.0	317	.05	0.1	.88	.74	617	209			
whole, dry	159	0.8	8.6	0.2	31	90	3	.39	.10	12	119	292	27	1.07	
¼ cup	32	8.4	12.3	5.4	0.0	295	.09	0.2	1.04	.73	426	248	.15		

MILK, OTHER

	KCAL	H₂O	FAT	PUFA	CHOL	A(RE)/A(IU)	C/B-1	B-2/NIA	B-6/B-12	FOL/PANT	Na/K	Ca/P	Mg/Fe	Zn/Cu	Mn
filled milk[b,c]	154	213.9	8.4	1.8	4	5	2	.30	.10	12	138	312	32	.88	
1 cup	244	8.1	11.6	1.9	0.0	17	.07	0.2	.83	.73	339	236	.12		
filled milk[b,d]	153	214.4	8.3	tr	4	5	2	.30	.10	12	138	312	32	.88	
1 cup	244	8.1	11.6	7.6	0.0	17	.07	0.2	.83	.73	339	236	.12		

[a] Reconstitutes to 1 qt fluid skim milk
[b] Filled milk contains fats or oils other than milk fat w/milk solids (milk, cream, or skim milk).
[c] Contains blend of hydrogenated soybean, cottonseed &/or safflower oils
[d] Contains lauric acid oil; lauric oils include modified coconut oil, hydrogenated coconut oil &/or palm kernel oil.

Vitamins / Minerals	KCAL / WT (g)	H2O / PRO (g)	FAT / CHO (g)	PUFA / SFA (g)	CHOL / FIBR (mg/g)	A (RE) / A (IU)	C / B-1 (mg)	B-2 / NIA (mg)	B-6 / B-12	FOL / PANT	Na / K (mg)	Ca / P (mg)	Mg / Fe (mg)	Zn / Cu (mg)	Mn (mg)
goat milk	168	212.4	10.1	0.4	28	137	3	.34	.11	1	122	326	34	.73	
1 cup	244	8.7	10.9	6.5	0.0	451	.12	0.7	.16	.76	499	270	.12		
human milk	21	27.0	1.4	0.2	4	20	1	.01	tr	2	5	10	1	.05	
1 fl oz	31	0.3	2.1	0.6	0.0	74	tr	0.1	.01	.07	16	4	.07		
imit milk[a,b]	150	215.2	8.3	1.2	tr	0	0	.22	.00	0	191	79	16	2.88	
1 cup	244	4.3	15.0	1.9	0.0	0	.03	0.0	.00	.00	279	181	.95		
imit milk[a,c]	150	215.2	8.3	tr	tr	0	0	.22	.00	0	191	79	16	2.88	
1 cup	244	4.3	15.0	7.4	0.0	0	.03	0.0	.00	.00	279	181	.95		
indian buffalo milk	236	203.5	16.8	0.4	46	129	6	.33	.06	14	127	412	76	.54	
1 cup	244	9.2	12.6	11.2	0.0	434	.13	0.2	.89	.47	434	286	.29		
reindeer milk	234	64.1	19.6								157	254			
3⅓ fl oz	100	10.8	4.1		0.0						159	198	.10		
sheep milk	264	197.7	17.2	0.8		103	10	.87			108	474	45		
1 cup	245	14.7	13.1	11.3	0.0	360	.16	1.0	1.74	1.00	334	387	.24		
soybean milk	87	243.0	4.0		0		0	.08	.28		55	55	57	.40	
1 cup	263	8.9	5.8		0.0	105	.02	0.5	.00	.28	340	126			
soybean milk, conc, sweetened	38	22.3	2.2		0		0	.01			13	9			
1 fl oz	30	1.4	3.7	0.3	tr		.02	tr			71	18	.20		
soybean milk, Soyamel	130		7.0		0						190				
1 cup		7.0	10.0								330				
soybean milk powder	120	1.2	5.7		0							77			
1 oz	28	11.7	7.8	0.8	tr										
soybean milk powder, sweetened	127	1.0	6.5		0		0	.07	.08		tr	32			
1 oz	28	5.7	13.6	2.8	0.1	6	.08	0.4	.00	.22	256	80	1.40		
soybean milk powder, Soyquik	101	1.8	0.3								78	73	87	.56	1.62
1 oz	28	14.6	9.7		1.0						518	182	3.64	.28	

MILK BEVERAGES

	KCAL / WT (g)	H2O / PRO (g)	FAT / CHO (g)	PUFA / SFA (g)	CHOL / FIBR (mg/g)	A (RE) / A (IU)	C / B-1 (mg)	B-2 / NIA (mg)	B-6 / B-12	FOL / PANT	Na / K (mg)	Ca / P (mg)	Mg / Fe (mg)	Zn / Cu (mg)	Mn (mg)
choc milk															
1% fat	158	211.3	2.5	0.1	7	148	2	.42	.10	12	152	287	33	1.02	
1 cup	250	8.1	26.1	1.5	0.2	500	.10	0.3	.86	.76	426	256	.60		
2% fat	179	209.0	5.0	0.2	17	142	2	.41	.10	12	150	284	33	1.02	
1 cup	250	8.0	26.0	3.1	0.2	500	.09	0.3	.85	.75	422	254	.60		
whole	208	205.8	8.5	0.3	30	72	2	.41	.10	12	149	280	33	1.02	.120
1 cup	250	7.9	25.9	5.3	0.2	302	.09	0.3	.84	.74	417	251	.60	.146	
w/malt (whole milk)	233	215.1	9.1	0.4	34	80	2	.43	.13	17	168	304	48	1.11	.095
1 cup	265	9.4	29.2	5.5	0.1	326	.14	0.7	.92	.77	500	265	.50	.066	
cocoa/hot choc (whole milk)	218	204.0	9.1	0.3	33	85	2	.44	.11	12	123	298	56	1.22	
1 cup	250	9.1	25.8	5.6	0.2	318	.10	0.4	.87	.81	480	270	.78		
cocoa, from mix, water added	110		3.0		2		2	.15	.03	tr	154	107	20	.60	.095
1 cup	240	4.1	20.0	2.8	0.1	23	.03	0.2	tr	.25	176	108	.60	.106	
eggnog, nonalcoholic	342	188.9	19.0	0.9	149	203	4	.48	.13	2	138	330	47	1.17	
1 cup	254	9.7	34.4	11.3	0.0	894	.09	0.3	1.14	1.06	420	278	.51		
instant breakfast, van, w/whole milk	280		8.0	0.4	27		26	.56	.51	10	242	407	115	3.70	
1 cup	276	14.9	35.1	5.7		1250	.40	5.2	1.53	2.66	711	386	4.60		
malted milk	236	215.2	9.9	0.6	37	93	2	.54	.18	22	215	347	52	1.14	.095
1 cup	265	10.8	26.6	6.0	0.1	376	.20	1.3	1.04	.77	529	307	.29	.066	
milkshake, homemade	421		17.9				4	.55				362			
1 cup	345	11.2	58.0		0.3	687	.10	0.5				321	1.00		
milkshake, choc, thick	356	216.6	8.1	0.3	32		0	.67	.08	15	333	396	48	1.44	
1 avg	300	9.2	63.5	5.0	0.8	258	.14	0.4	.95	1.09	672	378	.93		
milkshake, van, thick	350	233.0	9.5	0.4	37	88	0	.61	.13	21	299	457	37	1.22	
1 avg	313	12.1	55.6	5.9	0.2	357	.09	0.5	1.63		572	361	.31		
ovaltine, choc w/whole milk	227		8.8		34		29	.97	.77	29	228	392	52	1.13	.095
1 cup	265	9.5	29.2		tr	2343	.63	12.7	.87	.77	600	302	4.77	.134	
ovaltine, malt flavor w/whole milk	228		8.3				30	1.16	.75	29	201	371	47	1.08	.095
1 cup	265	9.9	29.0		tr	2561	.67	11.9	.87	.77	576	308	4.49	.084	

[a] Imit milk contains fats or oils other than milk fat w/food solids, excluding milk solids.
[b] Contains blend of hydrogenated soybean, cottonseed &/or safflower oils
[c] Contains lauric acid oil; lauric oils include modified coconut oil, hydrogenated coconut oil &/or palm kernel oil.

	KCAL / WT (g)	H_2O (g) / PRO (g)	FAT (g) / CHO (g)	PUFA (g) / SFA (g)	CHOL (mg) / FIBR (g)	A (RE) / A (IU)	C (mg) / B-1 (mg)	B-2 (mg) / NIA (mg)	B-6 (mg) / B-12 (mcg)	FOL (mcg) / PANT (mg)	Na (mg) / K (mg)	Ca (mg) / P (mg)	Mg (mg) / Fe (mg)	Zn (mg) / Cu (mg)	Mn (mg)
MILK BEVERAGE MIXES															
choc powder[a] for cocoa or choc milk	83		0.6			0	.04	tr			54	9	18	.270	.115
1 T	22	1.3	19.5		0.1	4	.00	0.1			168	31	.78	.122	
choc powder,[a] Hershey	76		0.4	0.0	0			.01			36	6	23	.38	.17
1 T	21	1.0	16.8	0.0	0.3	4	.01	.01			89	17	.69	.17	
choc syrup,[a] Bosco	50	5.9	0.1					.20			25				
1 T	20	0.2	13.4		0.1	1000		0.4					.40		
cocoa mix[b]	107		0.6			1	.19	.04	3		171	88	23	.45	.095
1 oz	28	3.5	22.4		0.1	3	.03	0.2	.44	.33	241	99	.28	.106	
cocoa mix,[b] Hershey	115		2.2	0.0	0			.09			141	90	25	.48	
1 oz	28	3.1	20.6	1.0	0.2	6	.02	0.1			77	87	.62	.11	
malt powder[a]	86	0.5	1.6	0.3	4	17	0	.19	.09	10	109	63	20	.21	.090
2–3 hp t (¾ oz)	21	2.3	16.0	0.9	tr	61	.08	1.1	.16		159	75	.14	.042	
malt powder, choc[a]	79	0.4	0.9	0.1	1	5	0	.04	.05	4	56	15	15	.19	.090
2–3 hp t (¾ oz)	21	1.5	18.0	0.5	tr	19	.03	0.4	.05		130	37	.65	.042	
ovaltine, choc powder[a]	77		0.6				27	.58	.66	17	108	101	19	.20	.090
¾ oz	21	1.5	17.8		tr	2036	.54	12.5			230	74	4.65	.110	
ovaltine, malt powder[a]	78		0.2				28	.76	.65	17	81	80	14	.15	.090
¾ oz	21	1.9	17.7		tr	2254	.58	11.7			206	80	4.37	.060	
strawberry powder,[a] Quik	90		0.0												
1 T	22	0.0	22.0												
YOGURT (from cow milk)															
plain															
lowfat w/nfdm	144	193.1	3.5	0.1	14	36	2	.49	.11	25	159	415	40	2.02	
1 cup	227	11.9	16.0	2.3	0.0	150	.10	0.3	1.28	1.34	531	326	.18		
skim w/nfdm	127	193.5	0.4	tr	4	5	2	.53	.12	28	174	452	43	2.20	
1 cup	227	13.0	17.4	0.3	0.0	16	.11	0.3	1.39	1.46	579	355	.20		
whole milk	139	199.5	7.4	0.2	29	68	1	.32	.07	17	105	274	26	1.34	
1 cup	227	7.9	10.6	4.8	0.0	279	.07	0.2	.84	.88	351	215	.11		
flavored, lowfat w/nfdm															
coffee/van flavor	194	179.3	2.8	tr	11	30	2	.46	.10	24	149	389	37	1.88	
1 cup	227	11.2	31.3	1.8	0.0	123	.10	0.2	1.20	1.25	498	306	.16		
fruit flavored	225	170.9	2.6	0.1	10	27	1	.37	.08	19	121	314	30	1.52	
1 cup	227	9.0	42.3	1.7	0.3	111	.08	0.2	.97	1.01	402	247	.14		
flavored, whole milk															
fruit flavored[c]	190		4.0								120				
6 oz	170	7.0	32.0												
fruit flavored,[c] custard style	180		4.0								105				
6 oz	170	7.0	30.0												
van, custard style	180		4.0								110				
6 oz	170	7.0	30.0												
w/honey, custard style	160		4.0							110					
6 oz	170	7.0	23.0												

NUTS, NUT PRODUCTS & SEEDS
NUTS & NUT PRODUCTS

	KCAL / WT (g)	H_2O (g) / PRO (g)	FAT (g) / CHO (g)	PUFA (g) / SFA (g)	CHOL (mg) / FIBR (g)	A (RE) / A (IU)	C (mg) / B-1 (mg)	B-2 (mg) / NIA (mg)	B-6 (mg) / B-12 (mcg)	FOL (mcg) / PANT (mg)	Na (mg) / K (mg)	Ca (mg) / P (mg)	Mg (mg) / Fe (mg)	Zn (mg) / Cu (mg)	Mn (mg)
almonds	90	1.1	8.1	1.6			tr	.10			tr	38			
12–15 nuts	15	2.8	2.9			0	.04	0.7			104	71	.70		
almonds, salted	93	1.1	8.5				tr	.10			24	38			
12–15 nuts	15	2.8	2.9	1.7		0	.04	0.7			106	71	.70		
almonds, roasted, salted	176	2.0	16.2				0	.26			55	66			
1 oz	28	5.2	5.5	0.7		0	.01	1.0			216	141	1.30		

[a] To be mixed w/milk
[b] Contains dry milk & needs only hot water for reconstitution
[c] Blueberry, lemon, raspberry, or strawberry

	KCAL	H₂O (g)	FAT (g)	PUFA (g)	CHOL (mg)	A (RE)	C (mg)	Vitamins B-2 (mg)	B-6 (mg)	FOL (mcg)	Na (mg)	Minerals Ca (mg)	Mg (mg)	Zn (mg)	Mn (mg)
	WT (g)	PRO (g)	CHO (g)	SFA (g)	FIBR (g)	A (IU)	B-1 (mg)	NIA (mg)	B-12 (mcg)	PANT (mg)	K (mg)	P (mg)	Fe (mg)	Cu (mg)	
almond paste	144		9.1	1.8			tr	.11			60	43			
1 oz	28	3.1	14.5			0	.04	0.8			116	80	.74		
almond powder, Nutquik	165	1.5	15.0	4.2			tr	.28	.01		4	64	77	1.09	
1 oz	28	7.2	3.6	1.6	1.3		.05	1.0			195	124	1.15	.36	
beechnuts	171	1.8	14.1	5.7											
1 oz	28	5.4	5.7		1.0										
brazil nuts	97	0.7	9.9	2.8			0				tr	28			
4 med	15	2.2	1.7		0.3	tr	.13				100	104	.50		
brazil nuts	646	4.6	65.9	18.4			10	.12			1	186			
⅓ cup	100	14.4	11.0		2.1	tr	1.09	7.7			670	693			
butternuts	96	0.6	9.2												
4–5 med	15	3.6	1.3										1.00		
cashews, roasted	84	0.8	6.9	0.4				.04			2	6	40		
6–8 nuts	15	2.6	4.4		0.2	15	.06	0.3			70	56	.60		
cashews, roasted	280	2.6	22.9	1.5				.13			8	19	134		
20–26 nuts	50	8.6	14.6		0.7	50	.22	0.9			232	186	1.90		
chestnuts															
fresh	29	7.9	0.2					.03			tr	4			
3 small	15	0.4	6.2				.03	0.1			62	13	.30		
fresh	191	52.5	1.5					.22			2	29			
½ cup	100	2.8	41.5		1.1		.23	0.5			410	87	1.70		
dried	377	8.4	4.1					.39			4	57			
½ cup	100	6.7	78.6		2.5		.34	0.8				170	3.30		
coconut															
dried, shredded, sweetened	53	1.5	3.6	0.1	tr		0	tr			29	2	5		
2 T	11	0.4	4.8	3.2	0.2	0	tr	tr	.00		36	11	.20	.034	
dried, shredded, sweetened	135	3.8	9.2	0.2	tr		0	.01			73	4	14		
⅓ cup	28	1.1	12.2	8.1	0.6	0	.01	0.1	.00		91	29	.52	.086	
dried, shredded, sweetened, cnd	114	6.1	8.2	0.2	tr		0	.01			5	4	13		
⅓ cup	26	1.0	10.5	7.2	0.6	0	.01	0.1	.00		84	27	.48	.080	
fresh meat	54	7.6	5.2	0.1			0	.01			3	3			
1 piece	15	0.5	2.1			0	.01	0.1			116	15	.30		
fresh, shredded	174	24.4	16.3	0.2			2	.01			8	10			
½ cup	48	1.6	6.8			0	.02	0.3			373	47	.95		
filberts (hazelnuts)	97	0.9	9.5	3.5			1	.08			tr	38			
10–12 nuts	15	1.6	3.0		2.3	16	.07	0.8			71	48	.50		
hickory nuts	101	0.5	10.1	1.9			0								
15 small	15	2.1	2.0		0.3	0							.40		
litchi nuts, dried	45		0.1				5				tr	4			
6 med	15	0.5	10.5			0					165		.30		
macadamia nuts, roasted	109	0.5	11.7				0	.02				8			
6 med	15	1.4	1.5			0	.03	0.2				36	.30		
mixed	94		8.9				tr	.02			2	14			
8–12 nuts	15	2.5	2.7			3	.09	0.6			84	67	.50		
mixed	313		29.6				tr	.07			7	47			
27–49 nuts	50	8.3	9.0			10	.30	2.0			280	223	1.70		
peanuts															
raw, w/skin	152	1.6	12.3	3.6			tr	.06			1	18	44	.92	.476
1 oz	28	7.1	6.0		1.2	4	.25	4.9			202	110	.84	.21	
raw, w/o skin	157	1.5	13.2	3.8			tr	.06				13	44	.92	.476
1 oz	28	7.5	4.9		0.5	1	.24	5.3				130	.90	.21	
roasted, w/skin	172	0.5	14.0	4.0			tr	.08				22			
1 oz	28	8.0	6.6		1.0	tr	.08	5.0			222	120	1.00		
roasted, w/skin, salted	158	0.5	13.1	3.8			0	.04			129	10			
1 oz	28	8.1	5.1		0.4	tr	.07	5.3			196	116	.90		
roasted, w/o skin, salted	170	0.5	14.0	4.0			tr	.04			138	10			
1 oz	28	8.6	5.4		0.4	tr	.08	5.6			210	124	1.00		
peanut butter	86	0.3	7.2	1.8			0	.02			18	11	22	.44	.212
1 T	15	3.9	3.2			0	.02	2.4			123	59	.30	.10	

	KCAL / WT (g)	H₂O (g) / PRO (g)	FAT (g) / CHO (g)	PUFA (g) / SFA (g)	CHOL (mg) / FIBR (g)	A (RE) / A (IU)	C (mg) / B-1 (mg)	B-2 (mg) / NIA (mg)	B-6 (mg) / B-12 (mcg)	FOL (mcg) / PANT (mg)	Na (mg) / K (mg)	Ca (mg) / P (mg)	Mg (mg) / Fe (mg)	Zn (mg) / Cu (mg)	Mn (mg)
peanut butter	576	1.7	47.8	11.9			0	.13			120	74	148	2.91	1.410
6–7 T	100	26.1	21.0		2.0	0	.12	16.2			820	393	1.90	.67	
peanut butter, creamy, Jif	186	0.4	15.7	5.0	0			.03			157	13	48	.736	
2 T	32	9.0	5.4	3.0	0.5		.02	3.8			234	99	.58	.192	
peanut butter, chunky, Jif	186	0.3	15.7	5.0	0			.03			131	12			
2 T	32	9.0	5.4	3.0	0.5		.02	3.8							
peanut butter, Skippy	95	0.2	8.2	2.6	0			.01			75	5	30	.50	
1 T	16	4.0	2.8	1.7	0.3		.01	2.2			110	60	.30		
peanut butter, old fashioned,[a] Skippy	95	0.2	8.1	2.7	0			.01			75	5	30	.50	
1 T	16	4.2	2.7	1.5	0.3		.01	2.3		.20	110	60	.30		
pecans	104	0.5	11.0	2.3			tr	.02			tr	11			
12 halves	15	1.4	2.0			8	.11	0.1			63	49	.40		
pignolia nuts	84	0.8	7.3												
2 T	15	4.7	1.7												
pili nuts	90	0.9	9.4				3	tr				23			
2 T	15	1.6	1.4		0.3	2	.10	0.1				9	.60		
pinon (pine) nuts	95	0.5	9.2				tr	.03				2			
2 T	15	2.3	2.5		0.4	2	.11	1.5				77	.70		
pistachios	88	0.8	8.0	1.6											
30 nuts	15	2.9	2.8		0.3										
soybean nuts	127		5.5					.07			19	68			
1 oz	28	13.3	6.6		1.0		.08				336	190	1.40		
walnuts, black	94	0.5	8.7	4.8			0								
8–10 halves	15	2.7	2.8			11							.90		
walnuts, english	98	0.5	9.7	7.2			tr	.02			tr	12			
8–15 halves	15	2.3	2.3		0.3	5	.07	0.2			68	57	.30		
walnuts, english, chopped	49	0.3	4.8	3.6			tr	.01			tr	6			
1 T	8	1.1	1.2		0.2	2	.04	1.0			36	28	.20		

SEEDS

	KCAL / WT (g)	H₂O (g) / PRO (g)	FAT (g) / CHO (g)	PUFA (g) / SFA (g)	CHOL (mg) / FIBR (g)	A (RE) / A (IU)	C (mg) / B-1 (mg)	B-2 (mg) / NIA (mg)	B-6 (mg) / B-12 (mcg)	FOL (mcg) / PANT (mg)	Na (mg) / K (mg)	Ca (mg) / P (mg)	Mg (mg) / Fe (mg)	Zn (mg) / Cu (mg)	Mn (mg)
pumpkin & squash kernels	155	1.2	13.1				20	.05				14			
1 oz	28	8.1	4.2		0.5		.07	0.7				320	3.14		
safflower seed kernels	172	1.4	16.7												
1 oz	28	5.3	3.5												
sesame seeds, decorticated	47	0.4	4.4		0	1		.01	.01		3	10	28	.82	
1 T	8	2.1	0.8		0.2	5	.06	0.4	.00	.05	33	62	.62		
sesame seeds, decorticated	167	1.3	15.5		0	4		.02	.04		11	35	99	2.91	
1 oz	28	7.5	2.7		0.9	18	.21	1.3	.00	.19	117	220	2.20		
sunflower seed kernels	157	1.3	13.2				14	.06			8	34			
1 oz	28	6.7	5.6		1.1		.55	1.5			258	234	1.99		

POULTRY[b]
CHICKEN

flesh & parts

broilers/fryers, light & dark meat

	KCAL / WT (g)	H₂O (g) / PRO (g)	FAT (g) / CHO (g)	PUFA (g) / SFA (g)	CHOL (mg) / FIBR (g)	A (RE) / A (IU)	C (mg) / B-1 (mg)	B-2 (mg) / NIA (mg)	B-6 (mg) / B-12 (mcg)	FOL (mcg) / PANT (mg)	Na (mg) / K (mg)	Ca (mg) / P (mg)	Mg (mg) / Fe (mg)	Zn (mg) / Cu (mg)	Mn (mg)
w/skin, fried, batter dipped	289	49.4	17.4	4.1	87	28	0	.19	.31	8	292	21	21	1.67	.057
3½ oz	100	22.5	9.4	4.6	0.0	93	.12	7.0	.28	.89	185	155	1.37	.07	
w/skin, fried, flour coated	269	52.4	14.9	3.4	90	27	0	.19	.41	6	84	17	25	2.04	.034
3½ oz	100	28.6	3.2	4.1	0.0	89	.09	9.0	.31	1.08	234	191	1.38	.08	
w/skin, roasted	239	59.5	13.6	3.0	88	47	0	.17	.40	5	82	15	23	1.94	.020
3½ oz	100	27.3	0.0	3.8	0.0	161	.06	8.5	.30	1.03	223	182	1.26	.07	
w/skin, stewed	219	63.9	12.6	2.7	78	42	0	.15	.22	5	67	13	19	1.76	.019
3½ oz	100	24.7	0.0	3.5	0.0	146	.05	5.6	.20	.67	166	139	1.16	.06	
w/o skin, fried	219	57.3	9.1	2.2	94	18	0	.20	.48	7	91	17	27	2.24	.028
3½ oz	100	30.6	1.7	2.5	0.0	59	.09	9.7	.34	1.17	257	205	1.35	.08	

[a] No added sweeteners or fats [b] Weights represent edible portions.

	KCAL	H₂O (g)	FAT (g)	PUFA (g)	CHOL (mg)	A (RE)	C (mg)	B-2 (mg)	B-6 (mg)	FOL (mcg)	Na (mg)	Ca (mg)	Mg (mg)	Zn (mg)	Mn (mg)
	WT (g)	PRO (g)	CHO (g)	SFA (g)	FIBR (g)	A (IU)	B-1 (mg)	NIA (mg)	B-12 (mcg)	PANT (mg)	K (mg)	P (mg)	Fe (mg)	Cu (mg)	
w/o skin, roasted	190	63.8	7.4	1.7	89	16	0	.18	.47	6	86	15	25	2.10	.019
3½ oz	100	28.9	0.0	2.0	0.0	53	.07	9.2	.33	1.10	243	195	1.21	.07	
w/o skin, stewed	177	66.8	6.7	1.5	83	15	0	.16	.26	6	70	14	21	1.99	.019
3½ oz	100	27.3	0.0	1.8	0.0	50	.05	6.1	.22	.75	180	150	1.17	.06	
broilers/fryers, light meat															
w/skin, fried	246	54.7	12.1	2.7	87	20	0	.13	.54	4	77	16	27	1.26	.026
3½ oz	100	30.5	1.8	3.3	0.0	68	.08	12.0	.33	.97	239	213	1.21	.06	
w/skin, roasted	222	60.5	10.9	2.3	84	32	0	.12	.52	3	75	15	25	1.23	.021
3½ oz	100	29.0	0.0	3.1	0.0	110	.06	11.1	.32	.93	227	200	1.14	.05	
w/skin, stewed	201	65.1	10.0	2.1	74	28	0	.11	.27	3	63	13	20	1.14	.018
3½ oz	100	26.1	0.0	2.8	0.0	96	.04	6.9	.20	.54	167	146	.98	.04	
w/o skin, fried	192	60.1	5.5	1.3	90	9	0	.13	.63	4	81	16	29	1.27	.020
3½ oz	100	32.8	0.4	1.5	0.0	30	.07	13.4	.36	1.03	263	231	1.14	.05	
w/o skin, roasted	173	64.8	4.5	1.0	85	9	0	.12	.60	4	77	15	27	1.23	.017
3½ oz	100	30.9	0.0	1.3	0.0	29	.07	12.4	34	.97	247	216	1.06	.05	
w/o skin, stewed	159	68.0	4.0	0.9	77	8	0	.12	.33	3	65	13	22	1.19	.018
3½ oz	100	28.9	0.0	1.1	0.0	27	.04	7.8	.23	.57	180	159	.93	.04	
broilers/fryers, dark meat															
w/skin, fried	285	50.8	16.9	3.9	92	31	0	.24	.32	8	89	17	24	2.60	.039
3½ oz	100	27.2	4.1	4.6	0.0	104	.10	6.8	.30	1.16	230	176	1.50	.09	
w/skin, roasted	253	58.6	15.8	3.5	91	58	0	.21	.31	7	87	15	22	2.49	.021
3½ oz	100	26.0	0.0	4.4	0.0	201	.07	6.4	.29	1.11	220	168	1.36	.08	
w/skin, stewed	233	63.0	14.7	3.2	82	54	0	.18	.17	6	70	14	18	2.26	.019
3½ oz	100	23.5	0.0	4.1	0.0	186	.05	4.5	.20	.77	166	133	1.31	.07	
w/o skin, fried	239	55.7	11.6	2.8	96	24	0	.25	.37	9	97	18	25	2.91	.033
3½ oz	100	29.0	2.6	3.1	0.0	79	.09	7.1	.33	1.26	253	187	1.49	.09	
w/o skin, roasted	205	63.1	9.7	2.3	93	22	0	.23	.36	8	93	15	23	2.80	.017
3½ oz	100	27.4	0.0	2.7	0.0	72	.07	6.6	.32	1.21	240	179	1.33	.08	
w/o skin, stewed	192	65.8	9.0	2.1	88	21	0	.20	.21	7	74	14	20	2.66	.021
3½ oz	100	26.0	0.0	2.5	0.0	69	.06	4.7	.22	.89	181	143	1.36	.08	
broilers/fryers, back w/skin, fried	238	31.7	14.9	3.5	64	27	0	.17	.22	6	65	17	17	1.78	.036
½ back	72	20.0	6.7	4.0	0.0	88	.08	5.3	.20	.79	163	119	1.17	.07	
broilers/fryers, breast															
w/skin, fried	218	55.5	8.7	1.9	88	15	0	.13	.57	4	75	16	29	1.07	.015
½ breast	98	31.2	1.6	2.4	0.0	49	.08	13.5	.34	.98	253	228	1.17	.06	
w/skin, roasted	193	61.2	7.6	1.6	83	26	0	.12	.54	3	69	14	27	1.00	.018
½ breast	98	29.2	0.0	2.2	0.0	91	.07	12.5	.32	.92	240	210	1.04	.05	
w/skin, stewed	202	72.8	8.2	1.7	83	26	0	.13	.32	3	68	14	24	1.06	.020
½ breast	110	30.1	0.0	2.3	0.0	90	.05	8.6	.23	.60	195	172	1.01	.05	
w/o skin, fried	161	51.8	4.1	0.9	78	6	0	.11	.55	4	68	14	27	.93	.018
½ breast	86	28.8	0.4	1.1	0.0	20	.07	12.7	.31	.89	237	212	.98	.05	
w/o skin, roasted	142	56.1	3.1	0.7	73	5	0	.10	.51	3	63	13	25	.86	.015
½ breast	86	26.7	0.0	0.9	0.0	18	.06	11.8	.29	.83	220	196	.89	.04	
w/o skin, stewed	144	64.9	2.9	0.6	73	6	0	.11	.32	3	59	12	22	.92	.017
½ breast	95	27.5	0.0	0.8	0.0	18	.04	8.0	.22	.54	178	157	.84	.04	
broilers/fryers, drumstick															
w/skin, fried	120	27.8	6.7	1.6	44	12	0	.11	.17	4	44	6	11	1.42	.014
1 drumstick	49	13.2	0.8	1.8	0.0	41	.04	3.0	.16	.60	112	86	.66	.04	
w/skin, roasted	112	32.6	5.8	1.3	48	15	0	.11	.18	4	47	6	12	1.49	.011
1 drumstick	52	14.1	0.0	1.6	0.0	52	.04	3.1	.17	.63	119	91	.69	.04	
w/skin, stewed	116	37.1	6.1	1.4	48	15	0	.11	.11	4	43	7	11	1.51	.011
1 drumstick	57	14.4	0.0	1.7	0.0	52	.03	2.4	.12	.49	105	80	.76	.04	
w/o skin, roasted	76	29.4	2.5	0.6	41	8	0	.10	.17	4	42	5	11	1.40	.009
1 drumstick	44	12.5	0.0	0.7	0.0	26	.03	2.7	.15	.57	108	81	.57	.04	
broilers/fryers, neck															
w/skin, fried	119	17.1	8.5	2.0	34	21	0	.09	.09	2	29	11	7	1.11	.019
1 neck	36	8.6	1.5	2.3	0.0	69	.03	1.9	.09	.35	65	48	.87	.05	

	KCAL	H₂O (g)	FAT (g)	PUFA (g)	CHOL (mg)	A (RE)	C (mg)	B-2 (mg)	B-6 (mg)	FOL (mcg)	Na (mg)	Ca (mg)	Mg (mg)	Zn (mg)	Mn (mg)
	WT (g)	PRO (g)	CHO (g)	SFA (g)	FIBR (g)	A (IU)	B-1 (mg)	NIA (mg)	B-12 (mcg)	PANT (mg)	K (mg)	P (mg)	Fe (mg)	Cu (mg)	
w/skin, simmered	94	23.5	6.9	1.5	27	18	0	.09	.04	1	20	10	5	1.03	.017
1 neck	38	7.5	0.0	1.9	0.0	61	.02	1.3	.05	.20	41	46	.87	.04	
w/o skin, simmered	32	12.1	1.5	0.4	14	7	0	.05	.03	1	12	8	3	.68	.009
1 neck	18	4.4	0.0	0.4	0.0	22	.01	0.7	.03	.12	25	23	.47	.02	
broilers/fryers, thigh															
w/skin, fried	162	33.6	9.3	2.1	60	18	0	.15	.21	5	55	8	5	1.56	.022
1 thigh	62	16.6	2.0	2.5	0.0	61	.06	4.3	.19	.74	147	116	.93	.06	
w/skin, roasted	153	36.8	9.6	2.1	58	30	0	.13	.19	4	52	8	14	1.46	.013
1 thigh	62	15.5	0.0	2.7	0.0	102	.04	3.9	.18	.69	137	108	.83	.05	
w/skin, stewed	158	42.9	10.0	2.2	57	30	0	.13	.12	4	49	8	13	1.53	.013
1 thigh	68	15.8	0.0	2.8	0.0	103	.04	3.3	.13	.53	115	94	.93	.05	
w/o skin, roasted	109	32.7	5.7	1.3	49	10	0	.12	.18	4	46	6	12	1.34	.010
1 thigh	52	13.5	0.0	1.6	0.0	34	.04	3.4	.16	.62	124	95	.68	.04	
broilers/fryers, wing															
w/skin, fried	103	15.6	7.1	1.6	26	12	0	.04	.13	1	25	5	6	.56	.009
1 wing	32	8.4	0.8	1.9	0.0	40	.02	2.1	.09	.28	57	48	.40	.02	
w/skin, roasted	99	18.7	6.6	1.4	29	16	0	.04	.14	1	28	5	7	.62	.006
1 wing	34	9.1	0.0	1.9	0.0	54	.01	2.3	.10	.31	62	51	.43	.02	
w/skin, stewed	100	24.9	6.7	1.4	28	16	0	.04	.09	1	27	5	6	.65	.007
1 wing	40	9.1	0.0	1.9	0.0	53	.02	1.8	.07	.20	56	48	.45	.02	
capon, w/skin, roasted	229	58.7	11.7	2.5	86	20	0	.17	.43	6	49	14	24	1.74	.021
3½ oz	100	29.0	0.0	3.3	0.0	68	.07	8.9	.33	1.10	255	246	1.49	.07	
roasters															
flesh w/skin, roasted	223	62.1	13.4	2.9	76	25	0	.14	.35	5	73	12	20	1.45	.018
3½ oz	100	24.0	0.0	3.7	0.0	83	.06	7.4	.27	.92	211	179	1.26	.06	
flesh w/o skin, roasted	167	67.4	6.6	1.5	75	12	0	.15	.41	5	75	12	21	1.52	.017
3½ oz	100	25.0	0.0	1.8	0.0	41	.06	7.9	.29	.97	229	192	1.21	.06	
light meat w/o skin, roasted	153	67.9	4.1	0.9	75	8	0	.09	.54	3	51	13	23	.78	.015
3½ oz	100	27.1	0.0	1.1	0.0	25	.06	10.5	.31	.91	236	217	1.08	.04	
dark meat w/o skin, roasted	178	67.1	8.8	2.0	75	16	0	.19	.31	7	95	11	20	2.13	.019
3½ oz	100	23.3	0.0	2.4	0.0	54	.06	5.7	.27	1.03	224	171	1.33	.07	
stewers															
flesh w/skin, stewed	285	53.1	18.9	4.2	79	39	0	.24	.25	5	73	13	20	1.77	.021
3½ oz	100	26.9	0.0	5.1	0.0	191	.09	5.8	.23	.75	182	180	1.37	.10	
flesh w/o skin, stewed	237	56.4	11.9	2.8	83	33	0	.28	.31	6	78	13	22	2.06	.022
3½ oz	100	30.4	0.0	3.1	0.0	112	.11	6.4	.26	.86	202	204	1.43	.12	
light meat w/o skin, stewed	213	57.8	8.0	1.9	70	22	0	.20	.39	4	58	14	23	.83	.020
3½ oz	100	33.0	0.0	2.0	0.0	73	.09	8.5	.27	.69	199	225	1.19	.09	
dark meat w/o skin, stewed	258	55.1	15.3	3.7	95	43	0	.35	.24	8	95	12	22	3.12	.023
3½ oz	100	28.1	0.0	4.1	0.0	145	.13	4.6	.25	1.01	204	187	1.64	.14	
chicken, cnd															
light meat w/broth	117	48.7	5.6	1.2			1	.09	.25		357	10	9		
½ can (2½ oz)	71	15.5	0.0	1.6	0.0		.01	4.5	.21	.60	98	110	1.12		
dark meat w/broth	120		7.0								432				
½ can (2½ oz)	71	15.0	0.0								135	102			
chicken frzn entrees															
chicken breast, baked, Stouffer's	385		24.0								715				
8½ oz	227	38.0	5.0								330				
chicken, creamed, Stouffer's	300		22.0								680				
6½ oz	184	20.0	6.0								225				
chicken divan, Stouffer's	335		22.0								830				
8½ oz	241	21.0	14.0								415				
chicken, fried, Banquet	650		38.9				0	.27			1630	380			
8 oz	227	44.8	29.3			46	.11	9.1			877	550	4.93		
chicken, fried, Campbell's	300		16.0				0	.16			595	35			
4 oz	112	21.0	18.0			0	.09	9.7			462	260	1.50		

	KCAL / WT (g)	H₂O (g) / PRO (g)	FAT (g) / CHO (g)	PUFA (g) / SFA (g)	CHOL (mg) / FIBR (g)	A (RE) / A (IU)	C (mg) / B-1 (mg)	B-2 (mg) / NIA (mg)	B-6 (mg) / B-12 (mcg)	FOL (mcg) / PANT (mg)	Na (mg) / K (mg)	Ca (mg) / P (mg)	Mg (mg) / Fe (mg)	Zn (mg) / Cu (mg)	Mn (mg)
chicken nibbles, Campbell's	310		20.0				0	.12			272	21			
3 oz	84	16.0	18.0			0	.18	4.1			130	98	1.50		
chicken w/white wine sce, Swanson	370		27.0								1060				
8¼ oz	234	24.0	10.0												
chicken roll, light meat	159	68.6	7.4	1.6	50			.13			584	43	19	.72	
3½ oz	100	19.5	2.5	2.0			.07	5.3			228	157	.97	.04	

TURKEY

flesh & parts

	KCAL / WT (g)	H₂O (g) / PRO (g)	FAT (g) / CHO (g)	PUFA (g) / SFA (g)	CHOL (mg) / FIBR (g)	A (RE) / A (IU)	C (mg) / B-1 (mg)	B-2 (mg) / NIA (mg)	B-6 (mg) / B-12 (mcg)	FOL (mcg) / PANT (mg)	Na (mg) / K (mg)	Ca (mg) / P (mg)	Mg (mg) / Fe (mg)	Zn (mg) / Cu (mg)	Mn (mg)
flesh w/skin, roasted	208	61.7	9.7	2.5	82	0	0	.18	.41	7	68	26	25	2.96	.021
3½ oz	100	28.1	0.0	2.8	0.0	0	.06	5.1	.35	.86	280	203	1.79	.09	
flesh w/o skin, roasted	170	64.9	5.0	1.4	76	0	0	.18	.46	7	70	25	26	3.10	.021
3½ oz	100	29.3	0.0	1.6	0.0	0	.06	5.4	.37	.94	298	213	1.78	.09	
light meat w/skin, roasted	197	62.8	8.3	2.0	76	0	0	.13	.47	6	63	21	26	2.04	.020
3½ oz	100	28.6	0.0	2.3	0.0	0	.06	6.3	.35	.63	285	208	1.41	.05	
light meat w/o skin, roasted	157	66.3	3.2	0.9	69	0	0	.13	.54	6	64	19	28	2.04	.020
3½ oz	100	29.9	0.0	1.0	0.0	0	.06	6.8	.37	.68	305	219	1.35	.04	
light & dark meat, roasted	155	67.8	5.8		53			.16	.27		680	5	22	2.54	
3½ oz	100	21.3	3.1				.05	6.3	1.52	.81	298	244	1.63	.06	
light & dark meat, smoked	120	73.0	5.0	1.0	44			.12	.37		983	6	19	1.98	
3½ oz	100	18.0	0.7	1.4			.05	6.6	.76		244	258	.45		
dark meat w/skin, roasted	221	60.2	11.5	3.1	89	0	0	.24	.32	9	76	33	23	4.16	.023
3½ oz	100	27.5	0.0	3.5	0.0	0	.06	3.5	.36	1.16	274	196	2.27	.15	
dark meat w/o skin, roasted	187	63.1	7.2	2.2	85	0	0	.25	.36	9	79	32	24	4.46	.023
3½ oz	100	28.6	0.0	2.4	0.0	0	.06	3.6	.37	1.29	290	204	2.33	.16	
breast, bbq, Louis Rich	135	70.0	5.0	1.0	57			.11	.38		568	6	25	1.25	
3½ oz	100	23.0	0.0	1.5			.05	9.7	.58		299	264	.43		
breast, oven roasted, Louis Rich	115	74.0	3.0	0.5	33			.12	.40		678	6	22	1.11	
3½ oz	100	21.0	0.0	0.7			.05	7.6	.71		226	276	.39		
breast, smoked, Louis Rich	120	72.0	4.0	0.4	31			.11	.46		959	6	23	1.22	
3½ oz	100	21.0	0.0	0.6			.06	8.5	.75		269	300	.42	.04	
drumsticks, ckd, Louis Rich	210	60.0	10.0	2.5	117			.26	.34		86	12	21	5.56	
3½ oz	100	29.0	0.0	3.5			.05	3.3	.37		162	152	2.40	.29	
drumsticks, smoked, Louis Rich	160	66.0	7.0	2.2				.29	.23		1340	23	18	3.56	
3½ oz	100	22.0	0.9	2.5			.07	4.9	2.13		223	247	1.42	.11	
wing, ckd, Louis Rich	190	64.0	9.0	2.3	94			.16	.42		74	8	21	3.51	
3½ oz	100	27.0	0.0	2.8			.03	3.6	.35		130	119	1.02	.13	
wing drumettes, smoked, Louis Rich	165	64.0	7.0	1.8	80			.17	.25		1082	13	19	2.66	
3½ oz	100	25.0	0.5	2.3			.04	6.6	1.07		185	208	.64		
cnd, light meat w/broth	116	46.9	4.9	1.2		0	1	.12			332	9			
½ can (2½ oz)	71	16.8	0.0	1.4	0.0	0	.01	4.7					1.32		
cnd, dark meat w/broth	120		7.0								382				
½ can (2½ oz)	71	15.0	0.0								192	121			

frzn entrees

	KCAL / WT (g)	H₂O (g) / PRO (g)	FAT (g) / CHO (g)	PUFA (g) / SFA (g)	CHOL (mg) / FIBR (g)	A (RE) / A (IU)	C (mg) / B-1 (mg)	B-2 (mg) / NIA (mg)	B-6 (mg) / B-12 (mcg)	FOL (mcg) / PANT (mg)	Na (mg) / K (mg)	Ca (mg) / P (mg)	Mg (mg) / Fe (mg)	Zn (mg) / Cu (mg)	Mn (mg)
sliced w/gravy	95	120.8	3.7	0.7				.18	.14		786	20	12	.99	
5 oz	142	8.4	6.6	1.2	0.4	59	.03	2.6				114	1.31		
sliced w/gravy, Banquet	141		4.3				tr	.16			1389	71			
8 oz	227	18.2	7.1			200	.05	6.4			298	189	2.20		
sliced w/gravy, bb, Banquet	98		3.8				tr	.09			836	36			
5 oz	142	10.5	5.3			74	.03	3.7			176	116	1.30		
sliced w/gravy, bb, Green Giant	100		2.8				6	.13			945	78			
5 oz	140	9.8	6.6			0	.06	2.5			183		.56		
sliced w/gravy, Swanson Hungry-Man—13¼ oz	380		13.0								1655				
	376	31.0	34.0												
ground, ckd	225	60.0	14.0	3.2	92			.27	.26		74	29	20	3.45	
3½ oz	100	25.0	0.0	4.5			.08	6.0	.25		260	193	1.66	.07	
turkey ham, cured thigh meat	128	71.4	5.1	1.5	62			.25	.28		996	10	21	3.06	
3½ oz	100	18.9	0.4	1.7			.05	3.5	2.27		325	191	2.76	.10	
turkey loaf, breast meat	110	71.9	1.6	0.3	41	0	0	.11	.36		1431	7	20	1.13	
3½ oz	100	22.5	0.0	0.5	0.0	0	.04	8.3	2.02	.59	278	229	.40	.05	

	KCAL / WT (g)	H₂O (g) / PRO (g)	FAT (g) / CHO (g)	PUFA (g) / SFA (g)	CHOL (mg) / FIBR (g)	A (RE) / A (IU)	C (mg) / B-1 (mg)	B-2 (mg) / NIA (mg)	B-6 (mg) / B-12 (mcg)	FOL (mcg) / PANT (mg)	Na (mg) / K (mg)	Ca (mg) / P (mg)	Mg (mg) / Fe (mg)	Zn (mg) / Cu (mg)	Mn (mg)
turkey patties, breaded, fried	266	46.7	16.9					.18			752	13			
1 patty	94	13.2	14.8				.09	2.2			259	254	2.07		
turkey roll, light meat	147	71.6	7.2	1.7	43			.23			489	40	16	1.56	
3½ oz	100	18.7	0.5	2.0			.09	7.0			251	183	1.28	.04	
turkey roll, light & dark meat	149	70.2	7.0	1.8	55			.28			58	32	18		
3½ oz	100	18.1	2.1	2.0			.09	4.8			270	168	1.35		
turkey sausage, ckd	50	12.4	3.4	0.9	17			.06	.06		163	4	5	.72	
1 oz	21	4.6	0.0	1.1			.02	1.1	.37		59	39	.39	.02	
turkey sausage, smoked, ckd	60	17.9	4.2	1.1	18			.06	.06		217	5	6	.71	
1 oz	28	4.8	0.3	1.4			.02	1.2	.56		55	39	.42	.03	
turkey sticks, breaded & fried	357	63.2	21.6					.23			1073	18			
2 sticks	128	18.2	21.8				.13	2.7			333	300	2.82		

OTHER POULTRY

	KCAL / WT (g)	H₂O (g) / PRO (g)	FAT (g) / CHO (g)	PUFA (g) / SFA (g)	CHOL (mg) / FIBR (g)	A (RE) / A (IU)	C (mg) / B-1 (mg)	B-2 (mg) / NIA (mg)	B-6 (mg) / B-12 (mcg)	FOL (mcg) / PANT (mg)	Na (mg) / K (mg)	Ca (mg) / P (mg)	Mg (mg) / Fe (mg)	Zn (mg) / Cu (mg)	Mn (mg)
duck w/skin, roasted	337	51.8	28.4	3.7	84	63	0	.27	.18	6	59	11	16	1.86	
3½ oz	100	19.0	0.0	9.7	0.0	210	.17	4.8	.30	1.10	204	156	2.70	.23	
duck w/o skin, roasted	201	64.2	11.2	1.4	89	23	0	.47	.25	10	65	12	20	2.60	
3½ oz	100	23.5	0.0	4.2	0.0	77	.26	5.1	.40	1.50	252	203	2.70	.23	
goose w/skin, roasted	305	52.0	21.9	2.5	91	21	0	.32	.37	2	70	13	22		
3½ oz	100	25.2	0.0	6.9	0.0	70	.08	4.2			329	270	2.83	.26	
goose w/o skin, roasted	238	57.2	12.7	1.5	96		0	.39	.47		76	14	25		
3½ oz	100	29.0	0.0	4.6	0.0		.09	4.1			388	309	2.87	.28	
guinea hen w/o skin, raw	110	74.4	2.5		63										
3½ oz	100	20.6	0.0		0.0										
pheasant w/o skin, raw	133	72.8	3.6	0.6		49	6	.15	.74		37	13	20	.97	.017
3½ oz	100	23.6	0.0	1.2	0.0	165	.08	6.8	.84	.96	262	230	1.15	.07	
quail w/o skin, raw	134	70.0	4.5	1.2		17	7	.29			51	13			
3½ oz	100	21.8	0.0	1.3	0.0	57	.28	8.2			237	307	4.50	.59	
squab (pigeon) w/o skin, raw	142	72.8	7.5	1.6	90										
3½ oz	100	17.5	0.0	2.0	0.0			6.9							

INTERNAL ORGANS

giblets

	KCAL / WT (g)	H₂O (g) / PRO (g)	FAT (g) / CHO (g)	PUFA (g) / SFA (g)	CHOL (mg) / FIBR (g)	A (RE) / A (IU)	C (mg) / B-1 (mg)	B-2 (mg) / NIA (mg)	B-6 (mg) / B-12 (mcg)	FOL (mcg) / PANT (mg)	Na (mg) / K (mg)	Ca (mg) / P (mg)	Mg (mg) / Fe (mg)	Zn (mg) / Cu (mg)	Mn (mg)
chicken, fried	277	47.9	13.5	3.4	446	3579	9	1.52	.61	379	113	18	25	6.27	.222
3½ oz	100	32.5	4.4	3.8	0.0	11929	.10	11.0	13.31	4.45	330	286	10.32	.42	
chicken, simmered	157	67.6	4.8	1.1	393	2229	8	.95	.34	376	58	12	20	4.57	.170
3½ oz	100	25.9	1.0	1.5	0.0	7431	.09	4.1	10.14	2.96	158	229	6.44	.26	
goose, raw	44	19.6	2.0												
1 oz	28	5.9	0.2		0.0										
guinea hen, raw	44	19.5	2.0												
1 oz	28	5.8	0.3		0.0										
pheasant, raw	39	20.0	1.4												
1 oz	28	5.8	0.4		0.0										
quail, raw	49	17.6	1.7												
1 oz	28	6.1	1.9		0.0										
squab (pigeon), raw	43	19.5	2.0												
1 oz	28	5.5	0.3		0.0										
turkey, simmered	167	65.4	5.1	1.1	418	1795	2	.90	.33	345	59	13	17	3.68	.175
3½ oz	100	26.6	2.1	1.5	0.0	6036	.05	4.5	24.03	3.46	200	204	6.71	.39	

gizzard

	KCAL / WT (g)	H₂O (g) / PRO (g)	FAT (g) / CHO (g)	PUFA (g) / SFA (g)	CHOL (mg) / FIBR (g)	A (RE) / A (IU)	C (mg) / B-1 (mg)	B-2 (mg) / NIA (mg)	B-6 (mg) / B-12 (mcg)	FOL (mcg) / PANT (mg)	Na (mg) / K (mg)	Ca (mg) / P (mg)	Mg (mg) / Fe (mg)	Zn (mg) / Cu (mg)	Mn (mg)
chicken, simmered	153	67.3	3.7	1.1	194	56	2	.24	.12	53	67	10	20	4.38	.062
3½ oz	100	27.2	1.1	1.0	0.0	188	.03	4.0	1.94	.71	179	155	4.15	.11	
goose, raw	39	20.4	1.5												
1 oz	28	6.0	0.0		0.0										
turkey, simmered	163	65.4	3.9	1.1	232	55	2	.33	.12	52	54	15	19	4.16	.098
3½ oz	100	29.4	0.6	1.1	0.0	185	.03	3.1	1.90	.85	211	128	5.44	.17	

	KCAL	H₂O (g)	FAT (g)	PUFA (g)	CHOL (mg)	A (RE)	C (mg)	B-2 (mg)	B-6 (mg)	FOL (mcg)	Na (mg)	Ca (mg)	Mg (mg)	Zn (mg)	Mn (mg)
	WT (g)	PRO (g)	CHO (g)	SFA (g)	FIBR (g)	A (IU)	B-1 (mg)	NIA (mg)	B-12 (mcg)	PANT (mg)	K (mg)	P (mg)	Fe (mg)	Cu (mg)	
heart															
chicken, simmered	185	64.9	7.9	2.3	242	9	2	.74	.32	80	48	19	20	7.30	.107
3½ oz	100	26.5	0.1	2.3	0.0	28	.07	2.8	7.29	2.65	132	199	9.03	.50	
turkey, simmered	177	64.2	6.1	1.8	226	8	2	.88	.32	79	55	13	22	5.27	.092
3½ oz	100	26.8	2.1	1.8	0.0	28	.07	3.3	7.15	2.72	183	205	6.89	.63	
liver															
chicken, simmered	157	68.3	5.5	0.9	631	4913	16	1.75	.58	770	51	14	21	4.34	.297
3½ oz	100	24.4	0.9	1.8	0.0	16375	.15	4.5	19.39	5.41	140	312	8.47	.37	
duck, raw	136	71.8	4.6	0.6		11946						11			
3½ oz	100	18.7	3.5	1.4	0.0	39907			54.00			269	30.53	5.96	
goose, raw	125	67.5	4.0	0.2		8728		.84	.72		132	40	23		
1 liver	94	15.4	5.9	1.5	0.0	29138	.53	6.1			216	245		7.07	
turkey, simmered	169	65.6	6.0	1.1	626	3741	2	1.42	.52	666	64	11	15	3.09	.250
3½ oz	100	24.0	3.4	1.9	0.0	12581	.05	5.9	47.50	5.96	194	272	7.80	.56	

SALAD DRESSINGS
REGULAR

	KCAL	H₂O (g)	FAT (g)	PUFA (g)	CHOL (mg)	A (RE)	C (mg)	B-2 (mg)	B-6 (mg)	FOL (mcg)	Na (mg)	Ca (mg)	Mg (mg)	Zn (mg)	Mn (mg)
	WT (g)	PRO (g)	CHO (g)	SFA (g)	FIBR (g)	A (IU)	B-1 (mg)	NIA (mg)	B-12 (mcg)	PANT (mg)	K (mg)	P (mg)	Fe (mg)	Cu (mg)	
blue (bleu) cheese	77	4.9	8.0	4.3		32	tr	.00				12			
1 T	15	0.7	1.1	1.5	0.0		.00	0.0				11	.00		
blue (bleu) cheese, from mix[a]	84	5.5	9.1	3.4	tr		0	tr	tr	tr	214	3	tr	.015	
1 T	16	0.4	0.3	1.4	tr	2	tr	tr	tr	tr	4	3	.02	.003	
buttermilk, from mix,[b] **Good Seasons**	58	7.9	5.8	2.9	5		tr	.02	.01	1	138	16	2	.054	
1 T	16	0.5	1.2	1.0	tr	31	.01	tr	.04	.05	24	14	.05	.001	
caesar	70		7.0												
1 T	15	0.0	1.0												
calif herb & cheese	182		20.0								647				
1 fl oz	31	0.2	0.3								21				
canadian-bacon flavored	78		1.5								300				
1 fl oz	31	0.5	16.0								20				
ckd, homemade	25	11.1	1.5	0.3		66	tr	.02			117	13			
1 T	16	0.7	2.4	0.5	0.0		.01	tr			19	14	.10		
farm style, from mix, Good Seasons	53	8.0	5.6	2.9	4		tr	.01	tr	tr	125	11	1	.045	
1 T	15	0.4	0.6	0.9	tr	23	tr	tr	.02	.02	15	9	.05	.003	
french	67	5.9	6.4	3.4							214	2			.01
1 T	16	0.1	2.7	1.5	0.1						12	2	.10		
french, from mix[a]	97	5.5	9.4	3.5	8		tr	.01	tr	1	206	7	1	.048	
1 T	19	0.4	2.9	1.4	tr	19	tr	tr	.05	.03	11	6	.07	.002	
french, creamy	70		6.9								125	1			
1 T	14	0.1	2.3		1.0	3					3	1	.00		
french, homemade	88	3.4	9.8	4.7		72	0	.00			92	1			
1 T	14	0.0	0.5	1.8	0.0		.00	0.0			3	tr	.00		
french, old fashioned, from mix,[a] **Good Seasons—***1 T*	84	5.5	9.2	3.5	0		tr	tr	tr		188	2	tr	.006	
	16	tr	0.5	1.4	tr	1	tr	tr	.00		2	1	.03	.001	
french, riviera, from mix,[a] **Good Seasons—***1 T*	91	5.5	9.2	3.5	0		tr	tr	tr	tr	273	2	1	.008	
	18	0.1	2.3	1.4	tr	15	tr	tr	.00	tr	11	2	.04	.004	
garlic, from mix[a]	83	5.5	9.2	3.4	0		tr	tr	tr		222	3	1	.017	
1 T	16	0.1	0.5	1.4	tr	23	tr	tr	.00		6	3	.05	.003	
garlic w/cheese, from mix[a]	85	5.5	9.2	3.4	tr		tr	tr	tr	tr	173	4	tr	.018	
1 T	16	0.2	0.5	1.4	tr	3	tr	tr	.01	.01	5	3		.002	
green goddess	68		7.0	4.0							150	2			
1 T	14	0.1	1.2								9	1			
green onion	130		13.6								296				
1 fl oz	31	0.3	1.7								24				
italian	69	5.6	7.1	4.1							116	1			.02
1 T	15	0.1	1.5	1.0	0.0						2	1	.00		
italian, from mix[a]	84	5.5	9.1	3.4	0		tr	tr	tr		172	1	tr	.006	
1 T	16	0.1	0.6	1.4	tr	31	tr	tr	.00	tr	6	2	.03	.002	
italian, creamy	52		4.5								105	0			
1 T	14	0.1	2.7		tr										

[a] Prep w/vinegar, water & hydrogenated soybean oil

[b] Prep w/whole milk & mayo

	KCAL	H₂O (g)	FAT (g)	PUFA (g)	CHOL (mg)	A (RE)	C (mg)	B-2 (mg)	B-6 (mg)	FOL (mcg)	Na (mg)	Ca (mg)	Mg (mg)	Zn (mg)	Mn (mg)
	WT (g)	PRO (g)	CHO (g)	SFA (g)	FIBR (g)	A (IU)	B-1 (mg)	NIA (mg)	B-12 (mcg)	PANT (mg)	K (mg)	P (mg)	Fe (mg)	Cu (mg)	
italian, mild, from mix[a]	84	5.4	8.9	3.3	0		tr	tr	tr		147	1	tr	.004	
1 T	16	tr	1.2	1.3	tr	3	tr	tr	.00	tr	4	1	.03	.001	
italian w/cheese from mix[a]	88	5.7	9.5	3.5	tr		tr	tr	tr	2	187	4	1	.012	
1 T	17	0.1	1.1	1.4	tr	3	tr	tr	tr	.01	6	4	.04	.003	
italian, zesty, from mix	85	5.6	9.2	3.5	0		tr	tr	tr		123	1	tr	.008	
1 T	16	0.1	0.6	1.4	tr	tr	tr	tr	.00	tr	6	2	.03	.017	
mayonnaise type	57	5.9	4.9	2.6	4	32					105	2	tr		
1 T	15	0.1	3.5	0.7	0.0						1	4	.00		
poppy seed russian	121		10.8								271				
1 fl oz	31	0.2	5.6								25				
oil & vinegar	69		7.5	4.7							244	2			
1 T	15	tr	0.6								4	1			
onion, from mix[a]	85	5.6	9.2	3.5	0		tr	tr	tr		140	2	1	.004	
1 T	16	0.1	0.6	1.4	tr	1	tr	tr	.00	tr	6	13	.03	.001	
ranch style, prep w/mayo	54		5.7								97				
1 T	15	0.4	0.6												
red wine vinegar & oil	103		8.5								423				
1 fl oz	31	0.1	6.6								12				
russian	76	5.3	7.8	4.5		106	1	.01			133	3		.07	
1 T	15	0.2	1.6	1.1	0.0		.01	0.1			24	6	.10		
san francisco	125		13.4								444				
1 fl oz	31	0.4	0.6								10				
sesame seed	68	6.0	6.9	3.8	0						153				
1 T	15	0.5	1.3	0.9	0.1										
spin blend	50	7.4	5.1	2.7	8			.00			110				
1 T	16	0.1	2.6	0.8	0.0		.00	0.0							
sweet & sour	29		0.3								68	1			
1 T	15	0.2	6.9								14	1			
thousand island	59	7.2	5.6	3.1		50					109	2		.02	
1 T	16	0.1	2.4	0.9	0.3						18	3	.10		
vinegar & oil, homemade	72	7.6	8.0	3.9							tr				
1 T	16	0.0	0.4	1.5							1				

LOW CALORIE

	KCAL	H₂O (g)	FAT (g)	PUFA (g)	CHOL (mg)	A (RE)	C (mg)	B-2 (mg)	B-6 (mg)	FOL (mcg)	Na (mg)	Ca (mg)	Mg (mg)	Zn (mg)	Mn (mg)
	WT (g)	PRO (g)	CHO (g)	SFA (g)	FIBR (g)	A (IU)	B-1 (mg)	NIA (mg)	B-12 (mcg)	PANT (mg)	K (mg)	P (mg)	Fe (mg)	Cu (mg)	
blue (bleu) cheese	11		0.8				tr	.01			155	9			
1 T	14	0.4	0.6		tr	24		tr			5	7	tr		
coleslaw	31		3.4								163				
1 T	15	0.1	0.0												
french	22	11.3	0.9	0.5	1						128	2		.03	
1 T	16	0.0	3.5	0.1	0.0						13	2	.10		
french, low Na, sugar-free	1		0.0								3				
1 T	14	0.0	0.0								6	2			
green goddess	27		2.0								57				
1 T	14	0.1	2.2												
herb & spice, low Na	6		0.0								5				
1 T	28	0.0	1.0								65				
italian	16	12.3	1.5	0.9	1						118	0			
1 T	15	0.0	0.7	0.2	0.0						2	1	.00		
italian, from mix[b]	8	15.5	tr	tr	0		tr	tr	tr		163	1	tr	.006	
1 T	18	0.1	1.8	tr	tr	tr	tr	tr	.00	tr	5	2	.02	.001	
italian, low Na, sugar-free	1		0.0								3	2			
1 T	14	0.0	0.0								6				
mayonnaise-type	19		1.8					tr			17	3			
1 T	14	0.2	0.7		0.1	31	tr	tr			1	4	tr		
russian	23	10.6	0.7	0.4	1						141	3			
1 T	16	0.1	4.5	0.1	0.1						26	6	.10		
russian, low Na, sugar-free	3		0.0								2	23			
1 T	14	0.1	0.0								33	3			
thousand island	24	10.6	1.6	1.0	2	49					153	2			
1 T	15	0.1	2.5	0.2	0.2						17	3	.10		

[a] Prep w/vinegar, water & hydrogenated soybean oil   [b] Prep w/vinegar & water

	KCAL	H₂O (g)	FAT (g)	PUFA (g)	CHOL (mg)	A (RE)	C (mg)	B-2 (mg)	B-6 (mg)	FOL (mcg)	Na (mg)	Ca (mg)	Mg (mg)	Zn (mg)	Mn (mg)
	WT (g)	PRO (g)	CHO (g)	SFA (g)	FIBR (g)	A (IU)	B-1 (mg)	NIA (mg)	B-12 (mcg)	PANT (mg)	K (mg)	P (mg)	Fe (mg)	Cu (mg)	
thousand island, low Na, sugar-free	10		1.2								2	19			
1 T	14	0.1	0.0								33	3			
vinegar, low Na, sugar-free	1		0.0								2				
1 T	14	0.0	0.0								5	1			
zero, low Na, sugar-free	1		0.0								3				
1 T	14	0.0	0.0								6	2			

SAUCES, CONDIMENTS & GRAVIES
SAUCES & CONDIMENTS

	KCAL	H₂O (g)	FAT (g)	PUFA (g)	CHOL (mg)	A (RE)	C (mg)	B-2 (mg)	B-6 (mg)	FOL (mcg)	Na (mg)	Ca (mg)	Mg (mg)	Zn (mg)	Mn (mg)
	WT (g)	PRO (g)	CHO (g)	SFA (g)	FIBR (g)	A (IU)	B-1 (mg)	NIA (mg)	B-12 (mcg)	PANT (mg)	K (mg)	P (mg)	Fe (mg)	Cu (mg)	
bbq sce	12	12.6	0.3	0.1	0	14	1	tr	.01	tr	127	3	1	.012	
1 T	16	0.3	2.0	tr	0.1	136	.01	0.1	0	tr	27	3	.14	.006	
béarnaise sce, from mix	263	58.5	25.6	1.1	71						474				
¼ pkt prep	96	3.1	6.6	15.7	tr										
burger sce, Big H	65	5.8	7.1	3.7	4			.00			145				
1 T	15	0.2	1.6	1.0	tr		.00	0.0							
catsup, tomato	16	10.3	0.1				2	.01			156	3	3		
1 T	15	0.3	3.8			210	.01	0.2			54	8	.10		
chili sce, tomato	16	10.2	tr				2	.01			201	3			
1 T	15	0.4	3.7			210	.01	0.2			56	8	.10		
curry sce, from mix	84	67.5	4.6	0.9	11						399	152			
¼ pkt prep	85	3.4	8.1	1.9	0.1							88			
enchilada dip, Fritos	35	20.9	1.2		1		1	.04			169	13	12	.14	.168
1 oz	28	1.8	4.3		0.2	123	.01	0.2			116	29	.53	.11	
hollandaise sce, homemade	180		18.5					tr	.04			23			
¼ cup	50	2.2	0.4			1027	.03	tr				78	.90		
hollandaise sce w/butterfat, from mix	47	42.7	3.9	0.2	10			.04			308	24			
¼ pkt prep	51	0.9	2.7	2.3	0.0			tr			25		.18		
hollandaise sce w/veg oil, from mix	264	58.5	25.6	1.1	71						425				
¼ pkt prep	96	3.1	6.7	15.7	tr										
horseradish, prep	7	15.7	tr								17	11			
1 T	18	0.2	1.7		0.2						52	6	.20		
jalapeno bean dip, Fritos	33	20.5	1.1		1		0	.03			163	7	9	.10	.160
1 oz	28	1.5	2.9		0.3	42	.02	1.1			77	23	.39	.09	
mushroom sce, from mix	71	67.4	3.2	0.4	11						479				
¼ pkt prep	83	3.5	7.4	1.7	0.1										
mustard, brown	14	11.7	0.9								196	19	6		
1 T	15	0.9	0.8		0.2						20	20	.27		
mustard, yellow	11	12.0	0.7								188	13			
1 T	15	0.7	1.0		0.1						20	11	.30		
mustard, yellow w/horseradish	16		1.0								265				
1 T	16	1.0	1.0												
mustard, yellow w/onion	25		1.0								190				
1 T	17	1.0	5.0												
picante sce, Tostitos	40	74.4	0.6		1		2	.07			480	18	14	.09	.327
6 T	85	1.0	7.7		0.4	628	.03	0.5			171	60	.48	.13	
sour cream sce, homemade	124	35.0	11.9	1.2	1966	82	0	.07	.05	23	7	23	3	.51	
¼ cup	52	2.8	1.9	6.1	0.0	274	.04	tr	.57	.66	13	75	.30		
sour cream sce, from mix	64	27.0	3.8	0.4	12			.09			126	68		.17	
¼ pkt prep	39	2.4	5.7	2.0				0.1			92		.08	.01	
soy sce	11	12.2	0.0	0.0	0	0	0	.02	.03	2	1029	3	8	.04	.00
1 T	18	1.6	1.5	0.0		0	.01	0.6	0	.06	64	38	.49	.02	
spaghetti sce, cnd	79		3.8				4	.04			925	18			
½ cup	125	1.3	10.0			1093	.08	0.9			413		.88		
steak sce	18		tr				11	.07			149	6			
1 T	15	tr	2.5		0.1	51	.01	tr			64	1	.40		
steak sce w/mushrooms	9		0.1				2	.02			157	2			
1 fl oz	30	0.3	1.9		0.2	4	tr	0.1			10	5	.12		
stroganoff sce, from mix	73	62.4	2.9	0.1	10			.21			493	141		.30	
¼ pkt prep	80	3.2	9.1	1.8	0.2		.23	0.2			181	81	.36	.02	

	KCAL	H₂O (g)	FAT (g)	PUFA (g)	CHOL (mg)	A (RE)	C (mg)	B-2 (mg)	B-6 (mg)	FOL (mcg)	Na (mg)	Ca (mg)	Mg (mg)	Zn (mg)	Mn (mg)
	WT (g)	PRO (g)	CHO (g)	SFA (g)	FIBR (g)	A (IU)	B-1 (mg)	NIA (mg)	B-12 (mcg)	PANT (mg)	K (mg)	P (mg)	Fe (mg)	Cu (mg)	
sweet & sour sce	131		0.2								320				
¼ cup	72	0.1	32.1												
sweet & sour sce, bbq	211		2.9								1560				
1 fl oz	30	1.3	45.0								244				
sweet & sour sce, from mix	55	44.7	tr	tr	0			.02			146	8		.02	
¼ pkt prep	59	0.2	13.6	tr			0				12		.30	.01	
tabasco sce	tr		0.0					.01			22				
1 t	5	0.1	0.1		0.0		tr	tr			3				
taco sce, chunky	4		tr								102				
2 t	10	0.2	0.7								25				
taco sce, hot/mild, bottled	4		0.0												
2 t	10	0.1	0.8												
taco sce & seasoner	7		0.1								112				
2 t	10	0.1	1.4								45				
tartar sce	70	5.3	7.9	4.2	5						185				
1 T	14	0.1	0.2	1.3	tr										
teriyaki sce, bottled	15	12.2	0.0	0.0	0	0	0	.01	.02	4	690	4	11	.02	.00
1 T	18	1.1	2.9	0.0		0	.01	0.2	0	.04	41	28	.31	.02	
teriyaki sce, from mix	8	14.8	0.1	tr	0						299	7			
1 T	18	0.3	1.7	tr				0.1	0		14		.17		
teriyaki bbq marinade	60		0.9								4550				
1 fl oz	30	3.0	10.0								77				
white sce, homemade															
thin	37	23.6	2.6				0	.05			105	37			
2 T	30	1.2	2.3			107	.01	tr			44	30	tr		
thin	74	48.0	5.2				tr	.10			214	73			
¼ cup	61	2.4	4.6			213	.02	0.1			89	59	.10		
medium	54	24.2	4.1				0	.05			125	37	5		
2 T	33	1.3	3.1			164	.01	0.1			46	31	.10		
medium	107	48.4	8.1				tr	.10			250	74	9		
¼ cup	66	2.6	6.1			328	.02	0.2			92	61	.20		
thick	65	22.4	5.2					.05			132	35			
2 T	33	1.3	3.6			188	.02	0.1			44	30	.10		
thick	131	44.8	10.3					.11			263	71			
¼ cup	66	2.6	7.3			376	.03	0.2			88	59	.20		
white sce, from mix	151	134.4	8.4	1.1	22			.28	.04		498	265	165	.34	
¼ pkt prep	165	6.4	13.4	4.0	tr		.05	0.3			277	160	.17	.03	
worcestershire sce	12		0.0				27	.03			147	15			
1 T	15	0.3	2.7			51	tr	tr			120	9	.90		

GRAVIES

	KCAL	H₂O (g)	FAT (g)	PUFA (g)	CHOL (mg)	A (RE)	C (mg)	B-2 (mg)	B-6 (mg)	FOL (mcg)	Na (mg)	Ca (mg)	Mg (mg)	Zn (mg)	Mn (mg)
	WT (g)	PRO (g)	CHO (g)	SFA (g)	FIBR (g)	A (IU)	B-1 (mg)	NIA (mg)	B-12 (mcg)	PANT (mg)	K (mg)	P (mg)	Fe (mg)	Cu (mg)	
au jus, cnd	24		0.3	tr	tr	0	1	.09			839	6			
½ can	149	1.8	3.7	0.1		0	.03	1.3			115	47	.89		
au jus, from mix	9	120.2	0.4	tr	0.4						289	5		.02	
½ cup	123	0.3	1.2	0.2	0.0									.005	
beef, cnd	77	127.3	3.4	0.1	4	0	0	.05	.01	tr	73	8		1.45	.29
½ can	145	5.4	7.0	1.7		0	.04	0.9			118	43	1.02	.14	
brown, homemade, thick	164		14.0	6.0			0	.03			720	0	1		
¼ cup	72	1.2	8.0		0.0	0	.04	0.0			76	8	.40		
brown, from mix	4	136.8	0.1	tr	tr			tr			66	4	tr	.01	.005
½ cup	138	0.1	0.8	tr	0.0		tr	tr			3	2	.01	tr	
brown w/onions, cnd	25		1.0						.02		349	9	6	.46	.12
2 oz	57	0.0	4.0						tr		34	12	.17	.06	
chicken, cnd	118	127.1	8.5	2.2	3	0	0	.06	.01		859	30		1.19	.30
½ can	149	2.8	8.1	2.1		550	.02	0.6			162	43	.70	.15	
chicken, from mix	41	118.7	0.9	0.2	1			.07			566	19		.16	
½ cup	130	1.3	7.1	0.2	tr									.01	
chicken giblet, cnd	35		2.0						.01		328	10	1	.59	.14
2 oz	57	1.0	3.0					tr			14	9	.17	.07	

	KCAL	H₂O (g)	FAT (g)	PUFA (g)	CHOL (mg)	A (RE)	C (mg)	B-2 (mg)	B-6 (mg)	FOL (mcg)	Na (mg)	Ca (mg)	Mg (mg)	Zn (mg)	Mn (mg)
	WT (g)	PRO (g)	CHO (g)	SFA (g)	FIBR (g)	A (IU)	B-1 (mg)	NIA (mg)	B-12 (mcg)	PANT (mg)	K (mg)	P (mg)	Fe (mg)	Cu (mg)	
home style, from mix	25		0.5					.03			332	9			
¼ cup	69	0.8	3.7								27				
mushroom, cnd	75	132.6	4.0	1.5	0	0	0	.09	.03	0	849	11		1.04	.445
½ can	149	1.9	8.1	0.6		0	.05	1.0			158	22	.98	.15	
mushroom, from mix	35	118.6	0.4	tr	tr						701	24		.16	
½ cup	129	1.0	6.9	0.2										.05	
onion, from mix	40	118.8	0.3	tr	tr						518	34		.10	
½ cup	130	1.1	8.4	0.2										.02	
pork, from mix	38	118.7	0.9	0.1	1			.03			617	16			
½ cup	129	0.9	6.7	0.4											
turkey, cnd	76	132.0	3.1	0.7	3	0	0	.12			868	6			
½ can	149	3.9	7.6	0.9		0	.03	1.9			154	60	1.04		
turkey, from mix	43	118.8	0.9	0.2	1			.05			749	25			
½ cup	130	1.4	7.5	0.3	tr										

SOUPS
CANNED SOUPS

	KCAL	H₂O (g)	FAT (g)	PUFA (g)	CHOL (mg)	A (RE)	C (mg)	B-2 (mg)	B-6 (mg)	FOL (mcg)	Na (mg)	Ca (mg)	Mg (mg)	Zn (mg)	Mn (mg)
	WT (g)	PRO (g)	CHO (g)	SFA (g)	FIBR (g)	A (IU)	B-1 (mg)	NIA (mg)	B-12 (mcg)	PANT (mg)	K (mg)	P (mg)	Fe (mg)	Cu (mg)	
asparagus, crm of, made w/milk	161	213.3	8.2	2.2	22	83	4	.28	.06		1041	175	20	.92	.379
1 cup	248	6.3	16.4	3.3	0.7	599	.10	0.9			359	153	.87	.14	
asparagus, crm of, made w/water	87	224.0	4.1	1.8	5	44	3	.08	.01		981	29	4	.88	.376
1 cup	244	2.3	10.7	1.0	0.7	445	.05	0.8			173	39	.80	.12	
bean, rts	66	197.7	2.0				tr	.02			249	59			
7½ oz	213	2.7	9.4			460	.04	0.3			42			.80	
bean w/bacon, made w/water	173	212.9	5.9	1.8	3	89	2	.03	.04	32	952	81	44	1.03	.670
1 cup	253	7.9	22.8	1.5	1.5	889	.09	0.6			403	132	2.05	.40	
bean w/franks, made w/water	187	207.6	7.0	1.6	12	87	1	.07	.13		1092	86	49	1.18	.788
1 cup	250	10.0	22.0	2.1	1.5	869	.11	1.0			477	166	2.34	.40	
bean w/ham, chunky, rts	231	191.1	8.5	1.0	22	395	4	.15			972	79			
1 cup	243	12.6	27.1	3.3		3950	.15	1.7					3.23		
beef & mushroom, chunky, low Na, rts	200		7.0								75				
10¾ oz	305	12.0	23.0												
beef broth/bouillon, rts	16	234.1	0.5	tr	tr	0	0	.05			782	15			
1 cup	240	2.7	0.1	0.3	tr	0	.01	1.9			130	31	.41		
beef, chunky, rts	171	200.0	5.1	0.2	14	261	7	.15	.13	13	867	31		2.64	.240
1 cup	240	11.7	19.6	2.6	0.7	2611	.06	2.7	.61		336	120	2.32	.24	
beef veg & barley, made w/water	64	183.4	1.1				2	.07			795	17			
7 oz	200	4.8	8.6		0.4	1138	.02	0.7			72		1.00		
beefy mushroom, made w/water	a		3.0	0.1	7	0	5	.06					5		
1 cup	244	5.8	a	1.5		0	.04	0.9					.88		
beef noodle, made w/water	84	224.5	3.1	0.5	5	63	tr	.06	.04	4	952	15	6	1.54	.273
1 cup	244	4.8	9.0	1.2	tr	629	.07	1.1	.20		99	46	1.10	.14	
black bean, made w/water	116	215.6	1.5	0.5	0	49	1	.05	.09	25	1198	45	42	1.41	.642
1 cup	247	5.6	19.8	0.4	1.3	506	.08	0.5	.02	.20	273	107	2.16	.39	
celery, crm of, made w/milk	165	214.4	9.7	2.7	32	68	1	.25	.06	9	1010	186	22	.20	.253
1 cup	248	5.7	14.5	4.0	0.4	461	.07	0.4			309	151	.69	.15	
celery, crm of, made w/water	90	225.1	5.6	2.5	15	31	tr	.05	.01	2	949	40	6	.15	.251
1 cup	244	1.7	8.8	1.4	0.4	306	.03	0.3			123	37	.62	.14	
cheese, cond	311	198.3	21.0	0.6	59	218	0	.27	.05		1920	284	8	1.29	.514
1 cup	257	10.9	21.1	13.3		2177	.03	0.8	0		308	272	1.49	.26	
cheese, made w/milk	230	206.9	14.6	0.4	48	147	1	.33	.08		1020	288	20	.69	.259
1 cup	251	9.5	16.2	9.1		1243	.06	0.5	.44		340	250	.81	.14	
cheese, made w/water	155	217.7	10.5	0.3	30	109	0	.14	.03		959	142	4	.64	.257
1 cup	247	5.4	10.5	6.7		1088	.02	0.4	.00		154	136	.75	.13	
chicken & dumplings, made w/water	97	221.2	5.5	1.3	34	52	0	.07	.04		861	15	4	.37	.489
1 cup	241	5.6	6.0	1.3		518	.02	1.8	.16		116	61	.62	.12	
chicken broth, made w/water	39	234.1	1.4	0.3	1	0	0	.07	.02		776	9	2	.25	.249
1 cup	244	4.9	0.9	0.4	tr	0	.01	3.3	.24		210	73	.51	.12	
chicken, chunky, rts	178	211.1	6.6	1.4	30	130	1	.17	.05	5	887	24		1.00	.251
1 cup	251	12.7	17.3	2.0	0.3	1299	.09	4.4	.25		176	113	1.73	.25	

[a] Kcal & cho not available

	KCAL / WT (g)	H₂O (g) / PRO (g)	FAT (g) / CHO (g)	PUFA (g) / SFA (g)	CHOL (mg) / FIBR (g)	A (RE) / A (IU)	C (mg) / B-1 (mg)	B-2 (mg) / NIA (mg)	B-6 (mg) / B-12 (mcg)	FOL (mcg) / PANT (mg)	Na (mg) / K (mg)	Ca (mg) / P (mg)	Mg (mg) / Fe (mg)	Zn (mg) / Cu (mg)	Mn (mg)
chicken, crm of, made w/milk	191	210.4	11.5	1.6	27	94	1	.26	.07	8	1046	180	18	.68	.379
1 cup	248	7.5	15.0	4.6	0.1	715	.07	0.9			273	152	.67	.14	
chicken, crm of, made w/water	116	221.1	7.4	1.5	10	56	tr	.06	.02	2	986	34	3	.63	.376
1 cup	244	3.4	9.3	2.1	0.1	560	.03	0.8			87	38	.61	.12	
chicken gumbo, made w/water	56	229.0	1.4	0.4	5	14	5	.05	.06		955	24	4	.38	.251
1 cup	244	2.6	8.4	0.3	0.2	136	.02	0.7			75	25	.89	.12	
chicken mushroom, made w/water	a		9.2	2.3	10	112	0	.11				29			
1 cup	244	4.4	a	2.4		1135	.02	1.6					.88		
chicken noodle, chunky, rts	a		6.0	1.5	18	122	0	.17				24			
1 cup	240	12.7	a	1.4		1222	.07	4.3					1.44		
chicken noodle,ᵇ made w/water	75	221.7	2.5	0.6	7	72	tr	.06	.03	2	1107	17	5	.40	.289
1 cup	241	4.0	9.4	0.7	0.2	711	.05	1.4			55	36	.78	.20	
chicken noodle w/meatballs, rts	99	225.0	3.6	0.8	10	233	8	.12			1039	30			
1 cup	248	8.1	8.4	1.1	0.6	2326	.12	2.15					1.74		
chicken rice, chunky, rts	127	208.3	3.2	0.7	12	586	4	.10		4	888	35			
1 cup	240	12.3	13.0	1.0		5858	.02	4.1					1.87		
chicken rice, made w/water	60	226.1	1.9	0.4	7	66	tr	.02	.02	1	814	17	1	.26	.366
1 cup	241	3.5	7.2	0.5	tr	660	.02	1.1			100	21	.75	.12	
chicken veg, chunky, rts	167	200.3	4.8	1.0	17	599	6	.17			1068	25			
1 cup	240	12.3	18.9	1.4		5991	.04	3.3					1.47		
chicken veg, chunky, low Na, rts	250		11.0								100				
10¾ oz	305	14.0	24.0												
chicken veg, made w/water	74	223.3	2.8	0.6	10	266	1	.06	.05		944	18	6	.40	.366
1 cup	241	3.6	8.6	0.9	0.1	2656	.04	1.2			154	41	.87	.12	
chicken w/noodles, chunky, low Na, rts	180		5.0								100				
10¾ oz	305	12.0	19.0												
chili beef, made w/water	169	211.7	6.6	0.3	12	151	4	.08	.16		1035	43	30	1.40	1.050
1 cup	250	6.7	21.5	3.3	1.5	1510	.06	1.1	.32		525	148	2.13	.40	
clam chowder															
manhattan, chunky, rts	133	206.5	3.4	0.1	14	329	12	.06	.26	9	1000	67		1.68	.240
1 cup	240	7.3	18.8	2.1	0.5	3292	.06	1.8	7.92		384	84	2.64	.24	
manhattan, made w/water	78	218.4	2.3	1.3	2	93	3	.05	.08	10	1808	34	10	.93	.376
1 cup	244	4.2	12.2	0.4	0.5	920	.06	1.3	2.19	.12	262	57	1.89	.15	
new england, made w/milk	163	211.4	6.6	1.1	22	40	4	.24	.13	10	992	187	23	.80	.253
1 cup	248	9.5	16.6	3.0		164	.07	1.0	10.25		300	157	1.48	.14	
new england, made w/water	95	220.9	2.9	1.1	5	1	2	.04	.08	4	914	43	7	.75	.251
1 cup	244	4.8	12.4	0.4	0.3	8	.02	1.0	8.01	32	146	54	1.48	.12	
consomme w/gelatin, made w/water	29	231.9	0.0	0.0	0	0	1	.03	.02	3	637	8	0	.37	.366
1 cup	241	5.4	1.8	0.0		0	.02	0.7	.00		153	32	.53	.25	
corn, low Na, rts	180		5.0									30			
10¾ oz	305	3.0	30.0												
crab, rts	76	223.3	1.5	0.4	10	50	0	.07	.12		1234	65			
1 cup	244	5.5	10.3	0.4	0.5	505	.20	1.3	.20	.29	326	88	1.22		
escarole, rts	27	240.3	1.8	0.4	2	217	5	.05			3865	32			
1 cup	248	1.5	1.8	0.5	0.7	2170	.08	2.3					.74		
gazpacho, rts	57	228.8	2.2	1.3	0	20	3	.02	.15		1183	24			
1 cup	244	8.7	0.8	0.3	0.8	200	.05	0.9	.00	.17	224	37	.98		
lentil w/ham, rts	140	212.7	2.8	0.3	7	36	4	.11	.22	50	1318	42			
1 cup	248	9.3	20.2	1.1	1.4	360	.17	1.4	.30	.35	356	184	2.64		
minestrone, chunky, rts	127	208.1	2.8	0.3	5	435	5	.12			864	61			
1 cup	240	5.1	20.7	1.5		4352	.06	1.2					1.77		
minestrone, made w/water	83	220.1	2.5	1.1		234	1	.04	.10	16	911	34	7	.74	.366
1 cup	241	4.3	11.2	0.5	0.7	2337	.05	0.9	.00		312	56	.92	.12	
mushroom barley, made w/water	a		2.3	0.7	0	20	0	.09		0		13			
1 cup	244	1.9	a	0.4		198	.02	0.9					.50		
mushroom, crm of, cond	313	247.7	23.1	10.8	3	0	3	.20	.03		2469	78	11	1.44	.610
1 can	305	4.9	22.6	6.3	-0.6	0	.07	2.0			203	102	1.28	.31	
mushroom, crm of, made w/milk	203	209.7	13.6	4.6	20	38	2	.28	.06		1076	178	20	.64	.253
1 cup	248	6.1	15.0	5.1	0.3	154	.08	0.9			270	156	.59	.14	
mushroom, crm of, made w/water	129	220.4	9.0	4.2	2	0	1	.09	.06		1031	46	5	.59	.251
1 cup	244	2.3	9.3	2.4	0.5	0	.05	0.7	.05	.29	101	50	.51	.12	

ᵃ Kcal & cho not available

ᵇ Includes chicken noodle o's, chicken w/stars, curly noodle & chicken, and chicken alphabet

	KCAL	H₂O (g)	FAT (g)	PUFA (g)	CHOL (mg)	Vitamins A (RE)	C (mg)	B-2 (mg)	B-6 (mg)	FOL (mcg)	Minerals Na (mg)	Ca (mg)	Mg (mg)	Zn (mg)	Mn (mg)
	WT (g)	PRO (g)	CHO (g)	SFA (g)	FIBR (g)	A (IU)	B-1 (mg)	NIA (mg)	B-12 (mcg)	PANT (mg)	K (mg)	P (mg)	Fe (mg)	Cu (mg)	
mushroom w/beef stock, made w/water	85	224.7	4.0	0.8	7	126	1	.10	.04	9	970	10	9	1.38	.376
1 cup	244	3.2	9.3	1.6		1255	.03	1.2	.00		158	36	.84	.25	
onion, made w/water	57	224.3	1.7	0.7	0	0	1	.02	.05	15	1053	26	2	.61	.246
1 cup	241	3.8	8.2	0.3	0.5	0	.03	0.6	.00		69	11	.67	.12	
onion, crm of, made w/milk	ᵃ		9.4	1.6	32	68	2	.27				180			
1 cup	248	6.8	ᵃ	4.0		451	.10	0.6					.69		
onion, crm of, made w/water	ᵃ		5.3	1.5	15	30	1	.08				34			
1 cup	244	2.8	ᵃ	1.5		296	.05	0.5					.63		
oyster stew, made w/milk	134	217.9	7.9	0.3	32	45	4	.23	.06		1040	167	21	10.33	.370
1 cup	245	6.1	9.8	5.1		225	.07	0.3	2.63		235	162	1.04	1.61	
oyster stew, made w/water	59	228.6	3.8	0.2	14	7	3	.04	.01		980	22	5	10.29	.366
1 cup	241	2.1	4.1	2.5		71	.02	0.2	2.19		49	48	.98	1.59	
pea, green, made w/milk	239	197.9	7.0	0.5	18	58	3	.27	.10	8	1048	173	55	1.76	.660
1 cup	254	12.6	32.2	4.0	0.7	356	.16	1.3	.44		377	238	2.01	.39	
pea, green, made w/water	164	208.7	2.9	0.4	0	20	2	.07	.05	2	987	27	39	1.71	.658
1 cup	250	8.6	26.5	1.4	0.7	202	.11	1.2	.00		190	124	1.95	.38	
pea, split, rts	58	198.0	0.5				tr	.03			145	21			
7½ oz	213	2.9	10.4			690	.09	0.3			230		.40		
pea, split, low Na, rts	220		4.0								25				
10¾ oz	305	11.0	35.0												
pea, split w/ham, chunky, rts	184	194.3	4.0	0.6	7	487	7	.09		5	965	33			
1 cup	240	11.1	26.8	1.6		4871	.12	2.5					2.14		
pea, split w/ham, made w/water	189	206.9	4.4	0.6	8	44	1	.08	.07	3	1008	22	48	1.32	.670
1 cup	253	10.3	28.0	1.8	0.7	444	.15	1.5	.00		399	213	2.28	.37	
pea, split w/ham & bacon, made w/water—7 oz	126	167.5	1.5				2	.07			927	17			
	200	7.9	20.4		1.0	388	.15	1.1			273		1.40		
pepperpot, made w/water	103	217.3	4.6	0.4	10	87	1	.05	.06		970	23	5	1.22	.612
1 cup	241	6.4	9.4	2.1	0.5	865	.05	1.2	.17		152	42	.89	.12	
potato, crm of,ᵇ made w/milk	148	215.0	6.5	0.6	22	67	1	.24	.09	9	1060	166	17	.68	.379
1 cup	248	5.8	17.2	3.8		443	.08	0.6			323	160	.54	.26	
potato, crm of, made w/water	73	225.7	2.4	0.4	5	29	0	.04	.04	3	1000	20	1	.63	.379
1 cup	244	1.7	11.5	1.2		288	.03	0.5			137	46	.48	.25	
scotch broth, made w/water	80	221.1	2.6	0.6	5	218	1	.05	.07		1012	15	4	1.59	.366
1 cup	241	5.0	9.5	1.1		2180	.02	1.2	.27		159	55	.83	.25	
shrimp, crm of, made w/milk	165	214.3	9.3	0.4	35	54	1	.23			1036	164		.80	
1 cup	248	6.8	13.9	5.8		313	.06	0.5					.59		
shrimp, crm of, made w/water	90	225.0	5.2	0.2	17	16	0	.03			976	18		.75	
1 cup	244	2.8	8.2	3.2		158	.02	0.4					.53		
stockpot, made w/water	100	223.7	3.9	1.8	5	398	2	.05	.09		1048	22	4	1.16	.257
1 cup	247	4.9	11.5	0.9	0.5	3980	.04	1.2	.00		238	54	.87	.13	
tomato, made w/milk	160	210.0	6.0	1.1	17	108	68	.25	.16	21	932	159	23	.29	.251
1 cup	248	6.1	22.3	2.9	0.5	849	.13	1.5	.44		450	148	1.82	.26	
tomato, made w/water	86	220.5	1.9	1.0	0	69	67	.05	.11	15	872	13	8	.24	.253
1 cup	244	2.1	16.6	0.4	0.5	688	.09	1.4	.00		263	34	1.76	.25	
tomato beef w/noodle, made w/water	140	211.5	4.3	0.7	5	53	0	.09	.09		917	18	8	.75	.251
1 cup	244	4.5	21.2	1.6		533	.08	1.9	.19		221	56	1.12	.12	
tomato bisque, made w/milk	198	204.6	6.6	1.2	22	110	7	.27	.14		1108	186	25	.63	.259
1 cup	251	6.3	29.4	3.1		879	.11	1.3	.44		604	174	.88	.14	
tomato bisque, made w/water	123	215.3	2.5	1.1	4	72	6	.07	.09		1048	40	9	.59	.257
1 cup	247	2.3	23.7	0.5		721	.07	1.1	.00		417	60	.82	.13	
tomato rice, made w/water	120	217.6	2.7	1.4	2	76	15	.05	.08		815	23	5	.51	.385
1 cup	247	2.1	21.9	0.5	0.6	755	.06	1.1	.00		330	33	.79	.13	
tomato w/tomato pieces, low Na, rts	200		6.0								90				
10½ oz	298	3.0	32.0												
turkey, chunky, rts	136	203.8	4.4	1.1	9	716	6	.11	.31	11	923	50		2.12	.236
1 cup	236	10.2	14.1	1.2	0.9	7156	.04	3.6	2.12		361	104	1.91	.24	
turkey noodle, made w/water	69	226.9	2.0	0.5	5	29	tr	.06	.04		815	12	5	.58	.251
1 cup	244	3.9	8.6	0.6	0.2	292	.07	1.4			75	48	.94	.12	
turkey veg, made w/water	74	223.9	3.0	0.7	2	244	0	.04	.05		905	17	4	.61	.246
1 cup	241	3.1	8.6	0.9		2445	.03	1.0	.17		175	40	.76	.12	
veg, chunky, rts	122	210.2	3.7	1.4	0	588	6	.07	.19	17	1010	56		3.12	.480
1 cup	240	3.5	19.0	0.6	1.2	5877	.07	1.2	.00		396	72	1.63	.24	

ᵃ Kcal & cho not available   ᵇ Includes vichyssoise

	KCAL	H$_2$O (g)	FAT (g)	PUFA (g)	CHOL (mg)	A (RE)	C (mg)	B-2 (mg)	B-6 (mg)	FOL (mcg)	Na (mg)	Ca (mg)	Mg (mg)	Zn (mg)	Mn (mg)
	WT (g)	PRO (g)	CHO (g)	SFA (g)	FIBR (g)	A (IU)	B-1 (mg)	NIA (mg)	B-12 (mcg)	PANT (mg)	K (mg)	P (mg)	Fe (mg)	Cu (mg)	
veg beef, chunky, low Na, rts	180		4.0								75				
10¾ oz	305	13.0	22.0												
veg, vegetarian, made w/water	72	222.5	1.9	0.7	0	300	1	.05	.06	11	823	21	7	.46	.460
1 cup	241	2.1	12.0	0.3	0.5	3005	.05	0.9	.00		209	35	1.08	.12	
veg w/beef,ᵃ made w/water	79	223.5	1.9	0.1	5	189	2	.05	.08	11	957	17	6	1.55	.315
1 cup	244	5.6	10.2	0.9	0.3	1891	.04	1.0	.31		173	40	1.11	.18	
veg w/beef broth, made w/water	81	220.5	1.9	0.8	2	209	2	.05	.06		810	18	7	.80	.337
1 cup	241	3.0	13.1	0.4	0.7	2091	.05	1.0	.00		192	39	.97	.15	
won ton, rts	92		2.0								2027				
1 cup	227	6.1	12.3												

DEHYDRATED RECONSTITUTED SOUPS

	KCAL	H$_2$O (g)	FAT (g)	PUFA (g)	CHOL (mg)	A (RE)	C (mg)	B-2 (mg)	B-6 (mg)	FOL (mcg)	Na (mg)	Ca (mg)	Mg (mg)	Zn (mg)	Mn (mg)
	WT (g)	PRO (g)	CHO (g)	SFA (g)	FIBR (g)	A (IU)	B-1 (mg)	NIA (mg)	B-12 (mcg)	PANT (mg)	K (mg)	P (mg)	Fe (mg)	Cu (mg)	
asparagus, crm of	59	235.5	1.7	0.7	tr						801				
1 cup	251	2.2	9.0	0.3	0.1										
bean w/bacon	105	237.7	2.2	0.2	3						928				
1 cup	265	5.5	16.4	1.0	1.5						326				
beef broth/bouillon	19	236.3	0.7	tr	1			.02			1358	5	4		.037
1 cup	244	1.3	1.9	0.3	0.0	4	.01	0.4			36	26			
beef noodleᵇ	41	239.2	0.8	0.2	2	1	1	.06	.04	2	1041	5	9	.10	
1 cup	251	2.2	6.0	0.3	0.1	9	.12	0.7			81	40	.33		
cauliflower	68	238.0	1.7	0.7	tr						843				
1 cup	256	2.9	10.7	0.3	0.2										
celery, crm of	63	237.4	1.6	0.6	1						839				
1 cup	254	2.6	9.8	0.2	0.2										
chicken broth/bouillonᶜ	21	236.2	1.1	0.4	1		tr	.03			1484	15	4	.01	
1 cup	244	1.3	1.4	0.3	0.0	40	.01	0.2			25	13	.08		
chicken, crm of	107	237.5	5.3	0.4	3			.20			1184	76			
1 cup	261	1.8	13.4	3.4	1.2						215	96			
chicken noodleᵈ	53	237.6	1.2	0.3	3	6	tr	.06	.01	1	1284	32	7	.20	.024
1 cup	252	2.9	7.4	0.3	0.1	63	.07	0.9			31	32	.50	.04	
chicken rice	60	237.2	1.4	0.4	3						980	8			
1 cup	253	2.4	9.3	0.3				0.4			10	10			
chicken veg	49	237.2	0.8	0.2	3	1	1	.05	.09		808		21	.21	
1 cup	251	2.7	7.8	0.2		14	.07	0.7			68	32	.59	.03	
clam chowder, manhattan	65		1.6	0.5	0						1336				
1 cup	250	2.1	10.9	0.3	0.6										
clam chowder, new england	95		3.7	1.2	1			.16			745	76			
1 cup	250	2.8	12.9	0.6	0.2						205	100			
consomme w/gelatin	17	236.5	0.0	tr	0						3299				
1 cup	249	2.2	2.1	tr	0.0										
leek	71	235.6	2.1	0.1	3						966			.24	
1 cup	254	2.1	11.4	1.0	0.3									.04	
minestrone	79	232.8	1.7	0.1	3						1026				
1 cup	254	4.4	11.9	0.8	0.4										
mushroom	96	231.9	4.9	1.5	1	1		.11			1019	67		.09	
1 cup	253	2.2	11.1	0.8	0.1	7	.28	0.5		.24	199	77		.03	
onionᵉ	28	236.9	0.6	0.1	0	tr	tr	.06		2	848	13	6	.06	.06
1 cup	246	1.1	5.1	0.1	0.2	2	.03	0.5			63	31	.14	.02	
oxtail	71	235.3	2.6	0.1	3						1210				
1 cup	253	2.8	9.0	1.3	0.1										
pea, green/splitᶠ	133	235.2	1.6	0.3	3	5	tr	.15	.05	15	1220	22	46	.59	.268
1 cup	271	7.7	22.7	0.4	0.7	49	.22	1.3		.26	238	134	1.01	.19	
tomatoᵍ	102	237.7	2.4	0.2	1	82	5	.05	.10	7	943	54	15	.21	
1 cup	265	2.5	19.4	1.1	0.4	832	.06	0.8			295	66	.42	.09	
tomato vegʰ	55	236.6	0.9	0.1	tr	20	6	.05			1146	8	20	.17	
1 cup	253	2.0	10.2	0.4	0.5	190	.06	0.8		.14	103	29	.63	.03	
veg beef	53	237.5	1.1	0.1	1	24		.04	.05		1000			.27	
1 cup	253	2.9	8.0	0.6	0.2	238	.03	0.5				37	.85	.03	

ᵃ Includes beef; beef veg; barley & veg beef
ᵇ Includes beef & macaroni & beef-flavored noodle
ᶜ Includes chicken consomme
ᵈ Includes chicken broth w/noodles
ᵉ Includes french onion
ᶠ Includes pea w/ham
ᵍ Includes crm of tomato
ʰ Includes italian veg & spring veg

	KCAL	H₂O (g)	FAT (g)	PUFA (g)	CHOL (mg)	A (RE)	C (mg)	B-2 (mg)	B-6 (mg)	FOL (mcg)	Na (mg)	Ca (mg)	Mg (mg)	Zn (mg)	Mn (mg)
	WT (g)	PRO (g)	CHO (g)	SFA (g)	FIBR (g)	A (IU)	B-1 (mg)	NIA (mg)	B-12 (mcg)	PANT (mg)	K (mg)	P (mg)	Fe (mg)	Cu (mg)	
veg, crm of	105	237.2	5.7	1.5	0	4	4	.11			1171				
1 cup	260	1.9	12.3	1.4	0.1	35	1.22	0.5			96	54			

DEHYDRATED SOUPS

	KCAL	H₂O	FAT	PUFA	CHOL	A	C	B-2	B-6	FOL	Na	Ca	Mg	Zn	Mn
beef broth cube	6	0.1	0.1	tr	tr			.01			864		2	.01	.014
1 cube	4	0.6	0.6	0.1			.01	0.1			15	8	.08		
chicken broth cube	9	0.1	0.2	0.1	1			.02			1152		3	.01	.018
1 cube	5	0.7	1.1	0.1			.01	0.2			18	9	.09		
onion soup mix	115	1.43	2.3	0.3	2	1	1	.24		6	3493	55	25	.23	.248
1 pkt	39	4.5	20.9	0.5	0.9	8	.11	2.0			260	126	.58	.064	

HOMEMADE SOUPS

	KCAL	H₂O	FAT	PUFA	CHOL	A	C	B-2	B-6	FOL	Na	Ca	Mg	Zn	Mn
bean	195		11.2				0	.07				52			
¾ cup	190	6.1	18.6		1.4	1364	.12	0.5				120	1.90		
bean w/ham	260		5.5	0.1	5		9	.18	.25		228	85	8	.29	
¾ cup	200	17.3	36.5	0.4	2.3	83	.43	2.3	1.20	.28	588	295	4.30		
beef barley	97		0.7				1	.04			367	13			
½ cup	113	5.6	18.1		0.2	10	.05	1.4			108	79	.90		
cauliflower, crm of	136		10.7				12	.15			517	98			
½ cup	113	4.1	6.3		0.2	555	.05	1.0			157	92	.40		
celery, crm of	157		10.5				1	.23				171			
¾ cup	155	5.4	10.9		0.2	425	.07	0.3				138	.50		
corn chowder	105		5.1				4	.10			379	53			
½ cup	116	3.4	11.0		0.2	212	.07	1.3			118	61	.40		
mulligatawny	64		3.5				tr	.01			421	8			
½ cup	125	2.2	6.0		tr	142	.03	1.1			39	20	.30		
onion, french	38		2.9				1	.01			744	8			
½ cup	113	0.8	2.8		0.1	117	.01	0.1			16	5	tr		
oyster stew (1 part oysters: 2 parts	97		6.4					.08			339	114			
milk)—½ cup	100	5.2	4.5		0.0	340	.06	0.9			133	111	1.90		
oyster stew (1 part oysters: 3 parts	86		5.3					.18			203	117			
milk)—½ cup	100	4.9	4.7			280	.06	0.7			138	109	1.40		
scotch broth	62		0.7				1	.03			714	13			
½ cup	120	4.3	9.8		0.2	729	.03	0.9			89	47	.70		

SPECIAL DIETARY FOODS
FORMULATED FOODS, MEAL REPLACEMENTS & DIET MEALS

	KCAL	H₂O	FAT	PUFA	CHOL	A	C	B-2	B-6	FOL	Na	Ca	Mg	Zn	Mn
breakfast bar, choc chip,[a] Carnation	200		11.0												
1.45-oz bar	41	6.0	21.0												
figurines,[b] Pillsbury	275		16.0								179				
2 bars	50	11.0	21.0												
figurines, yogurt,[c] Pillsbury	275		16.0								45				
2 bars	50	11.0	21.0												
inst breakfast,[d] dry	130		0.0								188				
1 pouch (1.26 oz)	36	5.5	26.5												
sego diet pudding[e]	250		5.5								347[f]				
8 oz	227	11.0	40.0								454[f]				

[a] Contains 25% of the U.S. RDA for vit B-1, vit B-2, niacin, vit D, vit E, vit B-6, folacin, vit B-12, pantothenic acid, Fe, P, Mg, Zn & Cu; 30% of the U.S. RDA for Ca & I; 40% of the U.S. RDA for vit A; and 50% of the U.S. RDA for vit C

[b] Caramel nut, choc, choc caramel, choc mint, double choc, raspberry or van; contains 25% of the U.S. RDA for vit A, vit C, vit B-1, vit B-2, niacin, vit B-6, vit B-12, folacin, pantothenic acid, vit D, Ca, P, Mg, Fe & I

[c] Strawberry, lemon, or honey flavored; contains 25% of the U.S. RDA for vit A, vit C, vit B-1, vit B-2, niacin, vit B-6, vit B-12, folacin, pantothenic acid, vit D, Ca, P, Mg, Fe & I

[d] Choc, choc malt, strawberry, or van; when mixed w/8 fl oz vit D fortified milk, contains 25% of the U.S. RDA for vit B-1, vit B-2, niacin, vit B-6, vit B-12, folacin, vit D, vit E, Ca, P, Mg & Fe & 30% of the U.S. RDA for vit A & vit C

[e] Banana, butterscotch, choc, choc fudge, choc marshmallow, or van

[f] Choc flavors have 378 mg Na & 642 mg K.

	KCAL	H_2O (g)	FAT (g)	PUFA (g)	CHOL (mg)	A (RE)	C (mg)	B-2 (mg)	B-6 (mg)	FOL (mcg)	Na (mg)	Ca (mg)	Mg (mg)	Zn (mg)	Mn (mg)
	WT (g)	PRO (g)	CHO (g)	SFA (g)	FIBR (g)	A (IU)	B-1 (mg)	NIA (mg)	B-12 (mcg)	PANT (mg)	K (mg)	P (mg)	Fe (mg)	Cu (mg)	
sego, liquid diet meal,[a] cnd	225		3.9								265[b]				
10 fl oz	c	11.0	36.7								506[b]				
sego lite, liquid diet meal, cnd															
choc	150		3.0		17						378				
10 fl oz	c	11.0	20.0								612				
dutch choc	150		3.0		17						423				
10 fl oz	c	11.0	20.0								583				
van	150		4.0		18						533				
10 fl oz	c	11.0	17.0								524				

LOW PROTEIN FOODS

	KCAL	H_2O (g)	FAT (g)	PUFA (g)	CHOL (mg)	A (RE)	C (mg)	B-2 (mg)	B-6 (mg)	FOL (mcg)	Na (mg)	Ca (mg)	Mg (mg)	Zn (mg)	Mn (mg)
	WT (g)	PRO (g)	CHO (g)	SFA (g)	FIBR (g)	A (IU)	B-1 (mg)	NIA (mg)	B-12 (mcg)	PANT (mg)	K (mg)	P (mg)	Fe (mg)	Cu (mg)	
bread, Henkel	83		1.8								10	3			
½ inch slice	32	0.3	15.8								13	6			
bread, Ener-G	228	23.7	10.0								10				
2 slices	57	0.3	36.0		0.3						7				
cereal, aproten semolina, ckd	68		0.1								4				
¾ cup	200	0.1	17.1								2				
cookies w/choc-flavored chips	70		4.0								30				
1 cookie	14	0.1	10.0								12	5			
gelled dessert (prono)	55		0.0												
⅓ cup	93	tr	14.0												
pasta															
aproten anellini, ckd	196		0.3								15				
1 cup	220	0.3	48.0								5				
aproten ditalini/rigatini, ckd	114		0.2								10				
1 cup	130	0.2	28.0								5				
aproten tagliotelle, ckd	214		0.4								15				
1 cup	240	0.3	53.0								5				
rusks	43	0.4	0.9								3				
1 rusk	10	0.1	8.0								5				
wheat starch	100	3.1	0.3								17	3			
1 oz	28	0.1	25.0		0.1						3	13			

PUREED FOODS

	KCAL	H_2O (g)	FAT (g)	PUFA (g)	CHOL (mg)	A (RE)	C (mg)	B-2 (mg)	B-6 (mg)	FOL (mcg)	Na (mg)	Ca (mg)	Mg (mg)	Zn (mg)	Mn (mg)
	WT (g)	PRO (g)	CHO (g)	SFA (g)	FIBR (g)	A (IU)	B-1 (mg)	NIA (mg)	B-12 (mcg)	PANT (mg)	K (mg)	P (mg)	Fe (mg)	Cu (mg)	
fruit, cnd															
apricots w/tapioca	108	203.5	1.1				3	.02			48	35		.02	
8⅛ oz	230	0.9	23.5			4752	.02	1.1			46		.69		
peaches	120	197.7	0.5				72	.05			39	27		.09	
8 oz	227	1.6	25.9			844	.05	1.0			241		.45		
pears	130	188.1	0.9				68	.04			40	20		.22	
7¾ oz	220	0.9	29.7			81	.02	1.1			97		.88		
meat, cnd															
beef w/beef broth	281	165.5	17.9				3	.21			102	9		5.22	
7½ oz	213	31.7				179	.04	9.2			334		2.56		
chicken w/chicken broth	285	161.9	18.5				1	.28			170	173		2.85	
7½ oz	213	29.6	3.2			32	.04	7.0			328		2.13		
lamb w/lamb broth	253	167.8	16.0				1	.30			111	11		5.71	
7½ oz	213	28.1	2.3			58	.04	5.2			360		2.77		
liver w/liver broth	187	171.0	5.3				40	3.81			117	13		2.58	
7½ oz	213	31.5	6.8			36800	.11	14.2			371		14.06		
turkey w/turkey broth	260	165.3	14.3				3	.26			124	53		3.32	
7½ oz	213	33.0	1.0			96	.04	7.8			356		1.70		
veal w/veal broth	245	167.2	13.4				3	.26			111	11		4.92	
7½ oz	213	30.9	0.0			68	.04	5.5			337		1.70		
veg, cnd															
beets	82	187.1	0.4				9	.04			226	36		1.67	
7⅜ oz	209	2.7	17.1			33	.04	0.4			380		1.67		

[a] French van, milk choc, choc fudge, van, strawberry, butterscotch, banana, cherry van, choc, dutch choc, choc malt, choc marshmallow & choc coconut

[b] Choc flavors have 509 mg Na & 693 mg K.

[c] Gram wt not available

	KCAL	H₂O (g)	FAT (g)	PUFA (g)	CHOL (mg)	A (RE)	C (mg)	Vitamins B-2 (mg)	B-6 (mg)	FOL (mcg)	Na (mg)	Minerals Ca (mg)	Mg (mg)	Zn (mg)	Mn (mg)
	WT (g)	PRO (g)	CHO (g)	SFA (g)	FIBR (g)	A (IU)	B-1 (mg)	NIA (mg)	B-12 (mcg)	PANT (mg)	K (mg)	P (mg)	Fe (mg)	Cu (mg)	
carrots	48	196.9	0.4				5	.06			44	63		.33	
7⅜ oz	209	1.3	10.2			3348	.04	0.5			130		1.25		
green beans	50	196.5	0.6				3	.13			19	75		.75	
7⅜ oz	209	1.9	9.6		2.1	1348	.06	0.6			146		1.88		
peas	136	176.2	0.6				9	.17			13	42		1.25	
7⅜ oz	209	9.0	21.9		3.8	1367	.23	2.3			286		2.30		
spinach	56	194.0	0.6				27	.29			138	153		.82	
7⅜ oz	209	4.2	8.4			12488	.06	0.6			399		2.30		
squash	66	196.8	0.4				5	.11			9	77		.64	
7½ oz	213	1.5	13.4			4492	.04	0.8			115		.85		

						Vitamins					Minerals				
	KCAL	H_2O (g)	FAT (g)	PUFA (g)	CHOL (mg)	A (RE)	C (mg)	B-2 (mg)	B-6 (mg)	FOL (mcg)	Na (mg)	Ca (mg)	Mg (mg)	Zn (mg)	Mn (mg)
	WT (g)	PRO (g)	CHO (g)	SFA (g)	FIBR (g)	A (IU)	B-1 (mg)	NIA (mg)	B-12 (mcg)	PANT (mg)	K (mg)	P (mg)	Fe (mg)	Cu (mg)	
			SAC (mg)	CAF (mg)	INOS (mg)	D (IU)	E (mg)	K (mcg)	BIO (mcg)	CHLN (mg)	Cl (mg)	I (mcg)	Mo (mg)	Se (mg)	Cr (mg)
	try (mg)	thr (mg)	iso (mg)	leu (mg)	lys (mg)	met (mg)	cys (mg)	phe (mg)	tyr (mg)	val (mg)	arg (mg)	his (mg)			

SPECIAL DIETARY FORMULAS, COMMERCIAL & HOSPITAL

Item	C1	C2	C3	C4	C5	C6	C7	C8	C9	C10	C11	C12	C13	C14	C15
amin-aid drink,[a] Am McGaw	665		15.7												
153 g pkt in 250 ml water	403	6.6	124.3												
	250	500	700	1100	790	1100		1100		800	250				
amin-aid pudding,[a] Am McGaw	695		15.7												
154 g pkt in 285 ml water	439	6.6	131.7												
	250	500	700	1100	790	1100		1100		800	250				
cal plus powder,[b] Henkel	128		1.9	0.0							35				
¼ cup	32	0.0	30.0								2				
casec powder,[c] Mead Johnson	17		0.3	tr							7	75			
1 T	5	4.0									38				
	56	181	250	440	375	125	13	242	250	315	177	138			
compleat-B,[d] Doyle	400		16.0				23	.65	.75	100	475	250	100	3.75	1.00
13.6 fl oz (400 ml)	[e]	16.0	48.0			1250	.56	5.0	1.50	2.5	525	500	4.50	.50	
						100	7.5[f]		75	75	325	37.5			
criticare HN (high nitrogen),[g] Mead Johnson—8 fl oz	250	211.4	0.8	0.6	0	188	38	.55	.62	50	150	125	50	2.50	.620
	260	9.0	52.5	0.1		625	.48	6.2	1.90	3.1	310	125	2.25	.25	
					14.5	50	9.5	31	40	62.5	250	19			
	145	440	550	920	780	400	35	430	235	680	360	270			
ensure,[h] choc, Ross	254	199.5	8.8				38	.43	.50	50	200	130	50	3.75	.50
8 fl oz	253	9.3	33.8			625	.38	5.0	1.50	1.25	370	130	2.25	.25	
					8.2	50	7.5[f]	35	38	130	340	19			
ensure,[h] van/strawberry/eggnog/coffee/black walnut, Ross—8 fl oz	254	199.5	8.8	5.1	3.3		38	.43	.50	50	200	130	50	3.75	.50
	253	8.8	34.3	1.3	0.0	625	.38	5.0	1.50	1.25	370	130	2.25	.25	
				[i]		50	7.5[f]	35	38	130	340	19			
	116	372	364	772	620	225	43	362	336	468	182				
ensure plus,[h] choc, Ross	355	182.0	12.6				38	.65	.72	75	270	150	75	5.63	.50
8 fl oz	259	13.5	46.8			890	.63	7.5	2.25	2.0	550	150	3.38	.38	
					10.2	70	10.7[f]	50	56	125	470	25			
ensure plus,[h] van/strawberry/eggnog/coffee, Ross—8 fl oz	355	182.0	12.6	2.6	4.4		38	.65	.72	75	270	150	75	5.63	.50
	259	13.0	47.3	1.7	0.0	890	.63	7.5	2.25	2.0	550	150	3.38	.38	
				[j]		70	10.7	50	56	56	470	25			
	136	539	642	1171	917	344	69	650	614	772	295				
forta pudding,[h] van, Ross	250	90.6	9.7	0.9	5.2		15	.28	.33	67	220	200	67	3.00	.66
5 oz	142	6.8	34.0	2.2		833	.25	3.3	1.00	1.66	300	200	3.00	.33	
						67	5.0[f]		50	30	210	60			
hepatic aid drink,[k] Am McGaw	560		12.3												
139 g pkt in 250 ml water	398	14.5	98.1												
	120	820	1640	2010	1120	180		180		1530	1100	440			

[a] Essential amino acid & cal supplement for acute or chronic renal failure
[b] Cal supplement consisting of glucose polymers from hydrolysis of corn starch
[c] Pro supplement for oral feedings, tube feedings, infant formulas, etc.
[d] Meat-based blenderized tube feeding
[e] Gram wt not available
[f] Vit E value in IUs
[g] Tube or oral feeding for impaired digestion or absorption
[h] Nutritionally complete oral feeding
[i] 5.6–10.7 mg 8 fl oz for coffee ensure
[j] 5.7–11.0 mg/8 fl oz for coffee ensure plus
[k] Amino acid supplement for chronic liver disease; also contains glucine, proline, alanine & serine

						Vitamins					Minerals				
	KCAL	H2O (g)	FAT (g)	PUFA (g)	CHOL (mg)	A (RE)	C (mg)	B-2 (mg)	B-6 (mg)	FOL (mcg)	Na (mg)	Ca (mg)	Mg (mg)	Zn (mg)	Mn (mg)
	WT (g)	PRO (g)	CHO (g)	SFA (g)	FIBR (g)	A (IU)	B-1 (mg)	NIA (mg)	B-12 (mcg)	PANT (mg)	K (mg)	P (mg)	Fe (mg)	Cu (mg)	
			SAC (mg)	CAF (mg)	INOS (mg)	D (IU)	E (mg)	K (mcg)	BIO (mcg)	CHLN (mg)	Cl (mg)	I (mcg)	Mo (mg)	Se (mg)	Cr (mg)
	try (mg)	thr (mg)	iso (mg)	leu (mg)	lys (mg)	met (mg)	cys (mg)	phe (mg)	tyr (mg)	val (mg)	arg (mg)	his (mg)			
hepatic aid pudding,[a] Am McGaw	585		12.3												
146 g pkt in 250 ml water	396	14.5	104.5												
	120	820	1640	2010	1120	180		180		1530	1110	440			
isocal,[b] Mead Johnson	250	210.8	10.5	5.3	3	188	38	.54	.62	50	125	150	50	2.50	.620
8 fl oz	250	8.0	31.2	1.3		625	.48	6.2	1.90	3.1	312	125	2.25	.25	
					22.0	50	9.5	31	40	62.5	250	19			
	148	320	430	780	580	200	40	400	375	550	303	218			
isocal HCN (high calorie & nitrogen),[c]	473	184.3	21.5	8.7	7	240	47	.68	.79	63	189	158	63	4.70	.80
Mead Johnson—*8 fl oz*	260	17.7	53.2	4.1		790	.60	7.8	2.40	4.0	331	158	2.80	.47	
					23.0	63	11.8	39	50	79.0	284	24			
	230	730	1010	1780	1510	500	52	970	989	1270	700	544			
lonalac,[d] Mead Johnson	20		1.1	tr	tr	9	.05				1	34	3		
1 fl oz	30	1.1	1.5	0.8		30	.01	tr			38	31	.03		
					0.9					2.0	16				
	13	49	60	106	91	30	3	59	35	75	24	20			
lytren,[e] Mead Johnson	72										160	19	11		
8 fl oz	240		18.4								230	21			
											210				
MCT (medium chain triglyceride) oil,[f]	115		14.0		0										
Mead Johnson—*1 T*	14	0.0	0.0		0.0										
meritene liquid,[g] van, Doyle	300		10.0				23	.65	.75	100	275	375	100	3.75	1.00
10 fl oz (300 ml)	[h]	18.0	34.5			1250	.56	5.0	1.50	2.5	500	375	4.50	.50	
						100	7.5[i]		75	25	500	37.5			
moducal,[j] Mead Johnson	236	80.0	0.0	0.0	0						41				
4 fl oz	[h]	0.0	59.0	0.0	0.0						3				
											101				
moducal powder,[j] Mead Johnson	30	0.4	0.0	0.0	0						6				
1 T	8	0.0	7.6	0.0	0.0						tr				
											14				
msud diet,[k] 20 cal/oz, Mead Johnson	20		0.9	0.5		15	2	.02	.01	3	8	21	2	.12	.031
1 fl oz	30	0.3	2.7	0.1			.02	0.3	.06	.09	21	11	.38	.02	
					0.9	13	0.3		2	2.7	16	1			
	8	23	0	0	42	11	11	23	27	0	21	11			
nutri-1000,[l] van, Cutter	1000	751.3	52.0				45	1.00	1.00	200	500	1150	200	7.50	1.25
32 fl oz (1 qt)	945	37.8	95.5			2500	1.00	10.0	3.00	5.00	1400	900	9.00	1.00	
						200	15.0[i]	150	150	190					
phenyl-free,[m] 25 cal/oz, Mead Johnson	25		0.4	0.3		38	3	.06	.03	6	16	38	4	.25	.063
1 fl oz	30	1.3	4.1	0.1			.04	0.5	.16	.20	44	28	.75	.04	
					1.9	25	0.6		2	5.3	31	3			
	18	58	68	106	116	39	21	0	58	78	43	29			
portagen,[n] 20 cal/oz, Mead Johnson	160		7.6	0.5	2	380	13	.30	.32	25	75	150	32	1.50	.480
8 fl oz	240	5.6	18.4	0.1		1250	.25	3.3	1.00	1.7	200	112	3.00	.25	
					tr	125	5.0[i]	25	13	21	138	11			
	70	230	320	560	480	160	18	310	318	400	224	176			

[a] Amino acid cal supplement for chronic liver disease; also contains glucine, proline, alanine & serine
[b] Tube feeding
[c] Tube feeding for hypermetabolic, fluid-restricted & volume-sensitive diets
[d] Low Na, high pro product
[e] Electrolyte & cho oral feeding for infants
[f] Used when conventional food fats are poorly digested, absorbed, or utilized
[g] Oral or tube total or supplemental feeding
[h] Gram wt not available

[i] Vit E value in IUs
[j] Refined cho used to increase the caloric density of diets
[k] For maple syrup urine disease
[l] Oral or tube feeding; nutri-1000 LF (lactose free) contains same nutrient values
[m] Phe-free formula for PKU patients past infancy
[n] Lactose-free oral feeding w/MCT for patients who do not digest or absorb conventional fats efficiently

Each product is listed across four data rows. Column headers stack four tiers per column: tier 1 · tier 2 · tier 3 · tier 4.

Product	KCAL · WT (g) · — · try (mg)	H2O (g) · PRO (g) · — · thr (mg)	FAT (g) · CHO (g) · SAC (mg) · iso (mg)	PUFA (g) · SFA (g) · CAF (mg) · leu (mg)	CHOL (mg) · FIBR (g) · INOS (mg) · lys (mg)	A (RE) · A (IU) · D (IU) · met (mg)	C (mg) · B-1 (mg) · E (mg) · cys (mg)	B-2 (mg) · NIA (mg) · K (mcg) · phe (mg)	B-6 (mg) · B-12 (mcg) · BIO (mcg) · tyr (mg)	FOL (mcg) · PANT (mg) · CHLN (mg) · val (mg)	Na (mg) · K (mg) · Cl (mg) · arg (mg)	Ca (mg) · P (mg) · I (mcg) · his (mg)	Mg (mg) · Fe (mg) · Mo (mg)	Zn (mg) · Cu (mg) · Se (mg)	Mn (mg) · Cr (mg)
portagen,[a] 30 cal/oz, Mead Johnson 8 fl oz	240		11.4	0.7	2	570	20	.45	.48	38	112	225	50	2.25	.72
	240	8.4	28.0	0.3		1875	.38	5.0	1.50	2.5	300	169	4.50	.38	
					tr	188	7.5	38	20	38	210	18			
	105	340	480	840	720	240	26	460	478	600	336	264			
product 3200-AB,[b] Mead Johnson 1 fl oz	20		0.8	0.5	tr	15	2	.02	.01	3	9	19	2	.12	.031
	30	0.7	2.6	0.1			.02	0.3	.06	.09	20	14	.38	.02	
					0.9	13	0.3		2	2.7	14	1			
	8	52	36	69	68	22	2	3		57	17	18			
product 3200-K,[c] Mead Johnson 1 fl oz	20		1.1			15	2	.02	.01	3	8	19	2	.12	.031
	30	0.6	2.0				.02	0.3	.06	.09	17	13	.28	.02	
					0.9	13	0.3		2	2.7	13	1			
	8	20	29	47	37	6	4	31	21	29	42	15			
product 3232-A (w/o added cho),[d] Mead Johnson—1 fl oz	13		0.8	0.1	tr	15	2	.02	.01	3	9	19	2	.12	.031
	30	0.7	0.9	tr			.02	0.3	.06	.09	20	14	.38	.02	
					0.9	13	0.3		2	2.7	14	1			
	7	32	39	66	56	20	2	32	12	49	22	18			
product 80056 (w/o added pro or Na),[e] Mead Johnson—1 fl oz	17		0.8	0.5		15	2	.02	.01	3	3	19	2	.12	.031
	30	0.0	2.5	0.1			.02	0.3	.06	.09	20	10	.38	.02	
					0.9	13	0.3		2	2.7	5	tr			
	0	0	0	0	0	0		0		0					
osmolite,[f] Ross 8 fl oz	254	199.1	9.1	3.0	2		38	.43	.50	50	130	130	50	3.70	.50
	253	8.8	34.3	4.3	0.0	625	.38	5.0	1.50	1.25	240	130	2.20	.25	
						50	7.5[g]	35	38	130	200	19			
	109	374	410	802	638	237	47	445	450	463		220			
precision high nitrogen diet,[h] Doyle 2.93 oz powder in 8 fl oz water	300		0.1				9	.26	.30	40	280	100	40	1.50	.40
		12.5	62.0			500	.22	2.0	.60	1.00	260	100	1.80	.20	
						40	3.0[g]	10	30	10	340	15			
precision isotonic diet,[j] Doyle 2.06 oz pkt in 8 fl oz water	250		7.8				15	.43	.50	67	200	167	67	2.50	.67
		7.5	37.5			833	.38	3.3	1.00	1.67	250	167	3.00	.33	
						67	5.0[g]	16.7	60	17	267	25			
precision LR (low residue) diet,[k] Doyle 3 oz powder in 8 fl oz water	317		0.2	.			15	.43	.50	67	200	167	67	2.50	.67
		7.5	71.2			833	.38	3.3	1.00	1.67	250	167	3.00	.33	
						67	5.0[g]	16.7	50	16.7	317	25			
sustacal,[l] Mead Johnson 8 fl oz	240	218.9	5.5	2.2	2	330	13	.40	.48	90	220	240	90	3.20	.680
	260	14.5	33.0	0.9		1110	.32	4.8	1.32	2.30	490	220	4.00	.48	
					26.0	89	6.8	23.5	67	55	370	33			
	145	550	750	1300	1020	330	60	720	757	900	666	416			
sustacal HC (high calorie),[m] Mead Johnson—8 fl oz	360	201.5	13.6	5.4	4	300	18	.51	.60	120	200	200	80	3.00	.600
	260	14.4	45.0	2.1		1000	.45	6.0	1.80	3.00	350	200	3.50	.40	
					11.5	80	6.0	50	90	50	300	30			
	1820	600	820	1450	1220	410	29	800	590	1020	419	325			
sustacal powder,[n] van, Mead Johnson 1.9 oz pkt	199		0.3				20	.20	.55	133	190	290	105	4.00	1.00
	54	12.7	36.4			1290	.40	6.8	1.00	2.70	560	250	6.00	.70	
						33	10			93	220	40			
sustacal powder,[o] van 1.9 oz pkt in 8 fl oz whole milk	360		8.8				20	.60	.70	133	330	580	135	5.00	
	290	21.7	48.4			1670	.50	7.0	2.00	3.50	910	480	6.00	.70	
						133	10			100	480				

[a] Lactose-free oral feeding w/MCT for patients who do not digest or absorb conventional fats efficiently

[b] Low phe, low tyr feeding for patients w/tyrosenemia

[c] Soy pro isolate formula w/no added met; for patients w/homocystinuria

[d] Pro hydrolysate formula base for use with added cho; may be used in the diagnosis & nutritional management of disaccharidase deficiency & impaired glucose transport

[e] Pro-free base for making infant diets w/specific mixtures of amino acids

[f] Liquid diet or supplement

[g] Vit E value in IUs

[h] Low-residue, high-pro tube or oral feeding

[i] Gram wt not available

[j] Oral or tube total or supplemental feeding

[k] Low-residue tube or oral feeding

[l] Oral or tube feeding

[m] Oral or tube feeding for hypermetabolic, fluid-restricted & volume-sensitive diets

[n] Choc powder contains 0.7 g fat, 35.4 g cho & 640 mg K/1.9-oz pkt; other values are the same as for van powder

[o] If made w/choc powder, fat is 9.3 g, cho is 47.4 g & K is 990 mg/8 fl oz; other values are the same as for van powder in whole milk

	KCAL / WT (g) / — / try (mg)	H₂O (g) / PRO (g) / — / thr (mg)	FAT (g) / CHO (g) / SAC (mg) / iso (mg)	PUFA (g) / SFA (g) / CAF (mg) / leu (mg)	CHOL (mg) / FIBR (g) / INOS (mg) / lys (mg)	A (RE) / A (IU) / D (IU) / met (mg)	C (mg) / B-1 (mg) / E (mg) / cys (mg)	B-2 (mg) / NIA (mg) / K (mcg) / phe (mg)	B-6 (mg) / B-12 (mcg) / BIO (mcg) / tyr (mg)	FOL (mcg) / PANT (mg) / CHLN (mg) / val (mg)	Na (mg) / K (mg) / Cl (mg) / arg (mg)	Ca (mg) / P (mg) / I (mcg) / his (mg)	Mg (mg) / Fe (mg) / Mo (mg)	Zn (mg) / Cu (mg) / Se (mg)	Mn (mg) / / Cr (mg)
sustacal pudding,[a] Mead Johnson	240	91.1	9.5	3.7	tr	225	9	.26	.30	60	120	225	60	2.25	.670
5 oz	142	6.8	32.0	1.5		750	.23	3.0	.90	1.50	320	225	2.70	.30	
					13.9	60	4.5		50	30	200	23			
	120	260	330	630	500	153	36	290	163	420	105	98			
sustagen,[b] Mead Johnson	440		4.0	0.1		375	75	1.08	1.25	89	300	800	100	5.00	1.25
8 fl oz	260	27.0	75.0	2.2		1114	.95	12.5	3.80	6.20	800	600	4.50	.50	
					30.0	100	11.2	60	80	30	680	38			
	440	1020	1380	2500	2100	640		1250		1720					
tram-aid HN drink,[c] Am McGaw	500		6.2				17	.28	.33	67	267	267	67	3.33	.667
143 g pkt in 420 ml water	563	21.7	90.1			833	.25	3.3	1.00	1.67	417	200	3.00	.333	
						67	10.0[d]	25	50	70	917	25			
	280	1080	1950	3420	1820	650	330	870	870	2430	1430	780			
traumacal,[e] Mead Johnson	355		16.2	7.5	1	180	35	.50	.60	47	280	178	47	3.5	.60
8 fl oz	260	19.5	33.7	1.9			.45	6.0	1.78	3.0	330	178	2.10	.35	
						47	9.0		40	60	380	18			
	250	800	1100	1950	1680	550		1075		1400					
vital high nitrogen,[f] van, Ross	300	252.4	3.3	1.2			18	.34	.44	80	120	200	80	3.00	.75
300 ml	327	12.5	56.5	1.4	0.0	1000	.30	4.0	1.20	2.00	350	200	3.60	.40	
						80	12.0[d]	56	60	40	200	30			
	140	491	592	103	690	290	120	582	491	719		330			
vivonex,[g] Norwich-Eaton	1800		2.6				60	1.70	2.00	400	843	1000	400	15.00	2.81
6 pkts	480	37.1	415.2			5000	1.50	20.0	6.00	10.00	2109	1000	18.00	2.00	
						400	30.0[d]	67	300	73.7	1300	150	.150	.150	.050
	87	281	281	445	334	288		320	58	310	548	137			
vivonex, high nitrogen,[g] Norwich-Eaton	3000		2.6				60	1.70	2.00	400	1586	1000	400	15.00	2.81
10 pkts	800	133.1	630.0			5000	1.50	20.0	6.00	10.00	3519	1000	18.00	2.00	
						400	30.0[d]	67	300	73.7	2446	150	.150	.150	.050
	1704	5537	5524	8745	6575	6096		9450	1118	6096	5417	3141			
vivonex, flavor packets, Norwich-Eaton	8		0.0												
lemon-lime	2.5	0.0	0.8												
.088 oz pkt			20												
orange-pineapple	8		0.0												
.088 oz pkt	2.5	0.0	0.9												
			20												
strawberry	8		0.0												
.088 oz pkt	2.5	0.0	1.7												
			20												
van	9		0.0												
.088 oz pkt	2.5	0.0	2.2												
			20												

[a] Nutritionally complete oral feeding
[b] High-cal, high-pro supplement for oral or tube feeding
[c] Oral or tube nutritionally complete, high-nitrogen diet for catabolic patients; also contains glutamic acid, proline, glycine, aspartic acid, serine & alanine
[d] Vit E value in IUs
[e] Oral or tube nutritionally complete, high-nitrogen feeding for traumatized patients
[f] Nutritionally complete oral feeding
[g] Nutritionally complete elemental diet for oral or tube feeding

	KCAL / WT (g)	H₂O (g) / PRO (g)	FAT (g) / CHO (g)	PUFA (g) / SFA (g)	CHOL (mg) / FIBR (g)	A (RE) / A (IU)	C (mg) / B-1 (mg)	B-2 (mg) / NIA (mg)	B-6 (mg) / B-12 (mcg)	FOL (mcg) / PANT (mg)	Na (mg) / K (mg)	Ca (mg) / P (mg)	Mg (mg) / Fe (mg)	Zn (mg) / Cu (mg)	Mn (mg)

SPICES, HERBS & FLAVORINGS

Item	KCAL/WT	H₂O/PRO	FAT/CHO	PUFA/SFA	CHOL/FIBR	A(RE)/A(IU)	C/B-1	B-2/NIA	B-6/B-12	FOL/PANT	Na/K	Ca/P	Mg/Fe	Zn/Cu	Mn
allspice, ground	5	0.2	0.2	tr	0	1	1	tr			1	13	3	.02	
1 t	2	0.1	1.4	0.1	0.4	10	tr	tr		.00	20	2	.13		
anise seed	7	0.2	0.3	0.1	0						tr	14	4	.11	
1 t	2	0.4	1.1		0.3					.00	30	9	.78		
basil, ground	4	0.1	0.1		0	13	1	tr			tr	30	6	.08	
1 t	1	0.2	0.9		0.3	131	tr	0.1		.00	48	7	.59		
bay leaf, crumbled	2	0.0	0.1	tr	0	4	tr	tr			tr	5	1	.02	
1 t	1	0.1	0.5	tr	0.2	37	tr	tr		.00	3	1	.26		
bbq seasoning, French's	6										70				
1 t	3		1.0												
beef flavor stock base, French's	8										500				
1 t	4		2.0												
caraway seed	7	0.2	0.3	0.1	0	1		.01			tr	14	5	.12	
1 t	2	0.4	1.1	tr	0.3	8	.01	0.1		.00	28	12	.34		
cardamon, ground	6	0.2	0.1	tr	0			tr			tr	8	5	.15	
1 t	2	0.2	1.4	tr	0.2		tr	tr		.00	22	4	.28		
celery seed	8	0.1	0.5	0.1	0	tr	tr				3	35	9	.14	
1 t	2	0.4	0.8	tr	0.2	1		0.0			28	11	.90		
chervil, dried	1	0.0	0.0		0				.01		tr	8	1	.05	
1 t	1	0.1	0.3		0.1					.00	28	3	.19		
chicken flavor stock base, French's	8										475				
1 t	3		1.0												
chili pepper, McCormick	9	0.1	0.3				1	.03			tr	2			
1 t	2	0.3	1.2		0.3	129	.01	0.3			44	9	.21		
chili powder[a]	8	0.2	0.4		0	91	2	.02			26	7	4	.07	
1 t	3	0.3	1.4		0.6	908	.01	0.2		.00	50	8	.37		
cinn, ground	6	0.2	0.1	tr	0	1	1	tr			1	28	1	.05	
1 t	2	0.1	1.8	tr	0.6	6	tr	tr		.00	11	1	.88		
cinn sugar, French's	16	0.0									0				
1 t	4	0.0	4.0												
cloves, ground	7	0.1	0.4		0	1	2	.01			5	14	6	.02	
1 t	2	0.1	1.3	0.1	0.2	11	tr	tr		.00	23	2	.18		
coriander leaf, dried	2	0.0	0.0		0		3	.01			1	7	4		
1 t	1	0.1	0.3		1.1		.01	0.1		.00	27	3	.25		
coriander seed	5	0.2	0.3	tr	0			.01			1	13	6	.08	
1 t	2	0.2	1.0	tr	0.5		tr	tr		.00	23	7	.29		
cumin seed	8	0.2	0.5		0	3	tr	.01			4	20	8	.10	
1 t	2	0.4	0.9		0.2	27	.01	0.1		.00	38	10	1.39		
curry powder	6	0.2	0.3		0	2	tr	.01			1	10	5	.08	
1 t	2	0.3	1.2		0.3	20	.01	0.1		.00	31	7	.59		
dill seed	6	0.2	0.3	tr	0	tr		.01			tr	32	5	.11	
1 t	2	0.3	1.2	tr	0.4	1	.01	0.1		.00	25	6	.34		
dill weed, dried	3	0.1	tr		0			tr	.02		2	18	5	.03	
1 t	1	0.2	0.6		0.1		tr	tr		.00	33	5	.49		
fennel seed	7	0.2	0.3	tr	0	tr		.01			2	24	8	.07	
1 t	2	0.3	1.1	tr	0.3	3	.01	0.1		.00	34	10	.37		
fenugreek seed	12	0.2	0.2		0		tr	.01		2	2	6	7	.09	
1 t	4	0.9	2.2		0.4		.01	0.1		.00	28	11	1.24		
garlic powder	9	0.2	tr		0			tr			1	2	2	.07	
1 t	3	0.5	2.0		0.1		.01	tr		.00	31	12	.08		
garlic powder w/parsley, Lawry's	11		0.1								5				
1 t	3	0.5	2.2		0.1						44				
ginger, ground	6	0.2	0.1	tr	0	tr		tr			1	2	3	.08	
1 t	2	0.2	1.3	tr	0.1	3	tr	0.1		.00	24	3	.21		
lemon & pepper seasoning, French's	6										805				
1 t	4		1.0												
lemon & pepper seasoning, McCormick	9		0.4				tr	tr			77	6	2	.02	
1 t	4	0.3	1.0			3	tr	tr			23	6	.17	.02	

[a] Contains red pepper, cumin, oregano, salt & garlic powder

	KCAL	H₂O (g)	FAT (g)	PUFA (g)	CHOL (mg)	A (RE)	C (mg)	B-2 (mg)	B-6 (mg)	FOL (mcg)	Na (mg)	Ca (mg)	Mg (mg)	Zn (mg)	Mn (mg)
	WT (g)	PRO (g)	CHO (g)	SFA (g)	FIBR (g)	A (IU)	B-1 (mg)	NIA (mg)	B-12 (mcg)	PANT (mg)	K (mg)	P (mg)	Fe (mg)	Cu (mg)	
mace, ground	8	0.1	0.6	0.1	0	1		.01			1	4	3	.04	
1 t	2	0.1	0.9	0.2	0.1	14	.01	tr	.00		8	2	.24		
marjoram, dried	2	0.0			0	5	tr	tr			tr	12	2	.02	
1 t	1	0.4			0.1	48	tr	tr	.00		9	2	.50		
mustard powder	9	tr	0.6				tr	.01			tr	5			
1 t	1.5	0.5	0.3		tr	3	.01	0.1			11	12	.12		
mustard seed, yellow	15	0.2	1.0	0.2	0	tr		.01			tr	17	10	.19	
1 t	3	0.8	1.2	0.1	0.2	2	.02	0.3	.00		23	28	.33		
nutmeg, ground	12	0.1	0.8	tr	0	tr		tr			tr	4	4	.05	
1 t	2	0.1	1.1	0.6	0.1	2	.01	tr	.00		8	5	.07		
onion powder	7	0.1	tr		0		tr	tr			1	8	3	.05	
1 t	2	0.2	1.7		0.1		.01	tr	.00		20	7	.05		
oregano, ground	5	0.1	0.2	0.1	0	10					tr	24	4	.07	
1 t	2	0.2	1.0	tr	0.2	104	.01	0.1	.00		25	3	.66		
paprika	6	0.2	0.3	0.2	0	127	1	.04			1	4	4	.08	
1 t	2	0.3	1.2	tr	0.4	1273	.01	0.3	.00		49	7	.50		
parsley, dried	4	0.1	0.1	0.1	0	30	2	.02	.01		6	19	3	.06	
1 T	1	0.3	0.7		0.1	303	tr	0.1	.00		49	5	1.27		
pepper, black	5	0.2	0.1	tr	0	tr		.01			1	9	4	.03	
1 t	2	0.2	1.4	tr	0.3	4	tr	tr	.00		26	4	.61		
pepper, red/cayenne	6	0.1	0.3	0.2	0	75	1	.02			1	3	3	.05	
1 t	2	0.2	1.0	0.1	0.5	749	.01	0.2	.00		36	5	.14		
pepper, seasoned	10	0.1									6				
1 t	3	0.3	2.1		0.2						33				
pepper, white	7	0.3	0.1		0			tr			tr	6	2	.03	
1 t	2	0.3	1.7		0.1		tr	tr	.00		2	4	.34		
pinch of herbs, Lawry's	18		0.9								495				
1 t	5	0.6	1.7		0.3						18				
pizza seasoning, French's	4		0.0								400				
1 t	4	0.0	1.0												
poppy seed	15	0.2	1.3	0.9	0			.01	.01		1	41	9	.29	
1 t	3	0.5	0.7	0.1	0.2		.02	tr	.00		20	24	.26		
poultry seasoning[a]	5	0.1	0.1		0	4	tr	tr			tr	15	3	.05	
1 t	2	0.1	1.0		0.2	39	tr	tr	.00		10	3	.53		
pumpkin pie spice[b]	6	0.1	0.2		0	tr	tr	tr			1	12	2	.04	
1 t	2	0.1	1.2		0.3	4	tr	tr	.00		11	2	.34		
rosemary, dried	4	0.1	0.2		0	4	1				1	15	3	.04	
1 t	2	0.1	0.8		0.2	38	.01	tr	.00		11	1	.35		
saffron	2	0.1	tr		0						1	1			
1 t	1	0.1	0.5		tr				.00		12	2	.08		
sage, ground	2	0.1	0.1	tr	0	4	tr	tr			tr	12	3	.03	
1 t	1	0.1	0.4	0.1	0.1	41	.01	tr	.00		7	1	.20		
salad seasoning, French's	6										630				
1 t	4		1.0												
salad sprinkles, Lawry's	16		0.6								445				
1 t	5	0.8	1.8		0.4						36				
salad supreme, McCormick	19		1.2				tr	.02			4790	34	19	.21	
1 t	5	1.2	0.8			65	.01	0.1			39	60	.34	.04	
savory, ground	4	0.1	0.1		0	7					tr	30	5	.06	
1 t	1	0.1	1.0		0.2	72	.01	0.1	.00		15	2	.53		
salt[c]	0		0.0	0.0	0						2300	2	0	.00	
1 t	6	0.0	0.0	0.0	0.0						tr	0	.00	.00	
salt & spice, McCormick	5		0.1				1	tr			1435	6	2	.02	
1 t	5	0.3	0.8			2	tr	tr			23	6	.22	.02	
salt, celery, French's	2										1505				
1 t	5														
salt, garlic, French's	4		0.0								2050				
1 t	6	0.0	1.0												
salt, garlic, parslied, French's	6										1125				
1 t	4		1.0												
salt, hickory smoke, French's	2										1145				
1 t	4														

[a] Contains white pepper, sage, thyme, marjoram, savory, ginger, allspice & nutmeg

[b] Contains cinn, ginger, nutmeg, allspice & cloves

[c] Contains 3.6 g Cl and 400 mcg I if iodized; contains less than 100 mcg I if not iodized

	KCAL	H2O (g)	FAT (g)	PUFA (g)	CHOL (mg)	A (RE)	C (mg)	B-2 (mg)	B-6 (mg)	FOL (mcg)	Na (mg)	Ca (mg)	Mg (mg)	Zn (mg)	Mn (mg)
	WT (g)	PRO (g)	CHO (g)	SFA (g)	FIBR (g)	A (IU)	B-1 (mg)	NIA (mg)	B-12 (mcg)	PANT (mg)	K (mg)	P (mg)	Fe (mg)	Cu (mg)	
salt, imit butter flavor, French's	8		1.0								1125				
1 t	4	0.0	0.0												
salt, onion, French's	6										1590				
1 t	5		1.0												
salt, onion, Lawry's	7		tr								1400				
1 t	5	0.2	1.3		0.1						9				
salt, season-all, McCormick	4		0.1				tr	.01			980	3	15	.02	
1 t	4	0.2	0.6			43	tr	tr			17	5	.18	.02	
salt, seasoning, French's	2		0.0								1280				
1 t	4	0.0	0.5												
salt, seasoning, Lawry's	3		tr								1164				
1 t	4	0.1	0.5		tr						111				
salt substitute															
Diamond crystal[a]	3										0				
1 pkt	0.5														
Morton[b]	0		0.0	0.0	0						tr	30	tr	.00	
1 t	6	0.0	0.1	0.0	0.0						2800	28	.00	.00	
Morton lite salt[c]	0		0.0	0.0	0						1100	3	4	.00	
1 t	6	0.0	0.0	0.0	0.0						1500	0	.00	.00	
noSalt,[d] Norcliff Thayer	0		0.0								0				
1 pkt	.75	0.0	0.0								385				
seafood seasoning, French's	2										1410				
1 t	5														
tarragon, ground	5	0.1	0.1		0	7		tr			1	18	6	.06	
1 t	2	0.4	0.8		0.1	67	tr	0.1	.00		48	5	.52		
thyme, ground	4	0.1	0.1	tr	0	5		.01			1	26	3	.09	
1 t	1	0.1	0.9	tr	0.3	53	.01	0.1	.00		11	3	1.73		
tumeric, ground	8	0.3	0.2		0		1	.01			1	4	4	.10	
1 t	2	0.2	1.4		0.2		tr	0.1	.00		56	6	.91		

SPREADS (BUTTER, MARGARINE, MAYONNAISE, ETC.)

	KCAL	H2O (g)	FAT (g)	PUFA (g)	CHOL (mg)	A (RE)	C (mg)	B-2 (mg)	B-6 (mg)	FOL (mcg)	Na (mg)	Ca (mg)	Mg (mg)	Zn (mg)	Mn (mg)
	WT (g)	PRO (g)	CHO (g)	SFA (g)	FIBR (g)	A (IU)	B-1 (mg)	NIA (mg)	B-12 (mcg)	PANT (mg)	K (mg)	P (mg)	Fe (mg)	Cu (mg)	
butter	36	0.8	4.1	0.2	11	38	0	.00	tr	tr	41	1	tr	tr	
1 t	5	0.0	tr	2.5	0.0	153	tr	0.0			1	1	.01		
butter	108	2.4	12.2	0.5	33	114	0	.01	tr	tr	123	3	tr	tr	
1 T	15	0.1	tr	7.6	0.0	459	tr	0.0			3	3	.03		
butter, sweet (unsalted)	36	0.8	4.1	0.2	11	38	0	.00	tr	tr	1	1	tr	tr	
1 t	5	0.0	tr	2.5	0.0	165	tr	0.0			1	1	.01		
butter, sweet (unsalted)	108	2.4	12.2	0.5	33	114	0	.01	tr	tr	2	3	tr	tr	
1 T	15	0.1	tr	7.6	0.0	495	tr	0.0			3	3	.03		
butter, whipped	27	0.6	3.1	0.1	8	29	0	.00	tr	tr	31	1	tr	tr	
1 t	4	0.0	tr	1.9	0.0	116	tr	0.0			1	1	.01		
butter, whipped	81	1.8	9.2	0.3	24	87	0	.00	tr	tr	93	3	tr	tr	
1 T	11	0.1	tr	5.7	0.0	319	tr	0.0			3	3	.03		
butter buds, liquid	12		0.0		0						220	12			
1 fl oz (2 t dry)	30		1.0			400					18	8			
margarine															
liquid, soybean & cottonseed	34	0.7	3.8	1.7		47	0	.00	.00	0	37	3	tr		
1 t	5	0.1	0.0	0.6		155	.00	0.0	.01	.01	4	2			
stick, corn	34	0.7	3.8	0.8		47	0	.00	.00	0	44[e]	1	tr		
1 t	5	0.0	0.0	0.6		155	.00	0.0	.00	.00	2	1			
stick, safflower & soybean	34	0.7	3.8	1.5		47	0	.00	.00	0	44[e]	1	tr		
1 t	5	0.0	0.0	0.6		155	.00	0.0	.00	.00	2	1			
stick, soybean	34	0.7	3.8	1.0		47	0	.00	.00	0	44[e]	1	tr		
1 t	5	0.0	0.0	0.8		155	.00	0.0	.00	.00	2	1			
stick, soybean & cottonseed	34	0.7	3.8	0.9		47	0	.00	.00	0	44[e]	1	tr		
1 t	5	0.0	0.0	0.8		155	.00	0.0	.00	.00	2	1			

[a] KCl, tricalcium phosphate, citric acid & glutamic acid
[b] Contains 2.5 g Cl & less than 100 mcg I
[c] Contains 3.2 mg Cl & 400 mcg I
[d] Contains 3.45 mg Cl
[e] Unsalted stick margarine contains 1 mg Na per t.

	KCAL / WT (g)	H2O / PRO (g)	FAT / CHO (g)	PUFA / SFA (g)	CHOL (mg) / FIBR (g)	A (RE) / A (IU)	C (mg) / B-1 (mg)	B-2 / NIA (mg)	B-6 (mg) / B-12 (mcg)	FOL (mcg) / PANT (mg)	Na / K (mg)	Ca / P (mg)	Mg / Fe (mg)	Zn / Cu (mg)	Mn (mg)
tub, corn	34	0.8	3.8	1.5		47	0	.00	.00	0	51ᵃ	1	tr		
1 t	5	0.0	0.0	0.7		158	.00	0.0	.00	.00	2	1			
tub, safflower	34	0.8	3.8	2.1		47	0	.00	.00	0	51ᵃ	1	tr		
1 t	5	0.0	0.0	0.4		155	.00	0.0	.00	.00	2	1			
tub, soybean	34	0.8	3.8	1.3		47	0	.00	.00	0	51ᵃ	1	tr		
1 t	5	0.0	0.0	0.6		155	.00	0.0	.00	.00	2	1			
tub, soybean & cottonseed	34	0.8	3.8	1.4		47	0	.00	.00	0	51ᵃ	1	tr		
1 t	5	0.0	0.0	0.8		155	.00	0.0	.00	.00	2	1			
margarine, imit, tub, corn	17	2.8	1.9	0.8		48	0	.00	.00	0	46	1	tr		
1 t	5	0.0	0.0	0.3		159	.00	0.0	.00	.00	1	1			
margarine, imit, tub, soybean & cottonseed—*1 t*	17	2.8	1.9	0.5		48	0	.00	.00	0	46	1	tr		
	5	0.0	0.0	0.3		159	.00	0.0	.00	.00	1	1			
mayonnaise, safflower & soybean	99	2.1	11.0	7.6		39	0				78	2		.02	
1 T	14	0.2	0.4	1.2	0.0		.00				5	4	.10		
mayonnaise, soybean	99	2.1	11.0	5.7	8	39	0				78	2		.02	
1 T	14	0.2	0.4	1.6	0.0		.00				5	4	.10		
mayonnaise, imit, soybean	35	9.4	2.9	1.6	4						75			.02	
1 T	15	0.0	2.4	0.5	0.0										
sandwich spread	60	6.2	5.2	3.1	12										
1 T	15	0.1	3.4	0.8	0.0										
spread, stick, soybean & palm	26	1.8	2.9	0.9		48	0	.00	.00	0	48	1	tr		
1 t	5	0.0	0.0	0.7		159	.00	0.0	.00	.00	1	1			
spread, tub, soybean & cottonseed	26	1.8	2.9	0.3		48	0	.00	.00	0	48	1	tr		
1 t	5	0.0	0.0	0.6		159	.00	0.0	.00	.00	1	1			

SUGARS, SYRUPS, JAMS, JELLIES & OTHER SWEET FOOD ITEMS

candied fruit															
apricot	101	3.6	0.1				tr	.01				4			
1 med	30	0.2	26.0	0.2		370	tr	0.2				6	.30		
cherry	51	1.8	tr				0								
3 large	15	0.1	13.0	0.1		30									
cherry, maraschino	19	11.2	tr												
2 med	16	tr	4.7	0.1											
citron	89	5.0	0.1								81	24			
1 oz	28	0.1	22.7	0.4							34	7	.20		
fig	90	6.3	0.1				30	tr				20			
1 piece	30	1.1	22.1	1.3		0	tr	0.1				12	.20		
ginger root	95	3.4	0.1												
1 oz	28	0.1	24.4	0.2											
grapefruit/lemon/orange peel	89	4.9	0.1								5				
1 oz	28	0.1	22.6	0.6							1				
pear	85	5.9	0.2												
1 oz	28	0.4	21.3	0.3											
pineapple	120	6.8	0.2				9	.01				12			
1 slice	38	0.3	30.4	0.3		40	.05	0.1				9	.20		
chutney, apple	41		tr								34	5	4		
1 T	20	0.2	10.5								43	7	.20		
chutney, tomato	31										26	5	4		
1 T	20	0.2	7.8								26	7	.18		
fruit butter, apple	37	10.3	0.2								tr	3			
1 T	20	0.1	9.1	0.2		0					50	4	.10		
fruit butter, guava	39		0.0				16								
1 T	20	0.0	10.0	0.0											
honey	61	3.4	0.0	0.0			tr	.01			1	1	1		
1 T	20	0.1	16.5	tr		0	.00	0.1			10	1	.10		
honey	306	17.2	0.0	0.0			4	.07			5	20	3		
5 T	100	0.2	78.0	0.1		tr	.01	0.2			51	16	.80		

ᵃ Unsalted tub margarine contains 2 mg Na per t.

	KCAL / WT (g)	H₂O (g) / PRO (g)	FAT (g) / CHO (g)	PUFA (g) / SFA (g)	CHOL (mg) / FIBR (g)	A (RE) / A (IU)	C (mg) / B-1 (mg)	B-2 (mg) / NIA (mg)	B-6 (mg) / B-12 (mcg)	FOL (mcg) / PANT (mg)	Na (mg) / K (mg)	Ca (mg) / P (mg)	Mg (mg) / Fe (mg)	Zn (mg) / Cu (mg)	Mn (mg)
jam															
all varieties	55	5.8	0.1				1	tr				2			
1 T	20	.01	14.2		0.1	2	tr	tr				2	.10		
all varieties, low cal	29		tr				tr	tr			16	1	1		
1 T	20	0.1	7.4			0	.00	tr			31	1	tr		
grape	59		tr				tr	.01				2			
1 T	20	0.1	15.0			6	tr	tr				2	.30		
plum	59		tr				2	tr				2			
1 T	20	0.1	15.0			64	tr	0.1				2	.30		
jelly															
all varieties	55	5.8	tr	0.0			1	.01			3	4	1		
1 T	20	tr	14.1		0.0	2	tr	tr			15	1	.30		
all varieties, low cal	27		0.0				tr	.01			tr	1	1		
1 T	20	0.1	7.0			0	tr	tr			13	1	.10		
blackberry	51		0.0				tr	.01			4	4	2		
1 T	20	0.1	13.2			13	.00	0.1			12	2	.10		
boysenberry	52		0.0				tr	.01			3	4	1		
1 T	20	0.0	13.4			13	.00	tr			12	2	.10		
cherry	52		tr				tr	.01			3	3	1		
1 T	20	0.1	13.2			0	tr	tr				3	.20		
currant	52		0.0				3	tr			8	4	1		
1 T	20	1.2	13.4			9	.00	0.0			19	2	.20		
grape	55		tr				1	.01			3	4	1		
1 T	20	tr	14.1		0.0	2	tr	tr			15	1	.30		
guava	52		tr				3	tr			3	3	1		
1 T	20	0.1	13.4			13	.00	0.1			13	3	.20		
quince	51		tr				tr	tr			2	2			
1 T	20	0.1	13.2			3	tr	tr			16	2	.20		
strawberry	51		0.0				tr	.01			2	3	1		
1 T	20	tr	13.2			5	.00	tr			13	2	.20		
marmalade, citrus	51	5.8	tr				1	tr			3	7	1		
1 T	20	0.1	14.0		0.1	0	tr	tr			7	2	.10		
marmalade, orange	56		0.1				2	tr			4	4			
1 T	20	0.2	14.0			0	tr	tr			9	3	.10		
marmalade, papaya	57		0.0				7								
1 T	20	0.0	14.6												
molasses															
first extraction, light	50	4.8	0.0		0.0				.01		16	33			
1 T	20	0.0	13.0					.01	tr		300	9	.90		
first extraction, light	252	24.0	0.0						.06		80	165			
5 T	100	0.0	65.0		0.0			.07	0.2		1500	45	4.30		
second extraction, med	46	4.8	0.0									58			
1 T	20	0.0	12.0		0.0							14	1.20		
second extraction, med	232	24.0	0.0									290			
5 T	100	0.0	60.0		0.0							69	6.00		
third extraction, blackstrap	43	4.8	0.0						.05			116			
1 T	20	0.0	11.0		0.0			.06	0.4			17	2.30		
third extraction, blackstrap	213	24.0	0.0						.25			579			
5 T	100	0.0	55.0		0.0			.28	2.1			85	11.30		
preserves															
apricot	51		tr				tr	tr			2	2	1		
1 T	20	0.1	13.0			42	.00	tr			19	2	.20		
apricot-pineapple	51		tr				tr	tr			3	3	1		
1 T	20	0.3	13.0			40	.02	tr			22	2	.20		
blackberry	55		tr				tr	.01			2	3	1		
1 T	20	0.3	13.8			13	.00	0.1			12	2	.10		
boysenberry	54		tr				tr	.01			6	4	1		
1 T	20	0.2	13.8			13	.00	0.1			12	3	.10		

	KCAL / WT (g)	H₂O (g) / PRO (g)	FAT (g) / CHO (g)	PUFA (g) / SFA (g)	CHOL (mg) / FIBR (g)	A (RE) / A (IU)	C (mg) / B-1 (mg)	B-2 (mg) / NIA (mg)	B-6 (mg) / B-12 (mcg)	FOL (mcg) / PANT (mg)	Na (mg) / K (mg)	Ca (mg) / P (mg)	Mg (mg) / Fe (mg)	Zn (mg) / Cu (mg)	Mn (mg)
peach	51		0.0				tr	tr			4	2	1		
1 T	20	0.1	13.2			0	.00	0.1			19	2	.20		
relish															
cranberry-orange	27		0.1				3	tr			tr	3			
1 T	15	0.1	6.8			11	.01	tr			11	1	.10		
strawberry	53		0.0				3	.01			2	3	1		
1 T	20	0.1	13.6			5	.00	tr			14	2	.20		
strawberry-pineapple	54		0.0				tr	tr			3	3	1		
1 T	20	1.0	14.0			5	tr	tr			14	2	.20		
tomato	53		tr				tr	tr			19	2	2		
1 T	20	0.2	13.6			0	tr	0.1			28	3	.20		
sugar															
brown	52	0.3	0.0					.00			3	11	9		
1 T	14	0.0	13.4	0.0		0	.00	0.0			32	5	.40		
brown	364	1.5	0.0					.02			17	53	43		
5 T	70	0.0	93.8	0.0		0	.01	0.1			161	26	1.82		
maple	52	1.2	0.0									27			
1 T	15	0.0	13.5	0.0								2	.50		
powdered	42	tr	0.0					.00							
1 T	11	0.0	10.9	0.0		0	.00	0.0							
powdered	385	0.5	0.0					.00							
9 T	100	0.0	99.5	0.0		0	.00	0.0							
white, granular	24	tr	0.0					.00				tr			
1 cube	6	0.0	6.0	0.0		0	.00	0.0							
white, granular	16	tr	0.0					.00				tr			
1 t	4	0.0	4.0	0.0		0	.00	0.0							
white, granular	46	0.1	0.0					.00				tr			
1 T	12	0.0	11.9	0.0		0	.00	0.0							
white, granular	385	0.5	0.0					.00			tr	5			
½ cup	100	0.0	99.5	0.0		0	.00	0.0			1	1	.10		
sugarcane jce	16		tr				tr	tr				3			
1 T	20	0.1	4.1			0	tr	tr				2	.10		
sugar substitute															
diamond crystal[a]	1		0.0								tr	2			
1 pkg	0.4	0.0	0.4												
equal[b]	4		0.0			0	0	.00	.00	0	0	0	0	.00	.00
1 pkg	1	tr	1.0			0	.00	0.0	.00	.00	0	0	.00	.00	
sprinkle sweet	2		0.0								1				
⅛ t	[c]	0.0	0.5												
sugartwin, white	3		0.0								2	8			
1 pkg[d]	0.8	0.0	0.8								tr				
sugartwin, white/brown	1		0.0								2	4			
1 t[e]	0.4	0.0	0.4								tr				
sweet & low[f]	4										4				
1 pkg[d]	1		0.9								3				
sweet 10	0		0.0								2				
⅛ t	[c]	0.0	0.0												
syrup															
cane	53	5.2	0.0				0	.01				12			
1 T	20	0.0	13.6	0.0		0	.03	tr			85	6	.70		
cane	263	26.0	0.0				0	.06				60			
5 T	100	0.0	68.0	0.0		0	.13	0.1			425	29	3.60		
corn	57	5.4	0.0				0	.00			30	9			
1 T	20	0.0	14.8	0.0		0	.00	0.0				3	.80		
corn	287	27.0	0.0				0	.01			150	46			
5 T	100	0.0	74.0	0.0		0	.00	0.1				16	4.10		
corn, dark	60	5.4	0.0	0.0				.00			40				
1 T	21	0.0	15.0	0.0	0.0	0	.00	0.0							

[a] Contains 360 mg lactose & 40 mg Ca saccharine
[b] Contains lactose, aspartame (17 mg aspartic acid & 21.2 mg phe) & silicon dioxide
[c] Gram wt not available
[d] Equivalent in sweetness to 2 t sugar
[e] Equivalent in sweetness to 1 t sugar
[f] Contains 0.9 g dextrose & 40 mg Na saccharine

	KCAL / WT (g)	H₂O (g) / PRO (g)	FAT (g) / CHO (g)	PUFA (g) / SFA (g)	CHOL (mg) / FIBR (g)	A (RE) / A (IU)	C (mg) / B-1 (mg)	B-2 (mg) / NIA (mg)	B-6 (mg) / B-12 (mcg)	FOL (mcg) / PANT (mg)	Na (mg) / K (mg)	Ca (mg) / P (mg)	Mg (mg) / Fe (mg)	Zn (mg) / Cu (mg)	Mn (mg)
maple	50	6.6	0.0			0					3	33	2		
1 T	20	0.0	12.8		0.0	0					26	3	.20		
maple	252	33.0	0.0			0					10	104	10		
5 T	100	0.0	65.0		0.0	0					176	8	1.20		
maple, imit	55	5.8	0.0				0	.00			35	2			
1 T	20	0.0	14.6		0.0	14	.00	0.0			1	1	.20		
maple, imit	275		0.0				0	.00			175	10			
5 T	100	0.0	73.0		0.0	70	.00	0.0			3	4	.90		
pancake/waffle															
Golden Griddle	50	6.5	0.0	0.0				.00			20				
1 T	20	0.0	13.4	0.0	0.0	0	.00	0.0							
Karo	60	5.5	0.0	0.0				.00			35				
1 T	21	0.0	14.9	0.0	0.0	0	.00	0.0							
Log Cabin	104	11.3	0.0	0.0	0		0	.00	.00	0	11	6			
1 fl oz	39	0.0	27.5	0.0	0.0	0	.00	0.0	.00		2	2	.48	.04	
Log Cabin, buttered	105	11.9	0.6	tr	2		0	tr	tr	tr	74	5	tr	.004	
1 fl oz	39	tr	26.1	0.4	0.0	24	tr	tr		.00	1	2	.41	.036	
Log Cabin, country kitchen	101	12.7	0.0	0.0	0		0	.00	.00	0	19	11	tr		
1 fl oz	39	0.0	26.1	0.0	0.0	0	.00	.00	.00	.00	1	4	.95	.083	
Log Cabin, maple honey	106	10.7	0.0	0.0	0		0	tr	tr		7	7	tr		
1 fl oz	39	tr	28.1	0.0	0.0	0	tr	tr		tr	6	2	.43	.05	
sorghum	52	4.6	0.0					.02			4	30			
1 T	20	0.0	13.4				.02				120	5	2.40		
table blend (cane & maple)	50	6.6	0.0				0	.00			tr	3			
1 T	20	0.0	13.0	0.0		0	.00	0.0			5	tr			
table blend (mainly corn)	57	4.8	0.0				0	tr			13	9	tr		
1 T	20	0.0	14.8		0.0	0	.00	tr			1	3	.80		
table blend (mainly corn)	286	24.0	0.0				0	.01			68	46	2		
5 T	100	0.0	74.0		0.0	0	.00	0.1			4	16	4.10		
treacle,ᵃ black	53		0.0								19	99			
1 T	20	0.2	13.4								297	6	1.80		
treacle,ᵃ black	265		0.0								96	495	144		
5 T	100	1.2	67.2		0.0						1470	31	9.20		

VEGETABLES & VEGETABLE SALADS

	KCAL / WT (g)	H₂O (g) / PRO (g)	FAT (g) / CHO (g)	PUFA (g) / SFA (g)	CHOL (mg) / FIBR (g)	A (RE) / A (IU)	C (mg) / B-1 (mg)	B-2 (mg) / NIA (mg)	B-6 (mg) / B-12 (mcg)	FOL (mcg) / PANT (mg)	Na (mg) / K (mg)	Ca (mg) / P (mg)	Mg (mg) / Fe (mg)	Zn (mg) / Cu (mg)	Mn (mg)
alfalfa sprouts, raw	41	88.3	0.6				16	.21				28		1.00	
3½ oz	100	5.1	5.5		1.7		.14						1.40		
artichoke,ᵇ ckd	44	86.5	0.2				8	.04			30	51			
1 large base & soft leaf ends	100	2.8	9.9		2.4	150	.07	0.7			301	69	1.10		
artichoke hearts,ᵇ frzn	32	75.2	0.4		0		5	.11	.08	85	40	16	25	.272	
½ cup	85	2.3	6.6		0.9	133	.04	0.7	.00	.15	210	50	.60	.051	
asparagus, cuts & spears															
ckd	20	93.6	0.2				26	.18			1	21			
⅔ cup pieces	100	2.2	3.6		0.7	900	.16	1.4			183	50	.60		
cnd	16	94.0	0.2				18	.12	.06	85	373	17	9	.50	
½ cup	100	1.8	2.6		0.5	645	.06	0.7		.20	193	43	.60	.14	
frzn	24	91.8	0.2	tr	0		30	.13	.13	191	7	22	14	.59	.203
³/₅ cup	100	3.3	4.2	tr	0.9	855	.14	1.3	.00	.19	271	65	.70	.14	
frzn bb, in butter sce, Green Giant	48		3.0				17	.09			414	20			
½ cup	100	2.2	3.1		1.4	826	.08	1.8			150	46	.40		
avocado, raw, calif	306	125.5	30.0	3.5	0	106	14	.21	.48	113	21	19	70	.73	.422
1 med	173	3.6	12.0	4.5	3.7	1059	.19	3.3	.00	1.68	1097	73	2.04	.46	
avocado, raw, florida	339	242.4	27.0	4.5	0	186	24	.37	.85	162	14	33	104	1.28	.517
1 med	304	4.8	27.1	5.3	6.4	1860	.33	5.8	.00	2.95	1484	119	1.60	.763	
bamboo shoots, raw	36	121.0	0.4				5	.09				17			
1 cup	133	3.5	6.9		0.9	27	.20	0.8			709	78	.70		

ᵃ Residual molasses left from sugar making.

ᵇ The cho in artichokes may be inulin, which is of doubtful availability. During storage, inulin is converted to sugars. Caloric values range from 9/100 g for freshly harvested to 47/100 g for stored.

	KCAL	H₂O (g)	FAT (g)	PUFA (g)	CHOL (mg)	A (RE)	C (mg)	B-2 (mg)	B-6 (mg)	FOL (mcg)	Na (mg)	Ca (mg)	Mg (mg)	Zn (mg)	Mn (mg)
	WT (g)	PRO (g)	CHO (g)	SFA (g)	FIBR (g)	A (IU)	B-1 (mg)	NIA (mg)	B-12 (mcg)	PANT (mg)	K (mg)	P (mg)	Fe (mg)	Cu (mg)	
bamboo shoots, cnd	21		0.1								5	14	6		
1 cup	133	1.9	3.5		0.9						128	20	.40		
bean salad, three bean, cnd, Green Giant—*²⁄₅ cup*	75		0.2				7	.05			440	27			
	100	2.2	16.5		2.5	128	.06	0.2					.90		
beans, cnd															
beans, bbq, Campbell's	270		4.0						.09		885	103	44	1.87	1.23
7¾ oz	220	10.0	42.0						tr				3.08	.64	
beans, brown sugar, Stokely van Camp—*1 cup*	330		6.0								800				
	260	14.0	58.0		4.1						630				
beans, chili, mex style, Stokely van Camp—*1 cup*	240		3.0								820				
	260	13.0	44.0		2.9						730				
beans, deep brown w/molasses sce, Libby—*3½ oz*	112		1.2				3	.11			235	65	34		
	100	5.5	20.3			tr	.04	0.3			285	114	1.67		
beans, deep brown w/tomato sce, Libby—*3½ oz*	109		1.0				2	.09			384	123	31		
	100	5.3	20.1			119	.06	0.4			274	109	1.29		
beans, deep brown & veg in tomato sce, Libby—*3½ oz*	106		0.5				2	.08			359	50	34		
	100	5.4	20.4			115	.06	0.4			268	110	1.48		
beans, homestyle, Campbell's	270		4.0						.20		1045	125	8	2.16	1.34
8 oz	227	11.0	48.0						tr		681	227	3.63	.66	
beans in molasses sce, Heinz	251	190.3	0.9				2	.13			812	178			
7¾ oz	220	12.8	47.7		3.5	141	.10	1.1			378	222	3.96		
beans in tomato sce, Heinz	232	166.8	1.8				3	.08			600	163			
8 oz	227	11.4	42.7		2.5	316	.08	0.7			173		3.63		
beans, vegetarian, Stokely van Camp	240		1.0								1100				
1 cup	260	13.0	49.0		2.4						700				
pork & beans in tomato sce, Campbell's—*8 oz*	255		4.0				3	.05	.07		900	131	74	3.18	.92
	224	11.0	44.0			345	.10	0.9	tr		608	268	3.70	.67	
pork & beans in tomato sce, Heinz	250	164.8	3.9				4	.10			884	152			
8 oz	227	11.4	42.7			359	.06	0.5			430		3.18		
pork & beans in tomato sce, Stokely van Camp—*1 cup*	250		2.0								1180				
	260	13.0	48.0		2.7						690				
beans & rice, mex style, cnd, Campbell's—*7½ oz*	179		4.0				19	.08			950	51			
	210	6.0	30.0			878	.06	1.5			490	90	2.80		
beans, white, ckd	118	69.0	0.6				0	.07			7	50			
½ cup	100	7.8	21.2		1.5	0	.14	0.7			416	148	2.70		
beets															
raw	43	87.3	0.1				10	.05			60	16	27		
2 med	100	1.6	9.9		0.8	20	.03	0.4			335	33	.70		
ckd, diced	27	75.5	0.1				5	.03			36	12			
½ cup	83	0.9	6.0		0.7	17	.03	0.3			172	19	.40		
cnd, harvard, Libby	73		0.1				2	.05			162	11	20		
²⁄₅ cup	100	0.8	18.2			tr	tr	0.1			164	17	.36		
cnd, harvard, Stokely van Camp	160		1.0								250				
1 cup	255	2.0	36.0		1.2						405				
cnd, shoestring	21		tr				2	.04			275	10	15		
3½ oz	100	0.6	5.0			tr	tr	0.1			124	12	.71		
cnd, sliced	27	91.7	0.1				3	.04	.05	29	282	11	13	.18	
³⁄₅ cup	100	0.9	6.2		0.6	4	.01	0.5		.10	168	13	.57	.11	
cnd, sliced, pickled	180		0.0								565				
1 cup	245	2.0	45.0		1.1						360				
cnd, whole	31	90.9	0.1				5	.05	.05	29	250	13	17	.28	
³⁄₅ cup	100	0.9	7.2		0.7		.02	0.6		.10	131	19	.49	.09	
cnd, whole, pickled	190		0.0								475				
1 cup	255	2.0	46.0		1.2						405				
beet greens, raw	24	90.9	0.3				30	.22			130	119	106		
3½ oz	100	2.2	4.6		1.3	6100	.10	0.4			570	40	3.30		
beet greens, ckd	18	93.6	0.2				15	.15			76	99			
½ cup	100	1.7	3.3		1.1	5100	.07	0.3			332	25	1.90		

	KCAL	H₂O (g)	FAT (g)	PUFA (g)	CHOL (mg)	A (RE)	C (mg)	B-2 (mg)	B-6 (mg)	FOL (mcg)	Na (mg)	Ca (mg)	Mg (mg)	Zn (mg)	Mn (mg)
	WT (g)	PRO (g)	CHO (g)	SFA (g)	FIBR (g)	A (IU)	B-1 (mg)	NIA (mg)	B-12 (mcg)	PANT (mg)	K (mg)	P (mg)	Fe (mg)	Cu (mg)	
black-eyed peas (cowpeas), immature seeds															
ckd	86	57.4	0.6				14	.09			1	19			
½ cup	80	6.5	14.5		1.4	280	.02	1.1			303	117	1.70		
cnd	70	81.0	0.3				3	.05			236	18			
½ cup	100	5.0	12.4		0.7	60	.09	0.5			352	112	1.50		
frzn	130	66.1	0.4	0.2			9	.11	.11	130	6	25	55	1.58	
⅔ cup	100	8.9	23.5	0.2	1.5	170	.40	1.4	.00	.24	337	168	2.80	.20	
frzn bb, w/sce, Green Giant	112		4.2				1	.03			610	19			
⅖ cup	100	5.2	13.5		0.6	25	.70	0.6			119	92	1.30		
broccoli															
raw	32	89.1	0.3				113	.23			15	103	24		
1 stalk	100	3.6	5.9		1.5	2500ᵃ	.10	0.9			382	78	1.10		
ckd	26	91.3	0.3				90	.20			10	88			
⅔ cup or 1 large stalk	100	3.1	4.5		1.5	2500	.09	0.8			267	62	.80		
frzn, chopped	27	91.3	0.3		0		57	.10	.14	130	21	55	17	.28	.336
½ cup	100	2.8	4.9		1.0	2040	.05	0.4	.00	.28	224	51	.84	.04	
frzn, cuts	26	86.4	0.2		0		57	.09	.14	132	21	37	15	.314	
⅔ cup	95	2.9	4.9		1.0	1376	.06	0.4	.00	.25	235	52	.67	.037	
frzn, florets	27	86.4	0.2		0		63	.09	.14		21	37	15	.31	
⅔ cup	95	2.9	4.9		1.0	1376	.06	0.4	.00	.25	235	52	.67	.04	
frzn, spears	27	91.0	0.2		0		67	.10	.15	142	17	38	16	.33	.255
½ cup	100	3.1	5.1		1.0	1296	.06	0.4	.00	.26	247	54	.70	.04	
frzn, au gratin, Stouffer's	170		12.0								470				
5 oz	142	7.0	9.0								240				
frzn, florentine, Stokely van Camp	25		0.0								30				
3⅕ oz	91	2.0	5.0		0.9						165				
frzn bb, pieces in butter sce, Green Giant—⅖ cup	54		2.3				11	.09			352	182			
	100	2.8	5.5		0.9	1580	.04	0.2			193	94	.40		
frzn, pieces w/almonds, Birds Eye	56	81.3	2.8	0.7	0		57	.10	.13	121	213	44	28	.468	
½ cup	95	3.7	6.0	0.3	1.0	1253	.06	0.6	tr	.23	249	70	1.03	.096	
frzn, pieces w/cheese sce, Birds Eye	166	111.6	11.6	1.8	4		35	.18	.11	110	665	119	18	.37	
½ cup	142	4.4	11.9	2.7	0.7	3186	.06	0.4	.17	.35	199	109	.55	.03	
frzn, pieces w/cheese sce, Green Giant—⅖ cup	96		6.4				30	.11				116			
	100	4.0	6.0		0.4	30	.03	0.1					.50		
frzn bb, spears in butter sce, Green Giant—½ cup	46		2.3				63	.11			470	31			
	100	2.2	4.0		1.3	828	.05	0.3			222	52	.40		
frzn, spears in hollandaise sce, Birds Eye—½ cup	105	78.8	8.6	1.6	55		41	.07	.11	106	117	24	10	.29	
	95	2.8	4.0	1.7	0.9	1047	.04	0.3	.14	.08	182	52	.59	.027	
broccoli & water chestnuts, frzn, Birds Eye—½ cup	33	84.2	0.2		0		55	.10	.12	114	214	33	14	.273	
	95	2.7	6.8		0.9	1185	.07	0.5	.00	.22	251	51	.64	.033	
broccoli, carrots & pasta twists in sce, frzn, Birds Eye—⅔ cup	88	76.5	4.4	0.8	0		26	.07	.06	60	263	30	13	.30	
	95	2.3	10.7	·0.8	0.7	7804	.07	0.6	tr	.15	184	41	.64	.04	
broccoli, carrots & water chestnuts, frzn, Birds Eye—⅔ cup	32	81.4	0.2		0		39	.09	.09	85	22	30	13	.258	
	91	2.1	6.6		0.9	5118	.06	0.5	.00	.18	247	45	.60	.037	
broccoli, cauliflower & carrots															
frzn	27	91.5	0.3		0		40	.03	.10	71	27	32	13	.27	
1 cup	100	1.9	4.5		1.2	2600	.02	0.3	.00	.18	210	40	.20	.041	
frzn, w/cheese sce, Birds Eye	128	116.7	8.4	1.3	3		43	.14	.12	72	479	94	20	.45	
½ cup	142	3.8	11.3	1.9	0.9	6645	:07	0.5	.13	.36	286	98	.62	.05	
frzn bb, w/cheese sce, Green Giant	55		2.2				30	.10				175			
⅖ cup	100	2.4	6.4		0.4	4880	.05	0.3					.40		
broccoli, cauliflower & red peppers, frzn, Birds Eye—⅔ cup	25	87.0	0.2		0		60	.08	.12		18	29	14	.23	
	95	2.4	4.8		0.9	770	.06	0.4	.00	.19	203	44	.60	.03	
broccoli, cauliflower, corn & pasta in parmesan cheese sce, frzn, Birds Eye—½ cup	108	72.1	5.8	1.0	2		38	.09	.11	60	418	70	16	.376	
	95	3.7	11.9	1.3	0.7	720	.07	0.7	.02	.19	181	83	.61	.038	
broccoli, corn & red peppers, frzn, Birds Eye—⅔ cup	49	76.5	0.4	0.1	0		40	.08	.14	82	11	20	16	.32	
	91	2.7	10.9	tr	0.8	736	.07	0.9	.00	.20	199	53	.55	.04	
broccoli, green beans, onion & red peppers, frzn, Birds Eye—⅔ cup	27	82.8	0.2		0		45	.07	.12	75	13	34	15	.23	
	91	2.0	5.5		0.9	774	.06	0.4	.00	.17	187	36	.66	.05	

ᵃ Vit A is 16,000 IU/100 g for leaves; 3000 IU/100 g for flower clusters; 400 IU/100 g for stalks.

						Vitamins					Minerals				
	KCAL	H_2O (g)	FAT (g)	PUFA (g)	CHOL (mg)	A (RE)	C (mg)	B-2 (mg)	B-6 (mg)	FOL (mcg)	Na (mg)	Ca (mg)	Mg (mg)	Zn (mg)	Mn (mg)
	WT (g)	PRO (g)	CHO (g)	SFA (g)	FIBR (g)	A (IU)	B-1 (mg)	NIA (mg)	B-12 (mcg)	PANT (mg)	K (mg)	P (mg)	Fe (mg)	Cu (mg)	
broccoli, shells, onions & mushrooms in	104	74.1	6.2	1.0	2		36	.13	.10	77	390	54	15	.33	
swiss cheese sce, frzn, Birds Eye *½ cup*	95	3.3	9.9	1.3	0.7	999	.07	0.8	.05	.38	209	73	.64	.116	
brussels sprouts															
ckd	36	88.2	0.4				87	.14			10	32			
6–8 med	100	4.2	6.4		1.6	520	.08	0.8			273	72	1.10		
frzn	37	87.9	0.3		0		69	.10	.19	150	14	27	20	.30	.288
3/5 cup	100	3.7	7.3		1.3	748	.10	0.6	.00	.36	344	58	.76	.03	
frzn, au gratin, Stouffer's	180		11.0								355				
5½ oz	156	6.0	16.0								330				
frzn bb, in butter sce, Green Giant	56		2.5				56	.10			458	24			
½ cup	100	3.1	5.3		1.1	491	.06	0.3			320	59	.60		
frzn, in cheese sce, Birds Eye	147	98.8	9.6	1.5	3		49	.16	.18	118	543	95	23	.45	
½ cup	128	4.6	12.7	2.2	0.9	2252	.10	0.5	.15	.47	335	113	.65	.04	
brussels sprouts, cauliflower & carrots,	30	81.6	0.2		0		46	.08	.14	86	18	25	14	.23	
frzn, Birds Eye—*⅔ cup*	91	2.3	6.1		1.0	3762	.07	0.5	.00	.22	248	44	.63	.03	
burdock, ckd	123		0.1									64			
½ cup	100	1.1	33.4									39			
butter beans, cnd	170		0.0								840				
1 cup	250	12.0	33.0		3.1						550				
butter beans, frzn	138	59.0	0.6	0.3	0		4	.05	.11	97	214	31	44	.73	
½ cup	95	7.5	26.3	0.1	1.8	63	.09	0.7	.00	.23	535	107	2.00	.13	
butter beans, speckled, frzn bb, w/sce,	111		4.0				2	.03			488	22			
Green Giant—*2/5 cup*	100	4.9	14.1		0.8	tr	.60	0.1			102	52	1.10		
cabbage															
chinese, raw	14	95.0	0.1				25	.04			23	43	14		
2¼ cup shredded	100	1.2	3.0		0.6	150	.05	0.6			253	40	.60		
chinese, ckd	8		0.0				26	.07				26			
½ cup	82	1.2	1.3			40	.07	0.8				32	.20		
green, raw	24	92.4	0.2				47	.05			20	49	13		
1 cup shredded	100	1.3	5.4		0.8	130	.05	0.3			233	29	.40		
green, ckd	20	93.9	0.2				33	.04			14	44			
3/5 cup	100	1.1	4.3		0.8	130	.04	0.3			163	20	.30		
red, raw	31	90.2	0.2				61	.06			26	42			
1 cup shredded	100	2.0	6.9		1.0	40	.09	0.4			268	35	.80		
savoy, raw	12	46.0	0.1				27	.04			11	33			
1 cup shredded	50	1.2	2.3		0.4	100	.02	0.2			134	27	.45		
spoon, raw	16	94.3	0.2				25	.10			26	165			
3½ oz	100	1.6	2.9		0.6	3100	.05	0.8			306	44	.80		
spoon, ckd	14	95.2	0.2				15	.08			18	148			
3½ oz	100	1.4	2.4		0.6	3100	.04	0.7			214	33	.60		
swamp, ckd	21		0.2				16	.08				55			
1 cup	100	2.2	3.9		0.9	5200	.05	0.5			88	32	1.50		
carrot															
raw	42	88.2	0.2				8	.05			47	37	23		
1 large	100	1.1	9.7		1.0	11000	.06	0.6			341	36	.70		
ckd	31	91.2	0.2				6	.05			33	33			
⅔ cup	100	0.9	7.1		1.0	10500	.05	0.5			222	31	.60		
cnd	25	92.4	0.2				4	.03	.03	6	281	26	12	.32	
3/5 cup	100	0.7	5.6		0.8	18211	.02	0.6		.13	222	23	.49	.09	
frzn	41	88.6	0.2	tr	0		5	.05	.15	24	46	32	12	.40	
3/5 cup	100	1.2	9.3	tr	1.1	19925	.04	0.7	.00	.28	194	29	.74	.06	
frzn bb, in butter sce, Green Giant	49		2.3				5	.04			482	24			
½ cup	100	0.7	6.4		0.8	10300	.03	0.4			141	28	.30		
frzn, w/brown sugar glaze, Birds Eye	82	74.8	2.2	0.4	0		5	.03	.05	20	510	23	11	.029	
½ cup	95	0.7	15.5	0.4	0.7	17900	.03	0.5	tr	.15	209	16	.23	.014	
carrots, peas & onions, frzn, Birds Eye	48	81.8	0.2	0.1	0		8	.05	.06	38	53	29	14	.379	
½ cup	95	2.1	10.1	tr	1.3	9344	.09	1.0	.00	.17	147	37	.85	.067	
carrot raisin salad, homemade	153		5.8				6	.08				48			
½ cup	134	1.9	27.9		0.7	4700	.08	0.5				65	1.50		

	KCAL / WT (g)	H₂O (g) / PRO (g)	FAT (g) / CHO (g)	PUFA (g) / SFA (g)	CHOL (mg) / FIBR (g)	A (RE) / A (IU)	C (mg) / B-1 (mg)	B-2 (mg) / NIA (mg)	B-6 (mg) / B-12 (mcg)	FOL (mcg) / PANT (mg)	Na (mg) / K (mg)	Ca (mg) / P (mg)	Mg (mg) / Fe (mg)	Zn (mg) / Cu (mg)	Mn (mg)
cauliflower															
raw	27	91.0	0.2				78	.10			13	25	24		
1 cup pieces	100	2.7	5.2		1.0	60	.11	0.7			295	56	1.10		
ckd	22	92.8	0.2				55	.08			9	21			
⅞ cup	100	2.3	4.1		1.0	60	.09	0.6			206	42	.70		
frzn	24	92.4	0.2		0		51	.07	.12	68	19	21	12	.17	.197
³/₅ cup	100	2.0	5.0		0.8	23	.05	0.4	.00	.14	195	37	.52	.02	
frzn, au gratin, Stouffer's	155		10.0								445				
5 oz	142	6.0	11.0								280				
frzn, w/almonds, Birds Eye	40	84.2	1.7	0.3	0		47	.08	.11	36	268	27	18	.161	
½ cup	95	2.7	5.1	0.1	0.9	28	.05	0.5	.00	.13	201	47	.64	.044	
frzn, w/cheese sce, Birds Eye	162	112.3	10.8	1.7	3		40	.17	.12	31	633	106	16	.34	
½ cup	142	3.4	13.1	2.5	0.7	2391	.07	0.3	.17	.53	243	99	.38	.026	
frzn, w/cheese sce, Green Giant	84		5.5				24	.08				82			
²/₅ cup	100	3.0	6.0		0.3	200	.03	0.1					.70		
frzn bb, w/cheese sce, Green Giant	52		2.3				6	.08			324	165			
²/₅ cup	100	2.3	5.6		1.0	1200	.03	0.2			178	83	.40		
cauliflower, green beans & corn, frzn, Birds Eye—⅔ cup	36	80.2	0.3	tr	0		27	.06	.10	36	9	21	14	.212	
	91	1.9	8.1	tr	0.8	195	.05	0.6	.00	.14	166	37	.55	.030	
celeriac root, raw	40	88.4	0.3				8	.06			100	43			
4–6 roots	100	1.8	8.5		1.3		.05	0.7			300	115	.60		
celery															
raw	8	47.0	0.1				5	.02			63	20	11		
1 stalk	50	0.4	2.0		0.3	120	.02	0.2			170	14	.20		
raw, diced	17	94.1	0.1				9	.03			126	39	22		
1 cup	100	0.9	3.9		0.6		.03	0.3			341	28	.30		
ckd, diced	14	95.3	0.1				6	.03			88	31			
⁴/₅ cup	100	0.8	3.1		0.6	230	.02	0.3			239	22	.20		
chard, raw	25	91.1	0.3				32	.17			147	88	65		
3½ oz	100	2.4	4.6		0.8	6500	.06	0.5			550	39	3.20		
chard, ckd	18	93.7	0.2				16	.11			86	73			
³/₅ cup	100	1.8	3.3		0.7	5400	.04	0.4			321	24	1.80		
chicory greens, raw	20		0.3				22	.10				86	13		
30–40 small leaves	100	1.8	3.8		0.8	4000	.06	0.5			420	40	.90		
chilies															
green, cnd	14		0.0												
2 oz	56	0.6	2.8												
red, raw	93		2.3				369	.36			9	29	27		
3½ oz	100	3.7	18.1		9.0	21600	.22	4.40			420	78	1.20		
red, dried	160		4.5				6	.66			186	65			
1¾ oz	50	6.4	29.9		3.1	38500	.11	5.2			600	120	3.90		
chives, raw, chopped	3	9.1	tr				6	.01				7	3		
1 T	10	0.2	0.6		0.1	581	.01	0.1			25	4	.20		
coleslaw, homemade	173	94.8	16.8				35	.06			144	53			
1 cup	120	1.6	5.8		0.8	190	.06	0.4			239	35	.50		
collard greens															
raw	40	86.9	0.7				92	.31			43	203	57		
3½ oz	100	3.6	7.2		0.9	6500	.20	1.7			401	63	1.00		
ckd	29	90.8	0.6				46	.20			25	152			
½ cup	100	2.7	4.9		0.8	5400	.14	1.2			234	39	.60		
frzn, chopped	27	91.3	0.4		0		40	.10	.12	59	48	204	29	.25	.633
³/₅ cup	100	2.8	4.6		1.0	5889	.05	0.6	.00	.11	253	27	1.09	.05	
corn, white															
cnd	60	82.3	0.3				10	.06			285	2	17	.38	
³/₅ cup	100	1.8	14.6		0.6	94	.04	1.0			177	49	.39	.10	
cnd, cream style	73	78.5	0.3				7	.07			294	3	16	.60	
²/₅ cup	100	1.9	18.3		0.8	7	.02	1.2			156	47	.43	.06	

	KCAL / WT (g)	H₂O (g) / PRO (g)	FAT (g) / CHO (g)	PUFA (g) / SFA (g)	CHOL (mg) / FIBR (g)	A (RE) / A (IU)	C (mg) / B-1 (mg)	B-2 (mg) / NIA (mg)	B-6 (mg) / B-12 (mcg)	FOL (mcg) / PANT (mg)	Na (mg) / K (mg)	Ca (mg) / P (mg)	Mg (mg) / Fe (mg)	Zn (mg) / Cu (mg)	Mn (mg)
frzn	88	75.3	0.9				7	.07	.21		4	4	15	.31	
½ cup	100	2.9	20.5		0.6	14	.09	1.9		.37	226	72	.33	.04	
frzn bb, in butter sce, Green Giant	95		2.3				8	.06			306	7			
½ cup	100	2.3	16.2		0.7	73	.05	1.3			167	58	.30		
corn, yellow															
on the cob, ckd	100	74.1	1.0				9	.10			tr	3			
4-inch ear	100	3.3	21.0		0.7	400	.12	1.4			196	89	.60		
on the cob, frzn	90	65.9	0.5	0.4	0		9	.06	.16	43	11	2	29	.62	
3-inch ear	90	2.4	18.8	0.1	0.3	214	.06	1.0	.00	.26	219	60	.40	.046	
on the cob, frzn	160	117.1	0.8	0.7	0		15	.11	.29	76	20	4	51	1.10	
5½-inch ear	160	4.2	32.9	0.1	0.6	234	.11	1.8	.00	.47	384	105	.70	.081	
cnd	60	82.1	0.4				6	.06		39	251	3	20	.46	
³⁄₅ cup	100	1.8	14.8		0.6	131	.04	0.8			166	56	.39	.08	
cnd, cream style	73	78.1	0.4				6	.06			272	2	24	.62	
²⁄₅ cup	100	1.9	18.6		0.7	150	.03	1.0			181	61	.44	.08	
frzn	88	74.6	0.7	0.4	0		6	.06	.16	48	4	5	21	.43	.096
½ cup	100	3.1	21.1	0.1	0.6	238	.08	1.6	.00	.19	196	72	.46	.04	
frzn, chuckwagon, Stokely van Camp	90		1.0								15				
3⅕ oz	91	3.0	18.0		0.6						170				
frzn, jubilee, Birds Eye	119	70.4	5.0	1.0	1		7	.12	.11	32	268	29	12	.195	
½ cup	95	2.5	16.2	1.0	0.7	2781	.06	0.8	.08	.37	221	50	.09	.016	
frzn bb, in butter sce, Green Giant	93		2.6				8	.06			331	8			
½ cup	100	2.1	15.1		0.8	318	.07	1.1			149	56	.40		
frzn, w/peppers, Green Giant	86		0.5				9	.08			309	5			
³⁄₅ cup	100	2.3	17.9		0.5	270	.03	0.8			162	64	.60		
frzn bb, w/peppers in butter sce, Green Giant—½ cup	93		2.6				6	.06			331	8			
	100	2.1	15.1		0.8	318	.07	1.1			149	56	.40		
corn, green beans & pasta twists in sce, frzn, Birds Eye—½ cup	108	71.1	4.9	0.8	1		10	.07	.08	30	283	53	18	.36	
	95	3.0	14.9	1.1	0.6	445	.07	0.9	.01	.13	137	68	.63	.04	
cornsalad,ª raw	21	92.8	0.4										13		
3½ oz	100	2.0	3.6		0.8										
cowpeas, mature seeds, ckd	76	80.0	0.3					.04			8	17			
3½ oz	100	5.1	13.8		1.0	10	.16	0.4			229	95	1.30		
crowder peas, frzn	126	58.8	0.9	0.4	0		2	.06			6	23			
⅔ cup	91	7.7	22.7	0.3	1.5	39	.26	0.7	.00		397		2.40		
cucumber w/skin, raw	8	47.5	0.1				6	.02			3	13	6		
½ med	50	0.5	1.7		0.3	125	.01	0.1			80	14	.60		
cucumber w/o skin, raw	7	47.8	0.1				6	.02			3	9	5		
½ med	50	0.3	1.6		0.2	tr	.01	0.1			80	9	.20		
dandelion greens, raw	45	85.6	0.7				35	.26			76	187	36		
3½ oz	100	2.7	9.2		1.6	14000	.19				397	66	3.10		
dandelion greens, ckd	33	89.8	0.6				18	.16			44	140			
½ cup	100	2.0	6.4		1.3	11700	.13				232	42	1.80		
dasheen (japanese taro), raw	98	73.0	0.2				4	.04			7	28			
1⅓ corms	100	1.9	23.7		0.8	20	.13	1.1			514	61	1.00		
dock (sorrel), raw	28	90.9	0.3				119	.22			5	66			
3½ oz	100	2.1	5.6		0.8	12900	.09	0.5			338	41	1.60		
dock (sorrel), ckd	19	93.6	0.2				54	.13			3	55			
½ cup	100	1.6	3.9		0.7	10800	.06	0.4			198	26	.90		
eggplant, raw, diced	25	92.4	0.2				5	.05			2	12	16		
½ cup	100	1.2	5.8		0.9	10	.05	0.6			214	26	.70		
eggplant, ckd, diced	19	94.3	0.2				3	.04			1	11			
½ cup	100	1.0	4.1		0.9	10	.05	0.5			150	21	.60		
endive (escarole), raw	20	93.1	0.1				10	.14			14	81	10		
20 long leaves	100	1.7	4.1		0.9	3300	.07	0.5			294	54	1.70		
fennel leaves, raw	28	90.0	0.4				31					100			
3½ oz	100	2.8	5.1		0.5	3500					397	51	2.70		
garbanzo beans (chick-peas), cnd	179		2.4				0	.07				75	54		
3½ oz	100	10.2	30.3			25	.15	1.0				165	3.00		
garden cress, raw	3	8.9	0.1				7	.03			1	8			
5-8 sprigs	10	0.3	0.6		0.1	930	.01	0.1			61	8	.10		

ª European herb widely cultivated as a salad plant & potherb

	KCAL / WT (g)	H_2O (g) / PRO (g)	FAT (g) / CHO (g)	PUFA (g) / SFA (g)	CHOL (mg) / FIBR (g)	A (RE) / A (IU)	C (mg) / B-1 (mg)	B-2 (mg) / NIA (mg)	B-6 (mg) / B-12 (mcg)	FOL (mcg) / PANT (mg)	Na (mg) / K (mg)	Ca (mg) / P (mg)	Mg (mg) / Fe (mg)	Zn (mg) / Cu (mg)	Mn (mg)
garden cress, ckd	23	92.5	0.6				34	.16			8	61			
3½ oz	100	1.9	3.8		0.9	7700	.06	0.8			353	48	.80		
ginger root, raw	49	87.0	1.0				4	.04			6	23			
3½ oz	100	1.4	9.5		1.1	10	.02	0.7			264	36	2.10		
green bean & mushroom casserole, frzn,	150		9.0								675				
Stouffer's—*4¾ oz*	135	4.0	12.0								215				
green beans, french style															
cnd	15		0.1				3	.05			295	23	12		
3½ oz	100	0.8	3.4			291	.02	0.1			83	15	.58		
frzn	26	90.8	0.1	tr	0		7	.08	.05	36	2	38	20	.25	
2/5 cup	100	1.6	6.0	tr	1.1	530	.06	0.3	.00	.10	136	30	.90	.052	
frzn bb, in butter sce, Green Giant	38		2.1				7	.05			421	27			
½ cup	100	1.0	3.5		0.8	469	.03	0.2			98	23	.70		
frzn, w/cheese sce, Birds Eye	156	110.6	10.5	3.3	3		7	.15	.06	3	598	115	26	.46	
½ cup	142	3.4	13.3	2.1	1.0	2291	.07	0.3	.15	.31	234	93	.80	.059	
frzn w/mushrooms, Birds Eye	29	76.1	0.3		0		7	.06	.05	29	188	26	14	.17	
½ cup	85	1.4	6.5		1.0	395	.04	0.3	.00	.04	133	19	.39	.03	
frzn, w/toasted almonds, Birds Eye	52	70.9	1.6	0.4	0		8	.06	.05	29	335	36	25	.28	
½ cup	85	2.5	8.4	0.2	1.0	372	.05	0.4	.00	.11	167	32	.52	.07	
green beans, italian, cnd	22	92.2	0.1				10	.07			448	19	14	.23	
2/3 cup	100	1.2	5.1		0.8	395	.04	0.4			152	26	1.07	.07	
green beans, italian, frzn	37	88.4	0.1	tr	0		18	.12	.06		4	41	23	.29	.371
2/3 cup	100	2.2	8.7	tr	1.1	454	.08	0.7	.00	.25	255	37	.89	.06	
green beans, snap															
ckd	31	115.5	0.2				15	.11			5	62			
1 cup	125	2.0	6.8		1.2	675	.09	0.6			189	46	.80		
cnd	15	94.6	0.1				3	.05	.04	18	397	26	12	.19	
2/3 cup	100	0.9	3.2		0.7	445	.02	0.3		.08	124	20	.65	.10	
frzn	29	91.0	0.2	tr	0		10	.08	.05	46	4	43	20	.22	.437
2/3 cup	100	1.6	6.8	tr	1.1	520	.06	0.3	.00	.13	162	25	.88	.05	
green beans, cauliflower & carrots, frzn,	26	83.2	0.2	tr	0		19	.06	.06	29	14	32	15	.22	
Birds Eye—*2/3 cup*	91	1.4	5.8	tr	1.0	4720	.05	0.4	.00	.11	175	27	.66	.04	
green beans, corn, carrots & onions, frzn,	42	78.8	0.3	tr	0		7	.06	.07	31	10	26	16	.249	
Birds Eye—*2/3 cup*	91	1.6	9.9	tr	0.8	4437	.05	0.6	.00	.13	163	35	.59	.045	
green beans, onions & bacon bits, frzn	37		1.6				5	.07			432	26			
bb, Green Giant—*½ cup*	100	1.5	4.2		1.1	265	.03	0.2			100	25	.50		
hominy, white, cnd	140		1.0								710				
1 cup	250	3.0	31.0		0.8						40				
hominy, yellow, cnd	120		1.0								730				
1 cup	245	3.0	28.0		0.8						25				
indian spinach (basella), raw	19		0.3				102					109			
3½ oz	100	1.8	3.4		0.7	8000	.05	0.5				52	1.20		
jerusalem artichoke, raw	[a]	79.8	0.1				4	.06				14	11		
4 small	100	2.3	16.7		0.8	20	.20	1.3				78	3.40		
kale															
raw	38	87.5	0.8				125				75	179	37		
3½ oz	100	4.2	6.0		1.3	8900					318	73	2.20		
ckd	28	91.2	0.7				62				43	134			
¾ cup	100	3.2	4.0		1.1	7400					221	46	1.20		
frzn, chopped	28	91.3	0.5		0		41	.10	.09		15	133	18	.17	.443
½ cup	100	2.6	4.9		0.8	6804	.06	0.6	.00	.05	333	29	.95	.05	
kidney beans, red															
ckd	118		0.5					.06			3	38			
2/5 cup	100	7.8	21.4		1.5	tr	.11	0.7			340	140	2.40		
cnd	90		0.4				tr	.04			300	29			
2/5 cup	100	5.7	16.4		0.9		.05	0.6			264	109	1.80		
cnd, baked, B & M	330		7.0								776				
7/8 cup	224	15.0	50.0												

[a] Kcal range from 7/100 g for freshly harvested to 75/100 g after long storage

	KCAL / WT (g)	H₂O (g) / PRO (g)	FAT (g) / CHO (g)	PUFA (g) / SFA (g)	CHOL (mg) / FIBR (g)	A (RE) / A (IU)	C (mg) / B-1 (mg)	B-2 (mg) / NIA (mg)	B-6 (mg) / B-12 (mcg)	FOL (mcg) / PANT (mg)	Na (mg) / K (mg)	Ca (mg) / P (mg)	Mg (mg) / Fe (mg)	Zn (mg) / Cu (mg)	Mn (mg)
cnd, new orleans style,	200		1.0								900				
Stokeley van Camp—1 cup	255	14.0	39.0		2.9						690				
kohlrabi, ckd	24	92.2	0.1				43	.03			6	33			
⅔ cup	100	1.7	5.3		1.0	20	.06	0.2			260	41	.30		
lambsquarters (pigweed), ckd	32	88.9	0.7				37	.26				258			
½ cup	100	3.2	5.0		1.8	9700	.10	0.9				45	.70		
leeks, raw	52	85.4	0.3				17	.06			5	52	23		
3-4 med	100	2.2	11.2		1.3	40	.11	0.5			347	50	1.10		
lentils, ckd	106	72.0	tr				0	.06				25			
⅔ cup	100	7.8	19.3		1.2	20	.07	0.6			249	119	2.10		
lettuce, raw															
butterhead	14	95.1	0.2				8	.06			9	35	11		
3½ oz	100	1.2	2.5		0.5	970	.06	0.3			264	26	2.00		
iceberg (crisphead)	13	95.5	0.1				6	.06			9	20	11		
3½ oz	100	0.9	2.9		0.5	330	.06	0.3			175	22	.50		
romaine (cos)	18	94.0	0.3				18	.08			9	68	11		
3½ oz	100	1.3	3.5		0.7	1900	.05	0.4			264	25	1.40		
lima beans, green															
ckd	111	71.1	0.5				17	.10			1	47			
⅝ cup	100	7.6	19.8		1.8	280	.18	1.3			422	121	2.50		
cnd	66	82.1	0.2				11	.05	.09	38	317	27	34	.65	
³⁄₅ cup	100	4.0	12.3		1.3	158	.03	0.5		.13	334	73	2.10	.19	
frzn, baby	128	61.6	0.5	0.2	0		18	.07	.15	90	125	33	46	.551	.345
½ cup	95	7.0	24.5	0.1	2.0	219	.09	1.1	.00	.08	470	97	1.87	.093	
frzn bb, baby, in butter sce, Green	114		2.8				13	.04			467	29			
Giant—½ cup	100	5.6	16.7		1.8	285	.05	0.6			322	95	1.20		
frzn, fordhook	106	71.9	0.3	0.2	0		20	.07	.15	87	75	25	38	.48	
³⁄₅ cup	100	6.4	20.0	0.1	1.9	228	.09	1.1	.00	.19	478	72	1.43	.06	
lima beans, mature, boiled	159	73.7	0.7					.07			2	33			
⅝ cup	115	9.4	29.4		2.0		.15	0.8			709	177	3.60		
lotus root, raw	69		0.1				75	.01				30			
⅔ segment	100	2.8	15.7			0	.14	0.3				103	.60		
mixed veg															
cnd; peas, carrots, lima beans, green	22	90.6	0.4				4	.06			279	26	18	.51	
beans—³⁄₅ cup	100	1.7	6.3		1.2	5810	.03	0.5			135	40	.74	.10	
frzn; corn, peas, carrots & green	59		0.4				7	.03			41	28			
beans—⅔ cup	100	2.6	11.1		1.0	3400	.10	0.9			150	51	.70		
frzn; corn, peas, carrots, green beans &	60	82.6	0.3				9	.04			39	27			
lima beans—⅔ cup	100	2.6	11.3		1.2	3120	.05	0.7			176	54	.70		
frzn, Birds Eye	63	77.6	0.4	0.2	0		10	.07	.12	48	39	25	21	.406	
½ cup	95	2.9	13.5	tr	1.1	5016	.09	1.1	.00	.20	197	53	.90	.062	
frzn bb, in butter sce, Green Giant	65		2.2				10	.04			352	20			
½ cup	100	2.3	9.0		0.9	3870	.06	0.5			137	44	.70		
frzn, w/onion sce, Birds Eye	107	54.4	5.3	1.0	1		6	.11	.09	30	332	33	13	.169	
⅓ cup	76	2.5	12.6	1.0	0.6	3675	.07	0.6	.10	.16	209	41	.25	.021	
mung bean sprouts, raw	35	88.8	0.2				19	.13			5	19			
3½ oz	100	3.8	6.6		0.7	20	.13	0.8			223	64	1.30		
mung bean sprouts, boiled	28	91.0	0.2				6	.10			4	17			
3½ oz	100	3.2	5.2		0.7	20	.09	0.7			156	48	.90		
mung bean sprouts, cnd	23		0.1								161				
1 cup	82	3.4	2.3												
mushrooms															
raw	28	90.4	0.5				3	.46			15	6	13		
10 small	100	2.7	4.4		0.8	tr	.10	4.2			414	116	.80		
cnd	17	93.1	0.2				0	.22			400	7	7		
⅓ cup	90	1.1	2.3		0.6		.02	1.8			197	81	.71		
fried/sauteed	78		7.4				tr	.27				8			
4 med	70	1.7	2.8		0.7		.05	2.9				81	.70		

	KCAL	H₂O (g)	FAT (g)	PUFA (g)	CHOL (mg)	A (RE)	C (mg)	B-2 (mg)	B-6 (mg)	FOL (mcg)	Na (mg)	Ca (mg)	Mg (mg)	Zn (mg)	Mn (mg)
	WT (g)	PRO (g)	CHO (g)	SFA (g)	FIBR (g)	A (IU)	B-1 (mg)	NIA (mg)	B-12 (mcg)	PANT (mg)	K (mg)	P (mg)	Fe (mg)	Cu (mg)	
frzn	23		0.2				2	.21			467	6			
3½ oz	100	1.8	3.0		0.6	15	.02	1.3			195	61	.50		
frzn, in butter sce, Green Giant	29		2.0				2	.11			118	3			
2 oz	56	0.8	1.7		0.3	100	.03	1.1			141	41	.22		
mustard greens															
raw	31	89.5	0.5				97	.22			32	183	27		
3½ oz	100	3.0	5.6		1.1	7000	.11	0.8			377	50	3.00		
ckd	23	92.6	0.4				48	.14			18	138			
½ cup	100	2.2	4.0		0.9	5800	.08	.06			220	32	1.80		
frzn, chopped	21	93.1	0.3		0		28	.06	.13		29	116	15	.23	.339
½ cup	100	2.6	3.4		0.8	5108	.05	0.3	.00	.02	170	30	1.30	.07	
mustard spinach, raw	22	92.2	0.3				130					210			
3½ oz	100	2.2	3.9		1.0	9900						28	1.50		
mustard spinach, ckd	16	94.5	0.2				65					158			
3½ oz	100	1.7	2.8		0.8	8200						18	.80		
new zealand spinach, raw	19	92.6	0.3				30	.17			159	58	40		
3½ oz	100	2.2	3.1		0.7	4300	.04	0.6			795	46	2.60		
new zealand spinach, ckd	13	94.8	0.2					.10			92	48			
3½ oz	100	1.7	2.1		0.6	3600	.03	0.5			463	28	1.50		
okra, ckd	29	91.1	0.3				20	.18			2	92			
8-9 pods	100	2.0	6.0		1.0	490	.13	0.9			174	41	.50		
okra, frzn, cut	26	87.0	0.2		0		9	.10	.04	25	2	72	39	.447	
½ cup	95	1.5	5.7		0.8	459	.07	0.6	.00	.12	178	30	.52	.070	
okra, frzn, whole	31	85.6	0.2		0		14	.10	.05	30	2	82	43	.551	
⅔ cup	95	1.7	6.8		0.8	420	.10	0.7	.00	.29	224	37	.56	.087	
okra gumbo, frzn bb, Green Giant	90		7.0				16	.05			356	43			
⅖ cup	100	0.9	5.6		0.6	345	.04	0.4			150	20	.60		
onions															
raw	38	89.1	0.1				10	.04			10	27	12		
1 med	100	1.5	8.7		0.6	40[a]	.03	0.2			157	36	.50		
raw, chopped	4	8.9	tr				1	tr			1	3	1		
1 T	10	0.2	0.9		0.1	4[a]	tr	tr			16	4	.10		
ckd	29	91.8	0.1				7	.03			7	24			
½ cup	100	1.2	6.5		0.6	40[a]	.03	0.2			110	29	.40		
cnd	29		0.0				7	.03			240	24			
3½ oz	100	1.2	5.9			40[a]	.03	0.2			110		.40		
dehydrated, instant flakes	15	0.2	0.1				1	.01			4	7	4		
1 T	4	0.3	3.3		0.2	8	.01	0.1			55	11	.12		
frzn	40	101.9	0.1	tr	0		9	.03	.10	25	11	40	12	.124	
½ cup	113	1.0	9.5	tr	0.8	18	.03	0.2	.00		160	26	.51	.112	
frzn, chopped	8	25.7	tr	tr	0		1	.01	.02	5	2	5	2	.02	
¼ cup	28	0.2	2.0	tr	0.1	4	.01	tr	.00	.03	35	6	.09	.006	
frzn bb, in cheese sce, Green Giant	52		2.8				5	.00			326	41			
⅖ cup	100	1.6	5.4		0.6	93	.02	0.2			161	60	.30		
frzn, w/cream sce, Birds Eye	105	64.9	6.1	1.1	1		7	.09	.06	10	332	52	9	.09	
½ cup	85	1.6	11.4	1.2	0.4	143	.03	0.2	.13	.12	169	32	.11	.015	
parsley, raw	44	85.1	0.6				172	.26			45	203	41		
3½ oz	100	3.6	8.5		1.5	8500	.12	1.2			727	63	6.20		
parsley, raw, chopped	4	8.5	tr				17	.02			4	20	4		
1 T	10	0.4	0.8		tr	850	.01	0.1			73	6	.60		
parsnips, diced, ckd	66	82.2	0.5				10	.08			8	45			
½ cup	100	1.5	14.9		2.0	30	.07	0.1			379	62	.60		
pea beans, baked, cnd	330		8.0								848				
⅞ cup	224	16.0	49.0												
peas															
raw	84	78.0	0.4				27	.14			2	26	35		
¾ cup	100	6.3	14.4		2.0	640	.35	2.9			316	116	1.90		
ckd	71	81.5	0.4				20	.11			1	23			
⅔ cup	100	5.4	12.1		2.0	540	.28	2.3			196	99	1.80		

[a] For yellow varieties; white varieties contain only a trace of Vit A.

	KCAL	H₂O (g)	FAT (g)	PUFA (g)	CHOL (mg)	A (RE)	C (mg)	B-2 (mg)	B-6 (mg)	FOL (mcg)	Na (mg)	Ca (mg)	Mg (mg)	Zn (mg)	Mn (mg)
	WT (g)	PRO (g)	CHO (g)	SFA (g)	FIBR (g)	A (IU)	B-1 (mg)	NIA (mg)	B-12 (mcg)	PANT (mg)	K (mg)	P (mg)	Fe (mg)	Cu (mg)	
cnd	47	87.3	0.3				11	.08	.05	29	291	17	14	.66	
³/₅ cup	100	2.9	8.6		1.4	407	.11	0.9		.15	112	55	1.03	.12	
frzn	81	79.0	0.5	0.2	0		20	.10	.14	87	98	24	25	.81	.310
³/₅ cup	100	5.4	14.3	0.1	2.0	696	.30	2.2	.00	.34	149	88	1.57	.11	
frzn, tiny	62	78.8	0.4	0.2	0		19	.09	.12		128	17	18	.551	
½ cup	95	4.5	10.8	0.1	1.9	818	.22	1.5	.00	.03	137	65	1.21	.080	
frzn, creamed w/bread crumbs, Green Giant—*²/₅ cup*	112		5.3				8	.09				91			
	100	4.4	11.9		0.8	349	.11	0.9					.60		
frzn bb, in butter sce, Green Giant	79		2.9				15	.09			425	24			
½ cup	100	3.9	9.2		1.9	706	.16	1.1			108	64	.90		
frzn, w/cream sce, Birds Eye	136	48.8	6.9	1.3	1		12	.18	.12	55	443	41	16	.36	
½ cup	76	4.5	14.2	1.4	1.1	669	.17	1.2	.14	.23	197	66	.54	.05	
peas & carrots, cnd	45	88.0	0.3				7	.06	.05		289	22	15	.58	
³/₅ cup	100	2.2	8.4		1.2	8572	.06	0.7		.20	120	46	.74	.10	
peas & carrots, frzn	59	84.3	0.3	0.1	0		13	.08	.11	62	82	26	18	.51	.234
³/₅ cup	100	3.4	11.4	0.1	1.6	10249	.19	1.4	.00	.20	192	59	1.09	.09	
peas & cauliflower w/cream sce, frzn, Birds Eye—*½ cup*	118	70.2	5.2	1.0	1		19	.13	.15	48	379	41	17	.397	
	95	4.4	13.7	1.0	1.4	597	.19	1.2	.08	.25	210	64	.66	.045	
peas & mushrooms, frzn	73	75.6	0.4	0.2	0		20	.11	.13	81	215	13	19	.55	
½ cup	95	5.0	13.1	0.1	2.0	744	.25	2.1	.00	.11	176	70	.93	.098	
peas & onions, frzn	71	75.6	0.2	0.1	0		19	.08	.13	73	312	15	18	.485	
½ cup	95	4.6	13.5	tr	1.7	636	.24	1.8	.00	.17	172	59	.85	.083	
peas & onions w/cheese sce, frzn, Birds Eye—*½ cup*	165	108.4	8.4	1.4	3		15	.15	.13	67	522	90	27	.75	
	142	5.5	17.7	1.9	1.5	2250	.22	1.5	.13	.43	215	122	1.20	.10	
peas & potatoes w/cream sce, frzn, Birds Eye—*½ cup*	140	47.6	7.4	1.3	1		13	.13	.10	41	485	43	14	.26	
	76	3.8	15.4	1.5	1.0	531	.15	1.0	.16	.19	236	62	.39	.017	
peas, carrots & onions, frzn, Birds Eye	54	76.8	0.3	0.1	0		12	.07	.09	56	60	26	17	.511	
⅔ cup	91	3.1	10.1	tr	1.4	6359	.17	1.3	.00	.22	158	56	1.03	.082	
peas, carrots, pasta & onions in parmesan sce, frzn, Birds Eye—*½ cup*	122	69.6	5.8	1.0	2		8	.08	.06	38	446	72	18	.53	
	95	4.0	14.1	1.3	1.0	5870	.14	1.1	.02	.02	151	87	.90	.069	
peas, onions & carrots in butter sce, frzn bb, Green Giant—*²/₅ cup*	71		2.8				13	.09			458	27			
	100	3.4	8.1		1.0	1100	.14	0.6			119	63	.90		
peas, pods & water chestnuts in sce, frzn bb, Green Giant—*²/₅ cup*	75		2.8				14	.09			350	30			
	100	3.4	9.5		1.2	672	.14	0.6			117	67	1.20		
peas, shells & corn w/crm sce, frzn, Birds Eye—*½ cup*	132	65.2	4.4	0.8	1		13	.12	.10	53	279	45	23	.61	
	95	4.7	19.4	0.8	1.0	525	.20	1.6	.08	.30	167	88	1.07	.07	
peas, shells & mushrooms w/crm sce, frzn, Birds Eye—*½ cup*	129	66.9	5.4	1.0	tr		14	.13	.11	68	459	36	22	.64	
	95	4.9	15.9	1.0	1.4	688	.24	1.9	.05	.43	161	87	1.26	.14	
peas, mature, split, ckd	104		0.3					.09			12	10			
½ cup	90	7.3	18.8		0.4	36	.22	0.9			268	81	1.50		
peas, mature, whole, ckd	102		0.4					.09			10	19	54		
½ cup	90	7.2	18.0		1.5	36	.22	0.9			301	102	1.50		
pepper, bell															
raw	22	93.4	0.2				128	.08			13	9	18		
1 large	100	1.2	4.8		1.4	420	.08	0.5			213	22	.70		
baked	17		0.1				64	.05				7			
1 med	65	0.8	3.9		1.0	481	.03	0.3				16	.30		
boiled	18	94.7	0.2				96	.07			9	9			
1 large	100	1.0	3.8		1.4	420	.06	0.5			149	16	.50		
pimentos, cnd	27	92.4	0.5				95	.06				7			
3 med	100	0.9	5.8		0.6	2300	.02	0.4				17	1.50		
poi, two finger	67		0.1				5	.01				11			
²/₅ cup	100	0.6	16.0				.04	0.3				22	.40		
potato, white															
raw	76	79.8	0.1				20	.04			3	7	34		
1 med	100	2.1	17.1		0.5	tr	.10	1.5			407	53	.60		
baked	95	75.1	0.1				20	.04			4	9			
1 med	100	2.6	21.1		0.6	tr	.10	1.7			503	65	.70		
baked	139	106.5	0.2				30	.06			6	14			
1 large	150	3.9	31.7		0.9	tr	.15	2.6			755	98	1.00		

	KCAL	H_2O (g)	FAT (g)	PUFA (g)	CHOL (mg)	A (RE)	C (mg)	B-2 (mg)	B-6 (mg)	FOL (mcg)	Na (mg)	Ca (mg)	Mg (mg)	Zn (mg)	Mn (mg)
	WT (g)	PRO (g)	CHO (g)	SFA (g)	FIBR (g)	A (IU)	B-1 (mg)	NIA (mg)	B-12 (mcg)	PANT (mg)	K (mg)	P (mg)	Fe (mg)	Cu (mg)	
boiled w/skin	76	79.8	0.1				16	.04				3	7			
1 med	100	2.1	17.1		0.5	tr	.09	1.5			407	53	.60		
boiled w/o skin	65	82.8	0.1				16	.03				2	6			
1 med	100	1.9	14.5		0.5	tr	.09	1.2			285	42	.50		
cnd, whole	40	88.3	0.1				14	.02	.10			366	25	14	.39	
³/₅ cup	100	1.4	8.7		0.2	0	.03	0.7			271	22	1.10	.07	
frzn, whole	67	82.4	0.1				19	.03				6	8	13	.30	.222
³/₅ cup	100	2.1	14.9		0.4	30	.07	1.2			355	32	.90	.09	
frzn, whole, peeled	57	75.6	tr	tr	0		5	.02	.15	13	65	18	12	.27	
3-4 potatoes	91	1.9	12.8	tr	0.4	tr	.05	1.0	.00	.23	323	29	.34	.085	
au gratin, frzn, Green Giant	150		8.8				4	.09					144			
²/₅ cup	100	4.8	12.9		0.2	110	.03	0.6					.60		
au gratin, frzn, Stouffer's	135		8.0									480				
3¾ oz	106	3.0	13.0								285				
au gratin, from mix, French's	153		4.4				2	.11				522	144			
1 serving	116	3.4	24.7			150	tr	0.8			287		.17		
creamed, from mix, General Mills	160		7.0									395				
½ cup	ᵃ	4.0	21.0												
fried	228	39.9	12.1					.16	.06			190	13			
½ cup	85	3.4	27.8		0.8	tr	.10	2.4			658	86	.90		
fries, homemade	137	22.3	6.6				10	.04				3	8			
10 pieces	50	2.1	18.0		0.5	tr	.06	1.6			427	56	.60		
fries, reg cut, frzn	142	68.6	5.0	1.8	0		11	.02	.13	15	30	5	17	.30	.242
³/₅ cup	100	2.4	23.2	0.7	0.5	tr	.07	1.1	.00	.38	364	64	.61	.11	
fries, cottage, frzn	116	54.7	4.7	1.8	0		3	.02	.11	16	14	2	12	.23	
²/₃ cup	79	2.0	17.1	0.7	0.4	tr	.05	1.1	.00	.34	310	36	.45	.11	
fries, crinkle cuts, frzn	117	60.0	4.0	1.4	0		8	.02	.11	16	23	9	17	.18	.10
²/₃ cup	85	1.9	18.4	0.6	0.7	tr	.08	1.1	.00	.34	309	75	.44	.06	
fries, shoestring, frzn	138	55.8	5.5	2.0	0		7	.02	.11	16	26	9	23	.26	.14
¾ cup	85	2.1	20.1	0.8	0.6	tr	.07	1.6	.00	.34	384	83	.50	.07	
fries, steak	121	58.2	3.6	1.3	0		11	.02	.11	15	20	8	19	.23	.13
¾ cup	85	2.1	20.0	0.5	0.4	tr	.08	1.3	.00	.32	304	60	.58	.05	
fries, tasti, frzn, Birds Eye	136	44.4	6.9	2.6	0		5	.02	.09	7	268	2	13	.234	
¾ cup	71	2.1	16.5	1.0	0.4	tr	.06	1.1	.00		307	54	.31	.023	
hash browns, homemade	229	54.2	11.7				9	.05				288	12			
½ cup	100	3.1	29.1		0.8	tr	.08	2.1			475	79	.90		
hash browns, frzn, Birds Eye	72	94.1	0.1	tr	0		4	.01	.09	17	54	3	12	.215	
¾ cup	113	1.8	16.4	tr	0.3	tr	.07	0.9	.00	.32	199	66	.35	.100	
hash browns, frzn, Lamb Weston	69	67.0	0.1				9	.01			14	10	17	.15	.09
3 oz	85	1.6	15.5		0.3		.06	1.2			269	43	.42	.04	
hash browns w/onions, from mix, General Mills—*½ cup*	150		6.0									460				
	ᵃ	2.0	23.0												
hickory smoked cheese, from mix, General Mills—*½ cup*	150		6.0									590				
	ᵃ	3.0	21.0												
julienne w/cheese sce, from mix, General Mills—*½ cup*	130		6.0									570				
	ᵃ	3.0	17.0												
mashed, from flakes/granules	83	84.8	2.3				3	.05				245	32			
½ cup	105	2.1	13.6			85	.03	0.8			352	46	.65		
mashed w/milk & margarine	94	79.8	4.3				9	.05				331	24			
½ cup	100	2.1	12.3		0.4	170	.08	1.0			250	48	.40		
puffs, frzn, Birds Eye	192	35.9	11.6	3.9	32		7	.05	.14	15	401	7	13	.21	
½ cup	71	2.5	19.4	1.9	0.4	tr	.06	1.1	.10	.32	324	45	.47	.044	
puffs, frzn, Lamb Weston	153	54.0	7.1				6	.03			260	12	18	.22	.10
3 oz	85	2.1	20.1		0.5		.08	1.6			347	70	.78	.034	
roundabouts (fried circles), frzn, Lamb Weston—*3 oz*	179	50.2	9.6				4	.02			333	14	16	.23	.09
	85	2.1	21.1		0.6		.08	1.4			343	77	.95	.04	
scalloped, homemade	255	187.9	9.6				27	.22				870	132			
1 cup	245	7.4	36.0		0.7	390	.15	2.5			801	181	1.00		
scalloped, from mix, French's	123		3.8				2	.11				406	93			
1 serving	127	2.6	20.0				.05	0.8			132		.24		
scalloped, frzn, Stouffer's	126		7.0									450				
4 oz	113	3.0	14.0								250				

ᵃ Gram wt not available

	KCAL · WT (g)	H₂O (g) · PRO (g)	FAT (g) · CHO (g)	PUFA (g) · SFA (g)	CHOL (mg) · FIBR (g)	A (RE) · A (IU)	C (mg) · B-1 (mg)	B-2 (mg) · NIA (mg)	B-6 (mg) · B-12 (mcg)	FOL (mcg) · PANT (mg)	Na (mg) · K (mg)	Ca (mg) · P (mg)	Mg (mg) · Fe (mg)	Zn (mg) · Cu (mg)	Mn (mg)
scalloped w/cheese, homemade	355	174.2	19.4				25	.29			1095	311			
1 cup	245	13.0	33.3		0.7	780	.15	2.2			750	299	1.20		
scalloped w/cheese, from mix, French's—1 serving	124		6.3				1	.14			423				
	127	3.7	24.8				.04	1.1			236		.30		
shoestring in butter sce, frzn bb, Green Giant—2/5 cup	129		6.8				6	.02			255	9			
	100	1.7	15.7		0.3	94	.08	0.5			160	34	.60		
slices in butter sce, frzn bb, Green Giant—2/5 cup	80		3.3				6	.01			395	11			
	100	1.2	11.6		0.2	68	.03	0.5			81	36	0.6		
sour cream & chives, from mix, French's—1 serving	132		6.9				1	.11			657	1			
	127	2.9	23.6			199	.04	1.0			246		.30		
sour cream & chives, frzn, Green Giant—5 oz	230		10.4				8	.08			546	42			
	140	4.3	29.5		0.6	111	.03	1.8			662	104	1.54		
tiny taters, frzn, Birds Eye	203	53.8	12.0	4.5	0.5		4	.02	.18	15	282	10	13	.208	
2/3 cup	91	2.0	22.1	1.8	0.5	tr	.04	1.0	.00	.28	250	34	.49	.041	
triangles, frzn, Birds Eye	143	59.8	10.2	3.8	0		4	.02	.12	10	334	15	9	.216	
2 patties	85	1.7	11.8	1.5	0.3	tr	.05	0.9	.00	.18	289	27	.63	.067	
vermicelli w/mushrooms & cheese sce, frzn, Green Giant—2/5 cup	144		6.8				4	.08				200			
	100	5.4	15.3		0.2	76	.04	0.6					.70		
wedges, farm style, frzn, Birds Eye	107	61.6	3.4	1.3	0		4	.02	.11	15	25	6	12	.187	
3 oz	85	1.6	17.8	0.5	0.4	tr	.05	0.7	.00	.32	237	47	.41	.039	
wedges, fried, frzn, Lamb Weston	163	57.8	8.7				7	.02			284	14	17	.24	.10
2 wedges	91	1.8	19.2		0.8		.07	1.3			365	76	.74	.05	
wedges w/skin, fried, frzn, Lamb Weston—3 oz	119	57.9	3.3				8	.04			16	11	23	.25	.14
	85	2.6	19.9		0.6		.09	1.5			405	69	.77	.06	
w/cheese topping, frzn, Green Giant	234		10.9				8	.11			693	45			
5 oz	140	4.3	29.5		0.6	53	.03	1.7			717	105	1.40		
w/sour cream sce, frzn, Green Giant	112		4.7				6	.07			575	33			
2/5 cup	100	2.3	15.5		0.2	94	.04	0.9			84	65	.60		
potato pancake, from mix, French's	127	45.8	5.0				3	.08			490	132			
3 pancakes	77	2.9	17.2					0.8			197		.60		
potato salad, german, cnd, General Mills—3½ oz	107		3.0								585				
	100	2.0	18.0				.05	0.7			205		.60		
potato salad w/ckd dressing, homemade—1 cup	248	190.0	7.0				28	.18			1320	80			
	250	6.8	40.8			350	.20	2.8			798	160	1.50		
potato salad w/mayo dressing, homemade—1 cup	363	181.0	23.0				28	.15			1200	48			
	250	7.5	33.5			450	.18	2.3			740	158	2.00		
potatoes & peas in bacon cream sce, frzn bb, Green Giant—2/5 cup	94		3.3				7	.05			375	37			
	100	2.6	13.4		0.3	140	.07	0.9			66	62	.70		
pumpkin, cnd	33	90.4	0.3				5	.06	.06		5	18	25	.17	
2/5 cup	100	0.9	7.9		1.4	33990	.02	0.4		.40	219	36	.74	.11	
purslane, raw	21	92.5	0.4				25	.10				103			
3½ oz	100	1.7	3.8		0.9	2500	.03	0.5				39	3.50		
purslane, ckd	15	94.7	0.3				12	.06				86			
3½ oz	100	1.2	2.8		0.8	2100	.02	0.4				24	1.20		
radish, red, raw	17	94.5	0.1				26	.03			18	30	15		
10 small	100	1.0	3.6		0.7	10	.03	0.3			322	31	1.00		
radish, oriental, raw	19	94.1	0.1				32	.02				35			
3½ oz	100	0.9	4.2		0.7	10	.03	0.4			180	26	.60		
rhubarb, frzn, raw	29	128.1	0.2		0	15	7	.04	.03	11	2	266	25	.14	.133
1 cup	137	0.8	7.0			147	.04	0.3	.00	.09	148	17	.39	.032	
rhubarb, frzn, ckd, sweetened	139	81.4	0.1			8	4	.03	.02	6	2	174	15	.10	.088
½ cup	120	0.5	37.4		1.0	83	.02	0.2	.00	.06	115	10	.25	.032	
rice, brown, ckd	178	105.5	0.9	0.1			0	.03				18	45		
4/5 cup	150	3.8	38.2		0.4		.14	2.1			105	110	.80		
rice, white															
all varieties, enr, ckd	164	108.9	0.2	0.2			0	.10			561[a]	15	12		
4/5 cup	150	3.0	36.3		0.2	0	.16	1.5			42	42	1.40		
all varieties, unenr, ckd	164	108.9	0.2	0.1			0	.01			561[a]	15	12		
4/5 cup	150	3.0	36.3		0.2	0	.03	0.6			42	42	.30		
long grain & wild rice, from inst, Minute Rice—½ cup	147	81.9	4.1	0.2	10	2		.02	.02	3	567	14	9	.292	
	115	2.8	24.7	2.4	0.1		.15	1.6	.01	.13	40	25	1.08	.046	

[a] Salt added according to package instructions; if cooked w/o added salt, value is negligible.

	KCAL / WT (g)	H_2O (g) / PRO (g)	FAT (g) / CHO (g)	PUFA (g) / SFA (g)	CHOL (mg) / FIBR (g)	A (RE) / A (IU)	C (mg) / B-1 (mg)	B-2 (mg) / NIA (mg)	B-6 (mg) / B-12 (mcg)	FOL (mcg) / PANT (mg)	Na (mg) / K (mg)	Ca (mg) / P (mg)	Mg (mg) / Fe (mg)	Zn (mg) / Cu (mg)	Mn (mg)
long grain, inst, enr, ckd	124	91.4	0.1	tr	0		0	.01	.01	1	268[a]	6	7	.368	
2/3 cup	122	2.4	27.3	tr	0.1	0	.15	1.2	.00	.09	tr	33	1.08	.044	
long grain, parboiled, enr, ckd	159	110.1	0.2	0.1			0				538[a]	29			
4/5 cup	150	3.2	35.0		0.2	0	.16	1.8			65	85	1.20		
beef flavored, from inst, Minute Rice	152	82.6	4.1	0.2	10		tr	.02	.01	2	723	9	9	.364	
1/2 cup	117	3.0	25.2	2.4	0.1	146	.30	1.6	.01	.08	25	37	1.09	.042	
chicken flavored, from inst, Minute Rice	153	72.7	4.2	0.3	10		tr	.01	.01	2	688	9	9	.386	
—1/2 cup	107	3.1	25.1	2.5	0.1	149	.23	1.6	.01	.07	20	39	1.09	.039	
chinese, fried, from inst, Minute Rice	159	62.0	4.8	1.8	0		tr	.01	.02	2	636	10	8	.368	
1/2 cup	97	3.2	25.3	0.7	0.1	1	.23	1.6	.00	.08	47	36	1.08	.045	
chinese, fried, La Choy	207		1.9								1225				
1/2 cup	114		42.8												
chinese, fried, frzn, Birds Eye	106	76.2	0.3	0.1	tr		10	.04	.12	12	424	15	10	.30	
1/2 cup	104	2.7	23.1	tr	0.4	88	.07	0.6	.00	.23	109	43	.61	.03	
french style, frzn, Birds Eye	118	73.6	0.4	tr	0		2	.02	.04	10	635	12	9	.41	
1/2 cup	104	3.2	25.0	tr	0.3	52	.05	0.6	.00	.07	36	45	1.03	.12	
italian style, frzn, Birds Eye	132	70.5	0.8	0.1	0		8	.02	.05	5	383	14	9	.38	
1/2 cup	104	3.4	28.3	0.1	0.4	348	.07	0.8	.00	.12	55	45	1.11	.11	
northern italian style, frzn, Birds Eye	111	75.6	1.0	tr	3		16	.04	.14	27	498	97	13	.49	
1/2 cup	104	3.9	21.3	0.6	0.3	268	.03	0.4	.00	.28	79	99	.37	.038	
oriental style, frzn, Birds Eye	125	71.9	0.5	tr	0		6	.02	.06	8	459	13	12	.35	
1/2 cup	104	3.2	27.0	tr	0.3	624	.07	0.7	.00	.12	65	39	.75	.078	
spanish, cnd, Heinz	150	169.5	4.1				2	.05			1091	35			
7¼ oz	206	2.7	26.0		1.6	707	.06				227		1.65		
spanish, cnd, Stokely van Camp	170		3.0								1480				
1 cup	250	3.0	32.0		0.6						280				
spanish, homemade	213	192.3	4.2				37	.07			774	34			
1 cup	245	4.4	40.7		1.2	1620	.10	1.7			566	96	1.50		
spanish, from inst, Minute Rice	150	113.1	4.1	0.2	10		13	.04	.08	1	841	16	15	.423	
1/2 cup	148	2.6	25.6	2.4	0.5	976	.15	1.2	.01	.24	186	43	1.08	.182	
spanish style, frzn, Birds Eye	124	72.7	0.5	0.1	0		27	.02	.07	16	493	9	8	.36	
1/2 cup	104	3.3	26.0	tr	0.5	442	.09	0.9	.00	.10	61	41	.77	.09	
rice & broccoli in cheese sce, frzn bb,	95		2.9				20	.02				48			
Green Giant—2/5 cup	100	2.8	14.5		0.2	1240	.02	0.6					.30		
rice & peas w/mushrooms, frzn, Birds	108	38.0	0.2	0.1	0		10	.14	.07	29	320	8	8	.34	
Eye—2/3 cup	66	3.5	23.0	tr	0.7	424	.16	1.8	.00	.04	68	39	.84	.04	
rice w/bean sprouts, pea pods & water	83		1.8				8	.03			425	8			
chestnuts, frzn, Green Giant—2/5 cup	100	2.2	14.5		0.2	94	.21	1.0			56	39	1.50		
rice w/bell peppers & parsley, frzn bb,	108		2.5				2	.05			480	8			
Green Giant—2/5 cup	100	1.8	20.5		0.6	68	.19	1.6			24	16	1.30		
rice w/green beans & almonds, frzn bb,	88		3.0				2	.03			432	20			
Green Giant—2/5 cup	100	1.7	13.7		0.2	162	.20	1.8			60	60	1.20		
rice w/mushrooms & onions, frzn bb,	90		1.0				2	.03			533	9			
Green Giant—2/5 cup	100	1.9	18.4		0.3	38	.18	1.6			44	26	1.60		
rice w/peas, celery, mushrooms &	119		4.4				2	.04			394	9			
almonds, frzn bb, Green Giant—2/5 cup	100	2.9	17.1		0.2	136	.27	2.0			11	53	2.00		
rice w/sweet peas & mushrooms, frzn bb,	86		1.9				2	.02			385	10			
Green Giant—2/5 cup	100	2.0	15.2		0.4	143	.24	1.9			34	28	1.50		
rice w/wild rice, from mix, Minute Rice	150		4.0								570				
1/2 cup		3.0	25.0		0.1						40				
rice w/wild rice, frzn bb, Green Giant	91		0.8				4	.05			461	12			
2/5 cup	100	2.2	18.8		0.5	77	.22	1.8			32	31	1.60		
rutabaga, diced, ckd	35	90.2	0.1				26	.06			4	59			
1/2 cup	100	0.9	8.2		1.1	550	.06	0.8			167	31	.30		
salsify, raw	16-94[b]	77.6	0.6				11	.04				47			
1 cup	100	2.9	18.0		1.0	10	.04	0.3			380	66	1.50		
sauerkraut, bottled, Claussen	15	69.8	0.2				8		.08		505	25	8	.10	
1/2 cup	75	0.8	2.8					0.1			112	12	.41		
sauerkraut, cnd	21	92.0	0.2				16	.02	.13		666	31	17	.19	
2/3 cup	100	0.9	4.6		1.1	25	.02	0.3		.09	197	19	1.60	.10	
scallions, raw	45	87.6	0.2				25	.04			5	40			
5 med	100	1.1	10.5		1.0	tr	.05	0.4			231	39	.60		

[a] Salt added according to package instructions; if cooked w/o salt, value is negligible.

[b] Caloric value ranges from 16 for freshly harvested to 94 for stored salsify. Much of the cho in freshly harvested salsify may be inulin (which is of doubtful availability). During storage inulin may be converted to sugars.

	KCAL / WT (g)	H_2O (g) / PRO (g)	FAT (g) / CHO (g)	PUFA (g) / SFA (g)	CHOL (mg) / FIBR (g)	Vitamins: A (RE) / A (IU)	C (mg) / B-1 (mg)	B-2 (mg) / NIA (mg)	B-6 (mg) / B-12 (mcg)	FOL (mcg) / PANT (mg)	Minerals: Na (mg) / K (mg)	Ca (mg) / P (mg)	Mg (mg) / Fe (mg)	Zn (mg) / Cu (mg)	Mn (mg)
shallot bulbs, raw	36	34.6	0.1				4	.01			6	18			
1¾ oz	50	1.2	8.4		0.4	tr	.03	0.1			167	30	.60		
shellie beans, cnd	70		0.0								845				
1 cup	245	4.0	15.0		1.5						270				
snow peas, chinese, frzn	90		0.3												
6 oz	168	5.8	20.4												
soybean curd (tofu)	72	84.8	4.2				0	.03			7	128	111		
3½ oz	100	7.8	2.4		0.1	0	.06	0.1			42	126	1.90		
soybean sprouts, raw	46	86.3	1.4				13	.20				48			
1 cup	100	6.2	5.3		0.8	80	.23	0.8				67	1.00		
soybean sprouts, ckd	38	89.0	1.4				4	.15				43			
¾ cup	100	5.3	3.7		0.8	80	.16	0.7				50	.70		
soybeans															
immature, ckd	118	73.8	5.1				17	.13				60			
⅔ cup	100	9.8	10.1		1.4	660	.31	1.2				191	2.50		
immature, cnd	103	76.7	5.0				2				236	67			
⅔ cup	100	9.0	7.4		1.4	340	.06					114	2.80		
mature, ckd	130	71.0	5.7				0	.09			2	73			
½ cup	100	11.0	10.8		1.6	30	.21	5.6			540	179	2.70		
fermented, miso	171	53.0	4.6				0	.10			2950	68			
3½ oz	100	10.5	23.5		2.3	40	.06	0.3			334	309	1.70		
fermented, natto	167	62.7	7.4				0	.50				103			
3½ oz	100	16.9	11.5		3.2	0	.07	1.1			249	182	3.70		
spinach															
raw	26	90.7	0.3				51	.20			71	93	88		
3½ oz	100	3.2	4.3		0.6	8100	.10	0.6			470	51	3.10		
ckd	21	82.8	0.5				25	.13			45	83			
½ cup	90	2.7	3.2		0.3	7300	.06	0.5			291	33	2.00		
cnd, leaf	19	92.8	0.4				13	.12	.07	58	356	122	46	.55	
½ cup	100	2.2	2.9		0.7	7235	.02	0.3		.07	317	34	1.39	.15	
frzn, chopped & leaf	23	91.8	0.3		0		25	.15	.14	153	77	107	55	.32	
½ cup	100	3.0	3.8		1.0	8120	.08	.43	.00	.09	332	39	2.11	.08	
frzn, creamed, Birds Eye	59	72.9	3.3	0.6	1		13	.11	.11	tr	277	56	22	.17	
⅓ cup	85	2.6	4.9	0.6	0.8	5527	.06	0.2	.07	.07	311	32	.57	.03	
frzn bb, creamed, Green Giant	74		3.2				14	.11			400	106			
⅖ cup	100	3.0	8.3		0.3	1685	.05	0.2			328	78	.90		
frzn bb, in butter sce, Green Giant	44		2.7				25	.12			360	90			
½ cup	100	2.5	2.5		0.6	3260	.05	0.2			319	38	1.30		
spinach & water chestnuts, frzn, Birds	29	85.1	0.3		0		18	.14	.08	25	257	87	39	.223	
Eye—*½ cup*	95	2.6	5.5		0.8	6582	.08	0.4	.00	.06	309	38	1.75	.065	
squash															
acorn,[a] baked	86	161.7	0.2				20	.20			2	61			
½ med	195	3.0	21.8		3.5	2180	.08	1.1			749	45	1.70		
acorn,[a] boiled, mashed	83	219.8	0.2				20	.25			2	69			
1 cup	245	2.9	20.6		3.4	2700	.10	1.0			659	49	2.00		
butternut,[a] baked, mashed	139	163.2	0.2				16	.27			2	82			
1 cup	205	3.7	35.9		3.7	13120	.10	1.4			1248	148	2.10		
butternut,[a] boiled, mashed	100	215.1	0.2				12	.25			2	71			
1 cup	245	2.7	25.5		3.4	13230	.10	1.0			835	120	1.70		
chayote,[b] raw	28		0.1				19	.03			5	13			
½ med	100	0.6	7.1		0.7	20	.03	0.4			102	26	.50		
hubbard,[a] baked, mashed	103	174.5	0.8				21	.27			2	49			
1 cup	205	3.7	24.0		3.7	9840	.10	1.4			556	80	1.60		
hubbard,[a] boiled, mashed	74	223.2	0.7				15	.25			2	42			
1 cup	245	2.7	16.9		3.4	10050	.10	1.0			372	64	1.20		
zucchini,[b] cnd	28	90.6	0.1				2	.04			374	17	14	.26	
⅔ cup	100	1.0	6.9		0.5	520	.04	0.5			274	29	.68	.10	
zucchini,[b] frzn	16	90.0	0.1	tr	0		4	.04	.05		2	17	13	.13	
½ cup	95	1.1	3.3	tr	0.5	459	.05	0.4	.00	.28	207	26	.50	.04	

[a] Winter varieties

[b] Summer varieties

	KCAL	H₂O (g)	FAT (g)	PUFA (g)	CHOL (mg)	A (RE)	C (mg)	B-2 (mg)	B-6 (mg)	FOL (mcg)	Na (mg)	Ca (mg)	Mg (mg)	Zn (mg)	Mn (mg)
	WT (g)	PRO (g)	CHO (g)	SFA (g)	FIBR (g)	A (IU)	B-1 (mg)	NIA (mg)	B-12 (mcg)	PANT (mg)	K (mg)	P (mg)	Fe (mg)	Cu (mg)	
squash, summer															
raw	19	94.0	0.1	0.1			22	.09			1	28	16		
½ cup	100	1.1	4.2		0.6	410	.05	1.0			202	29	.40		
boiled	14	95.5	0.1				10	.08			1	25			
½ cup	100	0.9	3.1		0.6	390	.05	0.8			141	25	.40		
frzn	20	93.7	0.1	tr	0		7	.04	.06	9	2	17	12	.16	.290
⅔ cup	100	1.5	4.3	tr	0.6	185	.05	0.4	.00	.11	193	26	.46	.05	
frzn bb, in cheese sce, Green Giant	43		1.4				12	.05				30			
⅓ cup	100	2.3	5.4			408	.04	0.6					.40		
squash, winter															
baked	63	81.4	0.4				13	.13			1	28			
½ cup	100	1.8	15.4		1.8	4200	.05	0.7			461	48	.80		
boiled, mashed	38	88.8	0.3				8	.10			1	20			
⅖ cup	100	1.1	9.2		1.4	3500	.04	0.4			258	32	.50		
frzn	39	88.5	0.2		0		11	.07	.11		2	21	14	.17	.152
⅖ cup	100	1.0	9.8		1.2	4334	.04	0.4	.80	.22	212	22	.59	.05	
succotash															
cnd	62		0.6				6	.07			230	11	19		
3½ oz	100	2.6	14.1			134	.03	0.5			176	55	.51		
cnd, cream style	74		0.5				6	.06			245	11	21		
3½ oz	100	2.6	17.6			141	.03	0.6			183	59	.55		
frzn	94	73.8	0.8	0.2	0		10	.07	.10	63	74	16	24	.47	.294
½ cup	100	4.4	20.2	0.1	1.0	229	.08	1.3	.00	.26	292	76	.84	.06	
sweet potato															
baked	141	63.7	0.5				22	.07			12	40			
1 small	100	2.1	32.5		0.9	8100	.09	0.7			300	58	.90		
baked	254	114.7	0.9				40	.13			22	72			
1 large	180	3.8	58.5		1.6	14600	.16	1.3			540	104	1.60		
boiled	172	127.1	1.3				26	.09			15	48			
1 large	180	2.6	39.8		0.6	11940	.14	0.9			367	71	1.10		
candied, homemade	168	60.0	3.3				10	.04			42	37			
3½ oz	100	1.3	34.3		0.6	6300	.06	0.4			190	43	.90		
cnd, solid pack	108	71.9	0.2			7800		.04			48	25			
⅖ cup	100	2.0	24.9		1.0	14	.05	0.6			200	41	.80		
cnd, syrup pack	114	70.7	0.2				8	.03			48	13			
1 small	100	1.0	27.5		0.6	3000	.03	0.6			120	29	.70		
frzn bb, glazed, Green Giant	128		2.9				26	.02				25			
⅖ cup	100	1.4	24.2			10770	.04	0.6					.50		
tampala leaves, raw	37		0.2				51					6			
3½ oz	100	2.1	8.4		0.9	12300	.16					229	3.40		
taro, hawaiian, corms, diced, raw	98	73.0	0.2				4	.04			7	28			
¾ cup	100	1.9	23.7		0.8	820	.13	1.1			514	61	1.00		
taro, hawaiian, leaves, raw	40	87.2	0.8				31					76			
8 leaves	100	3.0	7.4		1.4							59	1.00		
tomato, green, raw	24	93.0	0.2				20	.04			3	13			
1 small	100	1.2	5.1		0.5	270	.06	0.5			244	27	.50		
tomato, red															
raw	22	93.5	0.2				23				3	13	14		
1 small	100	1.1			0.5	900	.06	0.7			244	27	.50		
raw	33	140.3	0.3				34	.06			4	20	21		
1 med	150	1.6	7.0		0.8	1350	.09	1.0			366	40	.80		
raw	44	187.0	0.4				46	.08			6	26	28		
1 large	200	2.2	9.4		1.0	1800	.12	1.4			488	54	1.00		
boiled	26	92.4	0.2				24	.05			4	15			
½ cup	100	1.3	5.5		0.6	1000	.07	0.8			287	32	.60		
bottled, kosher, Claussen	5	25.8	tr				1		.02		336	3	2		
1 piece	28	0.3	1.1				.01	tr			39	4	.08		

	KCAL	H₂O (g)	FAT (g)	PUFA (g)	CHOL (mg)	A (RE)	C (mg)	B-2 (mg)	B-6 (mg)	FOL (mcg)	Na (mg)	Ca (mg)	Mg (mg)	Zn (mg)	Mn (mg)
	WT (g)	PRO (g)	CHO (g)	SFA (g)	FIBR (g)	A (IU)	B-1 (mg)	NIA (mg)	B-12 (mcg)	PANT (mg)	K (mg)	P (mg)	Fe (mg)	Cu (mg)	
cnd, stewed	27		0.1				13	.03			249	32	12		
3½ oz	100	0.8	6.4		0.4	459	.04	0.5			209	20	.11		
cnd, whole, peeled	19	93.8	0.2				18	.03	.09		157	27	11	.17	
2/5 cup	100	0.9	4.3		0.6	609	.05	0.7		.23	289	20	.48	.14	
tomato paste, cnd	215	196.5	1.0				128	.31			100	71			
1 cup	262	8.9	48.7			8650	.52	8.1			2237	183	9.20		
tomato puree, cnd	321	715.1	1.6				271	.41			3280	107			
29-oz can	822	14.0	73.2			13150	.74	11.5			3502	279	14.00		
tomato sce, cnd	31	89.1	0.3				18	.05			531	11	18	.25	
2/5 cup	100	1.3	7.3		0.7	1066	.08	1.1			389	34	.86	.20	
turnip, diced, ckd	23	93.6	0.2				22	.05			34	35			
2/3 cup	100	0.8	4.9		0.9	tr	.04	0.3			188	24	.40		
turnip greens															
raw	28	90.3	0.3				139	.39				246	58		
3½ oz	100	3.0	5.0		0.8	7600	.21	0.8				58	1.80		
ckd	20	93.2	0.2				69	.24				184			
2/3 cup	100	2.2	3.6		0.7	6300	.15	0.6				37	1.10		
cnd, chopped	35	220.2	1.0								650				
1 cup	235	3.0	6.0		1.4						330				
frzn, chopped	21	93.1	0.3	0			27	.08	.14	60	12	124	27	.17	.369
3/5 cup	100	2.5	3.6	0.8		6246	.04	0.4	.00	.05	184	27	1.51	.06	
frzn, w/turnips	19	88.8	0.3	0			21	.07	.11	47	15	98	24	.13	
½ cup	94	2.1	3.3	0.7		4625	.04	1.1	.00	.04	175	25	1.27	.051	
veg flakes, French's	12		0.0								20				
1 T		0.0	3.0												
veg combinations															
bavarian style beans & spaetzle, frzn,	108	70.5	6.3	1.1	12		4	.06	.05	28	420	41	15	.258	
Birds Eye—½ cup	95	2.4	11.5	1.2	0.5	627	.04	0.3	.09	.09	80	35	.75	.046	
cantonese style, stir-fry, frzn, Birds	53	79.5	0.2		0		44	.05	.10	46	475	16	11	.257	
Eye—½ cup	95	2.2	11.5		0.6	415	.06	0.6	.00	.20	136	45	.33	.042	
chinese, cnd, La Choy	35		0.2								144				
1 cup	265	5.9	2.3												
chinese, frzn, La Choy	72		0.9								1552				
10 oz	180	5.7	10.5												
chinese style, frzn, Birds Eye	79	78.5	4.7	0.8	tr		19	.05	.07	8	361	32	23	.241	
½ cup	95	2.3	8.4	0.8	0.3	1439	.05	0.4	.01	.09	140	33	.76	.043	
chinese style, frzn bb, Green Giant	48		1.6				14	.05				28			
2/5 cup	100	1.4	7.0			360	.03	0.3					.40		
chinese style, stir-fry, frzn, Birds Eye	31	84.3	0.2	tr	0		18	.07	.08	10	503	64	24	.127	
½ cup	95	1.9	7.0	tr	0.9	1777	.05	0.5	.00	.13	148	37	.92	.040	
chop suey, cnd, La Choy	53		0.2								1339				
1 cup	265	2.5	10.0												
danish style w/sce, frzn, Birds Eye	45		0.0								320				
3⅓ oz	94	2.0	9.0		0.8						165				
del sol frzn, Stokely van Camp	25		0.0								34				
3⅕ oz	91	2.0	5.0		0.8						200				
far eastern style, frzn, Birds Eye	80	78.2	4.7	0.8	tr		48	.07	.11	59	388	26	12	.195	
½ cup	95	2.4	8.4	0.8	0.8	1756	.05	0.4	tr	.16	185	38	.55	.031	
grande, frzn, Stokely van Camp	50		0.0								18				
3⅕ oz	91	2.0	11.0		0.4						190				
hawaiian, frzn bb, Green Giant	72		2.2				7	.03				32			
⅓ cup	100	0.8	12.2			2780	.03	0.3					.30		
hawaiian style w/sce, frzn, Birds Eye	50		0.0								265				
3⅓ oz	94	1.0	12.0		0.5						115				
italian style, frzn, Birds Eye	130	69.3	7.0	1.3	0		22	.06	.09	11	576	42	20	.383	
½ cup	95	2.9	14.0	1.2	0.8	913	.04	0.4	.01	.02	145	53	1.13	.124	
japanese, frzn, Stokely van Camp	25		0.0								34				
3⅕ oz	91	2.0	5.0		1.0						210				
japanese style, frzn, Birds Eye	98	75.0	5.8	1.1	tr		34	.07	.08	46	507	32	16	.235	
½ cup	95	2.1	10.5	1.1	0.7	853	.04	0.3	.01	.11	133	38	.57	.047	

	KCAL	H₂O (g)	FAT (g)	PUFA (g)	CHOL (mg)	A (RE)	C (mg)	B-2 (mg)	B-6 (mg)	FOL (mcg)	Na (mg)	Ca (mg)	Mg (mg)	Zn (mg)	Mn (mg)
WT (g)	WT (g)	PRO (g)	CHO (g)	SFA (g)	FIBR (g)	A (IU)	B-1 (mg)	NIA (mg)	B-12 (mcg)	PANT (mg)	K (mg)	P (mg)	Fe (mg)	Cu (mg)	
japanese style, frzn bb, Green Giant	46		0.8				26	.07				32			
⅓ cup	100	1.9	7.9			472	.03	0.3					.50		
japanese style, stir-fry, frzn, Birds Eye—*½ cup*	29	85.3	0.2	tr	0		26	.08	.09	34	537	24	11	.23	
	95	1.7	6.0	tr	0.7	720	.03	0.6	.00	.11	116	34	.78	.077	
la cariba, frzn, Stokely van Camp	20		0.0								33				
3⅕ oz	91	2.0	4.0		0.9						190				
mexicana style, frzn, Birds Eye	125	67.7	6.1	1.2	0		25	.06	.13	41	464	13	19	.39	
½ cup	95	3.4	16.1	1.1	1.0	417	.10	1.0	tr	.18	175	58	.97	.075	
milano, frzn, Stokely van Camp	45		0.0								32				
3⅕ oz	91	3.0	9.0		1.0						215				
new england style, frzn, Birds Eye	128	68.6	7.2	1.7	tr		22	.07	.09	52	464	32	17	.298	
½ cup	95	2.9	14.8	1.3	0.7	712	.07	0.7	.01	.15	161	46	.64	.044	
new orleans creole style, frzn, Birds Eye—*3⅓ oz*	70		0.0								360				
	94	3.0	14.0		0.3						270				
orient, frzn, Stokely van Camp	30		0.0								30				
3⅕ oz	91	2.0	6.0		0.9						150				
parisian, frzn, Stokely van Camp	30		0.0								24				
3⅕ oz	91	1.0	6.0		1.0						200				
pennsylvania dutch style, frzn, Birds Eye—*3⅓ oz*	45		1.0								355				
	94	2.0	7.0		0.5						160				
romano, frzn, Stokely van Camp	40		0.0								70				
3⅕ oz	91	2.0	9.0		1.0						170				
san francisco style, frzn, Birds Eye	99	74.2	5.5	1.0	tr		14	.09	.04	19	413	29	12	.103	
½ cup	95	2.7	11.2	1.0	0.7	374	.07	0.6	.01	.19	192	40	.80	.070	
wisconsin country style, frzn, Birds Eye—*3⅓ oz*	45		1.0								280				
	94	3.0	7.0		0.9						195				
veg marrow, ckd	16		0.1				11	.07				15			
½ cup	100	0.6	3.9		0.5	260	.04	0.6				15	.40		
veg, stew, frzn, Birds Eye	97	162.5	0.2	tr	0		24	.07	.01	22	48	38	25	.48	
6⅗ oz	189	3.0	22.0	tr	1.3	1196	.10	1.6	.00	.01	525	56	1.42	.15	
veg, stew, frzn, Stokely van Camp	60		1.0								50				
4 oz	113	2.0	12.0		0.7						290				
water chestnuts, cnd	80	78.3	0.2				4	.20			20	4	12		
16 med	100	1.4	19.0		0.8	0	.14	1.0			500	65	.60		
watercress, raw	2	9.3	tr				8	.01			5	15	2		
10 sprigs	10	0.2	0.3		0.1	490	.02	0.1			28	5	.20		
watercress, raw	19	93.3	0.3				79	.16			52	151	20		
3½ oz	100	2.2	3.0		0.7	4900	.08	0.9			282	54	1.70		
wax (yellow) beans, cut															
ckd	22	93.4	0.2				13	.09				50			
½ cup	100	1.4	4.6		1.0	230	.07	0.5			151	37	.60		
cnd	15	95.0	0.2				5	.05	.04		317	20	14	.15	
⅔ cup	100	0.7	3.1		0.7	33	.02	0.2			100	14	1.20	.07	
frzn	29	91.3	0.1	tr	0		12	.09	.08	35	2	41	27	.24	.225
⅔ cup	100	1.9	6.3	tr	1.7	135	.08	0.4	.00	.23	268	35	1.15	.06	
winged (goa) beans, ckd	10					0	.04					26			
1 cup	46	0.8	2.2			152	.10	0.3				17	.20		
yam,ᵃ ckd	210		0.4				18	.08				8			
1 cup	200	4.8	48.2		1.8	tr	.18	1.2				100	1.20		
yambean, raw	55	85.1	0.2				20	.03				15			
3½ oz	100	1.4	12.8		0.7	tr	.04	0.3				18	.60		
yautia (melanga/tanier), raw	136		0.4				11	.15				4			
1 corm	100	2.1	31.5		0.8	tr	.10	0.6				50	.60		
yellow eye beans, baked, cnd	330		7.0								968				
⅞ cup	224	15.0	50.0												

ᵃ The values for yam are for the true yam of tropical areas (*Dioscorea* species), rather than for the American "yam," which is really a sweet potato.

						Vitamins					Minerals			
KCAL	H₂O (g)	FAT (g)	PUFA (g)	CHOL (mg)	A (RE)	C (mg)	B-2 (mg)	B-6 (mg)	FOL (mcg)	Na (mg)	Ca (mg)	Mg (mg)	Zn (mg)	Mn (mg)
WT (g)	PRO (g)	CHO (g)	SFA (g)	FIBR (g)	A (IU)	B-1 (mg)	NIA (mg)	B-12 (mcg)	PANT (mg)	K (mg)	P (mg)	Fe (mg)	Cu (mg)	

MISCELLANEOUS

amaranth (red dye)														
4	8.7	0.1				8	.02				27			
2 t														
10	0.4	0.7		0.1	610	.01	0.1			41	7	.40		
baking powder														
home use, phosphate														
3	0.2	tr	tr	0		0	.00	.00	0	429	247	tr	.002	
1 t														
4	tr	0.6	tr	tr	0	.00	0.0	.00	.00	1	88	.84	tr	
home use, tartrate														
2	tr	tr				0	.00			219	0			
1 t														
3	tr	0.6			0	.00	0.0			114	0	.00		
commercial, pyrophosphate														
3	tr	tr				0	.00			486	27			
1 t														
3	tr	0.8			0	.00	0.0				367			
commercial, low Na														
5	tr	tr				0	.00			tr	145			
1 t														
3	tr	1.2			0	.00	0.0			328	219			
baking soda														
0		0.0								821				
1 t														
3	0.0	0.0												
chewing gum														
hubba bubba, original/fruit														
23		tr		0	0	0	.00	.00	0	tr	30	0	.00	
1 stick														
8	0.0	5.8			0	.00	0.0	.00	0	tr	0	.00	.00	
hubba bubba, strawberry/grape/														
raspberry—*1 stick*														
23		tr		0	0	0	.00	.00	0	tr	tr	0	.00	
8	0.0	5.8			0	.00	0.0	.00	0	tr	0	.00	.00	
orbit, sugar free, peppermint/														
spearmint—*1 stick*														
8[a]		0.0		0	0	0	.00	.00	0	tr	3	0	.00	
3	0.0	0.0			0	.00	0.0	.00	0	tr	0	.00	.00	
wrigley's[b]														
10		tr		0	0	0	.00	.00	0	tr	3	0	.00	
1 stick														
3	0.0	2.3			0	.00	0.0	.00	0	tr	0	.00	.00	
choc, baking, Baker's														
139	0.4	14.6	0.4	tr		0	.07	.01	3	1	23	85		
1 oz														
28	3.1	8.4	8.7	0.7	17	.01	0.4	.00	.05	242	112	2.00	.779	
choc, baking, Hershey														
185	0.6	15.8	1.0	0			.13			1	20	84	1.12	.56
1 oz														
28	4.0	6.7	10.0	0.7	6	.02	0.3			224	123	2.04	.56	
cocoa, dry														
115		3.6	0.0	0			.15			6	41	154	2.13	1.06
⅓ cup														
28	7.6	12.8	3.0	1.5	22	.02	0.6			476	221	4.54	1.01	
gelatin, dry														
23	0.9	tr				4	.00			8	0			
envelope														
7	6.0	0.0				.00	0.0			180	0	.40		
icing, decorator for cakes & cookies, all														
70		2.0								5				
colors—*1 t*														
c	0.0	12.0												
meat tenderizer														
2		tr					tr	tr		1695	11	2	.00	
1 t														
5	tr	tr			5		tr	tr		2		.14	.03	
meat tenderizer, seasoned														
6		0.1					tr	tr		1325	9	2	.03	
1 t														
5	0.3	1.0			7		tr	tr		22	6	.56	.02	
olives														
black														
37	14.6	4.0					tr			150	21			
2 large														
20	0.2	0.6		0.3	14	tr				5	3	.30		
greek														
67	8.8	7.1								658				
3 med														
20	0.4	1.7		0.8							6			
green														
15	10.2	1.6								312	8			
2 med														
13	0.2	0.2		0.2	40					7	2	.20		
oven fry,[d] General Foods														
77	1.7	0.5	0.3	0		tr	.02	.02	6	1001	14	13	.151	
¼ pkt														
23	1.7	16.1	0.1	0.2	257	.02	0.3	.00	.05	28	32	.31	.036	
pectin, Certo														
2	13.2	0.0	0.0	0		0	.00	.00	0	tr	0	0	.00	
1 T														
14	0.0	0.4	0.0	0.0	0	.00	0.0	.00	.00	33	0	tr	.00	
pectin, Sure-Jell														
37	1.0	0.0	0.0	0		0	.00	.00	0	3	tr	tr	tr	
¼ pkt														
12	0.0	10.3	0.0	0.0	0	.00	0.0	.00	.00	tr	tr	tr	tr	
pickle relish, sour														
3	14.0	0.1									4			
1 T														
15	0.1	0.4		0.2							3	.20		
pickle relish, sweet														
21	9.5	0.1								107	3			
1 T														
15	0.1	5.1		0.1							2	.10		
pickle relish, chow chow, sour														
8	24.5	0.4								375	9			
1 oz														
28	0.4	1.2		0.2							15	.70		

[a] Kcal are from 1.9 g polyols.
[b] Spearmint/doublemint/juicy fruit/big red/freedent
[c] Gram wt not available
[d] Coating mix for meat & poultry

	KCAL / WT (g)	H₂O (g) / PRO (g)	FAT (g) / CHO (g)	PUFA (g) / SFA (g)	CHOL (mg) / FIBR (g)	A (RE) / A (IU)	C (mg) / B-1 (mg)	B-2 (mg) / NIA (mg)	B-6 (mg) / B-12 (mcg)	FOL (mcg) / PANT (mg)	Na (mg) / K (mg)	Ca (mg) / P (mg)	Mg (mg) / Fe (mg)	Zn (mg) / Cu (mg)	Mn (mg)
pickle relish, chow chow, sweet	32	19.3	0.3								148	6			
1 oz	28	0.4	7.6		0.3							6	.40		
pickles															
bread & butter	18	21.4	0.1				2	.07			168	8			
4 slices	25	0.2	4.5		0.1	35	tr	tr			28	7	.40		
dill	11	93.3	0.2				6	.02			1428	26	12		
1 large	100	0.7	2.2		0.5	100	tr	0.1			200	21	1.00		
kosher	7	51.7	0.1				2	.01	.02		581	7	4	.04	
1 pickle	55	0.4	1.2				.01	0.1			51	7			
sour	10	99.5	0.2				7	.02			1353	17			
1 large	105	0.5	2.0		0.5	100	tr	tr				15	3.20		
sweet	146	60.7	0.4				6	.02			572	12	1		
1 large	100	0.7	36.5		0.5	90	.00					16	1.20		
sweet & sour, sliced	3	4.1	tr				tr	tr	tr		25	7	1	.05	
1 slice	5	tr	0.8				tr	tr			4	4	.01	tr	
rennin tablets	11	0.9	0.1				0	.00			2230	351			
0.35 oz	10	tr	2.4		0.0	0	.00	0.0				20			
shake & bake,[a] General Foods	69	0.8	2.6	tr	tr		tr	.11	.12	27	595	11	8	.209	
¼ pkt	17	1.5	10.5	1.4	0.2	371	.10	1.3	.36	.03	34	27	.43	.046	
soybean protein	32	0.8	tr				0				21	12			
0.35 oz	10	7.5	1.5		tr						18	67			
soybean proteinate	31	0.6	tr				0				120				
0.35 oz	10	8.1	0.8		tr										
tapioca, dry, inst	32	1.1	tr	0		0	.00	.00		0	tr	1	tr		
1 T	9	0.1	7.8	tr		0	.00	0.0	.00	.00	2	2	.04	.005	
vinegar															
cider	2	14.1	0.0								tr	1			
1 T	15	0.0	0.8		0.0	0					15	2	.10		
cider	14	112.6	0.0								1	8			
½ cup	120	0.0	6.0		0.0	0					120	12	.60		
distilled	2	14.3	0.0								tr	tr			
1 T	15	0.0	0.8		0.0						2				
whey															
acid, dry	10	0.1	tr	tr		tr	tr	.06	.02	1	28	59	6	.18	
1 T	3	0.3	2.1	tr	0.0	2	.02	tr	.07	.16	66	39	.04		
acid, fluid	59	229.8	0.2	tr		2	tr	.34	.10	5	118	253	24	1.06	
1 cup	246	1.9	12.6	0.1	0.0	17	.10	1.2	.44	.94	352	191	.20		
sweet, dry	26	0.2	0.1	tr	tr	1	tr	.17	.04	1	80	59	13	.15	
1 T	8	1.0	5.6	0.1	0.0	3	.04	0.1	.18	.42	155	70	.07		
sweet, fluid	66	229.1	0.9	tr	5	10	tr	.39	.08	2	132	115	20	.32	
1 cup	246	2.1	12.6	0.6	0.0	39	.09	0.2	.68	.94	396	112	.15		
yeast															
baker's, compressed, fortified	10	8.5	tr					.20			2	2	7		
1 cake	12	1.5	1.3				1.66	17.3			73	47	.60		
baker's, compressed, unfortified	10	8.5	tr					.20			2	2	7		
1 cake	12	1.5	1.3				.09	1.3			73	47	.60		
baker's, dry (active)	23	0.4	0.1					.43			4	4	5		
1 T	8	3.0	3.1				.19	2.9			160	103	1.30		
brewer's, debittered	28	0.5	0.1					.43			12	21	23		
1 T	10	3.9	3.8		.02		1.52	3.8			189	175	1.70		
torula	28	0.6	0.1					.51			2	42	17		
1 T	10	3.9	3.7		0.3		1.40	4.4			205	171	1.90		

[a] Coating mix for meat & poultry

Supplementary Tables

_____

_____

_____

_____

_____

_____

_____

_____

_____

Amino Acids[a] (mg)

	try	thr	iso	leu	lys	met	cys	phe	tyr	val	arg	his
CANDY & CANDY BARS												
milk choc—*1 oz (28 g)*	3	7	10	19	10	2		13		11		
CEREALS, COOKED												
barley, pearled, dry—*1 oz (28 g)*		81	112	202	87	81	34	160	62	154		64
buckwheat groats, dry—*1 oz (928 g)*	73	115	109	185	176	70	53	143	62	146		81
corn grits, reg/quick, enr, ckd—*1 cup (242 g)*	19	121	136	520	68	82	77	177	148	177	114	94
cream of rice, ckd—*¾ cup (183 g)*	24	81	27	134	68	48	27	68	90	104	132	48
cream of wheat, reg, ckd—*¾ cup (188 g)*	39	90	126	216	73	53	64	154	90	137	124	66
cream of wheat, quick, ckd—*¾ cup (179 g)*	38	86	120	206	70	50	61	147	86	132	118	63
cream of wheat, inst, ckd—*¾ cup (181 g)*	45	105	145	252	85	62	74	179	105	161	143	76
cream of wheat, mix n eat, prep—*1 pkg (142 g)*	38	86	120	208	72	51	62	149	88	135	122	62
cream of wheat, mix n eat, flavored, prep[b]—*1 pkg (150 g)*	34	78	106	186	64	46	55	132	78	118	109	57
farina, enr, ckd—*¾ cup (175 g)*	35	77	110	191	58	46	56	137	79	121	102	56
oats, reg/quick/inst, ckd—*¾ cup (175 g)*	61	158	207	345	184	75	112	247	161	264	338	102
CEREALS, READY-TO-EAT												
alpha bits—*1 oz (28 g)*	26	76	97	200	79	39	53	117	81	124	143	51
bran, 100%—*1 oz (28 g)*	55	115	113	210	137	50	69	136	101	166	248	97
bran flakes, 40%, Post—*1 oz (28 g)*	56	103	120	214	107	50	65	147	96	156	190	82
cap'n crunch—*1 oz (28 g)*	12	51	61	184	39	31	34	76	59	78	67	37
cap'n crunch's crunchberries—*1 oz (28 g)*	13	52	63	183	42	32	33	77	60	79	67	38
cap'n crunch's peanut butter—*1 oz (28 g)*	20	68	85	210	65	35	39	108	86	105	164	54
cheerios—*1 oz (28 g)*	58	149	196	327	175	71	107	233	153	251	320	97
cocoa pebbles—*1 oz (28 g)*	18	65	69	108	56	38	22	58	73	86	106	39
corn flakes, Post Toasties—*1 oz (28 g)*	14	80	89	343	45	54	51	117	97	117	75	62
crispy wheats n raisins—*1 oz (28 g)*	33	58	75	129	53	31	38	92	55	90	90	43
c.w. post—*1 oz (28 g)*	37	95	120	199	103	48	60	135	98	151	187	62
c.w. post w/raisins—*1 oz (28 g)*	34	89	112	185	96	45	56	125	91	140	173	57
fortified oat flakes—*1 oz (28 g)*	92	252	295	490	344	99	131	278	200	318	342	130
fruity pebbles—*1 oz (28 g)*	17	57	60	95	48	34	20	48	64	74	93	34
golden grahams—*1 oz (28 g)*	18	56	67	193	46	35	33	82	64	84	63	42
granola, homemade—*1 oz (28 g)*	42	127	153	249	151	60	71	168	110	189	311	87
granola, Nature Valley[c]—*1 oz (28 g)*	39	101	134	222	118	49	72	158	103	170	218	66
grape-nuts—*1 oz (28 g)*	60	106	136	235	101	56	66	168	102	166	169	80
grape-nuts flakes—*1 oz (28 g)*	55	97	124	215	93	51	60	154	93	152	155	73
honeycomb—*1 oz (28 g)*	14	57	67	207	43	35	38	85	66	87	75	42
honey-nut cheerios—*1 oz (28 g)*	79	114	136	367	145	54	75	160	108	177	240	76
king vitaman—*1 oz (28 g)*	12	52	62	191	39	33	34	77	61	79	67	38
kix—*1 oz (28 g)*	20	88	103	325	65	55	58	131	102	134	112	65
life, plain/cinn—*1 oz (28 g)*	75	210	277	446	297	96	107	284	206	313	368	133
lucky charms—*1 oz (28 g)*	35	90	119	198	105	43	64	141	92	151	193	58
puffed rice—*½ oz (14 g)*	13	45	48	75	38	27	15	38	50	58	74	27
puffed wheat—*½ oz (14 g)*	32	64	89	151	58	36	41	108	63	100	101	54
quaker 100% natural—*1 oz (28 g)*	46	123	167	273	160	62	63	174	125	197	227	82
quaker 100% natural w/apples & cinn—*1 oz (28 g)*	42	111	150	244	149	58	57	154	113	177	182	72
quaker 100% natural w/raisins & dates—*1 oz (28 g)*	40	106	143	234	138	53	53	149	106	169	192	71
quisp—*1 oz (28 g)*	12	50	60	179	38	31	33	75	57	76	66	36

[a] Amino acids for Infant Formula and Special Dietary Formulas, Commercial and Hospital are located in the main table.

[b] Apple w/cinn, banana & spice or maple & brown sugar
[c] Cinn & raisin, coconut & honey, fruit & nut, or toasted oat

167

	try	thr	iso	leu	lys	met	cys	phe	tyr	val	arg	his
raisin bran, Post—*1 oz (28 g)*	39	74	86	153	77	37	46	105	68	112	133	58
shredded wheat—*1 oz (28 g)*	60	104	123	215	96	54	60	150	91	154	162	72
shredded wheat—*1 biscuit (24 g)*	49	86	101	177	79	45	49	124	75	127	133	60
sugar sparkled flakes—*1 oz (28 g)*	9	52	58	223	29	35	33	76	63	76	48	40
super sugar crisp—*1 oz (28 g)*	28	56	78	133	50	32	36	95	56	88	89	47
team—*1 oz (28 g)*	26	77	87	156	69	44	36	87	84	109	127	50
total—*1 oz (28 g)*	54	94	111	195	87	49	54	136	83	139	147	66
trix—*1 oz (28 g)*	11	55	63	214	37	35	36	82	65	82	65	41
wheat germ, toasted—*1 oz (28 g)*	95	340	295	544	520	156	168	336	256	410	676	235
wheat germ, toasted w/brown sugar & honey	71	255	221	408	390	117	126	252	192	308	507	176
wheaties—*1 oz (28 g)*	51	90	106	186	83	47	51	130	79	133	140	62

CHEESE & CHEESE PRODUCTS
Natural Cheese

	try	thr	iso	leu	lys	met	cys	phe	tyr	val	arg	his
blue—*1 oz (28 g)*	89	223	319	545	526	166	30	309	368	442	202	215
brick—*1 oz (28 g)*	92	250	322	636	602	160	37	349	316	417	248	233
brie—*1 oz (28 g)*	91	213	288	547	525	168	32	328	340	380	208	203
camembert—*1 oz (28 g)*	87	203	275	522	501	160	31	313	325	362	199	194
cheddar—*1 oz (28 g)*	91	251	438	676	588	185	35	372	341	471	267	248
cheddar, grated—*1 cup (113 g)*	362	1001	1746	2695	2342	737	141	1482	1358	1879	1063	988
cheshire—*1 oz (28 g)*	85	236	411	635	551	173	33	349	320	442	250	233
colby—*1 oz (28 g)*	87	240	418	645	561	176	34	355	325	450	254	236
cottage cheese, creamed—*4 oz (113 g)*	157	626	830	1451	1141	425	131	761	752	874	644	469
cottage cheese, creamed—*1 cup (210 g)*	292	1163	1542	2697	2121	789	243	1414	1398	1624	1196	872
cottage cheese, creamed w/fruit—*1 cup (226 g)*	249	992	1315	2301	1810	673	207	1206	1192	1385	1021	743
cottage cheese, dry curd—*1 cup (145 g)*	279	1111	1472	2575	2025	754	232	1350	1334	1550	1142	832
cottage cheese, low fat, 1% fat—*1 cup (226 g)*	312	1242	1646	2879	2265	843	259	1510	1492	1734	1277	930
cottage cheese, low fat, 2% fat—*1 cup (226 g)*	346	1377	1825	3193	2511	934	287	1674	1655	1923	1416	1032
cream cheese—*1 oz (28 g)*	19	91	113	207	192	51	19	119	102	125	81	77
edam—*1 oz (28 g)*		264	371	728	754	204		406	413	513	273	293
gjetost—*1 oz (28 g)*	38	111	147	281	231	90	16	153	154	217	93	83
gouda—*1 oz (28 g)*		264	370	727	752	204		406	412	512	273	293
gruyère—*1 oz (28 g)*	119	309	457	880	768	233	86	494	503	636	276	317
liederkranz—*1 oz (28 g)*	64	170	308	451	336	120		248		331		
limburger—*1 oz (28 g)*	82	209	346	593	475	176		316	339	408	198	164
monterey—*1 oz (28 g)*	89	247	431	665	578	182	35	365	335	463	262	244
mozzarella—*1 oz (28 g)*		210	264	537	559	154	33	287	318	344	236	207
mozzarella, low moisture—*1 oz (28 g)*		233	294	597	622	171	36	320	354	383	263	230
mozzarella, part skim—*1 oz (28 g)*		262	330	671	699	192	41	359	398	430	295	259
mozzarella, part skim, low moisture—*1 oz (28 g)*		184	232	471	491	135	29	252	280	302	208	182
muenster—*1 oz (28 g)*	93	252	325	641	606	161	37	352	318	420	250	235
mysost[a]—*1 oz (28 g)*	85	85	92	131	97	24		41		81		
neufchatel—*1 oz (28 g)*	25	120	149	274	253	68	25	157	135	166	107	101
parmesan, grated—*1 T (5 g)*	28	77	110	201	192	56	14	112	116	143	77	80
parmesan, hard—*1 oz (28 g)*	137	373	537	979	937	272	67	545	566	696	373	392
port du salut—*1 oz (28 g)*	97	248	410	704	563	208		375	403	484	235	194
provolone—*1 oz (28 g)*		278	309	651	750	194	33	365	431	465	290	316
ricotta, part skim—*½ cup (124 g)*		649	739	1532	1678	352	124	697	739	868	793	576
ricotta, whole milk—*½ cup (124 g)*		641	731	1514	1659	348	123	689	731	858	783	569
swiss—*1 oz (28 g)*	114	294	436	839	733	222	82	471	480	606	263	302
tilsit, whole milk—*1 oz (28 g)*	100	255	421	722	578	214		385	413	497	241	200

Cheese Products

	try	thr	iso	leu	lys	met	cys	phe	tyr	val	arg	his
cheese sce, homemade—*2 T (38 g)*	42	110	194	289	217	76		156		213		
cheese sce, homemade—*¼ cup (76 g)*	82	220	388	578	434	152		312		426		
cheese spread, american—*1 oz (28 g)*		178	236	505	427	152		264		387		

[a] Scandinavian cheese made from whey

	try	thr	iso	leu	lys	met	cys	phe	tyr	val	arg	his
CHIPS & SNACKS												
popcorn—*1 cup (14 g)*	11	72	83	234	52	34		81		92		
potato chips—*10 pieces (20 g)*	11	45	48	55	58	13		48		58		
potato chips—*2 oz (56 g)*	30	121	130	148	157	36		130		157		
COMBINATION FOODS												
beef pie, frzn, Swanson—*8-oz pie (227 g)*		588	876	1296	1104	288		744		876	744	360
beef pie, frzn, Swanson Hungry-Man—*16-oz pie (454 g)*		1050	1470	2160	1950	480		1200		1470	1470	840
beef veg stew, cnd, Swanson—*7⅝ oz (216 g)*	36	504	648	936	972	264		480		684	720	252
beef veg stew, homemade—*1 cup (245 g)*	196	637	1152	1446	1152	368		858		931		
chicken fricassee, homemade—*7 oz (200 g)*	1580	460	2000	2680	3260	960		980		1840		
chicken pie, frzn, Swanson—*8-oz pie (227 g)*	56	434	616	896	784	224		504		588	686	336
chicken pie, frzn, Swanson Hungry-Man—*16-oz pie (454 g)*	224	1376	2048	2880	2752	928		1600		2048	1920	832
chicken stew, cnd, Swanson—*7⅝ oz (216 g)*	18	279	324	558	576	153		279		360	405	216
chow mein, chicken, homemade—*1 cup (220 g)*	264	968	1188	1760	1980	594		572		1100		
frzn breakfasts												
french toast & sausage, frzn, Swanson Hungry-Man—*4½-oz meal (127 g)*	32	576	880	1232	944	400		688		912	1024	320
pancakes & sausage, frzn, Swanson Hungry-Man—*6-oz meal (170 g)*	0	435	675	1020	795	240		585		750	630	315
scrambled eggs, sausage & hash browns, frzn, Swanson Hungry-Man—*6¼-oz meal (177 g)*	80	544	832	1200	1168	320		688		944	1024	320
frzn dinners												
beans & franks, Swanson—*11¼-oz meal (319 g)*	80	416	624	1008	800	208		624		672	624	336
beef, Swanson—*11-oz meal (312 g)*	162	1026	1539	2133	2430	648		1080		1539	1674	945
beef, 3 course, Swanson—*15-oz meal (425 g)*	232	957	1421	2177	2177	580		1131		1479	1479	899
chicken, fried breast, Swanson—*11-oz meal (312 g)*	128	928	1312	1952	2016	512		1120		1376	1696	704
chicken, fried, 3 course, Swanson—*15-oz meal (425 g)*	96	720	1032	1584	1536	504		864		1128	1128	552
german style, Swanson—*11¾-oz meal (333 g)*	0	1036	1400	2156	2212	532		1064		1400	1932	644
ham, Swanson—*10-oz meal (284 g)*	76	589	798	1273	1273	361		703		874	874	513
macaroni & beef, Swanson—*12-oz meal (340 g)*	36	288	456	708	600	180		420		492	528	252
macaroni & cheese, Swanson—*12½-oz meal (354 g)*	48	360	576	936	672	264		576		672	528	312
meatloaf, Swanson—*10¾-oz meal (305 g)*	95	437	627	1064	969	304		570		703	703	399
noodles & chicken, Swanson—*10¼-oz meal (291 g)*	42	392	630	924	770	238		532		630	630	336
pork loin, Swanson—*11¼-oz meal (319 g)*	192	768	1056	1704	1872	576		888		1128	1344	600
salisbury steak, 3 course, Swanson—*16-oz meal (454 g)*	46	621	851	1288	1288	391		736		943	1012	506
spaghetti & meatballs, Swanson—*12½-oz meal (354 g)*	30	200	290	490	400	110		290		340	340	140
swiss steak, Swanson—*10-oz meal (284 g)*	114	589	874	1311	1444	418		703		912	1064	323
turkey, Swanson—*11½-oz meal (326 g)*	42	609	840	1302	1449	399		693		882	1218	525
turkey, 3 course, Swanson—*16-oz meal (454 g)*	54	810	1107	1647	1728	486		918		1161	1161	540

	try	thr	iso	leu	lys	met	cys	phe	tyr	val	arg	his
veal parmigiana, Swanson—12¼-oz meal (347 g)	110	638	792	1408	1320	374		836		990	1254	528
hash, corned beef, cnd—3½ oz (100 g)	390	100	460	720	780	220		360		490		
hash, corned beef, homemade—1 cup (225 g)	251	941	1111	1681	1795	502		902		1199		
macaroni & cheese, cnd, Franco-Am—7⅜ oz (209 g)	30	138	192	108	216	84		216		246	162	108
sandwich, corned beef on rye bread—1 sandwich (130 g)	292	1069	1285	2071	2004	599		1114		1410		
sandwich, peanut butter & jelly on whole wheat bread—1 sandwich (114 g)	165	392	584	910	442	152		710		678		
spaghetti & tomato sce w/meatballs, cnd, Franco-Am—7⅜ oz (209 g)	40	310	400	690	520	150		400		440	560	210
tamales, cnd—2 tamales (155 g)	108	186	232	356	372	108		201		232		
turkey, gravy, dressing, whipped potatoes, frzn, Swanson Hungry-Man—8¾ oz (248 g)	80	600	860	1240	1280	400		640		860	1000	420
turkey pie, frzn, Swanson—8-oz pie (227 g)	65	442	559	949	832	234		507		585	715	260
turkey pie, frzn, Swanson Hungry-Man—16-oz pie (454 g)	150	1050	1410	2160	2010	480		1110		1410	1590	630

CREAMS, CREAM SUBSTITUTES AND WHIPPED TOPPINGS

	try	thr	iso	leu	lys	met	cys	phe	tyr	val	arg	his
cream, half & half—1 T (15 g)	6	20	27	43	35	11	4	21	21	30	16	12
cream, light (coffee/table)—1 T (15 g)	6	18	25	40	32	10	4	20	20	27	15	11
cream, med (25% fat)—1 T (15 g)	5	17	22	36	29	9	3	18	18	25	13	10
cream, sour, cultured—1 T (12 g)	4	15	20	32	25	8		15		22		
cream, whipped, pressurized—1 T (3 g)	1	4	6	9	8	2	1	5	5	6	3	3
cream, whipping, heavy, fluid—1 T (15 g)	4	14	19	30	24	8	3	15	15	21	11	8
cream, whipping, light, fluid—1 T (15 g)	5	15	20	32	26	8	3	16	16	22	12	9
cream sub,[a] liquid, frzn—½ fl oz (15 g)	2	7	8	13	10	2	3	8	6	8	12	4
cream sub,[b] liquid, frzn—½ fl oz (15 g)	2	6	9	15	12	5	1	8	9	11	6	4
cream, sub, powdered—1 t (2 g)	1	4	6	9	8	3	tr	5	5	7	4	3
whipped topping, frzn—1 T (4 g)	1	2	3	5	4	2	tr	3	3	4	2	1
whipped topping, from mix, prep w/whole milk—1 T (4 g)	2	6	9	14	11	4	1	7	7	10	5	4
whipped topping, pressurized—1 T (4 g)	1	2	2	4	3	1	tr	2	2	3	2	1

DESSERTS

	try	thr	iso	leu	lys	met	cys	phe	tyr	val	arg	his
cake, angel food, homemade—1 piece (60 g)	52	124	196	329	99	56		235		184		
danish pastry—1 pastry (42 g)	40	101	154	246	92	50		173		150		
doughnut, cake—1 avg (25 g)	16	44	67	106	46	23		71		66		
doughnut, cake w/sugar icing—1 avg (37 g)	27	72	108	171	75	36		115		107		
doughnut, cream filled—1 avg (35 g)	24	62	94	149	65	31		100		93		
doughnut, raised/yeast—1 avg (30 g)	24	65	97	154	67	32		104		96		
doughnut, raised, jelly center—1 avg (65 g)	44	116	174	276	120	58		186		172		
ice cream, french custard—1 cup (133 g)	83	271	378	585	462	139		283		408		
ice cream, french vanilla, soft serve—1 cup (173 g)	100	325	423	680	549	177	72	337	335	466	281	188
ice cream, van, reg (10% fat)—1 cup (133 g)	68	217	290	470	381	120	44	232	232	321	174	130
ice cream, van, rich (16% fat)—1 cup (148 g)	58	186	250	405	327	104	38	199	199	276	150	112

[a] Contains hydrogenated veg oil & soy pro; veg oils are usually soybean, cottonseed, safflower, or blends thereof.

[b] Contains lauric acid oil and Na caseinate; lauric oils include modified coconut oil, hydrogenated coconut oil, and/or palm kernel oil.

	try	thr	iso	leu	lys	met	cys	phe	tyr	val	arg	his
ice milk, choc—⅔ cup (90 g)	50	160	214	347	281	89		171		238		
ice milk, van—1 cup (131 g)	73	233	312	506	409	129	48	249	249	345	187	140
ice milk, van, soft serve—1 cup (175 g)	113	363	486	787	637	201	74	388	388	538	291	218
pie crust, graham cracker—1 serving (32 g)	1	4	5	9	7	2		4		6		
pudding, van, from inst mix (w/skim milk)—½ cup (148 g)	61	198	256	427	338	107		211		283		
pudding, van, from inst mix (w/whole milk)—½ cup (149 g)	58	225	242	399	326	105		193		267		
sherbet, orange—1 cup (193 g)	30	98	131	212	171	54	20	104	104	145	78	59
sweet roll—1 roll (42 g)	46	122	183	293	130	60		195		181		

EGGS, EGG DISHES & EGG SUBSTITUTES
Eggs, Chicken

	try	thr	iso	leu	lys	met	cys	phe	tyr	val	arg	his
boiled, hard/soft—1 large (50 g)	97	298	380	533	410	196	145	343	253	437	388	147
fried—1 large (46 g)	86	264	336	472	363	174	128	303	224	387	344	130
omelet, plain—1 large egg (64 g)	94	290	372	565	410	188	133	332	252	426	364	146
poached—1 large (50 g)	97	297	378	531	408	195	144	341	251	435	387	146
scrambled w/milk & fat—1 large egg (64 g)	94	290	372	565	410	188	133	332	252	426	364	146
white, fresh/frzn—1 large (33 g)	51	149	204	291	206	130	83	210	134	251	195	76
whole, dried, stabilized (glucose reduced)—1 T (5 g)	39	118	151	212	163	78	57	136	100	173	154	58
whole, fresh/frzn—1 large (50 g)	97	298	380	533	410	196	145	343	253	437	388	147
yolk, fresh/frzn—1 large (17 g)	41	151	160	237	189	71	50	121	120	170	193	67

Eggs, Other

	try	thr	iso	leu	lys	met	cys	phe	tyr	val	arg	his
duck, whole—1 egg (70 g)	182	515	419	768	666	403	199	588	429	620	535	224
turtle, whole—3–5 eggs (100 g)	139	554			882	315		580				

Egg Substitutes

	try	thr	iso	leu	lys	met	cys	phe	tyr	val	arg	his
scramblers, Morningstar Farms—¼ cup (57 g)	1	3	3	5	4		1	3	3	3	3	1

FATS, SHORTENINGS & OILS

	try	thr	iso	leu	lys	met	cys	phe	tyr	val	arg	his
salt pork, raw—1 oz (28 g)	2	39	31	103	89	15		44		47		
salt pork, fried—1 oz (28 g)	6	178	95	317	274	47		136		145		

FISH & SHELLFISH

	try	thr	iso	leu	lys	met	cys	phe	tyr	val	arg	his
alewife, raw—3½ oz (100 g)	194	834	989	1474	1707	563		718		1028		
alewife, cnd—3½ oz (100 g)	162	697	826	1231	1426	470		599		859		
anchovy, cnd—3 fillets (12 g)	23	99	117	175	202	67		85		122		
anchovy paste—1 t (7 g)	14	60	71	106	123	41		52		74		
anchovy, pickled—1 oz (28 g)	59	252	299	445	515	170		216		311		
bass, freshwater, smallmouth/largemouth, raw—3½ oz (100 g)	189	813	964	1436	1663	548		699		1002		
bass, saltwater, black, raw—3½ oz (100 g)	192	826	979	1459	1690	557		710		1018		
bass, saltwater, black, baked—1 serving (115 g)	212	1062	1227	1864	2384	661		897		1298		
bass, saltwater, black, baked, stuffed[a]—3½ oz (100 g)	162	687	826	1231	1426	470		599		859		
bass, saltwater, striped, raw—3½ oz (100 g)	189	813	964	1436	1663	548		699		1002		
bass, saltwater, striped, broiled—3½ oz (100 g)	231	992	1176	1751	2029	669		853		1222		
bass, saltwater, striped, oven-fried[b]—3½ oz (100 g)	215	924	1097	1634	1892	624		796		1140		
bluefish, raw—3½ oz (100 g)	205	882	1046	1558	1804	594		758		1086		
bluefish, baked fillet—1 fillet (125 g)	328	1410	1673	2493	2886	951		1214		1738		
bluefish, broiled—½ fish (122 g)	320	1376	1632	2432	2816	928		1184		1696		
bullhead, black, raw—3½ oz (100 g)	163	701	831	1239	1435	473		603		864		

[a] Stuffed w/bacon, butter, celery, onion & bread cubes [b] Prep w/milk, breadcrumbs, butter & salt

	try	thr	iso	leu	lys	met	cys	phe	tyr	val	arg	his
burbot, raw—3½ oz (100 g)	174	748	887	1322	1531	505		644		922		
burbot, fried—3½ oz (100 g)	370	1600	1900	2830	3300	1090		1370		2020		
butterfish, northern, raw—3½ oz (100 g)	181	778	923	1376	1593	525		670		959		
butterfish, gulf, raw—3½ oz (100 g)	162	697	826	1231	1426	470		599		859		
butterfish, fried—1 fish (50 g)	91	391	464	692	801	264		337		482		
carp, raw—3½ oz (100 g)	180	774	918	1368	1584	522		666		954		
catfish, raw—3½ oz (100 g)	176	757	898	1338	1549	510		651		933		
caviar, sturgeon, granular—1 rd t (10 g)	24	162	151	221	192	70		151		165		
caviar, sturgeon, pressed—1 rd t (10 g)	31	204	190	279	241	88		150		207		
cod, raw—3½ oz (100 g)	176	757	899	1338	1549	510		651		933		
cod, broiled—3⅓ oz (95 g)	260	1150	1330	1980	2300	760		960		1390		
cod, cnd—3½ oz (100 g)	192	826	979	1459	1690	557		710		1018		
cod, dried, salted—3½ oz (100 g)	290	1280	1480	2200	2550	840		1070		1550		
cod, dried, salted, creamed—4¾ oz (135 g)	304	1330	1556	2317	2690	893		1138		1634		
crab, cnd—½ cup (85 g)	237	770	696	1332	1317	444		710		740		
crab, fried—2⅓ oz (65 g)	171	556	503	963	952	321		514		535		
crab, steamed—3½ oz (100 g)	277	900	813	1557	1540	519		830		865		
crappie, white, raw—3½ oz (100 g)	168	722	857	1277	1478	487		622		890		
crayfish, freshwater, raw—3½ oz (100 g)	131	642	599	1256	1387	467		686		657		
croaker, atlantic, raw—3½ oz (100 g)	178	780	910	1350	1560	530		660		940		
croaker, atlantic, baked—3½ oz (100 g)	243	1080	1240	1850	2140	710	—	900		1300		
dolly varden, raw—3½ oz (100 g)	199	856	1015	1512	1751	577		736		1055		
drum, freshwater, raw—3½ oz (100 g)	173	744	882	1315	1522	502		640		917		
drum, red (redfish), raw—3½ oz (100 g)	180	792	918	1350	1584	522		666		954		
eel, am, raw—3½ oz (100 g)	159	700	811	1192	1399	461		588		843		
eel, am, smoked—1¾ oz (50 g)	93	409	474	698	818	270		344		493		
eulachon (smelt), raw—3½ oz (100 g)	146	642	745	1095	1285	423		540		774		
fish cakes, cnd—3½ oz (100 g)	247	1434	1385	2027	2398	668		940		1286		
fish sticks, frzn—4½ sticks (100 g)	170	720	840	1250	1460	480		620		880		
flatfishes, raw—3½ oz (100 g)	167	735	852	1252	1470	484		618		885		
flounder/sole, raw—3½ oz (100 g)	148	646	756	1125	1306	434		553		794		
flounder/sole, baked—3½ oz (100 g)	300	1290	1530	2250	2640	870		1110		1590		
haddock, raw—3½ oz (100 g)	183	787	933	1391	1610	531		677		970		
haddock, fried[a]—3½ oz (100 g)	196	843	1000	1491	1725	568		725		1039		
haddock, smoked/cnd—3½ oz (100 g)	232	998	1183	1763	2042	673		858		1230		
hake (including whiting), raw—3½ oz (100 g)	165	710	842	1254	1452	478		610		874		
halibut, atlantic/pacific, raw—3½ oz (100 g)	209	899	1066	1588	1839	606		773		1108		
halibut, atlantic/pacific, broiled—1 serving (125 g)	315	1354	1606	2394	2772	914		1166		1670		
halibut, atlantic/pacific, smoked—3½ oz (100 g)	208	894	1061	1581	1830	603		770		1102		
herring, atlantic, raw—3½ oz (100 g)	173	761	882	1315	1522	502		640		934		
herring, atlantic, broiled—1 fish (85 g)	208	915	1061	1581	1830	603		770		1123		
herring, atlantic, cnd, solids & liquid—3½ oz (100 g)	199	876	1015	1512	1751	577		736		1075		
herring, pacific, raw—3½ oz (100 g)	175	752	892	1312	1522	508		648		928		
herring, pacific, cnd, tomato sce—3½ oz (100 g)	158	679	806	1185	1375	458		585		837		
herring, pacific, pickled, bismarck type—3½ oz (100 g)	204	877	1040	1530	1775	592		755		1081		
lake herring (cisco), raw—3½ oz (100 g)	177	779	903	1545	1558	513		655		956		
lobster, northern, raw—3½ oz (100 g)	152	744	693	1453	1606	541		794		760		
lobster, northern, boiled/broiled w/butter—¾ lb (334 g)	180	880	820	1720	1900	640		940		900		

[a] Dipped in egg, milk & breadcrumbs

	try	thr	iso	leu	lys	met	cys	phe	tyr	val	arg	his
lobster, northern, cnd—½ cup (85 g)	139	678	631	1324	1463	493		724		693		
mackerel, atlantic, raw—3½ oz (100 g)	190	836	969	1444	1672	551		703		1026		
mackerel, atlantic, broiled fillet—1 fillet (130 g)	283	1245	1443	2151	2490	821		1047		1528		
mackerel, atlantic, cnd—½ cup (105 g)	202	889	1030	1535	1778	586		747		1091		
mackerel, pacific, raw—3½ oz (100 g)	219	964	1117	1664	1927	635		810		1183		
mackerel, pacific, cnd—3½ oz (100 g)	211	928	1076	1604	1857	612		781		1139		
mackerel, salted—3½ oz (100 g)	185	814	944	146	1628	536		684		999		
mackerel, smoked—3½ oz (100 g)	238	1047	1214	1809	2094	690		881		1285		
ocean perch, atlantic, raw—3½ oz (100 g)	190	817	969	1425	1672	557		703		1007		
ocean perch, pacific, raw—3½ oz (100 g)	190	817	969	1425	1672	557		703		1007		
perch, freshwater, yellow, raw—3½ oz (100 g)	195	838	994	1462	1716	566		721		1034		
pickerel, raw—3½ oz (100 g)	187	804	954	1402	1646	542		692		991		
pike, blue, raw—3½ oz (100 g)	191	821	974	1432	1681	554		707		1012		
pike, northern, raw—3½ oz (100 g)	183	787	933	1374	1610	531		677		970		
pike, walleye, raw—3½ oz (100 g)	193	830	984	1448	1698	560		714		1023		
pollack, raw—3½ oz (100 g)	204	877	1040	1530	1795	592		755		1081		
pompano, raw—3½ oz (100 g)	188	808	959	1410	1654	545		696		996		
pompano, broiled—3½ oz (100 g)	229	986	1170	1720	2018	665		849		1215		
porgy/scup, raw—3½ oz (100 g)	190	817	969	1425	1672	551		703		1007		
porgy/scup, fried—1 serving (93 g)	227	976	1158	1702	1998	658		840		1203		
red snapper, raw—3½ oz (100 g)	198	851	1010	1485	1742	574		733		1049		
redhorse, silver, raw—3½ oz (100 g)	180	774	918	1350	1584	522		666		954		
rockfish, raw—3½ oz (100 g)	189	813	964	1417	1663	548		699		1002		
rockfish, oven-steamed—3½ oz (100 g)	181	778	923	1357	1593	525		670		959		
roe, raw (salmon, sturgeon, turbot)—3½ oz (100 g)	227	1512	1411	2066	1789	655		1109		1537		
salmon, atlantic, raw—3½ oz (100 g)	225	968	1125	1688	1958	652		832		1192		
salmon, atlantic, cnd—3½ oz (100 g)	803	933	1085	1628	1888	629		803		1150		
salmon, chinook, raw—3½ oz (100 g)	191	821	955	1432	1662	554		707		1012		
salmon, chinook, cnd—⅖ cup (100 g)	196	843	980	1470	1705	568		725		1039		
salmon, pink (humpback), raw—3½ oz (100 g)	200	860	1000	1500	1740	590		740		1060		
salmon, pink (humpback), cnd—⅖ cup (100 g)	205	882	1025	1538	1784	595		758		1086		
salmon, sockeye (red), cnd—⅖ cup (100 g)	203	873	1015	1522	1766	589		751		1076		
salmon, broiled/baked—3½ oz (100 g)	270	1161	1350	2025	2349	783		999		1431		
sardines, atlantic, cnd in oil—8 med (100 g)	206	886	1030	1545	1792	597		762		1092		
sardines, pacific, raw—3½ oz (100 g)	192	826	960	1440	1670	557		710		1018		
sea bass, white, raw—3½ oz (100 g)	214	920	1091	1605	1883	621		792		1134		
shad, am, raw—3½ oz (100 g)	186	800	949	1395	1637	539		688		686		
shad, am, baked[a]—3½ oz (100 g)	232	998	1183	1740	2042	673		858		1230		
shad, am, cnd—3½ oz (100 g)	169	727	862	1268	1487	490		625		896		
sheepshead, atlantic, raw—3½ oz (100 g)	206	886	1051	1545	1813	597		762		1092		
shrimp, raw—3½ oz (100 g)	188	808	959	1429	1654	545		696		996		
shrimp, cnd, dry pack—3½ oz (100 g)	242	1041	1234	1839	2130	702		895		1283		
shrimp, cnd, wet pack—½ cup (100 g)	162	697	826	1231	1426	470		599		859		
smelt, atlantic, raw—4-5 med (100 g)	186	800	949	1395	1637	539		688		986		
smelt, atlantic, cnd—4-5 med (100 g)	184	791	938	1380	1619	534		681		975		
sole, raw—3½ oz (100 g)	148	646	756	1125	1306	434		553		794		
spanish mackerel, raw—3½ oz (100 g)	195	838	994	1462	1716	566		721		1034		
spot, raw—3½ oz (100 g)	176	757	898	1320	1549	510		651		933		
spot, baked—3½ oz (100 g)	228	980	1163	1710	2006	661		844		1208		

[a] Prep w/butter or margarine & bacon slices

	try	thr	iso	leu	lys	met	cys	phe	tyr	val	arg	his
sturgeon, raw—3½ oz (100 g)	181	778	923	1357	1593	525		670		959		
sturgeon, smoked—3½ oz (100 g)	312	1342	1591	2340	2746	905		1154		1654		
sturgeon, steamed—3½ oz (100 g)	254	1092	1295	1905	2235	737		940		1346		
swordfish, raw—3½ oz (100 g)	192	826	979	1440	1690	557		710		1018		
swordfish, broiled[a]—3½ oz (100 g)	280	1204	1428	2100	2464	812		1036		1484		
swordfish, cnd—3½ oz (100 g)	174	752	892	1312	1540	508		648		928		
tomcod, atlantic, raw—3½ oz (100 g)	172	740	877	1290	1514	499		636		912		
trout, brook, raw—3½ oz (100 g)	192	826	979	1440	1690	557		710		1018		
trout, rainbow, raw—3½ oz (100 g)	215	924	1096	1612	1892	624		796		1140		
tuna, albacore, raw—3½ oz (100 g)	253	1088	1290	1923	2226	734		936		1341		
tuna, bluefin, raw—3½ oz (100 g)	252	1084	1285	1890	2218	731		932		1336		
tuna, yellowfin, raw—3½ oz (100 g)	247	1062	1260	1852	2174	716		914		1309		
tuna, cnd, light in oil—6½ oz (184 g)	552	2208	2392	3680	4232	1472		1840		2576	2760	2944
tuna, cnd, light in water—6½ oz (184 g)	552	2208	2392	3680	4232	1472		1840		2576	2760	2944
tuna, cnd, white (albacore) in oil—6½ oz (184 g)	552	2392	2392	3496	4048	1472		1840		2576	2760	2944
tuna, cnd, white (albacore) in water—6½ oz (184 g)	552	2208	2392	3864	4416	1472		1840		2576	2760	2944
tuna, cnd, white (albacore) in water, low Na—6½ oz (184 g)	552	2208	2392	3864	4416	1472		1840		2576	2760	2944
weakfish (sea trout), raw—3½ oz (100 g)	165	710	842	1238	1452	478		610		874		
weakfish (sea trout), broiled—3½ oz (100 g)	246	1058	1255	1845	2165	713		910		1304		
whitefish, baked, stuffed[b]—3½ oz (100 g)	152	654	775	1140	1338	441		562		806		
whitefish, lake, raw—3½ oz (100 g)	189	813	964	1417	1663	548		699		1002		
whitefish, lake, smoked—3½ oz (100 g)	209	899	1066	1568	1839	606		773		1108		
wreckfish, raw—3½ oz (100 g)	184	791	938	1380	1619	534		681		975		
yellowtail, pacific, raw—3½ oz (100 g)	210	903	1071	1575	1848	609		777		1113		
FLOUR & GRAIN FRACTIONS												
barley flour—1 T (8 g)	9	29	37	62	19	8		48		42		
barley flour—1 cup (112 g)	125	410	524	878	274	114		672		593		
buckwheat flour, dark—1 oz (28 g)	56	134	129	213	171	62	50	160	67	168		78
buckwheat flour, light—1 oz (28 g)	31	72	68	111	106	34		75		100		
corn flour—1 cup sifted (110 g)	52	344	396	1118	249	163		387		439		
corn germ, toasted—1 oz (28 g)		190	168	522	304	76		149	100	275	442	170
corn meal, white/yellow, enr, dry—1 oz (3 T) (28 g)	14	96	111	313	70	46		108		123		
corn meal, white/yellow, enr, dry—3½ oz (100 g)	51	344	395	1118	249	163		387		439		
corn meal, white/yellow, enr, ckd—1 cup (240 g)	24	96	72	336	72	48		120		144		
corn meal, whole ground, dry—1 cup (118 g)	60	400	460	1300	290	190		450		510		
manioc (casava) flour—3½ oz (100 g)	21	49	45	66	66	10		45		49		
rice bran—1 oz (28 g)		186	151	300	232	92		192	165	219	454	144
rice flour—1 cup (125 g)	82	292	352	645	292	135		375		525		
rice polish—1 oz (28 g)		115	97	193	145	60		123	117	145	268	96
rye flour, light—3½ oz (100 g)	106	349	447	634	385	148		445		491		
rye flour, med—3½ oz (100 g)	130	423	487	768	466	180		539		596		
rye flour, dark—3½ oz (100 g)	179	602	684	1090	667	261		764		846		
soybean flour—3½ oz (100 g)	619	1775	2435	3508	4318	619		2229		2394		
soybean flour, defatted—3½ oz (100 g)	1344	3852	5284	7612	6180	1344		4837		7194		
wheat flour												
all-purpose, enr—1 T (7 g)	10	23	37	62	18	10		44		34		
all-purpose, enr—1 cup (112 g)	139	336	534	893	267	151		638		499		
all-purpose, unenr—1 T (7 g)	10	23	37	62	18	10		44		34		

[a] Prep w/butter or margarine

[b] Prep w/bacon, onion, celery & breadcrumbs

	try	thr	iso	leu	lys	met	cys	phe	tyr	val	arg	his
all-purpose, unenr—*1 cup (112 g)*	139	336	534	893	267	151		638		499		
bread flour, enr—*1 cup sifted (112 g)*	158	383	607	1016	304	172		726		568		
bread flour, unenr—*1 cup sifted (112 g)*	158	383	607	1016	304	172		726		568		
cake/pastry flour—*1 cup sifted (100 g)*	90	218	345	578	172	98		412		322		
gluten flour (55% white & 45% gluten)—*1 cup (140 g)*	638	1566	2668	4350	1102	986		3190		2726		
self-rising—*1 cup (112 g)*	125	302	479	802	240	136		573		448		
whole wheat—*1 cup (120 g)*	192	464	688	1072	432	240		784		736		
whole wheat, 80% extraction—*1 cup sifted (110 g)*	158	370	607	1016	304	172		726		568		
whole wheat, straight hard—*3½ oz (100 g)*	142	342	543	909	271	153		649		507		
whole wheat, straight soft—*3½ oz (100 g)*	16	281	446	747	223	126		534		417		
FRUITS												
amaranth (purple heart), raw—*3½ oz (100 g)*	38	56	164	206	141	25		96		136		
apples												
raw w/skin—*1 med (138 g)*	3	10	11	17	17	3	4	7	6	12	8	4
raw w/o skin—*1 med (128 g)*	1	6	8	12	12	3	3	5	4	9	6	3
boiled, w/o skin—*1 cup (171 g)*	3	15	17	27	27	5	7	12	9	21	14	7
cnd, sliced, sweetened—*½ cup (102 g)*	2	6	7	11	11	2	2	5	3	8	6	3
dried, sulfured—*10 rings (64 g)*	6	21	24	36	37	6	8	17	11	28	19	10
micro ckd, w/o skin—*1 cup (170 g)*	5	17	19	29	31	5	7	14	9	22	15	7
applesce, cnd, sweetened—*½ cup (128 g)*	3	9	9	14	14	3	3	6	4	10	8	4
applesce, cnd, unsweetened—*½ cup (122 g)*	2	7	7	12	12	2	2	6	4	10	6	4
apricots												
raw—*3 med (106 g)*	16	50	43	82	103	6	3	55	31	50	48	29
cnd, heavy syrup—*4 halves (90 g)*	8	16	14	27	32	3	2	19	11	17	18	7
cnd, jce pack—*3 halves (84 g)*	9	19	16	31	37	3	2	22	13	19	20	8
cnd, light syrup—*3 halves (85 g)*	8	16	14	26	31	3	2	19	10	16	18	8
cnd, water pack—*4 halves (90 g)*	11	23	19	36	43	3	2	25	14	23	24	10
dried, sulfured—*10 halves (35 g)*	23	46	39	75	89	6	4	53	30	47	49	21
frzn, sweetened—*½ cup (121 g)*	10	29	24	47	59	4	2	31	18	29	27	16
banana, raw—*1 med (114 g)*	14	39	38	81	55	13	19	43	27	54	54	92
blueberries												
raw—*1 cup (145 g)*	4	26	30	58	17	16	10	35	12	41	49	15
cnd, heavy syrup—*½ cup (128 g)*	4	23	26	50	15	13	9	29	10	35	42	13
frzn, sweetened—*1 cup (230 g)*	5	25	28	53	16	14	9	32	12	39	46	14
breadfruit, raw—*¼ small (96 g)*		50	61	62	36	10	9	25	18	45		
carambola, raw—*1 med (127 g)*	5	29	29	51	51	14		24	29	33	14	5
crabapples, raw—*1 cup slices (110 g)*	4	15	18	28	28	4	6	12	9	21	14	7
custard apple, raw—*3½ oz (100 g)*	7				37	4						
dates, dried—*10 dates (83 g)*	42	43	39	73	50	18	37	46	25	55	55	25
elderberries, raw—*1 cup (145 g)*	19	39	39	87	38	20	22	58	74	48	68	22
figs, raw—*1 med (50 g)*	3	12	12	17	15	3	6	9	16	14	9	6
figs, cnd, heavy syrup—*3 figs (85 g)*	3	10	10	14	13	3	5	8	14	12	8	4
figs, dried—*10 figs (187 g)*	49	187	174	249	228	47	94	138	247	215	131	80
grapefruit												
raw, pink & red—*½ med (123 g)*	2				17	2						
raw, white—*½ med (118 g)*	2				21	2						
cnd, jce pack—*½ cup (124 g)*	2				22	2						
cnd, light syrup—*½ cup (127 g)*	3				18	3						
grapes												
american (slip skin), raw—*1 cup (92 g)*	3	16	5	12	13	19	9	12	10	16	42	21

	try	thr	iso	leu	lys	met	cys	phe	tyr	val	arg	his
european (adherent skin), raw—*1 cup (160 g)*	5	29	8	22	24	35	18	22	19	29	78	38
thompson seedless, cnd, heavy syrup—*½ cup (128 g)*	3	17	5	13	14	20	10	13	10	17	45	23
guava, raw—*1 med (90 g)*	6	28	27	50	21	5		2	9	25	19	6
guava, strawberry, raw—*1 cup (244 g)*	12	54	51	95	39	10		2	17	49	37	12
lime, raw—*1 med (67 g)*	2				9	1						
longans, raw—*31 fruits (100 g)*		34	26	54	46	13		30	25	58	35	12
longans, dried—*3½ oz (100 g)*		128	97	202	172	49		112	94	217	131	45
loquats—*10 med (100 g)*	5	15	15	26	23	4	6	14	13	21	14	7
lychees, raw—*10 med (100 g)*	7				41	9						
lychees, dried—*3½ oz (100 g)*	33				187	42						
mammy apple, raw—*⅛ med (100 g)*	5				37	6						
mandarin oranges, cnd, jce pack—*½ cup (124 g)*	7	12	21	19	38	16	7	25	12	32	53	14
mandarin oranges, cnd, syrup pack—*½ cup (126 g)*	5	9	15	14	29	13	6	19	10	24	39	10
mangos, raw—*1 med (207 g)*	17	39	37	64	85	10		35	21	54	39	25
orange, navel, raw—*1 med (140 g)*	14	24	39	36	73	31	15	48	24	62	101	27
orange, valencia—*1 med (121 g)*	12	21	34	31	64	27	13	41	22	53	88	24
papayas—*1 med (304 g)*	24	33	24	49	76	6		27	15	30	30	15
peach												
raw—*1 med (87 g)*	2	23	17	35	20	15	5	19	16	33	16	11
cnd, heavy syrup—*1 cup (256 g)*	3	46	33	67	38	28	10	36	31	64	31	20
cnd, heavy syrup, spiced—*1 peach (88 g)*	1	14	11	20	11	9	3	11	10	20	9	7
cnd, jce pack—*1 cup (248 g)*	5	62	45	89	50	37	12	50	40	84	40	30
cnd, light syrup—*1 cup (251 g)*	3	45	33	63	35	28	10	35	30	63	28	20
cnd, water pack—*1 cup (244 g)*	2	41	32	61	34	27	10	34	27	59	27	20
dried, sulfured—*10 halves (130 g)*	13	183	135	265	151	113	38	148	122	256	120	87
frzn, sweetened—*1 cup (250 g)*	5	60	45	88	50	38	13	50	40	85	40	30
pears												
raw—*1 med (166 g)*	17	18	33	23	8	7	17	5	23	12	7	22
cnd, heavy pack—*1 cup (255 g)*	13	15	26	18	5	5	13	5	18	8	5	18
cnd, jce pack—*1 cup (248 g)*	22	25	42	30	10	7	22	7	30	15	10	27
cnd, light syrup—*1 cup (251 g)*	13	15	25	18	5	5	13	5	18	8	5	15
cnd, water pack—*1 cup (244 g)*	12	12	22	17	5	5	12	5	17	7	5	15
dried, sulfured—*10 halves (175 g)*	86	95	165	116	39	32	86	28	116	56	35	109
persimmons, raw—*1 med (25 g)*	4	10	9	15	11	2	5	9	6	11	9	4
persimmons, japanese, raw—*1 med (168 g)*	17	50	42	71	55	8	22	44	27	50	42	20
persimmons, japanese, dried—*1 med (34 g)*	8	24	20	34	27	4	10	21	13	24	20	9
pineapple												
raw—*1 cup pieces (155 g)*	8	19	20	29	39	17	3	19	19	25	28	14
cnd, heavy syrup—*1 cup pieces (255 g)*	13	23	23	33	41	23	3	23	20	28	31	10
cnd, jce pack—*1 cup pieces (250 g)*	13	25	25	40	48	28	3	25	25	33	35	23
plantain, ckd—*1 cup slices (154 g)*	14	32	34	55	57	15	18	42	31	43	102	60
plum												
raw—*1 med (66 g)*		11	11	14	11	4	3	11	4	13	9	9
cnd, heavy syrup—*3 plums (133 g)*		11	9	13	11	4	3	11	4	12	8	8
cnd, jce pack—*3 plums (95 g)*		10	10	13	10	4	3	10	4	11	9	8
sapodilla, raw—*1 med (170 g)*	9	20	26	41	66	5		22	24	27	29	27
sapotes, raw—*1 med (225 g)*	52	131	104	189	216	36		119	124	173	124	95
soursop, raw—*1 cup (225 g)*	25				135	16						
strawberries												
raw—*1 cup (149 g)*	10	28	21	46	37	1	7	27	31	27	39	18
frzn, sweetened—*1 cup (255 g)*	15	41	31	69	56	3	13	38	46	38	59	26
frzn, unsweetened—*1 cup (149 g)*	7	19	15	33	25	1	6	18	21	18	27	12
sugar apples, raw—*1 med (155 g)*	16				85	11						

	try	thr	iso	leu	lys	met	cys	phe	tyr	val	arg	his
tamarinds, raw—*1 cup (120 g)*	22				167	17						
tangerines, raw—*1 med (84 g)*	5	8	14	13	27	11	6	18	9	23	37	10
watermelon, raw—*1 cup (160 g)*	11	43	30	29	99	10	3	24	19	26	94	10

GRAIN PRODUCTS

	try	thr	iso	leu	lys	met	cys	phe	tyr	val	arg	his
biscuit, from mix—*1 biscuit (28 g)*	24	58	92	153	46	26		109		85		
biscuit, from refrig dough—*1 biscuit (28 g)*	25	59	94	158	47	26		113		88		
bread												
corn bread w/enr cornmeal, homemade—*1 piece (83 g)*	37	243	280	789	177	116		280		309		
corn bread w/whole ground cornmeal, homemade—*1 piece (78 g)*	35	228	263	742	166	109		263		291		
corn pone[a] w/whole ground cornmeal—*1 cake (45 g)*	13	81	90	265	58	40		112		103		
cracked wheat—*1 slice (25 g)*	26	63	94	146	59	33		107		100		
french/vienna, enr—*1 slice (25 g)*	28	65	104	174	51	29		124		96		
italian, enr—*1 slice (20 g)*	22	52	83	139	41	23		99		77		
raisin—*1 slice (25 g)*	20	33	70	109	44	24		81		75		
rye, am—*1 slice (25 g)*	25	73	98	154	73	35		110		119		
rye, pumpernickel—*1 slice (32 g)*	32	107	125	194	119	46		136		151		
spoon bread[b] w/whole ground cornmeal—*3²/₅ oz (96 g)*	38	62	96	159	60	29		108		92		
white—*1 slice (24 g)*	25	64	100	165	62	30		112		96		
whole wheat—*1 slice (25 g)*	32	78	116	181	77	40		128		123		
bread crumbs—*1 cup (88 g)*	133	333	522	871	294	150		605		494		
crackers, graham—*2 squares (14 g)*	14	32	52	87	25	14		38		48		
crackers, saltines—*2 crackers (6 g)*	7	16	25	37	13	7		29		23		
macaroni, enr, ckd—*³/₅ cup[c] (90 g)*	54	175	225	297	144	67		234		257		
muffins												
blueberry, from mix—*1 muffin (40 g)*	38	106	155	243	122	53		157		157		
corn w/enr cornmeal, homemade—*1 muffin (45 g)*	35	138	177	437	153	73		151		195		
corn w/whole ground cornmeal, homemade—*1 muffin (45 g)*	35	138	177	347	153	73		151		195		
soy[d]—*1 muffin (40 g)*	54	152	217	332	199	69		211		219		
white—*1 muffin (40 g)*	41	133	166	260	131	57		168		168		
whole wheat—*1 muffin (40 g)*	52	142	206	320	165	74		209		215		
noodles, enr, ckd—*³/₅ cup[c] (92 g)*	42	159	185	251	125	64		182		224		
pancakes												
plain, homemade—*1 med (45 g)*	43	124	178	274	151	66		173		184		
buckwheat, from mix—*1 med (45 g)*	46	131	168	258	189	68		153		192		
cornmeal, homemade—*1 med (48 g)*	26	103	132	251	126	55		114		146		
soy[d]—*1 med (45 g)*	40	113	162	247	148	51		157		163		
popover, homemade—*1 popover (50 g)*	62	183	257	383	234	100		239		271		
rolls												
dinner/pan, enr—*1 roll (28 g)*	28	75	113	183	75	35		122		110		
hamburger—*1 roll (40 g)*	41	109	165	267	109	51		179		161		
raisin—*1 roll (60 g)*	49	119	189	316	94	53		226		176		
white, enr, homemade—*1 roll (35 g)*	36	96	145	234	96	44		156		141		
white, enr, hard, homemade—*1 roll (35 g)*	42	112	168	273	112	52		182		164		
spaghetti, enr, ckd—*1 cup (146 g)*	88	285	365	482	234	110		380		416		
spaghetti w/tomato cheese sce, cnd, Franco-Am—*7³/₈ oz (209 g)*	20	155	200	345	260	75		200		220	280	105

[a] Corn bread often made w/o milk or eggs, shaped in irregular ovals by the palm of the hand & baked or fried on a griddle
[b] Bread made of cornmeal w/ or w/o added rice & hominy & mixed w/milk, eggs, shortening & leavening to a consistency that must be served w/a spoon
[c] From 1 oz dry
[d] Soy flour replaces ¼ of the white flour

	try	thr	iso	leu	lys	met	cys	phe	tyr	val	arg	his
spaghetti w/tomato cheese sce, homemade—10⁷/₁₀ oz (302 g)	63	510	423	534	329	127		417		365		
stuffing, corn bread, from mix—½ cup (90 g)	49	125				57		222		181		
tortilla, corn, enr/unenr—1 tortilla (30 g)	8	60	88	242	38	28		64		78		
waffles, homemade—1 large waffle (75 g)	94	272	391	598	331	144		379		404		
waffles, frzn—1 waffle (34 g)		59	97	198	55	43		96		119		
INFANT, JUNIOR & TODDLER FOODS												
Baked Products												
teething biscuits—1 biscuit (11 g)	21	62	93	161	39	30	17	58	73	97	66	44
Cereals												
barley, dry—1 T (2.4 g)	3	9	10	19	9	5	6	16	10	14	14	6
barley, prep w/whole milk—1 oz (28 g)	17	53	67	114	79	29	19	68	57	80	54	33
cereal & egg yolks, str—1 jar (128 g)	35	105	128	220	163	65	36	118	108	156	133	58
cereal & egg yolks, jr—1 jar (213 g)	58	175	213	366	271	109	60	196	179	260	222	96
grits & egg yolks, str—1 jar (128 g)	28	92	111	234	142	69	35	125	114	136	108	72
high pro cereal, dry—1 T (2.4 g)	13	35	42	71	57	15	17	45	34	45	67	24
high pro cereal, prep w/whole milk— 1 oz (28 g)	37	103	129	213	172	48	41	126	103	138	158	68
mixed cereal, dry—1 T (2.4 g)	4	10	11	25	10	6	8	16	12	16	17	7
mixed cereal, prep w/whole milk—1 oz (28 g)	18	54	69	125	81	31	23	69	60	82	61	34
mixed cereal w/applesce & bananas, str—1 jar (135 g)	18	47	59	119	49	34	36	85	59	80	90	38
mixed cereal w/applesce & bananas, jr—1 jar (220 g)	29	75	95	189	77	53	57	136	95	128	143	59
mixed cereal w/bananas, dry—1 T (2.4 g)	3	9	10	23	11	5	5	13	11	14	12	8
mixed cereal w/bananas, prep w/whole milk—1 oz (28 g)	17	52	67	121	83	30	16	63	58	80	52	36
oatmeal, dry—1 T (2.4 g)	4	11	13	26	14	6	12	13	13	19	25	6
oatmeal, prep w/whole milk—1 oz (28 g)	19	57	73	126	88	32	29	63	63	88	76	32
oatmeal w/applesce & bananas, str— 1 jar (135 g)	23	62	66	134	72	41	39	89	70	92	126	46
oatmeal w/applesce & bananas, jr— 1 jar (220 g)	37	101	108	220	119	68	66	147	114	152	207	75
oatmeal w/bananas, dry—1 T (2.4 g)	4	10	12	23	13	6	7	15	12	17	17	9
oatmeal w/bananas, prep w/whole milk—1 oz (28 g)	18	55	70	122	88	32	20	67	61	84	61	38
rice, dry—1 T (2.4 g)	2	8	7	13	7	4	4	9	8	11	16	5
rice, prep w/whole milk—1 oz (28 g)	15	50	60	102	76	28	15	54	53	73	58	30
rice w/applesce & bananas, str—1 jar (135 g)	16	54	65	157	92	27	19	78	76	92	54	43
rice w/bananas, dry—1 T (2.4 g)	4	11	11	20	11	5	4	10	9	13	14	7
rice w/bananas, prep w/whole milk— 1 oz (28 g)	18	56	69	115	83	30	16	56	55	77	56	34
rice w/mixed fruit, jr—1 jar (220 g)	24	81	110	213	139	42	35	119	108	139	143	64
Desserts												
choc custard pudding, str—1 jar (128 g)		111	129	233	173	59		109	88	152	105	60
choc custard pudding, jr—1 jar (220 g)		196	229	411	304	103		191	154	268	185	106
cottage cheese w/pineapple, str—1 jar (135 g)		99	132	244	190	35		143	109	159	81	72
cottage cheese w/pineapple, jr—1 jar (220 g)		163	216	398	312	57		233	178	262	132	117
orange pudding, str—1 jar (135 g)		61	77	153	122	20		57	61	95	115	42
van custard pudding, str—1 jar (128 g)		76	96	76	146	59		93	76	113	79	52
van custard pudding, jr—1 jar (220 g)		130	167	130	251	101		163	130	196	139	90

	try	thr	iso	leu	lys	met	cys	phe	tyr	val	arg	his
Dinners												
beef & egg noodles, str—*1 jar (128 g)*	32	114	159	238	212	60	33	134	106	151	180	84
beef & egg noodles, jr—*1 jar (213 g)*	58	211	294	443	394	113	62	249	198	281	334	158
beef & rice, toddler—*1 jar (177 g)*	81	354	434	694	666	218	96	349	285	487	598	227
beef lasagna, toddler—*1 jar (177 g)*	83	289	365	573	526	145	85	322	234	409	448	181
beef stew, toddler—*1 jar (177 g)*	94	372	435	687	697	251	94	356	281	481	625	227
chicken & noodles, str—*1 jar (128 g)*	31	113	141	230	198	54	35	125	101	160	175	67
chicken & noodles, jr—*1 jar (213 g)*	47	173	213	351	300	83	51	190	153	243	266	100
chicken soup, crm of, str—*1 jar (128 g)*	38	136	156	264	236	65	35	137	119	183	197	76
chicken stew, toddler—*1 jar (170 g)*	97	376	437	689	697	190	88	362	292	496	563	218
macaroni & cheese, str—*1 jar (128 g)*	41	100	166	300	189	115	41	169	157	188	131	79
macaroni & cheese, jr—*1 jar (213 g)*	68	166	277	498	315	192	68	281	262	313	217	132
macaroni, tomato & beef, str—*1 jar (128 g)*	32	104	137	229	173	46	40	129	95	147	154	74
macaroni, tomato & beef, jr—*1 jar (213 g)*	60	192	251	422	317	83	72	239	175	271	283	136
spaghetti, tomato & meat, toddler—*1 jar (177 g)*	115	349	474	731	554	184	117	427	326	506	503	250
split peas & ham, jr—*1 jar (213 g)*	72	262	285	515	479	115	60	326	245	328	624	192
turkey & rice, str—*1 jar (128 g)*	26	100	122	195	196	67	26	102	87	137	178	58
turkey & rice, jr—*1 jar (213 g)*	40	158	192	307	309	104	40	162	138	217	281	92
veg & bacon, str—*1 jar (128 g)*	19	69	84	133	109	41	29	79	70	109	142	44
veg & bacon, jr—*1 jar (213 g)*	36	130	175	273	232	79	55	164	121	207	258	85
veg & beef, str—*1 jar (128 g)*	26	91	106	173	179	41	24	87	65	128	151	56
veg & beef, jr—*1 jar (213 g)*	49	181	213	345	358	81	49	175	130	256	302	113
veg & chicken, str—*1 jar (128 g)*	27	88	116	174	155	46	35	100	76	133	151	49
veg & chicken, jr—*1 jar (213 g)*	43	143	187	283	251	75	58	162	124	215	245	79
veg & ham, str—*1 jar (128 g)*	23	84	100	165	152	47	23	84	68	118	148	60
veg & ham, jr—*1 jar (213 g)*	55	194	232	381	354	109	55	194	158	271	343	141
veg & ham, toddler—*1 jar (177 g)*	101	301	370	575	540	143	83	320	251	405	471	202
veg & lamb, str—*1 jar (128 g)*	29	93	115	188	187	38	22	101	79	124	170	59
veg & lamb, jr—*1 jar (213 g)*	51	164	202	330	328	66	38	177	141	217	300	102
veg & liver, str—*1 jar (128 g)*	41	114	133	244	209	64	37	133	97	175	168	68
veg & liver, jr—*1 jar (213 g)*	58	158	183	339	290	89	51	183	134	243	232	94
veg & turkey, str—*1 jar (128 g)*	23	84	102	165	156	47	23	79	73	120	134	45
veg & turkey, jr—*1 jar (213 g)*	38	145	175	281	266	81	38	136	124	204	228	77
veg & turkey, toddler—*1 jar (177 g)*	106	329	441	689	586	156	92	354	308	492	522	202
Dinners, High Meat/Cheese												
beef w/veg, str—*1 jar (128 g)*	59	279	307	544	539	204	78	275	209	361	449	219
beef w/veg, jr—*1 jar (128 g)*	64	307	338	599	594	225	87	303	230	398	495	242
chicken w/veg, str—*1 jar (128 g)*	83	332	370	625	614	209	69	308	230	392	520	230
chicken w/veg, jr—*1 jar (128 g)*	93	375	417	705	694	237	78	348	261	442	588	261
cottage cheese w/pineapple, str—*1 jar (135 g)*	128	293	374	752	585	267	61	394	405	474	288	238
ham w/veg, str—*1 jar (128 g)*	78	312	353	599	626	198	92	284	224	371	494	287
ham w/veg, jr—*1 jar (128 g)*	79	317	360	608	636	201	93	288	227	378	502	291
turkey w/veg, str—*1 jar (128 g)*	77	303	352	571	567	187	74	294	230	364	472	247
turkey w/veg, jr—*1 jar (128 g)*	82	320	371	604	599	197	78	311	243	385	499	261
veal w/veg, str—*1 jar (128 g)*	78	307	343	596	608	174	91	294	221	378	520	244
veal w/veg, jr—*1 jar (128 g)*	79	312	351	608	620	178	93	301	227	385	529	250
Meat/Egg Yolks												
beef, str—*1 jar (99 g)*	136	591	613	1080	1122	414	157	522	448	681	919	457
beef, jr—*1 jar (99 g)*	145	629	652	1150	1194	441	167	555	477	726	978	487
beef w/beef hearts, str—*1 jar (99 g)*	125	506	613	1000	1040	326	129	518	361	683	824	336
chicken, str—*1 jar (99 g)*	154	609	639	1047	1133	363	178	552	435	682	947	411
chicken, jr—*1 jar (99 g)*	165	653	686	1125	1216	390	191	593	466	733	1018	441
chicken sticks, jr—*1 jar (71 g)*	83	406	518	811	824	229	90	478	353	542	712	328
egg yolks, str—*1 jar (94 g)*	101	433	532	795	737	255	161	389	389	603	658	199
ham, str—*1 jar (99 g)*	137	597	654	1100	1168	351	169	525	461	709	931	467

	try	thr	iso	leu	lys	met	cys	phe	tyr	val	arg	his
ham, jr—*1 jar (99 g)*	148	649	711	1196	1270	382	184	570	501	771	1012	509
lamb, str—*1 jar (99 g)*	139	636	655	1101	1237	437	192	548	488	707	914	352
lamb, jr—*1 jar (99 g)*	149	686	707	1188	1336	471	207	592	527	762	986	380
liver, str—*1 jar (99 g)*	220	676	694	1307	926	372	213	678	569	898	831	363
meat sticks, jr—*1 jar (71 g)*	65	413	474	740	734	219	52	431	370	491	618	327
pork, str—*1 jar (99 g)*	135	611	673	1116	1146	394	152	564	505	695	939	443
turkey, str—*1 jar (99 g)*	148	627	710	1127	1172	439	172	584	498	720	900	362
turkey, jr—*1 jar (99 g)*	158	674	764	1213	1261	472	185	628	536	774	969	389
turkey sticks, jr—*1 jar (71 g)*	72	388	447	760	835	216	87	433	343	462	627	261
veal, str—*1 jar (99 g)*	145	558	604	1034	1074	295	173	518	428	650	888	411
veal, jr—*1 jar (99 g)*	174	632	682	1168	1215	334	196	585	484	736	1004	464
Vegetables												
beans, green, str—*1 jar (128 g)*	19	70	74	109	83	24	14	68	59	91	92	46
beans, green, jr—*1 jar (206 g)*	29	105	111	161	122	37	21	101	87	134	136	68
beans, green, buttered, str—*1 jar (128 g)*	18	65	69	100	76	23	13	63	54	83	84	42
beans, green, buttered, jr—*1 jar (206 g)*	31	113	119	175	132	39	23	109	95	144	146	74
beans, green, creamed, jr—*1 jar (213 g)*	32	81	102	166	92	47	23	96	92	124	102	49
beets, str—*1 jar (128 g)*	15	41	49	59	44	13	9	23	45	58	38	27
carrots, str—*1 jar (128 g)*	14	28	31	41	26	12	8	31	24	38	64	15
carrots, jr—*1 jar (213 g)*	23	49	51	70	45	19	13	53	43	66	111	28
carrots, buttered, str—*1 jar (128 g)*	15	31	32	44	27	12	8	33	26	41	68	17
carrots, buttered, jr—*1 jar (213 g)*	23	49	51	70	45	19	13	53	43	66	111	28
corn, creamed, str—*1 jar (128 g)*	19	67	83	179	104	51	23	63	86	99	77	59
corn, creamed, jr—*1 jar (213 g)*	32	111	138	300	175	85	38	104	145	166	128	98
garden veg, str—*1 jar (128 g)*	35	93	110	183	148	55	26	113	122	127	251	58
mixed veg, str—*1 jar (128 g)*	17	49	60	99	51	23	31	60	56	74	101	33
mixed veg, jr—*1 jar (213 g)*	32	96	119	194	100	45	60	117	111	147	198	66
peas, str—*1 jar (128 g)*	44	174	193	301	300	51	33	183	152	216	498	96
peas, buttered, str—*1 jar (128 g)*	46	183	204	316	315	54	36	192	160	228	525	101
peas, buttered, jr—*1 jar (206 g)*	70	284	315	490	488	84	56	299	249	352	814	157
spinach, creamed, str—*1 jar (128 g)*	46	129	143	283	189	70	40	123	147	193	195	82
spinach, creamed, jr—*1 jar (213 g)*	94	258	288	564	379	141	79	247	294	386	388	162
squash, str—*1 jar (128 g)*	15	32	42	60	40	13	9	37	36	46	59	20
squash, jr—*1 jar (213 g)*	26	53	70	102	66	23	15	62	60	77	100	34
squash, buttered, str—*1 jar (128 g)*	12	24	32	46	29	10	8	28	28	36	45	15
squash, buttered, jr—*1 jar (213 g)*	21	45	60	87	55	19	13	53	51	66	85	28
sweet potatoes, str—*1 jar (135 g)*	30	73	69	105	59	32	20	84	55	99	73	35
sweet potatoes, jr—*1 jar (220 g)*	46	117	110	167	95	51	33	134	88	156	117	55
sweet potatoes, buttered, str—*1 jar (135 g)*	24	61	57	86	49	27	18	70	46	82	61	28
sweet potatoes, buttered, jr—*1 jar (220 g)*	33	84	79	121	68	37	24	97	64	114	84	40
JUICES, FRUIT & VEGETABLE												
grape jce, cnd/bottle—*8 fl oz (253 g)*		40	18	30	25	3		30	8	25	119	18
grape jce, from frzn conc, sweetened—*8 fl oz (250 g)*		13	5	10	8			10	3	8	40	5
orange jce, fresh—*8 fl oz (248 g)*	5	20	20	32	22	7	12	22	10	27	117	7
orange jce, cnd—*8 fl oz (249 g)*	5	17	15	27	20	7	10	17	7	22	100	7
orange jce, from frzn conc—*8 fl oz (249 g)*	5	20	17	32	22	7	12	20	10	27	112	7
tangerine jce, fresh—*8 fl oz (247 g)*	2	15	12	25	17	5	10	15	7	20	84	5
tangerine jce, cnd, sweetened—*8 fl oz (249 g)*	2	15	12	25	17	5	10	15	7	20	85	5
tangerine jce, from frzn conc, sweetened—*8 fl oz (241 g)*	2	12	12	19	14	5	7	12	5	17	70	5

	try	thr	iso	leu	lys	met	cys	phe	tyr	val	arg	his

MEATS
Beef

	try	thr	iso	leu	lys	met	cys	phe	tyr	val	arg	his
arm/blade, lean & marb, pot roasted— 2 slices (83 g)	319	1208	1433	2243	2391	679		1126		1519		
arm/blade, lean only, pot roasted— 2 slices (41 g)	169	637	755	1181	1259	357		593		801		
brisket, lean, marb & fat, ckd—3 slices (95 g)	201	763	904	1415	1509	428		710		959		
chipped—2 slices (28 g)	113	425	504	788	841	239		396		534		
chipped—3 oz (85 g)	341	1288	1526	2388	2547	723		1199		1618		
chipped, creamed—½ cup (120 g)	191	667	828	1312	1212	365		709		861		
chuck stew meat, raw—4 oz (113 g)	297	1125	1333	2088	2226	632		1048		1415		
club steak, lean, marb & fat, ckd— 1 steak (93 g)	278	1050	1244	1948	2079	590		978		1321		
club steak, lean only, ckd—1 steak (55 g)	187	706	836	1310	1397	397		658		888		
corned beef, cnd—2 oz (57 g)	148	560	664	1040	1110	314		522		706		
cubed steak, ckd—3½ oz (100 g)	379	1434	1700	2661	2838	806		1336		1804		
flank steak, lean & marb, ckd—1 steak (141 g)	551	2080	2465	3859	4117	1169		1938		2617		
flank steak, lean only, ckd—1 steak (75 g)	301	1135	1345	2106	2249	638		1057		1428		
hamburger, med fat, ckd—1 patty (85 g)	255	963	1141	1786	1906	541		897		1211		
hamburger, lean, ckd—1 patty (86 g)	303	1144	1355	2122	2264	643		1066		1439		
neck, lean & marb, pot roasted— 2 slices (132 g)	472	1780	2109	3302	3523	1001		1658		2239		
neck, lean only, pot roasted—2 slices (30 g)	121	455	539	844	900	256		424		572		
porterhouse steak, lean & marb, broiled—1 steak (100 g)	297	1122	1329	2081	2220	631		1045		1411		
porterhouse steak, lean only, broiled— 1 steak (54 g)	172	649	769	1204	1285	365		605		817		
rib roast, lean & marb, ckd—2 slices (106 g)	332	1254	1486	2327	2483	705		1168		1578		
rib roast, lean only, ckd—2 slices (41 g)	129	486	576	901	961	273		453		611		
rib steak, lean & marb, ckd—1 steak (94 g)	281	1060	1256	1966	2098	596		987		1333		
rib steak, lean only, ckd—1 steak (43 g)	144	543	644	1008	1075	305		506		683		
round, bottom, lean & marb, broiled— 1 slice (114 g)	474	1789	2119	3318	3541	1006		1666		2250		
round, bottom, lean only, broiled— 1 slice (86 g)	357	1341	1596	2499	2666	757		1255		1695		
round, top, lean & marb, broiled— 1 slice (111 g)	504	1904	2255	3531	3768	1070		1773		2395		
round, top, lean only, broiled—1 slice (80 g)	367	1387	1643	2573	2745	780		1292		1745		
round heel, lean & marb, pot roasted— 1 slice (118 g)	431	1625	1926	3015	3217	914		1514		2045		
round heel, lean only, pot roasted— 1 slice (53 g)	204	769	911	1426	1521	432		716		967		
round stew meat, raw—4 oz (113 g)	429	1621	1921	3007	3208	911		1510		2039		
rump, lean & marb, pot roasted— 2 slices (80 g)	300	1131	1340	2097	2238	636		1053		1422		
rump, lean only, pot roasted—2 slices (37 g)	140	530	628	983	1049	297		494		667		
short ribs, lean & marb, ckd—1 serving (72 g)	206	777	921	1442	1539	437		724		978		
short ribs, lean only, ckd—1 serving (17 g)	64	243	288	451	481	137		226		306		
sirloin, lean & marb, broiled— 1 slice (125 g)	373	1409	1669	2614	2789	792		1312		1772		
sirloin, lean only, broiled—1 slice (77 g)	243	919	1088	1704	1818	516		856		1156		

	try	thr	iso	leu	lys	met	cys	phe	tyr	val	arg	his
sirloin tip, lean & marb, roasted—*1 slice (76 g)*	261	985	1167	1827	1949	554		917		1239		
sirloin tip, lean only, roasted—*1 slice (44 g)*	157	592	701	1098	1171	333		551		745		
T-bone, lean & marb, broiled—*1 steak (95 g)*	281	1060	1256	1966	2098	596		987		1333		
T-bone, lean only, broiled—*1 steak (59 g)*	183	689	816	1278	1364	387		642		867		
tenderloin, lean & marb, broiled—*1 steak (66 g)*	201	760	900	1409	1504	427		708		956		
tenderloin, lean only, broiled—*1 steak (52 g)*	178	671	795	1245	1329	377		625		845		
Lamb												
arm chop, lean, marb & fat, ckd—*3½ oz (100 g)*	290	1025	1161	1734	1813	538		911		1104		
arm chop, lean & marb, ckd—*1 chop (57 g)*	189	668	757	1130	1182	350		593		719		
arm chop, lean & marb, ckd—*2 chops (114 g)*	379	1341	1519	2269	2372	703		1191		1444		
arm chop, lean only, ckd—*2 chops (59 g)*	214	755	855	1278	1336	396		671		813		
blade chop, lean, marb & fat, ckd—*3½ oz (100 g)*	319	1126	1275	1905	1991	590		1000		1212		
blade chop, lean & marb, ckd—*1 chop (93 g)*	329	1163	1316	1967	2056	610		1033		1251		
blade chop, lean only, ckd—*1 chop (56 g)*	211	746	845	1262	1319	391		663		803		
leg, lean, marb & fat, roasted—*3½ oz (100 g)*	267	943	1068	1595	1667	494		837		1015		
leg, lean & marb, roasted—*1 slice (49 g)*	179	632	715	1069	1117	331		561		680		
leg, lean & marb, roasted—*2 slices (98 g)*	357	1263	1431	2137	2234	662		1120		1360		
leg, lean only, roasted—*2 slices (61 g)*	228	806	912	1363	1425	422		715		867		
loin chop, lean, marb & fat, ckd—*3½ oz (100 g)*	298	1053	1192	1781	1862	552		935		1133		
loin chop, lean & marb, ckd—*1 chop (46 g)*	162	572	648	968	1012	300		508		616		
loin chop, lean & marb, ckd—*2 chops (92 g)*	322	1140	1291	1928	2015	598		1012		1227		
loin chop, lean only, ckd—*2 chops (70 g)*	254	897	1016	1518	1586	470		797		966		
rib chop, lean, marb & fat, ckd—*3½ oz (100 g)*	263	929	1052	1572	1643	487		825		1000		
rib chop, lean & marb, ckd—*1 chop (41 g)*	136	481	544	813	850	252		427		517		
rib chop, lean & marb, ckd—*2 chops (82 g)*	272	961	1088	1626	1700	504		854		1035		
rib chop, lean only, ckd—*2 chops (52 g)*	193	682	772	1154	1206	358		606		734		
Pork												
bacon, canadian, broiled/fried—*1 slice (21 g)*	60	254	309	479	521	151		237		323		
bacon, cured, raw—*1 slice (28 g)*	24	77	101	184	148	36		110		110		
bacon, cured, broiled/fried crisp—*1 slice (6 g)*	19	61	79	144	116	28		86		86		
bacon, cured, broiled/fried crisp—*3 slices (18 g)*	56	182	237	432	348	84		258		258		
bacon, cured, cnd, ckd—*1 oz (28 g)*	25	82	107	195	157	38		116		116		
blade, lean, marb & fat, ckd—*3½ oz (100 g)*	323	1155	1279	1833	2044	621		980		1295		
blade, lean & marb, ckd—*1 slice (54 g)*	204	728	806	1156	1289	392		618		816		
blade, lean & marb, ckd—*2 slices (108 g)*	406	1452	1608	2304	2570	781		1232		1628		

	try	thr	iso	leu	lys	met	cys	phe	tyr	val	arg	his
blade, lean only, ckd—*2 slices (61 g)*	244	872	966	1384	1543	469		740		978		
boston butt, lean, marb & fat, ckd—*3½ oz (100 g)*	292	1044	1156	1656	1847	561		886		1170		
boston butt, lean & marb, roasted—*1 slice (58 g)*	191	682	755	1082	1207	367		578		764		
boston butt, lean & marb, roasted—*2 slices (116 g)*	383	1369	1515	2172	2422	736		1161		1534		
boston butt, lean only, roasted—*2 slices (41 g)*	153	548	606	869	969	294		464		614		
ham, fresh, lean, marb & fat, ckd—*3½ oz (100 g)*	427	1527	1690	2422	2701	821		1295		1711		
ham, fresh, lean & marb, ckd—*1 slice (53 g)*	254	909	1007	1443	1609	489		771		1019		
ham, fresh, lean & marb, ckd—*2 slices (107 g)*	514	1837	2034	2915	3251	988		1559		2059		
ham, fresh, lean only, ckd—*2 slices (75 g)*	376	1346	1489	2135	2381	723		1141		1508		
ham, cured butt, lean, marb & fat, ckd—*3½ oz (100 g)*	216	922	1120	1739	1890	547		860		1170		
ham, cured butt, lean & marb, ckd—*1 slice (60 g)*	145	618	751	1167	1268	367		577		786		
ham, cured butt, lean & marb, ckd—*2 slices (120 g)*	290	1237	1503	2334	2537	734		1155		1571		
ham, cured butt, lean only, ckd—*2 slices (64 g)*	170	725	881	1368	1487	430		677		921		
ham, cured shank, lean, marb & fat, ckd—*3½ oz (100 g)*	196	836	1015	1577	1714	496		780		1061		
ham, cured shank, lean & marb, ckd—*1 slice (39 g)*	96	410	498	773	840	243		382		520		
ham, cured shank, lean & marb, ckd—*2 slices (79 g)*	194	827	1015	1561	1697	491		772		1050		
ham, cured shank, lean only, ckd—*2 slices (43 g)*	116	496	602	935	1016	294		463		629		
loin chop, lean & fat, ckd—*3½ oz (100 g)*	382	1364	1510	2164	2414	733		1157		1529		
loin chop, lean & fat, ckd—*1 chop (88 g)*	336	1202	1330	1907	2126	646		1019		1347		
loin chop, lean only, ckd—*1 chop (68 g)*	305	1090	1207	1730	1929	586		925		1222		
picnic shoulder, lean, marb & fat, ckd—*3½ oz (100 g)*	302	1081	1197	1715	1913	581		917		1212		
picnic shoulder, lean & marb, roasted—*1 slice (47 g)*	158	566	627	898	1002	304		480		634		
picnic shoulder, lean & marb, roasted—*2 slices (95 g)*	319	1141	1263	1811	2020	614		968		1279		
picnic shoulder, lean only, roasted—*2 slices (45 g)*	170	608	673	964	1076	327		516		681		
sausage, pork, cnd—*2 patties (100 g)*	131	631	747	1104	1239	325		562		774		
sausage, pork, fresh, ckd—*1 link (13 g)*	20	101	93	171	194	62	26	85	74	103	151	74
sausage, pork, fresh, ckd—*1 patty (27 g)*	42	210	194	356	403	129	53	177	153	213	313	153
sausage, pork & beef, fresh, ckd—*1 link (13 g)*	17	72	69	127	141	43	18	62	53	77	111	54
shoulder butt, cured, lean, marb & fat, ckd—*3½ oz (100 g)*	188	803	976	1515	1647	477		749		1020		
shoulder butt, cured, lean & marb, roasted—*1 slice (75 g)*	164	699	849	1318	1433	415		652		887		
shoulder butt, cured, lean & marb, roasted—*2 slices (150 g)*	327	1395	1695	2632	2860	829		1301		1771		
shoulder butt, cured, lean only, roasted—*2 slices (55 g)*	141	602	732	1136	1235	358		562		765		
sirloin, lean & marb, roasted—*3½ oz (100 g)*	356	1271	1406	2016	2248	683		1079		1425		
sirloin, lean & marb, roasted—*3 slices (71 g)*	278	991	1097	1572	1753	533		842		1112		

	try	thr	iso	leu	lys	met	cys	phe	tyr	val	arg	his
sirloin, lean only, roasted—*3 slices (46 g)*	186	664	735	1053	1174	357		564		745		
spareribs, roasted—*3 med ribs (45 g)*	99	356	394	565	630	191		302		399		
spareribs, roasted—*6 med ribs (90 g)*	198	712	788	1130	1260	382		604		798		
tenderloin, lean only, roasted—*3½ oz (100 g)*	398	1423	1575	2257	2517	765		1208		1595		
Veal												
arm steak, lean & fat, ckd—*3½ oz (100 g)*	389	1283	1562	2169	2476	677		1202		1530		
arm steak, lean only, ckd—*1 steak (90 g)*	422	1390	1692	2350	2676	734		1302		1656		
blade, lean & fat, ckd—*3½ oz (100 g)*	391	1288	1568	2177	2481	680		1207		1536		
blade, lean only, ckd—*1 steak (108 g)*	472	1558	1896	2632	3000	822		1460		1856		
breast, stew meat, raw—*3½ oz (100 g)*	365	1205	1468	2038	2323	637		1131		1438		
breast, stewed w/gravy—*4 pieces (74 g)*	269	888	1082	1502	1711	469		833		1060		
chuck, med fat, braised—*3½ oz (100 g)*	366	1209	1473	2045	2330	639		1133		1442		
cutlet, round, lean & fat, ckd—*3½ oz (100 g)*	435	1438	1751	2429	2769	758		1346		1714		
cutlet, round, lean only, ckd—*1 cutlet (70 g)*	370	1222	1488	2065	2354	644		1144		1457		
cutlet, breaded, ckd—*3½ oz (100 g)*	435	1438	1751	2429	2769	758		1346		1714		
foreshank, med fat, stewed—*3½ oz (100 g)*	255	841	1024	1422	1620	444		788		1003		
loin chop, lean & fat, ckd—*3½ oz (100 g)*	298	981	1195	1660	1889	517		920		1169		
loin chop, lean & fat, ckd—*1 chop (122 g)*	362	1197	1451	2022	2305	631		1121		1426		
loin chop, lean only, ckd—*1 chop (72 g)*	323	1066	1298	1801	2053	562		998		1270		
plate, med fat, stewed—*3½ oz (100 g)*	342	1131	1378	1913	2179	598		1061		1349		
rib, med fat, roasted—*3½ oz (100 g)*	362	1197	1457	2022	2305	631		1121		1426		
rib chop, lean & fat, ckd—*3½ oz (100 g)*	362	1197	1457	2022	2305	631		1121		1426		
rib chop, lean & fat, ckd—*1 chop (83 g)*	300	990	1205	1672	1906	522		927		1179		
rib chop, lean only, ckd—*1 chop (58 g)*	256	846	1030	1429	1629	446		792		1008		
round w/rump, med fat, broiled—*3½ oz (100 g)*	356	1176	1431	1986	2264	620		1101		1401		
rump, lean, marb & fat, ckd—*3½ oz (100 g)*	371	1227	1494	2072	2362	647		1148		1462		
rump, lean & marb, roasted—*2 slices (97 g)*	386	1272	1548	2151	2450	671		1192		1516		
rump, lean only, roasted—*2 slices (50 g)*	210	690	840	1167	1329	364		647		823		
sirloin, lean, marb & fat, ckd—*3½ oz (100 g)*	315	1041	1267	1758	2004	549		974		1240		
sirloin, lean & marb, roasted—*2 slices (98 g)*	362	1197	1457	2022	2305	631		1120		1426		
sirloin, lean only, roasted—*2 slices (59 g)*	226	798	911	1264	1441	394		700		891		
sirloin steak, lean & fat, ckd—*½ steak (88 g)*	334	1107	1348	1871	2133	583		1036		1319		
sirloin steak, lean only, ckd—*½ steak (68 g)*	213	1031	1254	1740	1984	544		964		1228		
stew meat, marb, raw—*3½ oz (100 g)*	367	1213	1478	2052	2338	641		1138		1447		
Organ Meats												
brains, all kinds, raw—*3 oz (85 g)*	117	420	428	718	646	187		430		456		
chitterlings (hog intestine), raw—*3½ oz (100 g)*	94	398	308	457	670	193		359		462		
heart, beef, lean, braised—*3½ oz (100 g)*	250	887	979	1725	1585	461		874		112		
heart, hog, braised—*3½ oz (100 g)*	401	1423	1571	2766	2543	739		1402		1784		

	try	thr	iso	leu	lys	met	cys	phe	tyr	val	arg	his
kidneys, beef, braised—3½ oz (100 g)	285	858	942	1678	1402	396		911		1130		
kidneys, hog, raw—3½ oz (100 g)	240	722	793	1414	1181	334		767		952		
kidneys, lamb, raw—3½ oz (100 g)	244	736	807	1440	1203	340		781		969		
liver, beef, raw—3½ oz (100 g)	296	936	1031	1819	1475	463		993		1239		
liver, calf, raw—3½ oz (100 g)	286	903	994	1754	1423	447		958		1195		
liver, calf, fried—3½ oz (100 g)	208	1069	1178	2078	1686	531		1133		1414		
liver, hog, raw—3½ oz (100 g)	296	936	1031	1819	1475	463		993		1239		
liver, hog, fried—3½ oz (100 g)	357	1230	1246	2197	1781	559		1200		1495		
liver, lamb, broiled—3½ oz (100 g)	378	1195	1316	2322	1881	592		1268		1581		
pancreas, beef, med fat, raw—3½ oz (100 g)	175	626	683	1054	996	244		562		724		
pancreas, calf, raw—3½ oz (100 g)	250	885	981	1500	1423	346		808		1038		
pancreas, hog, raw—3½ oz (100 g)	188	673	733	1132	1070	262		603		777		
tongue, beef, med fat, braised—3½ oz (100 g)	196	708	792	1286	1364	356		661		840		
tongue, hog, braised—3½ oz (100 g)	265	951	1063	1725	1831	479		887		1126		

Other Meats

	try	thr	iso	leu	lys	met	cys	phe	tyr	val	arg	his
rabbit, stewed—3½ oz (100 g)		1021	1082	1636	1818	541		793		1021		
snail, raw—3½ oz (100 g)	681			938	975	791						
whale meat, raw—3½ oz (100 g)	220	800			1880	520		1260				

MEATS: LUNCHEON MEATS/ FRANKS/SANDWICH SPREADS

	try	thr	iso	leu	lys	met	cys	phe	tyr	val	arg	his
beef, thinly sliced lunchmeat—5 slices (21 g)	42	173	198	337	352	106	59	165	150	202	284	146
berliner (pork & beef)—1 slice (23 g)	40	150	157	276	303	90	51	138	110	162	239	135
bockwurst (pork, veal, milk, etc.), raw—1 link (65 g)	88	358	378	610	681	208	96	320	278	396	528	259
bologna, beef—1 slice (23 g)	25	102	116	198	206	62	34	97	88	118	166	86
bologna, beef & pork—1 slice (23 g)	24	118	117	207	203	64	31	106	83	143	161	73
bologna, pork—1 slice (23 g)	34	147	152	269	277	95	39	135	111	170	231	111
bratwurst (pork), ckd—1 link (85 g)	96	473	437	802	910	291	121	400	345	481	706	345
braunschweiger (pork liver sausage)—1 slice (18 g)	26	96	87	186	164	56	45	100	77	111	138	58
brotwurst (pork & beef w/nfdm)—1 link (70 g)	92	419	424	756	797	258	114	379	310	473	662	305
chorizo (pork & beef)—1 link (60 g)	167	884	1324	1025	1448	282		689		548	1016	433
corned beef loaf, jellied—1 slice (28 g)	48	263	252	464	516	149	70	238	181	291	466	177
frankfurter, beef—1 frank (45 g)	46	192	219	373	389	118	65	183	166	223	314	162
frankfurter, beef & pork—1 frank (45 g)	37	183	218	369	407	103	58	162	141	212	382	158
ham, chopped, cnd—1 slice (21 g)	38	151	145	262	290	88	40	131	111	151	209	134
ham, chopped, packaged—1 slice (21 g)	44	160	162	289	322	95	54	145	112	168	252	146
ham, minced—1 slice (21 g)	33	154	147	264	286	96	40	135	113	157	215	127
ham, sliced, lean (5% fat)—1 slice (28 g)	67	244	247	441	490	145	82	221	170	256	385	223
ham, sliced, reg (11% fat)—1 slice (28 g)	61	221	225	400	445	132	75	201	155	233	350	202
ham & cheese loaf/roll—1 slice (28 g)	59	204	214	384	428	124	67	196	159	227	317	192
headcheese (pork)—1 slice (28 g)	24	126	154	286	274	75	63	172	132	187	325	84
honey loaf (pork & beef)—1 slice (28 g)	52	223	206	389	420	135	44	190	164	220	305	173
italian sausage (pork), ckd—1 link (67 g)	108	531	490	900	1020	326	135	449	387	539	792	387
kielbasa/kolbassy (pork & beef w/nfdm)—1 slice (26 g)	36	112	166	227	263	72	59	130	127	166	245	82
knackwurst/knockwurst (pork & beef)—1 link (68 g)	73	326	317	558	634	195	100	277	245	350	482	245
lebanon bologna (beef)—1 slice (23 g)	37	189	185	337	368	109	53	169	136	207	305	130

	try	thr	iso	leu	lys	met	cys	phe	tyr	val	arg	his
livercheese (pork liver)—*1 slice (38 g)*	78	247	240	506	448	130	125	272	177	306	318	149
liver pate, unspecified, cnd—*1 oz (28 g)*	45	161	157	298	238	81	48	165	129	218	254	84
liver sausage/liverwurst (pork)—*1 slice (18 g)*	28	122	119	207	210	52	27	112	66	156	147	81
luxury loaf (pork)—*1 slice (28 g)*	61	249	231	430	468	133	43	204	183	253	332	186
mortadella (beef & pork)—*1 slice (15 g)*	23	95	106	182	189	59	31	90	80	110	154	78
new england brand sausage (pork & beef)—*1 slice (23 g)*	44	174	175	313	348	103	57	157	123	185	276	150
old fashioned loaf (pork & beef)—*1 slice (28 g)*	42	175	158	305	305	91	30	145	126	175	227	117
olive loaf (pork)—*1 slice (28 g)*	29	134	119	246	229	85	41	119	109	144	165	83
peppered loaf (pork & beef)—*1 slice (28 g)*	56	216	222	393	428	127	69	197	156	234	332	184
pepperoni (pork & beef)—*1 slice (6 g)*	11	47	50	87	90	29	14	43	37	54	74	37
pickle & pimento loaf (pork)—*1 slice (28 g)*	33	148	139	269	254	72	33	124	111	158	189	97
picnic loaf (pork & beef)—*1 slice (28 g)*	41	186	165	325	338	107	46	152	130	182	252	124
polish sausage (pork)—*1 oz (28 g)*	39	168	173	305	315	107	45	153	126	192	262	126
pork & beef lunch meat—*1 slice (28 g)*	38	154	182	297	336	82	65	145	142	202	262	115
pork & beef luncheon sausage—*1 slice (23 g)*	37	153	181	294	333	81	65	143	141	200	260	114
pork lunch meat, cnd—*1 slice (21 g)*	26	104	121	203	198	71	45	104	81	139	184	76
salami, ckd, beef—*1 slice (23 g)*	31	128	146	248	259	78	43	122	110	149	209	108
salami, ckd, beef & pork—*1 slice (23 g)*	26	120	155	214	255	69	45	111	127	154	197	83
salami, dry/hard, pork—*1 slice (10 g)*	25	101	108	163	188	47	29	94	69	112	137	61
salami, dry/hard, pork & beef—*1 slice (10 g)*	21	96	97	173	182	59	26	87	71	108	152	70
salami for beer (beerwurst), beef—*1 slice (23 g)*	26	107	123	208	217	66	36	102	92	125	175	90
salami for beer (beerwurst), pork—*1 slice (23 g)*	26	130	112	217	237	82	25	104	93	117	186	96
sandwich spread, ham salad—*1 oz (28 g)*	25	116	114	206	219	65	14	100	79	127	168	99
smoked link sausage, pork—*1 link (68 g)*	147	632	653	1151	1187	405	169	577	475	726	989	475
smoked link sausage, pork & beef—*1 link (68 g)*	73	316	330	551	614	248	71	275	262	316	520	269
smoked link sausage, pork & beef w/am cheese—*1 link (43 g)*	64	233	266	472	498	154	65	243	222	298	360	203
smoked link sausage, pork & beef w/flour & nfdm—*1 link (68 g)*	95	389	422	732	734	244	110	367	312	460	591	295
smoked link sausage, pork & beef w/nfdm—*1 link (68 g)*	92	375	411	710	709	234	103	354	307	449	553	282
thuringer (cervelat/summer sausage), beef & pork—*1 slice (23 g)*	35	158	177	241	318	81	45	133	125	185	228	108
turkey breast meat—*1 slice (21 g)*	54	210	246	377	445	137	49	188	187	251	330	147
turkey ham (cured thigh meat)—*2 slices (57 g)*	122	477	558	855	1012	311	112	426	424	570	749	335
turkey pastrami—*2 slices (57 g)*	115	452	521	806	942	290	117	405	393	540	731	311
vienna sausage, cnd (beef & pork)—*1 sausage (16 g)*	17	57	89	128	127	42	28	68	55	92	113	44

MEAT ANALOGUES

	try	thr	iso	leu	lys	met	cys	phe	tyr	val	arg	his
breakfast links, Morningstar Farms—*5 links (68 g)*		526	597	1198	658		136	796	582	677	727	296
breakfast patties, Morningstar Farms—*2 patties (76 g)*		543	615	1225	682		195	777	554	667	757	313
grillers, Morningstar Farms—*1 patty (64 g)*		3	2	5	3		tr	3	3	3	3	1

MILK, MILK BEVERAGES & YOGURT
Milk, Cow

	try	thr	iso	leu	lys	met	cys	phe	tyr	val	arg	his
buttermilk, cultured—*1 cup (245 g)*	88	386	500	807	679	198	76	427	339	596	309	233
buttermilk, dry—*1 T (7 g)*	31	101	135	218	177	56	21	108	108	149	81	60

	try	thr	iso	leu	lys	met	cys	phe	tyr	val	arg	his
condensed, sweetened, cnd—*1 fl oz (38 g)*	43	136	183	296	240	76	28	146	146	202	109	82
evaporated, skim milk, cnd—*1 fl oz (32 g)*	34	109	146	236	191	60	22	116	116	161	87	65
evaporated, whole milk, cnd—*1 fl oz (32 g)*	30	97	130	210	170	54	20	104	104	144	78	58
evaporated, whole milk, cnd—*½ cup (126 g)*	121	387	519	841	681	215	79	414	414	574	311	233
lowfat, 1% fat—*1 cup (244 g)*	113	362	486	786	637	201	74	388	388	537	291	218
lowfat, 1% fat w/nfdm—*1 cup (245 g)*	120	385	516	835	676	214	79	412	412	571	309	231
lowfat, 1% fat, pro fortified—*1 cup (246 g)*	136	436	585	947	767	242	89	467	467	647	350	262
lowfat, 2% fat—*1 cup (244 g)*	115	367	492	796	644	204	75	392	392	544	294	220
lowfat, 2% fat w/nfdm—*1 cup (245 g)*	120	385	516	835	676	214	79	412	412	571	309	231
lowfat, 2%, pro fortified—*1 cup (246 g)*	137	439	588	952	771	244	90	469	469	650	352	263
skim—*1 cup (245 g)*	118	377	505	818	663	210	77	403	403	559	302	227
skim w/nfdm—*1 cup (245 g)*	123	395	529	857	694	219	81	422	422	585	317	237
skim, pro fortified—*1 cup (246 g)*	137	440	589	954	773	244	90	470	470	652	353	264
skim, dry—*¼ cup (30 g)*	153	490	656	1063	860	272	100	524	524	726	393	294
skim, dry, Ca reduced—*1 oz (28 g)*	142	454	609	986	798	252	93	486	486	674	364	273
skim, dry, inst—*1⅓ cup (3.2-oz envelope)*[a] *(91 g)*	451	1442	1932	3129	2533	801	295	1542	1542	2138	1156	866
whole, 3.3% fat—*1 cup (244 g)*	113	362	486	786	637	201	74	388	388	537	291	218
whole, 3.5% fat—*1 cup (244 g)*	119	391	544	842	663	204		408		586		176
whole, 3.7% fat—*1 cup (244 g)*	113	361	484	784	635	201	74	386	386	536	290	217
whole, low Na—*1 cup (244 g)*	107	341	458	741	600	190	70	365	365	506	274	205
whole, dry—*¼ cup (32 g)*	119	380	510	825	668	211	78	407	407	564	305	228
Milk, Other												
filled milk[b,c]—*1 cup (244 g)*	115	367	492	796	644	204	75	392	392	544	294	220
filled milk[b,d]—*1 cup (244 g)*	115	367	492	796	644	204	75	392	392	544	294	220
goat milk—*1 cup (244 g)*	106	398	505	765	708	196	113	377	437	585	291	218
human milk—*1 fl oz (31 g)*	5	14	17	29	21	6	6	14	16	19	13	7
imit milk[c,e]—*1 cup (244 g)*	59	181	262	422	344	130	18	229	244	305	169	126
imit milk[d,e]—*1 cup (244 g)*	59	181	262	422	344	130	18	229	244	305	169	126
indian buffalo milk—*1 cup (244 g)*	131	445	496	892	683	237	116	394	447	534	278	189
sheep milk—*1 cup (245 g)*	207	657	829	1438	1256	379	85	696	689	1098	485	409
soybean milk—*1 cup (263 g)*	134	463	460	802	708	142	187	513	508	489		318
soybean milk powder—*1 oz (28 g)*	176	609	597	1053	925	187		667		644		
soybean milk powder, Soyquic—*1 oz (28 g)*	428	1092	1487	2234	1862	392	280	1422	1204	1495	2162	652
Milk Beverages												
choc milk, 1% fat milk—*1 cup (250 g)*	114	366	490	793	642	203	75	391	391	542	293	220
choc milk, 2% fat milk—*1 cup (250 g)*	113	362	486	786	636	201	74	387	387	537	291	218
choc milk, whole milk—*1 cup (250 g)*	112	358	479	776	629	199	73	383	383	530	287	215
choc milk w/malt (whole milk)—*1 cup (265 g)*	38	124	162	265	209	68	28	136	131	187		75
cocoa/hot choc (whole milk)—*1 cup (250 g)*	128	411	551	891	722	228	84	439	439	609	329	247
cocoa, from mix, water added—*1 cup (240 g)*	44	148	195	303	235	76	32	156	159	218		80
eggnog, nonalcoholic—*1 cup (254 g)*	137	444	583	937	758	222	97	463	462	643	378	240
inst breakfast, van, w/whole milk—*1 cup (276 g)*	219	687	91	1524	1157	394	162	762	753	1008		434
malted milk—*1 cup (265 g)*	143	433	567	944	712	239	129	479	464	630		272
milkshake, choc, thick—*1 avg (300 g)*	129	413	554	896	726	229	85	442	442	612	331	248
milkshake, van, thick—*1 avg (313 g)*	170	545	731	1184	958	303	112	583	583	809	437	328

[a] Reconstitutes to 1 qt fluid skim milk
[b] Contains fats or oils other than milk fat w/milk solids (milk, cream, or skim milk)
[c] Contains blend of hydrogenated soybean, cottonseed, and/or safflower oils
[d] Contains lauric acid oil; lauric oils include modified coconut oil, hydrogenated coconut oil, and/or palm kernel oil
[e] Contains fats or oils other than milk fat w/food solids, excluding milk solids

	try	thr	iso	leu	lys	met	cys	phe	tyr	val	arg	his
Milk Beverage Mixes												
cocoa mix—*1 oz (28 g)*	44	164	192	300	232	75		154		216		
malt powder—*2–3 hp t (21 g)*	29	70	82	157	75	38	55	92	76	94		55
malt powder, choc—*2–3 hp t (21 g)*	9	37	39	73	39	17	16	52	35	47		55
Yogurt (From Cow Milk)												
plain, lowfat w/nfdm—*1 cup (227 g)*	67	489	650	1201	1068	351		650	601	986	359	295
plain, skim w/nfdm—*1 cup (227 g)*	73	534	709	1311	1166	383		709	656	1076	391	322
plain, whole milk—*1 cup (227 g)*	44	323	430	794	706	232		430	398	652	237	195
coffee/van flavored, lowfat w/nfdm—*1 cup (227 g)*	63	460	610	1128	1003	330		610	565	926	337	277
fruit flavored, lowfat w/nfdm—*1 cup (227 g)*	51	371	493	911	810	266		493	456	748	272	224
NUTS, NUT PRODUCTS & SEEDS												
Nuts & Nut Products												
almonds—*12–15 nuts (15 g)*	26	92	131	218	87	39		172		169		
almonds, salted—*12–15 nuts (15 g)*	26	92	131	218	87	39		172		169		
almond paste—*1 oz (28 g)*	30	103	147	245	98	44		193		190		
brazil nuts—*4 med (15 g)*	28	63	89	169	66	141		93		123		
cashews, roasted—*6–8 nuts (15 g)*	64	103	170	212	111	49		132		222		
cashews, roasted—*20–26 nuts (50 g)*	215	344	567	705	370	164		438		740		
coconut, fresh meat—*1 piece (15 g)*	5	19	27	40	23	11		26		32		
coconut, fresh, shredded—*½ cup (48 g)*	16	62	87	130	73	34		84		103		
filberts (hazelnuts)—*10–12 nuts (15 g)*	27	52	107	118	53	18		68		118		
mixed nuts—*8–12 nuts (15 g)*	71	111	183	228	119	53		142		239		
mixed nuts—*27–40 nuts (50 g)*	236	368	611	759	396	176		473		796		
peanuts, raw, w/skin—*1 oz (28 g)*	90	219	335	495	290	72		412		405		
peanuts, raw, w/o skin—*1 oz (28 g)*	94	230	351	519	305	75		431		425		
peanuts, roasted, w/skin—*1 oz (28 g)*	100	244	374	554	324	80		460		452		
peanuts, roasted, w/skin, salted—*1 oz (28 g)*	102	248	379	561	329	81		466		459		
peanuts, roasted, w/o skin, salted—*1 oz (28 g)*	110	266	406	600	352	88		500		492		
peanut butter—*1 T (15 g)*	50	120	184	272	160	39		227		223		
peanut butter—*6–7 T (100 g)*	330	803	1228	1816	1066	263		1510		1487		
pecans—*12 halves (15 g)*	21	58	83	116	65	23		85		79		
sesame seeds, decorticated—*1 T (8 g)*	38	94	103	172	66	72	42	122	90	118	266	54
sesame seeds, decorticated—*1 oz (28 g)*	135	333	365	609	234	255	149	432	319	418	942	191
soybean nuts—*1 oz (28 g)*	tr	1	1	2	2	tr		2		1		
walnuts, english—*8–15 halves (15 g)*	26	88	115	184	66	46		115		146		
walnuts, english, chopped—*1 T (8 g)*	14	47	61	98	35	24		61		78		
Seeds												
pumpkin & squash kernels—*1 oz (28 g)*	146	244	455	641	374	154		455		244		
safflower seed kernels—*1 oz (28 g)*	86	182	24	348	193	91		332		310		
sesame seeds, decorticated—*1 oz (28 g)*	87	188	250	443	153	168		387		234		
sunflower seed kernels—*1 oz (28 g)*	101	262	370	511	255	128		356		396		
POULTRY[a]												
Chicken												
Flesh & Parts												
broilers/fryers, light & dark meat w/skin, fried, batter dipped—*3½ oz (100 g)*	257	922	1125	1653	1765	591	311	899	732	1100	1378	655
w/skin, fried, flour coated—*3½ oz (100 g)*	323	1181	1439	2092	2320	762	382	1121	928	1392	1766	845
w/skin, roasted—*3½ oz (100 g)*	305	1128	1362	1986	2223	726	364	1061	879	1325	1711	802
w/skin, stewed—*3½ oz (100 g)*	276	1020	1233	1797	2011	657	329	959	796	1199	1545	726
w/o skin, fried—*3½ oz (100 g)*	358	1289	1612	2294	2583	844	393	1217	1031	1516	1839	947
w/o skin, roasted—*3½ oz (100 g)*	338	1222	1528	2171	2458	801	370	1148	977	1435	1745	898
w/o skin, stewed—*3½ oz (100 g)*	319	1153	1441	2048	2318	755	349	1083	921	1353	1646	847

[a] Gram weights are edible portions.

	try	thr	iso	leu	lys	met	cys	phe	tyr	val	arg	his
broilers/fryers, light meat												
w/skin, fried—3½ oz (100 g)	344	1262	1537	2231	2487	815	405	1192	991	1485	1888	904
w/skin, roasted—3½ oz (100 g)	326	1202	1458	2119	2374	776	385	1130	940	1412	1811	858
w/skin, stewed—3½ oz (100 g)	294	1084	1316	1910	2142	699	347	1019	848	1273	1629	774
w/o skin, fried—3½ oz (100 g)	383	1386	1732	2463	2784	908	420	1303	1108	1628	1978	1018
w/o skin, roasted—3½ oz (100 g)	361	1305	1632	2319	2626	855	396	1226	1043	1533	1864	959
w/o skin, stewed—3½ oz (100 g)	337	1220	1525	2167	2454	799	370	1146	975	1433	1742	896
broilers/fryers, dark meat												
w/skin, fried—3½ oz (100 g)	308	1123	1370	1994	2202	725	365	1071	884	1326	1681	804
w/skin, roasted—3½ oz (100 g)	289	1071	1288	1883	2105	688	348	1007	832	1258	1634	759
w/skin, stewed—3½ oz (100 g)	261	969	1167	1705	1906	623	314	911	754	1139	1477	687
w/o skin, fried—3½ oz (100 g)	340	1221	1528	2176	2441	799	375	1156	978	1438	1742	897
w/o skin, roasted—3½ oz (100 g)	320	1156	1445	2053	2325	757	350	1086	924	1357	1651	849
w/o skin, stewed—3½ oz (100 g)	303	1097	1371	1949	2206	719	322	1030	877	1288	1566	806
broilers/fryers, back w/skin, fried—½												
back (72 g)	266	822	1001	1463	1599	529	272	790	647	973	1235	587
broilers/fryers, breast												
w/skin, fried—½ breast (98 g)	357	1300	1599	2306	2581	845	410	1228	1028	1531	1915	940
w/skin, roasted—½ breast (98 g)	333	1219	1495	2154	2424	791	382	1146	960	1432	1800	879
w/skin, stewed—½ breast (110 g)	343	1257	1541	2221	2499	815	395	1181	990	1476	1858	906
w/o skin, fried—½ breast (86 g)	335	1214	1518	2158	2439	796	368	1142	970	1427	1733	892
w/o skin, roasted—½ breast (86 g)	311	1127	1409	2002	2266	739	341	1059	900	1324	1609	828
w/o skin, stewed—½ breast (95 g)	322	1163	1454	2066	2339	762	352	1093	929	1365	1661	855
broilers/fryers, drumsticks												
w/skin, fried—1 drumstick (49 g)	150	549	672	972	1085	355	174	518	432	646	815	395
w/skin, roasted—1 drumstick (52 g)	158	583	708	1028	1152	376	186	548	456	684	876	417
w/skin, stewed—1 drumstick (57 g)	163	599	730	1057	1187	388	191	563	470	704	897	429
w/o skin, roasted—1 drumstick (44 g)	145	526	657	934	1057	345	159	494	420	617	751	386
broilers/fryers, neck												
w/skin, fried—1 neck (36 g)	92	346	403	608	658	218	122	331	264	410	559	237
w/skin, simmered—1 neck (38 g)	76	295	331	510	557	183	107	278	218	347	500	196
w/o skin, simmered—1 neck (18 g)	52	187	233	332	375	122	57	175	149	219	267	137
broilers/fryers, thigh												
w/skin, fried—1 thigh (62 g)	187	685	835	1214	1345	442	222	652	539	808	1027	490
w/skin, roasted—1 thigh (62 g)	174	643	779	1133	1269	415	206	605	502	755	971	458
w/skin, stewed—1 thigh (68 g)	177	654	792	1153	1291	422	211	615	511	768	990	466
w/o skin, roasted—1 thigh (52 g)	158	570	712	1012	1146	373	173	535	456	669	814	419
broilers/fryers, wing												
w/skin, fried—1 wing (32 g)	90	338	396	592	650	214	116	321	258	398	538	233
w/skin, roasted—1 wing (34 g)	98	370	432	645	714	234	126	348	281	435	592	255
w/skin, stewed—1 wing (40 g)	98	370	434	646	716	235	125	348	282	435	588	256
capon, flesh w/skin, roasted—3½ oz (100 g)	325	1200	1455	2115	2370	774	384	1128	938	1409	1806	857
roasters												
flesh w/skin, roasted—3½ oz (100 g)	266	989	1191	1739	1945	636	320	929	769	1162	1506	701
flesh w/o skin, roasted—3½ oz (100 g)	292	1056	1321	1877	2125	693	320	993	844	1240	1509	776
light meat w/o skin, roasted—3½ oz (100 g)	317	1146	1433	2036	2305	751	347	1077	916	1346	1637	842
dark meat w/o skin, roasted—3½ oz (100 g)	272	982	1228	1745	1975	644	298	923	785	1153	1402	722
stewers												
flesh w/skin, stewed—3½ oz (100 g)	301	1113	1348	1961	2197	717	357	1046	869	1307	1680	793
flesh w/o skin, stewed—3½ oz (100 g)	356	1285	1606	2283	2585	842	389	1207	1027	1509	1835	944
light meat w/o skin, stewed—3½ oz (100 g)	386	1396	1744	2479	2807	914	423	1311	1115	1639	1993	1025
dark meat w/o skin, stewed—3½ oz (100 g)	329	1189	1486	2112	2391	779	360	1117	950	1396	1698	874
Chicken, Cnd, Light Meat w/Broth—½ can (2½ oz) (71 g)	173	635	770	1120	1252	408	211	598	496	747	962	452

	try	thr	iso	leu	lys	met	cys	phe	tyr	val	arg	his
Turkey												
flesh & parts												
flesh w/skin, roasted—3½ oz (100 g)	311	1227	1409	2184	2557	790	308	1100	1066	1464	1979	845
flesh w/o skin, roasted—3½ oz (100 g)	333	1304	1525	2336	2763	849	305	1164	1159	1557	2045	915
light meat w/skin, roasted—3½ oz (100 g)	315	1247	1432	2220	2599	803	314	1117	1084	1487	2013	859
light meat w/o skin, roasted—3½ oz (100 g)	340	1330	1555	2383	2818	866	311	1187	1182	1588	2086	933
dark meat w/skin, roasted—3½ oz (100 g)	304	1200	1379	2138	2503	774	302	1076	1044	1432	1936	828
dark meat w/o skin, roasted—3½ oz (100 g)	325	1271	1485	2276	2693	828	297	1134	1129	1518	1993	893
cnd, light meat w/broth—½ can (2½ oz) (71 g)	185	731	840	1301	1522	469	189	655	635	872	1181	503
turkey ham, cured thigh meat—3½ oz (100 g)	215	842	984	1508	1784	548	197	751	748	1006	1321	591
turkey loaf, breast meat—3½ oz (100 g)	256	1001	1170	1793	2120	652	234	893	889	1195	1570	702
Other Poultry												
duck w/skin, roasted—3½ oz (100 g)	232	773	872	1465	1486	475	299	752	640	938	1284	462
duck w/o skin, roasted—3½ oz (100 g)	327	1003	1206	1983	2009	635	361	984	894	1228	1499	620
goose w/skin, roasted—3½ oz (100 g)		1123	1183	2109	1988	608		1055	805	1232	1566	700
pheasant w/o skin, raw—3½ oz (100 g)	328	1180	1324	1995	2157	686	309	920	773	1305	1433	939
quail w/o skin, raw—3½ oz (100 g)	341	1090	1187	1866	1905	689	380	944	1010	1180	1379	825
Internal Organs												
giblets, chicken, fried—3½ oz (100 g)	373	1467	1630	2601	2348	810	437	1480	1067	1737	2159	759
giblets, chicken, simmered—3½ oz (100 g)	295	1172	1297	2066	1886	646	343	1170	848	1379	1727	602
giblets, turkey, simmered—3½ oz (100 g)	307	1204	1339	2140	1951	662	354	1207	877	1430	1768	625
gizzard, chicken, simmered—3½ oz (100 g)	243	1251	1281	1907	1877	712	356	1129	825	1216	1950	547
gizzard, turkey, simmered—3½ oz (100 g)	264	1356	1389	2067	2034	772	386	1224	895	118	2114	593
heart, chicken, simmered—3½ oz (100 g)	338	1196	1415	2303	2214	638	359	1183	946	1496	1694	693
heart, turkey, simmered—3½ oz (100 g)	343	1212	1435	2333	2243	646	364	1199	959	1516	1717	702
liver, chicken, simmered—3½ oz (100 g)	343	1083	1294	2198	1843	577	327	1212	857	1535	1493	647
liver, duck, raw—3½ oz (100 g)	264	833	995	1691	1418	444	252	932	660	1181	1148	498
liver, goose, raw—1 liver (94 g)	216	684	818	1388	1165	365	207	766	541	970	943	409
liver, turkey, simmered—3½ oz (100 g)	338	1066	1273	2163	1814	568	322	1193	844	1511	1469	637
SOUPS												
asparagus, crm of, made w/milk—1 cup (248 g)	84	260	340	558	432	144	67	290	270	384	231	159
asparagus, crm of, made w/water—1 cup (244 g)	29	78	98	163	112	41	29	95	76	115	85	49
bean w/bacon, made w/water—1 cup (253 g)	83	326	385	650	536	99	89	440	235	435	415	205
bean w/franks, made w/water—1 cup (250 g)	413	488	823	680	125	110	558	298	550	525	260	498
beef chunky, rts—1 cup (240 g)	465	592	898	929	248	123	481	353	636	609	275	725
beef noodle, made w/water—1 cup (244 g)	46	154	188	315	261	90	59	195	124	207	198	112
black bean, made w/water—1 cup (247 g)	64	249	287	422	415	62	59	311	173	284	331	163
celery, crm of, made w/milk—1 cup (248 g)	74	241	322	518	394	131	55	273	248	360	206	149
celery, crm of, made w/water—1 cup (244 g)	20	59	78	124	73	29	20	78	54	90	59	39
cheese, cond—1 cup (257 g)	144	380	645	1025	761	234	90	558	499	761	324	293
cheese, made w/milk—1 cup (251 g)	128	371	567	906	700	218	83	474	444	650	309	256

	try	thr	iso	leu	lys	met	cys	phe	tyr	val	arg	his
cheese, made w/water—*1 cup (247 g)*	72	190	321	511	380	116	44	279	249	380	163	146
chicken & dumplings, made w/water— *1 cup (241 g)*	53	193	243	407	378	108	72	224	142	277	292	137
chicken, chunky, rts—*1 cup (251 g)*	123	437	552	924	853	243	163	505	326	628	660	311
chicken, crm of, made w/milk—*1 cup (248 g)*	99	312	414	657	533	181	87	347	312	444	312	201
chicken, crm of, made w/water—*1 cup (244 g)*	41	129	171	264	215	81	51	154	117	173	166	93
chicken gumbo, made w/water—*1 cup (244 g)*	22	83	100	168	161	46	17	98	68	117	122	59
chicken noodle, chunky, rts—*1 cup (240 g)*		437	552	924	854	245	163	504	326	629	662	312
chicken noodle,[a] made w/water—*1 cup (241 g)*	39	128	159	265	219	77	46	164	106	176	166	94
chicken rice, made w/water—*1 cup (241 g)*	41	142	178	270	251	92	51	152	123	188	234	101
chicken veg, made w/water—*1 cup (241 g)*	31	113	135	231	222	60	24	133	94	159	169	80
chili beef, made w/water—*1 cup (250 g)*	70	275	328	553	455	85	73	373	200	368	350	175
clam chowder, New England, made w/milk—*1 cup (248 g)*	117	350	451	719	605	203	102	374	337	489	407	265
clam chowder, New England, made w/water—*1 cup (244 g)*	54	149	183	288	251	90	56	159	127	195	229	137
minestrone, made w/water—*1 cup (241 g)*	31	104	130	236	183	43	34	154	84	178	198	72
mushroom, crm of, cond—*1 can (305 g)*	70	189	235	384	265	95	61	226	183	262	204	113
mushroom, crm of, made w/milk— *1 cup (248 g)*	84	260	340	553	429	141	62	288	270	377	231	156
mushroom, crm of, made w/water— *1 cup (244 g)*	34	90	112	181	127	44	27	107	88	122	95	54
pea, green, made w/milk—*1 cup (254 g)*	130	485	541	1016	831	206	117	572	447	711	853	279
pea, green, made w/water—*1 cup (250 g)*	73	303	298	623	510	105	80	378	250	443	708	170
pea, split w/ham, chunky, rts—*1 cup (240 g)*	110	391	468	766	749	149	144	490	343	526	758	233
pea, split w/ham, made w/water—*1 cup (253 g)*	101	364	435	711	696	139	134	455	319	491	703	215
pepperpot, made w/water—*1 cup (241 g)*	41	195	234	402	311	92	60	234	157	299	494	92
potato, crm of,[b] made w/milk—*1 cup (248 g)*	82	243	320	513	402	131	64	278	255	362	221	149
potato, crm of, made w/water—*1 cup (244 g)*	24	61	76	117	83	29	27	83	61	93	76	39
scotch broth, made w/water—*1 cup (241 g)*	43	154	186	316	304	84	34	181	128	217	231	108
stockpot, made w/water—*1 cup (247 g)*	42	151	183	311	299	82	35	178	126	215	227	109
tomato, made w/milk—*1 cup (248 g)*	77	233	303	494	370	124	64	265	238	335	206	146
tomato, made w/water—*1 cup (244 g)*	20	51	59	100	51	22	27	71	41	66	61	37
tomato beef w/noodle, made w/water— *1 cup (244 g)*	41	144	171	290	242	83	54	181	115	193	183	102
tomato bisque, made w/milk—*1 cup (251 g)*	80	248	321	520	409	131	60	271	254	356	211	153
tomato bisque, made w/water—*1 cup (247 g)*	22	67	77	126	89	30	25	77	59	86	67	44
turkey, chunky, rts—*1 cup (236 g)*	99	404	514	781	809	215	106	418	307	552	531	238
turkey noodle, made w/water—*1 cup (244 g)*	37	124	151	254	212	73	46	156	102	168	159	90
turkey veg, made w/water—*1 cup (241 g)*	27	96	116	198	190	53	22	113	82	135	145	67

[a] Includes chicken noodle o's, chicken w/stars, curly noodle & chicken, and chicken alphabet

[b] Includes vichyssoise

	try	thr	iso	leu	lys	met	cys	phe	tyr	val	arg	his
veg, chunky, rts—*1 cup (240 g)*	26	108	161	271	190	26	26	161	82	190	190	82
veg vegetarian, made w/water—*1 cup (241 g)*	14	75	99	147	99	24	24	99	48	99	99	48
veg w/beef,[a] made w/water—*1 cup (244 g)*	49	173	210	359	344	95	39	205	146	246	261	122
veg w/beef broth, made w/water—*1 cup (241 g)*	22	72	92	164	125	31	24	106	58	125	137	51
SPICES, HERBS & FLAVORINGS												
basil, ground—*1 t (1 g)*	3	8	8	15	9	3	2	10	6	10	9	4
dill seed—*1 t (2 g)*		12	16	19	22	3		14		24	27	7
fennel seed—*1 t (2 g)*	5	12	14	20	15	6	4	13	8	18	14	7
fenugreek seed—*1 t (4 g)*	14	33	46	65	62	13	14	40	28	41	91	25
garlic powder—*1 t (3 g)*	6	13	18	29	16	9	5	14	6	20	47	9
ginger, ground—*1 t (2 g)*	1	3	5	7	5	1	1	4	2	7	4	3
mustard seed, yellow—*1 t (3 g)*	17	36	36	59	50	16	19	35	25	44	58	25
onion powder—*1 t (2 g)*	3	4	6	7	10	2	4	5	5	5	28	3
poppy seed—*1 t (3 g)*	7	25	25	42	31	13	13	25	19	36	56	15
thyme, ground—*1 t (1 g)*	3	4	7	6	3		4		7	7		
SPREADS (BUTTER, MARGARINE, MAYONNAISE)												
butter—*1 t (5 g)*	1	2	3	4	3	1	tr	2	2	3	2	1
butter—*1 T (15 g)*	3	6	9	12	9	3	tr	6	6	9	6	3
butter, sweet (unsalted)—*1 t (5 g)*	1	2	3	4	3	1	tr	2	2	3	2	1
butter, sweet (unsalted)—*1 T (15 g)*	3	6	9	12	9	3	tr	6	6	9	6	3
butter, whipped—*1 t (4 g)*	tr	1	2	3	3	1	tr	2	2	2	1	1
butter, whipped—*1 T (11 g)*	tr	3	6	9	9	3	tr	6	6	6	3	3
margarine, liquid, soybean & cottonseed—*1 t (5 g)*	1	4	5	9	7	2	1	4	4	6	3	2
margarine, stick, corn—*1 t (5 g)*	1	2	2	4	3	1	0	2	2	3	1	1
margarine, stick, safflower & soybean—*1 t (5 g)*	1	2	2	4	3	1	0	2	2	3	1	1
margarine, stick, soybean—*1 t (5 g)*	1	2	2	4	3	1	0	2	2	3	1	1
margarine, stick, soybean & cottonseed—*1 t (5 g)*	1	2	2	4	3	1	0	2	2	3	1	1
margarine, tub, corn—*1 t (5 g)*	1	2	2	3	3	1	0	2	2	2	1	1
margarine, tub, safflower—*1 t (5 g)*	1	2	2	3	3	1	0	2	2	2	1	1
margarine, tub, soybean—*1 t (5 g)*	1	2	2	3	3	1	0	2	2	2	1	1
margarine, tub, soybean & cottonseed—*1 t (5 g)*	1	2	2	3	3	1	0	2	2	2	1	1
margarine, imitation, corn—*1 t (5 g)*	0	1	1	2	2	1	0	1	1	2	1	1
margarine, imitation, soybean & cottonseed—*1 t (5 g)*	0	1	1	2	2	1	0	1	1	2	1	1
mayonnaise, safflower & soybean—*1 T (14 g)*	2	8	9	13	10	5	3	8	6	10	10	4
mayonnaise, soybean—*1 T (14 g)*	2	8	9	13	10	5	3	8	6	10	10	4
spread, stick, soybean & palm—*1 t (5 g)*	0	1	2	3	2	1	0	1	1	2	1	1
spread, tub, soybean & cottonseed—*1 t (5 g)*	0	1	2	3	2	1	0	1	1	2	1	1
VEGETABLES & VEGETABLE SALADS												
asparagus, ckd—*⅔ cup pieces (100 g)*	26	66	79	97	103	33		68		106		
asparagus, cnd—*½ cup (100 g)*	23	57	69	84	90	29		59		92		
asparagus, frzn—*³⁄₅ cup (100 g)*	40	100	119	145	155	50		102		158		
avocado, raw, calif—*1 med (173 g)*	38	121	130	227	173	67	38	125	90	178	109	52
avocado, raw, florida—*1 med (304 g)*	52	161	173	301	228	88	52	164	119	237	143	70
beans (pork & beans) w/tomato sce, cnd—*1 cup (260 g)*	116	559	740	1118	961	130		715		793		

[a] Includes beef, beef veg, & barley & veg beef

	try	thr	iso	leu	lys	met	cys	phe	tyr	val	arg	his
beans, white, ckd—*½ cup (100 g)*	70	335	445	671	577	78		429		476		
beets, raw—*2 med (100 g)*	14	34	51	54	86	6		27		50		
beets, ckd, diced—*½ cup (83 g)*	8	19	29	31	49	4		15		28		
beets, cnd, sliced—*⅗ cup (100 g)*	8	23	35	34	53	5		35		30		
beet greens, raw—*3½ oz (100 g)*	26	84	92	141	119	37		128		110		
beet greens, ckd—*½ cup (100 g)*	20	65	71	109	92	29		99		85		
black-eyed peas (cowpeas), ckd—*½ cup (80 g)*	65	254	312	488	422	98		338		436		
black-eyed peas (cowpeas), cnd—*½ cup (100 g)*	50	195	240	375	325	75		260		335		
black-eyed peas (cowpeas), frzn—*⅔ cup (100 g)*	89	347	427	668	578	134		463		596		
broccoli, raw—*1 stalk (100 g)*	40	133	137	176	158	54		130		184		
broccoli, ckd—*⅔ cup (100 g)*	34	115	118	152	136	46		112		158		
broccoli, frzn—*½ cup (100 g)*	32	107	110	142	128	44		104		148		
brussels sprouts, ckd—*6–8 med (100 g)*	42	147	176	185	189	42		139		185		
brussels sprouts, frzn—*⅗ cup (100 g)*	32	112	134	141	144	32		106		141		
cabbage, green, raw—*1 cup shredded (100 g)*	10	36	51	52	61	12		27		39		
cabbage, green, ckd—*⅗ cup (100 g)*	9	31	43	44	52	10		23		33		
cabbage, red, raw—*1 cup shredded (100 g)*	16	56	78	80	94	18		42		60		
carrots, raw—*1 large (100 g)*	9	40	42	59	48	9		38		51		
carrots, ckd—*⅔ cup (100 g)*	7	32	34	48	39	7		31		41		
carrots, cnd—*⅗ cup (100 g)*	6	29	30	43	34	6		28		37		
cauliflower, raw—*1 cup pieces (100 g)*	35	113	116	181	151	54		84		162		
cauliflower, ckd—*⅞ cup (100 g)*	30	97	99	154	129	46		71		138		
cauliflower, frzn—*⅗ cup (100 g)*	25	80	82	127	106	38		59		114		
celery, raw—*1 stalk (50 g)*	4				6	5						
celery, raw, diced—*1 cup (100 g)*	8				12	10						
celery, ckd, diced—*⅘ cup (100 g)*	8				12	10						
chard, raw—*3½ oz (100 g)*	24	98	103	130	94	7		79		94		
chard, ckd—*⅗ cup (100 g)*	18	74	77	97	70	5		97		70		
chicory greens, raw—*30–40 small leaves (100 g)*	28				58	18						
collard greens, raw—*3½ oz (100 g)*	50	104	112	202	187	43		115		180		
collard greens, ckd—*½ cup (100 g)*	38	78	84	151	140	32		86		135		
collard greens, frzn—*⅗ cup (100 g)*	41	84	90	162	151	35		93		145		
corn, yellow, on the cob, ckd—*4-inch ear (100 g)*	20	135	122	363	122	63		185		208		
corn, yellow, on the cob, frzn—*3-inch ear (90 g)*	19	130	117	347	117	59		176		198		
corn, yellow, cnd—*⅗ cup (100 g)*	11	78	70	209	70	36		106		120		
cowpeas, mature seeds, ckd—*3½ oz (100 g)*	51	199	244	382	332	76		265		342		
cucumber w/skin, raw—*½ med (50 g)*	4	14	16	23	22	5		12		17		
cucumber w/o skin, raw—*½ med (50 g)*	2	8	9	13	13	3		7		10		
eggplant, raw, diced—*½ cup (100 g)*	11	42	61	74	32	6		53		71		
eggplant, ckd, diced—*½ cup (100 g)*	9	35	51	62	27	5		44		59		
garbanzo beans (chick-peas), cnd—*3½ oz (100 g)*	82	369	594	758	707	133		502		502		
garden cress, raw—*5–8 sprigs (10 g)*	5	15	14	23	16	2		11		15		
garden cress, ckd—*3½ oz (100 g)*	30	93	86	146	101	11		68		93		
green beans, french style, frzn—*⅖ cup (100 g)*	22	61	72	93	83	24		38		77		
green beans, snap, ckd—*1 cup (125 g)*	28		90	116	104	30		48	76	96		
green beans, snap, cnd—*⅔ cup (100 g)*	15	42	50	64	57	16		26		53		
green beans, snap, frzn—*⅔ cup (100 g)*	22	61	72	93	83	24		38		77		
kale, raw—*3½ oz (100 g)*	46	151	143	273	130	38		172		197		
kale, ckd—*¾ cup (100 g)*	35	115	109	208	99	29		131		150		
kale, frzn, chopped—*½ cup (100 g)*	33	108	102	195	93	27		123		141		

	try	thr	iso	leu	lys	met	cys	phe	tyr	val	arg	his
kidney beans, red, ckd—*⅖ cup (100 g)*	70	335	437	671	577	78		429		468		
kidney beans, red, cnd—*⅖ cup (100 g)*	51	245	319	490	422	57		314		342		
lentils, ckd—*⅔ cup (100 g)*	70	273	413	554	476	55		359		421		
lettuce, raw, butterhead—*3½ oz (100 g)*	12				70	4						
lettuce, raw, iceberg (crisphead)—*3½ oz (100 g)*	12				70	4						
lettuce, raw, romaine (cos)—*3½ oz (100 g)*	13				75	4						
lima beans, green, ckd—*⅝ cup (100 g)*	68	357	441	631	509	122		448		479		
lima beans, green, cnd—*⅗ cup (100 g)*	49	253	313	448	361	86		318		340		
lima beans, green, baby, frzn—*½ cup (95 g)*	63	329	406	581	469	112		413		441		
lima beans, green, frzn, fordhook—*⅗ cup (100 g)*	67	348	429	614	496	118		437		466		
lima beans, mature, boiled—*⅝ cup (115 g)*	85	442	545	780	630	150		555		592		
mung bean sprouts, raw—*3½ oz (100 g)*	27	118	213	346	258	42		182		224		
mung bean sprouts, boiled—*3½ oz (100 g)*	22	99	179	291	218	35		154		189		
mushrooms, raw—*10 small (100 g)*	8		597	316		189				424		
mushrooms, cnd—*⅓ cup (90 g)*	3		243	129		77				173		
mushrooms, fried/sauteed—*4 med (70 g)*	8		597	316		189				424		
mustard greens, raw—*3½ oz (100 g)*	48	78	99	81	147	30		96		141		
mustard greens, ckd—*½ cup (100 g)*	35	57	73	59	108	22		70		103		
mustard greens, frzn, chopped—*½ cup (100 g)*	35	57	73	59	108	22		70		103		
okra, ckd—*8-9 pods (100 g)*	20	74	76	112	84	24		72		100		
okra, frzn, whole—*⅔ cup (95 g)*	17	63	65	95	71	20		61		85		
onions, raw—*1 med (100 g)*	22	24	22	39	69	14		42		33		
onions, raw, chopped—*1 T (10 g)*	3	3	3	5	9	2		6		4		
onions, ckd—*½ cup (100 g)*	18	19	18	31	55	11		43		26		
onions, dehydrated, instant flakes—*1 T (4 g)*	5	6	5	9	16	3		10		8		
parsley, raw—*3½ oz (100 g)*	72				230	18						
parsley, raw, chopped—*1 T (10 g)*	7				23	2						
peas, raw—*¾ cup (100 g)*	50	101	290	397	296	44		246		258		
peas, ckd—*⅔ cup (100 g)*	43	86	248	340	254	38		211		221		
peas, cnd—*⅗ cup (100 g)*	38	75	216	296	221	33		183		193		
peas, frzn—*⅗ cup (100 g)*	41	82	235	321	240	36		199		209		
peas, mature, split, ckd—*½ cup (90 g)*	80	285	409	606	532	87		365		409		
peas, mature, whole, ckd—*½ cup (90 g)*	79	281	403	598	526	86		360		403		
pepper, bell, raw—*1 large (100 g)*	8	50	46	46	50	16		55		32		
pepper, bell, baked—*1 med (65 g)*	6	34	30	30	34	10		37		22		
pepper, bell, boiled—*1 large (100 g)*	7	42	38	38	42	13		46		27		
potato, raw—*1 med (100 g)*	21	86	92	105	111	25		92		111		
potato, baked—*1 med (100 g)*	26	107	114	130	138	31		114		138		
potato, baked—*1 large (150 g)*	39	160	172	195	207	47		172		207		
potato, boiled w/skin—*1 med (100 g)*	21	86	92	105	111	25		92		111		
potato, boiled w/o skin—*1 med (100 g)*	19	78	84	95	101	23		84		101		
potato, cnd, whole—*⅗ cup (100 g)*	11	45	48	55	58	13		48		58		
potato, fried—*½ cup (85 g)*	34	139	150	170	180	41		150		180		
potato, fries, homemade—*10 pieces (50 g)*	21	86	92	105	111	25		92		111		
potato, fries, reg cut, frzn—*⅗ cup (100 g)*	36	149	159	180	191	43		159		191		
potato, hash browns, homemade—*½ cup (100 g)*	31	127	136	155	164	37		136		164		
potato, mashed w/milk & margarine—*½ cup (100 g)*	21	86	92	105	111	25		92		111		
pumpkin, cnd—*⅖ cup (100 g)*	13	30	56	79	46	19		56		54		

	try	thr	iso	leu	lys	met	cys	phe	tyr	val	arg	his
radish, red, raw—*10 small (100 g)*	4	49			28	2				25		
rice, brown, ckd—*⅘ cup (150 g)*	42	148	179	327	148	68		190		266		
rice, white, all varieties, enr/unenr, ckd—*⅘ cup (150 g)*	33	117	141	258	117	54		150		210		
rice, white, long grain, inst, ckd—*⅔ cup (122 g)*	26	94	113	207	94	43		120		168		
rice, white, parboiled, enr, ckd—*⅘ cup (150 g)*	35	125	150	275	125	58		160		224		
scallions, raw—*5 med (100 g)*	16	18	16	29	51	10		31		24		
soybean sprouts, raw—*1 cup (100 g)*		161	223	267	211	43		186		223		
soybean sprouts, ckd—*¾ cup (100 g)*		138	191	228	180	37		159				
soybeans, immature, ckd—*⅔ cup (100 g)*	147	421	578	833	676	147		529		568		
soybeans, immature, cnd—*⅔ cup (100 g)*	135	387	531	765	621	135		486		522		
soybeans, mature, ckd—*½ cup (100 g)*	165	423	649	935	759	165		594		638		
spinach, raw—*3½ oz (100 g)*	51	141	150	246	198	54		138		176		
spinach, ckd—*½ cup (90 g)*	43	119	127	208	167	46		116		148		
spinach, cnd—*½ cup (100 g)*	39	105	113	185	149	41		103		131		
spinach, frzn—*½ cup (100 g)*	48	132	141	231	186	51		129		165		
squash, chayote, raw—*½ cup (100 g)*	8				38	1						
squash, summer, raw—*½ cup (100 g)*	9	25	35	50	42	14		30		41		
squash, summer, boiled—*½ cup (100 g)*	7	21	29	41	34	12		24		33		
squash, summer, frzn—*⅔ cup (100 g)*	11	32	45	63	53	18		38		52		
squash, winter, baked—*½ cup (100 g)*	14	41	58	81	68	23		49		66		
squash, winter, boiled, mashed—*⅖ cup (100 g)*	9	25	35	50	42	14		30		41		
squash, winter, frzn—*⅖ cup (100 g)*	10	28	38	54	46	16		32		45		
sweet potato, baked—*1 small (100 g)*	36	99	101	120	99	38		116		157		
sweet potato, baked—*1 large (180 g)*	65	179	182	217	179	68		209		285		
sweet potato, candied—*3½ oz (100 g)*	22	61	62	74	61	23		72		98		
sweet potato, cnd—*1 small (100 g)*	34	94	96	114	94	36		110		150		
sweet potato, cnd, syrup pack—*1 small (100 g)*	17	47	48	57	47	18		55		75		
taro, hawaiian, corms, raw—*¾ cup diced (100 g)*	34	89	99	169	110	21		99		114		
taro, hawaiian, leaves, raw—*8 leaves (100 g)*	54	141	156	267	174	33		156		180		
tomato, red, raw—*1 small (100 g)*	10	36	32	45	46	8		31		31		
tomato, red, raw—*1 med (150 g)*	15	54	48	68	69	12		46		46		
tomato, red, raw—*1 large (200 g)*	20	72	64	90	92	16		62		62		
tomato, red, boiled—*½ cup (100 g)*	12	43	38	53	55	9		36		36		
tomato, red, cnd, whole, peeled—*⅖ cup (100 g)*	9	33	29	41	42	7		28		28		
tomato puree, cnd—*29-oz can (822 g)*	123	460	403	575	584	99		395		395		
turnip, ckd, diced—*⅔ cup (100 g)*		14			42	9		14				
turnip greens, raw—*3½ oz (100 g)*	48	129	111	213	135	54		150		153		
turnip greens, ckd—*⅔ cup (100 g)*	35	95	81	156	99	40		110		112		
turnip greens, cnd, chopped—*1 cup (235 g)*	56	150	132	249	160	63		176		179		
watercress, raw—*10 sprigs (10 g)*	4	11	10	17	12	1		8		11		
watercress, raw—*3½ oz (100 g)*	35	108	99	169	117	13		79		108		
wax beans, ckd—*½ cup (100 g)*	20	53	63	81	73	21		34		67		
wax beans, cnd—*⅔ cup (100 g)*	20	53	63	81	73	21		34		67		
wax beans, frzn—*⅔ cup (100 g)*	24	65	76	99	88	26		41		82		
yam, ckd[a]—*1 cup (200 g)*	82				254	76						
yautia (melanga/tanier), raw—*1 corm (100 g)*	29				82	19						

[a] The values are for the true yam of tropical areas (*Dioscorea* species), rather than for the American "yam," which is really a sweet potato.

	try	thr	iso	leu	lys	met	cys	phe	tyr	val	arg	his
MISCELLANEOUS												
amaranth (red dye)—*2 t (10 g)*	4	6	16	21	14	3		10		14		
pickle, bread & butter—*4 slices (25 g)*	1	6	7	8	10	2		5		8		
pickle, dill—*1 large (100 g)*	5	19	22	30	31	7		16		24		
pickle, sour—*1 large (105 g)*	4	14	16	22	22	5		12		17		
pickle, sweet—*1 large (100 g)*	5	19	22	30	31	7		16		24		
whey, acid, dry—*1 T (3 g)*	7	17	17	32	29	6	6	11	9	17	9	7
whey, acid, fluid—*1 cup (246 g)*	38	94	93	178	161	35	34	62	48	92	52	37
whey, sweet, dry—*1 T (8 g)*	15	61	54	88	77	18	19	30	27	52	28	18
whey, sweet, fluid—*1 cup (246 g)*	33	132	116	192	166	39	41	66	59	113	61	38
yeast, baker's, dry (active)—*1 T (8 g)*	35	182	182	318	253	68		167		232		
yeast, brewer's, debittered—*1 T (10 g)*	74	248	252	338	345	89		201		287		

Alcoholic Beverages—Caloric, Carbohydrate & Alcoholic Content

Beverage—Serving	Weight (g)	KCAL	CHO (g)	Alcohol (g)	Alcohol (% by wt)	Alcohol[a] (% by vol)
DISTILLED LIQUORS						
brandy—*1 brandy glass*	30	73		10.5	35.0	43.8
cider, fermented—*6 fl oz*	180	71	1.8	9.4	5.2	6.5
cordials[b] & liqueurs—*1 fl oz*	34	97	11.5	7.3	22.1	30.4
anisette—*1 cordial glass*	20	74	7.0	7.0	35.0	43.7
apricot brandy—*1 cordial glass*	20	64	6.0	6.0	30.0	37.5
benedictine—*1 cordial glass*	20	69	6.6	6.6	33.0	41.2
creme de menthe—*1 cordial glass*	20	67	6.0	7.0	35.0	43.7
curacao—*1 cordial glass*	20	54	6.0	6.0	30.0	37.5
gin, rum, vodka, whisky (rye/scotch)						
80 proof—*1½ fl oz*[c]	42	97	tr	14.0	33.4	38.9
86 proof—*1½ fl oz*[c]	42	105	tr	15.1	36.0	41.9
90 proof—*1½ fl oz*[c]	42	110	tr	15.9	37.9	44.2
94 proof—*1½ fl oz*[c]	42	116	tr	16.7	39.7	46.4
100 proof—*1½ fl oz*[c]	42	124	tr	17.9	42.5	49.7
WINES						
champagne, domestic—*1 wine glass*	120	84	3.0	11.0	9.2	11.5
champagne, dry—*1 champagne glass*	135	105	3.0	13.0	9.6	12.0
champagne, sweet—*1 champagne glass*	135	160	17.0	13.0	9.6	12.0
dessert, dry—*1 wine glass*	103	126	4.1	15.8	15.3	18.8
dessert, sweet—*1 wine glass*	103	153	11.4	15.8	15.3	18.8
madeira—*1 wine glass*	100	105	1.0	15.0	15.0	18.8
muscatel—*1 wine glass*	100	158	14.0	15.0	15.0	18.8
port—*1 sherry glass*	30	50	5.0	4.0	13.3	16.7
sauterne, calif—*1 wine glass*	100	84	4.0	10.5	10.5	13.1
sherry, dry, domestic—*1 wine glass*	60	84	4.8	9.0	15.0	18.8
table—*1 wine glass*	102	85	4.2	9.9	9.7	12.2
table, red—*1 wine glass*	102	76	2.5	9.5	9.3	11.5
table, red, calif—*1 wine glass*	100	85		10.0	10.0	12.5
table, white—*1 wine glass*	102	80	3.4	9.5	9.3	11.5
vermouth, dry (french)—*1 wine glass*	100	105	1.0	15.0	15.0	18.8
vermouth, sweet (italian)—*1 wine glass*	100	167	12.0	18.0	18.0	22.5

[a] Based on 24 g alcohol per fl oz
[b] 54 proof
[c] 1½ fl oz = 1 jigger

Beverage—Serving	Weight (g)	KCAL	CHO (g)	Alcohol (g)	Alcohol (% by wt)	Alcohol[a] (% by vol)
MALT LIQUORS (AMERICAN)						
ale, mild—*8 fl oz*	230	98	8.0	8.9	3.9	4.6
ale, mild—*12 fl oz*	345	147	12.0	13.4	3.9	4.6
beer—*8 fl oz*	240	99	9.0	8.7	3.6	4.5
beer—*12 fl oz*	360	148	13.2	13.1	3.6	4.5
beer, near—*12 fl oz*	360	65		1.3	0.4	0.5
COCKTAILS						
daiquiri—*1 cocktail*	100	122	5.2	15.1	15.1	18.9
eggnog—*4 fl oz punch cup*	123	335	18.0	15.0	12.2	15.6
gin rickey—*4 fl oz*	120	150	1.3	21.0	17.5	21.9
highball—*8 fl oz*	240	166		24.0	10.0	12.5
manhattan—*1 cocktail*	100	164	7.9	19.2	19.2	24.0
martini—*1 cocktail*	100	140	0.3	18.5	18.5	23.1
mint julep—*10 fl oz*	300	212	2.7	29.2	9.7	12.2
old-fashioned—*4 fl oz*	100	179	3.5	24.0	24.0	25.0
planter's punch—*4 fl oz*	100	175	7.9	21.5	21.5	22.4
rum sour—*4 fl oz*	100	165		21.5	21.5	22.4
tom collins—*10 fl oz*	300	180	9.0	21.5	7.2	9.0

[a] Based on 24 g alcohol per fl oz

Beef Cut Names

Names Commonly Used	Other Names Used Regionally
arm pot roast	cross rib roast/thick rib roast/thick end roast/round bone roast/shoulder roast/round shoulder roast
blade pot roast	chuck roast/blade cut chuck roast/square cut chuck roast/English cut roast/7 roast/7 bone roast/flat bone roast
boneless sirloin steak	top loin steak/hip steak/rump steak/top of Iowa steak/top sirloin butt steak/bottom sirloin butt steak
bottom/outside round	silverside/gooseneck/silver tip/Swiss steak
brisket	deckle/boneless brisket/bone-in brisket/fresh boneless brisket/beef breast/brisket pot roast/barbeque beef brisket/corned beef
chuck/short ribs	flanken/brust flanken
chuck tender	scotch tender/Jewish tender/kosher filet/round muscle/fish muscle/top eye pot roast/catfish pot roast
club steak	sirloin steak/sirloin strip steak/Delmonico steak/market steak/individual steak
english cut	Boston cut/bread & butter/boneless English cut
flank steak	London broil/cube steak/minute steak/flank steak filet/Swiss steak
fore shank	shin/fore shin/shank
heel of round	pike's peak/diamond wedge/gooseneck/horseshoe/upper round/lower round/Jew daube/Denver pot roast
loin strip steak	top loin steak/sirloin steak/boneless sirloin steak/New York steak/Kansas City steak/club steak/Delmonico steak/shell steak/strip steak/boneless top sirloin steak/boneless hotel steak/boneless hip steak/minute sirloin steak/key strip steak
mechanically tenderized steaks	cubed steak/chicken steak/minute steak/quick steak/sandwich steak
porterhouse steak	T-bone steak/large T-bone steak/tenderloin steak/king steak
rib eye steak	market steak/spencer steak/beauty steak/Delmonico steak/boneless Delmonico steak/center cut steak/boneless rib steak/club steak/boneless club steak/boneless rib club steak/country club steak/regular roll steak
round	bucket steak/top round/bottom round/eye of round/full cut round/Swiss steak
sirloin, loin end	hip/short hip/head loin/rump/K-style butt/sirloin butt bone-in/sirloin butt/sir butt/sirloin butt/family steak
sirloin tip/knuckle	short sirloin/top sirloin/sirloin butt/crescent/veiny/bell of knuckle/face/face rump/round/boneless sirloin/round tip/ball tip/loin tip/family steak/sandwich steak
short ribs	middle ribs/English short ribs
shoulder clod	scalped shoulder/shoulder roast/boneless shoulder/cross rib/rolled cross rib/clod roast/boneless clod roast/London broil
skirt steak	skirt steak filet
T-bone steak	porterhouse steak/small T-bone steak/club steak/tenderloin steak
tenderloin	filet mignon/petite filet/tenderloin roast/tenderloin tips/tips

Infant Formulas—Sources of Protein, Fat & Carbohydrate

Formula, Company Protein Source	Fat Source	Carbohydrate Source
Advance, Ross cow milk & soy isolate	soy & corn oils	corn syrup solids & lactose
Enfamil & Enfamil w/Fe, Mead Johnson reduced minerals, whey & nonfat milk	coconut & soy oils	lactose
Enfamil Premature Formula, Mead Johnson demineralized whey & nonfat milk	MCT, corn & coconut oils	corn syrup solids & lactose
Isomil 20, Ross soy protein	soy & coconut oils	corn syrup solids & sucrose
Isomil SF 20, Ross soy protein	soy & coconut oils	polycose glucose polymers
MBF (meat-base formula), Gerber beef heart	sesame oil	cane sugar & tapioca starch
Nursoy, Wyeth soy isolate	oleo, coconut, safflower & soy oils	sucrose
Nutramigen, Mead Johnson casein hydrolysate	corn oil	sucrose & modified tapioca starch
Pregestimil, Mead Johnson casein hydrolysate & amino acids	corn oil & MCT	corn syrup solids & modified tapioca starch
ProSobee, Mead Johnson soy isolate	coconut & soy oils	corn syrup solids
Ross CHO Free Soy Protein Formula Base, Ross soy protein	soy & coconut oils	none
Similac & Similac w/Fe (13, 20, 24 & 27 cal/oz), Ross cow milk	soy & coconut oils	lactose
Similac 24 LBW, Ross cow milk	MCT, corn & coconut oils	lactose & corn syrup solids
Similac PM 60/40, Ross cow milk & whey	coconut & corn oils	lactose
Similac Special Care (20 & 24 cal/oz), Ross cow milk & whey	MCT, corn & coconut oils	lactose & corn syrup solids
SMA (13, 20, 24 & 27 cal/oz), Wyeth cow milk & whey	oleo, coconut, safflower & soy oils	lactose
Soylac, Loma Linda soybean solids	soy oil	dextrins, maltose, dextrose & sucrose
L-Soyalac, Loma Linda soy isolate	soy oil	sucrose & tapioca starch

Margarine, Diet Margarines & Spreads (values/T)

Margarine or Spread	Form	KCAL	Fat (g)	SFA (g)	PUFA (g)	PUFA (%)	NA (mg)
Allsweet marg	cube	100	11		3	27	108
A&P marg	cube	100	11		4	32	96
A&P soft marg	tub	100	11		5	43	102
A&P corn oil table spread	cube	100	11		4	34	119
Blue Bonnet marg	cube	100	11		4	32	89
Blue Bonnet soft marg	tub	100	11		4	35	109
Blue Bonnet soft whipped marg	tub	65	7		2	33	55
Blue Bonnet liquid marg	plastic bottle	100	11				
Blue Bonnet soft diet imitation marg	tub	50	6		2	39	95
Blue Bonnet light tasty spread	tub	80	8		3	32	74
Blue Seal Brand marg	cube	100	11				
Bonnie Hubbard marg	cube	100	11	2	3	27	
Chiffon soft stick marg	cube	100	11		3	29	101
Chiffon soft marg	tub	100	11		5	44	99
Chiffon sweet unsalted marg	tub	100	11		5	43	1
Chiffon whipped marg	tub	70	8	1	3	42	60
Coldbrook oleomarg	cube	100	11				
Coldbrook soft marg	tub	100	11		4	34	108
Country Morning marg	pats	100	11	4	1		115
Country Morning whipped marg	tub	50	6	2	1		55
Empress marg	cube	100	11		4	33	95
Empress soft marg	tub	100	11		4	40	86
Fleischmann's marg	cube	100	11	2	4	35	92
Fleischmann's sweet unsalted marg	cube	100	11		4	37	4
Fleischmann's soft marg	tub	100	11	2	5	44	97
Fleischmann's diet imitation marg	tub	50	6	1	2	40	107
Hain marg	cube	100	11				
Holiday marg	cube	100	11	2	3	27	170
Hollywood marg	cube	100	11	2	5	45	
Imperial marg	cube	100	11	4	4	33	103
Imperial soft marg	tub	100	11	3	4	36	87
Imperial diet imitation marg	tub	50	6	1	2	33	102
Imperial light blend	cube					19	73
Individual Servings colored vegetable oleomarg	pats	100	11				
Instant Whip marg	tub	100	11	2	3	27	
Kitchen Craft marg	cube	100	11	2	6	55	
Kroger marg	cube	100	11		3	28	83
Lady Lee marg	cube	100	11	2	3	27	
Lady Lee soft marg	tub	100	11	2	4	36	
Land O Lakes marg, corn oil	cube	100	11	2	4		115
Land O Lakes marg, soy oil	cube	100	11	2	2		115
Land O Lakes soft marg (soy)	tub	100	11	2	4	37	115
Mazola marg	cube	100	11	2	4	36	115
Mazola sweet unsalted marg	cube	100	11	3	4	37	0
Mazola diet imitation marg	tub	50	6	1	2	45	135
Miracle Whip marg	tub	65	7		3	38	65
Mothers sweet unsalted marg	cube	100	11		4	33	1
Mrs. Filbert's Golden Quarters marg	cube	100	11		2	14	92
Mrs. Filbert's soft 100% corn oil marg	cube	100	11	2	5	44	97
Mrs. Filbert's soft golden marg	tub	100	11	2	4	32	99
Mrs. Filbert's spread	tub					32	73
Nucoa marg	cube	100	11	3	3	33	160

Margarine or Spread	Form	KCAL	Fat (g)	SFA (g)	PUFA (g)	PUFA (%)	NA (mg)
Nucoa no-burn marg	cube	100	11	2	3	27	160
Nucoa soft marg	tub	100	11	2	3	39	150
Nu-Maid soft marg	tub	100	11		5	43	116
Nuspread veg oil spread	cube	80	8				
Parkay marg	cube	100	11		2	19	96
Parkay soft marg	tub	100	11	2	4	38	106
Parkay soft corn oil marg	tub	100	11		5	44	97
Parkay whipped marg	tub	65	7		3	40	64
Parkay squeeze marg	plastic bottle	100	11	2	4	45	100
Parkay soft diet imitation marg	tub	50	6	1	2	40	85
Promise marg	cube	100	11		5	45	104
Promise marg	tub	100	11	2	10	85	96
Saffola marg	cube	100	11	2	5	42	103
Satin Gold marg	tub	100	11	2	4	36	
Shedd's liq marg	plastic bottle	100	11	2	6	55	
Southern Belle marg	cube	100	11	2	4	36	111
Southern Belle corn oil marg	cube	100	11	2	3	27	111
Sun Valley marg	cube	100	11	2	3	27	
Supreme Miami marg	cube	100	11	2	3	29	
Table Maid soft marg	tub	90	10				
Weight Watcher's imitation marg	tub	50	6	1	3	50	83
Willow Run marg	cube	100	11	2	3	27	
butter	cube	100	11	7	0	4	116
butter, sweet	cube	100	11	7	0	4	1
butter, whipped	cube	81	9	6	0	4	93

Explanatory Notes: Margarine is usually made from hydrogenated or partially hydrogenated vegetable oils, milk solids, emulsifiers, preservatives, artificial flavor, and artificial color (usually carotene). Margarine contains 80% fat, about 16.5% water, no protein or carbohydrate, and usually no cholesterol unless made with some animal fat. Of the brands listed here only one, Blue Seal, contained an animal fat (hydrogenated lard). Vitamin A is added at a level of 15,000 IU/lb or 10% of the USRDA/serving (1T). Vitamin D may be added at a level of 2,000 IU lb or 15% of the USRDA/serving (1T). Margarine is available in cubes, tubs and liquid form. Unsalted, whipped, diet, and imitation varieties are also available.

The caloric value of regular margarine is 100 kcal/T. Diet or im-

itation margarines and spreads contain less fat, more water, and fewer calories than regular margarine. Diet or imitation margarines usually contain 40% fat, 38–57% water and about 50 kcal/T. Spreads contain about 58% fat and about 74 kcal/T. Whipped margarine has about 65 kcal/T because air has replaced some of the volume.

This table lists various margarines and spreads by brand name with their content of fat, saturated fatty acids, polyunsaturated fatty acids, and sodium. For comparative purposes, butter is listed at the end of the table. Butter, like margarine, is 80% fat and has 100 kcal/T. The fat composition of butter is 65% saturated, 31% monounsaturated, and 4% polyunsaturated. The cholesterol content of butter is 31 mg/T.

Chromium (mcg)

CHEESE

american—*3½ oz (100 g)*	170
swiss—*3½ oz (100 g)*	11

CHIPS & SNACKS

cheese puffed balls, Cheetos—*1 oz (28 g)*	13
cheese puffs, Cheetos—*1 oz (28 g)*	30
cheese puffs w/bacon flavor, Cheetos—*1 oz (28 g)*	15
cheese snacks, Cheetos—*1 oz (28 g)*	10
corn chips, Fritos—*1 oz (28 g)*	31
corn chips, bbq flavor, Fritos—*1 oz (28 g)*	32
corn chips, king size, Fritos—*1 oz (28 g)*	21
corn chips, lights, Fritos—*1 oz (28 g)*	23
funyuns—*1 oz (28 g)*	37
pork rinds, fried, Frito-Lay—*1 oz (28 g)*	27
potato chips, Lay's—*1 oz (28 g)*	34
potato chips, Ruffles—*1 oz (28 g)*	39
potato chips, bacon & sour cream, Ruffles—*1 oz (28 g)*	44
potato chips, bbq flavor, Lay's—*1 oz (28 g)*	24
potato chips, bbq flavor, Ruffles—*1 oz (28 g)*	22
potato chips, cheese flavor, Lay's—*1 oz (28 g)*	26
potato chips, cheese flavor, Ruffles—*1 oz (28 g)*	15
potato chips, no salt added, Lay's—*1 oz (28 g)*	16
potato chips, salt & vinegar flavor, Lay's—*1 oz (28 g)*	17
potato chips, sour cream & onion, Lay's—*1 oz (28 g)*	29
potato chips, sour cream & onion, Ruffles—*1 oz (28 g)*	27
potato crisps, Munchos—*1 oz (28 g)*	34
pretzel rods, Rold Gold—*1 oz (28 g)*	27
pretzel sticks, Rold Gold—*1 oz (28 g)*	40
pretzel, tiny tim, Rold Gold—*1 oz (28 g)*	26
pretzel twists, Rold Gold—*1 oz (28 g)*	34
tortilla chips, Doritos—*1 oz (28 g)*	31
tortilla chips, cheese flavor, Doritos—*1 oz (28 g)*	21
tortilla chips, extra crispy, Doritos—*1 oz (28 g)*	31
tortilla chips, extra crispy, cheese flavor, Doritos—*1 oz (28 g)*	27
tortilla chips, round, Tostitos—*1 oz (28 g)*	42
tortilla chips, round, cheese, Tostitos—*1 oz (28 g)*	27
tortilla chips, taco flavor, Doritos—*1 oz (28 g)*	47

EGGS

chicken—*3½ oz (100 g)*	6

FAST FOODS

Kentucky Fried Chicken®

chicken keel, original recipe—*1 piece (95 g)*	9

FAST FOODS

chicken side breast, original recipe—*1 piece (69 g)*	7
chicken wing, extra crispy—*1 piece (53 g)*	11
chicken wing, original recipe—*1 piece (42 g)*	4
dinner[a]	
drumstick & thigh, extra crispy—*1 dinner (375 g)*	3
drumstick & thigh, original recipe—*1 dinner (346 g)*	3
wing & side breast, extra crispy—*1 dinner (348 g)*	14
wing & side breast, original recipe—*1 dinner (322 g)*	14
wing & thigh, extra crispy—*1 dinner (371 g)*	14
wing & thigh, original recipe—*1 dinner (341 g)*	7
roll—*1 roll (21 g)*	3

FATS & SPREADS

butter—*3½ oz (100 g)*	17
margarine, corn oil—*3½ oz (100 g)*	37
veg oil, corn—*3½ oz (100 g)*	47

FISH

clams, hard shell, raw—*3½ oz (100 g)*	44
clams, soft shell, raw—*3½ oz (100 g)*	36
haddock, raw—*3½ oz (100 g)*	2
halibut, raw—*3½ oz (100 g)*	1
lobster, claw/tail meat, raw—*3½ oz (100 g)*	0
oysters, cnd—*3½ oz (100 g)*	9
scallops, raw—*3½ oz (100 g)*	11
shrimp, raw—*3½ oz (100 g)*	1

FRUIT & FRUIT JUICE

apple, raw—*3½ oz (100 g)*	11
apple, cnd—*3½ oz (100 g)*	139
apricot, cnd—*3½ oz (100 g)*	4
blackberries, raw—*3½ oz (100 g)*	0
black currants, cnd—*3½ oz (100 g)*	3
grapefruit, cnd—*3½ oz (100 g)*	4
orange jce, frzn, reconstituted—*⅖ cup (100 g)*	12
orange, cnd—*3½ oz (100 g)*	2
peach, raw/stewed—*3½ oz (100 g)*	1
peach, cnd—*3½ oz (100 g)*	5
pear, raw—*3½ oz (100 g)*	18
pineapple, cnd—*3½ oz (100 g)*	4
plums, cnd—*3½ oz (100 g)*	104
prunes—*3½ oz (100 g)*	101
raisins—*3½ oz (100 g)*	2

GRAINS & GRAIN PRODUCTS

biscuit mix—*3½ oz (100 g)*	58
bread, white—*3½ oz (100 g)*	47
bread, whole wheat—*3½ oz (100 g)*	63

[a] Includes 2 pieces chicken, mashed potatoes, gravy, coleslaw & roll

GRAINS & GRAIN PRODUCTS

cake—*3½ oz (100 g)*	33
cereal, corn flakes—*3½ oz (100 g)*	4
cereal, shredded wheat—*3½ oz (100 g)*	56
cereal, wheat flakes—*3½ oz (100 g)*	53
cornmeal—*3½ oz (100 g)*	5
crackers—*3½ oz (100 g)*	32
crackers w/cheese, Frito-Lay—*1.5 oz (43 g)*	17
crackers, rye w/cheese, Frito-Lay—*1.5 oz (43 g)*	15
crackers, toast w/peanut butter, Frito-Lay—*1.5 oz (43 g)*	45
crackers, wheat w/cheese, Frito-Lay—*1.5 oz (43 g)*	14
crackers, wheat w/peanut butter, Frito-Lay—*1.5 oz (43 g)*	27
doughnut, cake—*3½ oz (100 g)*	23
farina, dry—*3½ oz (100 g)*	41
flour, all-purpose—*3½ oz (100 g)*	32
flour, cake—*3½ oz (100 g)*	29
macaroni, dry—*3½ oz (100 g)*	26
oatmeal, dry—*3½ oz (100 g)*	6
rice, white, dry—*3½ oz (100 g)*	5
roll, hamburger—*3½ oz (100 g)*	47
rye, whole—*3½ oz (100 g)*	4

MEAT/POULTRY

chicken breast, raw—*3½ oz (100 g)*	26
chicken gizzard, raw—*3½ oz (100 g)*	11
chicken skin, raw—*3½ oz (100 g)*	27
beef chuck, raw—*3½ oz (100 g)*	9
beef tripe, raw—*3½ oz (100 g)*	4
lamb chop, raw—*3½ oz (100 g)*	12
pork chop, raw—*3½ oz (100 g)*	10
partridge gizzard, raw—*3½ oz (100 g)*	13

MILK

cow milk, skim, dry—*3½ oz (100 g)*	7
cow milk, whole—*1 cup (244 g)*	2
human milk—*1 cup (248 g)*	3

NUTS

peanuts, raw—*3½ oz (100 g)*	160
peanut butter—*3½ oz (100 g)*	260

SAUCES & CONDIMENTS

enchilada dip, Fritos—*1 oz (28 g)*	18
jalapeno bean dip, Fritos—*1 oz (28 g)*	15
picante sce, Tostitos—*3 oz (85 g)*	69

SPICES & HERBS

chili powder—*3½ oz (100 g)*	86
cloves—*3½ oz (100 g)*	150
herbs, dried—*3½ oz (100 g)*	11
pepper, black—*3½ oz (100 g)*	370
salt, table—*3½ oz (100 g)*	0
thyme—*3½ oz (100 g)*	1000

VEGETABLES

asparagus, cnd—*3½ oz (100 g)*	11
beans, baked, cnd—*3½ oz (100 g)*	24
beetroot, raw—*3½ oz (100 g)*	8

VEGETABLES

beets, raw—*3½ oz (100 g)*	2
broad beans, frzn—*3½ oz (100 g)*	22
broccoli, raw—*3½ oz (100 g)*	19
brussels sprouts, raw—*3½ oz (100 g)*	14
brussels sprouts, frzn—*3½ oz (100 g)*	16
cabbage, raw—*3½ oz (100 g)*	15
carrots, raw—*3½ oz (100 g)*	8
cauliflower, raw—*3½ oz (100 g)*	2
celery, raw—*3½ oz (100 g)*	11
corn, cnd—*3½ oz (100 g)*	22
corn, frzn—*3½ oz (100 g)*	37
corn on the cob, raw—*3½ oz (100 g)*	2
cucumber, raw—*3½ oz (100 g)*	17
green beans, frzn—*3½ oz (100 g)*	22
kohlrabi, raw—*3½ oz (100 g)*	0
leeks, raw—*3½ oz (100 g)*	8
lentils, dry—*3½ oz (100 g)*	9
lettuce, raw—*3½ oz (100 g)*	17
mushrooms, raw—*3½ oz (100 g)*	25
mushrooms, cnd—*3½ oz (100 g)*	33
navy beans, dry—*3½ oz (100 g)*	8
onions, raw—*3½ oz (100 g)*	19
parsnip, raw—*3½ oz (100 g)*	13
peas, frzn—*3½ oz (100 g)*	38
pepper, green, raw—*3½ oz (100 g)*	19
pepper, red, hot, raw—*3½ oz (100 g)*	1
potatoes, raw—*3½ oz (100 g)*	15
potatoes, frzn, Lamb Weston	
fries, crinkle cuts—*3 oz (85 g)*	10
fries, shoestrings—*3 oz (85 g)*	10
fries, steak—*3 oz (85 g)*	10
hash browns—*3 oz (85 g)*	10
potato puffs—*3 oz (85 g)*	10
roundabouts (fried circles)—*3 oz (85 g)*	10
tater wedges—*2 wedges (91 g)*	10
tater wedges w/skin—*3 oz (85 g)*	10
radish, raw—*3½ oz (100 g)*	0
rhubarb, raw—*3½ oz (100 g)*	4
rhubarb, ckd—*3½ oz (100 g)*	5
rhubarb, cnd—*3½ oz (100 g)*	66
rutabaga (swede)—*3½ oz (100 g)*	9
sauerkraut—*3½ oz (100 g)*	3
spinach, raw—*3½ oz (100 g)*	20
spinach, cnd—*3½ oz (100 g)*	4
spinach, frzn—*3½ oz (100 g)*	6
squash, summer, raw—*3½ oz (100 g)*	2
swiss chard, raw—*3½ oz (100 g)*	6
tomatoes, raw—*3½ oz (100 g)*	24
tomatoes, cnd—*3½ oz (100 g)*	3
turnip greens, raw—*3½ oz (100 g)*	5
yellow-eye beans, dry—*3½ oz (100 g)*	5
watercress, raw—*3½ oz (100 g)*	16
wax beans, raw—*3½ oz (100 g)*	3

MISCELLANEOUS

coffee, inst, dry—*3½ oz (100 g)*	790
cocoa, dry—*3½ oz (100 g)*	60
jelly, cranberry—*3½ oz (100 g)*	0

Cobalt (mcg)

EGG SUBSTITUTE
scramblers, Morningstar Farms—¼ cup (57 g)   11.4

FISH
tuna, light/white, cnd in oil/water—6.5 oz
  (184 g)   110.4

FRUIT
apple, raw—3½ oz (100 g)   1
apricots, cnd—3½ oz (100 g)   1
black currants, cnd—3½ oz (100 g)   1
pears, raw—3½ oz (100 g)   3
pineapple, cnd—3½ oz (100 g)   1
plums, cnd—3½ oz (100 g)   1
prunes, cnd—3½ oz (100 g)   5

MEATS
sheep heart—3½ oz (100 g)   6
sheep kidney—3½ oz (100 g)   25
sheep liver—3½ oz (100 g)   15
sheep pancreas—3½ oz (100 g)   11
sheep spleen—3½ oz (100 g)   9

MEAT ANALOGUES
breakfast links, Morningstar Farms—5 links
  (68 g)   13.6
breakfast patties, Morningstar Farms—2 patties
  (76 g)   30.4
breakfast strips, Morningstar Farms—3 strips
  (24 g)   14.4
grillers, Morningstar Farms—1 patty (64 g)   12.8

NUT PRODUCTS
peanut butter—2 T (32 g)   31.0

VEGETABLES
asparagus, cnd—3½ oz (100 g)   3
asparagus, frzn—3½ oz (100 g)   3
beans, baked, cnd—3½ oz (100 g)   2
beetroot, raw—3½ oz (100 g)   3
broad beans, frzn—3½ oz (100 g)   6
broccoli, raw—3½ oz (100 g)   2
brussels sprouts, raw—3½ oz (100 g)   1
brussels sprouts, frzn—3½ oz (100 g)   3
cabbage, raw—3½ oz (100 g)   3
carrots, raw—3½ oz (100 g)   2
celery, raw—3½ oz (100 g)   2
corn, cnd—3½ oz (100 g)   3
corn, frzn—3½ oz (100 g)   3
cucumbers, raw—3½ oz (100 g)   1
green beans, frzn—3½ oz (100 g)   2
lettuce, raw—3½ oz (100 g)   1
mushrooms, raw—3½ oz (100 g)   3
mushrooms, cnd—3½ oz (100 g)   2
peas, frzn—3½ oz (100 g)   2
potatoes, raw—3½ oz (100 g)   2
rhubarb, cnd—3½ oz (100 g)   2
spinach, raw—3½ oz (100 g)   5
spinach, cnd—3½ oz (100 g)   3
spinach, frzn—3½ oz (100 g)   2
swedes, raw—3½ oz (100 g)   1
tomatoes, raw—3½ oz (100 g)   1
watercress, raw—3½ oz (100 g)   2

Fluoride[a] (mcg/100 g)

	mean	range		mean	range
BEVERAGES			**EGGS**		
beer		20–120	whole, raw	120	
coffee beverage		20–160	white, raw	150	
coffee, inst, dry	170		yolk, raw	59	
cola soda	7				
ginger ale		2–77	**FATS & SPREADS**		
tea, brewed		120–6300	butter	150	
tea, inst, dry	200		salt pork, raw		100–3300
wine		5–30			
			FISH		
CHEESE			cod, raw	700	
cheese		16–160	crab, cnd	200	

[a] The use of fluoridated water by food or beverage processors or in the home during food preparation will increase the fluoride content of foods.

	mean	range		mean	range
FISH			**NUTS**		
herring, smoked	350		almonds	90	
mackerel, raw	2700		hazelnuts	30	
mackerel, cnd	1200				
oysters, raw	65		**POULTRY**		
salmon, cnd		450–900	chicken, raw	140	
sardines, cnd		800–4000	chicken, cnd	63	
shrimp, cnd	44				
tuna, cnd	10		**VEGETABLES**		
			beans (pork & beans), cnd		27–77
FRUIT			beets, raw	20	
apple, raw		5–130	cabbage, raw	15	
apricots, raw		2–22	carrot, raw	40	22–200
banana, raw	23		carrot, cnd		19–61
cantaloupe, raw	20		celery, raw	14	
cherries, raw	25		corn, raw	62	
figs, raw	21		corn, cnd		20–56
gooseberries, raw		11–52	cucumber, raw	20	
grapefruit, raw	36		eggplant, raw	40	
grapes, raw	16		green beans, raw	13	
orange, raw		7–17	green beans, cnd		20–89
peach, raw	21		kale, raw		16–300
pear, raw	19		mixed veg, cnd		37–105
pineapple, raw	14		onion, raw	60	
plums, raw	21		parsley, raw		80–100
strawberries, raw	18		peas, raw	60	
			peas, green, cnd	10	
GRAINS			potato, raw		40–520
cornmeal, dry	22		potato, cnd		38–76
flour, wheat		27–35	radish, raw	80	
oats, dry	25		rhubarb, raw	40	
wheat germ		88–400	rice, white, raw		10–67
wheat, whole grain	70		soybeans, raw	130	
			spinach, raw		20–180
MEATS			tomato, raw	24	
beef, lean & fat, raw		29–200	turnip, raw	30	
beef liver, raw	99		watercress, raw	100	
beef round, raw	130		wax beans, cnd	60	
calf liver, raw	19				
frankfurter	170		**MISCELLANEOUS**		
lamb, raw	120		chocolate candy	50	
pork, raw		34–98	honey	100	
veal, raw	90		soup, tomato, cond, cnd		4–38
MILK					
cow milk, choc		50–200			
cow milk, whole		2–32			

Iodine[a] (mcg)

	mean	range		mean	range
CHEESE			**FAST FOODS**		
cheddar—3½ oz (100 g)	49	17–81	McDonald's®		
cheddar, processed—3½ oz (100 g)	57	21–119	cheeseburger—1 sandwich (115 g)	126	
cottage cheese—3½ oz (100 g)	33	17–68	filet-o-fish—1 sandwich (139 g)	153	
cottage cheese, dry curd—3½ oz (100 g)	38	31–42	hamburger—1 sandwich (102 g)	133	
cottage cheese, low fat—3½ oz (100 g)	36	25–68	quarter pounder—1 sandwich (166 g)	144	
feta—3½ oz (100 g)	7	5–9	quarter pounder w/cheese—1 sandwich (194 g)	130	
mozzarella—3½ oz (100 g)	122	81–157	desserts		
			cookies, chocolaty chip—1 box (69 g)	4	
DESSERTS			ice cream in cake cone—1 serving (115 g)	18	
ice cream—3½ oz (100 g)	39	18–50	ice cream in sugar cone—1 serving (93 g)	13	
ice milk—3½ oz (100 g)	47	28–56	pie, apple—1 snack pie (85 g)	25	
			pie, cherry—1 snack pie (88 g)	74	
EGGS			shake, choc—1 shake (291 g)	79	
chicken eggs—3½ oz (100 g)	26		shake, strawberry—1 shake (290 g)	61	
			shake, van—1 shake (291 g)	76	
FAST FOODS			sundae, caramel—1 sundae (165 g)	48	
Kentucky Fried Chicken®			sundae, hot fudge—1 sundae (164 g)	84	
chicken, drumstick, original recipe—1 piece (47 g)	2		sundae, strawberry—1 sundae (164 g)	18	
chicken, keel, extra crispy—1 piece (104 g)	7		**FISH, SHELLFISH & FISH PRODUCTS**		
chicken, keel, original recipe—1 piece (95 g)	8		cod, dried—3½ oz (100 g)	100	75–139
chicken, side breast, extra crispy—1 piece (85 g)	65		cod liver oil—3½ oz (100 g)	700	510–870
chicken, side breast, original recipe—1 piece (69 g)	104		crayfish—3½ oz (100 g)	44	38–49
chicken, thigh, extra crispy—1 piece (107 g)	7		haddock—3½ oz (100 g)	139	122–169
chicken, thigh, original recipe—1 piece (88 g)	8		octopus—3½ oz (100 g)	20	15–30
chicken, wing, extra crispy—1 piece (53 g)	4		oysters—3½ oz (100 g)	140	100–200
chicken, wing, original recipe—1 piece (42 g)	4		plaice—3½ oz (100 g)	51	9–107
dinners[b]			shrimp—3½ oz (100 g)	36	29–43
drumstick & thigh, extra crispy—1 dinner (375 g)	29		**MILK & CULTURED MILKS**		
drumstick & thigh, original recipe—1 dinner (346 g)	32		buttermilk, cultured—1 cup (245 g)	91	69–127
wing & side breast, extra crispy—1 dinner (348 g)	91		evaporated milk—½ cup (126 g)	105	54–227
wing & side breast, original recipe—1 dinner (322 g)	130		kefir—1 cup (245 g)	39	27–64
wing & thigh, extra crispy—1 dinner (371 g)	33		human colostrum—1 fl oz (31 g)		16–42
wing & thigh, original recipe—1 dinner (341 g)	34		human milk—1 fl oz (31 g)		12–25
gravy—1 serving (14 g)	1		nonfat dry milk—¼ cup (30 g)	167	11–298
mashed potatoes—1 serving (85 g)	6		whole milk—1 cup (244 g)	88	66–142
roll—1 med (21 g)	15		yogurt—1 cup (227 g)	104	48–134
McDonald's®			**NUTS & NUT PRODUCTS**		
breakfast			almond powder, Nutquik—1 oz (28 g)	4	
egg mcmuffin—1 sandwich (138 g)	70		**SPICES**		
english muffin w/butter—1 muffin (63 g)	19		salt—1 t (6 g)	<100	
hash brown potatoes—1 serving (55 g)	6		salt, iodized—1 t (6 g)	400	
pancakes w/butter & syrup—1 serving (214 g)	17		salt substitute, Morton Lite Salt—1 t (6 g)	400	
scrambled eggs—1 serving (98 g)	52		**MISCELLANEOUS**		
sausage—1 serving (53 g)	38		salt, table, iodized—1 g		8–76
big mac—1 sandwich (204 g)	147		sour cream—3½ oz (100 g)	28	22–48
			soy milk powder, Soyquick—1 oz (28 g)	140	
			sugar, brown—3½ oz (100 g)	3	
			sugar, white—3½ oz (100 g)	tr	

[a] The iodine concentrations of foods are exceedingly variable owing to differences in the content and availability of iodine in the soil and to the amount and nature of fertilizers applied. Adding iodine to feed rations greatly increases the iodine content of animal products such as milk and eggs. Foods of marine origin are much higher in iodine than are other classes of foods.

[b] Includes 2 pieces chicken, mashed potatoes, gravy, coleslaw & roll

Molybdenum (mcg)

CHIPS & SNACKS

cheese puffed balls, Cheetos—*1 oz (28 g)*	35
cheese puffs, Cheetos—*1 oz (28 g)*	52
cheese puffs w/bacon flavor, Cheetos—*1 oz (28 g)*	48
cheese snacks, Cheetos—*1 oz (28 g)*	28
corn chips, Fritos—*1 oz (28 g)*	63
corn chips, bbq flavor, Fritos—*1 oz (28 g)*	46
corn chips, king size, Fritos—*1 oz (28 g)*	40
corn chips, lights, Fritos—*1 oz (28 g)*	44
funyuns—*1 oz (28 g)*	47
pork rinds, fried, Frito-Lay—*1 oz (28 g)*	8
potato chips, Lay's—*1 oz (28 g)*	46
potato chips, Ruffles—*1 oz (28 g)*	33
potato chips, bacon & sour cream, Ruffles—*1 oz (28 g)*	40
potato chips, bbq flavor, Lay's—*1 oz (28 g)*	49
potato chips, bbq flavor, Ruffles—*1 oz (28 g)*	52
potato chips, cheese flavor, Lay's—*1 oz (28 g)*	21
potato chips, cheese flavor, Ruffles—*1 oz (28 g)*	30
potato chips, no salt added, Lay's—*1 oz (28 g)*	28
potato chips, sour cream & onion, Lay's—*1 oz (28 g)*	44
potato chips, sour cream & onion, Ruffles—*1 oz (28 g)*	41
potato crisps, Munchos—*1 oz (28 g)*	25
pretzel rods, Rold Gold—*1 oz (28 g)*	79
pretzel sticks, Rold Gold—*1 oz (28 g)*	87
pretzels, tiny tim, Rold Gold—*1 oz (28 g)*	62
pretzel twists, Rold Gold—*1 oz (28 g)*	73
tortilla chips, Doritos—*1 oz (28 g)*	58
tortilla chips, cheese flavor, Doritos—*1 oz (28 g)*	48
tortilla chips, extra crispy, Doritos—*1 oz (28 g)*	60
tortilla chips, extra crispy, cheese, Doritos—*1 oz (28 g)*	69
tortilla chips, round, Tostitos—*1 oz (28 g)*	49
tortilla chips, round, cheese, Tostitos—*1 oz (28 g)*	63
tortilla chips, taco flavor, Doritos—*1 oz (28 g)*	71

FATS & SPREADS

butter—*1 t (5 g)*	0

FISH

halibut, broiled—*3½ oz (100 g)*	4
shrimp, frzn, breaded—*3½ oz (100 g)*	3

FRUIT

strawberries, raw—*1 cup (149 g)*	20

GRAINS & GRAIN PRODUCTS

barley, pearled, dry—*1 oz (28 g)*	40
bread, white, enr—*1 slice (23 g)*	7
buckwheat, whole grain, raw—*1 oz (28 g)*	136
cereal, all-bran—*1 cup (56 g)*	154
cereal, puffed rice—*1 cup (14 g)*	26
crackers w/cheese, Frito-Lay—*1.5 oz (43 g)*	38
crackers, rye w/cheese, Frito-Lay—*1.5 oz (43 g)*	30
crackers, toast w/peanut butter, Frito-Lay—*1.5 oz (43 g)*	41
crackers, wheat w/cheese, Frito-Lay—*1.5 oz (43 g)*	51
flour, all purpose, enr—*1 cup (115 g)*	29
noodles, egg, enr, dry—*1 cup (73 g)*	34
rye, whole grain—*3½ oz (100 g)*	147
wheat germ—*1 T (7 g)*	36
wheat, whole grain—*3½ oz (100 g)*	48

MEATS

beef, lean, ckd—*3½ oz (100 g)*	7
kidney, beef, braised—*3½ oz (100 g)*	2140
kidney, hog, raw—*3½ oz (100 g)*	110
lamb, rib chop, broiled—*2 med (82 g)*	410
pork, lean, ckd—*3½ oz (100 g)*	368

MILK, COW

whole—*1 cup (244 g)*	17

SAUCES & CONDIMENTS

enchilada dip, Fritos—*1 oz (28 g)*	41
jalapeno bean dip, Fritos—*1 oz (28 g)*	62
picante sce, Tostitos—*3 oz (85 g)*	135

VEGETABLES

brussels sprouts, raw—*10 med (100 g)*	4
cabbage, green, raw—*1 cup (90 g)*	1
carrots, raw—*1 cup (81 g)*	7
celery, raw—*1 cup (120 g)*	2
cucumber w/skin—*1 med (105 g)*	1
green beans, raw—*1 cup (100 g)*	66
lentils, raw—*½ cup (95 g)*	66
lettuce, boston & bibb—*1 cup (55 g)*	1
lettuce, iceberg—*1 cup (75 g)*	2
sauerkraut—*1 cup (235 g)*	138
spinach, raw—*1 cup (55 g)*	14
squash, winter, butternut—*1 cup (200 g)*	18
tomato sce—*3½ oz (100 g)*	280
wax beans, raw—*1 cup (100 g)*	43
yam, raw—*1 cup (200 g)*	118

Nickel[a] (mcg/100 g)

	mean	range		mean	range
CEREALS, READY-TO-EAT			**FISH**		
all-bran	74		oysters, raw	150	
grape-nuts	13		sardines, cnd	21	
puffed rice	30		scallops, fresh frzn	4	
shredded wheat		26–64	shrimp, fresh frzn	3	
wheat flakes	71		swordfish, frzn	2	
			tuna, cnd	4	3–5
CHIPS & SNACKS					
cheese puffed balls, Cheetos	232		**FRUIT**		
cheese snacks, Cheetos	111		apple, raw		8–24
corn chips, Fritos	96		apple, cnd	7	
corn chips, bbq flavor, Fritos	79		apple skin, raw	1	
corn chips, king size, Fritos	75		apricot, raw	6	4–8
corn chips, lights, Fritos	100		apricot, cnd	19	
funyuns	214		banana, raw	34	
pork rinds, fried, Frito-Lay	0		black currants, cnd	13	
potato chips, Lay's	93		damsons, cnd	32	
potato chips, Ruffles	104		grapefruit, cnd	24	
potato chips, bacon & sour cream flavor, Ruffles	132		oranges, cnd	3	
potato chips, bbq flavor, Lay's	107		peaches, cnd	9	
potato chips, bbq flavor, Ruffles	125		pear, raw	16	
potato chips, cheese flavor, Lay's	125		pear skin, raw	15	
potato chips, cheese flavor, Ruffles	143		pineapple, cnd	85	
potato chips, no salt added, Lay's	186		plums, raw	15	
potato chips, salt & vinegar flavor, Lay's	93		plums, cnd	36	
potato chips, sour cream & onion flavor, Lay's	175		prunes, cnd	40	
potato chips, sour cream & onion flavor, Ruffles	186				
potato crisps, Munchos	107		**GRAINS & GRAIN PRODUCTS**		
pretzel rods, Rold Gold	111		biscuit mix	72	
pretzel sticks, Rold Gold	96		bread, white	58	
pretzels, tiny tim, Rold Gold	46		bread, whole wheat	82	
pretzel twists, Rold Gold	111		bread, whole wheat, stone-ground	133	
tortilla chips, Doritos	100		cake	82	
tortilla chips, cheese flavor, Doritos	50		crackers	81	
tortilla chips, extra crispy, Doritos	82		crackers, cheese w/peanut butter, Frito-Lay	98	
tortilla chips, extra crispy, cheese flavor, Doritos	118		crackers, toast w/peanut butter, Frito-Lay	167	
tortilla chips, round, Tostitos	79		crackers w/cheese, Frito-Lay	84	
tortilla chips, round, cheese flavor, Tostitos	93		doughnuts, cake	41	
tortilla chips, taco flavor, Doritos	114		farina, dry	28	
			flour, all-purpose	21	17–25
EGGS			flour, cake	18	
chicken, whole	3		macaroni, dry	15	
			oats, dry	235	
FATS			rice, white, dry	47	
veg shortening, hydrogenated	114		rolls, hamburger	52	
FISH			**MEATS**		
anchovies, cnd	72		pork chop, raw	22	
clams, raw	58				
crabmeat, cnd	3		**MILK**		
haddock, frzn	5		evaporated milk, cnd	3	
herring, kippered, cnd	170		nonfat dry milk	3	0–7
lobster, claw meat	66				

[a] Contact of foods with machinery or cans can contribute to dietary nickel. Therefore, processed and canned foods generally contain more nickel than do fresh foods. Low nickel levels are found in refined foods and most foods of animal origin, such as meats and milk. Considerable losses of nickel occur in milling wheat to white flour.

	mean	range		mean	range
SAUCES & CONDIMENTS			**VEGETABLES**		
dip, jalapeno bean, Fritos	125		green beans, frzn	35	
dip, enchilada, Fritos	164		kale	112	
picante sce, Tostitos	92		kidney beans, red, dry	259	
			leeks, raw	13	
SPICES			lettuce, raw	5	
allspice	79		mushrooms, raw	8	
bay leaves	88		mushrooms, cnd	20	
cinnamon	74		navy beans, dry	159	
cloves, whole	10		onions, raw	9	
herbs, dried	6		peas, cnd	46	
nutmeg	117		peas, frzn	35	
pepper, black	393		peas, split, dry	166	
salt, table	35		potato, raw	16	
			rhubarb, raw	9	
			rhubarb, cnd	49	
VEGETABLES			spinach, raw	11	8–16
asparagus, cnd	22		spinach, cnd	27	
asparagus, frzn	42		spinach, frzn	2	
beans, baked, cnd	31		swedes, raw	6	
beetroot, raw	17		swiss chard, raw	71	
broad beans, frzn	55		tomato, raw	17	
broccoli, raw	11		tomato, cnd	49	
broccoli, frzn	33		tomato jce, cnd	5	
brussels sprouts, raw	16		watercress, raw	19	
brussels sprouts, frzn	18		yellow-eyed beans, dry	69	
cabbage, green, raw	19				
cabbage, red, raw	24				
cabbage, white, raw		14–32	**MISCELLANEOUS**		
carrots, raw	3		baking powder	1340	
celery, raw	8		catsup	98	
chicory, raw	55		cocoa, dry	500	
corn, cnd	12		gelatin, dry	450	
corn, frzn	8		sugar, white, granulated	3	
cucumber, raw	8		tea, dry leaves	760	
escarole, raw	27		vinegar, cider	31	
green beans, cnd	17		yeast, active, dry	48	

Selenium (mcg)

	mean	range
CHEESE		
american, processed—3½ oz (100 g)	23	9–30
cheddar—3½ oz (100 g)	12	
cottage—3½ oz (100 g)	23	19–27
swiss—3½ oz (100 g)	10	
CHIPS & SNACKS		
corn chips, king size, Fritos—1 oz (28 g)	182	
potato chips, Ruffles—1 oz (28 g)	275	
potato chips, bacon & sour cream, Ruffles—1 oz (28 g)	386	
potato chips, bbq flavor, Lay's—1 oz (28 g)	301	
potato chips, bbq flavor, Ruffles—1 oz (28 g)	221	
potato chips, cheese flavor, Lay's—1 oz (28 g)	258	
potato chips, sour cream & onion, Ruffles—1 oz (28 g)	255	
tortilla chips, extra crispy, Doritos—1 oz (28 g)	224	
tortilla chips, round, Tostitos—1 oz (28 g)	284	
tortilla chips, round, cheese flavor, Tostitos—1 oz (28 g)	265	
tortilla chips, taco flavor, Doritos—1 oz (28 g)	303	
EGGS		
egg white—3½ oz (100 g)		5–6
egg yolk—3½ oz (100 g)		18–20
FISH, SHELLFISH & SEAFOOD		
blue whiting, raw—3½ oz (100 g)	31	25–43
cod, raw—3½ oz (100 g)	29	17–43
cod fillet, raw—3½ oz (100 g)	43	
eel, raw—3½ oz (100 g)	40	35–46
fish sticks—3½ oz (100 g)	12	
flounder fillet, raw—3½ oz (100 g)	34	
herring, raw—3½ oz (100 g)	61	
kipper—3½ oz (100 g)	32	
ling, raw—3½ oz (100 g)	34	31–36
lobster tail, raw—3½ oz (100 g)	66	
mackerel, raw—3½ oz (100 g)	35	22–44
mussel, raw—3½ oz (100 g)	48	46–51
oysters, raw—3½ oz (100 g)	65	
perch, raw—3½ oz (100 g)	24	12–66
pike, raw—3½ oz (100 g)	13	8–24
pike-perch, raw—3½ oz (100 g)	26	21–31
plaice, raw—3½ oz (100 g)	65	26–104
redfish, raw—3½ oz (100 g)	44	26–53
shrimp, raw—3½ oz (100 g)	31	28–59
sole, raw—3½ oz (100 g)	24	15–29
tuna, cnd—3½ oz (100 g)	115	90–139
FRUITS		
apple, raw—3½ oz (100 g)	0.4	
applesce, cnd—3½ oz (100 g)	0.2	
applesce, str—3½ oz (100 g)		0.0–5.0
banana, raw—3½ oz (100 g)	1.0	
cantaloupe, raw—3½ oz (100 g)	0.4	
grapes, white, raw—3½ oz (100 g)	0.2	
orange, raw—3½ oz (100 g)	1.3	
FRUITS		
pear, raw—3½ oz (100 g)	0.6	
peach, raw, peeled—3½ oz (100 g)	0.4	
peach, cnd—3½ oz (100 g)	0.3	
pineapple, raw—3½ oz (100 g)	0.6	
pineapple, cnd—3½ oz (100 g)	1.0	
GRAINS & GRAIN PRODUCTS		
barley cereal, dry—3½ oz (100 g)	66	
barley, pearled—3½ oz (100 g)	38	28–56
bread, rye—3½ oz (100 g)	28	21–39
bread, white—3½ oz (100 g)	28	17–42
bread, whole wheat—3½ oz (100 g)	45	37–54
cereal, infant—3½ oz (100 g)	28	
cereal, rte, breakfast		
cheerios—3½ oz (100 g)	43	
corn flakes—3½ oz (100 g)	3	
puffed rice—3½ oz (100 g)	3	
wheaties—3½ oz (100 g)	11	
crackers—3½ oz (100 g)	14	5–39
flour, bread—3½ oz (100 g)	42	
flour, soybean—3½ oz (100 g)	9	
flour, wheat, white—3½ oz (100 g)	36	23–44
flour, wheat, whole grain—3½ oz (100 g)		53–64
macaroni, dry—3½ oz (100 g)	61	47–74
macaroni, enr, ckd—³/₅ cup (90 g)	25	
noodles, egg, dry—3½ oz (100 g)	59	41–85
noodles, enr, ckd—³/₅ cup (92 g)	24	
noodles, lasagna, dry—3½ oz (100 g)	96	
oats, dry—3½ oz (100 g)		3–11
pancake mix, dry—3½ oz (100 g)	9	
popcorn, unpopped—3½ oz (100 g)	20	12–32
rice, brown, dry—3½ oz (100 g)	39	
rice, white, dry—3½ oz (100 g)	20	7–32
spaghetti, dry—3½ oz (100 g)	61	47–74
wheatena, dry—3½ oz (100 g)	24	
wheat, hard blends—3½ oz (100 g)		33–78
wheat, whole—3½ oz (100 g)	50	
wild rice, dry—3½ oz (100 g)	4	
INFANT FOODS		
cereals		
dry—3½ oz (100 g)	28	
oatmeal w/applesce & ban, str—3½ oz (100 g)	3.0	
rice w/applesce & ban, str—3½ oz (100 g)	2.1	
desserts		
van custard pudding, str—3½ oz (100 g)	1.5	
fruits		
peaches, str—3½ oz (100 g)	0.3	
pears, str—3½ oz (100 g)	0.3	
infant formula, dry—3½ oz (100 g)	8	
meats/poultry		
beef, str—3½ oz (100 g)	11.5	
chicken, str—3½ oz (100 g)	10.6	
lamb, str—3½ oz (100 g)	13.1	
liver, str—3½ oz (100 g)	25.8	
pork, str—3½ oz (100 g)	12.4	

	mean	range		mean	range
INFANT FOODS			**POULTRY**		
vegetables			chicken leg, raw—3½ oz (100 g)	14	
carrots, str—3½ oz (100 g)	0.2		chicken liver, raw—3½ oz (100 g)	71	65–81
green beans, str—3½ oz (100 g)	0.4		chicken skin, raw—3½ oz (100 g)	15	
			chicken thigh, raw—3½ oz (100 g)	40	35–45
MEATS			pheasant breast, raw—3½ oz (100 g)	54	26–138
beef, raw—3½ oz (100 g)	24	18–37	pheasant liver, raw—3½ oz (100 g)	108	60–170
beef, corned, raw—3½ oz (100 g)	25	14–37	pheasant thigh, raw—3½ oz (100 g)	48	32–98
beef, dried/jerky—3½ oz (100 g)	54	26–117			
beef, ground, raw—3½ oz (100 g)	24	17–43	**VEGETABLES**		
beef, round steak, raw—3½ oz (100 g)	34		beets, raw—3½ oz (100 g)	0.6	0.3–0.9
beef heart, raw—3½ oz (100 g)	38	22–57	carrot, raw—3½ oz (100 g)	2.2	
beef kidney, raw—3½ oz (100 g)	145	106–178	carrot, cnd—3½ oz (100 g)	1.3	
beef liver, raw—3½ oz (100 g)		20–79	cabbage, raw—3½ oz (100 g)	2.2	
lamb, raw—3½ oz (100 g)	32	15–54	cauliflower, raw—3½ oz (100 g)	0.6	
lamb chop, raw—3½ oz (100 g)	18		celery, raw—3½ oz (100 g)	0.3	
lamb heart, raw—3½ oz (100 g)	49	35–75	corn, raw—3½ oz (100 g)	0.4	
lamb kidney, raw—3½ oz (100 g)		136–145	corn, cnd—3½ oz (100 g)	0.4	
lamb liver, raw—3½ oz (100 g)	98	54–152	garlic, raw—3½ oz (100 g)	24.9	
pork, raw—3½ oz (100 g)	31	17–35	green beans, raw—3½ oz (100 g)	0.6	
pork bacon, raw—3½ oz (100 g)	26	19–38	green beans, cnd—3½ oz (100 g)	0.9	
pork chop, raw—3½ oz (100 g)	17		lettuce, raw—3½ oz (100 g)	0.8	
pork, ham, cured—3½ oz (100 g)	47	33–51	mushrooms, raw—3½ oz (100 g)	13.2	
pork heart, raw—3½ oz (100 g)	35	25–40	mushrooms, cnd—3½ oz (100 g)	10.4	
pork kidney, raw—3½ oz (100 g)	210	175–256	navy beans, dry—3½ oz (100 g)	13.0	11.0–14.0
pork liver, raw—3½ oz (100 g)	70	56–80	onion, white, raw—3½ oz (100 g)	1.5	
pork sausage, raw—3½ oz (100 g)	33	20–68	peas, dry—3½ oz (100 g)	1.5	
			pepper, green, raw—3½ oz (100 g)	0.7	
MEATS, LUNCHEON			potato, raw—3½ oz (100 g)	0.4	
bratwurst—3½ oz (100 g)	29	23–35	potato, cnd—3½ oz (100 g)	0.9	
frankfurter—3½ oz (100 g)	23	10–40	onion, raw—3½ oz (100 g)	3.4	0.7–6.1
salami—3½ oz (100 g)	35	20–67	radish, raw—3½ oz (100 g)	3.9	
summer sausage—3½ oz (100 g)	35	20–67	squash, summer, raw—3½ oz (100 g)	3.2	
			sweet potato, raw—3½ oz (100 g)	0.7	
MILK			tomato, raw—3½ oz (100 g)	0.5	0.4–1.2
evaporated, cnd—½ cup (126 g)	1.5		tomato, cnd—3½ oz (100 g)	1.0	
human milk—1 cup (248 g)	4.5	1.7–8.2	turnip, raw—3½ oz (100 g)	0.7	
skim milk—1 cup (245 g)	11.8				
skim milk, dry—¼ cup (30 g)	5.0		**MISCELLANEOUS**		
whole milk—1 cup (244 g)	2.9		coffee, instant, dry—3½ oz (100 g)	4.0	
			cream sub—3½ oz (100 g)	3.3	
NUTS			cream, table—3½ oz (100 g)	0.5	
almonds—3½ oz (100 g)	4		jalapeno bean dip, Fritos—1 oz (28 g)	6	
cashews—3½ oz (100 g)	68		molasses—3½ oz (100 g)	128	64–176
peanut butter—3½ oz (100 g)	12		saccharin—3½ oz (100 g)	0.5	
peanuts, fresh—3½ oz (100 g)	3		sugar, brown—3½ oz (100 g)	1.2	
peanuts, roasted—3½ oz (100 g)	38		sugar, white—3½ oz (100 g)	0.3	
walnuts—3½ oz (100 g)	19		tapioca, dry—3½ oz (100 g)	0.4	
			tea, instant, dry—3½ oz (100 g)	5.0	
POULTRY					
chicken breast, raw—3½ oz (100 g)		12–42			
chicken heart, raw—3½ oz (100 g)	49	46–50			

Sodium Content of Some Nonprescription Drugs (mg)

Alka-Seltzer—*2 tablets*	1064	Metamucil instant mix—*1 pkt*	250
Basaljel suspension—*15 ml*	27	Milk of magnesia—*30 ml*	36
Bisodol powder—*1 pkt*	1540	Mylanta II liquid—*10 ml*	20
Bromo-Seltzer—*1.25 g*	717	Phosphaljel suspension—*15 ml*	39
Creamalin—*2 tablets*	50	Riopan—*3 tablets*	2
Gelusil liquid—*15 ml*	21	Rolaids—*2 tablets*	100
Kolantyl—*2 tablets*	20	Tritralac liquid—*15 ml*	38
Maalox suspension—*15 ml*	18	Tums—*2 tablets*	40

Tin (mcg/100 g)

biscuit mix	1190	doughnut, cake	560
bread, white	890	farina, dry	780
bread, whole wheat	780	flour, all-purpose	400
cake	3220	flour, cake	370
cereal, shredded wheat	850	macaroni, dry	520
cereal, wheat flakes	1360	rolls, hamburger	880
crackers	2490		

Biotin (mcg)

CEREALS, COOKED

corn grits
    inst—*1 pkt prep (137 g)* 1.0
    w/imit bacon bits, inst—*1 pkt prep (141 g)* 2.0
    w/imit ham bits, inst—*1 pkt prep (141 g)* 1.0
farina, ckd—*¾ cup (175 g)* 1.0
oats
    reg, ckd—*¾ cup (175 g)* 4.0
    inst, prep—*1 pkt prep (177 g)* 1.0
    w/apples & cinn, inst—*1 pkt prep (149 g)* 3.0
    w/maple & brown sugar, inst—*1 pkt (155 g)* 7.0
    w/raisins & spice, inst—*1 pkt prep (158 g)* 6.0
ralston cereal, ckd—*¾ cup (190 g)* 2.0
whole wheat cereal, ckd, Quaker—*¾ cup (182 g)* 2.0

CEREALS, READY-TO-EAT

bran chex—*⅔ cup (28 g)* 2.0
bran flakes, 40%, Ralston Purina—*¾ cup (28 g)* 3.0
cap'n crunch—*¾ cup (28 g)* 1.0
cap'n crunch's crunchberries—*¾ cup (28 g)* 1.0
cap'n crunch's peanut butter crunch—*¾ cup (28 g)* 2.0
cookie crisp, choc chip/van—*1 cup (28 g)* 1.0
corn chex—*1 cup (28 g)* 2.0
crispy rice—*1 cup (28 g)* 1.0
honey bran—*⅞ cup (28 g)* 1.0
life, plain/cinn—*⅔ cup (28 g)* 7.0
puffed rice—*1 cup (14 g)* 0.0
puffed wheat—*1 cup (14 g)* 1.0
quaker 100% natural—*¼ cup (28 g)* 5.0
quaker 100% natural w/raisins & dates—*¼ cup (28 g)* 4.0
quisp—*1 cup (28 g)* 1.0
raisin bran, Ralston Purina—*¾ cup (38 g)* 3.0
shredded wheat—*2 small biscuits (37 g)* 4.0
tasteeos—*1¼ cup (28 g)* 3.0
wheat chex—*⅔ cup (28 g)* 2.0

CHEESE

blue—*3½ oz (100 g)* 4.6
brick—*3½ oz (100 g)* 2.2
brie—*3½ oz (100 g)* 6.2
camembert—*3½ oz (100 g)* 4.5
chantelle—*3½ oz (100 g)* 3.6
cheddar—*3½ oz (100 g)* 2.2
cheddar, processed—*3½ oz (100 g)* 2.6
colby—*3½ oz (100 g)* 1.6
cottage cheese—*3½ oz (100 g)* 2.0
cream cheese—*3½ oz (100 g)* 1.4
edam—*3½ oz (100 g)* 1.5
gorgonzola—*3½ oz (100 g)* 1.9
gouda—*3½ oz (100 g)* 1.7
gruyère—*3½ oz (100 g)* 1.3
liederkranz—*3½ oz (100 g)* 3.0
limburger—*3½ oz (100 g)* 8.6
limburger, processed—*3½ oz (100 g)* 3.6

CHEESE

mozzarella—*3½ oz (100 g)* 1.6
muenster—*3½ oz (100 g)* 1.2
neufchatel—*3½ oz (100 g)* 1.9
parmesan—*3½ oz (100 g)* 3.0
port du salut—*3½ oz (100 g)* 1.2
provolone—*3½ oz (100 g)* 1.8
romano—*3½ oz (100 g)* 1.3
roquefort—*3½ oz (100 g)* 2.5
swiss—*3½ oz (100 g)* 0.5
swiss, processed—*3½ oz (100 g)* 1.1
tilsiter—*3½ oz (100 g)* 1.5

CHIPS & SNACKS

corn chips, Fritos—*1 oz (28 g)* 0.6
potato chips, Lay's—*1 oz (28 g)* 0.5
tortilla chips, Doritos—*1 oz (28 g)* 0.9

DESSERTS

cookies, animal crackers—*15 cookies (28 g)* 0.2
piecrust, plain, unbaked—*3½ oz (100 g)* 1.0

EGGS

fresh—*1 egg* 10.8
fresh—*3½ oz (100 g)* 20.0
white, fresh—*1 white* 2.3
white, fresh—*3½ oz (100 g)* 7.0
yolk, fresh—*1 yolk* 8.5
yolk, fresh—*3½ oz (100 g)* 50.0

FAST FOODS

Kentucky Fried Chicken®
  chicken
    breast, extra crispy—*½ breast (85 g)* 1.8
    breast, orig recipe—*½ breast (69 g)* 2.4
    drumstick, extra crispy—*1 drumstick (58 g)* 2.0
    drumstick, orig recipe—*1 drumstick (47 g)* 4.1
    keel, extra crispy—*1 keel (104 g)* 2.7
    keel, orig recipe—*1 keel (95 g)* 2.4
    thigh, extra crispy—*1 thigh (107 g)* 2.7
    thigh, orig recipe—*1 thigh (88 g)* 4.7
    wing, extra crispy—*1 wing (53 g)* 1.3
    wing, orig recipe—*1 wing (42 g)* 1.5
  coleslaw—*1 serving (91 g)* 1.6
  corn on the cob—*5½ inch piece (135 g)* 3.0
  dinner[a]
    drumstick & thigh, extra crispy—*1 dinner (375 g)* 7.2
    drumstick & thigh, orig recipe—*1 dinner (346 g)* 11.7
    wing & breast, extra crispy—*1 dinner (348 g)* 5.6
    wing & breast, orig recipe—*1 dinner (322 g)* 9.0
    wing & thigh, extra crispy—*1 dinner (371 g)* 6.5
    wing & thigh, orig recipe—*1 dinner (341 g)* 11.3
  mashed potatoes—*1 serving (85 g)* 0.3
  roll—*1 roll (21 g)* 0.4

[a] Includes 2 pieces chicken, mashed potatoes, gravy, coleslaw & roll

FISH & SHELLFISH

clams, raw—*3½ oz (100 g)*	2.0
cod, raw—*3½ oz (100 g)*	3.0
crab, cnd/ckd—*3½ oz (100 g)*	5.0
haddock, raw—*3½ oz (100 g)*	5.0
halibut, raw—*3½ oz (100 g)*	5.0
herring, raw—*3½ oz (100g)*	10.0
lobster, raw—*3½ oz (100 g)*	5.0
mackerel, raw—*3½ oz (100 g)*	2.0
oysters, raw—*3½ oz (100 g)*	10.0
pike, raw—*3½ oz (100 g)*	2.0
salmon, atlantic, raw—*3½ oz (100 g)*	5.0
salmon, atlantic, cnd—*3½ oz (100 g)*	15.0
sardines, cnd in oil—*3½ oz (100 g)*	5.0
scallops, raw—*3½ oz (100 g)*	0.3
tunny, cnd—*3½ oz (100 g)*	3.0

FLOUR & GRAIN FRACTIONS

cornmeal, white/yellow, enr—*3 T (28 g)*	1.0
cornmeal, white, self-rising, bolted—*⅙ cup (28 g)*	2.0
flour, corn—*3½ oz (100 g)*	6.0
flour, corn, masa harina—*⅓ cup (36 g)*	3.0
flour, corn, masa trigo—*⅓ cup (37 g)*	1.0
flour, rye, dark—*3½ oz (100 g)*	6.0
flour, soybean, full-fat—*3½ oz (100 g)*	70.0
flour, wheat, white—*3½ oz (100 g)*	1.0
flour, wheat, whole—*3½ oz (100 g)*	7.0

FRUIT & FRUIT JUICES

apple, raw—*3½ oz (100 g)*	1.0
apple jce, fresh—*8 fl oz (248 g)*	1.2
applesce, sweetened—*3½ oz (100 g)*	0.2
banana, raw—*3½ oz (100 g)*	4.0
blackberries, raw—*3½ oz (100 g)*	0.4
cantaloupe, raw—*3½ oz (100 g)*	3.0
cherries, raw—*3½ oz (100 g)*	0.4
currants, black, raw—*3½ oz (100 g)*	2.4
currants, red & white, raw—*3½ oz (100 g)*	2.6
elderberries, raw—*3½ oz (100 g)*	2.0
fruit cocktail, cnd—*3½ oz (100 g)*	0.1
gooseberries, raw—*3½ oz (100 g)*	0.5
grapefruit, raw—*3½ oz (100 g)*	3.0
grapefruit, cnd, sweetened—*3½ oz (100 g)*	1.0
grapefruit jce, fresh—*8 fl oz (247 g)*	1.7
grape jce—*8 fl oz (253 g)*	0.8
grapes, raw—*3½ oz (100 g)*	2.0
lemon, raw—*3½ oz (100 g)*	0.5
orange, raw—*3½ oz (100 g)*	1.0
orange jce, fresh—*8 fl oz (248 g)*	2.0
peach, raw—*3½ oz (100 g)*	2.0
peach, cnd, sweetened—*3½ oz (100 g)*	0.2
pear, raw—*3½ oz (100 g)*	0.2
raisins, dried—*3½ oz (100 g)*	5.0
raspberries, raw—*3½ oz (100 g)*	1.9
strawberries, raw—*3½ oz (100 g)*	1.1
watermelon, raw—*3½ oz (100 g)*	4.0

GRAIN PRODUCTS

bread, whole wheat—*3½ oz (100 g)*	6.0
crackers	
cheese snacks, Dixie Belle—*25 crackers (28 g)*	0.3
graham—*2 squares (14 g)*	0.2

GRAIN PRODUCTS

oyster—*33 crackers (28 g)*	0.2
rich & crisp, Dixie Belle—*10 crackers (28 g)*	0.4
ryekrisp—*2 triple crackers (12 g)*	0.4
ryekrisp, seasoned—*2 triple crackers (13 g)*	0.5
ryekrisp, sesame—*2 triple crackers (15 g)*	0.6
soda (unsalted tops)—*10 crackers (28 g)*	0.1
wheat snacks, Dixie Belle—*15 crackers (28 g)*	0.5
french toast, frzn, Aunt Jemima—*2 slices (84 g)*	4.0
french toast, cinn swirl, frzn, Aunt Jemima— *2 slices (84 g)*	5.0
scone, enr—*3½ oz (100 g)*	2.0
waffle, reg/blueberry/buttermilk, frzn, Aunt Jemima—*1 waffle (35 g)*	1.0

MEAT

beef brain, raw—*3½ oz (100 g)*	7.0
beef heart, raw—*3½ oz (100 g)*	7.0
beef kidney, raw—*3½ oz (100 g)*	24.0
beef liver, raw—*3½ oz (100 g)*	100.0
beef lung, raw—*3½ oz (100 g)*	6.0
beef pancreas, raw—*3½ oz (100 g)*	14.0
beef, round, raw—*3½ oz (100 g)*	3.0
beef sausage, raw—*3½ oz (100 g)*	2.0
beef spleen, raw—*3½ oz (100 g)*	6.0
beef tongue, raw—*3½ oz (100 g)*	3.0
lamb kidney, raw—*3½ oz (100 g)*	37.0
lamb liver, raw—*3½ oz (100 g)*	41.0
lamb leg, med fat, raw—*3½ oz (100 g)*	6.0
pork cutlet, raw—*3½ oz (100 g)*	5.0
pork, ham, raw—*3½ oz (100 g)*	5.0
pork heart, raw—*3½ oz (100 g)*	20.0
pork kidney, raw—*3½ oz (100 g)*	32.0
pork liver, raw—*3½ oz (100 g)*	27.0
veal brain, raw—*3½ oz (100 g)*	2.0
veal cutlet, raw—*3½ oz (100 g)*	2.0
veal heart, raw—*3½ oz (100 g)*	15.0
veal liver, raw—*3½ oz (100 g)*	75.0

MEATS, PROCESSED

frankfurter—*3½ oz (100 g)*	2.0
salami—*3½ oz (100 g)*	3.0

MILK & CULTURED MILK

cow milk

buttermilk—*1 cup (245 g)*	2.7
buttermilk, dry—*1 T (7 g)*	2.0
condensed, cnd—*1 fl oz (38 g)*	1.5
evaporated, cnd—*½ cup (126 g)*	7.1
nonfat dry milk—*¼ cup (30 g)*	9.0
skim—*1 cup (245 g)*	4.9
whole—*1 cup (244 g)*	7.6
whole, dry—*¼ cup (32 g)*	3.2
yogurt—*1 cup (227 g)*	2.7
goat milk—*1 cup (244 g)*	4.9
human milk—*1 cup (248 g)*	2.5
sheep milk—*1 cup (245 g)*	22.0

NUTS & NUT PRODUCTS

almonds—*3½ oz (100 g)*	20.0
almond powder, Nutquik—*1 oz (28 g)*	15.0
chestnuts—*3½ oz (100 g)*	1.3
peanut butter—*3½ oz (100 g)*	40.0

NUTS & NUT PRODUCTS

peanuts—*3½ oz (100 g)*	34.0
walnuts—*3½ oz (100 g)*	37.0

POULTRY

chicken fryers, flesh & skin, raw—*3½ oz (100 g)*	11.0
chicken liver, raw—*3½ oz (100 g)*	210.0

VEGETABLES

asparagus, cnd—*3½ oz (100 g)*	2.0
beet greens, raw—*3½ oz (100 g)*	3.0
broccoli, raw—*3½ oz (100 g)*	0.5
brussels sprouts, raw—*3½ oz (100 g)*	0.4
cabbage, red, raw—*3½ oz (100 g)*	2.0
cabbage, savoy, raw—*3½ oz (100 g)*	0.1
cabbage, white, raw—*3½ oz (100 g)*	0.1
carrot, raw—*3½ oz (100 g)*	3.0
carrot, cnd—*3½ oz (100 g)*	2.0
cauliflower, raw—*3½ oz (100 g)*	17.0
cucumber, raw—*3½ oz (100 g)*	1.0
fennel, raw—*3½ oz (100 g)*	3.0
green beans, cnd—*3½ oz (100 g)*	1.0
kale, raw—*3½ oz (100 g)*	0.5
leek, raw—*3½ oz (100 g)*	1.4
lentils, dried—*3½ oz (100 g)*	13.0
lettuce, raw—*3½ oz (100 g)*	3.0
lima beans, raw—*3½ oz (100 g)*	10.0
maize, raw—*3½ oz (100 g)*	6.0
maize, cnd—*3½ oz (100 g)*	3.0
onion, raw—*3½ oz (100 g)*	4.0

VEGETABLES

parsley, raw—*3½ oz (100 g)*	0.4
parsnip, raw—*3½ oz (100 g)*	0.1
peas, green, unripe—*3½ oz (100 g)*	9.0
peas, green, cnd—*3½ oz (100 g)*	2.0
peas, split, dried—*3½ oz (100 g)*	2.0
potato, raw—*3½ oz (100 g)*	0.1
rice, white, dry—*3½ oz (100 g)*	3.0
rutabaga, raw—*3½ oz (100 g)*	0.1
soybeans, dried—*3½ oz (100 g)*	60.0
spinach, raw—*3½ oz (100 g)*	7.0
spinach, cnd—*3½ oz (100 g)*	2.0
sweet potato, raw—*3½ oz (100 g)*	4.0
tomato, raw—*3½ oz (100 g)*	4.0
tomato, cnd—*3½ oz (100 g)*	1.5
turnip root, raw—*3½ oz (100 g)*	0.1

MISCELLANEOUS

casein, crude—*3½ oz (100 g)*	5.2
marzipan—*3½ oz (100 g)*	2.0
mayonnaise—*3½ oz (100 g)*	12.0
molasses—*3½ oz (100 g)*	9.0
whey, condensed—*3½ oz (100 g)*	29.0
whey, dried—*3½ oz (100 g)*	37.0
whey, fluid—*3½ oz (100 g)*	1.4
wine—*(100 g)*	0.6
yeast, baker's, compressed—*3½ oz (100 g)*	400.0
yeast, brewer's, dried—*3½ oz (100 g)*	80.0
yeast, torula, dried—*3½ oz (100 g)*	100.0

Vitamin D (IU)

CANDY

choc covered almonds—*1 oz (28 g)*	10
choc, semisweet—*1 oz (28 g)*	10
choc w/almonds—*1 oz (28 g)*	20
choc w/crisped rice—*1 oz (28 g)*	20
milk choc—*1 oz (28 g)*	25
milk choc w/almonds—*1 oz (28 g)*	10

CEREALS, READY-TO-EAT

banana flavored frosted flakes—*1 oz (28 g)*	50
boo berry—*1 cup (28 g)*	40
bran flakes, 40%, Ralston Purina—*¾ cup (28 g)*	100
cocoa krispies—*¾ cup (28 g)*	50
cookie crisp, choc chip/van—*1 cup (28 g)*	100
corn flakes, Kellogg's—*1¼ cup (28 g)*	50
corn flakes, Ralston Purina—*1 cup (28 g)*	40
cracklin bran—*⅓ cup (28 g)*	50
crispy rice—*1 cup (28 g)*	40
frankenberry—*1 cup (28 g)*	40
froot loops—*1 cup (28 g)*	50
frosted mini-wheats—*4 biscuits (28 g)*	50
fruit & fibre, apples & cinn—*½ cup (28 g)*	49
fruit & fibre, dates, raisins & walnuts—*½ cup (28 g)*	49
fruit brute—*1 cup (28 g)*	40
graham crackos—*¾ cup (28 g)*	50
honey & nut corn flakes—*¾ cup (28 g)*	50
honey bran—*⅞ cup (28 g)*	100
marshmallow krispies—*1¼ cups (37 g)*	50
most—*⅔ cup (28 g)*	200
nutri-grain, corn—*⅔ cup (28 g)*	50
nutri-grain, wheat—*¾ cup (28 g)*	50
nutri-grain, wheat & raisins—*⅔ cup (40 g)*	50
product 19—*¾ cup (28 g)*	200
puffa puffa rice—*1 cup (28 g)*	49
raisin bran, Kellogg's—*¾ cup (37 g)*	50
raisin bran, Ralston Purina—*¾ cup (38 g)*	100
rice krispies, frosted—*1 cup (28 g)*	50
sir grapefellow—*1 oz (28 g)*	40
special K—*1⅓ cups (28 g)*	50
sugar corn pops—*1 cup (28 g)*	50
sugar frosted flakes, Kellogg's—*¾ cup (28 g)*	50
sugar frosted flakes, Ralston Purina—*¾ cup (28 g)*	40
sugar frosted rice—*1 cup (28 g)*	40
sugar puffs—*⅞ cup (28 g)*	40
sugar smacks—*¾ cup (28 g)*	50
tasteeos—*1¼ cup (28 g)*	100
toasty O's—*1¼ cups (28 g)*	40
waffelos—*1 cup (28 g)*	100

CHEESE

cottage, creamed—*1 cup (225 g)*	5
cottage, uncreamed—*1 cup (226 g)*	5
edam—*3½ oz (100 g)*	84
swiss—*3½ oz (100 g)*	100

CREAM

sour cream, cultured—*1 T (12 g)*	1
sour cream onion dip—*1 T (15 g)*	1
sour cream sce—*¼ cup (53 g)*	9
whipping cream, heavy, fluid—*1 T (15 g)*	15
whipping cream, light, fluid—*1 T (15 g)*	8

DESSERTS

cheesecake, from mix[a]—*⅛ cake (103 g)*	22
custard, from mix—*½ cup (143 g)*	55
ice cream sandwich—*1 sandwich (62 g)*	2
junket—*½ cup (135 g)*	1
pie filling	
banana cream, from mix[a]—*amt for ⅙ pie (96 g)*	33
coconut cream, from mix[a]—*amt for ⅙ pie (96 g)*	33
lemon w/meringue, from mix—*amt for ⅙ pie (145 g)*	9
pudding, from inst mix—*½ cup (149 g)*	50[a]
pudding, low cal, from mix—*½ cup (130 g)*	50[a]
pudding, rice, from mix—*½ cup (149 g)*	50[a]
pudding, tapioca, from mix—*½ cup (145 g)*	50[a]
pudding, tapioca, choc, from mix—*½ cup (147 g)*	50[a]

EGGS[b]

chicken, boiled—*1 med (48 g)*	23
chicken, fried w/1 t margarine—*1 med (50 g)*	27
chicken, omelet, plain—*1 med (62 g)*	31
chicken, poached—*1 med (48 g)*	27
chicken, scrambled—*1 med (65 g)*	31
chicken, whole, fresh/frzn—*1 med (48 g)*	27
chicken, yolk, fresh/frzn—*1 med (17 g)*	27[b]

EGG SUBSTITUTES

egg beaters, Fleischmann's—*¼ cup (60 g)*	26
scramblers, Morningstar Farms—*¼ cup (57 g)*	39

FAST FOODS

Arthur Treacher®

chicken, fried fillet—*1 serving (136 g)*	4
chicken sandwich—*1 sandwich (156 g)*	3
chips (fried potatoes)—*1 serving (113 g)*	6
coleslaw—*1 serving (82 g)*	2
fish chowder—*1 serving (170 g)*	19
fish, fried—*1 serving (147 g)*	15
fish, sandwich—*1 sandwich (156 g)*	11
krunch pup (frank in bun)—*1 serving (57 g)*	9
shrimp, fried—*1 serving (115 g)*	2

Dairy Queen®

cheese dog—*1 serving (113 g)*	23
cheese dog, super—*1 serving (203 g)*	44
chili dog—*1 serving (128 g)*	20
chili dog, super—*1 serving (210 g)*	32
fish sandwich—*1 serving (170 g)*	40
fish sandwich w/cheese—*1 serving (177 g)*	40
french fries, reg—*1 serving (71 g)*	16
french fries, large—*1 serving (113 g)*	24

[a] Made w/vit D fortified milk

[b] Vit D is found in egg yolk but not in egg white.

FAST FOODS

Dairy Queen®

hot dog—*1 serving (99 g)*	23
hot dog, super—*1 serving (182 g)*	44
onion rings—*1 serving (85 g)*	8
desserts	
ice cream in cone, large—*1 serving (213 g)*	8
ice cream in cone, dipped in choc, large—*1 serving (234 g)*	8
ice cream parfait—*1 serving (284 g)*	8
shake, small—*1 serving (241 g)*	60
shake, reg—*1 serving (418 g)*	100
shake, large—*1 serving (588 g)*	140
sundae, choc, large—*1 serving (248 g)*	8

Jack in the Box®

breakfast	
breakfast jack sandwich—*1 serving (121 g)*	51
french toast—*1 serving (180 g)*	22
omelette, double cheese—*1 serving (166 g)*	61
omelette, ham & cheese—*1 serving (174 g)*	64
omelette, ranchero style—*1 serving (196 g)*	78
pancakes—*1 serving (232 g)*	23
scrambled eggs—*1 serving (267 g)*	80
cheeseburger—*1 serving (109 g)*	20
cheeseburger, jumbo jack—*1 serving (272)*	41
hamburger—*1 serving (97 g)*	20
hamburger, jumbo jack—*1 serving (246 g)*	42
moby jack sandwich—*1 serving (141 g)*	24
shake, choc—*1 serving (317 g)*	38
shake, choc[a]—*1 serving (322 g)*	45
shake, strawberry—*1 serving (328 g)*	30
shake, strawberry[a]—*1 serving (328 g)*	43
shake, van—*1 serving (314 g)*	44
shake, van[a]—*1 serving (317 g)*	41
taco—*1 serving (83 g)*	6
taco, super—*1 serving (146 g)*	9
turnover, apple—*1 serving (119 g)*	1

Kentucky Fried Chicken®

chicken drumstick, extra crispy—*1 piece (58 g)*	10
chicken drumstick, original recipe—*1 piece (47 g)*	12
chicken keel, extra crispy—*1 piece (104 g)*	18
chicken keel, original recipe—*1 piece (95 g)*	7
chicken side breast, extra crispy—*1 piece (85 g)*	13
chicken side breast, original recipe—*1 piece (88 g)*	15
chicken thigh, extra crispy—*1 piece (107 g)*	26
chicken thigh, original recipe—*1 piece (88 g)*	23
chicken wing, extra crispy—*1 piece (53 g)*	11
chicken wing, original recipe—*1 piece (42 g)*	16
corn on the cob—*5½ inch ear (135 g)*	22
dinners[b]	
drumstick & thigh, extra crispy—*1 dinner (375 g)*	22
drumstick & thigh, original recipe—*1 dinner (346 g)*	39
wing & side breast, extra crispy—*1 dinner (348 g)*	28
wing & side breast, original recipe—*1 dinner (322 g)*	35
wing & thigh, extra crispy—*1 dinner (371 g)*	41
wing & thigh, original recipe—*1 dinner (341 g)*	43
gravy—*1 serving (14 g)*	4

[a] Formula for CA, AZ, TX & WA

FAST FOODS

McDonald's®

big mac—*1 sandwich (204 g)*	33
cheeseburger—*1 sandwich (115 g)*	13
cookies, chocolaty chip—*1 box (67 g)*	10
cookies, mcdonaldland—*1 box (69 g)*	10
egg mcmuffin—*1 sandwich (138 g)*	46
eggs, scrambled—*1 serving (98 g)*	65
english muffin, buttered—*1 muffin (63 g)*	14
filet o fish—*1 sandwich (139 g)*	25
french fries—*reg serving (68 g)*	1
hamburger—*1 sandwich (102 g)*	12
hash browns—*1 serving (55 g)*	1
ice cream in sugar cone—*1 serving (93 g)*	7
ice cream in cake cone—*1 serving (115 g)*	10
pancakes w/butter & syrup—*1 serving (214 g)*	5
pie, apple—*1 serving (85 g)*	2
pie, cherry—*1 serving (88 g)*	2
quarter pounder—*1 sandwich (166 g)*	23
quarter pounder w/cheese—*1 sandwich (194 g)*	25
sausage, pork—*1 serving (53 g)*	31
shake, choc—*1 shake (291 g)*	44
shake, strawberry—*1 shake (290 g)*	32
shake, van—*1 shake (291 g)*	26
sundae, caramel—*1 serving (165 g)*	14
sundae, hot fudge—*1 serving (164 g)*	16
sundae, strawberry—*1 serving (164 g)*	16

FATS & SPREADS

butter—*3½ oz (100 g)*	30
cod liver oil—*3½ oz (100 g)*	8500
margarine—*3½ oz (100 g)*	320
mayonnaise—*3½ oz (100 g)*	40

FISH & SEAFOOD

bass, baked—*1 piece (115 g)*	1
eel, raw—*3½ oz (100 g)*	5000
eel, smoked—*3½ oz (100 g)*	6400
herring, raw—*3½ oz (100 g)*	900
mackerel, raw—*3½ oz (100 g)*	700
oysters, raw—*3½ oz (100 g)*	5
salmon, atlantic, raw—*3½ oz (100 g)*	650
salmon, atlantic, cnd—*3½ oz (100 g)*	500
salmon patty—*3½ oz (100 g)*	42
sardines, cnd in oil—*3½ oz (100 g)*	300
shrimp, cnd—*3½ oz (100 g)*	105
tuna patty—*3½ oz (100 g)*	15

GRAIN PRODUCTS

bread, banana tea—*1 slice (49 g)*	3
corn pone w/whole cornmeal—*1 cake (45 g)*	7
french toast, homemade—*1 slice (65 g)*	10
stuffing, from mix, Stove Top—*½ cup (108 g)*	3
wheat germ—*⅓ oz (10 g)*	3

MEAT/POULTRY

beef breakfast strips, ckd, Oscar Mayer—*1 strip (9 g)*	4
beef, chipped & creamed—*½ cup (120 g)*	2
canadian bacon, raw—*1 oz (28 g)*	10
liver, beef, raw—*3½ oz (100 g)*	45

[b] Includes 2 pieces chicken, mashed potatoes, gravy, coleslaw & roll

MEAT/POULTRY

liver, calf, raw—*3½ oz (100 g)*	15
liver, calf, fried—*3½ oz (100 g)*	14
liver, chicken, raw—*3½ oz (100 g)*	50
liver, chicken, simmered—*3½ oz (100 g)*	67
liver, hog, raw—*3½ oz (100 g)*	45
liver, hog, fried—*3½ oz (100 g)*	51
liver, lamb, raw—*3½ oz (100 g)*	20
liver, lamb, broiled—*3½ oz (100 g)*	23
pork bacon, ckd, Oscar Mayer—*1 slice (6 g)*	3
pork bacon bits, Oscar Mayer—*¼ oz (7 g)*	4
pork, ham, sectioned & formed, cnd—*3½ oz (100 g)*	26
pork, ham, sectioned & formed, smoked—*3½ oz (100 g)*	25
pork, ham, smoked, ckd—*3½ oz (100 g)*	25
pork, ham steaks, sectioned & formed—*3½ oz (100 g)*	26
pork sausage patties—*1 patty (27 g)*	23

MEAT, LUNCHEON

barbeque loaf, pork & beef—*1 slice (23 g)*	10
beef, loaved—*1 slice (28 g)*	17
bologna, beef—*1 slice (28 g)*	8
bologna, beef & pork—*1 slice (28 g)*	9
bologna, beef & pork w/cheese—*1 slice (28 g)*	10
braunschweiger—*1 slice (18 g)*	6
canadian bacon—*1 slice (28 g)*	10
frank, beef—*1 frank (45 g)*	11
frank, beef & pork—*1 frank (45 g)*	16
frank, pork & beef w/cheese—*1 frank (45 g)*	22
frank, battered & fried—*1 frank (111 g)*	38
ham, chopped, cnd—*1 slice (21 g)*	10
ham, chopped, pkg—*1 slice (21 g)*	5
ham & cheese loaf/roll—*1 slice (28 g)*	12
ham roll sausage—*1 slice (23 g)*	8
headcheese, pork—*1 slice (28 g)*	12
honey loaf, pork & beef—*1 slice (28 g)*	10
honey roll sausage, beef—*1 slice (23 g)*	8
liver cheese, pork liver—*1 slice (23 g)*	12
liverwurst—*1 slice (28 g)*	4
luxury loaf, pork—*1 slice (28 g)*	8
new england brand sausage—*1 slice (23 g)*	9
old fashioned loaf/dutch loaf—*1 slice (28 g)*	11
olive loaf, pork—*1 slice (28 g)*	11
peppered loaf, pork & beef—*1 slice (28 g)*	10
pickle & pimento loaf, pork—*1 slice (28 g)*	11
picnic loaf, pork & beef—*1 slice (28 g)*	13

MEAT, LUNCHEON

salami, ckd, cotto, beef—*1 slice (23 g)*	11
salami, ckd, cotto, beef & pork—*1 slice (23 g)*	8
salami, dry/hard, pork & beef—*1 slice (10 g)*	6
salami for beer, beef—*1 slice (23 g)*	10
salami for beer, pork—*1 slice (23 g)*	9
sandwich spread, pork & beef—*1 oz (28 g)*	10
sandwich spread w/pickle—*1 T (20 g)*	8
smoked link sausage, beef—*1 link (43 g)*	18
smoked link sausage, pork & beef—*1 link (68 g)*	32
smoked link sausage w/cheese—*1 link (43 g)*	20
thuringer/cervelat, beef—*1 slice (23 g)*	15
thuringer/cervelat, beef & pork—*1 slice (23 g)*	11
turkey breast—*1 slice (21 g)*	4

MILK, MILK BEVERAGES & MILK MIXES

eggnog, alcoholic—*½ cup (123 g)*	21
eggnog, nonalcoholic—*1 cup (254 g)*	57
milk, evaporated, cnd—*2 T (32 g)*	28
milk, evaporated, cnd—*½ cup (100 g)*	88
milk, evaporated, cnd—*1 oz (30 g)*	26
milk, fortified w/vit D—*1 cup (244 g)*	100
milk, goat—*1 cup (244 g)*	5
milk, human—*1 cup (248 g)*	1–24
milk, choc, fort w/vit D—*1 cup (244 g)*	100
milkshake, homemade—*1 cup (345 g)*	3
ovaltine milk mix, dry—*1 serving (21 g)*	177

MIXED DISHES

beans & ham—*7 oz (200 g)*	4
spaghetti sce w/meat—*3½ oz (100 g)*	2

SALAD DRESSINGS, FROM MIX

buttermilk, Good Seasons—*1 T (16 g)*	3
french—*1 T (19 g)*	1

SOUPS

bean w/ham, homemade—*⅘ cup (200 g)*	4
celery, crm of, homemade—*¾ cup (155 g)*	1

VEGETABLES

bavarian style beans & spaetzle, frzn, Birds Eye—*½ cup (95 g)*	2
broccoli spears w/hollandaise sce, frzn, Birds Eye—*½ cup (95 g)*	5

MISCELLANEOUS

shake & bake, General Foods—*¼ pkt (17 g)*	12
whipped topping, from mix, Dream Whip—*1 T (5 g)*	2

Vitamin E (IU)

CANDY

choc flavored chips—¼ cup (43 g)	2
choc, german sweet—1 oz (28 g)	1
choc, semisweet, Baker's—1 oz (28 g)	1

CEREALS, CKD

oats, quick/inst, ckd—¾ cup (175 g)	1
oats, inst, prep—1 pkt prep—(177 g)	1
oats w/apples & cinn, inst, prep—1 pkt prep (149 g)	1

CEREALS, READY-TO-EAT

fruit & fibre, apples & cinn—½ cup (28 g)	1
fruit & fibre, dates, raisins & walnuts—½ cup (28 g)	1
king vitaman—1¼ cups (28 g)	15
most—⅔ cup (28 g)	30
nutri-grain, corn—⅔ cup (28 g)	8
nutri-grain, wheat—¾ cup (28 g)	8
nutri-grain, wheat & raisins—⅔ cup (40 g)	8
product 19—¾ cup (28 g)	30
quaker 100% natural—¼ cup (28 g)	1
quaker 100% natural w/raisins & dates—¼ cup (28 g)	1

CHIPS & SNACKS

cheese puffed balls, Cheetos—1 oz (28 g)	0.8
cheese puffs, Cheetos—1 oz (28 g)	0.7
cheese puffs w/bacon flavor, Cheetos—1 oz (28 g)	1.1
cheese snacks, Cheetos—1 oz (28 g)	0.5
corn chips, Fritos—1 oz (28 g)	1.8
corn chips, bbq flavor, Fritos—1 oz (28 g)	1.1
corn chips, king size, Fritos—1 oz (28 g)	1.6
corn chips, lights, Fritos—1 oz (28 g)	1.2
funyuns—1 oz (28 g)	0.7
pork rinds, fried, Frito-Lay—1 oz (28 g)	0.1
potato chips, Lay's—1 oz (28 g)	3.8
potato chips, Ruffles—1 oz (28 g)	2.8
potato chips, bacon & sour cream, Ruffles—1 oz (28 g)	2.5
potato chips, bbq flavor, Lay's—1 oz (28 g)	3.6
potato chips, bbq flavor, Ruffles—1 oz (28 g)	3.4
potato chips, cheese flavor, Lay's—1 oz (28 g)	2.5
potato chips, cheese flavor, Ruffles—1 oz (28 g)	1.6
potato chips, no salt added, Lay's—1 oz (28 g)	0.4
potato chips, sour cream & onion, Lay's—1 oz (28 g)	2.4
potato chips, sour cream & onion, Ruffles—1 oz (28 g)	2.2
potato crisps, Munchos—1 oz (28 g)	2.8
pretzel twists, Rold Gold—1 oz (28 g)	0.5
tortilla chips, Doritos—1 oz (28 g)	0.8
tortilla chips, cheese flavor, Doritos—1 oz (28 g)	0.7
tortilla chips, extra crispy, Doritos—1 oz (28 g)	0.3
tortilla chips, extra crispy, cheese flavor, Doritos—1 oz (28 g)	0.4
tortilla chips, round, Tostitos—1 oz (28 g)	0.5
tortilla chips, round, cheese, Tostitos—1 oz (28 g)	0.6
tortilla chips, taco flavor, Doritos—1 oz (28 g)	0.6

FAST FOODS—MCDONALD'S

breakfast

egg mcmuffin—1 sandwich (138 g)	1.3
english muffin w/butter—1 muffin (63 g)	0.3
pancakes w/butter & syrup—1 serving (214 g)	1.9
sausage—1 serving (53 g)	0.3
scrambled eggs—1 serving (98 g)	1.3
big mac—1 sandwich (204 g)	2.7
cheeseburger—1 sandwich (115 g)	0.8
filet o fish—1 sandwich (139 g)	2.2
hamburger—1 sandwich (102 g)	0.6
quarter pounder—1 sandwich (166 g)	1.3
quarter pounder w/cheese—1 sandwich (194 g)	1.6

dessert

cookies, chocolaty chip—1 box (69 g)	0.7
cookies, mcdonaldland—1 box (67 g)	0.5
sundae, caramel—1 sundae (165 g)	1.0
sundae, hot fudge—1 sundae (164 g)	0.7
sundae, strawberry—1 sundae (164 g)	0.8

FISH

tuna, light, cnd in oil—6½ oz (184 g)	5
tuna, light, cnd in water—6½ oz (184 g)	4
tuna, white (albacore), cnd in oil—6½ oz (184 g)	7
tuna, white (albacore), cnd in water—6½ oz (184 g)	2

FLOUR & GRAIN FRACTIONS

corn germ, toasted—1 oz (28 g)	2
cornmeal, white, self-rising, bolted—⅙ cup (28 g)	1
cornmeal, white/yellow, enr, dry—3 T (28 g)	1

GRAIN PRODUCTS

crackers, cheese w/peanut butter, Frito-Lay—1.5 oz (43 g)	0.8
crackers w/cheese, Frito-Lay—1.5 oz (43 g)	0.9
crackers, rye w/cheese, Frito-Lay—1.5 oz (43 g)	0.9
crackers, toast w/peanut butter, Frito-Lay—1.5 oz (43 g)	0.9
crackers, wheat w/cheese, Frito-Lay—1.5 oz (43 g)	1.5
french toast, cinn swirl—2 slices (84 g)	3

NUTS & NUT PRODUCTS

almond powder, Nutquik—1 oz (28 g)	4

SALAD DRESSINGS, FROM MIX[a]

blue (bleu) cheese—1 T (16 g)	2
buttermilk, Good Seasons—1 T (16 g)	4
farm style, Good Seasons—1 T (15 g)	4
french—1 T (19 g)	2
french, old fashioned, Good Seasons—1 T (16 g)	2
french, riviera, Good Seasons—1 T (18 g)	2
garlic—1 T (16 g)	2
garlic w/cheese—1 T (16 g)	2
italian—1 T (16 g)	2
italian, mild—1 T (16 g)	2
italian w/cheese—1 T (17 g)	2
italian, zesty—1 T (16 g)	2
onion—1 T (16 g)	2

[a] Prep w/vinegar, water & hydrogenated soybean oil except for buttermilk dressing, which is prep w/whole milk & mayo

VEGETABLES, FRZN, BIRDS EYE

broccoli, pieces w/almonds—½ cup (95 g)	1.1
broccoli, spears—½ cup (100 g)	0.7
broccoli & water chestnuts—½ cup (95 g)	0.6
broccoli, carrots & pasta twists in sce—⅔ cup (95 g)	1.8
broccoli, carrots & water chestnuts—⅔ cup (91 g)	0.6
broccoli, cauliflower, corn & pasta in parmesan cheese sce—½ cup (95 g)	1.8
broccoli, shells, onions & mushrooms in swiss cheese sce—½ cup (95 g)	2.1
carrots—⅗ cup (100 g)	0.7
carrots, peas & onions—½ cup (95 g)	0.5
cauliflower—⅗ cup (100 g)	0.1
cauliflower w/almonds—½ cup (95 g)	0.3
cauliflower, green beans & corn—⅔ cup (91 g)	0.1
corn—½ cup (100 g)	0.1
corn, green beans & pasta twists in sce—½ cup (95 g)	1.4
green beans—⅔ cup (100 g)	0.3
green beans, corn, carrots & onions—⅔ cup (91 g)	0.3
peas—⅗ cup (100 g)	0.4
peas & carrots—⅗ cup (100 g)	0.5
peas, carrots & onions—⅔ cup (91 g)	0.4
peas, carrots, pasta & onions in parmesan sce—½ cup (95 g)	1.8

VEGETABLES, FRZN, BIRDS EYE

peas, shells & corn in crm sce—½ cup (95 g)	1.3
peas, shells & mushrooms in crm sce—½ cup (95 g)	1.7
potatoes	
fries, tasti—¾ cup (71 g)	1.7
puffs—½ cup (71 g)	3.1
tiny taters—⅔ cup (91 g)	2.7
triangles—2 patties (85 g)	2.6
wedges, farm style—3 oz (85 g)	1.4
whole, peeled—3-4 potatoes (91 g)	0.1
rice, northern italian style—½ cup (104 g)	0.2
spinach, chopped/leaf—½ cup (100 g)	2.8
spinach & water chestnuts—½ cup (95 g)	2.3
veg combinations	
bavarian style beans & spaetzle—½ cup (95 g)	1.9
chinese style—½ cup (95 g)	2.2
far eastern style—½ cup (95 g)	1.7
italian style—½ cup (95 g)	2.2
japanese style—½ cup (95 g)	2.0
mexicana style—½ cup (95 g)	2.0
new england style—½ cup (95 g)	2.8
san francisco style—½ cup (95 g)	1.5

MISCELLANEOUS

choc, unsweetened, Baker's—1 oz (28 g)	1.4

Vitamin E as Alpha-Tocopherol[a] (mg)

CHEESE

cheddar—3½ oz (100 g)	0.8
cottage, uncreamed—3½ oz (100 g)	0.1
edam—3½ oz (100 g)	1.0
parmesan—3½ oz (100 g)	1.0
swiss—3½ oz (100 g)	1.0

COMBINATION FOODS

beef stew, cnd, Bounty—3½ oz (100 g)	0.17
beef stew, cnd, Nalley—3½ oz (100 g)	0.13
beef stew, homemade—3½ oz (100 g)	0.27
chicken & dumplings, homemade—3½ oz (100 g)	0.08
corned beef hash, cnd, Nalley—3½ oz (100 g)	0.05
corned beef hash, homemade—3½ oz (100 g)	0.06
enchilada, beef, cnd, Old El Paso—3½ oz (100 g)	0.12
lima beans & ham, homemade—3½ oz (100 g)	0.20
ravioli, chicken, cnd, Nalley—3½ oz (100 g)	0.16
sloppy joe sce, cnd, Nalley—3½ oz (100 g)	0.13
sandwiches	
bologna—1 sandwich (118 g)	0.15
bologna & cheese—1 sandwich (108 g)	0.04
cheeseburger—1 sandwich (136 g)	0.07

COMBINATION FOODS

sandwiches	
egg salad—1 sandwich (100 g)	0.09
frankfurter in roll—1 sandwich (89 g)	0.12
ham on dark bread—1 sandwich (85 g)	0.75
ham, spiced & cheese—1 sandwich (106 g)	0.08
turkey, sliced—1 sandwich (93 g)	0.04

DESSERTS

cake, plain—3½ oz (100 g)	0.85
cake, pound—3½ oz (100 g)	1.10
cake, cupcake, choc—3½ oz (100 g)	0.14
cookies, choc cream—3½ oz (100 g)	1.29
cookies, oatmeal—3½ oz (100 g)	6.00
cookies, shortbread—3½ oz (100 g)	0.46
cookies, wafer—3½ oz (100 g)	0.53
doughnut—3½ oz (100 g)	0.72
ice cream, choc—3½ oz (100 g)	0.37
ice cream, van—3½ oz (100 g)	0.06
pie, apple/blueberry/lemon cream—3½ oz (100 g)	1.59
pie crust—3½ oz (100 g)	0.49

[a] Alpha-tocopherol is the most active form of vitamin E. About 60% of the vitamin E in the U.S. diet comes from veg oils or products made w/veg oils (margarines, salad dressings, shortenings); another 10% comes from fruits & veg; & smaller percentages come from grains & other products. Animal fats such as butter & milk have negligible amounts of vitamin E.

EGGS
chicken egg
raw—3½ oz (100 g)	0.70
ckd—3½ oz (100 g)	0.77
white, raw—3½ oz (100 g)	0.00
yolk, raw—3½ oz (100 g)	2.05

FATS & SPREADS
beef tallow—1 T (13 g)	0.3
butter—3½ oz (100 g)	1.58
lard—3½ oz (100 g)	2.0
margarine	
imit, soybean & cottonseed—1 t (5 g)	0.4
liquid, soybean & cottonseed—1 t (5 g)	0.2
stick, safflower & soybean—1 t (5 g)	0.8
stick, soybean—1 t (5 g)	0.1
stick, soybean & cottonseed—1 t (5 g)	0.3
tub, corn—1 t (5 g)	0.5
tub, safflower—1 t (5 g)	0.6
tub, soybean—1 t (5 g)	0.1
tub, soybean & cottonseed—1 t (5 g)	0.3
mayonnaise, soybean—1 T (14 g)	2.9
pork fat—1 T (13 g)	0.2
vegetable & fish oils	
almond—1 T (14 g)	5.3
coconut—1 T (14 g)	0.1
cod liver—1 T (14 g)	2.8
corn—1 T (14 g)	1.9
cottonseed—1 T (14 g)	4.8
olive—1 T (14 g)	1.6
palm—1 T (14 g)	2.6
peanut—1 T (14 g)	1.6
safflower—1 T (14 g)	4.6
sesame—1 T (14 g)	0.2
soybean—1 T (14 g)	1.5
soybean, hydrogenated—1 T (14 g)	1.1
sunflower seed—1 T (14 g)	6.1
wheat germ—1 T (14 g)	20.3

FISH & SHELLFISH
carp, raw—3½ oz (100 g)	0.63
cod, raw—3½ oz (100 g)	0.23
flounder, frzn—3½ oz (100 g)	0.36
haddock, raw—3½ oz (100 g)	0.39
haddock, broiled—3½ oz (100 g)	0.60
halibut, raw—3½ oz (100 g)	0.85
herring, raw—3½ oz (100 g)	1.07
jack mackerel, raw—3½ oz (100 g)	0.36
limpet, raw—3½ oz (100 g)	14.00
ling, raw—3½ oz (100 g)	0.30
lobster, raw—3½ oz (100 g)	1.47
mackerel, raw—3½ oz (100 g)	1.52
mussel, raw—3½ oz (100 g)	0.74
ocean perch, raw—3½ oz (100 g)	1.25
oysters, raw—3½ oz (100 g)	0.85
periwinkle, raw—3½ oz (100 g)	3.90
pike, raw—3½ oz (100 g)	0.2
pollock, raw—3½ oz (100 g)	0.31
prawn, raw—3½ oz (100 g)	2.85
sablefish, frzn—3½ oz (100 g)	4.35
salmon, atlantic, cnd—3½ oz (100 g)	1.5
salmon, broiled—3½ oz (100 g)	1.35

FISH & SHELLFISH
sardines, cnd in oil—3½ oz (100 g)	0.3
shrimp, fried—3½ oz (100 g)	0.60
squid, raw—3½ oz (100 g)	1.2
tunny, cnd—3½ oz (100 g)	6.3
whelk, raw—3½ oz (100 g)	0.8
wolffish, raw—3½ oz (100 g)	2.1
wrasse, raw—3½ oz (100 g)	0.60
yellowtail, raw—3½ oz (100 g)	0.18

FRUIT & FRUIT JUICE
apple, raw—3½ oz (100 g)	0.31
apple, raw, peeled—3½ oz (100 g)	0.27
apple, stewed w/sugar—3½ oz (100 g)	0.05
apple jce, cnd/bottled—8 fl oz (248 g)	0.03
apple jce, fresh—8 fl oz (248 g)	0.10
applesce, cnd, sweetened—3½ oz (100 g)	0.09
apricot, cnd, sweetened—3½ oz (100 g)	0.89
banana, raw—1 med (114 g)	0.31
blackberries, raw—3½ oz (100 g)	0.35
cantaloupe, raw—1 cup pieces (160 g)	0.22
cherries, raw—3½ oz (100 g)	0.13
currants, black, raw—½ cup (56 g)	0.56
currants, red & white—½ cup (56 g)	0.06
damson, raw—3½ oz (100 g)	0.7
gooseberries, raw—1 cup (150 g)	0.56
grapes, raw—3½ oz (100 g)	0.7
grapefruit, raw—3½ oz (100 g)	0.25
grapefruit jce, cnd—8 fl oz (247 g)	0.10
grapefruit jce, fresh—8 fl oz (247 g)	0.10
mango, raw—1 med (207 g)	2.32
orange, raw—3½ oz (100 g)	0.23
orange jce, fresh—8 fl oz (248 g)	0.10
peach, raw—3½ oz (100 g)	0.1
pear, raw—1 med (166 g)	0.83
pineapple, raw—1 cup pieces (155 g)	0.16
pineapple, cnd—3½ oz (100 g)	0.1
plum, raw—3½ oz (100 g)	0.7
raspberries, raw—1 cup (123 g)	0.37
raisins, dried—3½ oz (100 g)	0.7
strawberries, raw—1 cup (149 g)	0.18
strawberries, frzn—3½ oz (100 g)	0.19

GRAIN & GRAIN FRACTIONS
barley, pearled—3½ oz (100 g)	0.02
barley, whole grain—3½ oz (100 g)	0.57
bulgur, dry—3½ oz (100 g)	0.06
corn grits, dry—3½ oz (100 g)	0.12
cornmeal, dry—3½ oz (100 g)	0.15
cornmeal, ckd—3½ oz (100 g)	0.08
flour, buckwheat—3½ oz (100 g)	0.32
flour, corn—3½ oz (100 g)	0.12
flour, rye, dark—3½ oz (100 g)	1.41
flour, rye, light—3½ oz (100 g)	0.43
flour, rye, med—3½ oz (100 g)	0.79
flour, triticale—3½ oz (100 g)	0.20
flour, wheat, white—3½ oz (100 g)	0.03
flour, wheat, whole—3½ oz (100 g)	0.82
flour, wheat, whole, durum—3½ oz (100 g)	0.26
hominy grits, ckd—3½ oz (100 g)	0.04
millet, pearled—3½ oz (100 g)	0.05

GRAIN & GRAIN FRACTIONS

oats, dry—*3½ oz (100 g)*	0.25
rye, whole grain—*3½ oz (100 g)*	1.28
semolina, boiled—*3½ oz (100 g)*	0.06
triticale, whole grain—*3½ oz (100 g)*	0.90
wheat, whole grain—*3½ oz (100 g)*	1.01
wheat, whole grain, durum—*3½ oz (100 g)*	0.89
wheat bran—*3½ oz (100 g)*	1.49
wheat germ—*3½ oz (100 g)*	14.07

GRAIN PRODUCTS

bread, white—*3½ oz (100 g)*	0.12
bread, whole wheat—*3½ oz (100 g)*	0.10
biscuit mix—*3½ oz (100 g)*	0.27
cereal, rte	
corn flakes—*3½ oz (100 g)*	0.10
puffed corn—*3½ oz (100 g)*	0.09
puffed rice—*3½ oz (100 g)*	0.06
puffed wheat—*3½ oz (100 g)*	0.67
shredded wheat—*3½ oz (100 g)*	0.36
wheat flakes—*3½ oz (100 g)*	0.42
cereal, whole wheat, dry—*3½ oz (100 g)*	1.06
cookies—*3½ oz (100 g)*	2.57
crackers—*3½ oz (100 g)*	0.37
macaroni, dry—*3½ oz (100 g)*	0.02
pretzels—*3½ oz (100 g)*	0.15
roll, plain, white—*3½ oz (100 g)*	0.78
roll, hamburger—*3½ oz (100 g)*	0.04
scone, enr—*3½ oz (100 g)*	1.3
spaghetti, dry—*3½ oz (100 g)*	0.2

INFANT FOODS

cereals, dry	
barley—*3½ oz (100 g)*	0.10
high pro—*3½ oz (100 g)*	0.27
mixed—*3½ oz (100 g)*	0.16
oat flakes—*3½ oz (100 g)*	0.90
oatmeal—*3½ oz (100 g)*	0.19
rice—*3½ oz (100 g)*	0.26
cereal w/fruit/egg, str—*3½ oz (100 g)*	0.25
desserts, str—*3½ oz (100 g)*	0.23
dinners, meat & veg, str—*3½ oz (100 g)*	0.22
egg yolk, str—*3½ oz (100 g)*	0.60
fruits, str—*3½ oz (100 g)*	0.58
meats, str—*3½ oz (100 g)*	0.39
vegs, str—*3½ oz (100 g)*	0.45

MEAT

beef, corned, cnd—*3½ oz (100 g)*	0.8
beef, ground, raw—*3½ oz (100 g)*	0.79
beef, ground, ckd—*3½ oz (100 g)*	0.37
beef heart, raw—*3½ oz (100 g)*	0.60
beef kidney, raw—*3½ oz (100 g)*	0.2
beef liver, raw—*3½ oz (100 g)*	0.67
beef liver, broiled—*3½ oz (100 g)*	0.63
beef loin, lean, raw—*3½ oz (100 g)*	0.5
beef roast, ckd—*3½ oz (100 g)*	0.14
beef sausage, fried—*3½ oz (100 g)*	0.15
beef sirloin, lean, raw—*3½ oz (100 g)*	0.6
beef steak, raw—*3½ oz (100 g)*	0.47
beef steak, broiled—*3½ oz (100 g)*	0.13
beef tripe, raw—*3½ oz (100 g)*	0.1

MEAT

lamb chop, raw—*3½ oz (100 g)*	0.62
lamb chop, broiled—*3½ oz (100 g)*	0.16
lamb cutlet, broiled—*3½ oz (100 g)*	0.22
lamb kidney, raw—*3½ oz (100 g)*	0.45
lamb leg, roasted—*3½ oz (100 g)*	0.05
lamb liver, raw—*3½ oz (100 g)*	0.46
mutton, lean & fat, raw—*3½ oz (100 g)*	0.43
pork, lean & fat, raw—*3½ oz (100 g)*	0.08
pork bacon, med fat, raw—*3½ oz (100 g)*	0.48
pork bacon, fried—*3½ oz (100 g)*	0.53
pork chop, fried—*3½ oz (100 g)*	0.16
pork ham, fried—*3½ oz (100 g)*	0.28
pork kidney, raw—*3½ oz (100 g)*	0.4
pork liver, raw—*3½ oz (100 g)*	1.69
pork loin, raw—*3½ oz (100 g)*	0.40
pork sausage, fried—*3½ oz (100 g)*	0.16
pork spareribs, raw—*3½ oz (100 g)*	0.6
rabbit, lean & fat, raw—*3½ oz (100 g)*	0.40
veal brain, raw—*3½ oz (100 g)*	1.2
veal cutlet, fried—*3½ oz (100 g)*	0.05
veal heart, raw—*3½ oz (100 g)*	0.33
veal liver, raw—*3½ oz (100 g)*	0.33

MEAT, LUNCHEON

bologna—*3½ oz (100 g)*	0.06
frankfurter—*3½ oz (100 g)*	0.3
frankfurter, cnd—*3½ oz (100 g)*	0.16
liverwurst—*3½ oz (100 g)*	0.35
salami—*3½ oz (100 g)*	0.11

MILK

cow milk, choc—*1 cup (250 g)*	0.23
cow milk, condensed, sweetened—*1 fl oz (38 g)*	0.11
cow milk, whole—*1 cup (244 g)*	0.15
cow milk, whole, dry—*¼ cup (32 g)*	0.19
human milk—*1 fl oz (31 g)*	0.27

NUTS, NUT PRODUCTS & SEEDS

almonds—*3½ oz (100 g)*	15.0
brazil nuts—*3½ oz (100 g)*	6.5
cashews—*3½ oz (100 g)*	0.19
chestnuts—*3½ oz (100 g)*	0.5
coconut, fresh—*3½ oz (100 g)*	0.7
filberts (hazelnuts)—*3½ oz (100 g)*	21.0
peanut butter—*3½ oz (100 g)*	6.0
peanuts—*3½ oz (100 g)*	6.5
pecans—*3½ oz (100 g)*	1.5
pistachios—*3½ oz (100 g)*	5.21
poppy seeds—*3½ oz (100 g)*	1.8
sunflower seeds—*3½ oz (100 g)*	44.0
walnuts—*3½ oz (100 g)*	1.5

POULTRY

chicken, cnd—*3½ oz (100 g)*	0.28
chicken, flesh & skin, raw—*3½ oz (100 g)*	0.29
chicken, flesh & skin, raw, frzn—*3½ oz (100 g)*	0.42
chicken, flesh & skin, ckd—*3½ oz (100 g)*	0.35
chicken, fried, frzn—*3½ oz (100 g)*	0.25
chicken, fried, frzn, oven heated—*3½ oz (100 g)*	0.19
chicken heart, raw—*3½ oz (100 g)*	1.19

POULTRY

chicken liver, raw—3½ oz (100 g)	0.25
pigeon breast, raw—3½ oz (100 g)	0.06
pigeon liver, raw—3½ oz (100 g)	1.54
turkey breast, raw—3½ oz (100 g)	0.09
turkey heart, raw—3½ oz (100 g)	0.16
turkey skin, raw—3½ oz (100 g)	0.40
turkey thigh, raw—3½ oz (100 g)	0.64

VEGETABLES

artichoke, raw—3½ oz (100 g)	0.15
artichoke, jerusalem, raw—3½ oz (100 g)	0.19
avocado, raw, calif—1 med (173 g)	2.32
asparagus, raw—3½ oz (100 g)	1.98
asparagus, frzn—3½ oz (100 g)	1.40
beet, cnd—3½ oz (100 g)	0.03
beet greens, raw—3½ oz (100 g)	1.5
broad beans, dry—3½ oz (100 g)	0.05
broccoli, raw—3½ oz (100 g)	0.46
brussels sprouts, raw—3½ oz (100 g)	0.88
brussels sprouts, ckd—3½ oz (100 g)	0.85
cabbage, chinese, raw—3½ oz (100 g)	0.12
cabbage, green, raw—3½ oz (100 g)	1.67
cabbage, red, raw—3½ oz (100 g)	0.2
cabbage, savoy, raw—3½ oz (100 g)	0.2
cabbage, white, raw—3½ oz (100 g)	0.7
carrot, raw—3½ oz (100 g)	0.44
carrot, cnd—3½ oz (100 g)	0.42
cauliflower, raw—3½ oz (100 g)	0.03
celery, raw—3½ oz (100 g)	0.7
celery root, raw—3½ oz (100 g)	0.2
corn, raw—3½ oz (100 g)	0.49
corn, cnd—3½ oz (100 g)	0.04
corn, frzn—3½ oz (100 g)	0.03
chard, raw—3½ oz (100 g)	1.5
cress, garden, raw—3½ oz (100 g)	0.7
cucumber, raw—3½ oz (100 g)	0.15
dandelion greens, raw—3½ oz (100 g)	2.5
eggplant, raw—3½ oz (100 g)	0.03
garlic, raw—3½ oz (100 g)	0.01
green beans, raw—3½ oz (100 g)	0.02
green beans, cnd—3½ oz (100 g)	0.03
kale, raw—3½ oz (100 g)	8.0
kidney beans, dry—3½ oz (100 g)	4.0
leek, raw—3½ oz (100 g)	0.92
lettuce, raw—3½ oz (100 g)	0.40
maize, raw—3½ oz (100 g)	0.1
mushrooms, raw—3½ oz (100 g)	0.08
mustard greens—3½ oz (100 g)	2.01

VEGETABLES

navy beans, dry—3½ oz (100 g)	0.34
onion, raw—3½ oz (100 g)	0.12
onion rings, frzn, heated—3½ oz (100 g)	0.69
onions, pickled in vinegar—3½ oz (100 g)	0.19
parsley, raw—3½ oz (100 g)	1.74
parsnip, raw—3½ oz (100 g)	1.0
peas, dried—3½ oz (100 g)	0.09
peas, green, raw—3½ oz (100 g)	0.13
peas, green, cnd—3½ oz (100 g)	0.02
peas, green, frzn—3½ oz (100 g)	0.12
pepper, green, raw—3½ oz (100 g)	0.68
potato, raw—3½ oz (100 g)	0.06
potato, baked/boiled—3½ oz (100 g)	0.03
potato, fries—3½ oz (100 g)	0.19
potato chips—3½ oz (100 g)	4.27
pumpkin, raw—3½ oz (100 g)	1.02
rhubarb, raw—3½ oz (100 g)	0.2
rutabaga, steamed—3½ oz (100 g)	0.15
rice, brown, dry—3½ oz (100 g)	1.2
rice, white, dry—3½ oz (100 g)	0.35
rice, white, ckd—3½ oz (100 g)	0.18
shallots, raw—3½ oz (100 g)	0.21
soybeans, raw—3½ oz (100 g)	0.85
spinach, raw—3½ oz (100 g)	1.88
spinach, cnd—3½ oz (100 g)	0.02
squash, steamed, raw—3½ oz (100 g)	0.12
sweet potato, raw—3½ oz (100 g)	4.56
tomato, raw—3½ oz (100 g)	0.27
tomato, cnd—3½ oz (100 g)	0.22
tomato jce, cnd—8 fl oz (243 g)	0.53
turnip greens, raw—3½ oz (100 g)	2.24
turnip root, raw—3½ oz (100 g)	0.02
watercress, raw—3½ oz (100 g)	1.0
wax beans, ckd—3½ oz (100 g)	0.29

MISCELLANEOUS

candy, toffee—3½ oz (100 g)	0.17
choc candy—3½ oz (100 g)	0.7
choc candy, milk choc—3½ oz (100 g)	1.1
cocoa, dry—3½ oz (100 g)	0.2
coffee, inst, dry—3½ oz (100 g)	0.00
jam/jelly—3½ oz (100 g)	0.09
marzipan—3½ oz (100 g)	9.1
molasses—3½ oz (100 g)	0.41
mustard, prep—3½ oz (100 g)	1.75
tomato catsup—3½ oz (100 g)	0.3
yeast, baker's, dried/compressed—3½ oz (100 g)	0.08

Vitamin K (mcg)

	Mean	Range		Mean	Range
BEVERAGES			**VEGETABLES**		
coffee—*6 fl oz (180 g)*	68		asparagus, raw—*5–6 spears (100 g)*	57	
tea, green—*8 fl oz (240 g)*	1709		broccoli, raw—*1 cup (126 g)*	252	
FATS			brussels sprouts, raw—*3½ oz (100 g)*		800–3000
oil, corn—*3½ oz (100 g)*	50		cabbage, raw—*1 cup (124 g)*	155	
oil, soybean—*3½ oz (100 g)*	500		cauliflower, raw—*3½ oz (100 g)*	3600	
MEAT			green beans, raw—*3½ oz (100 g)*	290	
beef, ground, ckd—*3½ oz (100 g)*	7		lettuce, raw—*1 cup (74 g)*	95	
beef, ground, ckd, gamma-irradiated—			peas, green, unripe—*3½ oz (100 g)*	300	
3½ oz (100 g)	0		peas, green, boiled—*½ cup (85 g)*	221	
beef, liver, raw—*3½ oz (100 g)*	92		potato, raw—*3½ oz (100 g)*	80	
liverwurst—*1 oz (28 g)*	34		spinach, raw—*3½ oz (100 g)*	89	40–3000
MILK			tomato, raw—*1 med (148 g)*	7	
cow milk, whole—*1 liter*	60		turnip greens, raw—*1 cup (54 g)*	351	
human milk—*1 liter*	15		watercress, raw—*25 sprigs (25 g)*	14	

Caffeine Content of Selected Foods and Drugs[a] (mg)

	Mean	Range		Mean	Range
COFFEE BEVERAGE			**TEA BEVERAGE**		
drip, automatic—*5 fl oz (150 g)*	137	110–164	black, imported, 5 min brew—*6 fl oz*		
drip, nonautomatic—*5 fl oz (150 g)*	124	106–145	*(180 g)*	65	63–67
instant—*5 fl oz (150 g)*	60	47–68	decaffeinated, 5 min brew—*6 fl oz (180 g)*	1	
instant, decaffeinated—*5 fl oz (150 g)*	3	2–5	green, 1 min brew—*5 fl oz (150 g)*	14	9–19
percolated, automatic—*5 fl oz (150 g)*	117	99–134	green, 3 min brew—*5 fl oz (150 g)*	27	20–33
percolated, nonautomatic—*5 fl oz (150 g)*	108	93–130	green, 5 min brew—*5 fl oz (150 g)*	31	26–36
			instant—*6 fl oz (180 g)*	33	32–35
COFFEE, FLAVORED, FROM INSTANT			mint flavor, 5 min brew—*6 fl oz (180 g)*	50	36–63
MIXES			orange & spice, 5 min brew—*6 fl oz (180 g)*	45	30–59
cafe amaretto—*6 fl oz (185 g)*	60		oolong, 1 min brew—*5 fl oz (150 g)*	13	
cafe francais—*6 fl oz (185 g)*	52		oolong, 3 min brew—*5 fl oz (150 g)*	30	
cafe vienna—*6 fl oz (187 g)*	57		oolong, 5 min brew—*5 fl oz (150 g)*	40	
irish mocha mint—*6 fl oz (185 g)*	27				
orange cappuccino—*6 fl oz (187 g)*	74		**TEA, INSTANT DRY POWDER**		
sunrise (coffee & grain)—*6 fl oz (180 g)*	37		regular—*1 t (1 g)*	32	
suisse mocha—*6 fl oz (185 g)*	40		lemon flavored—*1 t (1 g)*	38	
COFFEE, INSTANT DRY POWDER			**SOFT DRINKS CONTAINING**		
regular—*1 t (1 g)*	60	50–65	**CAFFEINE[b]**		
freeze-dried—*1 t (1 g)*		50–65	Aspen—*12 fl oz (370 g)*	36	
coffee w/grain—*1 t (1 g)*	56		Big Red—*12 fl oz (370 g)*	38	
decaffeinated—*1 t (1 g)*	3		Big Red, Diet—*12 fl oz (370 g)*	38	
			Canada Dry Jamaica cola—*12 fl oz (370 g)*	30	
TEA BEVERAGE			Coca-Cola—*12 fl oz (370 g)*	45	
Am black, 1 min brew—*5 fl oz (150 g)*	28	21–33	cola/pepper sodas—*12 fl oz (360 g)*		30–46
Am black, 3 min brew—*5 fl oz (150 g)*	42	35–46	cola soda, decaffeinated—*12 fl oz (360 g)*	tr	
Am black, 5 min brew—*5 fl oz (150 g)*	46	39–50			

[a] Caffeine is naturally present in coffee, tea, chocolate and cocoa. It may be added to soft drinks. It is present in many prescription and non-prescription drugs such as cold, pain, diuretic, stimulant and weight-control preparations.

[b] Current regulations specify that "cola" and "pepper" soft drinks contain caffeine from kola nut extract or other natural caffeine-containing extracts. Caffeine may also be added to any soft drink, but the total caffeine content cannot exceed 0.02% by weight of the beverage. There is no caffeine in regular or diet club soda, ginger ale, grape soda, fanta sodas, fresca, lemon lime, orange soda, RC 100, root beer, seltzer or sparkling water, seven-up, sprite, teem or tonic water.

	Mean	Range		Mean	Range
SOFT DRINKS CONTAINING CAFFEINE			**CHOCOLATE & FOODS CONTAINING CHOCOLATE**		
cola soda, decaffeinated, diet—*12 fl oz (360 g)*	tr		choc ice cream—*⅔ cup (89 g)*	5	
Diet Coke—*12 fl oz (370 g)*	45		choc fudge topping—*2 T (28 g)*	4	
Diet-Rite Cola—*12 fl oz (355 g)*	36		choc milk—*8 fl oz (250 g)*	5	2–7
Dr. Pepper—*12 fl oz (369 g)*	40		choc powder for milk—*1 T*	10	
Dr. Pepper, Diet—*12 fl oz (355 g)*	40		choc powder for milk, Hershey—*3 T (21 g)*	6	
Kick—*12 fl oz (370 g)*	31		choc powder for milk, Nestle Quik—*2 t (22 g)*	7	
Mountain Dew—*12 fl oz (370 g)*	54		choc pudding, from inst mix—*½ cup (151 g)*	6	
Mr. Pibb—*12 fl oz (370 g)*	41		choc pudding, low cal, D-Zerta—*½ cup (130 g)*	5	
Mr. Pibb, Diet—*12 fl oz (370 g)*	57		choc pudding pop—*1 pop (57 g)*	4	
Mello Yello—*12 fl oz (370 g)*	53		choc fudge pudding, from inst mix—*½ cup (151 g)*	8	
Pepsi Cola—*12 fl oz (370 g)*	38		choc fudge pudding pop—*1 pop (57 g)*	5	
Pepsi, Diet—*12 fl oz (355 g)*	36		choc tapioca pudding, from mix—*½ cup (147 g)*	9	
Pepsi Light—*12 fl oz (355 g)*	36		choc syrup—*2 T (28 g)*	4	
Royal Crown Cola—*12 fl oz (370 g)*	36		cocoa beverage—*6 fl oz*	5	2–8
Royal Crown Cola, Diet—*12 fl oz (355 g)*	33		cocoa, dry powder—*1 T (5 g)*	11	4–19
Royal Crown with a Twist—*12 fl oz (370 g)*	21		cocoa, dry, Hershey—*1 oz (28 g)*	70	
Shasta Cola—*12 fl oz (370 g)*	44		cocoa mix,[a] Hershey—*1 pkt (28 g)*	5	
Shasta Cherry Cola—*12 fl oz (370 g)*	44		cocoa mix,[a] Nestle—*1 oz (28 g)*	4	
Shasta Diet Cola—*12 fl oz (370 g)*	44		cocoa mix[a] w/marshmallows, Nestle—*1 oz (28 g)*	4	
Shasta Diet Cherry Cola—*12 fl oz (370 g)*	44				
Tab—*12 fl oz (356 g)*	45			mg/std dose	mg/tablet or capsule
CHOCOLATE & FOODS CONTAINING CHOCOLATE			**NON-PRESCRIPTION DRUGS**		
baking choc—*1 oz (28 g)*	35		Anacin Analgesic/Anacin max strength/ Anacin-3 (for pain)	64	32
baking choc, Baker's—*1 oz (28 g)*	25		Aqua-Ban (diuretic)	200	
baking choc, Hershey—*1 oz (28 g)*	26		Bromoquinine (for colds)		15
chocolate candy			Caffedrine Capsules (stimulant)	200	
choc flavored chips, Baker's—*¼ cup (43 g)*	12		Cenegisic (for cold/allergy)		15
choc, german sweet, Baker's—*1 oz (28 g)*	8		Cope (for pain)		32
choc kisses—*6 pieces (28 g)*	5		Coryban-D (for colds)	30	30
crunch bar, Nestle—*1.06 oz bar (30 g)*	7		Dexatrim (weight control)	200	200
golden almond—*1 oz (28 g)*	5		Dietac (weight control)	200	200
kit kat—*1.5 oz bar (43 g)*	5		Dristan/Dristan A-F (decongestant)	32	16
krackel bar—*1.2 oz bar (34 g)*	5		Excedrin (for pain)	130	65
milk choc—*1 oz (28 g)*	6	1–15	Goody's Headache Powder (for pain)	33	
milk choc, Hershey—*1.02 oz bar (29 g)*	5		Midol (for pain/diuretic)	64	32
milk choc, Nestle—*1.07 oz bar (30 g)*	8		No Doz (stimulant)	200	100
milk choc w/almonds, Hershey—*1.05 oz bar (29 g)*	5		Neo-synephrine (for cold/allergy)		15
milk choc w/almonds, Nestle—*1 oz (28 g)*	6		Permathene Water Off (diuretic)	200	
milk choc chips—*¼ cup (42 g)*	8		Pre-Mens Forts (diuretic)	100	
mr. goodbar—*1.65 oz bar (47 g)*	6		Prolamine (weight control)	280	140
reese's peanut butter cups—*2 pieces (34 g)*	4		Sinapils (for cold/allergy)		32
choc, german sweet, Baker's—*1 oz (28 g)*	8		Sinarest (for allergy)		30
rolo—*5 pieces (28 g)*	1		Triaminicin (for colds)	30	30
semi-sweet choc, Bakers—*1 oz (28 g)*	12		Vanquish (for pain)	66	33
semi-sweet choc chips, Hershey—*¼ cup (42 g)*	4		Vivarin tablets (stimulant)	200	200
semi-sweet choc chips, Nestle—*1 oz (28 g)*	17		**PRESCRIPTION DRUGS**		
sweet (dark) choc—*1 oz (28 g)*	20	5–35	Apectol tablets (sedative/analgesic)		40
special dark choc, Hershey—*1.02 oz bar (29 g)*	23		Cafergot capsules (migraine headaches)		100
thousand dollar bar—*1.5 oz bar (43 g)*	5		Darvon Compound (pain reliever)		32
whatchamacallit—*1.1 oz bar (32 g)*	1		Esgic tablets (sedative/analgesic)		40
choc brownie w/nuts—*1¼ oz (35 g)*	8		Fiorinal tablets (headaches)		40
choc cake—*¹/₁₆ of 9 inch cake (92 g)*	14		Migrol tablets (headaches)		50
choc covered candy—*1 oz (28 g)*	3		Migralam capsules (migraine headaches)		100
			Soma Compound (pain reliever/muscle relaxant)		32

[a] Contains dry milk & needs only hot water for reconstitution.

Choline[a] (mg)

EGGS
chicken egg—*1 large (48 g)*	253
chicken egg, white—*1 large (33 g)*	tr
chicken egg, yolk—*1 large (17 g)*	253

FATS & SPREADS
butter—*1 t (5 g)*	1
corn oil—*1 T (14 g)*	0
lard—*1 T (14 g)*	1
margarine—*1 t (5 g)*	0

FLOUR & GRAIN FRACTIONS
flour, soybean, full-fat—*1 cup (70 g)*	158
flour, soybean, low-fat—*1 cup (88 g)*	198
flour, soybean, defatted—*1 cup (100 g)*	225
flour, wheat, all purpose, enr—*1 cup (115 g)*	60
wheat bran—*1 T (9 g)*	13
wheat germ—*1 T (7 g)*	28
wheat, whole, dry—*½ cup (59 g)*	63
wheat, whole, ckd—*1 cup (245 g)*	230

MEAT
beef rib, choice, lean, ckd—*3½ oz (100 g)*	82
beef round, choice, raw—*3½ oz (100 g)*	68
bologna—*1 oz (28 g)*	17
frankfurter—*1 frank (50 g)*	29
lamb leg, raw—*3½ oz (100 g)*	84
lamb loin, raw—*3½ oz (100 g)*	76
pork sausage links—*1 piece (60 g)*	29

MILK & MILK MIXES
milk, evaporated—*½ cup (126 g)*	15
milk, skim, reconstituted from dry—*1 cup (245 g)*	25
milk, whole—*1 cup (244 g)*	49

MILK & MILK MIXES
milk, whole, reconstituted from dry—*1 cup (244 g)*	34
inst breakfast mix, choc—*1 pkt (62 g)*	22

NUTS
cashews—*1 oz (28 g)*	37

VEGETABLES
avocado, calif—*½ small (84 g)*	14
cabbage, green, raw—*1 cup (70 g)*	16
carrots, raw—*1 med (81 g)*	11
corn, sweet, white/yellow, raw—*3½ oz (100 g)*	61
cowpeas, young pods/seeds, raw—*1 cup (100 g)*	97
cowpeas, mature, raw—*½ cup (85 g)*	218
green beans—*1 cup (135 g)*	18
lentils, raw—*½ cup (95 g)*	212
mung beans, mature seeds, raw—*½ cup (105 g)*	220
mustard greens, raw—*1 cup (33 g)*	7
rice, brown, raw—*½ cup (100 g)*	112
rice, brown, ckd—*1 cup (195 g)*	218
rice, white, enr, raw—*½ cup (98 g)*	58
rice, white, enr, ckd—*1 cup (150 g)*	89
rice, white, enr, long grain, raw—*½ cup (62 g)*	60
rice, white, enr, long grain, ckd—*1 cup (150 g)*	147
soybean protein concentrate—*0.4 oz (10 g)*	10
soybeans, immature, raw—*3½ oz (100 g)*	315
soybeans, mature, raw—*3½ oz (100 g)*	340
tomato sce—*3½ oz (100 g)*	20
turnip greens, raw—*3½ oz (100 g)*	27
turnip greens, frzn—*1 cup (165 g)*	45

MISCELLANEOUS
molasses—*1 T (20 g)*	17
yeast, brewer's—*1 T (10 g)*	24

[a] Essential nutrient for some animal species, but not for humans. It contains three methyl groups and is synthesized in the body from the amino acid glycine. In the body, it is a structural component of some phospholipids (lecithin & sphingomyelin), and it provides methyl groups for the synthesis of creatine and epinephrine and for methylating certain substances for excretion in the urine.

Dietary Fiber[a] (g)

CEREALS, COOKED

corn grits, reg/quick, enr, ckd—*1 cup (242 g)*	0.6
oats, reg/quick/isnt, ckd—*¾ cup (175 g)*	1.6
ralston, ckd—*¾ cup (190 g)*	3.2

CEREALS, READY-TO-EAT

all bran—*⅓ cup (28 g)*	8.5
alpha bits—*1 cup (28 g)*	0.3
apple jacks—*1 cup (28 g)*	0.2
bran, 100%—*½ cup (28 g)*	8.4
bran buds—*⅓ cup (28 g)*	7.9
bran chex—*⅔ cup (28 g)*	4.6
bran flakes, 40%, Kellogg's—*¾ cup (28 g)*	4.0
bran flakes, 40%, Post—*⅔ cup (28 g)*	3.9
bran flakes, 40%, Ralston Purina—*¾ cup (28 g)*	3.5
cap'n crunch—*¾ cup (28 g)*	0.3
cap'n crunch's crunchberries—*¾ cup (28 g)*	0.3
cap'n crunch's peanut butter—*¾ cup (28 g)*	0.3
cheerios—*1¼ cup (28 g)*	1.1
cocoa krispies—*¾ cup (28 g)*	0.1
cocoa pebbles—*⅞ cup (28 g)*	0.1
cookie crisp, choc chip/van—*1 cup (28 g)*	0.2
corn bran—*⅔ cup (28 g)*	5.4
corn chex—*1 cup (28 g)*	0.5
corn flakes, Kellogg's—*1¼ cup (28 g)*	0.3
corn flakes, Post Toasties—*1 cup (28 g)*	0.5
corn flakes, Ralston Purina—*1 cup (28 g)*	0.6
cracklin bran—*⅓ cup (28 g)*	4.3
crispy rice—*1 cup (28 g)*	0.4
crispy wheats n raisins—*¾ cup (28 g)*	1.3
C.W. Post—*¼ cup (28 g)*	0.7
C.W. Post w/raisins—*¼ cup (28 g)*	0.5
fortified oat flakes—*⅔ cup (28 g)*	0.7
froot loops—*1 cup (28 g)*	0.2
frosted mini-wheats—*4 biscuits (28 g)*	2.1
frosted rice krinkles—*⅞ cup (28 g)*	0.0
fruity pebbles—*⅞ cup (28 g)*	0.0
golden grahams—*¾ cup (28 g)*	0.5
graham crackos—*¾ cup (28 g)*	1.7
granola, Nature Valley—*⅓ cup (28 g)*	1.0
grape-nuts—*¼ cup (28 g)*	1.4
grape-nuts flakes—*⅞ cup (28 g)*	1.8
heartland natural—*¼ cup (28 g)*	1.3
heartland natural w/coconut—*¼ cup (28 g)*	1.4
heartland natural w/raisins—*¼ cup (28 g)*	1.3
honey & nut corn flakes—*¾ cup (28 g)*	0.3
honey bran—*⅞ cup (28 g)*	3.1
honeycomb—*1⅓ cup (28 g)*	0.4
kix—*1½ cups (28 g)*	0.4
life, plain/cinn—*⅔ cup (28 g)*	0.9
lucky charms—*1 cup (28 g)*	0.6
most—*⅔ cup (28 g)*	3.5

CEREALS, READY-TO-EAT

nutri-grain, barley—*¾ cup (28 g)*	1.7
nutri-grain, corn—*⅔ cup (28 g)*	1.8
nutri-grain, rye—*¾ cup (28 g)*	1.8
nutri-grain, wheat—*¾ cup (28 g)*	1.8
nutri-grain, wheat & raisins—*⅔ cup (40 g)*	2.0
product 19—*¾ cup (28 g)*	0.3
puffed rice—*1 cup (14 g)*	0.1
puffed wheat—*1 cup (14 g)*	0.5
quaker 100% natural—*¼ cup (28 g)*	1.0
quaker 100% natural w/apples & cinn—*¼ cup (28 g)*	1.3
quaker 100% natural w/raisins & dates—*¼ cup (28 g)*	1.1
quisp—*1 cup (28 g)*	0.4
raisin bran, Kellogg's—*¾ cup (37 g)*	4.0
raisin bran, Post—*½ cup (28 g)*	3.0
raisin bran, Ralston Purina—*¾ cup (38 g)*	4.8
rice chex—*1⅛ cups (28 g)*	0.2
rice krispies—*1 cup (28 g)*	0.1
rice krispies, frosted—*1 cup (28 g)*	0.1
shredded wheat—*1 oz (28 g)*	2.6
shredded wheat—*1 biscuit (24 g)*	2.2
special K—*1⅓ cups (28 g)*	0.2
sugar corn pops—*1 cup (28 g)*	0.2
sugar frosted flakes, Kellogg's—*¾ cup (28 g)*	0.3
sugar frosted flakes, Ralston Purina—*¾ cup (28 g)*	0.4
sugar frosted rice—*1 cup (28 g)*	0.3
sugar smacks—*¾ cup (28 g)*	0.4
super sugar crisp—*⅞ cup (28 g)*	0.4
tasteeos—*1¼ cups (28 g)*	1.0
team—*1 cup (28 g)*	0.3
total—*1 cup (28 g)*	2.0
trix—*1 cup (28 g)*	0.1
waffelos—*1 cup (28 g)*	0.3
wheat chex—*⅔ cup (28 g)*	2.1
wheat & raisin chex—*¾ cup (38 g)*	2.4

DESSERTS

cookies, animal—*15 cookies (28 g)*	0.4

FLOUR & GRAIN FRACTIONS

corn germ—*1 oz (28 g)*	5.8

FRUITS

apple, raw, w/skin—*1 med (138 g)*	2.8
apple, raw, w/o skin—*1 med (128 g)*	2.9
apple, boiled, w/o skin—*1 cup (171 g)*	3.3
apple, micro ckd, w/o skin—*1 cup (170 g)*	4.0
apple, cnd, sliced, sweetened—*½ cup (102 g)*	1.9
applesce, cnd, sweetened—*½ cup (128 g)*	1.4
applesce, cnd, unsweetened—*½ cup (122 g)*	1.4
apricots, raw—*3 med (106 g)*	1.4
apricots, cnd, jce pack—*3 halves (84 g)*	0.4
banana, raw—*1 med (114 g)*	1.6

[a] Nondigestible plant carbohydrates (including cellulose, hemicellulose, and pectin) and lignin, a nondigestible noncarbohydrate substance found in woody materials. The fiber values in the main table are crude fiber.

FRUITS

blackberries, raw—*½ cup (72 g)*	3.3
blueberries, raw—*1 cup (145 g)*	4.4
cantaloupe, raw—*1 cup (160 g)*	0.5
carambola, raw—*1 med (127 g)*	1.5
cherries, sweet, raw—*10 cherries (68 g)*	1.1
cherries, sweet, cnd, jce pack—*½ cup (125 g)*	0.3
currants, european black, raw—*½ cup (56 g)*	3.0
dates, dried—*10 dates (83 g)*	4.2
grapefruit, cnd, jce pack—*½ cup (124 g)*	0.3
grapes, european (adherent skin), raw—*1 cup (160 g)*	2.6
mangos, raw—*1 med (207 g)*	2.2
papayas, raw—*1 med (304 g)*	2.8
peach, raw—*1 med (87 g)*	0.5
peach, cnd, jce pack—*1 cup (248 g)*	1.1
pear, raw—*1 med (166 g)*	4.1
pear, cnd, jce pack—*1 cup (248 g)*	2.3
pineapple, raw—*1 cup (155 g)*	2.4
pineapple, cnd, jce pack—*1 cup (250 g)*	1.9
plums, cnd, jce pack—*3 plums (95 g)*	0.4
raspberries, raw—*1 cup (123 g)*	5.8
sapodilla, raw—*1 med (170 g)*	9.0

FRUITS

strawberries, raw—*1 cup (149 g)*	2.8
watermelon, raw—*1 cup (160 g)*	0.3

GRAIN PRODUCTS
crackers

cheese snacks, Dixie Belle—*25 crackers (28 g)*	0.7
graham—*2 squares (14 g)*	0.4
oyster—*33 crackers (28 g)*	0.4
ryekrisp—*2 triple crackers (12 g)*	1.6
ryekrisp, seasoned—*2 triple crackers (13 g)*	1.5
ryekrisp, sesame—*2 triple crackers (15 g)*	1.7
snackers, Dixie Belle—*8 crackers (28 g)*	0.7
soda (unsalted tops)—*10 crackers (28 g)*	0.4
wheat snacks, Dixie Belle—*15 crackers (28 g)*	1.1
croutons, herb-seasoned—*⁷⁄₁₀ oz (20 g)*	0.2

JUICES, FRUIT

apricot nectar, cnd—*8 fl oz (251 g)*	0.8
peach nectar, cnd—*8 fl oz (249 g)*	0.4
pear nectar, cnd—*8 fl oz (250 g)*	1.6

VEGETABLES

avocado, raw, calif—*1 med (173 g)*	4.7

Gluten-Containing & Gluten-Free Cereals[a]

GLUTEN-CONTAINING CEREALS
barley
buckwheat
oats
rye
wheat

GLUTEN-FREE CEREALS AND SUBSTITUTES
corn flour
cornmeal

GLUTEN-FREE CEREALS AND SUBSTITUTES
cornstarch
gluten-free wheat starch
lima-bean flour
potato flour
rice
rice flour
soy flour

[a] Nontropical sprue and other malabsorption symptoms may be relieved by a restriction of gluten-containing cereals.

Myo-inositol[a] (mg/100 g)

BEVERAGES
coffee, inst, dry	646
coffee, reg grind, prep	5
fruit punch, cnd	17
lemonade	2
soda, reg/diet	1
tea leaves, dry	3

CEREAL, RTE
bran flakes, 40%	274
corn flakes	6
cracklin bran	67
puffed rice	5
puffed wheat	8
raisin bran	107
shredded wheat	35
team flakes	93

CEREAL, COOKED
barley, ckd	3
corn grits, ckd	10
cream of wheat, ckd	7
oatmeal, reg, ckd	42
oatmeal, inst, ckd	34

CHEESE
american	7
cheddar	9
cottage, creamed	2
cream	7
mozzarella	5
muenster	3
parmesan	6
swiss	5

DESSERTS
cake, angel food	2
cake, yellow w/sugar icing	5
cookies, van wafers	23
ice cream, van	9
sherbet	7

EGGS, CHICKEN
raw	9
scrambled	8
white, raw	5
yolk, raw	34

FISH
crab, raw	5
clam, raw	3
herring, cnd in oil	20
oysters, raw	25
sardines, cnd	12
shrimp, broiled	7
trout, broiled	11
tuna, cnd in oil	11

FISH
tuna, cnd in water	9
whitefish, broiled	2

FRUIT
apple, dried, ckd	9
apple, red, raw	10
apple, yellow, raw	24
applesce, cnd	18
apricot, cnd, water-pack	52
blackberries, cnd, water-pack	173
cantaloupe, raw	355
cherries, raw	14
cherries, dark, cnd, water-pack	127
cherries, red, raw	14
cherries, red, cnd, water-pack	5
cranberries, raw	15
dates, dried	152
figs, dried	91
fruit cocktail, cnd	19
fruit cocktail, cnd, water-pack	43
grapefruit, raw	199
grapefruit sections, cnd	117
grapes, green, raw	16
grapes, green, cnd	7
grapes, purple, raw	15
honeydew melon, raw	46
kiwi fruit, raw	136
lemon peel, raw	33
lime, raw	194
mandarin orange, cnd	149
mango, raw	99
mixed fruit, cnd	58
mixed fruit, cnd, water-pack	49
nectarine, raw	118
orange, raw	307
papaya, raw	8
pear, raw	73
pear, cnd, water-pack	46
peach, raw	58
peach, cnd, water-pack	34
peach, dried	164
pineapple, raw	33
pineapple, cnd, water-pack	16
plums, purple, raw	11
plums, red, raw	30
prune, dried	470
raisins, dried	20
strawberries, raw	13
watermelon, raw	31

FRUIT JUICES
apple, cnd	21
apple, frzn conc	33
apricot nectar, cnd	26

[a] A growth factor for some lower organisms, but not an essential nutrient for humans or other higher animals; important constituent of certain phospholipids

FRUIT JUICE

cranapple, cnd	1
cranberry, cnd	3
cranberry cocktail, cnd	7
grape, frzn conc	36
grapefruit, cnd	41
grapefruit, frzn conc	380
lemon, cnd	73
lemon, fresh	30
orange, cnd	200
orange, fresh	35
orange, frzn conc	204
peach nectar, cnd	1
pineapple, cnd	15
prune, cnd	26

GRAIN PRODUCTS

biscuit	31
bread, bran	81
bread, corn	14
bread, french	34
bread, mixed grain	47
bread, pumpernickel	160
bread, rye	47
bread, wheat, stone-ground	115
bread, white	26
bread, whole wheat	142
crackers, cheese nibs	246
crackers, escort	5
crackers, graham	10
crackers, saltines	47
crackers, soda	13
crackers, wheat thins	89
french toast	8
macaroni, ckd	5
melba toast	59
muffin	15
noodles, ckd	18
pancake	23
popcorn, popped	107
roll, dinner	23
roll, hamburger	478
roll, hot dog	115
spaghetti, ckd	31
waffle	22

MEAT

beef, corned	39
beef, ground, broiled	8
beef liver, raw	64
beef roast, raw	15
beef round, broiled	37
beef tips, braised	7
lamb chop, raw	37
pork bacon, raw	23
pork chop, barbequed	42
pork chop, broiled	14
pork liver, raw	17
pork roast, ckd	30

MEAT, LUNCHEON

bologna	94
corned beef	19

MEAT, LUNCHEON

frankfurter	16
ham, deviled, cnd	4
ham, spiced	6
liver cheese	346
liver loaf	22
luncheon loaf, spiced	39
luncheon meat, cnd	18
pastrami	28
salami	42
souse	54
vienna sausage	81

MILK & FERMENTED MILK

cow milk, buttermilk	1
cow milk, choc, low fat	19
cow milk, condensed, sweetened	26
cow milk, skim	4
cow milk, whole	4
yogurt, plain	6
yogurt, boysenberry	7
yogurt, coffee/van	9
yogurt, strawberry/raspberry	16

NUTS, NUT PRODUCTS & SEEDS

almonds	278
cashews	81
coconut, grated	33
peanut butter, chunky	128
peanut butter, creamy	304
peanuts	134
sunflower seeds	12
walnuts	198

POULTRY

chicken, baked	8
chicken liver, raw	131
turkey, baked	23

SALAD DRESSING

blue cheese	8
blue cheese, low cal	4
french, low cal	8
mayonnaise	4
mayonnaise, low cal	5
oil & vinegar	4
thousand island	50
thousand island, low cal	8
zero, low cal	5

VEGETABLES & VEGETABLE PRODUCTS

artichoke, raw	60
artichoke, frzn	80
artichoke heart, cnd	116
asparagus, green, raw	29
asparagus, green, frzn	15
asparagus spears, green, cnd	28
asparagus, white, cnd	38
avocado, raw	46
beans (pork & beans), cnd	86
beet, raw	12
beet, cnd	8
broccoli, raw	30
broccoli, frzn	11

VEGETABLES & VEGETABLE PRODUCTS	
brussels sprouts, frzn	81
butter beans, cnd	48
cabbage, chinese, raw	27
cabbage, purple, raw	9
cabbage, savoy, raw	70
cabbage, white, raw	21
carrot, raw	12
carrot, cnd	52
carrot, frzn	10
cauliflower, raw	18
cauliflower, frzn	15
celery, raw	5
collard greens, raw	64
collard greens, cnd	30
collard greens, frzn	16
corn, white, cream style, cnd	7
corn, yellow, cnd	24
corn, yellow, frzn	11
corn, yellow, cream style, cnd	20
corn, yellow, cream style, frzn	13
cucumber, raw	15
eggplant, raw	84
great northern beans, cnd	440
great northern beans, dried	327
green beans, raw	105
green beans, cnd	51
green beans, frzn	55
green beans, french style, cnd	87
green beans, french style, frzn	55
green beans, italian, cnd	35
hominy, white, cnd	43
hominy, yellow, cnd	17
kidney beans, dark red, cnd	249
kidney beans, light red, cnd	69
kidney beans, light red, dried	60
lentils, dried	45
lettuce, raw	18
lettuce, endive, raw	11
lettuce, red leaf, raw	22
lettuce, romaine, raw	17
lima beans, cnd	35
lima beans, dried	33
lima beans, frzn	48
lima beans, baby, cnd	110
lima beans, baby, dried	56
lima beans, baby, frzn	42
lima beans, speckled, dried	70
lima beans, speckled, frzn	55
mixed veg, cnd	5
mixed veg, frzn	13
mushrooms, raw	9
mushrooms, cnd	29
mustard greens, raw	23
mustard greens, cnd	9
mustard greens, frzn	17
navy beans, cnd	65
navy beans, dried	283
okra, raw	33
okra, cnd	117

VEGETABLES & VEGETABLE PRODUCTS	
okra, fried	37
okra, frzn	28
onion, green, raw	27
onion, purple, raw	41
onion, white, raw/ckd	23
onion, yellow, raw	44
onion, yellow, ckd	16
parsley, raw	22
peas, black-eyed, raw	116
peas, black-eyed, cnd	117
peas, black-eyed, dried	39
peas, crowder, frzn	70
peas, green, raw	40
peas, green, cnd	76
peas, green, frzn	85
peas, split, dried	128
peas & carrots, frzn	99
pepper, hot, raw	59
pepper, green, banana, raw	135
pepper, green, bell, raw	57
pepper, jalapeno, cnd	30
pinto beans, cnd	23
poke, raw	43
potato, baked	97
potato chips	73
potato, cnd	47
potatoes, hash browns	57
potatoes, inst, dry	30
potatoes, mashed	19
pumpkin, cnd	62
radish, raw	10
rice, brown, ckd	30
rice, white, ckd	15
rice, white, inst, ckd	2
rutabaga, raw	24
rutabaga, cnd	252
sauerkraut, cnd	11
soybeans, dried	88
spinach, raw	8
spinach, cnd	25
spinach, frzn	6
squash, acorn, raw	22
squash, acorn, frzn	66
squash, green, raw	17
squash, hubbard, raw	66
squash, yellow, raw	32
squash, yellow, cnd	6
squash, yellow, frzn	25
squash, zucchini, raw	53
sweet potato, baked	92
tomato, raw	54
tomato, cnd	38
tomato, cherry, raw	41
tomato jce, cnd	48
tomato paste, cnd	51
tomato puree, cnd	77
tomato sce, cnd	81
turnip greens, raw	43
turnip greens, cnd	12

			MISCELLANEOUS	
turnip greens, frzn	8		cranberry sce, sweetened, cnd	2
turnip greens w/turnips, cnd	8		cream sub	1
veg jce, cnd	29		gelatin, dry	7
wax beans, cnd	144		honey	33
wild rice, ckd	27		hot sce	25
			olives, black	10
MISCELLANEOUS			sour cream	76
catsup	38		syrup, pancake	1
cocoa mix, inst, dry	31			

Nitrite and Nitrate[a] (mg/100 g)

	Mean	Range		Mean	Range
NITRITE			**NITRITE**		
bacon	1.3	0.5–3.0	cucumber, raw	2.4	
bacon, smoked	3.1	0.2–6.0	green beans, raw	25.3	
luncheon meat	0.3		eggplant, raw	30.2	
ham, smoked	3.0		lettuce, raw	85.0	
salami		0.2–0.4	lima beans, raw	5.4	
salami, kosher	38.0		melon, raw	43.3	
			onion, raw	13.4	
NITRATE			peas, raw	2.8	
asparagus, raw	2.1		pepper, sweet, raw	12.5	
beet, raw	276.0		pickles	5.9	
beans, dry	1.3		potato, raw	11.9	
broccoli, raw	78.3		pumpkin, raw	41.3	
cabbage, raw	63.5		sauerkraut	19.1	
carrot, raw	11.9		spinach, raw	186.0	
cauliflower, raw	84.7		sweet potato, raw	5.3	
corn, raw	4.5		tomato, raw	6.2	

[a] Nitrates are compounds that occur naturally in leafy vegetables, root vegetables, and water; nitrites are used commercially to cure meats. Nitrates may be converted to nitrites by bacteria in the mouth and intestine. Nitrites may combine with secondary and tertiary amines to form nitrosamines, which are considered to be carcinogenic in test animals.

Oxalic Acid[a] (mg/100 g)

BEVERAGES

beer	1.7
coffee, brewed	1.0
coffee, inst, dry	143.0
tea, brewed	12.5
wine	3.1

EGGS, CHICKEN

boiled	0.45

FISH

flounder, boiled	0.3
haddock, boiled	0.2
sardines, cnd	1.6

FRUIT & FRUIT JUICES

apple, raw	1.5
apricot, raw	6.8
apricot, cnd, sweetened	2.8
banana, raw	0.7
blackberries, raw	12.4
blueberries, raw	0.0
cantaloupe, raw	2.7
cherries, raw	7.2
currants, black, raw	4.3
currants, red, raw	9.9
gooseberries, raw	19.3
gooseberries, stewed	2.6
grapes, raw	7.9
grapefruit, raw	3.3
lemon jce, fresh	1.5
orange, raw	6.2
orange jce, fresh	1.2
peach, raw	0.0
peach, cnd, sweetened	2.5
pear, raw	6.2
pear, cnd, sweetened	1.5
pineapple, cnd, sweetened	1.5
plums, raw	11.9
plums, stewed	2.2
raspberries, raw	2.2
strawberries, raw	6.7

GRAIN PRODUCTS

bread, white	6.9
bread, whole wheat	20.9
cereal, rte, corn flakes	5.0

MEAT & POULTRY

beef, corned, cnd	0.2
beef kidney, braised	3.2
beef liver, braised	4.3
beef, roasted	1.6
chicken, roasted	1.1
lamb, roasted	1.6

MEAT & POULTRY

pork, ham, ckd	1.0
pork, roasted	1.7

MILK

cow milk	0.7

VEGETABLES

artichoke, raw	8.8
asparagus, raw	0.0
asparagus, boiled	1.7
beet, raw	72.2
beet, boiled	109.0
brussels sprouts, raw	6.1
brussels sprouts, boiled	2.8
cabbage, red, raw	7.4
cabbage, savoy, raw	4.9
cabbage, white, raw	0.0
cabbage, white, boiled	1.2
carrot, raw	6.1
carrot, boiled	14.5
cauliflower, raw	6.6
cauliflower, boiled	1.1
celery, raw	6.8
chives, raw	1.1
cucumber, raw	0.0
eggplant, raw	9.5
endive, raw	2.5
fennel, raw	5.0
garlic, raw	5.0
green beans, raw	43.7
green beans, boiled	29.7
kale, raw	7.2
kohlrabi, raw	2.8
leek, raw	0.0
lettuce, raw	2.2
onion, raw	3.0
parsley, raw	5.7
peas, green, raw	0.0
peas, green, boiled	1.1
pepper, green, raw	0.0
potato, raw	0.0
potato, boiled	5.2
pumpkin, raw	0.5
radish, raw	0.3
rhubarb, raw	537.0
rhubarb, stewed	447.0
rutabaga, raw	0.0
salsify, raw	0.0
spinach, boiled	571.0
tomato, raw	3.9

MISCELLANEOUS

butter	0.0
cocoa, dry	623.0
marmalade	5.7
ovaltine, powder	45.9

[a] Organic acid that may bind with minerals in the gastrointestinal tract & hinder their absorption

Phytic Acid[a] (mg)

	Mean	Range		Mean	Range
FRUIT			**NUTS, NUT PRODUCTS & SEEDS**		
apple, raw—*1 med (150 g)*	94		walnuts—*3½ oz (100 g)*	760	
blackberries, raw—*3½ oz (100 g)*	14		sesame seeds, raw—*1 oz (28 g)*	1319	
figs, dried—*3½ oz (100 g)*	62		**VEGETABLES**		
			black gram beans, raw—*3½ oz (100 g)*	1460	
GRAINS & GRAIN FRACTIONS			broad beans, boiled—*3½ oz (100 g)*	18	
barley, whole grain—*3½ oz (100 g)*	970		carrot, raw—*1 med (81 g)*	8	
barley, pearl, raw—*3½ oz (100 g)*	491		corn, raw—*3½ oz (100 g)*	890	
cornmeal, whole kernel—*3½ oz (100 g)*	610		corn, yellow, cnd—*½ cup (82 g)*	26	
millet, raw—*3½ oz (100 g)*	750		cowpeas, raw—*3½ oz (100 g)*	440	
milo—*3½ oz (100 g)*	990		garbanzo beans, mature, boiled—*½ cup (62 g)*	129	
oats, raw—*3½ oz (100 g)*	943	790–1010	garbanzo beans, raw—*3½ oz (100 g)*	280	
rye flour—*3½ oz (100 g)*	919		great northern beans, raw—*3½ oz (100 g)*		560–1630
rye, whole grain—*3½ oz (100 g)*	970		green beans, snap, cnd—*½ cup (62 g)*	56	
sorghum—*3½ oz (100 g)*		570–960	green gram beans, raw—*3½ oz (100 g)*	660	
soy flour, full fat—*3½ oz (100 g)*	704		haricot beans, raw—*3½ oz (100 g)*	802	
soy flour, low fat—*3½ oz (100 g)*	660		jerusalem artichoke, boiled—*3½ oz (100 g)*	29	
triticale—*3½ oz (100 g)*		500–1890	kidney beans, raw—*3½ oz (100 g)*		1200–2060
wheat flour, all-purpose—*1 cup (137 g)*	386		lentils, raw—*3½ oz (100 g)*	434	
wheat flour, whole wheat—*1 cup (120 g)*	1014		lima beans, mature, raw—*3½ oz (100 g)*	890	
wheat grain—*3½ oz (100 g)*		620–1350	navy beans, mature, raw—*3 T (48 g)*	295	
wheat grain, hard red winter—*3½ oz (100 g)*	840		navy beans, mature, boiled—*½ cup (85 g)*	294	
wheat grain, soft—*3½ oz (100 g)*	1140		parsnips, raw—*3½ oz (100 g)*	76	
wheat bran, crude—*1 oz (28 g)*	843		peas, green, raw—*3½ oz (100 g)*	39	
wheat germ—*1 T (6 g)*	244		peas, green, cnd—*½ cup (85 g)*	24	
wheat gluten—*1 oz (28 g)*	596		peas, dried, raw—*3½ oz (100 g)*	851	
			peas, split, raw—*3½ oz (100 g)*	546	
GRAIN PRODUCTS			pinto beans, raw—*3½ oz (100 g)*		610–1950
bread, rye—*1 slice (25 g)*	235		potato w/o skin, boiled—*½ cup (78 g)*	63	
bread, white, enr—*1 slice (27 g)*	30	19–33	red mexican beans, raw—*3½ oz (100 g)*		540–1100
bread, whole wheat—*1 slice (28 g)*	163	49–179	rice, brown, raw—*3½ oz (100 g)*	890	
cereal, rte			rice, white, long grain, raw—*3½ oz (100 g)*	340	
all bran—*1 oz (28 g)*	679		rice, white, med grain, raw—*3½ oz (100 g)*		140–190
corn flakes—*1 oz (28 g)*	14		rice, white, short grain, raw—*3½ oz (100 g)*	140	
granola—*1 oz (28 g)*	175		soybeans, raw—*3½ oz (100 g)*		1000–1470
rice flakes—*1 oz (28 g)*	65		tomato, raw, sliced—*½ cup (100 g)*	15	
shredded wheat—*1 oz (28 g)*	415		tomato, cnd—*½ cup (120 g)*	8	
wheat flakes—*1 oz (28 g)*	411		white beans, raw—*3½ oz (100 g)*	1030	
corn chips—*1 oz (28 g)*	178		white beans, small, raw—*3½ oz (100 g)*		550–750
crackers, saltines—*4 crackers (11 g)*	19		wild rice, raw—*3½ oz (100 g)*	2200	
farina, reg, ckd—*½ cup (122 g)*	5		**MISCELLANEOUS**		
macaroni, ckd—*½ cup (70 g)*	57		cake, white—*1 square (104 g)*	18	
oatmeal, ckd—*½ cup (120 g)*	133		cocoa, dry—*1 T (5 g)*	94	
popcorn, popped—*1 cup (6 g)*	37		coffee beverage, brewed—*6 fl oz (188 g)*	10	
roll, white—*1 med*	19		milk chocolate—*1 oz (28 g)*	43	
			pie, peach—*1 slice (118 g)*	4	
NUTS, NUT PRODUCTS & SEEDS			soybean meal—*3½ oz (100 g)*		1400–1600
almonds—*3½ oz (100 g)*	1280		soybean pro concentrate—*3½ oz (100 g)*		1240–2170
barcelona nuts—*3½ oz (100 g)*	883		soybean pro isolate—*3½ oz (100 g)*		430–1170
brazil nuts—*3½ oz (100 g)*	1799		tomato soup—*½ cup (122 g)*	8	
chestnuts—*3½ oz (100 g)*	47				
coconut, raw—*3½ oz (100 g)*	270				
hazelnuts—*3½ oz (100 g)*	604				
peanut butter—*1 T (16 g)*	200				
peanuts—*3½ oz (100 g)*	748				

[a] A strong acid that may form salts with minerals in the intestine and thus hinder mineral absorption. The concentration of phytic acid in plant materials varies according to plant part and state of maturity at harvest. The chemical name is myo-inositol 1, 2, 3, 4, 5, 6-hexakis (dihydrogen phosphate).

Phytosterol (mg)

FRUITS

apricots, raw—*3 med (106 g)*	19
banana, raw—*1 med (114 g)*	18
cantaloupe, raw—*1 cup pieces (160 g)*	16
cherries, sweet, raw—*10 cherries (68 g)*	8
figs, raw—*1 med (50 g)*	16
grapefruit, white, raw—*½ med (118 g)*	20
grapes, european (adherent skin), raw—*1 cup (160 g)*	6
lemon peel, raw—*1 T (6 g)*	2
loquats, raw—*10 med (100 g)*	2

FRUITS

orange, navel, raw—*1 med (140 g)*	34
orange peel, raw—*1 T (6 g)*	2
peach, raw—*1 med (87 g)*	9
pears, raw—*1 med (166 g)*	13
persimmons, japanese, raw—*1 med (168 g)*	7
pineapple, raw—*1 cup pieces (155 g)*	9
plum, raw—*1 med (66 g)*	5
pomegranates, raw—*1 med (154 g)*	26
strawberries, raw—*1 cup (149 g)*	18
watermelon, raw—*1 cup (160 g)*	3

Purine-Yielding Foods[a]

FOODS HIGHEST IN PURINES (150–825 mg/100 g)
anchovies (363 mg/100 g)
brains
kidney (beef—200 mg/100 g)
game meats
gravies
herring
liver (calf/beef—233 mg/100 g)
mackerel
meat extracts (160–400 mg/100 g)
sardines (295 mg/100 g)
scallops
sweetbreads (825 mg/100 g)

FOODS HIGH IN PURINES (50–150 mg/100 g)
asparagus
breads & cereals, whole grain
cauliflower
eels
fish, fresh & saltwater
legumes, beans/lentils/peas
meat—beef/lamb/pork/veal
meat soups & broths

FOODS HIGH IN PURINES (50–150 mg/100 g)
mushrooms
oatmeal
peas, green
poultry—chicken/duck/turkey
shellfish—crab/lobster/oysters
spinach
wheat germ & bran

FOODS LOWEST IN PURINES (0–50 mg/100 g)
beverages—coffee/tea/sodas
breads & cereals except whole grain
cheese
eggs
fats
fish roe
fruits & fruit juices
gelatin
milk
nuts
sugars, syrups, sweets
vegetables (except those listed above)
vegetable & cream soups

[a] Purines are normally formed in the body during the metabolic breakdown of nucleoproteins. In certain genetic disorders, including gout, the relatively insoluble purine *uric acid* tends to accumulate and deposit in the toes and in other joints. Drug treatment is generally prescribed for patients with gout; however, dietary restriction of purine-yielding foods may also be advised.

Saccharin[a] Content of Beverages

Beverage	mg/fl oz	mg/12 fl oz	Beverage	mg/fl oz	mg/12 fl oz
Alba '77 fit & frosty	4.2[b]		diet root beer	6.7–11.8	80.4–141.6
cranberry apple jce, low cal, bottled	7.5	90.0	diet root beer, A&W	10.5	126.0
cranberry jce cocktail, low cal, bottled	8.8	105.6	diet root beer, Hires	6.7	80.4
Diet Coke	10.8	129.0	diet root beer, Ramblin	11.3	135.6
diet cola/pepper	8.4–12.0	100.8–144.0	Diet Seven-Up	7.3	87.6
diet cola, decaffeinated	8.4–12.0	100.8–144.0	diet soda, various flavors	6.1–10.7	73.2–128.4
diet lemon-lime	6.5–12.0	78.0–144.0	Diet Sprite	7.1	85.5
Diet Mr. Pibb	9.5	114.0	Fresca	6.8	81.0
Diet Pepsi	10.4	124.8	Pepsi Light	9.0	108.0
Diet Rite	12.0	144.0	Tab	9.3	111.0

[a] Artificial sweetener
[b] 33.6 mg per 8 fl oz

Saccharin[a] Content of Sugar Substitutes

Sugar Substitute	Saccharin Content	Sugar Substitute	Saccharin Content
Diamond Crystal	40.0 mg Ca saccharin/0.4-g packet	Sugartwin, white/brown	14.0 mg/1 t (0.4 g)
Sucaryl Liquid	7.6 mg/t	Sweet & Low	40.0 mg Na saccharin/1-g packet
Sugartwin, white	28.2 mg/0.8-g packet		

[a] Artificial sweetener

Foods High in Salicylates[a]

FRUITS
apples
apricots
blackberries
boysenberries
cherries
currants
dewberries
gooseberries
grapefruit
grapes
lemons
melons
nectarines
oranges
peaches
plums

FRUITS
prunes
raisins
raspberries
strawberries

VEGETABLES
cucumbers
peppers, green bell
peppers, tabasco
potatoes
tomatoes

MISCELLANEOUS
almonds
aspirin
root beer
tartrazine (yellow no. 5)

[a] Some individuals are sensitive to salicylates and develop salicylate-induced urticaria (hives) after ingestion of aspirin or foods containing salicylates.

Sugars[a] (g)

BEVERAGES, CARBONATED		**CEREALS, READY-TO-EAT**		
cola soda—*12 fl oz (369 g)*	40.7	cocoa krispies—*¾ cup (28 g)*	12.0	
ginger ale—*12 fl oz (366 g)*	29.0	cocoa puffs—*1 cup (28 g)*	11.0	
lemon-lime soda—*12 fl oz (360 g)*	39.6	cookie crisp, choc chip—*1 cup (28 g)*	12.0	
orange soda—*12 fl oz (372 g)*	45.8	cookie crisp, van—*1 cup (28 g)*	14.0	
pepper-type soda—*12 fl oz (369 g)*	40.7	corn chex—*1 cup (28 g)*	2.0	
tonic water—*4 fl oz (122 g)*	10.4	corn flakes, Kellogg's—*1¼ cup (28 g)*	2.0	
		corn flakes, Post Toasties—*1 cup (28 g)*	3.0	
BEVERAGES, NONCARBONATED		corn flakes, Ralston Purina—*1 cup (28 g)*	2.0	
awake,[b] from frzn conc—*6 fl oz (186 g)*	20.3	corn total—*1 cup (28 g)*	3.0	
coffee, from inst		count chocula—*1 cup (28 g)*	13.0	
cafe amaretto—*6 fl oz (185 g)*	6.1	cracklin bran—*⅓ cup (28 g)*	8.0	
cafe francais—*6 fl oz (185 g)*	5.9	crazy cow, choc/strawberry—*1 cup (28 g)*	12.0	
cafe vienna—*6 fl oz (187 g)*	9.6	crispy rice—*1 cup (28 g)*	3.0	
irish mocha mint—*6 fl oz (185 g)*	6.5	crispy wheats & raisins—*¾ cup (28 g)*	10.0	
orange cappuccino—*6 fl oz (187 g)*	9.4	donutz, choc—*1 cup (28 g)*	9.0	
suisse mocha—*6 fl oz (185 g)*	6.6	donutz, powdered—*1 cup (28 g)*	10.0	
kool-aid, all flavors,[c] from mix—*8 fl oz (246 g)*	24.2	frankenberry—*1 cup (28 g)*	13.0	
lemonade, cnd—*12 fl oz (368 g)*	34.3	froot loops—*1 cup (28 g)*	13.0	
lemonade, from frzn conc—*8 fl oz (246 g)*	23.1	frosted mini-wheats—*4 biscuits (28 g)*	7.0	
lemonade, from mix—*8 fl oz (244 g)*	21.9	fruit & fibre w/apples & cinn—*½ cup (28 g)*	7.4	
lemon-lime, from mix—*8 fl oz (244 g)*	22.5	fruit & fibre w/dates, raisins & walnuts—*½ cup (28 g)*	7.1	
orange plus,[b] from frzn conc—*6 fl oz (187 g)*	19.2	fruit brute—*1 cup (28 g)*	12.0	
tang, grape—*3 rd t in 6 fl oz water (186 g)*	22.7	golden grahams—*¾ cup (28 g)*	10.0	
tang, grapefruit—*3 rd t in 6 fl oz water (186 g)*	20.9	graham crackos—*¾ cup (28 g)*	10.0	
tang, orange—*3 rd t in 6 fl oz water (186 g)*	21.7	granola, Nature Valley—*⅓ cup (28 g)*	7.0	
		honey & nut corn flakes—*¾ cup (28 g)*	9.0	
CANDY & CANDY BARS		honey bran—*⅞ cup (28 g)*	7.0	
choc chips, semi-sweet—*1 oz (28 g)*	17.0	honey nut cheerios—*¾ cup (28 g)*	10.0	
choc flavored chips—*¼ cup (43 g)*	11.7	kaboom—*1 cup (28 g)*	6.0	
choc, german sweet—*1 oz (28 g)*	8.3	kix—*1½ cups (28 g)*	2.0	
choc, semi-sweet—*1 oz (28 g)*	12.2	lucky charms—*1 cup (28 g)*	11.0	
crunch bar, Nestle—*1¹⁄₁₆ oz bar (30 g)*	15.0	marshmallow krispies—*1¼ cup (37 g)*	10.0	
kit kat—*1½ oz bar (43 g)*	20.0	most—*⅔ cup (28 g)*	6.0	
krackel—*1.45 oz bar (41 g)*	21.0	nutri-grain, corn—*⅔ cup (28 g)*	2.0	
milk choc—*1.07 oz bar (30 g)*	17.0	nutri-grain, wheat—*¾ cup (28 g)*	2.0	
milk choc—*1.45 oz bar (41 g)*	22.0	nutri-grain, wheat & raisins—*⅔ cup (40 g)*	8.0	
milk choc w/almonds—*1 oz (28 g)*	14.0	product 19—*¾ cup (28 g)*	3.0	
milk choc w/almonds—*1.45 oz bar (41 g)*	20.0	puffed rice—*1 cup (14 g)*	0.0	
mr. goodbar—*1.65 oz bar (47 g)*	19.0	puffed wheat—*1 cup (14 g)*	0.0	
mr. goodbar, big block—*2 oz bar (57 g)*	24.0	raisin bran, Kellogg's—*¾ cup (37 g)*	12.0	
peanut butter cup—*1.6 oz (45 g)*	21.0	raisin bran, Ralston Purina—*¾ cup (38 g)*	10.0	
reese's pieces—*1 oz (28 g)*	16.0	raisins, rice & rye—*1 cup (37 g)*	10.0	
reese's pieces—*1 pkg (49 g)*	28.0	rice chex—*1⅛ cups (28 g)*	2.0	
thousand dollar bar—*1.5 oz bar (43 g)*	21.0	rice krispies—*1 cup (28 g)*	3.0	
whatchamacallit—*1.4 oz bar (40 g)*	15.0	rice krispies, frosted—*1 cup (28 g)*	10.0	
		shredded wheat—*1 oz (28 g)*	0.0	
CEREALS, READY-TO-EAT		special K—*1⅓ cups (28 g)*	2.0	
banana flavored frosted flakes—*1 oz (28 g)*	10.0	sugar corn pops—*1 cup (28 g)*	12.0	
body buddies—*1 cup (28 g)*	6.0	sugar frosted flakes—*¾ cup (28 g)*	11.0	
boo berry—*1 cup (28 g)*	13.0	sugar frosted rice—*1 cup (28 g)*	11.0	
bran chex—*⅔ cup (28 g)*	5.0	sugar puffs—*⅞ cup (28 g)*	14.0[d]	
bran flakes, 40%, Ralston Purina—*¾ cup (28 g)*	5.0	sugar smacks—*¾ cup (28 g)*	16.0	
buc wheats—*¾ cup (28 g)*	9.0	tasteeos—*1¼ cups (28 g)*	1.0	
cheerios—*1¼ cup (28 g)*	1.0			

[a] Includes all mono- and disaccharides unless otherwise indicated
[b] Imit orange jce

[c] Avg of 12 flavors
[d] Sucrose rather than total sugars

CEREALS, READY-TO-EAT

toasty O's—*1¼ cups (28 g)*	1.0[a]
total—*1 cup (28 g)*	3.0
trix—*1 cup (28 g)*	12.0
waffelos—*1 cup (28 g)*	13.0
wheat chex—*⅔ cup (28 g)*	2.0
wheat & raisin chex—*¾ cup (38 g)*	11.0
wheaties—*1 cup (28 g)*	3.0

COMBINATION FOODS

frzn entrees, Stouffer's Lean Cuisine	
beef oriental in sce w/veg & rice—*9⅛ oz (259 g)*	2.0
chicken & veg w/vermicelli—*12¾ oz (361 g)*	5.0
chicken, glazed w/veg rice—*8½ oz (241 g)*	4.0
chow mein, chicken w/rice—*11¼ oz (319 g)*	2.0
lasagna, zucchini—*11 oz (312 g)*	8.0
meatball stew—*10 oz (284 g)*	8.0
scallops, oriental & veg w/rice—*11 oz (312 g)*	4.0
spaghetti w/beef & mushroom sce—*11½ oz (326 g)*	5.0

DESSERTS

cheesecake, from mix—*⅛ cake (103 g)*	29.3
custard, from mix—*½ cup (143 g)*	22.8
gelatin dessert, all flavors—*½ cup (140 g)*	18.6
pie filling	
banana cream, from mix—*amt for ⅙ pie (96 g)*	14.0
coconut cream, from mix—*amt for ⅙ pie (96 g)*	13.1
lemon w/meringue, from mix—*amt for ⅙ pie (145 g)*	31.3
pudding	
banana cream, from inst mix—*½ cup (149 g)*	26.0
butter pecan, from inst mix—*½ cup (148 g)*	24.7
butterscotch, from inst mix—*½ cup (149 g)*	25.9
butterscotch, low cal, from mix—*½ cup (130 g)*	7.1
choc, from inst mix—*½ cup (151 g)*	26.5
choc fudge, from inst mix—*½ cup (151 g)*	25.9
choc, low cal, from mix—*½ cup (130 g)*	6.6
coconut cream, from inst mix—*½ cup (149 g)*	23.3
french van, from inst mix—*½ cup (149 g)*	26.1
lemon, from inst mix—*½ cup (149 g)*	26.7
pineapple cream, from inst mix—*½ cup (149 g)*	26.2
pistachio, from inst mix—*½ cup (149 g)*	25.6
rice, from mix—*½ cup (149 g)*	19.0
tapioca, from mix—*½ cup (145 g)*	21.1
tapioca, choc, from mix—*½ cup (147 g)*	21.1
van, from inst mix—*½ cup (149 g)*	26.7
van, low cal, from mix—*½ cup (130 g)*	7.3
pudding pops	
banana—*1 pop (57 g)*	14.2
butterscotch—*1 pop (57 g)*	14.2
choc—*1 pop (57 g)*	14.8
choc fudge—*1 pop (57 g)*	14.7
van—*1 pop (57 g)*	14.2
toaster pastry	
blueberry—*1 pastry (52 g)*	13.0
blueberry, frosted—*1 pastry (52 g)*	15.0
brown sugar cinn—*1 pastry (50 g)*	12.0
brown sugar cinn, frosted—*1 pastry (50 g)*	14.0
cherry—*1 pastry (52 g)*	13.0
cherry, frosted—*1 pastry (52 g)*	15.0
choc chip—*1 pastry (50 g)*	15.0

[a] Sucrose rather than total sugars

DESSERTS

toaster pastry	
choc fudge—*1 pastry (52 g)*	18.0
choc van creme, frosted—*1 pastry (52 g)*	19.0
concord grape, frosted—*1 pastry (52 g)*	16.0
dutch apple, frosted—*1 pastry (52 g)*	16.0
raspberry, frosted—*1 pastry (52 g)*	17.0
strawberry—*1 pastry (52 g)*	13.0
strawberry, frosted—*1 pastry (52 g)*	15.0

FISH, STOUFFER'S LEAN CUISINE

fillet of fish divan, frzn—*12⅜ oz (351 g)*	6.0
fillet of fish florentine, frzn—*9 oz (255 g)*	3.0

FRUIT & FRUIT JUICES

apple, raw—*3½ oz (100 g)*	9.9
apricot, raw—*3½ oz (100 g)*	7.4
banana, raw—*3½ oz (100 g)*	14.0
blackberries, raw—*3½ oz (100 g)*	5.5
blueberries, raw—*3½ oz (100 g)*	5.8
cantaloupe/honeydew, raw—*3½ oz (100 g)*	11.1
cherries, raw—*3½ oz (100 g)*	11.9
currants, raw—*3½ oz (100 g)*	8.0
dates, dried—*3½ oz (100 g)*	66.0
gooseberries, raw—*3½ oz (100 g)*	8.4
grapes, raw—*3½ oz (100 g)*	13.6
grapefruit, raw—*3½ oz (100 g)*	6.8
lemon jce, fresh—*(100 g)*	1.6
mixed fruit, frzn, sweetened—*1 cup (250 g)*	54.3
orange, raw—*3½ oz (100 g)*	8.2
peach, raw—*3½ oz (100 g)*	6.7
peach, frzn, sweetened—*1 cup (250 g)*	54.2
pear, raw—*3½ oz (100 g)*	8.0
plums, raw—*3½ oz (100 g)*	8.6
raspberries, raw—*3½ oz (100 g)*	5.4
raspberries, frzn, sweetened—*⅖ cup (100 g)*	22.0
strawberries, raw—*3½ oz (100 g)*	5.2
strawberries, frzn, sweetened—*1 cup (255 g)*	47.9
tangerine, raw—*3½ oz (100 g)*	7.5

GRAIN & GRAIN PRODUCTS

corn-flake crumbs—*1 oz (28 g)*	2.0
croutons, herb-seasoned—*7/19 oz (20 g)*	1.0
rice bran—*1 oz (28 g)*	0.6
rice flour—*1 oz (28 g)*	0.1
rice polish—*1 oz (28 g)*	1.2
stuffing, from mix, Stove Top—*½ cup (108 g)*	3.3

MILK MIXES

choc powder, Nestle Quik—*2 t (22 g)*	18.0
choc syrup, Bosco—*1 T (20 g)*	9.9[a]
cocoa mix, Hershey—*1 oz (28 g)*	20.0
cocoa mix, Nestle—*1 oz (28 g)*	23.0
cocoa mix w/marshmallows, Nestle—*1 oz (28 g)*	22.0

NUTS & NUT PRODUCTS

almond powder, Nutquik—*1 oz (28 g)*	1.6[a]
coconut	
dried, shredded, sweetened—*2 T (11 g)*	4.1
dried, shredded, sweetened—*⅓ cup (28 g)*	10.3
dried, shredded, sweetened, cnd—*⅓ cup (26 g)*	9.3

SALAD DRESSINGS, FROM MIX
buttermilk, Good Seasons—*1 T (16 g)*	0.9
farm style, Good Seasons—*1 T (15 g)*	0.4
french—*1 T (19 g)*	2.7
french, old fashioned, Good Seasons—*1 T (16 g)*	0.5
french, riviera, Good Seasons—*1 T (18 g)*	2.1
garlic—*1 T (16 g)*	0.2
garlic w/cheese—*1 T (16 g)*	0.2
italian—*1 T (16 g)*	0.4
italian, low cal—*1 T (18 g)*	1.4
italian, mild—*1 T (16 g)*	1.0
italian w/cheese—*1 T (17 g)*	0.8
italian, zesty, Good Seasons—*1 T (16 g)*	0.3
onion—*1 T (16 g)*	0.4

SOUPS, CND, LOW NA, RTS
beef & mushroom, chunky—*10¾ oz (305 g)*	3.0
chicken veg, chunky—*10¾ oz (305 g)*	4.0
chicken w/noodles, chunky—*10¾ oz (305 g)*	3.0
corn—*10¾ oz (305 g)*	11.0
pea, split—*10¾ oz (305 g)*	5.0
tomato w/tomato pieces—*10½ oz (298 g)*	22.0
veg beef, chunky—*10¾ oz (305 g)*	7.0

SPICES, HERBS & FLAVORINGS
lemon & pepper seasoning, McCormick—*1 t (4 g)*	0.3
salt & spice, McCormick—*1 t (5 g)*	0.1

SYRUP
corn, dark—*1 T (21 g)*	0.6[a]
pancake/waffle	
Log Cabin—*1 fl oz (39 g)*	25.2
Log Cabin, buttered—*1 fl oz (39 g)*	22.7
Log Cabin, country kitchen—*1 fl oz (39 g)*	19.6
Log Cabin, maple honey—*1 fl oz (39 g)*	24.6

VEGETABLES
asparagus, raw—*3½ oz (100 g)*	2.8
beet, raw—*3½ oz (100 g)*	8.7
broccoli, raw—*3½ oz (100 g)*	1.8
brussels sprouts, raw—*3½ oz (100 g)*	2.8
cabbage, red, raw—*3½ oz (100 g)*	3.5
cabbage, white, raw—*3½ oz (100 g)*	4.3
carrot, raw—*3½ oz (100 g)*	4.7
cauliflower, raw—*3½ oz (100 g)*	2.4
celery root, raw—*3½ oz (100 g)*	2.6
chicory, red, raw—*3½ oz (100 g)*	1.6
chicory, white, raw—*3½ oz (100 g)*	3.1
corn, raw—*3½ oz (100 g)*	3.7
cucumber, raw—*3½ oz (100 g)*	1.9
dandelion greens—*3½ oz (100 g)*	1.2
eggplant, raw—*3½ oz (100 g)*	3.3
fennel, raw—*3½ oz (100 g)*	2.6
green beans, raw—*3½ oz (100 g)*	2.7
jerusalem artichoke, raw—*3½ oz (100 g)*	2.4
kohlrabi, raw—*3½ oz (100 g)*	3.9
leek, raw—*3½ oz (100 g)*	3.4
lettuce, raw—*3½ oz (100 g)*	1.1
okra, raw—*3½ oz (100 g)*	2.9
onion, raw—*3½ oz (100 g)*	5.6
peas, green, raw—*3½ oz (100 g)*	4.6

VEGETABLES
peas, green, cnd—*3½ oz (100 g)*	0.7
pepper, green, raw—*3½ oz (100 g)*	2.8
potato, raw—*3½ oz (100 g)*	3.9
pumpkin, raw—*3½ oz (100 g)*	4.4
radish, raw—*3½ oz (100 g)*	2.2
rhubarb, raw—*3½ oz (100 g)*	0.9
salsify, raw—*3½ oz (100 g)*	1.4
spinach, raw—*3½ oz (100 g)*	0.5
squash, summer, raw—*3½ oz (100 g)*	2.2
sweet potato, raw—*3½ oz (100 g)*	4.0
swiss chard, raw—*3½ oz (100 g)*	1.5
tomato, raw—*3½ oz (100 g)*	2.9

VEGETABLES, FRZN, BIRDS EYE
artichoke hearts—*½ cup (85 g)*	5.6
asparagus, cuts—*³⁄₅ cup (100 g)*	2.8
asparagus, spears—*³⁄₅ cup (100 g)*	2.7
black-eyed peas—*⅔ cup (100 g)*	8.6
broccoli, chopped—*½ cup (100 g)*	1.6
broccoli, cuts—*⅔ cup (95 g)*	1.8
broccoli, in cheese sce—*½ cup (142 g)*	5.1
broccoli, pieces w/almonds—*½ cup (95 g)*	2.5
broccoli, spears—*½ cup (100 g)*	1.9
broccoli, spears in hollandaise sce—*½ cup (95 g)*	1.5
broccoli & water chestnuts—*½ cup (95 g)*	3.1
broccoli, carrots & pasta twists in sce—*⅔ cup (95 g)*	2.5
broccoli, carrots & water chestnuts—*⅔ cup (91 g)*	3.1
broccoli, cauliflower & carrots—*1 cup (100 g)*	2.7
broccoli, cauliflower & carrots in cheese sce—*½ cup (142 g)*	5.6
broccoli, cauliflower, corn & pasta in parmesan cheese sce—*½ cup (95 g)*	3.1
broccoli, corn & red peppers—*⅔ cup (91 g)*	2.5
broccoli, green beans, onions & red peppers—*⅔ cup (91 g)*	2.5
broccoli, shells, onions & mushrooms in swiss cheese sce—*½ cup (95 g)*	2.3
brussels sprouts—*³⁄₅ cup (100 g)*	1.9
brussels sprouts, in cheese sce—*½ cup (128 g)*	4.7
brussels sprouts, cauliflower & carrots—*⅔ cup (91 g)*	2.3
butter beans—*½ cup (95 g)*	4.7
carrots—*³⁄₅ cup (100 g)*	5.7
carrots, w/brown sugar glaze—*½ cup (95 g)*	12.8
carrots, peas & onions—*½ cup (95 g)*	5.1
cauliflower—*³⁄₅ cup (100 g)*	2.5
cauliflower w/almonds—*½ cup (95 g)*	2.4
cauliflower w/cheese sce—*½ cup (142 g)*	6.0
cauliflower, green beans & corn—*⅔ cup (91 g)*	2.6
collard greens—*½ cup (100 g)*	0.0
corn, frzn—*½ cup (100 g)*	3.8
corn on the cob—*3 inch ear (90 g)*	3.5
corn on the cob—*5½ inch ear (160 g)*	6.2
corn jubilee—*½ cup (95 g)*	5.0
corn, green beans & pasta twists in sce—*½ cup (95 g)*	3.3
crowder peas—*⅔ cup (90 g)*	7.9
green beans—*⅔ cup (100 g)*	3.3
green beans, corn, carrots & onions—*⅔ cup (91 g)*	3.9
green beans, french style—*⅖ cup (100 g)*	3.3
green beans, french style w/almonds—*½ cup (85 g)*	4.2

[a] Sucrose rather than total sugars

VEGETABLES, FRZN, BIRDS EYE

green beans, french style w/cheese sce—½ cup (142 g)	3.6
green beans, french style & mushrooms—½ cup (85 g)	3.4
green beans, french style, cauliflower & carrots—⅔ cup (91 g)	2.9
green beans, italian—⅔ cup (100 g)	4.2
kale, chopped—½ cup (100 g)	0.4
lima beans, baby—⅝ cup (100 g)	4.6
lima beans, fordhook—³/₅ cup (100 g)	3.2
mixed veg—½ cup (95 g)	4.1
mixed veg w/onion sce—⅓ cup (76 g)	5.2
mustard greens, chopped—½ cup (100 g)	0.0
okra, cut—½ cup (95 g)	2.1
okra, whole—⅔ cup (95 g)	2.6
onions—½ cup (113 g)	6.0
onions, chopped—¼ cup (28 g)	1.3
peas—³/₅ cup (100 g)	4.6
peas, tiny—½ cup (95 g)	3.3
peas, w/crm sce—½ cup (76 g)	7.3
peas & cauliflower w/crm sce—½ cup (95 g)	6.7
peas & carrots—³/₅ cup (100 g)	5.0
peas & mushrooms—½ cup (95 g)	4.6
peas & onions—½ cup (95 g)	5.6
peas & onions, w/cheese sce—½ cup (142 g)	7.3
peas & potatoes w/crm sce—½ cup (76 g)	7.3
peas, carrots & onions—⅔ cup (91 g)	4.2
peas, carrots, pasta & onions in parmesan cheese sce—½ cup (95 g)	5.0
peas, shells & corn in crm sce—½ cup (95 g)	5.0
peas, shells & mushrooms in crm sce—½ cup (95 g)	4.8
potatoes	
fries, reg cut—³/₅ cup (100 g)	0.2
fries, cottage—⅔ cup (79 g)	0.2
fries, crinkle cuts—⅔ cup (85 g)	0.2
fries, shoestring—¾ cup (85 g)	0.2
fries, steak—¾ cup (85 g)	0.2
fries, tasti—¾ cup (71 g)	4.0
hash browns—½ cup (113 g)	3.9
puffs—½ cup (71 g)	5.0
tiny taters—⅔ cup (91 g)	5.6
triangles—2 patties (85 g)	2.8
wedges, farm style—3 oz (85 g)	0.2
whole, peeled—3–4 potatoes (91 g)	3.1
rice, chinese fried—½ cup (104 g)	3.2
rice, french style—½ cup (104 g)	1.6
rice, italian style—½ cup (104 g)	1.8

a Coating mix for meat & poultry

VEGETABLES, FRZN, BIRDS EYE

rice, northern italian style—½ cup (104 g)	2.0
rice, oriental style—½ cup (104 g)	1.8
rice, spanish style—½ cup (104 g)	2.1
rice, peas & mushrooms—⅔ cup (66 g)	1.7
succotash—½ cup (100 g)	4.0
spinach, chopped/leaf—½ cup (100 g)	0.2
spinach, creamed—⅓ cup (85 g)	1.7
spinach & water chestnuts—½ cup (95 g)	1.7
squash, summer—⅔ cup (100 g)	1.6
squash, zucchini—½ cup (95 g)	1.4
turnip greens, chopped—³/₅ cup (100 g)	0.0
turnip greens w/turnips—½ cup (95 g)	0.2
veg combinations	
bavarian style beans & spaetzle—½ cup (95 g)	2.7
cantonese stir fry—½ cup (95 g)	2.5
chinese style—½ cup (95 g)	2.7
chinese style, stir fry—½ cup (95 g)	2.8
far eastern style—½ cup (95 g)	2.6
italian style—½ cup (95 g)	4.3
japanese stir fry—½ cup (95 g)	2.8
japanese style—½ cup (95 g)	3.9
mexicana style—½ cup (95 g)	2.9
new england style—½ cup (95 g)	2.8
san francisco style—½ cup (95 g)	3.0
veg, stew—6³/₅ oz (189 g)	7.7
wax (yellow) beans—⅔ cup (100 g)	1.8

VEG, RICE, FROM INST, MINUTE RICE

regular—⅔ cup (123 g)	0.3
beef flavored—½ cup (117 g)	1.6
chicken flavored—½ cup (107 g)	0.8
chinese fried—½ cup (97 g)	1.5
long grain & wild rice—½ cup (115 g)	1.0
spanish style—½ cup (148 g)	3.6

MISCELLANEOUS

barbecue sce—1 T (16 g)	4.0
choc, unsweetened, baking—1 oz (28 g)	4.0
oven fry,a General Foods—¼ pkt (23 g)	0.8
pectin, Certo—1 T (14 g)	0.2
pectin, Sure-Jell—¼ pkt (12 g)	9.2
shake & bake,a General Foods—¼ pkt (17 g)	1.5
whipped topping	
Cool Whip, frzn—1 T (4 g)	1.0
Dover Farms, frzn—1 T (5 g)	1.3
Dream Whip, from mix—1 T (5 g)	1.0
low cal, D-Zerta, from mix—1 T (3 g)	0.3

Theobromine[a] (mg)

	Mean[b]	Range		Mean[b]	Range
TEA BEVERAGES			**CHOCOLATE & FOODS CONTAINING CHOCOLATE**		
black,[c] 3-min brew—*6 fl oz*	2		chocolate candy		
from inst[c]—*6 fl oz*	2		reese's peanut butter cups—*2 pieces (34 g)*	37	
mint flavor—*6 fl oz*	2		rolo—*5 pieces (28 g)*	19	
orange spice—*6 fl oz*	2		semi-sweet choc chips—*1 oz (28 g)*	101	62–139
			semi-sweet choc chips, Hershey—*1 oz (28 g)*	62	
CHOCOLATE & FOODS CONTAINING CHOCOLATE			special dark choc, Hershey—*1 oz (28 g)*	115	
baking choc, Hershey—*1 oz (28 g)*	55		sweet (dark) choc—*1 oz (28 g)*	129	101–176
chocolate candy			whatchamacallit—*1.13 oz bar (32 g)*	29	
choc kisses—*6 pieces (28 g)*	52		choc fudge topping, Hershey—*2 T (28 g)*	25	
crunch bar, Nestle—*1.06 oz bar (30 g)*	48		choc milk—*8 fl oz (250 g)*	58	35–99
golden almond—*1 oz (28 g)*	64		choc powder, inst, Hershey—*3 T (21 g)*	67	
kit kat—*1.5 oz bar (43 g)*	43		choc powder, inst, Quik—*2 t (22 g)*	88	
krackel—*1.2 oz bar (34 g)*	50		choc syrup, Hershey—*2 T (28 g)*	68	
milk choc—*1 oz (28 g)*	42	38–52	cocoa beverage—*6 fl oz*	78	65–237
milk choc chips, Hershey—*¼ cup (42 g)*	84		cocoa, dry powder—*1 T (5 g)*	102	79–114
milk choc, Hershey—*1.02 oz bar (29 g)*	54		cocoa, dry, Hershey—*1 oz (28 g)*	409	
milk choc w/almonds—*1 oz (28 g)*	45	42–48	cocoa mix[d], Hershey—*1 oz (28 g)*	56	
milk choc w/almonds, Hershey—*1 oz (28 g)*	48		cocoa mix[d]—*1 pkt (28 g)*	67	
mr. goodbar—*1.65 oz bar (47 g)*	58		cocoa mix[d] w/marshmallows—*1 oz (28 g)*	55	
thousand dollar bar—*1.5 oz bar (43 g)*	32				

[a] Theobromine, along with theophylline and caffeine, are xanthines found in coffee, tea, and cocoa. All three compounds are stimulants.
[b] May vary due to growing conditions and variety of cocoa beans

[c] Also contains about 1 mg theophylline per 6 fl oz
[d] Contains dry milk & needs only hot water for reconstitution

Foods High in Tyramine[a]

ale	game
banana, green, stewed	herring, pickled
beans, italian broad (fava beans)	liver, beef & chicken
beer	soy sauce
cheese, aged (brie, camembert, cheddar, emmentaler, gouda, gruyère, mozzarella, parmesan, provolone, romano, roquefort, stilton)	vanilla
chocolate	wine (chianti, reisling, sauterne, sherry)
fish, dried (caplin, cod, herring)	yeast & yeast extract
	yogurt

[a] A strong vasoconstrictor that raises blood pressure when administered intravenously. Patients on monoamine oxidase inhibitor therapy may experience a hypertensive crisis if they consume foods containing tyramine or other amines.

Data Sources[a]

Appledorf, H. and L.S. Kelly, Proximate and mineral content of fast foods, J. Am. Dietet. Assoc. 74(1):35, 1978.

Baetz, R.A. and C.T. Kenner, Determination of heavy metals in foods, Agr. and Food Chem. 21(3):436, 1973.

Baetz, R.A. and C.T. Kenner, Determination of trace metals in foods using chelating ion exchange concentration, Agr. and Food Chem. 23(1):41, 1975.

Blauch, J.L. and S.M. Tarka, Jr., HPLC determination of caffeine and theobromine in coffee, tea and instant hot cocoa mixes, J. Food Sci. 48:745, 1983.

Bruhn, J.C. and A.A. Franke, An indirect method for the estimation of the iodine content of raw milk, J. Dairy Sci. 61:1557, 1978.

Bruhn, J.C., A.A. Franke, R.B. Bushnell, H. Weisheit, G.H. Hutton and G.C. Gurtle, Sources and content of iodine in California milk and dairy products, J. Food Protection 46(1):41, 1983.

Bunker, M.L. and M. McWilliams, Caffeine content of common beverages, J. Am. Dietet. Assoc. 74(1):28, 1979.

Burg, A.W., Effects of caffeine in the human system, Tea and Coffee Trade J. 147:40, 1975.

Bunnell, R.H., J. Keating, A. Quaresimo and G.K. Parman, Alpha-tocopherol content of foods, Am. J. Clin. Nutr. 17:1, 1965.

Caffeine and Pregnancy, U.S. Dept. Health and Human Services, HHS Pub. No. (FDA) 81-1081, Rockville, MD, 1981.

Clements, R.S., Jr. and B. Darnell, Myo-inositol content of common foods: development of a high-myo-inositol diet, Am. J. Clin. Nutr. 33:1954, 1980.

Composition of Foods, Raw. Processed. Prepared, USDA Handbook No. 8, Washington, D.C.
8-1 Dairy & Egg Products, November 1976
8-2 Spices & Herbs, January 1977
8-3 Baby Foods, December 1978
8-4 Fats & Oils, June 1979
8-5 Poultry Products, August 1979
8-6 Soups, Sauces & Gravies, February 1980
8-7 Sausages & Luncheon Meats, September 1980
8-8 Breakfast Cereals, July 1982
8-9 Fruits & Fruit Juices, August 1982

Crosby, N.T., J.K. Foreman, J.F. Palframan and R. Sawyer, Estimation of steam-volatile N-nitrosamines in foods at the 1 mcg/kg level, Nature 238:342, 1972.

Douglass, J.S. and R.H. Matthews, Nutrient content of pasta products. Cereal Foods World 27(11):558, 1982.

Evans, R.J. and J.A. Davidson, The choline content of fresh and stored shell eggs, Poultry Sci. 30:29, 1951.

Evans, R.J., J.A. Davidson, D. Brauer and H.A. Butts, The biotin content of fresh and stored shell eggs, Poultry Sci. 32:680, 1953.

Evans, W.H., J.I. Read and B.E. Lucan, Evaluation of a method for the determination of total cadmium, lead and nickel in foodstuffs using measurement by flame atomic-absorption spectrophotometry, Analyst 103:580, 1978.

Fletcher, D.C., Do clotting factors in vitamin K-rich vegetables hinder anticoagulant therapy, J. Am. Med. Assoc. 237(17):1871, 1977.

Galvao, L.C.A., A. Lopex and H.L. Williams, Essential mineral elements in peanuts and peanut butter, J. Food Sci. 41:1305, 1976.

Geigy Scientific Tables, Volume 1, Units of Measurement, Body Fluids, Composition of the Body, Nutrition, 8th ed., CIBA-GEIGY, 1981.

Gormican, A., Inorganic elements in foods used in hospital menus, J. Am. Dietet. Assoc. 56(5):397, 1970.

Graham, D.M., Caffeine—its identity, dietary sources, intake and biological effects, Nutrition Reviews 36(4):97, 1978.

Hartman, A.M. and L.P. Dryden, Vitamins in Milk and Milk Products, Am. Dairy Science Foundation, Oct. 1965.

Herting, D.C. and E.E. Drury, Alpha-tocopherol content of cereal grains and processed cereals, Agr. and Food Chem. 17(4):785, 1969.

Hodge, H.C. and F.A. Smith, Minerals: fluorine and dental caries, in Advances in Chemistry, Series 94, Washington, D.C., American Chemical Society, 1970.

Holak, W., Analysis of foods for lead, cadmium, copper, zinc, arsenic and selenium, using closed system sample digestion: Collaborative study, J.A.O.A.C. 63(3):485, 1980.

Human Nutrition Information Service, Hyattsville, Maryland, USDA Provisional Tables on the Nutrient Content of:
Bakery Foods & Related Items, August 1981
Beverages, September 1981
Frozen Vegetables, April 1979

Institute of Food Technologists' Expert Panel on Food Safety and Nutrition, Caffeine, Food Technology 37(4):87, 1983.

Koehler, H.H., H.C. Lee and M. Jacobson, Tocopherols in canned entrees and vended sandwiches, J. Am. Dietet. Assoc. 70:616, 1977.

Lambertsen, G., H. Myklestad and O.R. Braekkan, Tocopherols in nuts, J. Sci. Food Agric. 13:617, 1962.

Luten, J.B., A. Ruiter, T.M. Ritskes, A.B. Rauchbaar and G. Richwel-Booy, Mercury and selenium in marine- and freshwater fish, J. Food Sci. 45(3):416, 1980.

Marier, J.R. and D. Rose, The fluoride content of some foods and beverages—a brief survey using a modified Zr-SPADNS method, J. Dental Res. 31:941, 1966.

Matschiner, J.T. and E.A. Doisy, Vitamin K content of ground beef, J. Nutr. 90:331, 1966.

[a] Data were generously supplied by various food companies and trade associations. Data from previous editions of Bowes & Church were also used.

McLaughlin, P.J. and J.L. Weihrauch, Vitamin E content of foods, J. Am. Dietet. Assoc. 75:647, 1979.

McNutt, K.W., Perspective—fiber, J. Nutr. Ed. 8:150, 1976.

Morris, V.C. and O.A. Levander, Selenium content of foods, J. Nutr. 100:1383, 1970.

Oberleas, D. and B.F. Harland, Phytate content of foods: Effect on dietary zinc bioavailability, J. Am. Dietet. Assoc. 79(4):433, 1981.

Olson, O.E., I.S. Palmer and Sr. M. Howe, Selenium in foods consumed by South Dakotans, Proc. S.D. Acad. Sci. 57:113, 1978.

O'Neill, I.K., M. Sargent and M.L. Trimble, Determination of phytate in foods by phosphorus-31 fourier transform nuclear magnetic resonance spectrometry, Anal. Chem. 52:1288, 1980.

Ophaug, R.H., L. Singer and B.F. Harland, Estimated fluoride intake of 6-month-old infants in four dietary regions of the United States, Am. J. Clin. Nutr. 33:324, 1980.

Paul, A.A. and D.A.T. Southgate, McCance and Widdowson's The Composition of Foods, 4th edition, Elsevier/North-Holland Biomedical Press, N.Y., 1978.

Pilac, L.M., I.C. Abdon and E.P. Mandap, Oxalic acid content and its relation to the calcium present in some Philippine plant foods, Philippine J. Nutr 24(1):21, 1971.

Reddy, N.R., S.K. Sathe and D.K. Salunkhe, Phytates in legumes and seeds, In Advances in Food Res., vol. 28, pages 1–92, edited by C.O. Chichester, E.M. Mrak and F.G. Stewart, Academic Press, New York, 1982.

Schroeder, H.A., J.J. Balassa and I.H. Tipton, Abnormal trace metals in man—chromium, J. Chron. Dis. 15:941, 1962.

Schroeder, H.A., J.J. Balassa and I.H. Tipton, Abnormal trace metals in man—nickel, J. Chron. Dis. 15:51, 1962.

Seigel, A., A. Bhumiratana and D.R. Lineback, Development, acceptability and nutritional evaluation of high-protein, soy-supplemented rice noodles for Thai children, Cereal Chem. 52:801, 1975.

Solomons, N.W., F. Viteri, T.R. Shuler and F.H. Nielson, Bioavailability of nickel in man: effects of foods and chemically-defined dietary constituents on the absorption of inorganic nickel, J. Nutr. 112(1):39, 1982.

Tangkongchitr, U., P.A. Seib and R.C. Hoseney, Phytic acid II. Its fate during breadmaking, Cereal Chem. 58(3):229, 1981.

Tarone, C.M. and R.H. Matthews, Proximate and mineral content of selected baked products, Cereal Foods World 27(7):308, 1982.

Thomas, B., J.A. Roughan and E.D. Watters, Cobalt, chromium and nickel content of some vegetable food stuffs, J. Sci. Fd. Agric. 25:771, 1974.

Thorn, J., J. Robertson and D.H. Buss, Trace elements. Selenium in British foods, Brit. J. Nutr. 39:391, 1978.

Underwood, E.J., Trace Elements in Human and Animal Nutrition, 4th ed., Academic Press, New York, 1977.

Waldbott, G.L., Fluoride in food, Am. J. Clin. Nutr. 12:455, 1963.

What's in Soft Drinks, National Soft Drink Association, Washington, D.C., Sept. 1982.

White, J.W., Relative significance of dietary sources of nitrate and nitrite, J. Agr. Food Chem. 23(5):886, 1975.

Young, E.A., E.H. Brennan and G.I. Irving, Update: Nutritional analysis of fast foods, Public Health Currents 21(3):9, 1981, Ross Laboratories, Columbus, Ohio 43216.

Zook, E.G., F.E. Green and E.R. Morris, Nutrient composition of selected wheats and wheat products. VI. Distribution of manganese, copper, nickel, zinc, magnesium, lead, tin, chromium and selenium as determined by atomic absorption spectroscopy and colorimetry, Cereal Chem. 47:720, 1970.

Zoumas, B.L., W.R. Kreiser and R.A. Martin, Theobromine and caffeine content of chocolate products, J. Food Sci. 45(2):314, 1980.

Index

Page references refer to the food listings in the main nutrient table. For references to specific substances in the supplementary tables (*i.e.*, vitamins, minerals, and other substances of nutritional concern), see the particular substance.

A

abalone, 63
acerola, 74
acerola juice, 98
acorn squash, 158
Advance formula, 95
albacore, 71
alcoholic beverages, 3, 196–197
ale, 3
alewife, 63
alfalfa sprouts, 145
All Bran, 12
alligator meat, 108
allspice, 139
almond(s), 117
    chocolate-covered, 8
    sugar-coated, 9
almond chocolate bar, 9
almond coffee cake, 38
Almond Joy, 9
almond mocha, 4
almond oil, 62
almond paste, 118
almond powder, 118
Alpen, 12
Alpha-Bits, 12
alpha-tocopherol content of foods, 219–222
amaranth, 74, 162
amaretto cafe, 4
American cheese, 17–18
Amin-aid, 135
amino acid content of foods, 167–196
anchovy, 63
angel food cake, 35
animal cookies, 41
anise seed, 139
apple, 74
    custard, 75
    mammy, 77
    sugar, 79
apple Bavarian dessert, 44
apple Betty, 43
    infant, 88
apple butter, 142
apple cake, 35
apple chutney, 142
apple cinnamon oats, 11

apple coffee cake, 38
apple crepe, 53
apple crisp, 43
apple dessert, infant, 88
apple dumpling, 43
Apple Jacks, 12
apple juice, 98
    infant, 92–93
apple juice drink, 6
apple pastry, 42
apple pie, 45, 48
    Burger King, 55
    McDonald's, 60
applesauce, 74
    infant, 91–92
apple strudel, 50
apple sweet roll, 50
apple toaster pastry, 51
apple turnover, 51
    Jack in the Box, 58
apricot, 74
    candied, 142
    infant, 92
    pureed, 133
apricot nectar, 98
apricot preserves, 143
Aproten diet foods, 133
Arby's, 54
armadillo meat, 108
arm steak, veal, 105
arrowroot cookies, 41, 87
arrowroot flour, 72
Arthur Treacher, 54
artichoke, 145
asparagus, 145
asparagus souffle, 53
asparagus soup, 128, 131
au jus gravy, 127
avocado, 145
Awake, 6

B

baby cookies, 87
baby foods. *See* infant foods
baby pretzels, 87
Bac-O-Bits, 112

Bac-O-Chips, 19
bacon, 103
    Canadian, 109
    imitation, 112
bacon dinners, infant, 90
bacon fat, 62
bacon-lettuce, tomato sandwich, 31
Bacon Nips, 19
bagel, 80
baked beans, 146, 153
baking chocolate, 162
baking powder, 162
baking soda, 162
bamboo shoots, 145–146
banana, 74
    infant, 92–93
banana cake, 35
banana cream pie, 45
banana cream pie filling, 48
banana custard, 42
banana custard pie, 45
banana dessert, infant, 88
banana pudding pop, 49
banana snack cake, 39
banana split, Dairy Queen, 56
barbeque loaf, 109
barbeque sauce, 60, 126
barbeque seasoning, 139
barley, 11
    Nutri-grain, 14
barley cereal, infant, 87
barley flour, 72
barley snack, 19
barracuda, 63
basella, 151
basil, 139
bass, 63–64, 70
Bavarian gelatin dessert, 45
Bavarian mint coffee, 4
Bavarian-style beans, 160
bay leaf, 139
beans, 146
    beef, tomato sauce and, 21
    butter, 148
    chili and, 23
    franks and, 21, 25
    garbanzo, 150

vanilla icing, 40
vanilla milkshake, 116
vanilla pie filling, 48
vanilla pudding, 49
vanilla pudding pop, 50
vanilla wafers, 42
veal, 105–106
  infant, 93
  pureed, 133
veal dinner, infant, 91
veal frozen dinner, 33
veal parmigiana, 27, 106
veal scallopini, 33
veal stew, 33
Veelets, 114
Vegelona, 114
vegetable(s), 145–161
  infant, 94
  pureed, 133–134
vegetable chow mein, 24
vegetable dinners, infant, 90–91
vegetable flakes, 160
vegetable juice, 98–99
vegetable marrow, 161
vegetable oil, 62
vegetable soup, 130–132
vegetable stew, 161
vegetarian burger, 114
vegetarian foods. *See* meat, analogues of
vegetarian stew, 32
Veja-Links, 114
venison, 108
vermouth, 3
Vernors, 5
Vienna bread, 80
Vienna cafe, 4
Vienna Dream Bar, 42
Vienna Finger cookies, 42
Vienna sausage, 112
vinegar, 125–126, 163
vinegar and oil dressing, 125
Vital high nitrogen formula, 138
Vitamin D content of foods, 215–217
Vitamin E content of foods, 218–222
Vitamin K content of foods, 223
Vivonex, 138
vodka, 3

W
Waffelos, 16
waffle syrup, 145
waffles, 86
walleye pike, 68
walnut cake, 38
walnuts, 119
  in syrup, 52
water
  mineral, 6
  sparkling, 6
water chestnuts, 161
watercress, 161
watermelon, 80
Waverly Wafers, 83
wax beans, 161
weakfish, 72
weiner wrap, 86
Welsh rarebit, 33
Wendy's, 61
Western frozen dinner, 27–28
Whatchamacallit, 10
Wham, 114
wheat
  bulgar, 11
  cream of, 11
  Nutri-grain, 14
  puffed, 15
  shredded, 15
Wheat and Raisin Chex, 16
wheatberry bread, 81
wheat cereal, 12
wheat Chex, 16
wheat crackers, 83
Wheatena, 12
wheat flour, 73
wheat germ, 16
wheat germ oil, 63
wheat hearts, 12
Wheaties, 16
Wheat Snacks, 83
wheat starch, dietary, 133
Wheat Thins, 83
whey, 163
whipped cream, 34
whipped topping, 34
whiskey, 3

whiskey sour, 3
white beans, 146
white bread, 81
white cake, 38
whitefish, 72
white mustard cabbage. *See* spoon cabbage
white perch, 72
white potato. *See* potato
white sauce, 127
white sugar, 14
whiting, 66
whole wheat bread, 81
whole wheat cereal, 12
whole wheat flour, 73
whole wheat muffin, 83
whole wheat rolls, 85
wild berry juice drink, 7
wild rice, 156
wine, 3
winged beans, 161
Wink, 5
winter squash, 159
Wisconsin country-style vegetables, 161
won ton soup, 131
Worcestershire sauce, 127
wreckfish, 72

Y
yam, 161
yam beans, 161
yautia, 161
yeast, 163
yellow beans, 161
yellow cake, 38
yellow cupcake, 39
yellow eye beans, 161
yogurt, 117
yolk. *See* egg yolk

Z
Zante currants, 75
Zero, 10
Zero dressing, 126
zucchini, 150
zwieback, 83, 87